Texts in Computing

Volume 14

Java: Just in Time

Texts in Computing Series Editor
Ian Mackie

mackie@lix.polytechnique.fr

Java: Just in Time

John Latham

ISBN 978-1-84890-025-7
First printing January 2011 (L21)
Second printing (revised) September 2011 (A?J)
Third printing (revised) September 2012 (A30)
Fourth printing (revised)September 2013 (AJ1)
Fifth printing (revised) September 2014 (AJ2)

College Publications
Scientific Director: Dov Gabbay
Managing Director: Jane Spurr
Department of Computer Science
King's College London, Strand, London WC2R 2LS, UK

http://www.collegepublications.co.uk

Original cover design by Richard Fraser
Cover produced by Laraine Welch
Printed by Lightning Source, Milton Keynes, UK

Preface

Why yet another Java book? I think it's fair to say that we Computer Science (or whatever we call ourselves) teachers have been struggling since the outset to find the best way to teach first programming using Java. Objects first was thought by many to be exciting, and moreover, appropriate – I suspect because those holding that view were themselves relatively new to object orientation, and were revitalized by it. Of course, it wasn't 'first' for them, but it seemed natural enough.

We tried objects first for a number of years at Manchester, and it became clear, quite quickly, that the most successful students were those who had programmed before – almost invariably not object oriented, and so it wasn't 'first' for them either. The most amusing memory of that time is *separate incident*s of students asking me: "Mammal, Lion, Leo: I don't get it – is it because zoos have computers?" Most students new to programming do not see the world as a collection of interacting objects. Rather, they have a self-centric perspective – any previous experience even remotely close to programming has been expressed in terms of what *they* must do to solve the 'problem'. This is our old friend the non-object oriented imperative paradigm.

So, I pondered about the features of an *ideal* first object oriented programming course, which starts where students new to programming *really* are, and takes them on a *staged* journey through the concepts, permitting them to grow understanding, skill, and above all, confidence, in unison. The first and main principle was **basics first, objects soon, inheritance later**, from which came another dozen or so principles. I take credit for believing I have found those ideals, but in defence of my humility I must add I have been teaching first programming since about 1982, so it has taken me a while to get it, and I have the advantage of both being taught badly when I was a student and being naturally cynical about new trends.

The next step was to convince my colleagues who were set to teach with me on our planned new course – all of us keen to improve on the previous objects first course. To my delight, the principles sold themselves. To our dismay, we found no book that came close to delivering them – thanks are due, by the way, for the sheer sweat of publishing reps who also failed to find one, and for the free copies of those they found instead!

The rest, as they say, is history: it has taken nearly seven years to create, during which time it has been used and abused, has evolved much of its detail but not though, its core principles: they have stood the test of that time. In all my experience the only programming course I recall as successful as this was back when we taught SML – somewhat less of a challenge.

So what are those principles? Take a look at the next section, aimed at students of the book, where most of them are expressed. Or you can find a more formal coverage on the book's website, http://www.cs.man.ac.uk/~jtl/JJIT. Perhaps the second most important pair of principles is that the learning is all based on full program examples, and that all the Java and programming concepts are introduced **just in time** to support that. Hence the name of the book.

Speaking of the website, the answers to the coursework tasks in the book are only available to bona-fide course teachers. This is because they form effective assessed material which, together with formative feedback, support that steady and staged growth of confidence in programming for the student.

I decided to include a chapter to introduce graphical user interfaces, but am aware that many teachers prefer not to cover that topic in a first programming course. So, I have written it in such a way that it may be skipped without significant impact on subsequent chapters. However, I will say that I think teaching GUIs is a good thing to do, because it completes the link between what students have come to learn programming is, and the kind of programs they use everyday, albeit with much less sophisticated examples. Perhaps those who prefer to omit it do so because when previously it has been included, their students found it too tricky. I like to think that I have made the ideas accessible, mainly by taking the bull by the horns and talking about the 'GUI event thread'; this demystifies event driven programming. Among the extra material on the book's website is another chapter on more advanced GUIs, and sophistications such as anonymous classes are held back until that.

One last thing: the process of producing the book is novel. In the master, the discussion text is embedded in Java program comments inside the source code of the example programs. And where we see the programs being run, they really have been run during document production, with the real results being placed at that point. (All this is done by a combination of shell scripts and LaTeX.) The upshot is that the example programs are *guaranteed* to work.

John Latham, December 2010

Dear student: why should you use this book?

Thank you for wanting to learn programming! You will soon find that it is an enjoyable and brilliantly creative craft. And thank you for choosing to learn the most modern style of **object oriented programming**. And thank you again for choosing Java – a serious and widely used programming language, not a noddy one specifically designed for teaching.

Ah, but therein lies the rub – Java is a tricky language to use as a learning vehicle for programming *because* it is a real one. So there has been much debate on how to do it, with many conflicting views and failed experiments. As a result there are a great number of Java books for you to choose from, all different in various ways from each other, and from this one. But arguably, this one is more different than most!

What's more, it has been shown to work.

- This book is genuinely aimed at people who have never programed before – it starts where you are now, based on your previous perceptions and relevant non-programming experience, rather than expecting you to somehow leap ahead.

- It is all based on a large number of example programs (well over a hundred), so the emphasis is on gradual acquisition of programming and problem solving skill, rather than the simpler, but less useful, topic of programming *language*. It does not assume that just by being shown Java concepts you can instantly be a programmer. Instead it shows you how to design code and gives you plenty of practice.

- Also, this means that the introduction of every programming concept is motivated by us wanting to use it in a real program straight away – part of the **just in time** idea.

- Despite the above, the examples are arranged into chapters that focus on particular major topics, so each stage has clearly stated coherent aims.

- It never uses the 'boiler plate' approach of telling you to ignore parts of Java that cannot be explained to you just yet. That leads to confusion and uncertainty. Neither does it go for the approach in which everything is explained right now in all its gory detail. Instead, it adopts the **just in time** principle: everything is explained when you first meet it, but only to a level of understanding that is appropriate for that stage of the learning process. Concepts are elaborated upon later in the book as required.

- It is not **objects first** – meaning that it does not assume you naturally view the real world as a collection of interacting objects. Instead it recognizes that you probably have a 'self centric' view, i.e. you see the world in terms of how it interacts with you, and the steps you must take to achieve a particular outcome. So our starting point is *task oriented*, rather than object oriented. For example, how do you view the process of running a bath? Do you: 1) put the plug in, 2) turn on the tap, 3) wait until full, 4) turn it off, and finally 5) get in. Or do you regard the plug, the plug hole, the tap, the bath and yourself as objects such that the plug interacts with the plug hole, and the tap interacts with the bath by passing water to it, and ...?

- It is not **objects late** either – that approach spends a long time permitting you to learn programming without using objects, and then, just when you have gained your confidence, destroys it by changing the rules.

- Instead it has a **basics first, objects soon, inheritance later** order to the learning. This has proved to be most successful for students new to programming, allowing them to start from where they are, build up plenty of confidence, and then, **just in time**, meet objects and **object oriented programming** before the habit of not using objects becomes too ingrained.

- When objects are introduced, it is done by revisiting a previous program example and gradually simplifying its implementation by using object technology. Thus, there is never a point when the idea of objects lacks motivation – their benefit is immediately obvious, which readily leads to seeing them as natural! In other words, you are painlessly taken to the point where objects first books assume you already are.

- When you do meet objects, you get an **open box** coverage of them, that is, your objects are created from code *you* have written, rather than from something hidden away. This means you see at the same time how objects are defined as well as how they are created and used – so you properly understand an important principle called **encapsulation**.

- The presentation of the book is such that the need to flip back to previous pages is minimized. For example, when we have a program which is a variant of a previous one, the parts of the code which have not been changed are presented again, but using a small font. This also emphasizes the new parts, whilst being able to see their proper context clearly.

- The book recognizes that programming is at least 51% confidence, and reflects this by providing coursework exercises which collectively mean you write a huge number of programs.

- It has no end of chapter exercises – they are too easily ignored because they all come in one lump. Instead coursework tasks are more usefully, and carefully, located at the end of examples within the chapters. This means you can practise the new skills and concepts in a timely and paced manner.

- Coffee time questions, sprinkled throughout the text, are designed to invite you to think more deeply about what you have just read.

- All the concepts introduced in a chapter are listed at its end, each with a self assessment question (and a reference back to the page it appeared on). So you can check your learning from each stage before moving onto the next one.

- There is a consolidation chapter just before we start talking about objects. This provides an opportunity to cement and review the foundations for those who were new to programming, but is also a possible entry point for those who already have *significant* (non-object oriented) programming experience.

- A collection of all the concepts covered, in an order suitable for reference and revision, is available on the website at `http://www.cs.man.ac.uk/~jtl/JJIT`.

- The book does not depend on a particular programming environment, which makes it usable in any. However, it recommends reliance on the absolute minimum of programming tools to start with. Otherwise, confidence built during learning can be too centred on the particular environment used, and thus may disappear if you are placed in a different one.

- Further, it does not depend on the use of any non-standard library code to hide the grubby details early on to get you started. That would create another unhealthy dependency, and confuse you about what is standard Java and what is not. Instead, the book carefully avoids the need to hide things from you in the first place!

- The book is not unnecessarily rigid. For example, it does not incorporate a strangulating code style on the program code, such as using unhelpful systematic naming conventions or being obsessed with presenting named parts in, say, alphabetical order. Where there is a variety of approaches, such as in the way programs handle erroneous situations, the book does not arbitrarily choose one, but exposes you to different strategies in different examples.

- The important, but simple, topic of producing on-line program documentation is covered in appropriate places, but the overall learning process is not cluttered by it appearing everywhere.

- On the other hand, program testing, another important, and more complex topic, is centrally visible throughout the text. Every program is tested, but not in a way that encourages a reluctant view of testing, nor one that obscures the learning of other principles.

Dear student: how should you use this book?

If you have not programmed before you should start at Chapter 1 and work through. If you have done a lot of previous programming, but not in Java, you might try skipping to Chapter 9 which contains a consolidation of all the concepts introduced in the preceding chapters.

Just in time learning

Each chapter focuses on a particular topic of programming, and is divided into a number of sections, most of which contain an example program. Programming and Java concepts are introduced and explained in appropriate detail just as they are needed for each example. This is a key principle of the **just in time** learning approach, making it easy to pick up the complexities in 'layers'.

Chapter aims

The start of each chapter contains a discussion of its aims. You should read this so that you know what to expect from the chapter. This is followed by a table of the chapter sections, with their particular aims and a summary of their associated coursework.

The parts in each example

The text in each section contains a mixture of parts.

- General discussion, introducing and explaining the example, and acting as a glue around the other parts.

- Introduction and explanation of programming and java concepts, such as this.

> *Concept* **System.out.println()**. The simplest way to print a message is to use:
>
>   System.out.println("This text will appear on the screen");

- Code listing of the example, which appears like this.

```
001: public class HelloWorld
002: {
003:   public static void main(String[] args)
004:   {
005:     System.out.println("Hello world!");
006:   }
007: }
```

- Thought provoking questions like the following. You should stop and ponder these for a while as you get to them, so that they might help deepen your understanding.

Coffee time: Soon you will know what all the code listed above means, but right now, what do you think that program will do?

0.0.1

- Runs of commands, especially runs of the current example.

Console Input / Output
| ```
$ java HelloWorld
Hello world!
$ _
``` |

These might appear anywhere, but in particular after we have developed each example, we show it being run with appropriate test data. If you take notice of this, you will also gradually and naturally pick up the skill of designing good test data for your programs.

Revisits to previous examples, or similar ones

Two key observations about programming are that there are many ways to solve a particular task, and that many programs are in fact similar to others. In this book when you meet later versions of previous programs, or new programs which are similar to previous ones, you will be invited to focus more on the different parts of the code, by us showing the similar parts in a smaller font.

```
001: public class HelloMum
002: {
003:   public static void main(String[] args)
004:   {
005:     System.out.println("Hello mum!");
006:   }
007: }
```

This is better than showing you the new code only, which would make you have to flick back to previous pages in order to see the context.

Coursework

At the end of most sections you will find a piece of coursework. If you want to get the most from the book then you ought to undertake these as you get to them. They have been carefully created for you to try out the ideas covered in the section, get a deeper understanding of them, and thus become able to *write* programs, rather than just read them!

Please organize your work carefully. For example, you will find some pieces of coursework ask you to make a new version of a program you have written before, and yet these will have the same file name. Clearly you should keep all versions – especially if they are being used as part of some formal assessment of your progress. So, you should undertake the coursework for each section in a separate folder or directory. A good structure is to have a folder for each chapter, within which there is a folder for each section, and you can download this from the book's website, http://www.cs.man.ac.uk/~jtl/JJIT.

Getting the most from the coursework

Some coursework tasks, especially early on, are deliberately similar to their associated example and thus the simplest way to tackle them is to start with the example and make changes. *Don't do this!!!* Resist the temptation as much as you can. If you can do the coursework without needing to look at the corresponding example, it will prove to you that the ideas and the way you need to express them are *in your head*, or not.... Whereas if you always look at the example while doing the coursework, you will become dependent on that, learn less and have more difficulty when you get to the parts for which the coursework is *not* similar to the example!

So, I recommend you read the section containing the example just before undertaking the associated coursework, and then try your best to not need to look at it while you do the coursework.
```

Maybe you should keep a logbook?

You will learn a lot from this book, but from time to time you will want to keep your own notes, or listings of things you don't properly understand when you first meet them. In addition, when you undertake the coursework you may need to scribble your thoughts somewhere before you start typing. Perhaps this won't be necessary for the early tasks, but sooner or later you'll need to. And some coursework asks you to design test data for the program – where should you scribble that as you think it through? You could use a scrap of paper each time you need to write something, but then you'd probably end up throwing them away. This book invites you to be a little more professional than that by buying yourself a (cheap) hardback bound notebook, and calling it your logbook. Many of the coursework descriptions remind you of this idea by suggesting specific things you should record, but even where they don't, the suggestion is implicitly there. You should record the date and time you start each logbook entry, and perhaps give it a title too.

End of chapter concepts list

As you get to the end of each chapter, you will find a handy list of all the concepts that were introduced in it. Each of these has a quick 'self assessment' question to help you decide whether you should go back and reread that bit. You are strongly encouraged to spend the time going through these lists when you get to them: it will either be a short time, in which case no harm is done, or it will be time very well spent avoiding misunderstanding in the following chapters.

Finally, supporting reference tools

As you read through the book you may from time to time wish to look back at something you have previously met. To help you with this there are three supporting tools.

- On the book's website, `http://www.cs.man.ac.uk/~jtl/JJIT`, you will find reference documents containing the concepts that have been introduced. There is a version of this for each chapter, containing the concepts that have been covered by all chapters up to the end of that one.

- The table of contents in the book lists major concept names, as well as chapter and section names.

- There is a comprehensive index at the back of the book.

The personal bit

I would like to thank my mum, for her persistent prayers and appropriate mix of encouragement, gentle nagging and pride, during this lengthy writing process. And my late dad too – I only wish he had been able to see its final product. And my siblings, and their families, too numerous to mention(!). A million thanks to be shared by you all.

To my daughter Lizzy – again for encouragement, and tolerance of me being too busy too many times, and for letting me use your photo in Chapter 18, the grand sum of one thousand thanks.

And friends, perhaps less numerous than siblings(?), but still I can't list you all here: a few hundred thanks each – you know who you are. Especially Dave Thorne.

To my co-lecturers at the University of Manchester: Howard Barringer, Alan Williams and Sean Bechhofer; many thanks for all those discussions on principles, and for helping with the development of some of the material.

To the 1000 or so students who have completed their study of this course since September 2004 at that dear place: one thank each – two if you ever told me about an error you found. ;-)

And then there's the commissioning editors at various publishing houses, and their appointed reviewers, yet again too numerous to list, who have been so encouraging – thanks to you all. But especially the team at College Publications: Dov Gabbay, Jane Spurr and Ian Mackie – thank you for your enthusiasm, vision and hard work.

But most of all, to Alison, probably the best critic in the world, with a sharp eye for typos and clumsy wording (so blame her if she missed any!): a billion thanks for all that proof reading, support, ideas, coffee, tolerance, more coffee, more proof reading and for letting me do so little housework, for so long.[1]

---

[1] Now I need a new excuse!

List of chapters

Contents

Chapter 1

Introduction

Do not search for the start of your journey:
you are already there.
Endeavour instead to discover where *that* is!

1.1   Chapter aims

In this chapter we introduce the principle of programming using an abstract scenario. We then take a brief look at what a computer is and the distinction between such things as **hardware** and **software**. Next we focus on what a program is, and how it is produced. Finally, before taking a look at some specific example programs, we talk about the **operating environment** in which programs are developed and **run**.

The chapter contains the following sections.

Section	Aims	Associated Coursework
1.2 What is programming? (p.2)	To explore what we mean by programming, by using a non-computing analogy.	(None.)
1.3 What is a computer? (p.2)	To take a brief look at the components of a computer, including **hardware**, **software** and **data**.	(None.)
1.4 What is a program? (p.5)	To look at what we mean by a computer program, particularly in Java, and how it is produced and processed.	(None.)
1.5 Operating environment (p.6)	To explore the relationship between a program and the **operating system** it is **run** on. We see that programs are commands, with **command line arguments**, and meet **standard output**.	(None.)
1.6 Our first Java program (p.8)	To show the mechanics of processing a finished Java source program so that it can be **run**, through to actually running it.	To **compile** and **run** the `HelloWorld` program. (p.11)
1.7 Our second Java program (p.11)	To reinforce the process of the **compile** and **run** cycle of a Java program.	To **compile** and **run** the `HelloSolarSystem` program. (p.12)

1.2   What is programming?

AIM:
To explore what we mean by programming, by using a non-computing analogy.

You are about to start learning to program in Java, and this book assumes you have no prior experience of programming. Before we start, it might be helpful to draw on an analogy.

Suppose in your garden you have a maze with a number of routes through it. Also, you have a new puppy, Spike, and for reasons we shall not question, you have the bright idea of training him to walk efficiently and apparently intelligently through the maze. It is unlikely you would succeed if you tried to teach him to treat the whole maze as a problem to be solved, but you do know that dogs can be taught much simpler actions like, sitting, walking and turning.

So, for the first few months you would train Spike to appropriately respond to your voice when given the basic commands "sit", "stand", "walk", "stop", "left" and "right". During this process, *you* would in effect be designing a language of instructions for *your* dog, which would probably not work well with any other. You are not really using English (or whatever is your natural language) because Spike does not understand that – for example you could not say "go" as an alternative, if you had trained him to respond to "walk". Indeed, you might have, perhaps bizarrely from your point of view, trained him to walk when hearing the word "stop".

Once this training was complete, you would be able to direct Spike through the maze by shouting the instructions at exactly the right time for him to respond immediately. Now, to make him *appear* to be acting autonomously, you might sneakily record your voice onto a small mp3 player and hang it around his neck! (With special canine headphones for subtlety?) You would make several tracks, one for each path through the maze from each starting point.

One view of this then, is that you would have created a machine (Spike) which can follow very simple instructions, and can be programmed to solve a complex task via a program (an audio track). This is essentially like computer programming, the main difference is that you as a programmer do not design the instruction language – it is a standard which has already been created, and the instructions work for many dogs, not just yours, and they are already trained to obey that standard.

Programming is the process of **design**ing and expressing in an appropriate language, a set of instructions to solve a particular task, that a machine will obey sometime *later*, whenever that task is needed to be done.

Coffee time: 1.2.1   What do you think would be the kind of problems that might make your dog machine unreliable and sometimes not work?

Coffee time: 1.2.2   Apart from any previous computer programming experience you may have, which we are assuming is none, what previous experience of more general programming do you have? That is, in what situations have you done something which will cause some 'programmed' things to happen at a later stage?

1.3   What is a computer?

AIM:
To take a brief look at the components of a computer, including **hardware**, **software** and **data**.

You have probably used computers for much of your life, but you might not know a lot about them. They are dumb machines that are capable of obeying simple instructions, reliably and without question or distraction. If they have been given the correct instructions they will do the right thing, if not then they'll still do what they have been told to!

If you haven't already, it's a good idea some time to take the lid off the main component of your computer and and have a peep inside – while the power is off of course!

Concept **Computer basics: hardware.** The physical parts of a computer are known as **hardware**. You can see them, and touch them.

It is likely you have used lots of computer **software** and **data**, but may not have taken the time to think about the difference between these and **hardware**.

Concept **Computer basics: software.** One part of a computer you cannot see is its **software**. This is stored on **computer media**, such as **DVD ROM**s, and ultimately inside the computer, as lots of numbers. It is the instructions that the computer will obey. The closest you get to seeing it might be if you look at the silver surface of a DVD ROM with a powerful magnifying glass!

Concept **Computer basics: data.** Another part of the computer that you cannot see is its **data**. Like **software** it is stored as lots of numbers. Computers are processing and producing data all the time. For example, an image from a digital camera is data. You can only see the picture when you display it using some image displaying or editing software, but even this isn't showing you the actual data that makes up the picture. The names and addresses of your friends is another example of data.

In order to understand programming, it is very useful to have at least a brief idea of what a computer is doing beneath the lid, and how it is structured.

Concept **Computer basics: hardware: processor.** The **central processing unit** (**CPU**) is the part of the **hardware** that actually obeys instructions. It does this dumbly – computers are not inherently intelligent.

Concept **Computer basics: software: machine code.** The instructions that the **central processing unit** obeys are expressed in a language known as **machine code**. This is a very **low level language**, meaning that each instruction gets the computer to do only a very simple thing, such as the **addition** of two numbers, or sending a **byte** to a printer.

Concept **Computer basics: hardware: memory.** The **computer memory** is part of the computer which is capable of storing and retrieving **data** for short term use. This includes the **machine code** instructions that the **central processing unit** is obeying, and any other data that the computer is currently working with. For example, it is likely that an image from a digital camera is stored in the computer memory while you are editing or displaying it, as are the machine code instructions for the image editing program.

The computer memory requires electrical power in order to remember its data – it is **volatile memory** and will forget its contents when the power is turned off.

An important feature of computer memory is that its contents can be accessed and changed in any order required. This is known as **random access** and such memory is called **random access memory** or just **RAM**.

Concept **Computer basics: hardware: persistent storage.** For longer term storage of **data**, computers use **persistent storage** devices such as **hard discs** and **DVD ROM**s. These are capable of holding much more information than **computer memory**, and are persistent in that they do not need power to remember the information stored on them. However, the time taken to store and retrieve data is *much* longer than for computer memory. Also, these devices cannot as easily be accessed in a random order.

Concept **Computer basics: hardware: input and output devices.** Some parts of the **hardware** are dedicated to receiving input from or producing output to the outside world. Keyboards and mice are examples of **input devices**.

Displays and printers are examples of **output device**s.

The following diagram shows how the pieces of hardware fit together to make a computer. The **central processing unit** (**CPU**) is the key part that connects to everything else. The arrows show the flow of data and instructions around the computer.

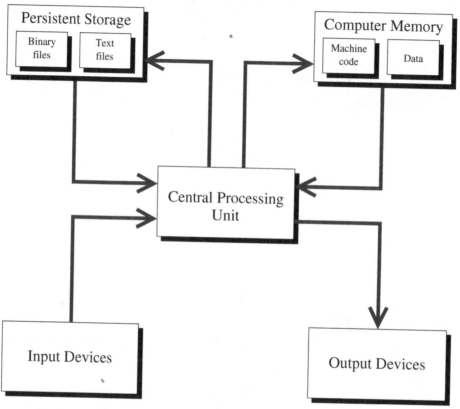

You will have used an **operating system** and various **application program**s, but thanks to modern integrated environments, it is possible you have not appreciated the difference. In this book you are going to learn how to write application programs.

Concept **Computer basics: software: operating system.** A collection of **software** which is dedicated to making the computer generally usable, rather than being able to solve a *particular* task, is known as an **operating system**. The most popular examples for modern personal computers are Microsoft Windows, Mac OS X and Linux. The latter two are implementations of Unix, which was first conceived in the early 1970s. The fact it is still in widespread use today, especially by computer professionals, is proof that it is a thoroughly stable and well **design**ed and integrated platform for the expert (or budding expert) computer scientist.

Concept **Computer basics: software: application program.** A piece of **software** which is dedicated to solving a particular task, or application, is known as an **application program**. For example, an image editing program.

Computers typically produce and process **file**s, but what are they?

Concept **Computer basics: data: files.** When **data** is stored in **persistent storage**, such as on a **hard disc**, it is organized into chunks of related information known as **files**. Files have names and can be accessed by the computer through the **operating system**. For example, the image from a digital camera would probably be stored in a jpeg file, which is a particular type of image file, and the name of this file would probably end in .jpg or .jpeg.

Concept **Computer basics: data: files: text files.** A **text file** is a type of **file** that contains **data** stored directly as **character**s in a human readable form. This means if you were to send the raw contents directly to the printer, you would (for most printers) be immediately able to read it. Examples of text files include README.txt that sometimes comes with **software** you are installing, or source text for a document to be processed by the LATEX[6] document processing system, such as the ones used to produce this book. As you will see shortly, a more interesting example for you right now, is computer program **source code** files.

Concept **Computer basics: data: files: binary files.** A **binary file** is another kind of **file** in which **data** is stored as **binary** (base 2) numbers, and so is not human readable. For example, the image from a digital camera is probably stored as a jpeg file, and if you were to look directly at its contents, rather than use some **application program** to display it, you would see what appears to be nonsense! An interesting example of a binary file is the **machine code** instructions of a program.

1.4 What is a program?

AIM: To look at what we mean by a computer program, particularly in Java, and how it is produced and processed.

If you have not programmed before, then your idea of a computer program might be that it is something that comes on a **DVD ROM**, you install it on your computer and then you can **run** or **execute** it. When you run it, it does something and finally it ends – perhaps when you exit from its **user interface**. This is a good starting point for what a computer program is.

How does a computer program get onto that DVD? A programmer must first write the program in a programming language, such as Java. This essentially involves creating pieces of text that express the meaning of the program and storing them in one or more **text file**s. These are the **source code file**s for the program.

Concept **Java tools: text editor.** A **text editor** is a program that allows the user to type and edit **text file**s. You may well have used notepad under Microsoft Windows; that is a text editor. More likely you have used Microsoft Word. If you have, you should note that it is not a text editor, it is a **word processor**. Although you can save your documents as text files, it is more common to save them as .doc **files**, which is actually a **binary file** format. Microsoft Word is not a good tool to use for creating program **source code** files.

If you are using an **integrated development environment** to support your programming, then the text editor will be built in to it. If not, there are a plethora of text editors available which are suited to Java programming.

In its simplest perspective, a program consists of a sequence of instructions that the programmer wishes the computer to obey or execute. The **source code** files written by the programmer are processed by another, special, computer program called a **compiler**. A compiler checks the program it is given to process, and if it satisfies the various rules of the programming language, it produces a version of the program that can be executed, or run, by the computer.

For many programming languages, this **compiled** form of the instructions in the program is expressed in **machine code**. This is the kind of **low level language** that the processor of the computer can execute directly. Modern programming languages are **high level languages** which means that one instruction in the source program is typically translated (compiled) into many simpler instructions in machine code.

Different kinds of processors have different machine code languages, so, for example, it is not possible for a program that was compiled for Intel X86 processors to run on a SUN UltraSPARC processor. Java gets around this portability problem by having a low level language that is processor independent. This language is called **byte code**. The Java compiler creates a byte code version of a Java program from its source text, and then this byte code is executed by another special program called an **interpreter** or **virtual machine**. Such a program acts like a computer processor executing low level instructions: hence the name *virtual* machine.

The following diagram shows the steps of a Java program being created by a programmer, and being run by an end user.

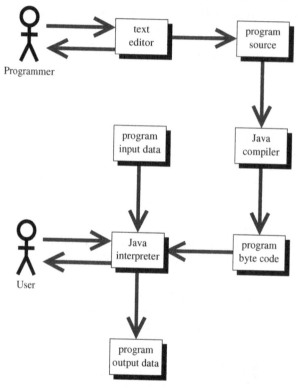

1.5 Operating environment

AIM:
> To explore the relationship between a program and the **operating system** it is **run** on. We see that programs are commands, with **command line arguments**, and meet **standard output**.

Regardless of which **operating system** you are using, and whether or not you are using an **integrated development environment** to support your Java programming, it is essential that you appreciate what happens when a program is **executed**.

Concept **Operating environment: programs are commands.** When a program is **execute**d, the name of it is passed to the **operating system** which finds and loads the **file** of that name, and then starts the program. This might be hidden from you if you are used to starting programs from a menu or browser interface, but it happens nevertheless.

Under Microsoft Windows we can best appreciate this principle by **run**ning a program from within a **Command Prompt** window.

The following screen dump shows a run of a program called date which displays the current date and then prompts for the user to change it.

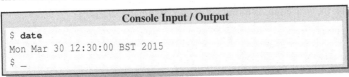

After the prompt (C:\>) the user has typed the command name date. This causes the operating system to find the program with that name (actually date.exe), load it and then run it.

Throughout this book we use a Unix, or more precisely, a Linux environment to run programs because that is the preferred choice of the author. It really doesn't matter though, as the fundamental concepts involved in programming are independent of the **operating environment**. So, as another example of running a program, let us briefly look at a similar program called date which typically comes as standard with Unix. We can run this by typing the command into the Unix command interface, or **shell**. (This is rather like a Command Prompt window on Microsoft Windows.) For simplicity, we are assuming the prompt given by the Unix shell is a simple dollar ($) followed by a space. What the user types after this we show in **bold face**. Lines which follow such **command line**s are the output from that command.

Console Input / Output
$ **date**
Mon Mar 30 12:30:00 BST 2015
$ _

You can see that when the program is run it simply prints the current date and time on its **standard output**, i.e. on the screen.

Concept **Operating environment: standard output.** When programs **execute**, they have something called the **standard output** in which they can produce text results. If they are **run** from some kind of **command line interface**, such as a Unix **shell** or a Microsoft Windows **Command Prompt**, then this output appears in that interface while the program is running. (If they are invoked through some **integrated development environment**, browser, or menu, then this output might get displayed in some pop-up box, or special console window.)

The Unix date program accepts a wide variety of possible **command line argument**s which vary its behaviour.

For example, we can ask it to print just today's date in day/month/year format.

Console Input / Output
$ **date "+%d/%m/%Y"**
30/03/2015
$ _

We can even get the date in a rather verbose form if we wish.

Console Input / Output
$ **date "+Today is %A, day %d of %B in the year %Y"**
Today is Monday, day 30 of March in the year 2015
$ _

If you are using Unix, you can find out more about the date program by looking at its documentation (e.g. by typing man date).

The idea of command line arguments is not specific to Unix.

For example, the Microsoft Windows date command can be given the /t argument which tells it not to prompt for a new date.

> *Concept* **Operating environment: command line arguments.** Programs can be, and often are, given **command line arguments** to vary their behaviour.

This is typical of computer programs: they have a purpose, but exactly what they do often depends on what arguments they are given. In the next section you will meet the standard Java tools for processing programs. These act on the program named by a given argument. In the next chapter, you will see how to *write* Java programs which vary their behaviour based on arguments!

As another example of a program that takes a command line argument, and to prove that this principle applies as much to Microsoft Windows as it does to Unix, let us consider what happens in Windows when the user clicks on an icon that represents a **text file**, e.g. one called MyText.txt. At that moment, a command line is created, which by default would be notepad "MyText.txt" and this is then executed.[1] The program notepad is thus started with the command line argument which is the name of the **file** that notepad should open. If you wish to check what will actually happen on your Windows XP computer then do the following. (Unfortunately, the procedure is more obscure on Windows Vista/7.)

- Open a file browser (e.g. start My Computer).

- Click on the Tools menu and select Folder options...

- In the resulting window, select the File Types tab.

- In the Registered file types list, scroll down and select the line for the extension TXT.

- Click on Advanced.

- In the new window, select open and click on Edit....

- In the text field entitled Application used to perform action: you might see something like C:\WINDOWS\system32\NOTEPAD.EXE %1. This is the command that is executed, except that %1 is replaced by the path and name of the file that the user clicked on.

- Presumably you do not want to change this, so click on Cancel, then on Cancel on each of the two previous windows.

1.6 Example: Our first Java program

AIM:
> To show the mechanics of processing a finished Java source program so that it can be **run**, through to actually running it.

---
[1]Actually, this filename is preceded by the path of the folder containing the file.

Our first example program is one which simply prints the message Hello world! on the **standard output**. Here is its **source code**. The line numbers are not part of the **file** – they are just used in code listings in this book to save you having to count the lines when you want to locate a particular one.

 Coffee time: [1.6.1] We shall study this source code in detail in the next chapter, however for now you should try and guess which line of code is the instruction that makes the message appear on the standard output.

```
001: public class HelloWorld
002: {
003:    public static void main(String[] args)
004:    {
005:       System.out.println("Hello world!");
006:    }
007: }
```

This source code would be typed by the programmer and saved in a file called HelloWorld.java. Depending on the **text editor** being used, certain words might be shown as highlighted in some way, like in the example above. In this book we present the programs as though the programmer is using a stand alone text editor to produce the source code, and then invoking the **compiler** and **virtual machine** from a **command line**. This is because the author believes that is the best environment in which to get a good grasp of what is going on. (However, see Section 1.6.3 on page 11 if you are planning to use an **integrated development environment**.)

Having produced the source code, the next step is to get the Java **compiler** to process it.

Concept **Java tools: javac compiler.** The Java **compiler** is called javac. Java program source is saved by the programmer in a **text file** that has the suffix .java. For example, the text file HelloWorld.java might contain the source text of a program that prints Hello world! on the **standard output**. This text file can then be **compiled** by the Java compiler, by giving its name as a **command line argument**. Thus the command

```
javac HelloWorld.java
```

will produce the **byte code** version of it in the **file** HelloWorld.class. Like **machine code** files, byte code is stored in **binary file**s as numbers, and so is not human readable.

Then to **run** the program, we invoke the Java **interpreter** or **virtual machine** with the program name as its **command line argument**.

Concept **Java tools: java interpreter.** When the end user wants to run a Java program, he or she invokes the java **interpreter** with the name of the program as its **command line argument**. The program must, of course, have been **compiled** first! For example, to run the HelloWorld program we would issue the following command.

```
java HelloWorld
```

This makes the **central processing unit** run the interpreter or **virtual machine** java, which itself then **execute**s the program named as its first argument. Notice that the suffix .java is needed when compiling the program, but no suffix is used when **run**ning it. In our example here, the virtual machine finds the **byte code** for the program in the **file** HelloWorld.class which must have been previously produced by the **compiler**.

1.6.1 Trying it

We enter the program **source code** into our **text editor** and save it in the **text file** `HelloWorld.java`.

Remember, we are assuming the prompt given by the Unix **shell** is a simple dollar ($) followed by a space. So lines starting with that prompt are commands typed by the user, and lines which follow are the **standard output** from that command.

On Unix we can see that the text file has been created, using the `ls` command, and the `-l` **command line argument** makes `ls` show us when the file was changed or created, along with other information about it.

```
                    Console Input / Output
$ ls -l HelloWorld.java
-rw-------   1 jtl jtl 117 Mar 30 12:30 HelloWorld.java
$ _
```

Then we **compile** the program by **run**ning the Java **compiler**, `javac`.

```
                    Console Input / Output
$ javac HelloWorld.java
$ _
```

This has produced an extra **file** for us, as is shown by running the `ls` command again, this time with an argument that will show all files whose names start with `HelloWorld..`

```
                    Console Input / Output
$ ls -l HelloWorld.*
-rw-------   1 jtl jtl 426 Mar 30 12:30 HelloWorld.class
-rw-------   1 jtl jtl 117 Mar 30 12:30 HelloWorld.java
$ _
```

Now we can run the program and see that it does simply say `Hello World!` on its **standard output**.

```
                    Console Input / Output
$ java HelloWorld
Hello world!
$ _
```

1.6.2 Running under Microsoft Windows

If you are using Microsoft Windows instead of Linux, then the process really is much the same, as this screen dump of a **Command Prompt** window shows.

```
Command Prompt                                                  - □ ×
D:\JJIT\Example 1.6>dir HelloWorld.java
 Volume in drive D is DATA
 Volume Serial Number is 5C90-0C33

 Directory of D:\JJIT\Example 1.6

30/03/2015  12:30                    125 HelloWorld.java
               1 File(s)             125 bytes
               0 Dirs(s)   8,389,459,968 bytes free

D:\JJIT\Example 1.6>javac HelloWorld.java

D:\JJIT\Example 1.6>dir HelloWorld.*
 Volume in drive D is DATA
 Volume Serial Number is 5C90-0C33

 Directory of D:\JJIT\Example 1.6

30/03/2015  12:30                    125 HelloWorld.java
30/03/2015  12:30                    426 HelloWorld.class
               2 File(s)             551 bytes
               0 Dirs(s)   8,389,459,968 bytes free

D:\JJIT\Example 1.6>java HelloWorld
Hello World!

D:\JJIT\Example 1.6>
```

1.6.3 Using an integrated development environment

If you choose to use an **integrated development environment** instead of the **command line** the process is still much the same, however it may be a little obscured from you. The following screen dump shows the **Eclipse** integrated development environment with the HelloWorld source code in its text editor.

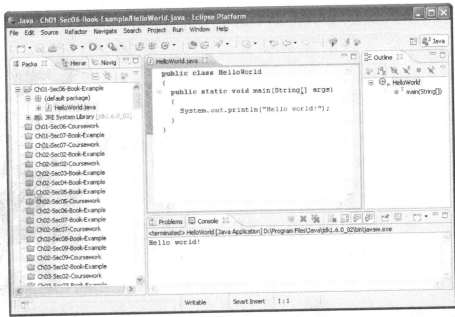

In such environments, the compiler is invoked simply by pressing a button, or even automatically. If you are using one, it is important for you to realize that underneath this convenience the environment is actually running javac. In this book we shall keep the fundamental principles exposed by showing the compiler being run explicitly by the programmer.

The same is true about running the program during development – in an integrated development environment this is probably achieved by pressing a button. In this book we shall keep exposed the fundamental step of invoking the Java **virtual machine**.

1.6.4 Coursework: Compile and run HelloWorld

Carefully type in the **source code** for the HelloWorld program, and save it in the appropriately named **file**. Check it to make sure you have not made any typing errors – otherwise you may get error messages that will alarm you! (Try to get the **indentation** right – e.g. line 3 has two spaces at the front, and line 5 has four.) Now **compile** and **run** it. Record your progress and any observations you make, in your logbook.

1.7 Example: Our second Java program

AIM: To reinforce the process of the **compile** and **run** cycle of a Java program.

Our second program says hello (or goodbye, as appropriate...) to all nine planets! This too will be covered in detail in the next chapter.

```
001: public class HelloSolarSystem
002: {
003:   public static void main(String[] args)
004:   {
```

```
005:        System.out.println("Hello Mercury!");
006:        System.out.println("Hello Venus!");
007:        System.out.println("Hello Earth!");
008:        System.out.println("Hello Mars!");
009:        System.out.println("Hello Jupiter!");
010:        System.out.println("Hello Saturn!");
011:        System.out.println("Hello Uranus!");
012:        System.out.println("Hello Neptune!");
013:        System.out.println("Goodbye Pluto!");
014:    }
015: }
```

1.7.1   Trying it

We enter the program **source code** into our **text editor** and save it in the **text file** HelloSolarSystem.java.

We can see that this **file** has been created, using the ls command.

```
                          Console Input / Output
$ ls -l HelloSolarSystem.java
-rw-------  1 jtl jtl 452 Mar 30 12:30 HelloSolarSystem.java
$ _
```

Then we **compile** the **class** by **run**ning the Java **compiler**, javac.

```
                          Console Input / Output
$ javac HelloSolarSystem.java
$ _
```

This has produced an extra file for us.

```
                          Console Input / Output
$ ls -l HelloSolarSystem.*
-rw-------  1 jtl jtl 687 Mar 30 12:30 HelloSolarSystem.class
-rw-------  1 jtl jtl 452 Mar 30 12:30 HelloSolarSystem.java
$ _
```

Now we can run the program and see the results on its **standard output**.

```
                          Console Input / Output
$ java HelloSolarSystem
Hello Mercury!
Hello Venus!
Hello Earth!
Hello Mars!
Hello Jupiter!
Hello Saturn!
Hello Uranus!
Hello Neptune!
Goodbye Pluto!
$ _
```

1.7.2   Coursework: Compile and run HelloSolarSystem

Carefully type in the **source code** for the HelloSolarSystem program, and save it in the appropriately named **file**. Check it to make sure you have not made any typing errors – otherwise you may get error messages that will alarm you! (Try to get the **indentation** right – e.g. line 3 has two spaces at the front, and line 5 has four.) Now **compile** and **run** it. Record your progress and any observations in your logbook.

1.8 Concepts covered in this chapter

Here is a list of the concepts that were covered in this chapter, each with a self-test question. You can use this to check you remember them being introduced, and perhaps re-read some of them before going on to the next chapter.

Computer basics	
– data (p.3)	List two examples of data.
– data: files (p.5)	What are files used for?
– data: files: text files (p.5)	What are text files used for? What is the most interesting example of a text file in the context of Java programming?
– data: files: binary files (p.5)	What are binary files used for? What is the most interesting example of a binary file in the context of programming?
– hardware (p.3)	What can you do to hardware that you cannot do to software?
– hardware: processor (p.3)	What does the central processing unit actually do, and how clever is it?
– hardware: memory (p.3)	Why is computer memory called RAM and what is the consequence of it being volatile?
– hardware: persistent storage (p.3)	What does persistent storage have that RAM does not, and vice versa?
– hardware: input and output devices (p.3)	Name two input devices and two output devices.
– software (p.3)	Where does software live?
– software: machine code (p.3)	Give two examples of what a machine code instruction might be.
– software: operating system (p.4)	Name two operating systems.
– software: application program (p.4)	What is the difference between an application program and an operating system?

Java tools	
– text editor (p.5)	In the context of Java programming, what is a text editor used for?
– javac compiler (p.9)	What files are produced by the javac compiler?
– java interpreter (p.9)	Which filename suffix is *not* needed when using `java`?

Operating environment	
– programs are commands (p.7)	What happens when a program is executed?
– standard output (p.7)	What is the standard output used for?
– command line arguments (p.8)	What are command line arguments used for? Give an example of one.

Chapter 2

Sequential execution and program errors

> One long distance
> is simply a lot of short steps
> in the right direction.

2.1 Chapter aims

In this chapter we introduce some very basic Java concepts, including the idea that a program embodies the principle of **sequential execution** of a list of instructions.

We also look at the kinds of errors we can have in our programs. This is necessary because, whether you like it or not, you will make errors – especially early on! By explicitly exploring them at this stage you will be less afraid of them when they happen, and see them as simply part of the programming experience.

The chapter contains the following sections.

Section	Aims	Associated Coursework
2.2 Hello world (p.16)	To introduce some very basic Java concepts, including the **main method** and System.out.println().	Write a program to greet the whole world, in French! (p.20)
2.3 Hello world with a syntactic error (p.20)	To introduce the principle of program errors, in partic- ular **syntactic errors**. We also see that a **string literal** must be ended on the same line its starts on.	Take a given program that has **syntac- tic error**s in it, and get it working. (p.21)
2.4 Hello world with a semantic error (p.22)	To introduce **semantic errors** and note that these and **syntactic errors** are **compile time errors**.	Take a given program that has **seman- tic error**s in it, and get it working. (p.22)
2.5 Hello solar system (p.23)	To introduce the principle of **sequential execution**.	Write a program to greet some of your family. (p.24)
2.6 Hello solar system with a run time error (p.24)	To introduce the principle of **run time errors**.	Take a given program that has **run time error**s in it, and get it working. (p.26)
2.7 Hello anyone (p.26)	To introduce the principle of making Java programs per- form a variation of their task based on **command line arguments**, which can be accessed via an **index**. We also meet string **concatenation**.	Write a program to say how wonderful the user is. (p.29)

Section	Aims	Associated Coursework
2.8 Hello anyone with a logical error (p.29)	To introduce the principle of **logical errors**.	Take a given program that has **logical errors** in it, and get it working. (p.30)
2.9 Hello solar system, looking at the layout (p.31)	To begin to explore the decisions behind the way we lay out the **source code** for a program.	Take a given program and lay it out properly. (p.32)

2.2 Example: Hello world

AIM:
To introduce some very basic Java concepts, including the **main method** and `System.out.println()`.

Our first example program is one which simply prints the message `Hello World!` on the **standard output**.

Concept **Class: programs are divided into classes.** In Java, the source text for a program is separated into pieces called **class**es. The source text for each class is (usually) stored in a separate **file**. Classes have a name, and if the name is `HelloWorld` then the text for the class is saved by the programmer in the **text file** `HelloWorld.java`.

One reason for dividing programs into pieces is to make them easier to manage – programs to perform complex tasks typically contain thousands of lines of text. Another reason is to make it easier to share the pieces between more than one program – such **software reuse** is beneficial to programmer productivity.

Every program has at least one class. The name of this class shall reflect the intention of the program. By convention, class names start with an upper case letter.

There are further reasons for dividing a program into separate **class**es which we shall meet later, but to start with, our programs will have just one.

Concept **Class: public class.** A **class** can be declared as being **public**, which means it can be accessed from anywhere in the running Java environment; in particular the **virtual machine** itself can access it. The source text for a public class definition starts with the **reserved word `public`**. A reserved word is one which is part of the Java language, rather than a word chosen by the programmer for use as, say, the name of a program.

Concept **Class: definition.** After stating whether it has **public** access, a **class** next has the **reserved word `class`**, then its name, then a left brace ({), its body of text and finally a closing right brace (}).

```
public class MyFabulousProgram
{
   ... Lots of stuff here.
}
```

The heading for our `HelloWorld` class is as follows.

```
001: public class HelloWorld
```

Then we have the opening bracket.

```
002: {
```

16

Inside the brackets of the **class** we have the **source code** for the **main method**.

Concept **Method: main method: programs contain a main method.** All Java programs contain a section of code called main, and this is where the computer will start to **execute** the program. Such sections of code are called **method**s because they contain instructions on how to do something. The **main method** always starts with the following heading.

```
public static void main(String[] args)
```

The main method is a section of code called main, but what is the meaning of the three words that appear before that name?

Concept **Method: main method: is public.** The **main method** starts with the **reserved word public**, which means it can be accessed from anywhere in the running Java environment. This is necessary – the program could not be **run** by the **virtual machine** if the starting point was not accessible to it.

```
public
```

Concept **Method: main method: is static.** The **main method** of the program has the **reserved word static** which means it is allowed to be used in the **static context**. A context relates to the use of **computer memory** during the **run**ning of the program. When the **virtual machine** loads a program, it creates the static context for it, allocating computer memory to store the program and its **data**, etc.. A **dynamic context** is a certain kind of allocation of memory which is made later, during the running of the program. The program would not be able to start if the main method was not allowed to run in the static context.

```
public static
```

Concept **Method: main method: is void.** In general, a **method** (section of code) might calculate some kind of **function** or formula, and **return** the answer as a result. For example, the result might be a number. If a method returns a result then this must be stated in its heading. If it does not, then we write the **reserved word void**, which literally means (among other definitions) 'without contents'. The **main method** does not return a value.

```
public static void
```

Concept **Method: main method: is the program starting point.** The starting part, or **main method**, of the program is always called main, because it is the main part of the program.

```
public static void main
```

Okay, so what is the meaning of the words in the brackets following the name? You will recall from the last chapter that, in general, programs are given **command line arguments**.

Concept **Command line arguments: program arguments are passed to main.** Programs can be given **command line argument**s which typically affect their behaviour. Arguments given to a Java program are strings of text **data**, and there can be any number of them in a **list**. In Java, String[] means 'list of strings'. We have to give a name for this list, and usually we call it args. The chosen name allows us to refer to the given data from within the program, should we wish to.

```
public static void main(String[] args)
```

17

Concept **Method: main method: always has the same heading.** The **main method** of a Java program must always have a heading like this.

```
public static void main(String[] args)
```

This is true even if we do not intend to use any **command line arguments**. So a typical single **class** program might look like the following.

```
public class MyFabulousProgram
{
  public static void main(String[] args)
  {
    ... Stuff here to perform the task.
  }
}
```

Continuing with our `HelloWorld` program, the main method has the usual heading, and then we have a left brace({) to mark the start of the body of the **method**.

```
003:  public static void main(String[] args)
004:  {
```

Inside this body, we want to make the program print a **string literal** on the standard output.

Concept **Type: String: literal.** In Java, we can have a **string literal**, that is a fixed piece of text to be used as **data**, by enclosing it in double quotes. It is called a string literal, because it is a **type** of data which is a string of **characters**, exactly as listed. Such a piece of data might be used as a message to the user.

```
"This is a fixed piece of text data -- a string literal"
```

Concept **Standard API: System: out.println().** The simplest way to print a message on **standard output** is to use:

```
System.out.println("This text will appear on standard output");
```

`System` is a **class** (that is, a piece of code) that comes with Java as part of its **application program interface (API)** – a large number of classes designed to support our Java programs. Inside `System` there is a thing called `out`, and this has a **method** (section of code) called `println`. So overall, this method is called `System.out.println`. The method takes a string of text given to it in its brackets, and displays that text on the standard output of the program.

So the body of our `HelloWorld` main method contains one **statement** or instruction.

```
005:    System.out.println("Hello world!");
```

Did you spot the semi-colon (;) at the end of the line?

Concept **Statement.** A command in a programming language, such as Java, which makes the computer perform a task is known as a **statement**. `System.out.println("I will output whatever I am told to")` is an example of a statement.

Concept **Statement: simple statements are ended with a semi-colon.** All simple **statements** in Java must be ended by a semi-colon (;). This is a rule of the Java language **syntax**.

Coffee time: 2.2.1 Can you think of a reason why Java insists on the programmer putting a semi-colon at the end of statements?

To mark the end of the body of the main method, we have a closing right brace (}).

```
006:    }
```

Finally, the class is ended with its closing brace!

```
007: }
```

2.2.1 The full `HelloWorld` code

```
001: public class HelloWorld
002: {
003:    public static void main(String[] args)
004:    {
005:      System.out.println("Hello world!");
006:    }
007: }
```

2.2.2 Trying it

We enter the program **source code** into our **text editor** and save it in the **text file** HelloWorld.java.

Let us check that the text file has been created.

```
                       Console Input / Output
$ ls -l HelloWorld.java
-rw-------   1 jtl jtl 117 Mar 30 12:30 HelloWorld.java
$ _
```

Then we **compile** the **class** by **run**ning the Java **compiler**, javac.

```
                       Console Input / Output
$ javac HelloWorld.java
$ _
```

This has produced an extra **file** for us.

```
                       Console Input / Output
$ ls -l HelloWorld.*
-rw-------   1 jtl jtl 426 Mar 30 12:30 HelloWorld.class
-rw-------   1 jtl jtl 117 Mar 30 12:30 HelloWorld.java
$ _
```

Now we can run the program and see that it does simply say Hello world! on its **standard output**.

```
                       Console Input / Output
$ java HelloWorld
Hello world!
$ _
```

19

2.2.3   Coursework: `HelloWorld` in French

Write a new version of `HelloWorld` which gives its greeting in French (or any other language of your choice, apart from English). You will learn most if you try to do this without looking at the original version. Your program should still be called `HelloWorld`, as only the message **data** is in French. Type the program in and save it in the appropriately named **file**. Check it against the original to see you have not made any mistakes – otherwise you may get error messages that will alarm you. Then **compile** and **run** it.

2.3   Example: Hello world with a syntactic error

AIM:
> To introduce the principle of program errors, in particular **syntactic error**s. We also see that a **string literal** must be ended on the same line its starts on.

We are now going to look at a version of the `HelloWorld` program that has a **syntactic error** in it.

Concept **Error.** When we write the **source code** for a Java program, it is very easy for us to get something wrong. In particular, there are lots of rules of the language that our program must obey in order for it to be a valid program.

Concept **Error: syntactic error.** One kind of error we might make in our programs is **syntactic error**s. This is when we break the **syntax** rules of the language. For example, we might miss out a closing bracket, or insert an extra one, etc.. This is rather like missing out a word in a sentence of natural language, making it grammatically incorrect. The sign below, seen strapped to the back of a poodle, contains bad grammar – it has an `is` missing.

My other dog an Alsatian.

Syntactic errors in Java result in the **compiler** giving us an error message. They can possibly confuse the compiler, resulting in it thinking many more things are wrong too!

Here is our program code.

```
001: public class HelloWorld
002: {
003:   public static void main(String[] args)
004:   {
005:     System.out.println("Hello world!");
006:   }
007: }
```

 Coffee time: Can you spot the **syntactic error**?

2.3.1

2.3.1   Trying it

We **compile** the **class**.

```
Console Input / Output
$ javac HelloWorld.java
HelloWorld.java:5: unclosed string literal
    System.out.println("Hello world!);

HelloWorld.java:5: ';' expected
    System.out.println("Hello world!);
                                      ^
HelloWorld.java:7: reached end of file while parsing
}
^
3 errors
$ _
```

Error messages from the **compiler** can look very daunting at first. However, if you read them carefully you can work out what their meaning is. They start with the name of the **source code text file**, the line number at which the compiler thinks the error is situated, and then a message indicating the nature of the error.

In this case, the compiler has spotted the absence of a closing quote for the **string literal** – it has scanned to the end of the line and not found it.

> *Concept* **Type: `String`: literal: must be ended on the same line.** In Java, **string literal**s must be ended on the same line they are started on.

The compiler can be pretty stupid at figuring out what is wrong with bad code. Having complained about the missing quote, it then has become confused – it thinks the semi-colon is part of the string literal, and so complains that it is missing! And then it gets more confused, causing a third error message.[1]

2.3.2   Coursework: `Fortune` syntactic errors

Carefully type in the following program *exactly*. It contains some deliberate mistakes – type them in anyway even if you spot them as you read the code.

```
001: public class Fortune
002: {
003:   public static void main[String() args]
004:   {
005:     System.out,println('Sometimes having a fortune is too expensive!");
006:   }
007: }
```

Now **compile** the program and examine the error messages. Record these in your logbook, each along with your best attempt to explain the meaning and the cause of it. Can you see any errors which appear not to have caused a message? If so, record these too.

Now fix the errors *one at a time*, and compile the program in between. Record any new error messages that appear, along with your explanation for them.

Optional extra: Make the smallest number of edits to your `HelloWorld` program so as to have `javac` produce the largest number of **syntactic errors**! For example, what happens if you simply delete a space between two words of the program?

---

[1]Depending on the exact version of Java you are using, you may get different error messages – the compiler may be more, or less, confused.

2.4 Example: Hello world with a semantic error

AIM:
To introduce **semantic errors** and note that these and **syntactic errors** are **compile time errors**.

We are now going to look at a version of the `HelloWorld` program that has a **semantic error** in it.

> *Concept* **Error: semantic error.** Another kind of error we might make is a **semantic error**, when we obey the rules of the **syntax** but what we have written does not make any sense – it has no semantics (meaning). Another sign on a different poodle might say
>
> > My other dog is a Porsche.
>
> which is senseless because a Porsche is a kind of car, not a dog.

> *Concept* **Error: compile time error.** Java **syntactic errors** and many **semantic errors** can be detected for us by the **compiler** when it processes our program.[2] Errors that the compiler can detect are called **compile time errors**.

Here is our program code.

```
001: public class HelloWorld
002: {
003:   public static void main(Text[] args)
004:   {
005:     System.out.println("Hello world!");
006:   }
007: }
```

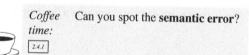

Coffee time: Can you spot the **semantic error**?
2.4.1

2.4.1 Trying it

We **compile** the **class**.

```
                    Console Input / Output
$ javac HelloWorld.java
HelloWorld.java:3: cannot find symbol
symbol  : class Text
location: class HelloWorld
  public static void main(Text[] args)
                         ^
1 error
$ _
```

In this case, the **compiler** has complained that the symbol `Text` does not make sense to it (`cannot find symbol`). Of course, the kind or **type** of the **command line arguments** in Java is called `String[]` rather than `Text[]`. The compiler is not clever enough to 'know what you mean' when you get this sort of thing wrong.

2.4.2 Coursework: `ManchesterWeather` semantic errors

Carefully type in the following program *exactly*. It contains some deliberate mistakes – type them in anyway even if you spot them as you read the code.

---

[2]Semantic errors which are detectable by the compiler are sometimes called **static semantic errors**.

```
001: public class ManchesterWeather
002: {
003:   public static avoid main(spring[] args)
004:   {
005:     Cistern.flush.printline("Rainfalls keep dropping on my head!");
006:   }
007: }
```

Now **compile** the program and examine the error messages. Record these in your logbook, each along with your best attempt to explain the meaning and the cause of it. Can you see any errors which appear not to have caused a message? If so, record these too.

Now fix the errors *one at a time*, and compile the program in between. Record any new error messages that appear, along with your explanation for them.

2.5   Example: Hello solar system

AIM: To introduce the principle of **sequential execution**.

This second program says hello to all eight planets, and goodbye to Pluto. As you may know, poor Pluto is now officially recognized as not being a planet!

Concept **Execution: sequential execution.**   Programs generally consist of more than one **statement**, in a list. We usually place these on separate lines to enhance human readability, although Java does not care about that. Statements in such a list are **executed** sequentially, one after the other. More correctly, the Java **compiler** turns each one into corresponding **byte code**s, and the **virtual machine** executes each collection of byte codes in turn. This is known as **sequential execution**.

```
001: public class HelloSolarSystem
002: {
003:   public static void main(String[] args)
004:   {
005:     System.out.println("Hello Mercury!");
006:     System.out.println("Hello Venus!");
007:     System.out.println("Hello Earth!");
008:     System.out.println("Hello Mars!");
009:     System.out.println("Hello Jupiter!");
010:     System.out.println("Hello Saturn!");
011:     System.out.println("Hello Uranus!");
012:     System.out.println("Hello Neptune!");
013:     System.out.println("Goodbye Pluto!");
014:   }
015: }
```

2.5.1 Trying it

First we **compile** the **class**.

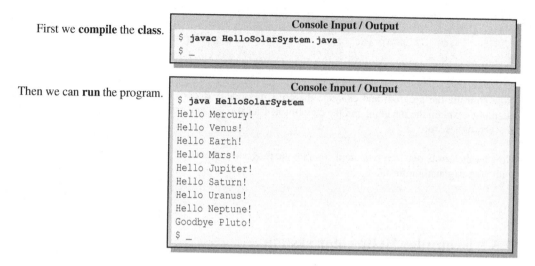

```
                    Console Input / Output
$ javac HelloSolarSystem.java
$ _
```

Then we can **run** the program.

```
                    Console Input / Output
$ java HelloSolarSystem
Hello Mercury!
Hello Venus!
Hello Earth!
Hello Mars!
Hello Jupiter!
Hello Saturn!
Hello Uranus!
Hello Neptune!
Goodbye Pluto!
$ _
```

2.5.2 Coursework: `HelloFamily`

Preferably without looking at `HelloSolarSystem`, write a program called `HelloFamily` which greets your maternal grand parents and all their descendants. Don't forget to include yourself. If you have a lot of relatives, then you may limit your program to around 12 of them if you wish. The greeting must be done in alphabetical order by name – so you had better plan the output before you start typing.

(Hint: one approach would be to type the names into a **text file**, one name per line, and then use some program which **sorts** lines of text – for example the `sort` program. After this the resulting text could be edited to become the final program.)

2.6 Example: Hello solar system with a run time error

AIM:
To introduce the principle of **run time errors**.

We are now going to see an example of a **run time error**.

Concept **Error: run time error.** Another kind of error we can get with programs is **run time errors**. These are errors which are detected when the program is **run** rather than when it is **compiled**.[3] In Java this means the errors are detected and reported by the **virtual machine**, `java`.

Java calls run time errors **exceptions**. Unfortunately, the error messages produced by `java` can look very cryptic to novice programmers. A typical one might be as follows.

```
Exception in thread "main" java.lang.NoSuchMethodError: main
```

You can get the best clue to what has caused the error by just looking at the words either side of the colon (`:`). In the above example, the message is saying that `java` cannot find the **method** called `main`.

---

[3]Runtime errors are sometimes called **dynamic semantic errors**.

Here is the `HelloSolarSystem` program again, this time with an error which is not detectable by the **compiler**.

```
001: public class HelloSolarSystem
002: {
003:   public static void Main(String[] args)
004:   {
005:     System.out.println("Hello Mercury!");
006:     System.out.println("Hello Venus!");
007:     System.out.println("Hello Earth!");
008:     System.out.println("Hello Mars!");
009:     System.out.println("Hello Jupiter!");
010:     System.out.println("Hello Saturn!");
011:     System.out.println("Hello Uranus!");
012:     System.out.println("Hello Neptune!");
013:     System.out.println("Goodbye Pluto!");
014:   }
015: }
```

Coffee time: Can you spot what will cause the **run time error**?

`2.6.1`

2.6.1 Trying it

We **compile** the class.

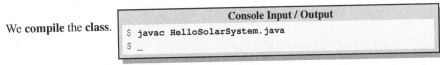

Console Input / Output
`$ javac HelloSolarSystem.java`
`$ _`

This produces no errors from the **compiler**. Now we **run** the program.

Console Input / Output
`$ java HelloSolarSystem`
`Exception in thread "main" java.lang.NoSuchMethodError: main`
`$ _`

The Java **virtual machine** is telling us (rather cryptically) that our program does not contain a **main method**, so the program cannot start. If you look at the source, you will see we called it `Main` – Java names are case sensitive.

An even more obvious example of a **run time error** is when we try to run a program that does not exist.

Console Input / Output
`$ java HelloMum`
`Exception in thread "main" java.lang.NoClassDefFoundError: HelloMum`
`$ _`

Coffee time: Imagine a version of `HelloSolarSystem` which is the same as in Section 2.5 on page 23, with a lower case m on `main`, except that `String[] args` has been omitted. Let us call this version `HelloSolarSystemNoArgs`. Below are the results of compiling and running that program – can you explain them?

`2.6.2`

Console Input / Output
`$ javac HelloSolarSystemNoArgs.java`
`$ java HelloSolarSystemNoArgs`
`Exception in thread "main" java.lang.NoSuchMethodError: main`
`$ _`

2.6.2 Coursework: Quote run time errors

Carefully type in the following program *exactly*. It contains some deliberate mistakes – type them in anyway even if you spot them as you read the code.

```
001: public class Quote
002: {
003:   public void Main(String args)
004:   {
005:     System.out.println("Programming is about making the stupid seem clever.");
006:     System.out.println("                    _ ^ _                    ");
007:     System.out.println(                    0 / 0                    );
008:     System.out.println("                     =                     ");
009:     System.out.println("        (At least, to the dumb user!)        ");
010:   }
011: }
```

Now **compile** the program, and if you have typed it correctly it should compile without errors. However, when you **run** the program you will get an error message. Record this in your logbook, along with your best attempt to explain the meaning and the cause of it.

Now fix the error and run the program again. Record any new error messages that appear, along with your explanation for them.

2.7 Example: Hello anyone

AIM:
To introduce the principle of making Java programs perform a variation of their task based on **command line arguments**, which can be accessed via an **index**. We also meet string **concatenation**.

This program will take a single **command line argument**, for example the name of a person, and then print the message "Hello " (including the space) followed by that name, on the **standard output**.

Concept **Command line arguments: program arguments are accessed by index.** The **command line arguments** given to the **main method** are a **list** of strings. These are the **text data string** arguments supplied on the **command line**. The strings are **index**ed by **integer**s (whole numbers) starting from zero. We can access the individual strings by placing the index value in square brackets after the name of the list. So, assuming that we call the list args, then args[0] is the first command line argument given to the program, if there is one.

Concept **Type: String: concatenation.** The + **operator**, when used with two string **operand**s, produces a string which is the **concatenation** of the two strings. For example "Hello " + "world" produces a string which is Hello (including the space) concatenated with the string world, and so has the same value as "Hello world".

There would not be much point concatenating together two **string literal**s like this, compared with having one string literal which is already the text we want. We would be more likely to use concatenation when at least one of the operands is not a fixed value, i.e. is a **variable** value. For example, "Hello " + args[0] produces a string which is Hello (including the space) concatenated with the first **command line argument** given when the program is **run**.

The resulting string can be used anywhere that a single string literal could be used. For example System.out.println("Hello " + args[0]) would print the resulting string on the **standard output**.

Coffee time: 2.7.1   Can you think of a situation when we would wish to use **concatenation** to join two **string literals** together?

```
001: public class HelloAnyone
002: {
003:   public static void main(String[] args)
004:   {
005:     System.out.println("Hello " + args[0]);
006:   }
007: }
```

2.7.1 Trying it

First we **compile** the class.

> **Console Input / Output**
> ```
> $ javac HelloAnyone.java
> $ _
> ```

Then we can **run** the program with various **command line argument**s.

> **Console Input / Output**
> ```
> $ java HelloAnyone John
> Hello John
> $ java HelloAnyone Lizzy
> Hello Lizzy
> $ _
> ```

If we do not supply an argument, we will get a **run time error** when the program tries to access the first item in the **list** of arguments.

> **Console Input / Output**
> ```
> $ java HelloAnyone
> Exception in thread "main" java.lang.ArrayIndexOutOfBoundsException: 0
>         at HelloAnyone.main(HelloAnyone.java:5)
> $ _
> ```

Notice that java has told us the source **file** name and line number corresponding to the point in the **byte code** at which it detected the error.

We might want to run the program with an argument that contains a space. We can achieve this by putting quotes around the string on the command line.

> **Console Input / Output**
> ```
> $ java HelloAnyone "John Latham"
> Hello John Latham
> $ _
> ```

If we did not write the quotes, then the string would be treated as two arguments instead of one. For this program, the second argument would simply be ignored.

> **Console Input / Output**
> ```
> $ java HelloAnyone John Latham
> Hello John
> $ _
> ```

Finally, let us try the program with an empty string as its argument. Note that this is different from running the program with no argument.

> **Console Input / Output**
> ```
> $ java HelloAnyone ""
> Hello
> $ _
> ```

If we were using Microsoft Windows instead of Linux, then the process really would be much the same, as this screen dump of a **Command Prompt** window shows.

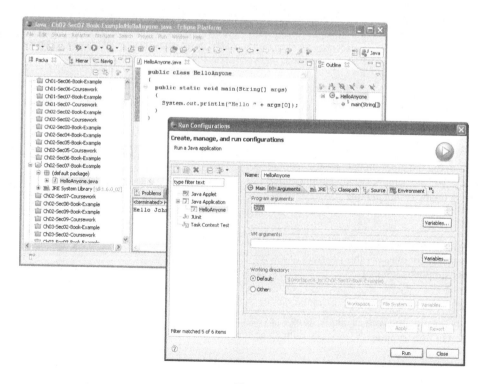

When using an **integrated development environment** we may need to enter command line arguments in a separate window. The following shows **Eclipse** with the `HelloAnyone` **source code** in its **text editor**, and the Run Configurations window being used to set the program argument.

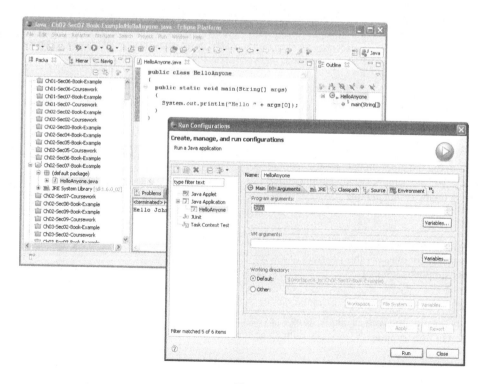

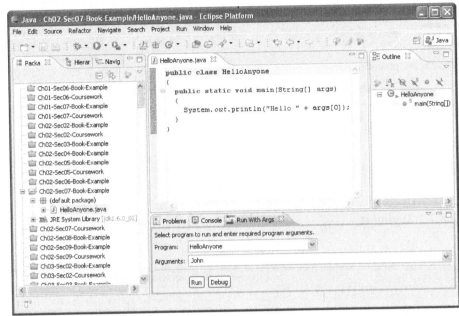

If you are using Eclipse, you may wish to download a plug-in from the book's website which makes this easier, as illustrated here.

From now on in this book we shall show only the Linux **command line** environment when running the examples, and you should be able to translate this to whatever environment you are using.

2.7.2 Coursework: `FlatterMe`

Without looking at `HelloAnyone`, write a program called `FlatterMe` which flatters the person named as the first **command line argument**, three times. The first comment should start with the person's name, the second should end with it, and the third should have some text either side of the name. (Hint: you will need to use two **concatenation operator**s for that.)

2.8 Example: Hello anyone with a logical error

AIM: To introduce the principle of **logical errors**.

We are now going to look at a version of the `HelloAnyone` program that has a **logical error** in it.

Concept **Error: logical error.** The most tricky kind of error we can make in our programs is a **logical error**. For these mistakes we do not get an error message from the **compiler**, nor do we get one at **run time** from the **virtual machine**. These are the kind of errors for which the Java program we have written is meaningful as far as Java is concerned, it is just that our program does the wrong thing compared with what we wanted. There is no way the compiler or virtual machine can help us with these kinds of error: they are far, far too stupid to understand the *problem* we were trying to solve with our program.

For this reason, many logical errors, especially very subtle ones, manage to slip through undetected by human program testing, and end up as **bug**s in the final product – we have all heard stories of computer generated demands for unpaid bills with *negative* amounts, etc..

Coffee time: [2.8.1] Search on the internet to find the most notorious examples of **software bugs**.

Here is our program code.

```
001: public class HelloAnyone
002: {
003:   public static void main(String[] args)
004:   {
005:     System.out.println("Hello + args[0]");
006:   }
007: }
```

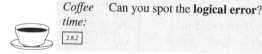

Coffee time: [2.8.2] Can you spot the **logical error**?

2.8.1   Trying it

First we **compile** the class.

Console Input / Output
$ **javac HelloAnyone.java**
$ _

It compiles okay. Then we **run** the program.

Console Input / Output
$ **java HelloAnyone John**
Hello + args[0]
$ _

If you didn't spot it before, then perhaps you can now see our not very subtle **logical error**.

2.8.2   Coursework: **Birthday** logical errors

Carefully type in the following program *exactly*. It contains some deliberate mistakes – type them in anyway even if you spot them as you read the code.

```
001: public class Birthday
002: {
003:   public static void main(String[] args)
004:   {
005:     System.out.print("Name: + args[1] + , " + args[2] + ";");
006:     System.out.println("Born: " + args[0]);
007:   }
008: }
```

Now **compile** the program, and if you have typed it correctly it should compile without errors. Next you should **run** the program with *three* **command line arguments** – the first should be your personal name, the second should be your surname or family name, and the third should be your date of birth, e.g. 24/04/1959.

It is *intended* to print a result like the following.

Console Input / Output
$ **java Birthday John Latham 24/04/1959**
Name: Latham, John; Born: 24/04/1959
$ _

Note the position of spaces and punctuation in the desired output. However you will see that the output you actually get is wrong! Record the errors in your logbook, along with your best attempt to explain the cause of them.

Now fix the errors and run the program again. Record any new errors that appear, along with your explanation for them.

During this process you should have learnt about a **method** which is similar to `System.out.println()`. Record what this method is called and what it does.

2.9 Hello solar system, looking at the layout

AIM: To begin to explore the decisions behind the way we lay out the **source code** for a program.

Before finishing this chapter, we are going to take a closer look at how we lay out the **source code** of our programs to make them easy to read by programmers.

Concept **Code clarity: layout.** Java does not care how we lay our code out, as long as we use some **white space** to separate adjacent symbols that would otherwise be treated as one symbol if they were joined. For example `public void` with no space between the words would be treated as the single symbol `publicvoid` and no doubt cause a **compile time error**. So, if we were crazy, we could write all our program **source code** on one line with the minimum amount of space between symbols!

```
public class HelloSolarSystem{public static void main(String[]args){System.out.println("Hello Mercury!");System.out.println("Hello Venus
```

Oh dear – it ran off the side of the page (and that was with a smaller font too). Let us split it up into separate lines so that it fits on the page.

```
public class HelloSolarSystem{public static void main(String[]args){
System.out.println("Hello Mercury!");System.out.println(
"Hello Venus!");System.out.println("Hello Earth!");System.out.println
("Hello Mars!");System.out.println("Hello Jupiter!");System.out.
println("Hello Saturn!");System.out.println("Hello Uranus!");System.
out.println("Hello Neptune!");System.out.println("Goodbye Pluto!");}}
```

Believe it or not, this program would still **compile** and **run** okay, but hopefully you will agree that it is not very easy for *us* to read. Layout is very important to the human reader, and programmers must take care and pride in laying out their programs as they are written. So we split our program *sensibly*, rather than arbitrarily, into separate lines, and use **indentation** (i.e. spaces at the start of some lines), to maximize the readability of our code.

Let us look at the `HelloSolarSystem` program again.

```
001: public class HelloSolarSystem
```

A **new line** here makes the start of the **class** easily seen.

```
002: {
```

A new line here, plus **indentation**, makes the **main method** easily seen. Two or three spaces is a good choice for indentation – any less makes it too subtle, and any more leads to us having insufficient room on the line when we come to have many levels of indentation.

```
003:   public static void main(String[] args)
```

A new line here, with the same indentation, makes the start of the **method** body easily seen.

```
004:   {
```

A new line here, plus more indentation, helps us see what is inside the method.

```
005:     System.out.println("Hello Mercury!");
```

We put each **statement** on a separate line so they are easily seen, all at the same level of indentation.

```
006:     System.out.println("Hello Venus!");
007:     System.out.println("Hello Earth!");
008:     System.out.println("Hello Mars!");
009:     System.out.println("Hello Jupiter!");
010:     System.out.println("Hello Saturn!");
011:     System.out.println("Hello Uranus!");
012:     System.out.println("Hello Neptune!");
013:     System.out.println("Goodbye Pluto!");
```

A new line here, with spaces to line up with the opening brace of the method, makes it easy to see the end of the method.

```
014:   }
```

A new line here, lining up with the opening brace of the class, makes it easy to see the end of the class.

```
015: }
```

Now that we have analysed the layout of a particular program, let us look at the general principle of indentation.

Concept **Code clarity: layout: indentation.** A **class** contains structures **nested** within each other. The outer-most structure is the class itself, consisting of its heading and then containing it's body within the braces. The body contains items such as the **main method**. This in turn consists of a heading and a body contained within braces.

The idea of **indentation** is that the more nested a part of the code is, the more space it has at the start of its lines. So the class itself has no spaces, but its body, within the braces, has two or three. Then the body of the main method has two or three more. You should be consistent: always use the same number of spaces per nesting level. It is also a good idea to avoid using **tab character**s as they can often look okay on your screen, but not line up properly when the code is printed.

In addition, another rule of thumb is that opening braces ({) should have the same amount of indentation as the matching closing brace (}). You will find that principle being used throughout this book. However, some people prefer a style where opening braces are placed at the end of lines, which this author believes is less clear.

```
public class HelloWorld {

  public static void main(String[] args) {
    System.out.println("Hello world!");
  }
}
```

2.9.1 Coursework: `Limerick` layout

Carefully type in the following program *exactly*. It contains very poor layout – type it in anyway even if you can see how it should be laid out as you read the code.

```
001: public class Limerick{public static void main(String[]args){System.out.
002: println("There was a young user of Java");System.out.println(
003: "Whose coding was such a palava!");System.out.println(
004: "His layout was pooh!");System.out.println(
005: "So what did we do?");System.out.println(
006: "We told him to stick to making coffee!");}}
```

You should **compile** the program, and if you have typed it correctly it should compile and **run** without errors. Record all the instances of poor layout you can see, in your logbook.

Now fix the layout!

2.10   Concepts covered in this chapter

Here is a list of the concepts that were covered in this chapter, each with a self-test question. You can use this to check you remember them being introduced, and perhaps re-read some of them before going on to the next chapter.

Class	
– programs are divided into classes (p.16)	What are two reasons why programs are divided into classes?
– public class (p.16)	What is the first word in the source of a public class?
– definition (p.16)	What is the general form of a class definition?

Code clarity	
– layout (p.31)	What aspect of layout matters to the compiler?
– layout: indentation (p.32)	What is the basic principle behind the way we indent our programs?

Command line arguments	
– program arguments are passed to main (p.17)	What does `String[]` mean?
– program arguments are accessed by index (p.26)	What is the index of the first command line argument and how is that argument accessed?

Error	
Error (p.20)	What is the source of errors?
– syntactic error (p.20)	What is the cause of syntactic errors?
– semantic error (p.22)	What is the cause of semantic errors?
– compile time error (p.22)	What are the two kinds of compile time error?
– run time error (p.24)	Why can the compiler not detect run time errors?
– logical error (p.29)	Why can neither the compiler nor the virtual machine detect logical errors for us?

Execution	
– sequential execution (p.23)	What is the relationship between Java statements being executed sequentially, and byte codes being executed sequentially?

Method	
– main method: programs contain a main method (p.17)	What heading does the main method always have?
– main method: is public (p.17)	Why does the main method have to be public?

Method	
– main method: is static (p.17)	What would be the consequence if the main method was not static?
– main method: is void (p.17)	Does the main method return a value?
– main method: is the program starting point (p.17)	Why is the main method called `main`?
– main method: always has the same heading (p.18)	What is the general form of a single class program?
Standard API	
– System: `out.println()` (p.18)	What is `System`?
Statement	
Statement (p.18)	What does a statement do?
– simple statements are ended with a semi-colon (p.18)	Why?
Type	
– `String`: literal (p.18)	What kind of quotes are used for string literals?
– `String`: literal: must be ended on the same line (p.21)	How is a string literal ended?
– `String`: concatenation (p.26)	What operator is used for concatenation?

Chapter 3

Types, variables and expressions

Precise expression
is the key to clear meaning.

3.1 Chapter aims

In this chapter we introduce the idea that programs process different kinds of values, known as **type**s. We see that such values can be stored in **variable**s, placed there by **assignment statement**s. We also study **arithmetic expression**s, composed from the common **arithmetic operator**s, and observe that these have **operator precedence** and **operator associativity**.

The chapter contains the following sections.

Section	Aims	Associated Coursework
3.2 Age next year (p.36)	To introduce the concepts of **type**, **int**, **variable**, **expression** and **assignment statement**. We also find out how to convert a number to a string, and discover what it means for **data** to be **hard coded**.	Write a program to determine how many years *you* have before you retire! (p.39)
3.3 Age next year – a common misconception (p.39)	To clarify the relationship between **variable**s and **assignment statement**s.	(None.)
3.4 Age next year with a command line argument (p.40)	To introduce the idea of converting a **command line argument** into an **int** and using the value in a program.	Write a program to determine how many years the user has before he or she retires. (p.42)
3.5 Finding the volume of a fish tank (p.42)	To reinforce the use of **command line argument**s and **expression**s, and introduce the idea of splitting up lines of code which are too long, whilst maintaining their readability. We also see that a **variable** can be given a value when it is declared.	Write a program to determine how much fence is needed to surround a rectangular field. (p.44)
3.6 Sum the first N numbers – incorrectly (p.45)	To introduce the principle of **operator precedence**, and have a program containing a **bug**.	Take a program with **bug**s in it, and fix them. (p.47)
3.7 Disposable income (p.47)	To introduce **operator associativity**. We also take a look at the **string literal escape sequence**s.	Write a program to show what weights can be weighed using a balance scale and three given weights. (p.50)

Section	Aims	Associated Coursework
3.8 Sum the first N numbers – correctly (p.52)	To introduce the fact that **integer division** produces a truncated result. We then look at the interaction between that and **operator associativity**.	Write a program to help a child determine whether she has enough pennies to go shopping! (p.53)
3.9 Temperature conversion (p.54)	To introduce the **double type** and some associated concepts, including converting to and from strings, and **double division**.	Write a program to convert a temperature from Fahrenheit to Celsius. (p.57)

3.2 Example: Age next year

AIM:
To introduce the concepts of **type**, `int`, **variable**, **expression** and **assignment statement**. We also find out how to convert a number to a string, and discover what it means for **data** to be **hard coded**.

Our first program knows my age – it is **hard coded** in. When we **run** it, it will compute my age next year and tell me what it will be.

Concept **Design: hard coding.** Programs typically process input **data**, and produce output data. The input data might be given as **command line arguments**, or it might be supplied by the user through some **user interface** such as a **graphical user interface** or **GUI**. It might be obtained from **files** stored on the computer.

Sometimes input data might be built into the program. Such data is said to be **hard coded**. This can be quite common while we are developing a program and we haven't yet written the code that obtains the data from the appropriate place. In other cases it might be appropriate to have it hard coded in the final version of the program, if such data only rarely changes.

The **source code** starts with the usual headings.

```
001: public class AgeNextYear
002: {
003:   public static void main(String[] args)
004:   {
```

The program will process an age, which is a whole number – a particular **type** of **data**.

Concept **Type.** Programs can process various different kinds of **data**, such as numbers, text data, images etc.. The kind of a data item is known as its **type**.

Concept **Type: `int`.** One of the **type**s of **data** we can use in Java is called `int`. A data item which is an `int` is an **integer** (whole number), such as 0, -129934 or 982375, etc..

Concept **Variable.** A **variable** in Java is an entity that can hold a **data** item. It has a name and a value. It is rather like the notion of a variable in algebra (although it is not quite the same thing). The name of a variable does not change – it is carefully chosen by the programmer to reflect the meaning of the entity it represents in relation to the problem being solved by the program. However, the *value* of a variable can (in general) be changed – we can vary it. Hence the name of the concept: a **variable** is an entity that has a (possibly) varying value.

The Java **compiler** implements variables by mapping their names onto **computer memory** locations, in which the values associated with the variables will be stored at **run time**.

So one view of a variable is that it is a box, like a pigeon hole, in which a value can be placed. If we wish, we can get the program to place a different value in that box, replacing the previous; and we can do this as many times as we want to.

Variables only have values at run time, when the program is **run**ning. Their names, created by the programmer, are already fixed by the time the program is **compile**d. Variables also have one more attribute – the **type** of the data they are allowed to contain. This too is chosen by the programmer.

Concept **Variable: int variable.** In Java, **variable**s must be declared in a **variable declaration** before they can be used. This is done by the programmer stating the **type** and then the name of the variable. For example the code

```
int noOfPeopleLivingInMyStreet;
```

declares an **int variable**, that is a variable the value of which will be an **int**, and which has the name noOfPeopleLivingInMyStreet. Observe the semi-colon (;) which, according to the Java **syntax** rules, is needed to terminate the variable declaration. At **run time**, this variable is allowed to hold an **integer** (whole number). Its value can change, but it will always be an **int**. The name of a variable should reflect its intended meaning. In this case, it would seem from its name that the programmer intends the variable to always hold the number of people living in his or her street. The programmer would write code to ensure that this meaning is always reflected by its value at run time.

By convention, variable names start with a lower case letter, and consist of a number of words, with the first letter of each subsequent word capitalized.

In our program for computing my age next year, we want to have two **variable**s.

```
005:    int myAgeNow;
006:    int myAgeNextYear;
```

Our code will need to give a value to these variables.

Concept **Statement: assignment statement.** An **assignment statement** is a Java **statement** which is used to give a value to a **variable**, or change its existing value. This is only allowed if the value we are assigning has a **type** which matches the type of the variable.

Concept **Statement: assignment statement: assigning a literal value.** We can assign a **literal value**, that is a constant, to a **variable** using an **assignment statement** such as the following.

```
noOfPeopleLivingInMyStreet = 47;
```

We use a single **equal sign** (=), with the name of the variable to the left of it, and the value we wish it to be given on the right. In the above example, the **integer literal** 47 will be placed into the variable noOfPeopleLivingInMyStreet. Assuming the variable was declared as an **int variable** then this assignment would be allowed because 47 is an **int**.

In our program for computing my age next year, we wish to give the variable myAgeNow the value of my age, which let us say for sake of some nostalgia, is 18. In doing this, we have hard coded my age into the program.

```
007:    myAgeNow = 18;
```

We shall obtain the value of myAgeNextYear from myAgeNow using an **arithmetic expression**.

Concept **Expression: arithmetic.** We can have **arithmetic expression**s in Java rather like we can in mathematics. These can contain **literal values**, that is constants, such as the **integer literal**s 1 and 18. They can also contain **variable**s which have already been declared, and **operator**s to combine sub-expressions together. Four common **arithmetic operator**s are **addition** (+), **subtraction** (−), **multiplication** (*) and **division** (/). Note the use of an asterisk for multiplication, and a forward slash for division – computer keyboards do not have multiply or divide symbols.

These four operators are **binary infix operator**s, because they take two **operand**s, one on either side of the operator. + and − can also be used as the **unary prefix operator**s, **plus** and **minus** respectively, as in −5.

When an **expression** is **evaluate**d (**expression evaluation**) Java replaces each variable with its current value and works out the result of the expression depending on the meaning of the operators. For example, if the variable noOfPeopleLivingInMyStreet had the value 47 then the expression noOfPeopleLivingInMyStreet + 4 would evaluate to 51.

Concept **Statement: assignment statement: assigning an expression value.** More generally than just assigning a **literal value**, we can use an **assignment statement** to assign the value of an **expression** to a **variable**. For example, assuming we have the variable

```
int noOfPeopleToInviteToTheStreetParty;
```

then the code

```
noOfPeopleToInviteToTheStreetParty = noOfPeopleLivingInMyStreet + 4;
```

when **execute**d, would **evaluate** the expression on the right of the **equal sign** (=) and then place the resulting value in the variable noOfPeopleToInviteToTheStreetParty.

In our program for computing my age next year, we wish to add one to the value of the variable myAgeNow and place the result in our other variable.

```
008:    myAgeNextYear = myAgeNow + 1;
```

In order to print the two ages, we shall need the numbers to be converted into text.

Concept **Type: String: conversion: from int.** The Java **operator** + is used for both **addition** and **concatenation** – it is an **overloaded operator**. If at least one of the **operand**s is a **text data string**, then Java uses concatenation, otherwise it uses addition. When only one of the two operands is a string, and the other is some other **type** of **data**, for example an **int**, the Java **compiler** is clever enough to understand the programmer wishes that data to be converted into a string before the concatenation takes place. It is important to note the difference between an **integer** and the decimal digit string we usually use to represent it. For example, the **integer literal** 123 is an **int**, a number; whereas the **string literal** "123" is a text data string – a string of 3 separate **character**s.

Suppose the **variable** noOfPeopleToInviteToTheStreetParty had the value 51, then the code

```
System.out.println("Please invite " + noOfPeopleToInviteToTheStreetParty);
```

would print out the following text.

```
Please invite 51
```

The number 51 would be converted to the string "51" and then concatenated to the string "Please invite " before being processed by System.out.println().

Furthermore, for our convenience, there is a separate version of `System.out.println()` that takes a single `int` rather than a string, and prints its decimal representation. Thus, the code

```
System.out.println(noOfPeopleToInviteToTheStreetParty);
```

has the same effect as the following.

```
System.out.println("" + noOfPeopleToInviteToTheStreetParty);
```

In our program for computing my age next year, we wish to print out two messages.

```
009:     System.out.println("My age now is " + myAgeNow);
010:     System.out.println("My age next year will be " + myAgeNextYear);
011:   }
012: }
```

3.2.1   The full `AgeNextYear` code

```
001: public class AgeNextYear
002: {
003:   public static void main(String[] args)
004:   {
005:     int myAgeNow;
006:     int myAgeNextYear;
007:     myAgeNow = 18;
008:     myAgeNextYear = myAgeNow + 1;
009:     System.out.println("My age now is " + myAgeNow);
010:     System.out.println("My age next year will be " + myAgeNextYear);
011:   }
012: }
```

3.2.2   Trying it

We can **compile** and **run** the code.

```
                    Console Input / Output
$ javac AgeNextYear.java
$ java AgeNextYear
My age now is 18
My age next year will be 19
$ _
```

3.2.3   Coursework: Hard coded `YearsBeforeRetirement`

Preferably without looking at `AgeNextYear`, write a program called `YearsBeforeRetirement`, which has your age **hard coded** into it, along with the age you expect to retire at (probably 68 – although that may well change before you get there!). Your program will need two **variables** for these values. It should then compute the difference between them and store it in a third variable, for which you should choose an *appropriate* name. Finally, it should produce three lines of output, similar to the following.

```
                    Console Input / Output
$ java YearsBeforeRetirement
My age now is 55
I will retire at the age of 68
Years left working is 13
$ _
```

3.3   Example: Age next year – a common misconception

AIM: To clarify the relationship between **variables** and **assignment statements**.

A common misconception held by some new programmers is that **assignment statement**s are like mathematical equations which remain true for the duration of the program. Java's use of an **equal sign** unfortunately helps encourage this wrong view! Instead, they are instructions which cause the computer to simply **evaluate** the **expression** and store the result in the **variable**, when, *and only when*, the **statement** is obeyed.

To illustrate this, let us try to swap the order of the two assignment statements from the previous program.

```
001: public class AgeNextYear
002: {
003:   public static void main(String[] args)
004:   {
005:     int myAgeNow;
006:     int myAgeNextYear;
007:     myAgeNextYear = myAgeNow + 1;
008:     myAgeNow = 18;
009:     System.out.println("My age now is " + myAgeNow);
010:     System.out.println("My age next year will be " + myAgeNextYear);
011:   }
012: }
```

3.3.1 Trying it

We can **compile** the code.

```
                              Console Input / Output
$ javac AgeNextYear.java
AgeNextYear.java:7: variable myAgeNow might not have been initialized
     myAgeNextYear = myAgeNow + 1;
                     ^
1 error
$ _
```

You can see that the **compiler** has complained – it is clever enough to check that the **variable** will already have been given a value before it is used in any **expression**.

3.3.2 Changing my age

Recall that variables can have their value changed, so we can have a second **assignment statement** for one if we wish.

```
001: public class AgeNextYear
002: {
003:   public static void main(String[] args)
004:   {
005:     int myAgeNow;
006:     int myAgeNextYear;
007:     myAgeNow = 18;
008:     myAgeNextYear = myAgeNow + 1;
009:     myAgeNow = 55;
010:     System.out.println("My age now is " + myAgeNow);
011:     System.out.println("My age next year will be " + myAgeNextYear);
012:   }
013: }
```

Of course, that doesn't seem the right thing to do for this example!

Coffee time: 3.3.1
What do you think would be the result of the above program?

3.4 Example: Age next year with a command line argument

AIM:
To introduce the idea of converting a **command line argument** into an **int** and using the value in a program.

In this example we have another version of the AgeNextYear program. This time the age is not **hard coded**, instead it is supplied by the user as a **command line argument**. Even though this example is still rather contrived, you can see that this change makes the program more general and hence usable to more people.

The argument supplied by the user is a **text data string**, so we need our program to convert it into an `int`.

Concept **Standard API: `Integer`: `parseInt()`.** One simple way to turn a **text data string**, say `"123"` into the **integer** (whole number) it represents is to use the following.

```
Integer.parseInt("123");
```

`Integer` is a **class** (that is, a piece of code) that comes with Java. Inside `Integer` there is a **method** (section of code) called `parseInt`. This method takes a text data string given to it in its brackets, converts it into an `int` and **return**s that number. A **run time error** will occur if the given string does not represent an `int` value.

For example

```
int firstArgument;
firstArgument = Integer.parseInt(args[0]);
```

would take the first **command line argument** and, assuming it represents a number (i.e. it is a string of digits with a possible sign in front), would turn it into the number it represents, then store that number in `firstArgument`. If instead the first argument was some other text data string, it would produce a run time error.

```
001: public class AgeNextYear
002: {
003:   public static void main(String[] args)
004:   {
005:     int ageNow;
006:     int ageNextYear;
007:
008:     ageNow = Integer.parseInt(args[0]);
009:     ageNextYear = ageNow + 1;
010:
011:     System.out.println("Your age now is " + ageNow);
012:     System.out.println("Your age next year will be " + ageNextYear);
013:   }
014: }
```

3.4.1 Trying it

We **compile** the program.

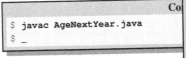

```
$ javac AgeNextYear.java
$ _
```

Then we can **run** it with various **command line argument**s.

Console Input / Output
| ```
$ java AgeNextYear 55
Your age now is 55
Your age next year will be 56
$ java AgeNextYear 18
Your age now is 18
Your age next year will be 19
$
``` |

We might accidentally run it with an argument which does not represent a number. This will produce a **run time error**.

Console Input / Output
| ```
$ java AgeNextYear John
Exception in thread "main" java.lang.NumberFormatException: For input string: "J
ohn"
        at java.lang.NumberFormatException.forInputString(NumberFormatException.
java:48)
        at java.lang.Integer.parseInt(Integer.java:449)
        at java.lang.Integer.parseInt(Integer.java:499)
        at AgeNextYear.main(AgeNextYear.java:8)
$ _
``` |

Notice that java gives us a list of **source code** line positions at which the error was detected. The error was found inside the parseInt() **method** in the Integer **class**, which was called by our program. It is the first and last lines of the error message which are most useful to us.

3.4.2 Coursework: Command line `YearsBeforeRetirement`

Here you will write another version of YearsBeforeRetirement, which is similar to the fully **hard coded** version of the program, but takes the user's age as its first **command line argument**. The retirement age is still to be hard coded as 68.

Before implementing the program, you should design **test data** for various tests which do the following.

- Make the program behave sensibly.

- Make the program behave inappropriately (i.e. a silly input resulting in a silly output).

- Make the program crash.

You should record this data in your logbook along with what you expect from each test.

Then copy your previous version of the program and alter it to suit the new requirement. You will learn most if you try not to look at the latest version of AgeNextYear while you do this. Finally, **run** it with your pre-planned tests and record whether the outcome was as you expected.

3.5 Example: Finding the volume of a fish tank

AIM:
To reinforce the use of **command line arguments** and **expressions**, and introduce the idea of splitting up lines of code which are too long, whilst maintaining their readability. We also see that a **variable** can be given a value when it is declared.

Our next example is a program to compute the volume of a rectangular box-shaped fish tank, from its three dimensions given as **command line arguments**.

Concept **Variable: a value can be assigned when a variable is declared.** Java permits us to assign a value to a **variable** at the same time as declaring it. You could regard this as a kind of **assignment statement** in which the variable is also declared at the same time. For example

```
int noOfHousesInMyStreet = 26;
```

 Coffee time: 3.5.1 Look back through the examples in this chapter, and spot the places where we might have assigned a value to a **variable** as soon as it was declared, rather than later.

In our fish tank program, we want four variables, all of which can have their value assigned straight away.

```
001: public class FishTankVolume
002: {
003:   public static void main(String[] args)
004:   {
005:     int width = Integer.parseInt(args[0]);
006:     int depth = Integer.parseInt(args[1]);
007:     int height = Integer.parseInt(args[2]);
008:     int volume = width * depth * height;
```

Concept **Code clarity: layout: splitting long lines.** One of the features of good layout is to keep our **source code** lines from getting too long. Very long lines cause the reader to have to work harder in horizontal eye movement to scan the code. When code with long lines is viewed on the screen, the reader either has to use a horizontal scroll bar to see them, or make the window so wide that other windows cannot be placed next to it. Worst of all, when code with long lines is printed on paper there is a good chance that the long lines will disappear off the edge of the page! At very least, they will be wrapped onto the next line making the code messy and hard to read.

So a good rule of thumb is to keep your source code lines shorter than 80 **characters** long. You can do this simply in most **text editors** by never making the text window too wide and never using the horizontal scroll bar while writing the code.

When we do have a **statement** that is quite long, we simply split it into separate lines at carefully chosen places. When we choose such places, we bear in mind that most human readers scan down the left hand side of the code lines, rather than read every word. So, if a line is a continuation of a previous line, it is important to make this obvious at the start of it. This means using an appropriate amount of **indentation**, and choosing the split so that the first symbol on the continued line is not one which could normally start a statement.

A little thought at the writing stage quickly leads to a habit of good practise which seriously reduces the effort required to read programs once they are written. Due to **bug** fixing and general maintenance over the lifetime of a real program, the code is read many more times than it is written!

We split the next **statement** into three lines so it is not too long. The positions at which we split the lines are chosen carefully.

- We cannot split the line inside a **string literal** – they must all end on the same line on which they start.

- It is better to split a line *before* an **operator** rather than after, so it is more obvious to the human reader that the next line is a continuation of the previous one.

- We indent the continued lines to make it clear that they are part of the argument to System.out.println().

```
009:    System.out.println("The volume of a tank with dimensions "
010:                    + "(" + width + "," + depth + "," + height + ") "
011:                    + "is " + volume);
012:    }
013: }
```

3.5.1   The full FishTankVolume code

```
001: public class FishTankVolume
002: {
003:    public static void main(String[] args)
004:    {
005:       int width = Integer.parseInt(args[0]);
006:       int depth = Integer.parseInt(args[1]);
007:       int height = Integer.parseInt(args[2]);
008:       int volume = width * depth * height;
009:       System.out.println("The volume of a tank with dimensions "
010:                       + "(" + width + "," + depth + "," + height + ") "
011:                       + "is " + volume);
012:    }
013: }
```

3.5.2 Trying it

After we have **compiled** the program, we can **run** it with various **command line arguments**.

We can devise tests to help show that the order of the arguments is not important.

```
                           Console Input / Output
$ java FishTankVolume 10 20 30
The volume of a tank with dimensions (10,20,30) is 6000
$ java FishTankVolume 10 30 20
The volume of a tank with dimensions (10,30,20) is 6000
$ java FishTankVolume 20 10 30
The volume of a tank with dimensions (20,10,30) is 6000
$ java FishTankVolume 20 30 10
The volume of a tank with dimensions (20,30,10) is 6000
$ java FishTankVolume 30 10 20
The volume of a tank with dimensions (30,10,20) is 6000
$ java FishTankVolume 30 20 10
The volume of a tank with dimensions (30,20,10) is 6000
$ _
```

These tests show the effect of one dimension being zero.

```
                           Console Input / Output
$ java FishTankVolume 0 20 30
The volume of a tank with dimensions (0,20,30) is 0
$ java FishTankVolume 10 0 30
The volume of a tank with dimensions (10,0,30) is 0
$ java FishTankVolume 10 20 0
The volume of a tank with dimensions (10,20,0) is 0
$ _
```

Coffee time: 3.5.2
How about this next test? Is the result correct? Is it meaningful?

```
                           Console Input / Output
$ java FishTankVolume 10 -20 -30
The volume of a tank with dimensions (10,-20,-30) is 6000
$ _
```

Coffee time: 3.5.3
If we are taking program testing seriously, then the whole point of it is to try and find situations that break the program, rather than 'prove' that it works. In what sense are the next two tests successful?

```
                           Console Input / Output
$ java FishTankVolume 10.75 20.25 30.5
Exception in thread "main" java.lang.NumberFormatException: For input string: "1
0.75"
        at java.lang.NumberFormatException.forInputString(NumberFormatException.
java:48)
        at java.lang.Integer.parseInt(Integer.java:458)
        at java.lang.Integer.parseInt(Integer.java:499)
        at FishTankVolume.main(FishTankVolume.java:5)
$ java FishTankVolume 10.0 20.0 30.0
Exception in thread "main" java.lang.NumberFormatException: For input string: "1
0.0"
        at java.lang.NumberFormatException.forInputString(NumberFormatException.
java:48)
        at java.lang.Integer.parseInt(Integer.java:458)
        at java.lang.Integer.parseInt(Integer.java:499)
        at FishTankVolume.main(FishTankVolume.java:5)
$ _
```

3.5.3 Coursework: `FieldPerimeter`

Here you will write a program called `FieldPerimeter` which takes the length and width of a field as its two **command line arguments**, and computes the length of fence needed to enclose the field. (The simplest way to compute this is $length + length + width + width$).

Before implementing the program, you should design **test data** for various tests which do the following.

- Make the program behave sensibly.
- Make the program behave inappropriately (i.e. a silly input resulting in a silly output).
- Make the program crash.

You should record this data in your logbook along with what you expect from each test.

You will learn most if you try not to look at FishTankVolume while writing your program. Afterwards, **run** it with your pre-planned tests and record whether the outcome was as you expected.

3.6 Example: Sum the first N numbers – incorrectly

AIM: To introduce the principle of **operator precedence**, and have a program containing a **bug**.

Our next example is a program to compute the sum of the first n positive whole numbers, where n is given as a **command line argument**. Our first attempt is going to have a **bug** in it.

```
001: public class SumFirstN
002: {
003:   public static void main(String[] args)
004:   {
005:     int n = Integer.parseInt(args[0]);
```

The formula for computing the sum of the first *n* positive whole numbers is based on the idea of finding their average and then multiplying that by the number of numbers. The average of the numbers between 1 and *n* is given by $\frac{1+n}{2}$. Hence the sum of the numbers must be $\frac{1+n}{2}n$.

Concept **Expression: brackets and precedence.** In addition to **operators** and **variables**, **expressions** in Java can have round brackets in them. As in mathematics, brackets are used to define the structure of the expression by grouping parts of it into sub-expressions. For example, the following two expressions have different structures, and thus very different values.

```
(2 + 4) * 8
2 + (4 * 8)
```

The value of the first expression is made from the **addition** of 2 and 4 and then **multiplication** of the resulting 6 by 8 to get 48. The second expression is **evaluate**d by multiplying 4 with 8 to get 32 and then adding 2 to that result, ending up with 34.

To help us see the structure of these two expressions, let us draw them as **expression tree**s.

What if there were no brackets?

```
2 + 4 * 8
```

Java allows us to have expressions without any brackets, or more generally, without brackets around *every* sub-expression. It provides rules to define what the structure of such an expression is, i.e., where the missing brackets should go. If you look at the 4 in the above expression, you will see that it has an operator on either side of it. In a sense, the + operator and the * operator are both fighting to have the 4 as an **operand**. Rather like a tug of war, + is pulling the 4 to the left, and * is tugging it to the right. The question is, which one wins? Java, as in mathematics, provides the answer by having varying levels of **operator precedence**. The * and / operators have a higher precedence than + and –, which means * fights harder than +, so it wins! 2 + 4 * 8 evaluates to 34.

If Java **operator**s were simply **evaluated** left to right as on a basic (non-scientific) calculator, we could code the **expression** we want as 1 + n / 2 * n. However, this would not work in Java because the **division** and **multiplication** operators have a higher precedence than the **addition** operator. So, we shall code the expression to compute the sum as (1 + n) / 2 * n.

```
006:     int sumOfFirstN = (1 + n) / 2 * n;
007:     System.out.println("The sum of the first " + n + " numbers is "
008:                         + sumOfFirstN);
009:   }
010: }
```

Coffee time: When computing the value of sumOfFirstN, do you think the division is done before the multiplication, or vice versa? Does it matter?

3.6.1 The full SumFirstN code

```
001: public class SumFirstN
002: {
003:   public static void main(String[] args)
004:   {
005:     int n = Integer.parseInt(args[0]);
006:     int sumOfFirstN = (1 + n) / 2 * n;
007:     System.out.println("The sum of the first " + n + " numbers is "
008:                         + sumOfFirstN);
009:   }
010: }
```

3.6.2 Trying it

After we have **compiled** the program, we can **run** it with various **command line arguments**.

Console Input / Output
$ **java SumFirstN 1**
The sum of the first 1 numbers is 1
$ **java SumFirstN 2**
The sum of the first 2 numbers is 2
$ **java SumFirstN 3**
The sum of the first 3 numbers is 6
$ _

Console Input / Output
$ **java SumFirstN 4**
The sum of the first 4 numbers is 8
$ **java SumFirstN 5**
The sum of the first 5 numbers is 15
$ **java SumFirstN 10**
The sum of the first 10 numbers is 50
$ **java SumFirstN 11**
The sum of the first 11 numbers is 66
$ **java SumFirstN 50**
The sum of the first 50 numbers is 1250
$ **java SumFirstN 51**
The sum of the first 51 numbers is 1326
$ _

Some of these results are wrong!

Coffee time: 3.6.2 Figure out which ones are right and which are wrong, and see if you can spot a pattern, leading you to suggest what the problem might be. We know the formula is right, so you can still use it to work out what the answers should have been. The error lies somewhere in our implementation of the formula – maybe something there doesn't behave as you might expect it to?

3.6.3 Coursework: `FishTankMaterials`

Suppose you want to build fish tanks. Each tank has five pieces of glass – two sides, a front, a back and a bottom. It also has twelve pieces of metal angle-strip to form the edges. Below is a program which computes the surface area and the length of the edges for a tank with dimensions given by three **command line argument**s.

Design some **test data** for the program, predicting what the surface area and edge length should be if the program worked correctly. For simplicity, you do not need to worry about missing or meaningless arguments for this program. Record your planned test data in your logbook.

Then carefully type in the program, as is, and **run** it with your tests. Record the actual results, and attempt to explain the **bug**s, in your logbook.

```
001: public class FishTankMaterials
002: {
003:    public static void main(String[] args)
004:    {
005:      int width = Integer.parseInt(args[0]);
006:      int depth = Integer.parseInt(args[1]);
007:      int height = Integer.parseInt(args[2]);
008:
009:      int surfaceArea = width + height * depth + height + 2 * width + depth;
010:
011:      int edgesLength = height * width * depth + 4;
012:
013:      System.out.println("The surface area of a tank with dimensions "
014:                  + "(" + width + "," + depth + "," + height + ") "
015:                  + "is " + surfaceArea);
016:
017:      System.out.println("The length of the edges of a tank with dimensions "
018:                  + "(" + width + "," + depth + "," + height + ") "
019:                  + "is " + edgesLength);
020:    }
021: }
```

Now fix the program and test it again, making a record of your bug corrections. Does the program now produce the results you originally predicted, or is it still wrong, or were your original predictions wrong?

3.7 Example: Disposable income

AIM: To introduce **operator associativity**. We also take a look at the **string literal escape sequences**.

Suppose you have a job for which you get paid. You also have two regular expenditures – your mortgage and your standing bills, such as council tax and energy. You obviously need a program to compute your disposable income – that little bit of your salary left over for your life.

Let us express all the amounts in whole pounds.

```
001: public class DisposableIncome
002: {
003:    public static void main(String[] args)
004:    {
005:       int salary   = Integer.parseInt(args[0]);
006:       int mortgage = Integer.parseInt(args[1]);
007:       int bills    = Integer.parseInt(args[2]);
```

Let us assume your salary has already had tax and other deductions removed from it. Your disposable income is the difference between this net salary and the sum of your mortgage and your bills. We can compute this in one **assignment statement**, but we need to take care to ensure the **operators** are **evaluated** in the right order.

Concept **Expression: associativity.** The principle of **operator precedence** is insufficient to disambiguate all **expressions** which are not fully bracketed. For example, consider the following expressions.

```
10 + 7 + 3
10 + 7 - 3
10 - 7 + 3
10 - 7 - 3
```

In all four expressions, the 7 is being fought over by two **operators** which have the same precedence: either two +, two -, or one of each. So where should the missing brackets go? The **expression trees** could have one of the two following structures, where OP1 is the first operator, and OP2 is the second.

Let us see whether it makes a difference to the results of the expressions.

Expression	Value
(10 + 7) + 3	20
10 + (7 + 3)	20
(10 + 7) - 3	14
10 + (7 - 3)	14
(10 - 7) + 3	6
10 - (7 + 3)	0
(10 - 7) - 3	0
10 - (7 - 3)	6

As you can see, it does make a difference sometimes – in these cases when the first operator is **subtraction** (–). So how does Java resolve this problem? As in mathematics, Java operators have an **operator associativity** as well as a precedence. The operators +, –, * and / all have **left associativity** which means that when two of these operators of

48

equal precedence are both fighting over one **operand**, it is the left operator that wins. If you like, the tug of war takes place on sloping ground with the left operator having the advantage of being lower down than the right one!

Expression	Implicit brackets	Value
10 + 7 + 3	(10 + 7) + 3	20
10 + 7 - 3	(10 + 7) - 3	14
10 - 7 + 3	(10 - 7) + 3	6
10 - 7 - 3	(10 - 7) - 3	0

The operators * and / also have equal precedence (but higher than + and -) so similar situations arise with those too.

Coffee time: Figure out why `"I earn " + 1 + 2 + 3 + 4 + 5 + 6` evaluates to `"I earn 123456"`, whereas `"I am " + (1 + 2 + 3 + 4 + 5 + 6)` becomes `"I am 21"`.

To compute your disposable income, we subtract the sum of your mortgage and your bills from your salary.

```
008:    int disposableIncome = salary - (mortgage + bills);
```

Coffee time: Alternatively, we could have written our **expression** as `salary - mortgage - bills`. Convince yourself that this would produce the same result, whereas the expression `salary - mortgage + bills` would be wrong.

Let's display our results neatly using **tab character**s, and while we're at it, let's use just a single `System.out.println()` **statement** to get four lines of output.

Concept **Type: `String`: literal: escape sequences.** We can have a **new line character** embedded in a **string literal** by using the **escape sequence** `\n`. For example, the following code will print out three lines on **standard output**.

```
System.out.println("This text\nspans three\nlines.");
```

It will generate the following.

```
This text
spans three
lines.
```

There are other escape sequences we can use, including the following.

Sequence	Name	Effect
\b	Backspace	Moves the cursor back one place, so the next **character** will over-print the previous.
\t	Tab (horizontal tab)	Moves the cursor to the next 'tab stop'.
\n	New line (line feed)	Moves the cursor to the next line.
\f	Form feed	Moves to a new page on many (text) printers.
\r	Carriage return	Moves the cursor to the start of the current line, so characters will over-print those already printed.
\"	Double quote	Without the backslash escape, this would mark the end of the string literal.
\'	Single quote	This is just for consistency – we don't need to escape a single quote in a string literal.
\\	Backslash	Well, sometimes you want the backslash character itself.

49

Note: `System.out.println()` always ends the line with the platform dependent **line separator**, which on Linux is a new line character but on Microsoft Windows is a **carriage return character** followed by a new line character. In practice you may not notice the difference, but the above code is not strictly the same as using three separate `System.out.println()` calls and is not 100% portable.

```
009:    System.out.println("Your salary:\t" + salary
010:                        + "\nYour mortgage:\t" + mortgage
011:                        + "\nYour bills:\t" + bills
012:                        + "\nDisposable:\t" + disposableIncome);
013:  }
014: }
```

3.7.1 The full `DisposableIncome` code

```
001: public class DisposableIncome
002: {
003:   public static void main(String[] args)
004:   {
005:     int salary  = Integer.parseInt(args[0]);
006:     int mortgage = Integer.parseInt(args[1]);
007:     int bills   = Integer.parseInt(args[2]);
008:     int disposableIncome = salary - (mortgage + bills);
009:     System.out.println("Your salary:\t" + salary
010:                         + "\nYour mortgage:\t" + mortgage
011:                         + "\nYour bills:\t" + bills
012:                         + "\nDisposable:\t" + disposableIncome);
013:   }
014: }
```

3.7.2 Trying it

After we have **compiled** the program, we can **run** it.

You'll survive. ;-) But the guy below needs a better job – perhaps Java programming?

```
                Console Input / Output
$ java DisposableIncome 38356 24317 4665
Your salary:     38356
Your mortgage:   24317
Your bills:      4665
Disposable:      9374
$ _
```

```
                Console Input / Output
$ java DisposableIncome 19178 12875 3665
Your salary:     19178
Your mortgage:   12875
Your bills:      3665
Disposable:      2638
$ _
```

In later examples we shall see two ways of addressing the **line separator** portability issue without needing to use separate `System.out.println()` **statements** for each line.

3.7.3 Coursework: `ThreeWeights`

In the days before accurate mechanical spring weighing scales (let alone digital ones), gold merchants were quite clever in their use of a small number of brass or lead weights, and a balance scale. (Indeed, many still use these in preference to inferior modern technology!) They would place the gold to be weighed in the left pan of the balance scale, and then place known weights in the right pan, and maybe also in the left pan, until the scales balanced. For example, suppose an unknown amount of gold was placed in the left pan. The merchant might experiment with a number of weights until he or she managed to make it balance with a known weight of R ounces in the right pan, and L ounces in the left pan along with the gold. This would show that the gold weighed $R - L$ ounces. In order to be able to weigh different amounts of gold, each merchant would carry a small number of known weights. When making a particular weighing, each weight could be placed in one of three positions: in the left pan with the gold, in the right one or not used.[1]

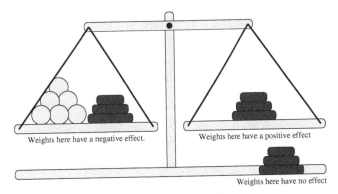

Weights here have a negative effect.   Weights here have a positive effect

Weights here have no effect

Suppose then that a merchant carries just three known brass or lead weights. Each of the three weights has three positions, thus giving rise to 3^3 combinations. These 27 combinations are listed below.

	Position of				Position of				Position of		
	Wt 1	Wt 2	Wt 3		Wt 1	Wt 2	Wt 3		Wt 1	Wt 2	Wt 3
1	Left	Left	Left	10	Off	Left	Left	19	Right	Left	Left
2	Left	Left	Off	11	Off	Left	Off	20	Right	Left	Off
3	Left	Left	Right	12	Off	Left	Right	21	Right	Left	Right
4	Left	Off	Left	13	Off	Off	Left	22	Right	Off	Left
5	Left	Off	Off	14	Off	Off	Off	23	Right	Off	Off
6	Left	Off	Right	15	Off	Off	Right	24	Right	Off	Right
7	Left	Right	Left	16	Off	Right	Left	25	Right	Right	Left
8	Left	Right	Off	17	Off	Right	Off	26	Right	Right	Off
9	Left	Right	Right	18	Off	Right	Right	27	Right	Right	Right

Not all of these are useful. For example, at least one of them results in a weighing of zero – the one in which none of the weights are used. In fact, *any* combination in which the total of the known weights in the two pans is **equal**, results in a weighing of zero amount of gold. Then also, any combination for which the total known weight in the left pan is **greater than** that of the right pan is not useful – this would need a negative weight of gold in the left pan in order to balance!

Smart gold merchants chose the weights they would carry in such a way as to maximize their usefulness – that is, to enable the greatest range of weighings for a given number of carried weights. Suppose the number of weights carried is to be three. To maximize their effectiveness, there must be only one way of weighing zero, that is, the sum of any two weights must not equal the third. Also, of the 26 non-zero weighing combinations, for each that totals a positive weight, i.e., where the sum of the weights in the right pan exceeds that in the left, there is a corresponding negative weighing – formed by simply swapping the weights in the left and right pans over. This means there will be 13 combinations giving positive weighings, and 13 which give the opposite negative weighings. These negative weighings are of no use, and some of the positive weighings could add up to the same amount, which would not be efficient. The maximum effectiveness is achieved when the 13 positive weighings are the numbers 1 to 13.

You are going to write a program to help you experiment with this scenario, and by a mixture of trial and error with your grasp of number theory, discover which three weight values gives the ability to weigh whole amounts from 1 to 13 inclusive.

Your program should be called `ThreeWeights`, and will take the three weights as **command line arguments**. It should then print out all 27 possible weighing values. Each value will appear on one line of the output. You will use 27 calls to `System.out.println()`.

Attempt to derive which three weights are the best to use, that is, the three values which produce weighing values from -13 through to 13 inclusive. If you are **run**ning in a Unix environment, and the first, or only, item on each output line is the weighing value, then the following command may help you assess your output.

```
                    Console Input / Output
$ java ThreeWeights 1 2 3 | sort -n
 (Output shown using multiple columns to save space.)
 -6  | -4  | -2  | -1  | 0  | 1  | 2  | 3  | 4
 -5  | -3  | -2  | -1  | 0  | 1  | 2  | 3  | 5
 -4  | -3  | -2  | -1  | 0  | 1  | 2  | 4  | 6
$ _
```

This runs your program and pipes the output of it into the input of `sort`, for which the `-n` option means 'sort numerically'.

On Microsoft Windows, the nearest equivalent is `java ThreeWeights 1 2 3 | sort` which sorts the lines lexicographically (alphabetically), rather than numerically – e.g. 10 comes before 2. Nevertheless, even this is helpful.

As you can see from the above output, there are duplicate values in the 27 listed, so 1 2 3 is not the right answer. (They don't even add up to 13...) You will substitute the arguments you think the weights should be instead. If you are successful, attempt to explain why your values are the best three weights, in your logbook.

Coffee time: 3.7.3 When weighing food, one would not wish to place weights in the pan containing the food, and so grocers did not use a three state, negative weighing scheme. What *four* weights did they use to weigh units of 1 to 15 inclusive? What is the connection between this and your answer for the gold merchants?

3.8 Example: Sum the first N numbers – correctly

AIM:
To introduce the fact that **integer division** produces a truncated result. We then look at the interaction between that and **operator associativity**.

The error we made in our previous attempt to compute the sum of the first n numbers, in Section 3.6 on page 45, is perhaps one of the most common errors that novice programmers, and occasionally even expert programmers, make.

Concept **Expression: arithmetic: `int` division truncates result.** The four **arithmetic operators**, +, -, * and / of Java behave very similarly to the corresponding operators in mathematics. There is however one serious difference to look out for. When the **division operator** is given two **integers** (whole numbers) it uses **integer division** which always yields an integer as its result, by throwing away any fractional part of the answer. So, 8 / 2 gives the answer 4 as you might expect, but 9 / 2 also gives 4 – not 4.5 as it would in mathematics. It does not round to the nearest whole number, it always rounds towards zero. In mathematics 15 / 4 gives 3.75. In Java it yields 3 not 4.

If you spotted the cause of the problem when you analysed the test results you should feel very pleased with yourself. In our previous version of the program, the implementation of the formula was (1 + n) / 2 * n. This only worked properly if n was an odd number – making 1 + n an even number. In the other cases, the fractional 0.5 was being thrown away.

To avoid this problem, we must ensure that the **multiplication** by n is done before the **division** by 2. This must work, because the sum of the first n whole numbers is a whole number!

This leads us to ask again the question, of the division and multiplication **operators** in our previous version, which was **evaluated** first, and why did this cause the answer to be wrong?

Concept **Expression: arithmetic: associativity and `int` division.** Like the **operators** + and -, the operators * and / have equal **operator precedence** (but higher than + and -) and also have **left associativity**.

However, there is an extra complication to consider because the Java / operator truncates its answer when given two **integer**s. Consider the following two **arithmetic expression**s.

Expression	Implicit brackets	Value
9 * 4 / 2	(9 * 4) / 2	18
9 / 2 * 4	(9 / 2) * 4	16

In mathematics one would expect to get the same answer from both these **expression**s, but not in Java!

The simplest solution to our **bug** is to swap the order of the divide and multiply.

```
001: public class SumFirstN
002: {
003:   public static void main(String[] args)
004:   {
005:     int n = Integer.parseInt(args[0]);
006:     int sumOfFirstN = (1 + n) * n / 2;
007:     System.out.println("The sum of the first " + n + " numbers is "
008:                          + sumOfFirstN);
009:   }
010: }
```

Coffee time: Convince yourself that this will always avoid the problem for this program.

3.8.1

3.8.1 Trying it

After we have **compiled** the program, we can **run** it with the same **command line arguments** as before.

```
Console Input / Output

$ java SumFirstN 1
The sum of the first 1 numbers is 1
$ java SumFirstN 2
The sum of the first 2 numbers is 3
$ java SumFirstN 3
The sum of the first 3 numbers is 6
$ java SumFirstN 4
The sum of the first 4 numbers is 10
$ java SumFirstN 5
The sum of the first 5 numbers is 15
$ java SumFirstN 10
The sum of the first 10 numbers is 55
$ java SumFirstN 11
The sum of the first 11 numbers is 66
$ java SumFirstN 50
The sum of the first 50 numbers is 1275
$ java SumFirstN 51
The sum of the first 51 numbers is 1326
$ _
```

Convince yourself that these results are all correct now.

3.8.2 Coursework: RoundPennies

Imagine there is a child who collects pennies in a piggy bank. Her mother tells her she is allowed to spend some of it when she has saved "about X pounds", where X varies depending on what her mother thinks the girl is likely to want to buy. Your job is to write a program that helps the girl convert a number of pennies, which she is able to count up, into "about pounds" – i.e. round the number of pennies to the nearest pound. The program will take the number of pennies as its **command line argument**, and report how many pounds it rounds to. So, any non-negative number **less than** 50 will round to zero, but 50 through to 149 will round to 1. The value 749 rounds to 7, but 750 and 751 round to 8. And so on.

Start by designing **test data** and expected results in your logbook. You do not need to worry about arguments which are missing or are not **integer** numbers, but you should consider what the program will do for negative numbers, even though they are not really valid inputs.

Now write the program, calling it RoundPennies. You will learn most if you try to avoid looking at any other program while you do this. To get you thinking, the calculation will exploit the fact that **integer division** truncates its result. However that is not enough. For example, 750 / 100 will yield 7, not 8 as we want here. There is some value you must add to the numerator before the **division** by 100.

Then, after implementing the program, you should **run** it with your pre-planned tests and record whether the outcome was as you expected. Record comments about the negative cases – is this the behaviour of a more general round-to-the-nearest-whole-number function? If not, what could we do to make it so?

3.9 Example: Temperature conversion

AIM:
   To introduce the **double type** and some associated concepts, including converting to and from strings, and **double division**.

The program in this example converts a given Celsius temperature to Fahrenheit. The values do not have to be whole numbers.

Concept **Type: double.**   Another of the **types of data** we can use in Java is known as **double**. A data item which is a **double** is a **real** (fractional decimal number), such as 0.0, -129.934 or 98.2375, etc.. The type is called **double** because it uses a means of storing the numbers called **double precision**. On computers, real numbers are only approximated, because they have to be stored in a finite amount of memory space, whereas in mathematics we have the notion of infinite decimals. The double precision storage approach uses twice as much memory per number than the older **single precision** technique, but gives numbers which are much more precise.

Concept **Variable: double variable.**   We can declare **double variables** in Java, that is **variables** which have the **type double**. For example the code

```
double meanAgeOfPeopleLivingInMyHouse;
```

declares a **variable** of type **double**, with the name meanAgeOfPeopleLivingInMyHouse. At **run time**, this variable is allowed to hold a **double data** item, that is a **real** (fractional decimal number). The value of this variable can change, but it will always be a **double**, including of course, approximations of *whole* numbers such as 43.0.

Concept **Standard API: Double: parseDouble().**   One simple way to turn a **text data string**, say "123.456" into the **real** (fractional decimal number) it represents is to use the following.

```
Double.parseDouble("123.456");
```

Double is a **class** (that is, a piece of code) that comes with Java. Inside Double there is a **method** (section of code) called parseDouble. This method takes a text data string given to it in its brackets, converts it into an **double** and **returns** that number. A **run time error** will occur if the given string does not represent a number. For example

```
double firstArgument = Double.parseDouble(args[0]);
```

would take the first **command line argument** and, assuming it represents a number, would turn it into the number it represents, then store that number in firstArgument. To represent a number, the string must be a sequence of digits, possibly with a decimal point and maybe a negative sign in front. If instead the first argument was some other text data string, it would produce a run time error.

Our program to convert temperatures starts in the usual way.

```
001: public class CelsiusToFahrenheit
002: {
003:   public static void main(String[] args)
004:   {
005:     double celsiusValue = Double.parseDouble(args[0]);
```

Concept **Expression: arithmetic: double division.** The Java **division operator**, /, uses **double division** and produces a **double** result if at least one of its **operand**s is a **double**. The result will be the best approximation to the actual answer of the division.

Expression	Result	Type of Result
8 / 2	4	int
8 / 2.0	4.0	double
9 / 2	4	int
9 / 2.0	4.5	double
9.0 / 2	4.5	double
9.0 / 2.0	4.5	double

The relationship between Celsius and Fahrenheit can be expressed as $F = \frac{9}{5}C + 32$.

```
006:     double fahrenheitValue = celsiusValue * 9 / 5 + 32;
```

Concept **Type: String: conversion: from double.** The Java **concatenation operator**, +, for joining **text data strings** can also be used to convert a **double** to a string. For example, the **expression** "" + 123.4 has the value "123.4".

```
007:     System.out.println("Temperature " + celsiusValue + " Celsius"
008:                        + " in Fahrenheit is " + fahrenheitValue + ".");
009:   }
010: }
```

Coffee time: What do you think would happen if we declared the **variable** fahrenheitValue as an **int** instead of a **double**?

3.9.1 The full CelsiusToFahrenheit code

```
001: public class CelsiusToFahrenheit
002: {
003:   public static void main(String[] args)
004:   {
005:     double celsiusValue = Double.parseDouble(args[0]);
006:     double fahrenheitValue = celsiusValue * 9 / 5 + 32;
007:     System.out.println("Temperature " + celsiusValue + " Celsius"
008:                        + " in Fahrenheit is " + fahrenheitValue + ".");
009:   }
010: }
```

3.9.2 Trying it

After we have **compiled** the program, we can **run** it with various **command line argument**s.

The freezing point of water.

Console Input / Output
```
$ java CelsiusToFahrenheit 0
Temperature 0.0 Celsius in Fahrenheit is 32.0.
$ _
```

Classic healthy human body temperature.

Console Input / Output
```
$ java CelsiusToFahrenheit 37.0
Temperature 37.0 Celsius in Fahrenheit is 98.6.
$ _
```

The boiling point of water.

Console Input / Output
```
$ java CelsiusToFahrenheit 100
Temperature 100.0 Celsius in Fahrenheit is 212.0.
$ _
```

The next test reminds us that **real** numbers stored on computers are only approximated.

See that our input **data** is not exactly reported back to us.

Console Input / Output
```
$ java CelsiusToFahrenheit -17.777777777777777
Temperature -17.77777777777778 Celsius in Fahrenheit is 0.0.
$ _
```

One less decimal place on the input permits the number to be repeated back exactly.

Also, see how the Fahrenheit result is presented in exponent notation.

Console Input / Output
```
$ java CelsiusToFahrenheit -17.77777777777777
Temperature -17.77777777777777 Celsius in Fahrenheit is 1.0658141036401503E-14.
$ _
```

This next test reminds us that computers are stupid – any intelligence they *appear* to have is an effect of the programming they have been given.

No doubt if you gave this input data to an intelligent being, e.g. the programmer who wrote the program, you would get a sensible answer. Alas, such intelligence was not coded into the program!

Console Input / Output
```
$ java CelsiusToFahrenheit Freezing
Exception in thread "main" java.lang.NumberFormatException: For input string: "F
reezing"
        at sun.misc.FloatingDecimal.readJavaFormatString(FloatingDecimal.java:12
24)
        at java.lang.Double.parseDouble(Double.java:510)
        at CelsiusToFahrenheit.main(CelsiusToFahrenheit.java:5)
$ _
```

3.9.3 Coursework: `FahrenheitToCelsius`

In this task you will write a program called `FahrenheitToCelsius` which converts a given Fahrenheit temperature into its Celsius equivalent.

Start by designing **test data** and expected results in your logbook. You do not need to worry about arguments which are missing or not **real** numbers.

Now **design** your program. You can derive the formula by manipulating the one given for converting the other way. Show your working in your logbook. There is a temperature at which the Fahrenheit and Celsius measurements are the same. Figure out what this is, showing your working in your logbook, and add it to your tests.

As always, you will learn most if you try to avoid looking at any other program while writing this one. Afterwards, **run** it with your pre-planned tests and record whether the outcome was as you expected.

3.10 Concepts covered in this chapter

Here is a list of the concepts that were covered in this chapter, each with a self-test question. You can use this to check you remember them being introduced, and perhaps re-read some of them before going on to the next chapter.

Code clarity	
– layout: splitting long lines (p.43)	What principles do we apply to keep our source lines short and readable?

Design	
– hard coding (p.36)	What are two reasons for hard coding data?

Expression	
– arithmetic (p.38)	Name four binary infix operators and give their Java spellings. Two of these can also be used in another way – what do we call that sort of operator?
– arithmetic: `int` division truncates result (p.52)	What is the value of `-15 / 4` (in Java!)?
– arithmetic: associativity and `int` division (p.52)	What is the value of `9 * 4 / 2 - 9 / 2 * 4` (in Java!)?
– arithmetic: `double` division (p.55)	What is the value and type of `9.0 / 2` (in Java!)?
– brackets and precedence (p.45)	Why is the value of `10 - 6 / 2` not 2?
– associativity (p.48)	In general, operators could have right or left associativity. Which would `/` need to have in order for `16 / 4 / 2` to equal 8? What value does that expression have in Java?

Standard API	
– `Double: parseDouble()` (p.54)	What does `Double.parseDouble()` do?
– `Integer: parseInt()` (p.41)	What does `Integer.parseInt()` do?

Statement	
– assignment statement (p.37)	What property must some value have in order for it to be assignable to a particular variable?
– assignment statement: assigning a literal value (p.37)	What is a literal value? Give an example of an integer literal.

Statement	
– assignment statement: assigning an expression value (p.38)	Apart from bits of syntax, what two main parts does an assignment statement consist of?
Type	
Type (p.36)	Name three kinds of data.
– String: conversion: from int (p.38)	What is the difference between 51 and "51"?
– String: conversion: from double (p.55)	What is the value of 1234.0 + 0.5 + ""? What about "" + 1234.0 + 0.5?
– String: literal: escape sequences (p.49)	What is an escape sequence? How do we include a double quote in a string literal?
– int (p.36)	Give three examples of an **int** value.
– double (p.54)	Why is this type called double? Why does System.out.println(0.7 + " is equal to " + (1 - 0.1 - 0.1 - 0.1)); print 0.7 is equal to 0.7000000000000001?
Variable	
Variable (p.36)	What three things does a variable have?
– int variable (p.37)	When we declare a variable, what two things do we write, and in what order do we write them?
– a value can be assigned when a variable is declared (p.42)	Write a single line of Java that declares a variable, x, which is a double, and gives it the value 123.4
– double variable (p.54)	If the double variable x has the value 10.0, what is the value of x / 2? How would this be different if x was an int?

Chapter 4

Conditional execution

```
001: if (conditions are right)
002:    your program will work
003: else
004:    you'll be sorry.
```

4.1 Chapter aims

This chapter is concerned with the simple principle that not every part of every program need be **execute**d every time the program is **run** – certain parts are needed only under certain **condition**s. This facility can be achieved through the use of **if statement**s and **if else statement**s.

The chapter contains the following sections.

Section	Aims	Associated Coursework
4.2 Oldest spouse 1 (p.59)	To introduce the idea of **conditional execution**, implemented by the **if else statement**, and controlled by **boolean expression**s based on the use of **relational operator**s.	Write a program to find the maximum of two given numbers, using an **if else statement**. (p.61)
4.3 Oldest spouse 2 (p.62)	To introduce the idea of nesting **if else statement**s.	Write a program to report the degree category of a given mark. (p.64)
4.4 Film certificate age checking (p.64)	To introduce the **if statement** without a **false part**.	Write a program to report the pass or fail status of an exam candidate, giving a message of distinction if appropriate using an **if statement**. (p.65)
4.5 Absolute difference (p.65)	To introduce the **compound statement**.	(None.)

4.2 Example: Oldest spouse 1

AIM: To introduce the idea of **conditional execution**, implemented by the **if else statement**, and controlled by **boolean expression**s based on the use of **relational operator**s.

In this first example, we shall have a program that takes the age (in whole years) of a husband, and then that of his wife, as two **command line argument**s. It reports whether or not the husband is older than the wife (ignoring the possibility that he may be the same age in whole years, but is actually a few months older).

Concept **Execution: conditional execution.**   Having a computer always obey a list of instructions in a certain order is not sufficient to solve many problems. We often need the computer to do some things only under certain circumstances, rather than every time the program is **run**. This is known as **conditional execution**, because we get the computer to **execute** certain instructions **condition**ally, based on the values of the **variable**s in the program.

Concept **Expression: boolean.**   An **expression** which when **evaluate**d yields either **true** or **false** is known as a **condition**, and is typically used for controlling **conditional execution**. Conditions are also called **boolean expression**s.

Concept **Expression: boolean: relational operators.**   Java gives us six **relational operator**s for comparing values such as numbers, which we can use to make up **conditions**. These are all **binary infix operator**s, that is they take two **operand**s, one either side of the **operator**. They yield **true** or **false** depending on the given values.

Operator	Title	Description
==	Equal	This is the **equal** operator, which provides the notion of **equality**. a == b yields **true** if and only if the value of a is the same as the value of b.
!=	Not equal	This is the **not equal** operator, providing the the notion of not equality. a != b yields **true** if and only if the value of a is *not* the same as the value of b.
<	Less than	This is the **less than** operator. a < b yields **true** if and only if the value of a is less than the value of b.
>	Greater than	This is the **greater than** operator. a > b yields **true** if and only if the value of a is greater than the value of b.
<=	Less than or equal	This is the **less than or equal** operator. a <= b yields **true** if and only if the value of a is less than value of b, or is equal to it.
>=	Greater than or equal	This is the **greater than or equal** operator. a >= b yields **true** if and only if the value of a is greater than value of b, or is equal to it.

Coffee time:

Which of the following **conditions** are true?

a)	5 < 4	b)	5 < 5	c)	5 < 6
d)	5 > 4	e)	5 > 5	f)	5 > 6
g)	5 <= 4	h)	5 <= 5	i)	5 <= 6
j)	5 >= 4	k)	5 >= 5	l)	5 >= 6
m)	5 == 4	n)	5 == 5	o)	5 == 6
p)	5 != 4	q)	5 != 5	r)	5 != 6
s)	5 > 4 == 9 < 15	t)	5 < 4 != 9 > 15

Do the last two examples above suggest that == and != have a different **operator precedence** from the other **relational operator**s? If so, are they higher or lower?

Concept **Statement: if else statement.**   The **if else statement** is one way in Java of having **conditional execution**. It essentially consists of three parts: a **condition** or **boolean expression**, a **statement** which will be **execute**d when the condition is **true** (the **true part**), and another statement which will be executed when the condition is **false** (the **false part**). The whole statement starts with the **reserved word if**. This is followed by the condition, written in brackets. Next comes the statement for the true part, then the reserved word **else** and finally the statement for the false part.

For example, assuming we have the **variable** noOfPeopleToInviteToTheStreetParty containing the number suggested by its name, then the code

```
if (noOfPeopleToInviteToTheStreetParty > 100)
  System.out.println("We will need a big sound system!");
else
  System.out.println("We should be okay with a normal HiFi.");
```

will cause the computer to compare the current value of noOfPeopleToInviteToTheStreetParty with the number 100, and if it is greater then print out the message We will need a big sound system! or otherwise print out the message We should be okay with a normal HiFi. – it will never print out both messages. Notice the brackets around the condition and the semi-colons at the end of the two statements inside the if else statement. Notice also the way we lay out the code to make it easy to read, splitting the lines at sensible places and adding more **indentation** at the start of the two inner statements.

Our program to report whether or not the husband is older than the wife essentially consists of a single **if else statement**.

```
001: public class OldestSpouse
002: {
003:   public static void main(String[] args)
004:   {
005:     int husbandsAge = Integer.parseInt(args[0]);
006:     int wifesAge = Integer.parseInt(args[1]);
007:
008:     if (husbandsAge > wifesAge)
009:       System.out.println("The husband is older than the wife");
010:     else
011:       System.out.println("The husband is not older than the wife");
012:   }
013: }
```

4.2.1 Trying it

After we have **compiled** the program, we can **run** it with various **command line arguments**.

```
Console Input / Output
$ java OldestSpouse 55 32
The husband is older than the wife
$ java OldestSpouse 37 36
The husband is older than the wife
$ java OldestSpouse 35 35
The husband is not older than the wife
$ java OldestSpouse 33 34
The husband is not older than the wife
$ java OldestSpouse 22 27
The husband is not older than the wife
$ _
```

4.2.2 Coursework: **MaxTwoDoubles**

In this task you will write a program called MaxTwoDoubles which takes two **command line arguments**, interprets them as **double** values, and reports both numbers along with which one of the two is the greatest, on the **standard output**. You will use an **if else statement**.

Start by designing **test data** and expected results in your logbook. You do not need to worry about arguments which are missing or are not **real** numbers.

Now **design** your program, preferably without looking at OldestSpouse. After implementing the program, you should **run** it with your pre-planned tests and record whether the outcome was as you expected.

4.3 Example: Oldest spouse 2

AIM:
To introduce the idea of nesting **if else statement**s.

In this example, we shall have a program that is a variation of the previous. It takes the age of a husband, and then that of his wife like before, but it produces one of *three* messages depending on whether the husband is older than the wife, they are the same age, or the husband is younger (based only on whole years).

Concept **Statement: if else statement: nested.** The **true part** or **false part** statements inside an **if else statement** may be any valid Java **statement**, including other if else statements. When we place an if else statement inside another, we say they are **nested**.

For example, study the following code.

```
if (noOfPeopleToInviteToTheStreetParty > 300)
    System.out.println("We will need a Mega master 500 Watt amplifier!");
else
  if (noOfPeopleToInviteToTheStreetParty > 100)
    System.out.println("We will need a Maxi Master 150 Watt amplifier!");
  else
    System.out.println("We should be okay with a normal HiFi.");
```

Depending on the value of noOfPeopleToInviteToTheStreetParty, this will report one of *three* messages. Notice the way we have laid out the code above – this is following the usual rules that inner statements have more **indentation** than those they are contained in, so the second if else statement has more spaces because it lives inside the first one. However, typically we make an exception to this rule for if else statements nested in the false part of another, and we would actually lay out the code as follows.

```
if (noOfPeopleToInviteToTheStreetParty > 300)
    System.out.println("We will need a Mega master 500 Watt amplifier!");
else if (noOfPeopleToInviteToTheStreetParty > 100)
    System.out.println("We will need a Maxi Master 150 Watt amplifier!");
else
    System.out.println("We should be okay with a normal HiFi.");
```

This layout reflects our *abstract* thinking that the collection of statements is *one* construct offering three choices, even though it is implemented using two if else statements. This idea extends to cases where we want many choices, using many nested if else statements, without the indentation having to increase for each choice.

Coffee time: 4.3.1 If we wanted some program code to **execute** one out of *N* choices, how many **if else statements** would we need?

Coffee time: 4.3.2 What would be output by the following?

```
int x = 1; int y = 2; int z = 3;
if (x < y)
    System.out.println("x is less than y");
else if (y < z)
    System.out.println("y is less than z");
else
    System.out.println("I believe in Father Christmas!");
```

Our new version of the OldestSpouse program essentially consists of a single pair of **nested** if else statements.

```
001: public class OldestSpouse
002: {
003:   public static void main(String[] args)
004:   {
005:     int husbandsAge = Integer.parseInt(args[0]);
006:     int wifesAge = Integer.parseInt(args[1]);
007:
008:     if (husbandsAge > wifesAge)
009:       System.out.println("The husband is older than the wife");
010:     else if (husbandsAge == wifesAge)
011:       System.out.println("The husband is the same age as the wife");
012:     else
013:       System.out.println("The husband is younger than the wife");
014:   }
015: }
```

4.3.1 Trying it

After we have **compiled** the program, we can **run** it with various **command line arguments**.

```
                    Console Input / Output
$ java OldestSpouse 55 32
The husband is older than the wife
$ java OldestSpouse 37 36
The husband is older than the wife
$ java OldestSpouse 35 35
The husband is the same age as the wife
$ java OldestSpouse 33 34
The husband is younger than the wife
$ java OldestSpouse 22 27
The husband is younger than the wife
$ _
```

Coffee time: `4.3.3`
What do you think of the following code as an alternative to the **if else statements** we wrote in our program? Would it work? Is it as easy to read?
```
if (husbandsAge <= wifesAge)
  if (husbandsAge != wifesAge)
    System.out.println("The husband is younger than the wife");
  else
    System.out.println("The husband is the same age as the wife");
else
  System.out.println("The husband is older than the wife");
```

Coffee time: `4.3.4`
What about the following code instead? What makes it better than the code above?
```
if (husbandsAge < wifesAge)
  System.out.println("The husband is younger than the wife");
else if (husbandsAge == wifesAge)
  System.out.println("The husband is the same age as the wife");
else
  System.out.println("The husband is older than the wife");
```

Coffee time: `4.3.5`
And finally, what about the following code? What makes it *less* good than the one above?
```
if (husbandsAge == wifesAge)
  System.out.println("The husband is the same age as the wife");
else if (husbandsAge < wifesAge)
  System.out.println("The husband is younger than the wife");
else
  System.out.println("The husband is older than the wife");
```

63

4.3.2   Coursework: `DegreeCategory`

In this task you will write a program called `DegreeCategory` which takes a student mark (e.g. final year, total assessment mark) and reports what degree category it is worth. The input is a single number, which might have decimal places in it, entered as a **command line argument**.

Input	Required output
$input \geq 70$	Honours, first class
$70 > input \geq 60$	Honours, second class, division one
$60 > input \geq 50$	Honours, second class, division two
$50 > input \geq 40$	Honours, third class
$40 > input \geq 32$	Pass / ordinary degree
$input < 32$	Fail

Start by designing your **test data** and expected output in your logbook. You do not need to worry about input which is invalid. Then **design** and implement your program, preferably without looking at `OldestSpouse`. Finally, **run** it with your pre-planned tests and record whether your outcome was as you expected.

4.4   Example: Film certificate age checking

AIM:
To introduce the **if statement** without a **false part**.

This next example is a program which takes two **command line argument**s – the minimum age a person is required to be to watch a certain film, and the age of a person wishing to watch it. It produces a message if, and only if, the person is too young. Otherwise it does nothing.

Concept **Statement: if statement.** Sometimes we want the computer to **execute** some code depending on a **condition**, but do nothing if the condition is **false**. We could implement this using an **if else statement** with an empty **false part**. For example, consider the following code.

```
if (noOfPeopleToInviteToTheStreetParty > 500)
  System.out.println("You may need an entertainment license!");
else ;
```

This will print the message if the **variable** has a value **greater than** 500, or otherwise execute the **empty statement** between the **reserved word** `else` and the semi-colon. Such empty statements do nothing, as you would probably expect!

It is quite common to wish nothing to be done when the condition is **false**, and so Java offers us the **if statement**. This is similar to the if else statement, except it simply does not have the word `else`, nor a false part.

```
if (noOfPeopleToInviteToTheStreetParty > 500)
  System.out.println("You may need an entertainment license!");
```

Our program to check the age of a person against the minimum age required to watch the film, essentially consists of a single **if statement**.

```
001: public class FilmAgeCheck
002: {
003:   public static void main(String[] args)
004:   {
005:     int minimumAge = Integer.parseInt(args[0]);
006:     int ageOfPerson = Integer.parseInt(args[1]);
007:     if (ageOfPerson < minimumAge)
008:       System.out.println("The person is too young to watch the film!");
009:   }
010: }
```

4.4.1 Trying it

After we have **compiled** the program, we can
run it with various **command line arguments**.

```
                          Console Input / Output
$ java FilmAgeCheck 18 14
The person is too young to watch the film!
$ java FilmAgeCheck 18 17
The person is too young to watch the film!
$ java FilmAgeCheck 15 15
$ java FilmAgeCheck 15 16
$ java FilmAgeCheck 12 21
$ _
```

Coffee time: Under what **condition** will the following code print the message?

    4.4.1

```
if (noOfPeopleToInviteToTheStreetParty > 500);
    System.out.println("You may need an entertainment license!");
```
(Hint: count the semi-colons.)

Coffee time: When do we get the quiet party message with this code?

    4.4.2

```
if (noOfPeopleToInviteToTheStreetParty > 100)
    if (noOfPeopleToInviteToTheStreetParty > 500)
        System.out.println("You may need an entertainment license!");
else
    System.out.println("It will be a fairly quiet party.");
```
(Hint: which **if** does the **else** match?)

4.4.2 Coursework: `PassFailDistinction`

In this task you will write a program called `PassFailDistinction` which takes a postgraduate student mark and reports whether it is a pass or fail; and then, possibly, that it is a distinction. You will use an **if else statement** followed by an **if statement**. Here is the specification of the required output for a given input.

The input is a single number, which might have decimal places in it, entered as a **command line argument**.

Input	First line of output
$input \geq 50$	Pass
$input < 50$	Fail

Input	Second line of output
$input \geq 70$	Distinction
$input < 70$	(no second line)

Start by designing your **test data** and expected output in your logbook. You do not need to worry about input which is invalid. Then **design** and implement your program, preferably without looking at any others. Finally, **run** it with your pre-planned tests and record whether your outcome was as you expected.

4.5 Example: Absolute difference

AIM: To introduce the **compound statement**.

This next example is a program to compute the absolute difference between two given numbers, i.e. the smallest subtracted from the largest. It also reports which of the numbers is the largest, or whether they are **equal**.

We wish to have more than one **statement** in the bodies of our **if else statements**, and to achieve this we shall use a **compound statement**.

Concept **Statement: compound statement.** The Java **compound statement** is simply a list of any number of **statement**s between an opening left brace ({) and a closing right brace (}). You could think of the body of a **method**, e.g. main(), as being a compound statement if that is helpful. The meaning is straightforward: when the computer **executes** a compound statement, it merely executes each statement inside it, in turn. More precisely of course, the Java **compiler** turns the **source code** into **byte code** that has this effect when the **virtual machine** executes the **compiled** program.

We can have a compound statement wherever we can have any kind of statement, but it is most useful when combined with statements which have another statement within them, such as **if else statement**s and **if statement**s.

For example, the following code reports three messages when the **variable** has a value **greater than** 500.

```
if (noOfPeopleToInviteToTheStreetParty > 500)
{
  System.out.println("You may need an entertainment license!");
  System.out.println("Also hire some street cleaners for the next day?");
  System.out.println("You should consider a bulk discount on lemonade!");
}
```

When the **condition** of the if statement is **true**, the body of the if statement is executed. This single statement is itself a compound statement, and so the three statements within it are executed. It is for this sort of purpose that the compound statement exists.

Note how we lay out the compound statement, with the opening brace at the same **indentation** as the if statement, the statements within it having extra indentation, and the closing brace lining up with the opening one.

Less usefully, a compound statement can be empty, as in the following example.

```
if (noOfPeopleToInviteToTheStreetParty > 500)
{
  System.out.println("You may need an entertainment license!");
  System.out.println("Also hire some street cleaners for the next day?");
  System.out.println("You should consider a bulk discount on lemonade!");
}
else {}
```

As you might expect, the meaning of an empty compound statement is the same as the meaning of an **empty statement**!

Here is our program.

```
001: public class AbsoluteDifference
002: {
003:   public static void main(String[] args)
004:   {
005:     double firstNumber = Double.parseDouble(args[0]);
006:     double secondNumber = Double.parseDouble(args[1]);
007:
008:     double absoluteDifference;
009:
010:     if (firstNumber > secondNumber)
011:     {
012:       System.out.println("The first number is larger than the second");
013:       absoluteDifference = firstNumber - secondNumber;
014:     }
```

```
015:    else if (firstNumber == secondNumber)
016:    {
017:      System.out.println("The two numbers are equal");
018:      absoluteDifference = 0;
019:    }
020:    else
021:    {
022:      System.out.println("The second number is larger than the first");
023:      absoluteDifference = secondNumber - firstNumber;
024:    }
025:    System.out.println("The absolute difference is " + absoluteDifference);
026:  }
027: }
```

4.5.1 Trying it

Let us test the program with some obvious cases
– note that this is not an exhaustive set of tests.

Console Input / Output
```
$ java AbsoluteDifference 123.4 123.45
The second number is larger than the first
The absolute difference is 0.04999999999999716
$ _
```

Coffee time: [4.5.1]
Are you surprised by the inaccuracy of the above
result?

Console Input / Output
```
$ java AbsoluteDifference 123.45 123.45
The two numbers are equal
The absolute difference is 0.0
$ java AbsoluteDifference 123.45 123.4
The first number is larger than the second
The absolute difference is 0.04999999999999716
$ _
```

The next test reminds us that **equality**
is a somewhat dangerous notion in the
context of computer approximations of
real numbers!

Console Input / Output
```
$ java AbsoluteDifference 123.45 123.450000000000001
The two numbers are equal
The absolute difference is 0.0
$ _
```

4.6 Concepts covered in this chapter

Here is a list of the concepts that were covered in this chapter, each with a self-test question. You can use this to check you
remember them being introduced, and perhaps re-read some of them before going on to the next chapter.

Execution	
– conditional execution (p.60)	What do we mean by conditional execution?

Expression	
– boolean (p.60)	How many possible values does a boolean expression have?
– boolean: relational operators (p.60)	How many relational operators are there, and what are they?

Statement	
– if else statement (p.60)	What are the three parts of an if else statement?

Statement	
– if else statement: nested (p.62)	What is special about the way we lay out if else statements contained within the false part of another?
– if statement (p.64)	What is the relationship between the if statement and the if else statement?
– compound statement (p.66)	What is the point of putting a list of statements inside a compound statement?

Chapter 5

Repeated execution

Many beads
make a necklace
when strung in a loop.

5.1 Chapter aims

Most programs require some parts of their code to be **execute**d more than once, and such **repeated execution** or **iteration** is the main focus of this chapter. We look in particular at Java's **while loop** and **for loop statement**s. As is often the case from now on, we also introduce some more general concepts.

The chapter contains the following sections.

Section	Aims	Associated Coursework
5.2 Minimum tank size (p.70)	To introduce the idea of **repeated execution**, implemented by the **while loop**. We also meet the notion of a **variable update**.	Write a program which calculates the minimum size of cubic tanks to hold given required volumes, where the possible sizes are in steps of 0.5 metre. (p.72)
5.3 Minimum bit width (p.72)	To introduce the idea of using **pseudo code** to help us **design** programs. We also meet Math.pow().	Write a program to find the largest square number which is **less than or equal** to a given number. (p.75)
5.4 Special note about design (p.75)	To make sure the process of **design** does not get forgotten!	(None.)
5.5 Compound interest one (p.75)	To reinforce the **while loop** and the **compound statement**.	Write a program to find the minimum **bit** width needed to support a given number of values, by doubling. (p.76)
5.6 Compound interest two (p.76)	To introduce the **for loop**.	Write a program to raise a given number to the power of a second given number, without using Math.pow(). (p.78)
5.7 Average of a list of numbers (p.78)	To show how to get the length of a **list**, note that an **index** can be a **variable**, and introduce **type casting**.	Write a program to produce the variance of some given numbers. (p.80)
5.8 Single times table (p.81)	To reinforce the **for loop**.	Write a program to produce a sin table. (p.81)

Section	Aims	Associated Coursework
5.9 Age history (p.82)	To introduce the idea of documenting programs using **comments**.	Write a program to print out all the years from the present day until the user retires. (p.84)
5.10 Home cooked Pi (p.85)	To introduce various **shorthand operators** for **variable updates**, have another example where we reveal the **pseudo code design**, and meet `Math.abs()` and `Math.PI`.	Go through all the programs before this point to see where **shorthand operators** could have been used. (p.89)

5.2 Example: Minimum tank size

AIM:
To introduce the idea of **repeated execution**, implemented by the **while loop**. We also meet the notion of a **variable update**.

Suppose you are a manufacturer of tanks for storing central heating oil, and typically specialize in making cubic shaped tanks from square pieces of metal in any size from $1M^2$ upwards, but due to some artifact of your cutting and assembly process, always a whole number of metres in each dimension. You would like to have a program that computes the dimensions of the smallest tank that is big enough to hold a given amount of oil.

One approach would be to start off with the smallest tank, that is a one metre cube, and keep making it one metre bigger in each dimension, while it is too small. This will require **repeated execution** of some part of the program.

Concept **Execution: repeated execution.** Having a computer always obey instructions just once within the **run** of a program is not sufficient to solve many problems. We often need the computer to do some things more than once. In general, we might want some instructions to be **executed**, zero, one or many times. This is known as **repeated execution**, **iteration**, or **looping**. The number of times a loop of instructions is executed will depend on some **condition** involving the **variables** in the program.

Concept **Statement: assignment statement: updating a variable.** Java **variables** have a name and a value, and this value can change. For example, the following code is one way of working out the maximum of two numbers.

```
int x;
int y;
int z;
... Code here that gives values to x, y and z.

int maximumOfXYandZ = x;
if (maximumOfXYandZ < y)
  maximumOfXYandZ = y;
if (maximumOfXYandZ < z)
  maximumOfXYandZ = z;
```

See that the variable `maximumOfXYandZ` is given a value which then might get changed, so that after the end of the second **if statement** it holds the correct value.

A very common thing we want the computer to do, typically inside a **loop**, is to perform a **variable update**. This is when a variable has its value changed to a new value which is based on its current one. For example, the code

```
count = count + 1;
```

will add one to the value of the variable `count`. Such examples remind us that an **assignment statement** is *not* a definition of **equality**, despite Java's use of the single **equal sign**!

Concept **Statement: while loop.** The **while loop** is one way in Java of having **repeated execution**. It essentially consists of two parts: a **condition**, and a **statement** which will be **execute**d repeatedly while the condition is `true`. The whole statement starts with the **reserved word** `while`. This is followed by the condition, written in brackets. Next comes the statement to be repeated, known as the **loop body**.

For example, the following code is a long winded and inefficient way of giving the **variable** x the value 21.

```
int x = 1;
while (x < 20)
  x = x + 2;
```

The variable starts off with the value 1, and then repeatedly has 2 added to it, until it is no longer **less than** 20. This is when the **loop** ends, and x will have the value 21.

Notice the brackets around the condition and the semi-colon at the end of the statement inside the loop. Notice also the way we lay out the code to make it easy to read, splitting the lines at sensible places and adding more **indentation** at the start of the inner statement.

Observe the similarity between the while loop and the **if statement** – the *only* difference in **syntax** is the first word. There is a similarity in meaning too: the while loop executes its body zero or *more* times, whereas the if statement executes its body zero or *one* time. However, **if statement**s are *not* loops and you should avoid the common novice phrase "if loop" when referring to them!

Our program to compute the minimum tank dimension will first obtain the required volume from the **command line argument**. Then it will compute the dimension of each side in the **variable** sideLength. It will do this by starting off with a value of 1, and then use a **while loop** to repeatedly add 1 to it, while a cubic tank of that side length is too small to hold the required volume. Finally it will report the computed side length.

```
001: public class MinimumTankSize
002: {
003:   public static void main(String[] args)
004:   {
005:     double requiredVolume = Double.parseDouble(args[0]);
006:     int sideLength = 1;
007:     while (sideLength * sideLength * sideLength < requiredVolume)
008:       sideLength = sideLength + 1;
009:     System.out.println("You need a tank of " + sideLength
010:                        + " metres per side to hold the volume "
011:                        + requiredVolume + " cubic metres");
012:   }
013: }
```

5.2.1 Trying it

After we have **compiled** the program, we can **run** it with various **command line argument**s.

```
                          Console Input / Output
$ java MinimumTankSize 1
You need a tank of 1 metres per side to hold the volume 1.0 cubic metres
$ java MinimumTankSize 1.001
You need a tank of 2 metres per side to hold the volume 1.001 cubic metres
$ java MinimumTankSize 8
You need a tank of 2 metres per side to hold the volume 8.0 cubic metres
$ java MinimumTankSize 8.001
You need a tank of 3 metres per side to hold the volume 8.001 cubic metres
$ java MinimumTankSize 100
You need a tank of 5 metres per side to hold the volume 100.0 cubic metres
$ _
```

What about some inappropriate values, such as zero, or a negative amount?

Console Input / Output
`$ java MinimumTankSize 0`
`You need a tank of 1 metres per side to hold the volume 0.0 cubic metres`
`$ java MinimumTankSize -10`
`You need a tank of 1 metres per side to hold the volume -10.0 cubic metres`
`$ _`

Coffee time: A common error made by novice programmers is to place a semi-colon (;) at the end of lines which shouldn't have one. What do you think would happen if the **while loop** of our program was as follows?

```
while (sideLength * sideLength * sideLength < requiredVolume);
    sideLength = sideLength + 1;
```

(Hint: remember the **empty statement**).

5.2.2   Coursework: `MinimumTankSize` in half measures

In this task you will write a program called `MinimumTankSize` which is the same as the one we have just covered, except that the tanks can be made with side lengths which are any positive whole multiple of 0.5 metre, instead of whole metres. (Hint: use **double** for the side length.)

Use the same **test data** as was used for the whole metres version of the program. Start by planning the expected output, in your logbook.

Then **design** and implement your program, preferably without looking at the previous version while you do this. When completed, **run** it with your pre-planned tests and record whether your outcome was as you expected.

Now change your program so that it has increments of 0.1 metres and test it again with the same data. Are there some surprises due to the accuracy of **real** numbers? Would you go so far as to say that some of them are wrong, rather than just inaccurate?

5.3   Example: Minimum bit width

AIM:
To introduce the idea of using **pseudo code** to help us **design** programs. We also meet `Math.pow()`.

Numbers are represented inside computers in **binary** form. This is base 2 representation, in which each number is a sequence of **binary digit**s or **bit**s, each bit being either 0 or 1.

This next example is a program to calculate how many bits would be needed to represent a given number of different values. One bit can represent two values (0, 1), two bits can represent four values (00, 01, 10, 11), three bits can represent eight values (000, 001, 010, 011, 100, 101, 110, 111), and so on. Each time we add one more bit, we double the number of values we can represent.

 Coffee time: Convince yourself that the number of values representable using N bits is 2^N.

Our program will first obtain the number of values from the **command line argument**. Then it will compute the number of bits needed, in the **variable** `noOfBits`. It will do this by starting off its value as 0, and using a **while loop** to add 1 to it, while it is too small to represent the number of values we want.

Before we write the code, we should scribble some **pseudo code** for it.

Concept **Design: pseudo code.** As our programs get a little more complex, it becomes hard to write them straight into the **text editor**. Instead we need to **design** them *before* we implement them.

We do not design programs by starting at the first word and ending at the last, like we do when we implement them. Instead we can start wherever it suits us – typically at the trickiest bit.

Neither do we express our designs in Java – that would be a bad thing to do, as Java forces our mind to be cluttered with trivia which, although essential in the final code, is distracting during the design.

Instead, we express our **algorithm** designs in **pseudo code**, which is a kind of informal programming language that has all unnecessary trivia ignored. So, for example, we do not bother writing the semi-colons at the end of **statement**s, or the brackets round **condition**s etc.. We might not bother writing the **class** heading, nor the **method** heading, if it is obvious to us what we are designing. And so on.

Also, during design in pseudo code, we can vary the level of **abstraction** to suit us – we do not have to be constrained to use only the features that are available in Java.

Here is the pseudo code for our minimum bit width program.

```
get numberOfValues from command line
noOfBits = 0
while noOfBits is too small
  increment noOfBits
output noOfBits
```

How do we know whether noOfBits is too small? It will be big enough when $2^{noOfBits} \geq numberOfValues$. So, we should continue incrementing it while $2^{noOfBits} < numberOfValues$. Let us rewrite our pseudo code, taking it closer to Java code.

```
numberOfValues = args[0]
noOfBits = 0
while 2^noOfBits < numberOfValues
  noOfBits = noOfBits + 1
s.o.p noOfBits
```

See how we have abbreviated System.out.println to just s.o.p in the pseudo code. See also the lack of semi-colons, and **condition** brackets. There really is no need to waste time during the **design** writing the exact code required for the final program.

Concept **Standard API: Math: pow().** Java does not have an **operator** to compute powers. Instead, there is a standard **class** called Math which contains a collection of useful **method**s, including pow(). This takes two numbers, separated by a comma, and gives the value of the first number raised to the power of the second.

For example, the **expression** Math.pow(2, 10) produces the value of 2^{10} which is 1024.

Our code for the finished program is as follows.

```
001: public class MinimumBitWidth
002: {
003:   public static void main(String[] args)
004:   {
005:     int numberOfValues = Integer.parseInt(args[0]);
006:     int noOfBits = 0;
```

```
007:     while (Math.pow(2, noOfBits) < numberOfValues)
008:        noOfBits = noOfBits + 1;
009:     System.out.println("You need " + noOfBits + " bits to represent "
010:                        + numberOfValues + " values");
011:  }
012: }
```

5.3.1 Trying it

After we have **compile**d the program, we can **run** it with various **command line argument**s.

Console Input / Output
```
$ java MinimumBitWidth 0
You need 0 bits to represent 0 values
$ java MinimumBitWidth 1
You need 0 bits to represent 1 values
$ _
```

Coffee time: ⌗5.3.2⌗ What do you think of the last result above – that you can represent one value using no bits? For example, how much memory would be needed to store the gender of each member of a club that only allows women to join?

Console Input / Output
```
$ java MinimumBitWidth 2
You need 1 bits to represent 2 values
$ java MinimumBitWidth 3
You need 2 bits to represent 3 values
$ java MinimumBitWidth 4
You need 2 bits to represent 4 values
$ java MinimumBitWidth 5
You need 3 bits to represent 5 values
$ java MinimumBitWidth 255
You need 8 bits to represent 255 values
$ java MinimumBitWidth 256
You need 8 bits to represent 256 values
$ java MinimumBitWidth 257
You need 9 bits to represent 257 values
$ _
```

Console Input / Output
```
$ java MinimumBitWidth 65535
You need 16 bits to represent 65535 values
$ java MinimumBitWidth 65536
You need 16 bits to represent 65536 values
$ java MinimumBitWidth 65537
You need 17 bits to represent 65537 values
$ java MinimumBitWidth 536870911
You need 29 bits to represent 536870911 values
$ java MinimumBitWidth 536870912
You need 29 bits to represent 536870912 values
$ java MinimumBitWidth 536870913
You need 30 bits to represent 536870913 values
$ java MinimumBitWidth 1073741823
You need 30 bits to represent 1073741823 values
$ java MinimumBitWidth 1073741824
You need 30 bits to represent 1073741824 values
$ java MinimumBitWidth 1073741825
You need 31 bits to represent 1073741825 values
$ _
```

Console Input / Output
```
$ java MinimumBitWidth 2147483647
You need 31 bits to represent 2147483647 values
$ java MinimumBitWidth 2147483648
Exception in thread "main" java.lang.NumberFormatException: For input string: "2
147483648"
        at java.lang.NumberFormatException.forInputString(NumberFormatException.
java:48)
        at java.lang.Integer.parseInt(Integer.java:465)
        at java.lang.Integer.parseInt(Integer.java:499)
        at MinimumBitWidth.main(MinimumBitWidth.java:5)
$ _
```

Coffee time: ⌗5.3.3⌗ Can you guess what has caused the **exception** in the last test? (Hint: **int** uses 32 **bits** to represent numbers, and needs to store negative as well as non-negative values.)

5.3.2 Coursework: `LargestSquare`

A square number is a whole number which is the square of another (or the same) whole number. Examples are 0, 1, 4, 9, 16, 25, 36, 49, 64, 81, 100, 121, 144, 169, etc.. In this task you will write a program called `LargestSquare` which takes a given positive **integer** as its **command line argument** and finds the largest square number which is **less than or equal** to that given number.

Start by planning your **test data** and expected results in your logbook. You do not need to worry about invalid inputs.

Now think about the **design** of your program. Perhaps the simplest approach to use is to focus on the square roots, rather than their squares. Start with a value which is **equal** to the given number, and keep decrementing it until its square is not **greater than** the number. So, for example, if the given number was 99, then we would start at 99 and count down until we finally get to 9 – this being the first number we find whose square is less than or equal to 99.

Express this **algorithm** in **pseudo code** in your logbook.

Finally, implement the program and test it with your test data, recording the results in your logbook.

Optional extra: Would it be quicker for the program to **loop** upwards from 0, rather than downwards from the given command line argument? Write that version as a program called `LargestSquare2`.

Optional extra: Look in the on-line Java documentation for the Java `Math` **class**, and find out how to obtain the square root of a number. Use this to speed up your program by making it start at a number which is much closer to the answer than the given command line argument is.

5.4 Special note about design

AIM: To make sure the process of **design** does not get forgotten!

There is not enough room in this book to show the **pseudo code** for every example, so we will only show it from time to time. However, it is most important that you do not get the wrong impression: all programs require some amount of **design** work, how much depends on the complexity of the program and the experience of the programmer. If you are new to programming, then it is safe to say that all the examples from now on would require you to produce pseudo code if you were writing the programs: even if you already knew the Java concepts being used in them. A common mistake that novice programmers make is to start writing each new program by immediately loading up the **text editor** and trying to simply type the code from start to end. You wouldn't do that with an essay would you? (I hope not!) Well, programs typically have a more complex structure than essays do, and so need more planning.

Remember that behind every example from now on there is some pseudo code design, even where it is not shown.

5.5 Example: Compound interest one

AIM: To reinforce the **while loop** and the **compound statement**.

This next example is a program to compute the minimum number of years we need to invest a given sum of money at a given interest rate, in order to achieve a balance of at least a given target amount.

We shall use a **while loop** for this, accumulating the balance within the **loop** while it is **less than** the target. We shall need the computer to perform two **statements** within the **loop body**, and so we use a **compound statement** – the name of which has nothing to do with compound interest! The while loop will both accumulate the balance and count the number of years in its body.

```
001: public class CompoundInterestKnownTarget
002: {
003:   public static void main(String[] args)
004:   {
005:     double initialInvestment = Double.parseDouble(args[0]);
006:     double interestRate = Double.parseDouble(args[1]);
007:     double targetBalance = Double.parseDouble(args[2]);
008:     int noOfYearsInvested = 0;
009:     double currentBalance = initialInvestment;
010:
011:     while (currentBalance < targetBalance)
012:     {
013:       noOfYearsInvested = noOfYearsInvested + 1;
014:       currentBalance = currentBalance + currentBalance * interestRate / 100;
015:     }
016:
017:     System.out.println(initialInvestment + " invested at interest rate "
018:                        + interestRate + "%");
019:     System.out.println("After " + noOfYearsInvested + " years,"
020:                        + " the balance will be " + currentBalance);
021:   }
022: }
```

5.5.1 Trying it

```
                          Console Input / Output
$ java CompoundInterestKnownTarget 100.0 12.5 1000.0
100.0 invested at interest rate 12.5%
After 20 years, the balance will be 1054.50938424492
$ java CompoundInterestKnownTarget 100.0 4.5 1000.0
100.0 invested at interest rate 4.5%
After 53 years, the balance will be 1030.7738533669428
$ _
```

5.5.2 Coursework: MinimumBitWidth by doubling

In this task you will write a variation of the MinimumBitWidth program which works a little more efficiently. Instead of computing a power of 2 in the **loop condition** on each **iteration**, your version will accumulate 2 to the power of noOfBits in a separate **variable**. This can be done by initializing your new variable to 1, and simply doubling its value each time you increment noOfBits.

You will use the same **test data** as used for the previous version of the program – except, do not try higher than 1073741824, otherwise your program will not end!

First think about the **design** of your program and plan in your logbook the changes you need to make to the original version.

Finally, implement the program and test it with your test data, recording the results in your logbook.

Optional extra: Explain why an input of, say, 1073741825 will cause a never ending **infinite loop**. Is there a solution?

5.6 Example: Compound interest two

AIM:
To introduce the **for loop**.

This next program is similar to the previous, except that this time we know the number of years of investment and wish to calculate the end balance.

We could use a **while loop** in this program, but it is actually more appropriate to use a **for loop** instead.

Concept **Statement: for loop.** Another kind of **loop** in Java is the **for loop**, which is best suited for situations when the number of **iterations** of the **loop body** is known before the loop starts. We shall describe it using the following simple example.

```java
for (int count = 1; count <= 10; count = count + 1)
    System.out.println("Counting " + count);
```

The **statement** starts with the **reserved word for**, which is followed by three items in brackets, separated by semi-colons. Then comes the loop body, which is a single statement (often a **compound statement** of course). The first of the three items in brackets is a **for initialization**, which is performed once just before the loop starts. Typically this involves declaring a **variable** and giving an initial value to it, as in the above example int count = 1. The second item is the **condition** for continuing the loop – the loop will only **execute** and will continue to execute while that condition is **true**. In the example above the condition is count <= 10. Finally, the third item, a **for update**, is a statement which is executed at the *end* of each iteration of the loop, that is *after* the loop body has been executed. This is typically used to change the value of the variable declared in the first item, as in our example count = count + 1.

So the overall effect of our simple example is: declare count and set its value to 1, check that it is **less than** 10, print out Counting 1, add one to count, check again, print out Counting 2, add one to count, check again, and so on until the condition is **false** when the value of count has reached 11.

We do not really need the for loop, as the **while loop** is sufficient. For example, the code above could have been written as follows.

```java
int count = 1;
while (count <= 10)
{
    System.out.println("Counting " + count);
    count = count + 1;
}
```

However you will see that the for loop version has placed together all the code associated with the control of the loop, making it easier to read, as well as a little shorter.

There is one very subtle difference between the for loop and while loop versions of the example above, concerning the **scope** of the variable count, that is the area of code in which the variable can be used. Variables declared in the initialization part of a for loop can only be used in the for loop – they do not exist elsewhere. This is an added benefit of using for loops when appropriate: the variable, which is used solely to control the loop, cannot be accidentally used in the rest of the code.

Our program to calculate the end balance after a known number of years will use a for loop that accumulates the balance once for each year.

```java
001: public class CompoundInterestKnownYears
002: {
003:     public static void main(String[] args)
004:     {
005:         double initialInvestment = Double.parseDouble(args[0]);
006:         double interestRate = Double.parseDouble(args[1]);
007:         int noOfYearsInvested = Integer.parseInt(args[2]);
008:         double currentBalance = initialInvestment;
009:
010:         for (int year = 1; year <= noOfYearsInvested; year = year + 1)
011:             currentBalance = currentBalance + currentBalance * interestRate / 100;
```

77

```
012:
013:        System.out.println(initialInvestment + " invested at interest rate "
014:                          + interestRate + "%");
015:        System.out.println("After " + noOfYearsInvested + " years,"
016:                          + " the balance will be " + currentBalance);
017:    }
018: }
```

Coffee time: **5.6.1** Could we have written the first line of the for loop as follows?
   `for (int year = 0; year < noOfYearsInvested; year = year + 1)`
If so, which is better? What if we wanted to use the value of `year` inside the **loop** – would that affect your choice of which is best?

Coffee time: **5.6.2** Could we have written it as this?!!
   `for (int year = 0; year < 2 * noOfYearsInvested; year = year + 2)`

5.6.1 Trying it

```
                          Console Input / Output
$ java CompoundInterestKnownYears 100.0 12.5 5
100.0 invested at interest rate 12.5%
After 5 years, the balance will be 180.2032470703125
$ java CompoundInterestKnownYears 100.0 4.5 12
100.0 invested at interest rate 4.5%
After 12 years, the balance will be 169.5881432767867
$ _
```

5.6.2 Coursework: `Power`

What would you do if you needed to compute powers, and somebody had not already written the **method** Math.pow()? You would write the code yourself, and perhaps make it available for others to use.

In this task you will write a program, called `Power`, that takes two **integer** values as **command line argument**s and prints out the result of the first number raised to the power of the second. You may not use the Math.pow() method – somebody had to write that code, and let us pretend it is you! However, for simplicity, you may assume that both arguments exist and represent integers, and that the second number is non-negative.

Start by planning your **test data** and expected results in in your logbook.

Now think about the **design** of your program. One approach is to have a **variable** to accumulate the result, which starts off with the value 1. Then, using a **loop**, this result is multiplied by the first number as many times as the value of the second number. A **for loop** is appropriate for this task. Write **pseudo code** in your logbook.

Finally implement the program, (ideally without looking at CompoundInterestKnownYears!), test it with your preplanned tests and record the results in your logbook.

5.7 Example: Average of a list of numbers

AIM:
To show how to get the length of a **list**, note that an **index** can be a **variable**, and introduce **type cast**ing.

This next program is one which takes a **list** of **integer**s from the **command line argument**s, and calculates their mean average. This is done by computing their sum in a **for loop**, and dividing it by the number of numbers.

Our program will need to find the length of the list of command line arguments, that is, the number of them. It also needs to access them using a **variable** as the **index**.

Concept **Command line arguments: length of the list.** The **command line arguments** passed to the **main method** are a **list** of strings. We can find the length of a list by writing a dot followed by the word `length`, after the name of the list. For example, `args.length` yields an **int** value which is the number of items in the list `args`.

Concept **Command line arguments: list index can be a variable.** The **index** used to access the individual items from a **list** of strings does not have to be an **integer literal**, but can be an **int variable** or indeed an **arithmetic expression**. For example, the following code adds together a list of **integers** given as **command line arguments**.

```
int sumOfArgs = 0;
for (int argIndex = 0; argIndex < args.length; argIndex = argIndex + 1)
  sumOfArgs = sumOfArgs + Integer.parseInt(args[argIndex]);
System.out.println("The sum is " + sumOfArgs);
```

The benefit of being able to use a **variable**, rather than an integer literal is that the access can be done in a **loop** which controls the value of the variable: thus the actual value used as the index is not the same each time.

Back in our `MeanAverage` program, the sum of the numbers is an integer, as is the number of them. So, if we are not careful, when we come to do the **division**, Java will throw away the remainder and give us the wrong result! We can ensure that Java uses **double division**, by turning at least one of the two integers into a **double** using a **type cast**.

Concept **Type: casting an int to a double.** Sometimes we have an **int** value which we wish to be regarded as a **double**. The process of conversion is known as **cast**ing, and we can achieve it by writing `(double)` in front of the **int**. For example, `(double)5` is the **double** value `5.0`. Of course, we are most likely to use this feature to cast the value of an **int variable**, rather than an **integer literal**.

It does not make sense to ask for the mean average of no numbers, so we shall assume there is at least one number. Our program will start by making the sum **equal** to the first number, and then use a for loop to add on the remaining numbers.

Here is our code.

```
001: public class MeanAverage
002: {
003:   public static void main(String[] args)
004:   {
005:     int sumSoFar = Integer.parseInt(args[0]);
006:
007:     for (int index = 1; index < args.length; index = index + 1)
008:       sumSoFar = sumSoFar + Integer.parseInt(args[index]);
009:
010:     System.out.println("The mean average is "
011:                         + sumSoFar / (double) args.length);
012:   }
013: }
```

Coffee time: 5.7.1 Recall that list indices start at 0. Convince yourself that we are correctly accessing the numbers in the list: should the for loop index start from 0? Why not? Would the following code for the for loop work? Is it better code?

```
for (int index = 1; index <= args.length - 1; index = index + 1)
```

Coffee time: *5.7.2* What would happen if there were no numbers given on the command line? What sort of **exception** would be reported? What if we had started the value of sumSoFar at 0 and dealt with the first number inside the **loop**, instead of separately before the loop. What sort of exception would we *expect* to get now, if there were no command line arguments? Try it and see!

5.7.1   Trying it

After we have **compile**d the program, we can **run** it with various **command line arguments**.

```
                      Console Input / Output
$ java MeanAverage 100
The mean average is 100.0
$ java MeanAverage 100 500
The mean average is 300.0
$ java MeanAverage 34 67 12 904 -5 8375 -1249
The mean average is 1162.5714285714287
$ java MeanAverage 60 -100 40
The mean average is 0.0
$ _
```

Note that we get a **run time error** if we run the program with no arguments.

```
                      Console Input / Output
$ java MeanAverage
Exception in thread "main" java.lang.ArrayIndexOutOfBoundsException: 0
        at MeanAverage.main(MeanAverage.java:5)
$ _
```

5.7.2   Coursework: Variance

In statistics, the variance of a **set** of numbers is one way of measuring the spread of them. It is the sum of the squares of the deviations (differences) between each number and the mean average of the numbers, all divided by the number of numbers.

For example, a set of student marks $\{2,4,6,8,10\}$ (out of 10) has a mean of 6 (which also happens to be one of the marks). The deviations from the mean are $\{-4,-2,0,2,4\}$ and the squares of such are $\{16,4,0,4,16\}$. The variance is thus $(16+4+0+4+16)/5$, which is 8. Whereas, the results $\{4,5,6,7,8\}$ share the same mean but have a variance of only 2.

One approach to computing the variance is as follows. First compute the mean average of the numbers. Then, go through each number and compute the deviation between it and the mean, squaring this difference and accumulating the sum of all these squared deviations. Finally, divide that sum by the number of numbers.

In this task you will write a program, called Variance that takes a **list** of **integer** values as **command line arguments** and prints out the mean average and the variance of them. You may assume that there is at least one number, and that all the arguments represent integers.

Here is an example **run** of the program.

```
                      Console Input / Output
$ java Variance 2 4 6 8 10
The mean average is 6.0
The variance is 8.0
$ _
```

Start by planning your **test data** and expected results in in your logbook.

Now think about the **design** of your program. You can copy the code for computing the mean of the numbers from the example in this section. This will then be followed by a second **for loop** to compute the sum of the squares of the deviations between each number and the mean. You will need more **variables**, including one to hold the mean of the numbers, and another for the sum of the squares of the deviation between each number and the mean. Then the variance can be computed and output.

Write **pseudo code** in your logbook.

Finally, implement the program, test it with your preplanned tests and record the results in your logbook.

5.8   Example: Single times table

AIM:
To reinforce the **for loop**.

Our next example is a program that prints out the times table for a given number. We shall attempt to make the output pretty using lines of hyphens and vertical bar **character**s.

```
001: public class TimesTable
002: {
003:   public static void main(String[] args)
004:   {
005:     int multiplier = Integer.parseInt(args[0]);
006:
007:     System.out.println("------------------------------");
008:     System.out.println("| Times table for " + multiplier);
009:     System.out.println("------------------------------");
010:     for (int thisNumber = 1; thisNumber <= 10; thisNumber = thisNumber + 1)
011:       System.out.println("| " + thisNumber + " x " + multiplier
012:                               + " = " + thisNumber * multiplier);
013:     System.out.println("------------------------------");
014:   }
015: }
```

5.8.1   Trying it

After we have **compiled** the program, we can **run** it with various **command line arguments**.

Console Input / Output
$ **java TimesTable 3**

| Times table for 3

| 1 x 3 = 3
| 2 x 3 = 6
| 3 x 3 = 9
| 4 x 3 = 12
| 5 x 3 = 15
| 6 x 3 = 18
| 7 x 3 = 21
| 8 x 3 = 24
| 9 x 3 = 27
| 10 x 3 = 30

$ _

Console Input / Output
$ **java TimesTable 5**

| Times table for 5

| 1 x 5 = 5
| 2 x 5 = 10
| 3 x 5 = 15
| 4 x 5 = 20
| 5 x 5 = 25
| 6 x 5 = 30
| 7 x 5 = 35
| 8 x 5 = 40
| 9 x 5 = 45
| 10 x 5 = 50

$ _

5.8.2   Coursework: `SinTable`

In the days before scientific calculators, students of trigonometry used to use mathematical tables to look up values of **function**s, such as sin, cosin and tan.

In this task you will write a program, called `SinTable` to produce a sin table. It will take three **integer command line arguments**: the starting point of the table, the increment and the ending point. You can assume these arguments represent whole numbers of degrees.

Here is an example **run**.

```
          Console Input / Output
$ java SinTable 0 10 90
-----------------------------------------------
| Sin table from 0 to 90 in steps of 10
-----------------------------------------------
| sin(0)  = 0.0
| sin(10) = 0.17364817766693033
| sin(20) = 0.3420201433256687
| sin(30) = 0.49999999999999994
| sin(40) = 0.6427876096865393
| sin(50) = 0.766044443118978
| sin(60) = 0.8660254037844386
| sin(70) = 0.9396926207859083
| sin(80) = 0.984807753012208
| sin(90) = 1.0
-----------------------------------------------
$ _
```

In Java, in order to compute the sin of a value, d, which is expressed in degrees, we can use the following **expression**.

```
Math.sin(Math.toRadians(d))
```

The **method** `sin()` is available in the standard **class** `Math`. It takes a value, expressed in radians, and **returns** the sin of that value. The method `toRadians()`, in the same class, converts a given value in degrees to the corresponding value in radians.

Start by planning your **test data** and expected results in in your logbook.

Now think about the **design** of your program. It should use a **for loop**. Write **pseudo code** in your logbook. You will learn most if you try not to look at `TimesTable` while designing – perhaps you should compare the two programs after you have completed the task?

Finally, implement the program, test it with your preplanned tests and record the results in your logbook.

5.9   Example: Age history

AIM:
To introduce the idea of documenting programs using **comments**.

Our next example is a program that produces the birthday history of a person, given the present year and their birth year as **command line arguments**. We shall use it for exploring the principle of writing **comments** to make our programs more readable to humans.

Concept **Code clarity: comments.** In addition to having careful layout and **indentation** in our programs, we can also enhance human readability by using **comments**. These are pieces of text which are ignored by the **compiler**, but help describe to the human reader what the program does and how it works.

For example, every program should have comments at the start saying what it does and briefly how it is used. Also, **variables** can often benefit from a comment before their declaration explaining what they are used for. As appropriate, there should be comments in the code too, *before* certain parts of it, explaining what these next **statements** are going to do.

One form of comment in Java starts with the symbol //. The rest of that source line is then the text of the comment. For example

```
// This is a comment, ignored by the compiler.
```

82

Concept **Code clarity: comments: marking ends of code constructs.**   Another good use of **comment**s is to mark every closing brace (}) with a comment saying what code construct it is ending. The following skeleton example code illustrates this.

```
public class SomeClass
{
  public static void main(String[] args)
  {
    ...
    while (...)
    {
      ...
      ...
      ...
    } // while
    ...
  } // main

} // class SomeClass
```

Here is our code for the age history program.

```
001: // Program to print out the history of a person's age.
002: // First argument is an integer for the present year.
003: // Second argument is the birth year, which must be less than the present year.
004: public class AgeHistory
005: {
006:   public static void main(String[] args)
007:   {
008:     // The year of the present day.
009:     int presentYear = Integer.parseInt(args[0]);
010:
011:     // The year of birth: this must be less than the present year.
012:     int birthYear = Integer.parseInt(args[1]);
013:
014:     // Start by printing the event of birth.
015:     System.out.println("You were born in " + birthYear);
016:
017:     // Now we will go through the years between birth and last year.
018:
019:     // We need to keep track of the year we are considering
020:     // starting with the year after the birth year.
021:     int someYear = birthYear + 1;
022:
023:     // We keep track of the age, starting with 1.
024:     int ageInSomeYear = 1;
025:
026:     // We deal with each year while it has not reached the present year.
027:     while (someYear != presentYear)
028:     {
029:       // Print out the age in that year.
030:       System.out.println("You were " + ageInSomeYear + " in " + someYear);
031:
```

```
032:        // Add one to the year and to the age.
033:        someYear = someYear + 1;
034:        ageInSomeYear = ageInSomeYear + 1;
035:    } // while
036:
037:    // At this point someYear will equal presentYear.
038:    // So ageInSomeYear must be the age in the present year.
039:    System.out.println("You are " + ageInSomeYear + " this year");
040:    } // main
041:
042: } // class AgeHistory
```

> *Coffee time:* 5.9.1
> What would happen if we ran the program with a birth year which is not **less than** the present year?

5.9.1 Trying it

After we have **compil**ed the program, we can **run** it with various **command line argument**s.

> **Console Input / Output**
> ```
> $ java AgeHistory 2015 2014
> You were born in 2014
> You are 1 this year
> $ _
> ```

> **Console Input / Output**
> ```
> $ java AgeHistory 2015 1996
> ```
> (Output shown using multiple columns to save space.)
> ```
> You were born in 1996 | You were 7 in 2003  | You were 14 in 2010
> You were 1 in 1997    | You were 8 in 2004  | You were 15 in 2011
> You were 2 in 1998    | You were 9 in 2005  | You were 16 in 2012
> You were 3 in 1999    | You were 10 in 2006 | You were 17 in 2013
> You were 4 in 2000    | You were 11 in 2007 | You were 18 in 2014
> You were 5 in 2001    | You were 12 in 2008 | You are 19 this year
> You were 6 in 2002    | You were 13 in 2009 |
> $ _
> ```

Let us try the program with inappropriate **data**, where the birth year is **greater than** the present year. In this test we use some Unix commands to run the program in the background, and then force it to stop running after one second (a long time for a computer to be doing some work), and then show only the last 3 lines of the resulting output.[1]

> **Console Input / Output**
> ```
> $ (java AgeHistory 2015 2016 & PID=${!}; sleep 1; kill $PID) | tail -3
> You were 30043 in 32059
> You were 30044 in 32060
> You were 30045 in 32061
> $ _
> ```

>
> *Coffee time:* 5.9.2
> Can you explain the program behaviour?

Let us repeat that experiment.

> **Console Input / Output**
> ```
> $ (java AgeHistory 2015 2016 & PID=${!}; sleep 1; kill $PID) | tail -3
> You were 28780 in 30796
> You were 28781 in 30797
> You were 28782 in 30798
> $ _
> ```

> *Coffee time:* 5.9.3
> Why is the result different? What would happen if we let the program run indefinitely? (Hint: is there a maximum value for someYear?)

5.9.2 Coursework: WorkFuture

In this task you will write a program, called WorkFuture, which shows the future working time of a user, assuming he or she retires at 68. The program will take two **command line argument**s, which you may assume are valid. The first is the present year, the second is the birth year of the user.

---

[1] Unfortunately, there is no simple way of running this experiment using standard commands in a Microsoft Command Prompt.

An example use of the program might be as follows.

Console Input / Output
```
$ java WorkFuture 2015 1959
You have 12 years left to work
In 2016 you will have 11 years left to work
In 2017 you will have 10 years left to work
In 2018 you will have 9 years left to work
In 2019 you will have 8 years left to work
In 2020 you will have 7 years left to work
In 2021 you will have 6 years left to work
In 2022 you will have 5 years left to work
In 2023 you will have 4 years left to work
In 2024 you will have 3 years left to work
In 2025 you will have 2 years left to work
In 2026 you will have 1 years left to work
You will retire in 2027
$ _
```

Start by planning your **test data** and expected results in your logbook. Next, **design** the program, writing **pseudo code** in your logbook. As is generally true, you will learn most if you can avoid referring to the associated example while you do this, and only compare the two programs when you have finished.

Finally, implement the program – including suitable **comment**s in the text, and test it. Record your results in the usual way.

5.10   Example: Home cooked Pi

AIM: To introduce various **shorthand operator**s for **variable update**s, have another example where we reveal the **pseudo code design**, and meet `Math.abs()` and `Math.PI`.

Whether or not geometry is your cup of tea, you will appreciate that the constant π (Pi) plays an important role, and many people have spent much of their life trying to calculate its value to more and more accuracy.

The 15th century Indian mathematician Madhava of Sangamagrama (or one of his successors) discovered the following, which was rediscovered in 1673 by Gottfried Leibniz[15].

$$\pi = 4 - \frac{4}{3} + \frac{4}{5} - \frac{4}{7} + \frac{4}{9} - \cdots$$

The result gets more accurate as more terms are included in the sum. However, one cannot achieve an exact answer – no matter how many terms we include, there are always more. Each one is smaller than the previous and they are alternately added and subtracted from the sum. So the result jumps either side of true π getting closer to it, but never actually reaches it. It does not matter if you do not understand why the formula works – it is sufficient to trust Leibniz and merely implement it correctly.

So, as another example program, we are here going to write an implementation of this formula. It is not the fastest **algorithm** for calculating π, but it is an interesting example from a programming point of view. Our program will start off with the value 4, then subtract $\frac{4}{3}$, then add $\frac{4}{5}$, and so on. The denominator of each term is two more than the previous one, and the sign keeps alternating between + and –. Our estimation will stop when the difference between two successive sums is **less than or equal** to some tolerance given as a **command line argument**. In other words, we will stop including terms when we have a result which is close enough as an estimate of π.

Let us write some **pseudo code** for the program. Our basic approach is to have two results: the latest one, and the previous one. Our **loop** will stop when the difference between these satisfies the tolerance.

```
obtain tolerance from command line
set up previousEstimate as value from no terms
set up latestEstimate as value from one term
while previousEstimate is not within tolerance of latestEstimate
  previousEstimate = latestEstimate
  add next term to latestEstimate
end-while
print out latestEstimate
print out the number of terms used
print out the standard known value of Pi for comparison
```

We next make some of the code more concrete, and add a **variable** to count the number of terms.

```
double tolerance = args[0]
double previousEstimate = 0
double latestEstimate = 4
int termCount = 1
while previousEstimate is not within tolerance of latestEstimate
  previousEstimate = latestEstimate
  add next term to latestEstimate
  termCount = termCount + 1
end-while
s.o.p latestEstimate
s.o.p termCount
s.o.p the standard known value of Pi for comparison
```

In order to find the next term to add in the loop, we could use two variables: one for the denominator and one for the sign of the numerator. The first keeps growing by two each time, and the second alternates between 1 and −1.

 Coffee time: 5.10.1   What simple operation can we do to a variable to make it change the sign of its value?

```
double tolerance = args[0]
double previousEstimate = 0
double latestEstimate = 4
int termCount = 1
int nextDenominator = 3
int nextNumeratorSign = -1
while previousEstimate is not within tolerance of latestEstimate
  previousEstimate = latestEstimate
  latestEstimate = latestEstimate + nextNumeratorSign * 4 / nextDenominator
  termCount = termCount + 1
  nextNumeratorSign = nextNumeratorSign * -1
  nextDenominator = nextDenominator + 2
end-while
s.o.p latestEstimate
s.o.p termCount
s.o.p the standard known value of Pi for comparison
```

Now there is only two pieces of pseudo code left to make more concrete before we can write the Java code. Do you agree?

Our loop **condition** must see if the **absolute value** of the difference between the latest and previous results, is still **greater than** the tolerance.

Concept **Standard API: Math: abs ().** Java does not have an **operator** to yield the **absolute value** of a number, that is, its value ignoring its sign. Instead, the standard **class** called `Math` contains a **method**, called `abs`. This method takes a number and gives its absolute value.

For example, the **expression** `Math.abs(-2.7)` produces the value `2.7`, as does the expression `Math.abs(3.4 - 0.7)`.

We will code the loop condition as follows.

```
Math.abs(latestEstimate - previousEstimate) > tolerance
```

That just leaves the question: where can we find a standard known value of π?

Concept **Standard API: Math: PI.** The standard **class** called `Math` contains a constant value called `PI` that is set to the most accurate value of π that can be represented using the **double** number **type**. We can refer to this value using `Math.PI`, as in the following example.

```
double circleArea = Math.PI * circleRadius * circleRadius;
```

Before we present the final code of our π estimating program, we are going to introduce a number of **shorthand operators** which can be used for updating the value of a variable.

Concept **Statement: assignment statement: updating a variable: shorthand operators.** The need to undertake a **variable update** is so common, that Java provides various **shorthand operators** for certain types of update.

Here are some of the most commonly used ones.

Operator	Name	Example	Longhand meaning
++	postfix increment	x++	x = x + 1
--	postfix decrement	x--	x = x - 1
+=	compound assignment: add to	x += y	x = x + y
-=	compound assignment: subtract from	x -= y	x = x - y
*=	compound assignment: multiply by	x *= y	x = x * y
/=	compound assignment: divide by	x /= y	x = x / y

The point of these **postfix increment**, **postfix decrement** and **compound assignment** operators is not so much to save typing when a program is being written, but to make the program easier to read. Once you are familiar with them, you will benefit from the shorter and more obvious code.

There is also a historical motivation. In the early days of the programming language C, from which Java inherits much of its **syntax**, these shorthand **operators** caused the **compiler** to produce more efficient code than their longhand counterparts. The modern Java compiler with the latest optimization technology should remove this concern.

 Coffee time: [5.10.2] How many of these shorthand operators can be used in this program? Where? If we had known about them before this point, do you think we would have used them in our pseudo code?

Here is the final code.

```
001: // A program to estimate Pi using Leibniz's formula.
002: // Argument is desired tolerance between successive terms.
003: // Reports the estimate, the number of terms
004: // and the library constant for comparison.
005: public class PiEstimation
006: {
007:   public static void main(String[] args)
008:   {
009:     // The tolerance is the minimum difference between successive
010:     // terms before we stop estimating.
011:     double tolerance = Double.parseDouble(args[0]);
012:
013:     // The result from our previous estimate, initially 0 for 0 terms.
014:     double previousEstimate = 0;
015:
016:     // The result from our latest estimate, eventually the final result.
017:     double latestEstimate = 4;
018:
019:     // We count the terms, initially 1 for the 4.
020:     int termCount = 1;
021:
022:     // The value of the next term denominator, initially 3.
023:     int nextDenominator = 3;
024:
025:     // The sign of the next term, initially -ve.
026:     int nextNumeratorSign = -1;
027:
028:     // Keep adding terms until change is within tolerance.
029:     while (Math.abs(latestEstimate - previousEstimate) > tolerance)
030:     {
031:       previousEstimate = latestEstimate;
032:       latestEstimate += nextNumeratorSign * 4.0 / nextDenominator;
033:       termCount++;
034:       nextNumeratorSign *= -1;
035:       nextDenominator += 2;
036:     } // while
037:
038:     System.out.println("The estimated value of Pi to tolerance " + tolerance
039:                         + " is " + latestEstimate);
040:     System.out.println("The estimate used " + termCount + " terms");
041:     System.out.println("The library value of Pi is " + Math.PI);
042:   } // main
043:
044: } // class PiEstimation
```

> **Coffee time:**
> *5.10.3*
>
> What would happen if we wrote 4 instead of 4.0 when computing the next term to add to the result? Without trying it, can you say what the output would be?

5.10.1   Trying it

Let us try the program with some large tolerances first.

Console Input / Output

```
$ java PiEstimation 0.1
The estimated value of Pi to tolerance 0.1 is 3.189184782277596
The estimate used 21 terms
The library value of Pi is 3.141592653589793
$ java PiEstimation 0.01
The estimated value of Pi to tolerance 0.01 is 3.1465677471829556
The estimate used 201 terms
The library value of Pi is 3.141592653589793
$ _
```

```
                    Console Input / Output
$ java PiEstimation 0.001
The estimated value of Pi to tolerance 0.0010 is 3.1420924036835256
The estimate used 2001 terms
The library value of Pi is 3.141592653589793
$ _
```

See how the number of terms is growing rapidly as we ask for more accuracy – we did say this was not the fastest **algorithm** for computing π!

```
                    Console Input / Output
$ java PiEstimation 0.00001
The estimated value of Pi to tolerance 1.0E-5 is 3.141597653564762
The estimate used 200001 terms
The library value of Pi is 3.141592653589793
$ java PiEstimation 0.000001
The estimated value of Pi to tolerance 1.0E-6 is 3.1415931535894743
The estimate used 2000001 terms
The library value of Pi is 3.141592653589793
$ _
```

You may observe above that Java prints out small **double** values using **scientific notation**. 1.0E-6 means 1.0×10^{-6} which is of course 0.000001.

Coffee time: 5.10.4   How many decimal places accuracy would you expect to get from the tolerance **command line argument** given in that last test? Does this tally with the results?

Let us see what happens when we ask for more decimal places.

```
                    Console Input / Output
$ java PiEstimation 0.0000001
The estimated value of Pi to tolerance 1.0E-7 is 3.1415927035898146
The estimate used 20000001 terms
The library value of Pi is 3.141592653589793
$ _
```

Coffee time: 5.10.5
Did you notice that the number of terms from the last test has broken the pattern from the previous ones? Might this suggest something about accuracy?

```
                    Console Input / Output
$ java PiEstimation 0.00000001
The estimated value of Pi to tolerance 1.0E-8 is 3.1415926485894077
The estimate used 199999998 terms
The library value of Pi is 3.141592653589793
$ _
```

Coffee time: 5.10.6   As we ask for more accuracy, the program takes longer to **run**: about 10 times more terms for each extra decimal place! What is the specific danger if we ask for too much accuracy? (Hint: is there a maximum value for nextDenominator? Also, remember that **double**s are only approximations of **real** numbers.)

5.10.2   Coursework: Shorthand operators

Now that you know about the **shorthand operators** for updating **variable**s, in this task you will go through all the examples in this chapter and identify all the places where they could have been used, recording your analysis in your logbook.

Optional extra: Take the program from this section and try it with one more decimal place. Then try to improve it to extend its accuracy.

5.11 Concepts covered in this chapter

Here is a list of the concepts that were covered in this chapter, each with a self-test question. You can use this to check you remember them being introduced, and perhaps re-read some of them before going on to the next chapter.

Code clarity	
– comments (p.82)	Where should we write comments?
– comments: marking ends of code constructs (p.83)	Why is this a good idea?
Command line arguments	
– length of the list (p.79)	What does it mean if `args.length` is zero?
– list index can be a variable (p.79)	What is the benefit of being able to use a variable as a list index?
Design	
– pseudo code (p.73)	What is the difference between Java and pseudo code?
Execution	
– repeated execution (p.70)	What does iteration mean?
Standard API	
– `Math: pow()` (p.73)	What is the value of `Math.pow(10, 2)` – is it `100` or `1024`?
– `Math: abs()` (p.87)	What is the value of `Math.abs(-2.7)`?
– `Math: PI` (p.87)	What type does the value of `Math.PI` have?
Statement	
– assignment statement: updating a variable (p.70)	What is the effect of `x = x * 10;`?

– assignment statement: updating a variable: shorthand operators (p.87)	What is the shorthand way of writing each of the following?
	`x = x + 1;   x = x - 1;   x = x + y;`
	`x = x - y;   x = x * y;   x = x / y;`

– while loop (p.71)	What is the similarity between the while loop and the if statement?
– for loop (p.77)	What are the four parts of a for loop? When should a for loop be used instead of a while loop?
Type	
– casting an `int` to a `double` (p.79)	If the **int** variable `x` has the value 4, what is the value of `10 / (double)x`?

Chapter 6

Control statements nested in loops

Many stones
can make a wall.
Many walls
can make a castle.

6.1 Chapter aims

The principle concern of this chapter is to explore the idea of nesting **statement**s within one another, in order to build appropriately complex **algorithm** structures capable of solving significant problems.

The chapter contains the following sections.

Section	Aims	Associated Coursework
6.2 Film certificate age checking the whole queue (p.92)	To introduce the ideas of nesting an **if statement** within a **for loop**, and declaring a **variable** inside a **compound statement**. We also introduce the **conditional operator**.	Write a program to find the maximum of a given **list** of numbers. (p.95)
6.3 Dividing a cake (GCD) (p.95)	To introduce the idea of nesting an **if else statement** within a **while loop**.	Write a program to compute the **greatest common divisor** of three numbers. (p.97)
6.4 Printing a rectangle (p.97)	To introduce the idea of nesting a **for loop** within a **for loop**. We also meet System.out.print() and revisit System.out.println().	Write a program to print out a rectangle with a hole in it. (p.99)
6.5 Printing a triangle (p.100)	To reinforce the idea of nesting a **for loop** within a **for loop**.	Write a program to print out an isosceles right angled triangle, with a straight right edge, and the longest side at the top. (p.101)
6.6 Multiple times table (p.101)	To reinforce the idea of having **nested statement**s within each other, and explore the idea of using multiple **loop**s in sequence.	Write a program to produce a table showing pairs of numbers which share common factors. (p.103)
6.7 Luck is in the air: dice combinations (p.104)	To introduce the idea of using **nested loop**s to generate combinations.	Write a program that determines which 3 digit decimal whole numbers are **equal** to the sum of the cubes of their digits. (p.105)

6.2 Example: Film certificate age checking the whole queue

AIM:
To introduce the ideas of nesting an **if statement** within a **for loop**, and declaring a **variable** inside a **compound statement**. We also introduce the **conditional operator**.

Our first example is one which checks the age validity of a whole queue of people wishing to see a film. The program takes the age limit of the film as the first **command line argument**, and then a **list** of ages of people in the queue. For each person under age, the program reports the position in the queue of that person. At the end, the program reports the number of under age people found.

Our program will have an **if statement nested** inside a **for loop**.

Concept **Statement: statements can be nested within each other.** Statements that control execution flow, such as **loops** and **if else statement**s have other **statements** inside them. These inner statements can be any kind of statement, including those that control the flow of execution. This allows quite complex **algorithm**s to be constructed with unlimited nesting of different and same kinds of control statements.

For example, one simple (but inefficient) way to print out the non-negative multiples of x which lie between y (≥ 0) and z inclusive, is as follows.

```
for (int number = 0; number <= z; number += x)
  if (number >= y)
    System.out.println("A multiple of " + x + " between " + y
                        + "and " + z + " is " + number);
```

Coffee time: 6.2.1 Whilst the code in the above concept description is a simple way to achieve its aim, what is the inefficiency inherent in it?

In our `FilmAgeCheck` program, we shall declare a **variable** within the body of the for loop, to store the age of the person currently being considered.

Concept **Variable: can be defined within a compound statement.** We can declare a **variable** within the body of a **method**, such as `main()`, (practically) anywhere where we can have a **statement**. The variable can then be used from that point onwards within the method body. The area of code in which a variable may be used is called its **scope**.

However, if we declare a variable within a **compound statement**, its scope is restricted to the compound statement: it does not exist after the end of the compound statement. This is a good thing, as it allows us to localize our variables to the exact point of their use, and so avoid cluttering up other parts of the code with variables available to be used but which have no relevance.

Consider the following symbolic example.

```
public static void main(String[] args)
{
  ...
  int x = ...
  ... x is available here.
  while (...)
  {
    ... x is available here.
```

```
        int y = ...
        ... x and y are available here.
    } // while
    ... x is available here, but not y,
    ... so we cannot accidentally refer to y instead of x.
} // main
```

The variable x can be used from the point of its definition onwards up to the end of the method, whereas the variable y can only be used from the point of its definition up to the end of the compound statement which is the body of the **loop**.

Here is the code for our program.

```
001: // Program to check the ages of a queue of film goers.
002: // First argument is the minimum age required.
003: // Remaining arguments is the ages of people in the queue.
004: public class FilmAgeCheck
005: {
006:   public static void main(String[] args)
007:   {
008:     // The minimum age required to watch the film.
009:     int minimumAge = Integer.parseInt(args[0]);
010:
011:     // The number of underage people found so far, initially 0.
012:     int underAgeCountSoFar = 0;
013:
014:     // We loop through the queue, checking each age.
015:     for (int queuePosition = 1; queuePosition < args.length; queuePosition++)
016:     {
017:       int ageOfPersonAtQueuePosition = Integer.parseInt(args[queuePosition]);
018:       if (ageOfPersonAtQueuePosition < minimumAge)
019:       {
020:         System.out.println("The person at position " + queuePosition
021:                            + " is only " + ageOfPersonAtQueuePosition
022:                            + ", which is less than " + minimumAge);
023:         underAgeCountSoFar++;
024:       } // if
025:     } // for
026:
027:     // Now report how many underage were found.
028:     if (underAgeCountSoFar == 1)
029:       System.out.println("There is 1 under age");
030:     else
031:       System.out.println("There are " + underAgeCountSoFar + " under age");
032:   } // main
033:
034: } // class FilmAgeCheck
```

Notice that the variable ageOfPersonAtQueuePosition is only in **scope** within the body of the for loop. Any reference to it after the for loop would be meaningless, and thus accidental. Thanks to us defining it where we have, we are protected from that mistake – the **compiler** would produce a **semantic error**.

Coffee time: 6.22
What do you think is the scope of the variable queuePosition?

Notice also in the last part of the **main method** above the amount of fuss needed just to make the message correctly use the word "is" or "are". In examples up to this point we have not bothered with such polishing. Java actually provides a handy **operator** which is ideal for situations like this.

Concept **Expression: conditional expression.**   The **conditional operator** in Java permits us to write **conditional expressions** which have different sub-expressions **evaluate**d depending on some **condition**. The general form is

```
c ? e1 : e2
```

where c is some condition, and e1 and e2 are two **expressions** of some **type**. The condition is evaluated, and if the value is **true** then e1 is evaluated and its value becomes the result of the expression. If the condition is **false** then e2 is evaluated and its value becomes the result instead.

For example

```
int maxXY = x > y ? x : y;
```

is another way of achieving the same effect as the following.

```
int maxXY;
if (x > y)
  maxXY = x;
else
  maxXY = y;
```

Coffee time: `6.2.3`   Convince yourself that the last **if else statement** of the main method of `FilmAgeCheck` could be replaced with the following.

```
System.out.println("There "
             + (underAgeCountSoFar == 1 ? "is" : "are")
             + " " + underAgeCountSoFar + " under age");
```

Coffee time: `6.2.4`   The brackets around the **conditional expression** in the code above are necessary – what does that tell you about the **operator precedence** of the **conditional operator**?

6.2.1   Trying it

After we have **compiled** the program, we can **run** it with various carefully chosen **command line argument**s to test it.

```
                  Console Input / Output
$ java FilmAgeCheck 18
There are 0 under age
$ java FilmAgeCheck 15 15
There are 0 under age
$ java FilmAgeCheck 12 10
The person at position 1 is only 10, which is less than 12
There is 1 under age
$ java FilmAgeCheck 18 19
There are 0 under age
$ java FilmAgeCheck 18 20 19 21
There are 0 under age
$ java FilmAgeCheck 12 9 19 21
The person at position 1 is only 9, which is less than 12
There is 1 under age
$ java FilmAgeCheck 18 20 17 21
The person at position 2 is only 17, which is less than 18
There is 1 under age
$ _
```

```
                        Console Input / Output
$ java FilmAgeCheck 15 20 19 13
The person at position 3 is only 13, which is less than 15
There is 1 under age
$ java FilmAgeCheck 12 12 11 9
The person at position 2 is only 11, which is less than 12
The person at position 3 is only 9, which is less than 12
There are 2 under age
$ java FilmAgeCheck 18 17 18 12
The person at position 1 is only 17, which is less than 18
The person at position 3 is only 12, which is less than 18
There are 2 under age
$ java FilmAgeCheck 15 10 14 15
The person at position 1 is only 10, which is less than 15
The person at position 2 is only 14, which is less than 15
There are 2 under age
$ java FilmAgeCheck 18 17 14 16
The person at position 1 is only 17, which is less than 18
The person at position 2 is only 14, which is less than 18
The person at position 3 is only 16, which is less than 18
There are 3 under age
$ _
```

Test plan

- No people.
- 1 person:
  - right age.
  - too young.
  - older.
- 3 people:
  - all old enough.
  - one too young:
    * first.
    * second.
    * third.
  - two too young:
    * not first.
    * not second.
    * not third.
  - all too young.

Coffee time: 6.2.5   Was that a good set of tests? Are there significant combinations of input conditions that have been overlooked, or would you trust the program now?

6.2.2 Coursework: `MaxList`

In this task you will write a program, called `MaxList`, which finds the maximum of a given **list** of numbers. The numbers are supplied as **command line arguments**. The program should report the number together with its **index** in the list (counting from zero). If two or more are jointly the maximum, it should report the one with the lowest index.

You may assume that the arguments all represent valid **double** numbers.

To find the maximum of a list of numbers, your program can start by regarding the first number as the maximum found so far, and then **loop**ing through the remaining numbers, comparing each with the maximum found so far and updating it as necessary.

Take the usual steps of planning **test data** and expected results, and **design**ing **pseudo code** in your logbook, before implementing the program, including suitable **comment**s, and recording your results back in your logbook.

6.3 Example: Dividing a cake (GCD)

AIM: To introduce the idea of nesting an **if else statement** within a **while loop**.

Two sisters of different ages share the same birthday and are given a huge cake between them, but they squabble over who should have how much of it. To shut them up, their mother says they should each have a number of equal sized portions, that number being in proportion to their ages. The mother knows, or at least hopes, the cake will not be eaten all in one go and wants it to be cut into the largest portions possible to reduce the amount it will dry out. So she tells the girls to work out the minimum number of portions needed, or she will eat it all herself!

This program accepts the ages of the two girls as **command line arguments** and reports how many pieces the cake should be cut into, and how many each girl should receive. With a little thought, you should agree that the key to the solution is finding the **greatest common divisor** of the two ages, that is, the largest whole number which divides both ages without remainder.

To find the GCD of two numbers, we can repeatedly subtract the smallest one from the largest until they are **equal**. The idea here is that, both numbers, by definition, are a multiple of their GCD, and so the difference between them also is a multiple of their GCD. For example, suppose we wish to find the GCD of 25 and 20.

$$GCD(25, 20)$$
$$= GCD(25 - 20, 20) \quad = GCD(5, 20)$$
$$= GCD(5, 20 - 5) \quad = GCD(5, 15)$$
$$= GCD(5, 15 - 5) \quad = GCD(5, 10)$$
$$= GCD(5, 10 - 5) \quad = GCD(5, 5)$$
$$= 5$$

Here is the code for the program.

```
001: // Program to decide how to divide a cake in proportion to the age of two
002: // persons, using the minimum number of equal sized portions.
003: // The two arguments are the two positive integer ages.
004: public class DivideCake
005: {
006:   public static void main(String[] args)
007:   {
008:     // Both ages must be positive.
009:     // First person's age.
010:     int age1 = Integer.parseInt(args[0]);
011:     // Second person's age.
012:     int age2 = Integer.parseInt(args[1]);
013:
014:     // This is a multiple of the GCD, initially age1.
015:     int multiple1OfGCD = age1;
016:     // This is a multiple of the GCD, initially age2.
017:     int multiple2OfGCD = age2;
018:
019:     // Compute the GCD of multiple1OfGCD and multiple2OfGCD.
020:     // While the two multiples are not the same, the difference
021:     // between them must also be a multiple of the GCD.
022:
023:     // E.g. X = x * d, Y = y * d, (X - Y) = (x - y) * d
024:
025:     // So we keep subtracting the smallest from the largest
026:     // until they are equal.
027:     while (multiple1OfGCD != multiple2OfGCD)
028:       if (multiple1OfGCD > multiple2OfGCD)
029:         multiple1OfGCD -= multiple2OfGCD;
030:       else
031:         multiple2OfGCD -= multiple1OfGCD;
032:
033:     // Now multiple1OfGCD == multiple2OfGCD
034:     // which is also the GCD of age1 and age2.
035:     System.out.println("The GCD of " + age1 + " and " + age2
036:                        + " is " + multiple1OfGCD);
037:
```

```
038:    // Calculate the number of portions for each person.
039:    int noOfPortions1 = age1 / multiple1OfGCD;
040:    int noOfPortions2 = age2 / multiple1OfGCD;
041:
042:    // Report the total number of portions.
043:    System.out.println("So the cake should be divided into "
044:                        + (noOfPortions1 + noOfPortions2));
045:
046:    // Report the number of portions for each person.
047:    System.out.println
048:        ("The " + age1 + " year old gets " + noOfPortions1
049:        + " and the " + age2 + " year old gets " + noOfPortions2);
050:  } // main
051:
052: } // class DivideCake
```

Coffee time:

6.3.1

Why did we need to put brackets around noOfPortions1 + noOfPortions2? (Hint: + has **left associativity** and has the same precedence when used as **concatenation** that it does when used as **addition**.)

6.3.1 Trying it

After we have **compile**d the program, we can **run** it with various **command line arguments**.

Console Input / Output

```
$ java DivideCake 10 15
The GCD of 10 and 15 is 5
So the cake should be divided into 5
The 10 year old gets 2 and the 15 year old gets 3
$ java DivideCake 9 12
The GCD of 9 and 12 is 3
So the cake should be divided into 7
The 9 year old gets 3 and the 12 year old gets 4
$ java DivideCake 4 8
The GCD of 4 and 8 is 4
So the cake should be divided into 3
The 4 year old gets 1 and the 8 year old gets 2
$ _
```

6.3.2 Coursework: `DivideCake3`

Suppose the mother has three daughters who share their birthday. In this task you will write a program, called `DivideCake3`, which finds the greatest common divisor of the three ages given as **command line arguments** and reports the number of portions the cake should be divided into, and the number of portions each girl should get.

You may assume that the arguments all represent positive **int** numbers.

To find the **greatest common divisor** of three numbers, your program can find the greatest common divisor of two of them, and then find the greatest common divisor of that result and the third one.

Take the usual steps of planning **test data** and expected results, and **design**ing **pseudo code** in your logbook, before implementing the program, including suitable **comments**, and recording your results back in your logbook.

6.4 Example: Printing a rectangle

AIM: To introduce the idea of nesting a **for loop** within a **for loop**. We also meet `System.out.print()` and revisit `System.out.println()`.

This next example is a program which prints a little 'ASCII art', that is a picture made from text **characters** (so named because ASCII is a standard coding for text characters[9]). In this case the picture is to be a single rectangle made up of cells of

the string "[_]". The width and height dimensions are to be given as **command line arguments** to the program. For example, a three by four rectangle would be printed as follows.

Console Input / Output

```
$ java PrintRectangle 3 4
[_][_][_]
[_][_][_]
[_][_][_]
[_][_][_]
$ _
```

To achieve this, we shall have a **loop nested** inside another loop. The outer of these **nested loop**s will deal with lines of text, and will **execute** as many times as the height of the rectangle. The inner loop will produce single cells of the rectangle, and will execute as many times as the width of the rectangle. Here is our **pseudo code**.

```
get width and height
for row = 1 to height
  for column = 1 to width
    output a cell with no new line
  output a new line
end-for
```

For the above sample output, the outer loop will have executed four times to produce the four lines. For *each* execution of the outer loop, the inner loop will have executed three times to produce the three cells. This means the code which outputs a single cell will have executed four multiplied by three, i.e. twelve, times.

Before we write the code, we need to find a way of printing text without producing a **new line** after it, and a way of producing a new line without printing any text!

Concept **Standard API: System: `out.print()`.** The **class** System contains a **method** `out.print()` which is almost the same as `out.println()`. The only difference is that `out.print()` does not produce a **new line** after printing its output. This means that any output printed after this will appear on the same line. For example

```
System.out.print("Hello");
System.out.print(" ");
System.out.println("world!");
```

would have the same effect as the following.

```
System.out.println("Hello world!");
```

`System.out.print()` is most useful when the output is being generated a piece at a time, often within a **loop**.

Concept **Standard API: System: `out.println()`: with no argument.** The **class** System also contains a version of the `out.println()` **method** which takes no arguments. This outputs nothing except a **new line**. It has the same effect as calling `System.out.println()` with an empty string as its argument, that is

```
System.out.println();
```

has the same effect as the following.

```
System.out.println("");
```

So, for example

```
System.out.print("Hello world!");
System.out.println();
```

would have the same effect as the following.

```
System.out.println("Hello world!");
```

`System.out.println()` with no argument is most useful when we need to end a line which has been generated a piece at a time, or when we want to have a blank line.

Here is our rectangle printing program.

```
001: // Program to print out a rectangle.
002: // The width and then the height are given as arguments.
003: // We assume the arguments represent positive integers.
004: public class PrintRectangle
005: {
006:   public static void main(String[] args)
007:   {
008:     // The width of the rectangle, in cells.
009:     int width = Integer.parseInt(args[0]);
010:     // The height of the rectangle, in cells.
011:     int height = Integer.parseInt(args[1]);
012:
013:     // Print out height number of rows.
014:     for (int row = 1; row <= height; row++)
015:     {
016:       // Print out width number of cells, on the same line.
017:       for (int column = 1; column <= width; column++)
018:         System.out.print("[_]");
019:       // End the line.
020:       System.out.println();
021:     } // for
022:   } // main
023:
024: } // class PrintRectangle
```

6.4.1 Trying it

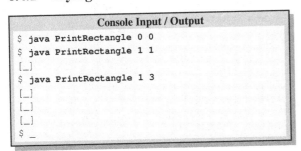

6.4.2 Coursework: PrintHoledRectangle

In this task you will write a program, called PrintHoledRectangle, which prints a rectangle with a hole at the centre. This just means missing out one cell, printing spaces for it instead. The program takes the width and height arguments as before, but in order to ensure there is a centre cell, each of these have one added to them if necessary to make them an odd number.

You may assume that the arguments represent positive int numbers.

To ensure an **integer** number is odd you can simply divide it by two, multiply it by two and then add one! The simplest way to miss out the centre cell is to count all the cells as you print them, and check the sequence number of a cell just before you print it. The centre cell will have a sequence number which is the width times the height, divided by two, plus one.

Take the usual steps of planning **test data** and expected results, and **design**ing **pseudo code** in your logbook, before implementing the program, including suitable **comments**, and recording your results back in your logbook.

6.5 Example: Printing a triangle

AIM:
To reinforce the idea of nesting a **for loop** within a **for loop**.

This next program is very similar to the previous, except this time to make it trickier, we want an isosceles right angled triangle of a height given as the **command line argument**. The first line of text has one cell, the second has two, and so on, until the last line has as many cells as the height. For example, a triangle of height four would be printed as follows.

Here is the code, which you should compare with that for printing a rectangle.

```
001: // Program to print out an isosceles right angled triangle.
002: // The height is given as an argument.
003: // We assume the argument represents a positive integer.
004: public class PrintTriangle
005: {
006:     public static void main(String[] args)
007:     {
008:         // The height of the triangle.
009:         int height = Integer.parseInt(args[0]);
010:
011:         // Print out height number of rows.
012:         for (int row = 1; row <= height; row++)
013:         {
014:             // Print out row number of cells, on the same line.
015:             for (int column = 1; column <= row; column++)
016:                 System.out.print("[_]");
017:             // End the line.
018:             System.out.println();
019:         } // for
020:     } // main
021:
022: } // class PrintTriangle
```

Console Input / Output

```
$ java PrintTriangle 4
[_]
[_] [_]
[_] [_] [_]
[_] [_] [_] [_]
$ _
```

6.5.1 Trying it

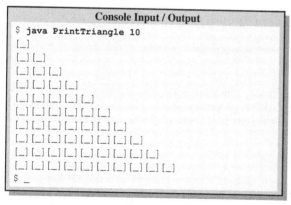

Console Input / Output

```
$ java PrintTriangle 10
[_]
[_] [_]
[_] [_] [_]
[_] [_] [_] [_]
[_] [_] [_] [_] [_]
[_] [_] [_] [_] [_] [_]
[_] [_] [_] [_] [_] [_] [_]
[_] [_] [_] [_] [_] [_] [_] [_]
[_] [_] [_] [_] [_] [_] [_] [_] [_]
[_] [_] [_] [_] [_] [_] [_] [_] [_] [_]
$ _
```

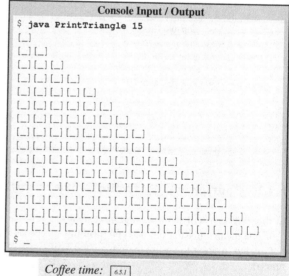

Console Input / Output

```
$ java PrintTriangle 15
[_]
[_] [_]
[_] [_] [_]
[_] [_] [_] [_]
[_] [_] [_] [_] [_]
[_] [_] [_] [_] [_] [_]
[_] [_] [_] [_] [_] [_] [_]
[_] [_] [_] [_] [_] [_] [_] [_]
[_] [_] [_] [_] [_] [_] [_] [_] [_]
[_] [_] [_] [_] [_] [_] [_] [_] [_] [_]
[_] [_] [_] [_] [_] [_] [_] [_] [_] [_] [_]
[_] [_] [_] [_] [_] [_] [_] [_] [_] [_] [_] [_]
[_] [_] [_] [_] [_] [_] [_] [_] [_] [_] [_] [_] [_]
[_] [_] [_] [_] [_] [_] [_] [_] [_] [_] [_] [_] [_] [_]
[_] [_] [_] [_] [_] [_] [_] [_] [_] [_] [_] [_] [_] [_] [_]
$ _
```

Coffee time: 6.5.1
What would happen if we changed the outer **for loop** to the following?
```
for (int row = 0; row < height; row++)
```

Coffee time: 6.5.2
What would happen if we changed the inner **for loop** to the following?
```
for (int column = 1; column <= height - row + 1; column++)
```

100

6.5.2 Coursework: `PrintTriangleMirror`

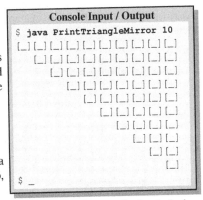

In this task you will write a program, called `PrintTriangleMirror`, which prints an isosceles right angled triangle with its longest row at the top and the right hand side straight. The program is given the height as its argument – here is an example **run**.

You may assume that the argument represents a positive **int** number.

Each row will consist of a number of space cells (each 3 spaces) followed by a number of brick cells ("[_]"). This will require two **loops** inside the outer loop, one after the other.

Take the usual steps of planning **test data** and expected results, and **design**ing **pseudo code** in your logbook, before implementing the program, including suitable **comment**s, and recording your results back in your logbook.

6.6 Example: Multiple times table

AIM: To reinforce the idea of having **nested statement**s within each other, and explore the idea of using multiple **loop**s in sequence.

This example is a program which prints out the **multiplication** tables for the first ten numbers, in a ten by ten square, with neat layout, row and column headings, and a box around the whole thing made out of hyphens and vertical bar **character**s. Here is what the final output will look like.

```
Console Input / Output
$ java TimesTable
|-----|--------------------------------------|
|     |  1   2   3   4   5   6   7   8   9  10 |
|-----|--------------------------------------|
|   1 |  1   2   3   4   5   6   7   8   9  10 |
|   2 |  2   4   6   8  10  12  14  16  18  20 |
|   3 |  3   6   9  12  15  18  21  24  27  30 |
|   4 |  4   8  12  16  20  24  28  32  36  40 |
|   5 |  5  10  15  20  25  30  35  40  45  50 |
|   6 |  6  12  18  24  30  36  42  48  54  60 |
|   7 |  7  14  21  28  35  42  49  56  63  70 |
|   8 |  8  16  24  32  40  48  56  64  72  80 |
|   9 |  9  18  27  36  45  54  63  72  81  90 |
|  10 | 10  20  30  40  50  60  70  80  90 100 |
|-----|--------------------------------------|
$ _
```

Our initial **design** in **pseudo code** is as follows.

```
print the box top line
print column headings
print headings underline
for row = 1 to 10
  print a row
print the box bottom line
```

We refine this first draft into a second one.

```
print the box top line
print column headings
print headings underline
for row = 1 to 10
  print box left side
  print row label
  print separator
  for column = 1 to 10
    print row * column
  print box right side and new line
end-for
print the box bottom line
```

101

Next we refine each of the steps identified in this second draft of the design, but for brevity we do not show that process here. Instead let us go straight to the final code.

```
001: // Program to print out a neat 10 by 10 multiplication table.
002: public class TimesTable
003: {
004:   public static void main(String[] args)
005:   {
006:     // Top line.
007:     // Left side, 5 characters for row labels, separator.
008:     System.out.print("|-----|");
009:     // Above the column headings.
010:     for (int column = 1; column <= 10; column++)
011:       // 4 characters for each column.
012:       System.out.print("----");
013:     // The right side.
014:     System.out.println("-|");
015:
016:     // Column headings.
017:     System.out.print("|     |");
018:     for (int column = 1; column <= 10; column++)
019:       // Need to make column number always occupy 4 characters.
020:       if (column < 10)
021:         System.out.print("   " + column);
022:       else
023:         System.out.print("  " + column);
024:     System.out.println(" |");
025:
026:     // Underline headings -- same as Top line.
027:     System.out.print("|-----|");
028:     for (int column = 1; column <= 10; column++)
029:       System.out.print("----");
030:     System.out.println("-|");
031:
032:     // Now the rows.
033:     for (int row = 1; row <= 10; row++)
034:     {
035:       // Need to make row number always occupy 7 characters
036:       // including vertical lines.
037:       if (row < 10)
038:         System.out.print("|   " + row + " |");
039:       else
040:         System.out.print("|  " + row + " |");
041:
042:       // Now the columns on this row.
043:       for (int column = 1; column <= 10; column++)
044:       {
045:         int product = row * column;
046:         // Need to make product always occupy 4 characters.
047:         if (product < 10)
048:           System.out.print("   " + product);
049:         else if (product < 100)
050:           System.out.print("  " + product);
051:         else
```

```
052:                System.out.print(" " + product);
053:        } // for
054:
055:        // The right side.
056:        System.out.println(" |");
057:     } // for
058:
059:     // Bottom line -- same as Top line.
060:     System.out.print("|-----|");
061:     for (int column = 1; column <= 10; column++)
062:        System.out.print("----");
063:     System.out.println("-|");
064:  } // main
065:
066: } // class TimesTable
```

6.6.1 Trying it

After we have **compiled** the program, we can **run** it – we have already seen its result on page 101.

Coffee time: **6.6.1** What if when we show the output to the end user, perhaps a primary school teacher, she tells us she wanted a 12 by 12 table? What changes would we have to make to our program? What would happen if we just changed every 10 to 12? Is there something we could have done to make the program more flexible in this respect?

6.6.2 Coursework: `CommonFactorsTable`

In this task you will write a program, called `CommonFactorsTable`, which prints a 19 times 19 labelled table indicating which of all the pairs made up of **integers** between 2 and 20, inclusive, have common factors other than one. (That is, their **greatest common divisor** is **greater than** one.)

The program's output will be as follows.

A `"--#"` at the intersection of two numbers shows that their greatest common divisor is bigger than one, a `"--|"` shows otherwise.

This program may reasonably be developed by making changes to the `TimesTable` program. Plan these changes in your logbook, before taking the usual steps of implementing the program, including suitable **comment**s, and recording your results back in your logbook.

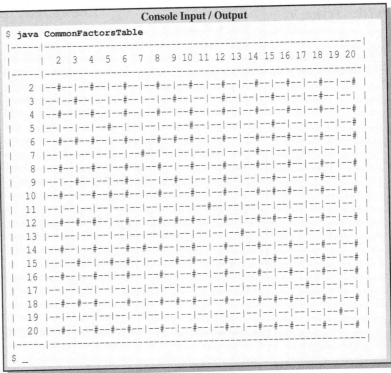

103

6.7   Example: Luck is in the air: dice combinations

AIM:
To introduce the idea of using **nested loops** to generate combinations.

Suppose we wished to design a board game in which each player throws *three* dice on each move, moving forwards a number of places on the board equal to the sum of the dice values thrown. To help us get the balance of play just right, we would want to have a chart of all the total values obtainable by throwing three dice.

The final program in this chapter uses **nested loops** to produce such a chart. Each **loop** represents one die, and goes through the values from one to six, and so the centre of the nesting is **executed** six multiplied by six multiplied by six times, with the three loop control **variables** together holding one of the 216 combinations.

```
001: // Program to output all 216 combinations of three six sided dice.
002: public class DiceThrows
003: {
004:   public static void main(String[] args)
005:   {
006:     // Nested loops produce all 216 combinations of die1 to die3.
007:     for (int die1 = 1; die1 <= 6; die1++)
008:       for (int die2 = 1; die2 <= 6; die2++)
009:         for (int die3 = 1; die3 <= 6; die3++)
010:           System.out.println(die1 + die2 + die3 + " from "
011:                       + die1 + "+" + die2 + "+" + die3);
012:   } // main
013:
014: } // class DiceThrows
```

Coffee time: Why do we *not* need brackets around die1 + die2 + die3 to avoid the + **operator** being interpreted as **concatenation**?

6.7.1

6.7.1   Trying it

After we have **compiled** the program, we can **run** it.

Console Input / Output

```
$ java DiceThrows
(Output shown using multiple columns to save space.)
```

3 from 1+1+1	9 from 1+6+2	10 from 2+5+3	11 from 3+4+4	12 from 4+3+5	13 from 5+2+6	9 from 6+2+1
4 from 1+1+2	10 from 1+6+3	11 from 2+5+4	12 from 3+4+5	13 from 4+3+6	9 from 5+3+1	10 from 6+2+2
5 from 1+1+3	11 from 1+6+4	12 from 2+5+5	13 from 3+4+6	9 from 4+4+1	10 from 5+3+2	11 from 6+2+3
6 from 1+1+4	12 from 1+6+5	13 from 2+5+6	9 from 3+5+1	10 from 4+4+2	11 from 5+3+3	12 from 6+2+4
7 from 1+1+5	13 from 1+6+6	9 from 2+6+1	10 from 3+5+2	11 from 4+4+3	12 from 5+3+4	13 from 6+2+5
8 from 1+1+6	4 from 2+1+1	10 from 2+6+2	11 from 3+5+3	12 from 4+4+4	13 from 5+3+5	14 from 6+2+6
4 from 1+2+1	5 from 2+1+2	11 from 2+6+3	12 from 3+5+4	13 from 4+4+5	14 from 5+3+6	10 from 6+3+1
5 from 1+2+2	6 from 2+1+3	12 from 2+6+4	13 from 3+5+5	14 from 4+4+6	10 from 5+4+1	11 from 6+3+2
6 from 1+2+3	7 from 2+1+4	13 from 2+6+5	14 from 3+5+6	10 from 4+5+1	11 from 5+4+2	12 from 6+3+3
7 from 1+2+4	8 from 2+1+5	14 from 2+6+6	10 from 3+6+1	11 from 4+5+2	12 from 5+4+3	13 from 6+3+4
8 from 1+2+5	9 from 2+1+6	5 from 3+1+1	11 from 3+6+2	12 from 4+5+3	13 from 5+4+4	14 from 6+3+5
9 from 1+2+6	5 from 2+2+1	6 from 3+1+2	12 from 3+6+3	13 from 4+5+4	14 from 5+4+5	15 from 6+3+6
5 from 1+3+1	6 from 2+2+2	7 from 3+1+3	13 from 3+6+4	14 from 4+5+5	15 from 5+4+6	11 from 6+4+1
6 from 1+3+2	7 from 2+2+3	8 from 3+1+4	14 from 3+6+5	15 from 4+5+6	11 from 5+5+1	12 from 6+4+2
7 from 1+3+3	8 from 2+2+4	9 from 3+1+5	15 from 3+6+6	11 from 4+6+1	12 from 5+5+2	13 from 6+4+3
8 from 1+3+4	9 from 2+2+5	10 from 3+1+6	6 from 4+1+1	12 from 4+6+2	13 from 5+5+3	14 from 6+4+4
9 from 1+3+5	10 from 2+2+6	6 from 3+2+1	7 from 4+1+2	13 from 4+6+3	14 from 5+5+4	15 from 6+4+5
10 from 1+3+6	6 from 2+3+1	7 from 3+2+2	8 from 4+1+3	14 from 4+6+4	15 from 5+5+5	16 from 6+4+6
6 from 1+4+1	7 from 2+3+2	8 from 3+2+3	9 from 4+1+4	15 from 4+6+5	16 from 5+5+6	12 from 6+5+1
7 from 1+4+2	8 from 2+3+3	9 from 3+2+4	10 from 4+1+5	16 from 4+6+6	11 from 5+6+1	13 from 6+5+2
8 from 1+4+3	9 from 2+3+4	10 from 3+2+5	11 from 4+1+6	7 from 5+1+1	13 from 5+6+2	14 from 6+5+3
9 from 1+4+4	10 from 2+3+5	11 from 3+2+6	7 from 4+2+1	8 from 5+1+2	14 from 5+6+3	15 from 6+5+4
10 from 1+4+5	11 from 2+3+6	7 from 3+3+1	8 from 4+2+2	9 from 5+1+3	15 from 5+6+4	16 from 6+5+5
11 from 1+4+6	7 from 2+4+1	8 from 3+3+2	9 from 4+2+3	10 from 5+1+4	16 from 5+6+5	17 from 6+5+6
7 from 1+5+1	8 from 2+4+2	9 from 3+3+3	10 from 4+2+4	11 from 5+1+5	17 from 5+6+6	13 from 6+6+1
8 from 1+5+2	9 from 2+4+3	10 from 3+3+4	11 from 4+2+5	12 from 5+1+6	8 from 6+1+1	14 from 6+6+2
9 from 1+5+3	10 from 2+4+4	11 from 3+3+5	12 from 4+2+6	8 from 5+2+1	9 from 6+1+2	15 from 6+6+3
10 from 1+5+4	11 from 2+4+5	12 from 3+3+6	8 from 4+3+1	9 from 5+2+2	10 from 6+1+3	16 from 6+6+4
11 from 1+5+5	12 from 2+4+6	8 from 3+4+1	9 from 4+3+2	10 from 5+2+3	11 from 6+1+4	17 from 6+6+5
12 from 1+5+6	8 from 2+5+1	9 from 3+4+2	10 from 4+3+3	11 from 5+2+4	12 from 6+1+5	18 from 6+6+6
8 from 1+6+1	9 from 2+5+2	10 from 3+4+3	11 from 4+3+4	12 from 5+2+5	13 from 6+1+6	

```
$ _
```

The results would be more useful if they were **sort**ed by total. Examples in later chapters will show us how to achieve sorted output from within Java, but for now we can sort them by simply piping the output through the sort program! (If you are running on Microsoft Windows then you cannot use the -n option to sort numerically, but the result from sort is still helpful.)

Console Input / Output

```
$ java DiceThrows | sort -n
(Output shown using multiple columns to save space.)
3 from 1+1+1    7 from 3+3+1    9 from 2+2+5    10 from 3+4+3   11 from 4+5+2   12 from 6+1+5   14 from 4+6+4
4 from 1+1+2    7 from 4+1+2    9 from 2+3+4    10 from 3+5+2   11 from 4+6+1   12 from 6+2+4   14 from 5+3+6
4 from 1+2+1    7 from 4+2+1    9 from 2+4+3    10 from 3+6+1   11 from 5+1+5   12 from 6+3+3   14 from 5+4+5
4 from 2+1+1    7 from 5+1+1    9 from 2+5+2    10 from 4+1+5   11 from 5+2+4   12 from 6+4+2   14 from 5+5+4
5 from 1+1+3    8 from 1+1+6    9 from 2+6+1    10 from 4+2+4   11 from 5+3+3   12 from 6+5+1   14 from 5+6+3
5 from 1+2+2    8 from 1+2+5    9 from 3+1+5    10 from 4+3+3   11 from 5+4+2   13 from 1+6+6   14 from 6+2+6
5 from 1+3+1    8 from 1+3+4    9 from 3+2+4    10 from 4+4+2   11 from 5+5+1   13 from 2+5+6   14 from 6+3+5
5 from 2+1+2    8 from 1+4+3    9 from 3+3+3    10 from 4+5+1   11 from 6+1+4   13 from 2+6+5   14 from 6+4+4
5 from 2+2+1    8 from 1+5+2    9 from 3+4+2    10 from 5+1+4   11 from 6+2+3   13 from 3+4+6   14 from 6+5+3
5 from 3+1+1    8 from 1+6+1    9 from 3+5+1    10 from 5+2+3   11 from 6+3+2   13 from 3+5+5   14 from 6+6+2
6 from 1+1+4    8 from 2+1+5    9 from 4+1+4    10 from 5+3+2   11 from 6+4+1   13 from 3+6+4   15 from 3+6+6
6 from 1+2+3    8 from 2+2+4    9 from 4+2+3    10 from 5+4+1   12 from 1+5+6   13 from 4+3+6   15 from 4+5+6
6 from 1+3+2    8 from 2+3+3    9 from 4+3+2    10 from 6+1+3   12 from 1+6+5   13 from 4+4+5   15 from 4+6+5
6 from 1+4+1    8 from 2+4+2    9 from 4+4+1    10 from 6+2+2   12 from 2+4+6   13 from 4+5+4   15 from 5+4+6
6 from 2+1+3    8 from 2+5+1    9 from 5+1+3    10 from 6+3+1   12 from 2+5+5   13 from 4+6+3   15 from 5+5+5
6 from 2+2+2    8 from 3+1+4    9 from 5+2+2    11 from 1+4+6   12 from 2+6+4   13 from 5+2+6   15 from 5+6+4
6 from 2+3+1    8 from 3+2+3    9 from 5+3+1    11 from 1+5+5   12 from 3+3+6   13 from 5+3+5   15 from 6+3+6
6 from 3+1+2    8 from 3+3+2    9 from 6+1+2    11 from 1+6+4   12 from 3+4+5   13 from 5+4+4   15 from 6+4+5
6 from 3+2+1    8 from 3+4+1    9 from 6+2+1    11 from 2+3+6   12 from 3+5+4   13 from 5+5+3   15 from 6+5+4
6 from 4+1+1    8 from 4+1+3    10 from 1+3+6   11 from 2+4+5   12 from 3+6+3   13 from 5+6+2   15 from 6+6+3
7 from 1+1+5    8 from 4+2+2    10 from 1+4+5   11 from 2+5+4   12 from 4+2+6   13 from 6+1+6   16 from 4+6+6
7 from 1+2+4    8 from 4+3+1    10 from 1+5+4   11 from 2+6+3   12 from 4+3+5   13 from 6+2+5   16 from 5+5+6
7 from 1+3+3    8 from 5+1+2    10 from 1+6+3   11 from 3+2+6   12 from 4+4+4   13 from 6+3+4   16 from 5+6+5
7 from 1+4+2    8 from 5+2+1    10 from 2+2+6   11 from 3+3+5   12 from 4+5+3   13 from 6+4+3   16 from 6+4+6
7 from 1+5+1    8 from 6+1+1    10 from 2+3+5   11 from 3+4+4   12 from 4+6+2   13 from 6+5+2   16 from 6+5+5
7 from 2+1+4    9 from 1+2+6    10 from 2+4+4   11 from 3+5+3   12 from 5+1+6   13 from 6+6+1   16 from 6+6+4
7 from 2+2+3    9 from 1+3+5    10 from 2+5+3   11 from 3+6+2   12 from 5+2+5   14 from 2+6+6   17 from 5+6+6
7 from 2+3+2    9 from 1+4+4    10 from 2+6+2   11 from 4+1+6   12 from 5+3+4   14 from 3+5+6   17 from 6+5+6
7 from 2+4+1    9 from 1+5+3    10 from 3+1+6   11 from 4+2+5   12 from 5+4+3   14 from 4+4+6   17 from 6+6+5
7 from 3+1+3    9 from 1+6+2    10 from 3+2+5   11 from 4+3+4   12 from 5+5+2   14 from 4+5+5   18 from 6+6+6
7 from 3+2+2    9 from 2+1+6    10 from 3+3+4   11 from 4+4+3   12 from 5+6+1   14 from 4+6+4
$ _
```

We can get a useful result if we cut out just the totals, sort them and then make each total unique, but add on to the front of it a count of how many times it occurred. We could do this by hand in a **text editor**, or, if we are running on Unix, we can use a combination of the the cut, sort and uniq programs.

In the following output, the second number of each pair is a possible dice throw total, and the first number is the count of the occurrences of that total in the original program output.[1]

Console Input / Output

```
$ java DiceThrows | cut -f1 -d' ' | sort -n | uniq -c
(Output shown using multiple columns to save space.)
     1  3            15  7           27  11          10  15
     3  4            21  8           25  12           6  16
     6  5            25  9           21  13           3  17
    10  6            27  10          15  14           1  18
$ _
```

This shows that with three dice, you are 27 times more likely to get a total of 10 or 11 than 3 or 18!

6.7.2 Coursework: SumOfCubedDigits

There are four numbers in the range 100 to 999 which have the property that the sum of the cubes of the three digits in the number is **equal** to the number itself. 153 is such a number because $1^3 + 5^3 + 3^3$ is equal to $1 + 125 + 27$ which is 153. In this task you will write a program, called SumOfCubedDigits, that finds all four such numbers. [2]

---

[1] Unfortunately, there is no simple way of doing this using standard commands in a Microsoft Command Prompt.

Your program will work by **loop**ing through the numbers 100 to 999 using three **nested loop**s, one for each digit. In the centre of the loops, your program can calculate the number represented by the three digits, and the sum of their cubes, and print out the number if these are equal.

Take the usual steps of **design**ing **pseudo code** in your logbook, before implementing the program, including suitable **comment**s, and recording your results back in your logbook.

6.8 Concepts covered in this chapter

Here is a list of the concepts that were covered in this chapter, each with a self-test question. You can use this to check you remember them being introduced, and perhaps re-read some of them before going on to the next chapter.

Expression	

– conditional expression (p.94)	What is printed by the following code?
	`int x = 10;`
	`int y = 20;`
	`System.out.println(x + y > 30 ? x : y);`

Standard API	
– System: out.println(): with no argument (p.98)	What is the effect of the following code? `System.out.println();` `System.out.println();` `System.out.println();`
– System: out.print() (p.98)	What do you think is the effect of the following code? `System.out.print("");`

Statement	
– statements can be nested within each other (p.92)	What limit is there on the nesting of statements within other statements?

Variable	

– can be defined within a compound statement (p.92)	What is wrong with the following code?
	`int x = ...`
	`int y = ...`
	`if (x > y)`
	`    { int large = x; int small = y; }`
	`else`
	`    { int large = y; int small = x; }`
	`System.out.println`
	`    (large + " is greater than " + small);`

Chapter 7

Additional control statements

7.1 Chapter aims

This chapter presents two more Java **statement**s for controlling execution, which, whilst being less commonly used than those we have seen so far, are appropriate in certain **algorithm**s.

There is no coursework in this chapter, but the concepts will be exercised in coursework contained in later chapters.

The chapter contains the following sections.

Section	Aims	Associated Coursework
7.2 Birthday greeting (p.107)	To introduce the **switch statement** with **break statement**s.	(None.)
7.3 Descending through decades (p.110)	To introduce the **switch statement** without **break statement**s.	(None.)
7.4 Pi reheated (p.112)	To introduce the **do while loop**.	(None.)

7.2 Example: Birthday greeting

AIM: To introduce the **switch statement** with **break statement**s.

Our first example is a program which prints out an appropriate birthday greeting, depending on the age of the user, which is given as a **command line argument**. The program will give a specific message for certain ages, and a generic one for all others.

We could use lots of **nested if else statement**s for this purpose, but Java provides us with another **conditional execution statement**, and it is ideal for this program.

Concept **Statement: switch statement with breaks.** Java provides a **conditional execution statement** which is ideal for situations where there are many choices based on some value, such as a number, being **equal** to specific fixed values for each choice. It is called the **switch statement**. The following example code will applaud the user when they have correctly guessed the winning number of 100, encourage them when they are one out, or insult them otherwise.

```
int userGuess = Integer.parseInt(args[0]);

switch (userGuess)
{
  case 99: case 101:
    System.out.println("You are close!");
    break;
  case 100:
    System.out.println("Bingo! You win!");
    System.out.println("You have guessed correctly.");
    break;
  default:
    System.out.println("You are pathetic!");
    System.out.println("Have another guess.");
    break;
} // switch
```

The switch statement starts with the **reserved word switch** followed by a bracketed **expression** of a **type** that has discrete values, such as **int** (notably not **double**). (From Java 7.0, String values are allowed.) The body of the statement is enclosed in braces, ({ and }), and consists of a list of entries. Each of these starts with a list of labels, comprising the reserved word **case** followed by a value and then a colon (:). After the labels we have one or more statements, typically ending with a **break statement**. One (at most) label is allowed to be the reserved word **default** followed by a colon – usually written at the end of the list.

When a switch statement is **execute**d, the expression is **evaluate**d and then each label in the body is examined in turn to find one whose value is equal to that of the expression. If such a match is found, the statements associated with that label are executed, down to the special **break statement** which causes the execution of the switch statement to end. If a match is not found, then instead the statements associated with the **default** label are executed, or if there is no **default** then nothing is done.

Here is the code for our birthday greeting program.

```
001: // Program to produce birthday greetings appropriate to the age of the user
002: // which is given as an argument.
003: public class BirthdayGreeting
004: {
005:   public static void main(String[] args)
006:   {
007:     // The user's age.
008:     int ageToday = Integer.parseInt(args[0]);
009:
010:     // Give a message appropriate to the user's age.
011:     System.out.print(ageToday + " today! ");
012:     switch (ageToday)
013:     {
014:       case 100:
015:         System.out.println("Your telegram is in the post!");
016:         break;
```

Coffee time: Why do you think the **expression** in a **switch statement** cannot be of type **double**?

[7.2.1]

```
017:        case 99: case 89: case 79: case 69: case 59: case 49: case 39: case 29:
018:        case 19: case 9:
019:            System.out.println("One more year to a mile stone!");
020:            break;
021:        case 90: case 80: case 70: case 60: case 50: case 20: case 10:
022:            System.out.println("Another mile stone!");
023:            break;
024:        case 40:
025:            System.out.println("Life begins today.");
026:            System.out.println("(Or so they say.)");
027:            break;
028:        case 30:
029:            System.out.println("Time to get flirty!");
030:            System.out.println("(Before it's too late!)");
031:            break;
032:        case 18:
033:            System.out.println("Hooray -- you can vote!");
034:            System.out.println("(But will you bother?)");
035:            break;
036:        case 17:
037:            System.out.println("Get cracking on that driving licence!");
038:            break;
039:        case 16: case 15: case 14:
040:            System.out.println("IT'S STILL NOT FAAAAIIIR!");
041:            break;
042:        case 13:
043:            System.out.println("IT'S NOT FAAAAIIIR!");
044:            break;
045:        case 7:
046:            System.out.println("From now on you must act your age.");
047:            System.out.println("(Not your shoe size!)");
048:            break;
049:        default:
050:            System.out.println("Happy birthday!");
051:            break;
052:        } // switch
053:    } // main
054:
055: } // class BirthdayGreeting
```

7.2.1 Trying it

```
                    Console Input / Output
$ java BirthdayGreeting 100
100 today! Your telegram is in the post!
$ java BirthdayGreeting 99
99 today! One more year to a mile stone!
$ _
```

```
                    Console Input / Output
$ java BirthdayGreeting 13
13 today! IT'S NOT FAAAAIIIR!
$ java BirthdayGreeting 17
17 today! Get cracking on that driving licence!
$ java BirthdayGreeting 18
18 today! Hooray -- you can vote!
(But will you bother?)
$ java BirthdayGreeting 5
5 today! Happy birthday!
$ _
```

If we are using an environment in which we can run *programs* in a **loop**, then this program is one where we might test every possible reasonable input, rather than carefully think of just a few **test cases**. On Unix, for example, we can run the program in a **shell** for loop. Here we try it with all the numbers from one to 110.

```
Console Input / Output

$ for age in `seq 1 110`; do java BirthdayGreeting $age; done
(Output shown using multiple columns to save space.)
1 today! Happy birthday!               94 today! Happy birthday!
2 today! Happy birthday!               95 today! Happy birthday!
3 today! Happy birthday!               96 today! Happy birthday!
4 today! Happy birthday!               97 today! Happy birthday!
5 today! Happy birthday!               98 today! Happy birthday!
6 today! Happy birthday!               99 today! One more year to a mile stone!
7 today! From now on you must act your age.   100 today! Your telegram is in the post!
(Not your shoe size!)                  101 today! Happy birthday!
8 today! Happy birthday!               102 today! Happy birthday!
9 today! One more year to a mile stone!   103 today! Happy birthday!
10 today! Another mile stone!          104 today! Happy birthday!
(...lines removed to save space.)      105 today! Happy birthday!
89 today! One more year to a mile stone!   106 today! Happy birthday!
90 today! Another mile stone!          107 today! Happy birthday!
91 today! Happy birthday!              108 today! Happy birthday!
92 today! Happy birthday!              109 today! Happy birthday!
93 today! Happy birthday!              110 today! Happy birthday!
$ _
```

On Microsoft Windows, you can achieve the same effect with the following command (on one line).

```
for /L %a in (1,1,110) do java
BirthdayGreeting %a
```

Coffee time: `7.2.2`
What would happen if we gave the program a negative age?

7.3 Example: Descending through decades

AIM:
To introduce the **switch statement** without **break statement**s.

In this next example we have a program which when given a user's age as its **command line argument**, reports the decade birthdays that the user has had. We shall achieve this using a form of the **switch statement** that has no **break statement**s.

Concept **Statement: switch statement without breaks.** A less common form of the **switch statement** is when we omit the **break statement**s at the end of the list of **statement**s associated with each set of **case** labels. This, perhaps surprisingly, causes execution to "fall through" to the statements associated with the next set of **case** labels. Most of the time we do *not* want this to happen – so we have to be careful to remember the break statements.

We can also mix the styles – having break statements for some entries, and not for some others. The following code is a bizarre, but interesting way of doing something reasonably simple. It serves as an illustration of the switch statement, and as a puzzle for you. It takes two **integer**s, the second of which is meant to be in the range one to ten, and outputs a result which is some **function** of the two numbers. What is that result?

```
int value = Integer.parseInt(args[0]);
int power = Integer.parseInt(args[1]);

int valueToThePower1 = value;
int valueToThePower2 = valueToThePower1 * valueToThePower1;
int valueToThePower4 = valueToThePower2 * valueToThePower2;
int valueToThePower8 = valueToThePower4 * valueToThePower4;

int result = 1;

switch (power)
{
  case 10: result *= valueToThePower1;
  case 9:  result *= valueToThePower1;
  case 8:  result *= valueToThePower8;
           break;
  case 7:  result *= valueToThePower1;
```

```
case 6:   result *= valueToThePower1;
case 5:   result *= valueToThePower1;
case 4:   result *= valueToThePower4;
          break;
case 3:   result *= valueToThePower1;
case 2:   result *= valueToThePower2;
          break;
case 1:   result *= valueToThePower1;
          break;
} // switch

System.out.println(result);
```

If you find the semantics of the switch statement somewhat inelegant, then do not worry – you are not alone! Java inherited it from C, where it was designed more to ease the work of the **compiler** than to be a good construct for the programmer. You will find the switch statement is less commonly used than the **if else statement**, and the majority of times you use it, you will want to have break statements on every set of **case** labels. Unfortunately, due to them being optional, accidentally missing them off does not cause a **compile time error**.

Here is the code for our decade birthdays program.

```
001: // Program to report the list of decade birthdays the user has had.
002: // The age of the user is given as the argument.
003: public class DecadeDescending
004: {
005:   public static void main(String[] args)
006:   {
007:     // Age is assumed to be a valid non-negative whole number.
008:     int ageOfUser = Integer.parseInt(args[0]);
009:
010:     // Convert age to decades completed.
011:     ageOfUser /= 10;
012:
013:     System.out.println("You've had the following decade birthdays:");
014:     // A switch without breaks, to exploit fall through.
015:     switch (ageOfUser)
016:     {
017:       case 10 : System.out.println("your hundredth, and");
018:       case 9  : System.out.println("your ninetieth, and");
019:       case 8  : System.out.println("your eightieth, and");
020:       case 7  : System.out.println("your seventieth, and");
021:       case 6  : System.out.println("your sixtieth, and");
022:       case 5  : System.out.println("your fiftieth, and");
023:       case 4  : System.out.println("your fortieth, and");
024:       case 3  : System.out.println("your thirtieth, and");
025:       case 2  : System.out.println("your twentieth, and");
026:       case 1  : System.out.println("your tenth.");
027:     } // switch
028:   } // main
029:
030: } // class DecadeDescending
```

7.3.1   Trying it

Console Input / Output

```
$ java DecadeDescending 21
You've had the following decade birthdays:
your twentieth, and
your tenth.
$ _
```

Console Input / Output

```
$ java DecadeDescending 103
You've had the following decade birthdays:
your hundredth, and
your ninetieth, and
your eightieth, and
your seventieth, and
your sixtieth, and
your fiftieth, and
your fortieth, and
your thirtieth, and
your twentieth, and
your tenth.
$ _
```

Note that our program does not always work sensibly for every possible input.

```
          Console Input / Output
$ java DecadeDescending 8
You've had the following decade birthdays:
$ java DecadeDescending 110
You've had the following decade birthdays:
$ _
```

Coffee time: 7.3.1
How could we improve it so it gives a message to the user when the age is not in range? (Hint: **default** and **break**?)

7.4 Example: Pi reheated

AIM:
To introduce the **do while loop**.

In our final example, we are going to re-implement the π estimating program from Section 5.10 on page 88, using the third kind of **loop** available in Java.

Concept **Statement: do while loop.** The **do while loop** is the third way in Java of having **repeated execution**. It is similar to the **while loop** but instead of having the **condition** at the start of the **loop**, it appears at the end. This means the condition is **evaluated** *after* the **loop body** is **executed** rather than before. The whole **statement** starts with the **reserved word do**. This is followed by the statement to be repeated, then the reserved word **while** and finally the condition, written in brackets.

For example, the following code is a long winded and inefficient way of giving the **variable** x the value 21.

```
int x = 1;
do
   x += 2;
while (x < 20);
```

Observe the semi-colon that is needed after the condition.

Of course, the body of the do while loop might be a **compound statement**, in which case we might lay out the code as follows.

```
int x = 0;
int y = 100;
do
{
  x++;
  y--;
} while (x != y);
```

Coffee time: 7.4.1
If you were designing Java, would you have made the body of a **do while loop** have to be a single **statement**, or would you have enabled it to be a list of statements without the programmer having to use a **compound statement**?

The above is a long winded and inefficient way of giving both the variables x and y the value 50.

Note that, because the condition is evaluated *after* the body is executed, the body is executed at least once. This is in contrast to the while loop, which might have have its body executed zero times.

Here is the code of this version of the π program – you should compare it with the previous one. You will recall that the process involves computing a series of ever decreasing terms which are added together. The main change here is that we do not keep the previous estimate of π, instead we keep the value of just the latest term. We use a **do while loop** because we want the body to **execute** at least once, and it is convenient to test the **condition** at the end of the loop.

```
001: // A program to estimate Pi using Leibniz's formula.
002: // Argument is desired tolerance between successive terms.
003: // Reports the estimate, the number of terms
004: // and the library constant for comparison.
005: public class PiEstimation
006: {
007:   public static void main(String[] args)
008:   {
009:     // The tolerance is the minimum difference between successive
010:     // terms before we stop estimating.
011:     double tolerance = Double.parseDouble(args[0]);
012:
013:     // The value of the latest term.
014:     double latestTerm;
015:
016:     // The result from our latest estimate, eventually the final result.
017:     double latestEstimate = 4;
018:
019:     // We count the terms, initially 1 for the 4.
020:     int termCount = 1;
021:
022:     // The value of the next term denominator, initially 3.
023:     int nextDenominator = 3;
024:
025:     // The sign of the next term, initially -ve.
026:     int nextNumeratorSign = -1;
027:
028:     // Keep adding terms until latest term is within tolerance.
029:     do
030:     {
031:       latestTerm = nextNumeratorSign * 4.0 / nextDenominator;
032:       latestEstimate += latestTerm;
033:       termCount++;
034:       nextNumeratorSign *= -1;
035:       nextDenominator += 2;
036:     } while (Math.abs(latestTerm) > tolerance);
037:
038:     System.out.println("The estimated value of Pi to tolerance " + tolerance
039:                        + " is " + latestEstimate);
040:     System.out.println("The estimate used " + termCount + " terms");
041:     System.out.println("The library value of Pi is " + Math.PI);
042:   } // main
043:
044: } // class PiEstimation
```

Coffee time: 7.4.2
Will this version of the program be significantly different from the other in terms of its **run time** performance?

7.4.1 Trying it

We can try the program with the same **test data** as previously, to ensure it has the same behaviour, which it nearly does. In fact, it produces the same results with larger tolerances, but is *slightly* more accurate with the smallest one we tried earlier, because it is better at determining the difference between the last two estimates. This has nothing to do with the fact we used a different kind of **loop** – it is due to the other changes in the program.

Coffee time: 7.4.3
Compare the two programs carefully, and figure out why the second one is slightly more accurate for 0.00000001.

```
Console Input / Output
$ java PiEstimation 0.00000001
The estimated value of Pi to tolerance 1.0E-8 is 3.1415926585894076
The estimate used 200000001 terms
The library value of Pi is 3.141592653589793
$ _
```

7.5 Concepts covered in this chapter

Here is a list of the concepts that were covered in this chapter, each with a self-test question. You can use this to check you remember them being introduced, and perhaps re-read some of them before going on to the next chapter.

Statement	

– switch statement with breaks (p.107)	What would be the result of running the following code when noOfBedrooms has the value 3?
	
	``java
	// noOfBedrooms is assumed to be non-negative.
	switch (noOfBedrooms)
	{
	  case 0:
	    System.out.println("I hope you have a car!");
	    break;
	  case 1:
	    System.out.println("Nice and cosy.");
	    break;
	  case 2: case 3: case 4:
	    System.out.println("Room for a family...");
	    break;
	  case 5:
	    System.out.println("You should get a lodger!");
	  default:
	    System.out.println("Woah -- too much cleaning!");
	    break;
	} // switch
	``

– switch statement without breaks (p.110)	Consider the following fragment of code.
	
	``java
	int count = Integer.parseInt(args[0]);
	switch (count)
	{
	  case 5: System.out.println("Got 5");
	  case 4: System.out.println("Got 4");
	  case 3: System.out.println("Got 3");
	  case 2: System.out.println("Got 2");
	  case 1: System.out.println("Got 1");
	  case 0: System.out.println("Got 0");
	} // switch
	``
	Why are *five* lines output if the first command line argument is 4?

– do while loop (p.112)	With respect to how many times the loop body might be executed, what is the difference between the do while loop and the while loop?

Chapter 8

Separate methods and logical operators

> A complex problem
> is made less so when we see its parts –
> not least because some of them are the same.

8.1   Chapter aims

Up to this point all our example programs have had all their code contained in their **main method**. There are two reasons why we don't always want that to be the case. One is that often we would like to reuse certain parts of the code instead of copying it – you may recall that in a previous example in Section 6.6 on page 102 we experienced the need to duplicate some pieces of code. The second reason is simply that as our programs get bigger, we wish to split them up into separate, manageable, parts; using separate **method**s is one way of achieving that.

In addition to these ideas, this chapter introduces the **logical operator**s and some other new Java concepts.

The chapter contains the following sections.

Section	Aims	Associated Coursework
8.2 Age history with two people (p.116)	To further illustrate the inconvenience of having to copy a chunk of code which is used in different parts of a program, and thus motivate the need for separate **method**s.	Write a program to print out all the years from the present day until retirement, for two people. (p.117)
8.3 Age history with a separate method (p.118)	To introduce the idea of dividing a program into separate **method**s to enable the reuse of some parts of it. We meet the concepts **private**, **method parameter**, **method call** and **void method**.	Write a program, with a separate **method**, to print out all the years from the present day until retirement, for four people. (p.122)
8.4 Dividing a cake with a separate method for GCD (p.122)	To introduce the idea of using **method**s merely to split the program into parts, making it easier to understand and develop. We also meet the **return statement** for use in **non-void method**s, and see that altering a **method parameter** does not change its argument.	Write a program to compute the **greatest common divisor** of *four* numbers, using a separate **method**. (p.124)
8.5 Multiple times table with separate methods (p.124)	To introduce the concept of **class variable**s, compared with **local variable**s, and reinforce the ideas of using separate **method**s for reuse and for dividing a program into manageable chunks. We also meet `System.out.printf()`.	Write a program, with separate **method**s, to produce a table showing pairs of numbers which share common factors. (p.127)

Section	Aims	Associated Coursework
8.6 Age history with day and month (p.128)	To introduce the **logical operators**. We also see that a group of **variables** can be declared together.	Do some reasoning to show that two different **conditions** have the same value. (p.132)
8.7 Truth tables (p.132)	To introduce the **boolean type**, and reinforce **logical operators**. We also meet the String type and see that a **for update** can have multiple **statements**.	Write a program to test the equivalence of three **propositional expressions**, each having four **variables**. (p.137)
8.8 Producing a calendar (p.137)	To reinforce much of the material presented in this chapter. We also revisit System.out.printf().	Modify a calendar month printing program to produce a larger calendar format and to highlight a certain date. (p.141)

8.2 Example: Age history with two people

AIM:
To further illustrate the inconvenience of having to copy a chunk of code which is used in different parts of a program, and thus motivate the need for separate **methods**.

Recall our program to report the age history of a person, from Section 5.9 on page 83. Suppose we wish the program to report the age history of two people rather than just one. The obvious approach is to simply make a second copy of the code we already have, change the messages a bit, and add a 1 or a 2 to most **variable** names.

```
001: // Print out an age history of two people.
002: // Arguments: present year, first birth year, second birth year.
003: public class AgeHistory2
004: {
005:   public static void main(String[] args)
006:   {
007:     // The year of the present day.
008:     int presentYear = Integer.parseInt(args[0]);
009:
010:     // The two birth years, which must be less than the present year.
011:     int birthYear1 = Integer.parseInt(args[1]);
012:     int birthYear2 = Integer.parseInt(args[2]);
013:
014:     // PERSON 1
015:     // Start by printing the event of birth.
016:     System.out.println("Pn 1 was born in " + birthYear1);
017:
018:     // Now we will go through the years between birth and last year.
019:     int someYear1 = birthYear1 + 1;
020:     int ageInSomeYear1 = 1;
021:     while (someYear1 != presentYear)
022:     {
023:       System.out.println("Pn 1 was " + ageInSomeYear1 + " in " + someYear1);
024:       someYear1++;
025:       ageInSomeYear1++;
026:     } // while
027:
028:     // Finally, the age of the person this year.
029:     System.out.println("Pn 1 is " + ageInSomeYear1 + " this year");
030:
031:     // PERSON 2
```

```
032:     // Start by printing the event of birth.
033:     System.out.println("Pn 2 was born in " + birthYear2);
034:
035:     // Now we will go through the years between birth and last year.
036:     int someYear2 = birthYear2 + 1;
037:     int ageInSomeYear2 = 1;
038:     while (someYear2 != presentYear)
039:     {
040:       System.out.println("Pn 2 was " + ageInSomeYear2 + " in " + someYear2);
041:       someYear2++;
042:       ageInSomeYear2++;
043:     } // while
044:
045:     // Finally, the age of the person this year.
046:     System.out.println("Pn 2 is " + ageInSomeYear2 + " this year");
047:   } // main
048:
049: } // class AgeHistory2
```

Coffee time: 8.2.1 While this approach works, what are the problems with it? E.g., could we be careless with our editing? What if we wanted to make it work for 10 people?

8.2.1 Trying it

After we have **compiled** the program, we can **run** it with various **command line arguments**.

8.2.2 Coursework: `WorkFuture2`

In this task you will write a program, called `WorkFuture2`, which shows the future working time of two people, assuming they retire at 68. The program will take three **command line arguments**, which you may assume are valid. The first is the present year, and the second and third are the birth years of the two people.

```
                 Console Input / Output
$ java AgeHistory2 2015 1996 1982
Pn 1 was born in 1996
Pn 1 was 1 in 1997
Pn 1 was 2 in 1998
(... lines removed to save space.)
Pn 1 was 18 in 2014
Pn 1 is 19 this year
Pn 2 was born in 1982
Pn 2 was 1 in 1983
Pn 2 was 2 in 1984
(... lines removed to save space.)
Pn 2 was 32 in 2014
Pn 2 is 33 this year
$ _
```

In case you have been reading ahead, you should *not* use a separate **method** – write all your code in the **main method**.

An example use of the program might be as follows.

```
                 Console Input / Output
$ java WorkFuture2 2015 1959 1996
Pn 1 has 12 years left to work
In 2016 pn 1 will have 11 years left to work
In 2017 pn 1 will have 10 years left to work
(... lines removed to save space.)
In 2026 pn 1 will have 1 years left to work
Pn 1 will retire in 2027
Pn 2 has 49 years left to work
In 2016 pn 2 will have 48 years left to work
In 2017 pn 2 will have 47 years left to work
(... lines removed to save space.)
In 2063 pn 2 will have 1 years left to work
Pn 2 will retire in 2064
$ _
```

Undertake the usual tasks of planning **test data**, **design**ing the program, implementing and testing it, and finally recording your results.

8.3 Example: Age history with a separate method

AIM:
To introduce the idea of dividing a program into separate **method**s to enable the reuse of some parts of it. We meet the concepts **private, method parameter, method call** and **void method**.

What if we wanted to report the age of four people? Ten? The obvious approach of copying a big chunk of code is not very appealing. For a start, the program is getting quite big and yet large parts of it are the same. Secondly, it would be nice to have the repeated part of the code existing in just one place to save maintaining it more than once: any change we would like to make to it in the future, such as rewording the messages, would have to be made as many times as there are copies of the code.

A better approach is to place the repeated part of the code in a separate **method**, which we can then use as many times as we like. So far, we have only written **main method**s.

Concept **Method.** A **method** in Java is a section of code, dedicated to performing a particular task. All programs have a **main method** which is the starting point of the program. We can have other methods too, and we can give them any name we like – although we should always choose a name which suits the purpose. By convention, method names start with a lower case letter. For example, System.out.println() is a method which prints a line of text. Apart from its slightly strange spelling, the name println does reflect the meaning of the method.

In the AgeHistory4 program we are about to write, the separate method for printing the age history of one person is too specific to be of general use in any other program. It is intended for use only within this program, and so we shall declare it as having **private** visibility.

Concept **Method: private.** A **method** should be declared with a **private** visibility **modifier** if it is not intended to be usable from outside the **class** it is defined in. This is done by writing the **reserved word private** instead of **public** in the heading.

Our method will be used to print the age history of different people, who will have different birth years. It will also need to know the current year. These values will be passed to it as **method parameters**.

Concept **Method: accepting parameters.** A **method** may be given **method parameter**s which enable it to vary its effect based on their values. This is similar to a program being given **command line argument**s, indeed the arguments given to a program are passed as parameters to the **main method**.

Parameters are declared in the heading of the method. For example, main methods have the following heading.

```
public static void main(String[] args)
```

The text inside the brackets is the declaration of the parameters. A method can have any number of parameters, including zero. If there is more than one, they are separated by commas (,). Each parameter consists of a **type** and a name. For example, the following method is given two parameters, a **double** and an **int**.

```
private static void printHeightPerYear(double height, int age)
{
    System.out.println("At age " + age + ", height per year ratio is "
                    + height / age);
} // printHeightPerYear
```

You should think of parameters as being like **variables** defined inside the method, except that they are given initial values before the method body is **executed**. For example, the single parameter to the main method is a variable which is given a **list** of strings before the method begins execution, these strings being the command line arguments supplied to the program.

The names of the parameters are not important to Java – as long as they all have different names! The names only mean something to the human reader, which is of course important. The above method could easily have been written as follows.

```
private static void printHeightPerYear(double howTall, int howOld)
{
  System.out.println("At age " + howOld + ", height per year ratio is "
                      + howTall / howOld);
} // printHeightPerYear
```

You might think the first version is subjectively nicer than the second, but clearly both are better than this next one!

```
private static void printHeightPerYear(double d, int i)
{
  System.out.println("At age " + i + ", height per year ratio is "
                      + d / i);
} // printHeightPerYear
```

And that is only marginally better than calling the parameters, say x and y. However, Java does not care – it is not clever enough to be able to, as it can have no understanding of the problem being solved by the code.

In the `AgeHistory4` program, our main method will have four **statement**s which are **method call**s to the separate method. At these points, the **method argument**s to be used for the parameters will be supplied.

Concept **Method: calling a method.** The body of a **method** is **executed** when some other code refers to it using a **method call**. For example, the program calls a method named `println` when it executes `System.out.println("Hello world!")`. For another example, if we have a method, named `printHeightPerYear`, which prints out a height to age ratio when it is given a height (in metres) and an age, then we could make it print the ratio between the height 1.6 and the age 14 using the following method call.

```
printHeightPerYear(1.6, 14);
```

When we call a method we supply a **method argument** for each **method parameter**, separating them by commas (,). These argument values are copied into the corresponding parameters of the method – the first argument goes into the first parameter, the second into the second, and so on.

The arguments passed to a method may be the current values of **variables**. For example, the above code could have been written as follows.

```
double personHeight = 1.6;
int personAge = 14;

printHeightPerYear(personHeight, personAge);
```

As you may expect, the arguments to a method are actually **expression**s rather than just **literal value**s or variables. These expressions are **evaluate**d at the time the method is called. So we might have the following.

```
double growthLastYear = 0.02;

printHeightPerYear(personHeight - growthLastYear, personAge - 1);
```

Our separate method in the AgeHistory4 program will print out the age history of one person, based on the details given to it as parameters. It will not **return** a result to the code that calls it, so it will be a **void method**.

> *Concept* **Method: void methods.** Often, a **method** might calculate some kind of **function** or formula, perhaps based on its **method parameter**s, and **return** the answer as a result. The result might be an **int** or a **double** or some other **type**. If a method returns a result then the **return type** of the result must be stated in its heading. If it does not, then we write the word **void** instead, which literally means (among other definitions) 'without contents'. For example, the **main method** of a program does not return a result – it is always a **void method**.
>
> ```
> public static void main(String[] args)
> ```

Our AgeHistory4 program contains two items – the separate method followed by the main method. The first of these is a private void method to print the age history of a single person. It will be given the present year, the number of the person (for identification in the messages) and his or her birth year, as three parameter values of **type int**.

```
001: // Print out an age history of four people.
002: // Arguments: present year, first birth year, second, third, fourth.
003: public class AgeHistory4
004: {
005:   // Print the age history of one person, identified as personNumber.
006:   // Birth year must be less than present year.
007:   private static void printAgeHistory(int presentYear,
008:                                       int personNumber, int birthYear)
009:   {
010:     // Start by printing the event of birth.
011:     System.out.println("Pn " + personNumber + " was born in " + birthYear);
012:
013:     // Now we will go through the years between birth and last year.
014:     int someYear = birthYear + 1;
015:     int ageInSomeYear = 1;
016:     while (someYear != presentYear)
017:     {
018:       System.out.println("Pn " + personNumber + " was "
019:                         + ageInSomeYear + " in " + someYear);
020:       someYear++;
021:       ageInSomeYear++;
022:     } // while
023:
024:     // Finally, the age of the person this year.
025:     System.out.println("Pn " + personNumber + " is "
026:                       + ageInSomeYear + " this year");
027:   } // printAgeHistory
```

We could have decided to put the main method first had we wished to – the order does not matter to Java.

```
030:   // The main method: get arguments and call printAgeHistory.
031:   public static void main(String[] args)
032:   {
033:     // The year of the present day.
034:     int presentYear = Integer.parseInt(args[0]);
035:
036:     // The four birth years, which must be less than the present year.
037:     int birthYear1 = Integer.parseInt(args[1]);
038:     int birthYear2 = Integer.parseInt(args[2]);
039:     int birthYear3 = Integer.parseInt(args[3]);
040:     int birthYear4 = Integer.parseInt(args[4]);
```

```
041:
042:     // Now print the four age histories.
043:     printAgeHistory(presentYear, 1, birthYear1);
044:     printAgeHistory(presentYear, 2, birthYear2);
045:     printAgeHistory(presentYear, 3, birthYear3);
046:     printAgeHistory(presentYear, 4, birthYear4);
047:   } // main
048:
049: } // class AgeHistory4
```

Coffee time: Why did we need to write the **reserved word static** in the heading of `printAgeHistory()`? What do you think would happen if we omitted it?

Console Input / Output
`$ java AgeHistory4 2015 1996 1982 1959 2014`
`Pn 1 was born in 1996`
`Pn 1 was 1 in 1997`
(... lines removed to save space.)
`Pn 1 is 19 this year`
`Pn 2 was born in 1982`
`Pn 2 was 1 in 1983`
(... lines removed to save space.)
`Pn 2 is 33 this year`
`Pn 3 was born in 1959`
`Pn 3 was 1 in 1960`
(... lines removed to save space.)
`Pn 3 is 56 this year`
`Pn 4 was born in 2014`
`Pn 4 is 1 this year`
`$ _`

8.3.1 Trying it

After we have **compiled** the program, we can **run** it with various **command line arguments**.

8.3.2 Warning: do not forget `static`

Finally, a little warning. You will have noticed that we declared `printAgeHistory()` with the **reserved word static**. This is because it is being called directly from the **main method**, which itself is **static**. At some point you will make an error in one of your own programs, and forget to put that word when it is needed. So, for illustration, we have made a copy of the `AgeHistory4` program called `AgeHistoryOops` and then deleted the word **static** from the `printAgeHistory()` **method** in this copy. This is what we get when we try to compile it.

Console Input / Output
`$ javac AgeHistoryOops.java`
`AgeHistoryOops.java:43: non-static method printAgeHistory(int,int,int) cannot be`
`  referenced from a static context`
`    printAgeHistory(presentYear, 1, birthYear1);`
`     ^`
`AgeHistoryOops.java:44: non-static method printAgeHistory(int,int,int) cannot be`
`  referenced from a static context`
`    printAgeHistory(presentYear, 2, birthYear2);`
`     ^`
`AgeHistoryOops.java:45: non-static method printAgeHistory(int,int,int) cannot be`
`  referenced from a static context`
`    printAgeHistory(presentYear, 3, birthYear3);`
`     ^`
`AgeHistoryOops.java:46: non-static method printAgeHistory(int,int,int) cannot be`
`  referenced from a static context`
`    printAgeHistory(presentYear, 4, birthYear4);`
`     ^`
`4 errors`
`$ _`

8.3.3   Coursework: `WorkFuture4`

In this task you will write another version of the work future program, called `WorkFuture4`, which shows the future working time of four people. The program will take five **command line argument**s, which you may assume are valid. The first is the present year, and the others are the birth years of the four people.

Your program should use a separate **method** to print the work future for one person, and call it four times.

Undertake the usual tasks of planning **test data**, **design**ing the program, implementing and testing it, and finally recording your results.

8.4   Example: Dividing a cake with a separate method for GCD

AIM:
To introduce the idea of using **method**s merely to split the program into parts, making it easier to understand and develop. We also meet the **return statement** for use in **non-void method**s, and see that altering a **method parameter** does not change its argument.

We can make the code for the cake division example more readable by introducing a separate **method** to compute the GCD. This will be given the two numbers as **method arguments** for its two **method parameters**, and it will **return** the **greatest common divisor** as a result.

Concept **Method: returning a value.**   A **method** may **return** a result back to the code that called it. If this is so, we declare the **return type** of the result in the method heading, in place of the **reserved word** `void`. Such methods are often called **non-void method**s. For example, the following method takes a Celsius temperature, and returns the corresponding Fahrenheit value.

```
private static double celsiusToFahrenheit(double celsiusValue)
{
  double fahrenheitValue = celsiusValue * 9 / 5 + 32;
  return fahrenheitValue;
} // celsiusToFahrenheit
```

The method is declared with a return type of `double`, by writing that **type** name before the method name.

The **return statement** is how we specify what value is to be returned as the result of the method. The **statement** causes the execution of the method to end, and control to transfer back to the code that called the method.

The result of a non-void method can be used in an **expression**. For example, the method above might be used as follows.

```
double celsiusValue = Double.parseDouble(args[0]);
System.out.println("The Fahrenheit value of "
                + celsiusValue + " Celsius is "
                + celsiusToFahrenheit(celsiusValue) + ".");
```

The return statement takes any expression after the reserved word `return`. So our method above could be implemented using just one statement.

```
private static double celsiusToFahrenheit(double celsiusValue)
{
  return celsiusValue * 9 / 5 + 32;
} // celsiusToFahrenheit
```

Here is the code for the new `DivideCake` program.

```
001: // Program to decide how to divide a cake in proportion to the age of two
002: // persons, using the minimum number of equal sized portions.
003: // The two arguments are the two positive integer ages.
004: public class DivideCake
005: {
006:    // Find the GCD of two positive integers.
007:    private static int greatestCommonDivisor(int multiple1OfGCD,
008:                                             int multiple2OfGCD)
009:    {
010:       // Both multiple1OfGCD and multiple2OfGCD must be positive.
011:       // While the two multiples are not the same, the difference
012:       // between them must also be a multiple of the GCD.
013:       // So we keep subtracting the smallest from the largest
014:       // until they are equal.
015:       while (multiple1OfGCD != multiple2OfGCD)
016:         if (multiple1OfGCD > multiple2OfGCD)
017:            multiple1OfGCD -= multiple2OfGCD;
018:         else
019:            multiple2OfGCD -= multiple1OfGCD;
020:
021:       // Now multiple1OfGCD == multiple2OfGCD
022:       // which is also the GCD of their original values.
023:       return multiple1OfGCD;
024:    } // greatestCommonDivisor
025:
026:
027:    // Obtain arguments, get GCD, compute portions and report it all.
028:    public static void main(String[] args)
029:    {
030:       // Both ages must be positive.
031:       int age1 = Integer.parseInt(args[0]);
032:       int age2 = Integer.parseInt(args[1]);
033:
034:       int agesGCD = greatestCommonDivisor(age1, age2);
035:       System.out.println("The GCD of " + age1 + " and " + age2
036:                          + " is " + agesGCD);
037:       int noOfPortions1 = age1 / agesGCD;
038:       int noOfPortions2 = age2 / agesGCD;
039:
040:       System.out.println("So the cake should be divided into "
041:                          + (noOfPortions1 + noOfPortions2));
042:       System.out.println
043:         ("The " + age1 + " year old gets " + noOfPortions1
044:          + " and the " + age2 + " year old gets " + noOfPortions2);
045:    } // main
046:
047: } // class DivideCake
```

Coffee time:

8.4.1

Did you notice that inside the `greatestCommonDivisor()` method, the code changes the values of both `multiple1OfGCD` and `multiple2OfGCD`? These start off as being the ages of the two people, but end up being the GCD of the two ages. Then, after the method has finished executing, the `main()` method prints out the values of `age1` and `age2` in its message.

So, will `age1` and `age2` have had their value changed, causing the program to wrongly report both ages as being the GCD of the original values?

8.4.1 Trying it

After we have **compile**d the program, we can **run** it with various **command line argument**s, and we get the same results as we did for the previous version in Section 6.3.1 on page 97.

8.4.2 Changing values of method parameters

Concept **Method: changing parameters does not affect arguments.** We can think of **method parameters** as being like **variables** defined inside the **method**, but which are given their initial value by the code that calls the method. This means the method can change the values of the parameters, like it can for any other variable defined in it. Such changes have no effect on the environment of the code that called the method, regardless of where the **method argument** values came from. An argument value, be it a literal constant, taken straight from a variable, or the result of some more complex **expression**, is simply copied into the corresponding parameter at the time the method is called. This is known as **call by value**.

So, when the `greatestCommonDivisor()` **method** is called, the values of the **variables** `age1` and `age2` are *copied* into the **method parameters** `multiple1OfGCD` and `multiple2OfGCD`. Then when these parameters are changed within the method, it is the value of just these variables which is changed.

8.4.3 Coursework: `DivideCake4`

In this task you will write a version of the cake dividing program for those very rare families that have four daughters sharing a birthday! This should be called `DivideCake4`. You may assume that the four arguments all represent positive **int** numbers. You should use a separate **method** to compute the **greatest common divisor** of two numbers.

Undertake the usual tasks of planning **test data**, **design**ing the program, implementing and testing it, and finally recording your results.

8.5 Example: Multiple times table with separate methods

AIM:
To introduce the concept of **class variables**, compared with **local variables**, and re-inforce the ideas of using separate **methods** for reuse and for dividing a program into manageable chunks. We also meet `System.out.printf()`.

Recall the program to print a multiple times table from Section 6.6 on page 102. In this example we give another version of it, using separate **methods** to avoid duplicated code and make the program more manageable.

We are also going to improve the program by making it more flexible. We will put the size of the table in a **variable** so that it can easily be changed if required. This variable needs to be accessed by code inside some of the separate methods as well as by the **main method**, and so we shall use a **class variable**.

Concept **Variable: local variables.** When we declare **variables** inside a **method**, they are local to that method and only exist while that method is running – they cannot be accessed by other methods. They are known as **local variables** or **method variables**. Also, different methods can have variables with the same name – they are different variables.

Concept **Variable: class variables.** We can declare **variables** directly inside a **class**, outside of any **methods**. Such **class variables** exist from the moment the class is loaded into the **virtual machine** until the end of the program, and they can be accessed by any method in the class. For example, the following are three class variables which might be used to store the components of today's date.

```
private static int presentDay;
private static int presentMonth;
private static int presentYear;
```

Notice that we use the **reserved word static** in their declaration. Also, class variables have a visibility **modifier** – the above have all been declared as being **private**, which means they can only be accessed by code inside the class which has declared them.

In our new TimesTable program we have a single **private** class variable to store the size of the table.

```
001: // Program to print out a neat multiplication table.
002: public class TimesTable
003: {
004:   // The size of the table -- the number of rows and columns.
005:   private static int tableSize = 12;
```

Our main method calls the separate methods as required. Notice the direct access to the class variable tableSize.

```
008:   // The main method implements the top level structure of the table.
009:   public static void main(String[] args)
010:   {
011:     // Top line.
012:     printLine();
013:
014:     // Column headings.
015:     printColumnHeadings();
016:
017:     // Underline headings.
018:     printLine();
019:
020:     // Now the rows.
021:     for (int row = 1; row <= tableSize; row++)
022:       printRow(row);
023:
024:     // Bottom line.
025:     printLine();
026:   } // main
```

The **method** printLine() also uses the value of the class variable tableSize.

```
029:   // Print a line across the table.
030:   private static void printLine()
031:   {
032:     // Left side, 5 characters for row labels, separator.
033:     System.out.print("|-----|");
034:     // Across each column.
035:     for (int column = 1; column <= tableSize; column++)
036:       System.out.print("----");
037:     // The right side.
038:     System.out.println("-|");
039:   } // printLine
```

As does printColumnHeadings().

```
042:   // Print the line containing the column headings.
043:   private static void printColumnHeadings()
044:   {
045:     System.out.print("|     |");
046:     for (int column = 1; column <= tableSize; column++)
047:       printNumber(column);
048:     System.out.println("  |");
049:   } // printColumnHeadings
```

And `printRow()` too!

```
052:   // Print one row of the table.
053:   private static void printRow(int row)
054:   {
055:     // The left side.
056:     System.out.print("|");
057:     printNumber(row);
058:     // Separator.
059:     System.out.print("  |");
060:
061:     // Now the columns on this row.
062:     for (int column = 1; column <= tableSize; column++)
063:       printNumber(row * column);
064:
065:     // The right side.
066:     System.out.println("  |");
067:   } // printRow
```

Whereas, `printNumber()` merely has a **method parameter**. This is how we *could* write it, following the style we used previously.

```
private static void printNumber(int n)
{
  if (n < 10)
    System.out.print("    " + n);
  else if (n < 100)
    System.out.print("   " + n);
  else
    System.out.print("  " + n);
} // printNumber
```

Writing this code in a separate method would avoid the need to write it more than once like we did before, but there is a simpler way to write it in the first place.

Concept **Standard API: System: out.printf().** The **class** System contains a **method** out.printf(), introduced in Java 5.0, which is similar to out.print() except that we can use it to produce formatted output of values.

A simple use of this is to take an **integer** value and have it printed with **space padding** to a given positive integer field width. This means the output contains leading spaces followed by the usual representation of the integer, such that the number of **characters** printed is at least the given field width.

The following code fragment includes an example which prints a string representation of 123, with leading spaces so that the result has a width of ten characters.

```
System.out.println("1234567890");
System.out.printf("%10d%n", 123);
```

Here is the effect of these two **statement**s.

```
1234567890
       123
```

The first % tells out.printf() that we wish it to format something, the 10 tells it the minimum total width to produce, and the following letter says what kind of conversion to perform. A d tells it to produce the representation of a decimal whole number, which is given after the **format specifier** string, as the second **method argument**. The %n tells out.printf() to output the platform dependent **line separator**.

The method can be asked to format a floating point value, such as a **double**. In such cases we give the minimum total width, a dot (.), the number of decimal places, and an f conversion. For example,

```
System.out.printf("%1.2f%n", 123.456);
```

needs more than the given minimum width of 1, and so produces the following.

```
123.46
```

Whereas, the format specifier in

```
System.out.println("1234567890");
System.out.printf("%10.2f%n", 123.456);
```

prints a total of ten characters for the number, two of which are decimal places.

```
1234567890
    123.46
```

Coffee	Are you tempted to pop back to previous example programs and improve
time:	their output using System.out.printf()?

For our printNumber() method we do not wish out.printf() to produce a **new line** so we omit the %n from the **format specifier** string.

```
070:    // Print a number using exactly 4 characters, with leading spaces.
071:    private static void printNumber(int n)
072:    {
073:        System.out.printf("%4d", n);
074:    } // printNumber
075:
076: } // class TimesTable
```

8.5.1 Trying it

After we have **compile**d the program, we can **run** it.

```
                        Console Input / Output
$ java TimesTable
|-----|------------------------------------------------|
|     |  1   2   3   4   5   6   7   8   9  10  11  12 |
|-----|------------------------------------------------|
|  1  |  1   2   3   4   5   6   7   8   9  10  11  12 |
|  2  |  2   4   6   8  10  12  14  16  18  20  22  24 |
|  3  |  3   6   9  12  15  18  21  24  27  30  33  36 |
|  4  |  4   8  12  16  20  24  28  32  36  40  44  48 |
|  5  |  5  10  15  20  25  30  35  40  45  50  55  60 |
|  6  |  6  12  18  24  30  36  42  48  54  60  66  72 |
|  7  |  7  14  21  28  35  42  49  56  63  70  77  84 |
|  8  |  8  16  24  32  40  48  56  64  72  80  88  96 |
|  9  |  9  18  27  36  45  54  63  72  81  90  99 108 |
| 10  | 10  20  30  40  50  60  70  80  90 100 110 120 |
| 11  | 11  22  33  44  55  66  77  88  99 110 121 132 |
| 12  | 12  24  36  48  60  72  84  96 108 120 132 144 |
|-----|------------------------------------------------|
$ _
```

8.5.2 Coursework: CommonFactorsTable with methods

In this task you will write a new version of the CommonFactorsTable program from Section 6.6.2 on page 103. This will use separate **method**s to avoid repeated code, and may reasonably be developed by making changes to the previous one. Plan these changes in your logbook, before taking the usual steps of implementing the program and recording your results.

8.6 Example: Age history with day and month

AIM:
To introduce the **logical operators**. We also see that a group of **variables** can be declared together.

We now elaborate on our program to print the age history of people, by adding the day and month to dates in it. This requires the code to compare dates based on three values, rather than just one, and so the **loop condition** is more complex than in the previous version of the program which only needed to compare years. To achieve this, we use **logical operators**.

Concept **Expression: boolean: logical operators.** For some **algorithms**, we need **conditions** on **loops** etc. that are more complex than can be made simply by using the **relational operators**. Java provides us with **logical operators** to enable us to glue together simple conditions into bigger ones. The three most commonly used logical operators are **conditional and**, **conditional or** and **logical not**.

Operator	Title	Posh title	Description
&&	and	**conjunction**	c1 && c2 is **true** if and only if both conditions c1 and c2 **evaluate** to **true**. Both of the two conditions, known as **conjunct**s, must be **true** to satisfy the combined condition.
||	or	**disjunction**	c1 || c2 is **true** if and only if at least one of the conditions c1 and c2 evaluate to **true**. The combined condition is satisfied, unless both of the two conditions, known as **disjunct**s, are **false**.
!	not	**negation**	!c is **true** if and only if the condition c evaluates to **false**. This operator negates the given condition.

We can define these **operators** using **truth table**s, where ? means the **operand** is not evaluated.

c1	c2	c1 && c2	c1	c2	c1 || c2	c	!c
true	true	true	true	?	true	true	false
true	false	false	false	true	true	false	true
false	?	false	false	false	false		

Using these operators, we can make up complex conditions, such as the following.

```
age1 < age2 || age1 == age2 && height1 <= height2
```

As with the **arithmetic operators**, Java defines **operator precedence** and **operator associativity** to disambiguate complex conditions that are not fully bracketed, such as the one above. && and || have a lower precedence than the relational operators which have a lower precedence than the arithmetic ones. ! has a very high precedence (even more so than the arithmetic operators) and && has a higher precedence than ||. So the above example **expression** has implicit brackets as follows.

```
(age1 < age2) || ((age1 == age2) && (height1 <= height2))
```

This might be part of a program that **sort**s people standing in a line by age, but when they are the same age, it sorts them by height. Assuming that the **int variables** age1 and height1 contain the age and height of one person, and the other two variables similarly contain that **data** for another, then the following code might be used to tell the pair to swap their order if necessary.

```
if (age1 < age2 || age1 == age2 && height1 <= height2)
   System.out.println("You are in the correct order.");
else
   System.out.println("Please swap over.");
```

We might have, perhaps less clearly, chosen to write that code as follows.

```
if (!(age1 < age2 || age1 == age2 && height1 <= height2))
  System.out.println("Please swap over.");
else
  System.out.println("You are in the correct order.");
```

You might find it tricky, but it's worth convincing yourself: yet another way of writing code with the same effect would be as follows.

```
if (age1 > age2 || age1 == age2 && height1 > height2)
  System.out.println("Please swap over.");
else
  System.out.println("You are in the correct order.");
```

In mathematics, we are used to writing expressions such as $x \leq y \leq z$ to mean true, if and only if y lies in the range x to z, inclusive. In Java, such expressions need to be written as x <= y && y <= z.

Also, in everyday language we are used to using the words 'and' and 'or' where they have very similar meanings to the associated Java operators. However, we say things like "my mother's age is 46 or 47". In Java, we would need to write myMumAge == 46 || myMumAge == 47 to capture the same meaning. Another example, "my brothers are aged 10 and 12", might be coded as myBrother1Age == 10 && myBrother2Age == 12.

However, there are times in everyday language when we say "and" when we really mean "or" in logic, and hence would use || in Java. For example, "the two possible ages for my dad are 49 *and* 53" is really the same as saying "my dad's age is 49 *or* my dad's age is 53".

As before, we shall have a separate **method** to print the age history of one person. Previously this was given three **method parameter**s, the present year, the person number, and the birth year. Now, the two dates are each expressed as three **variable**s, so this suggests that there should be seven parameters. However, the present date is the same for all the people, so instead of passing it as three parameters, we are going to store it in **class variables**. We shall define these on the same line.

Concept **Variable: a group of variables can be declared together.** Java permits us to declare a group of **variable**s which have the same **type** in one declaration, by writing the type followed by a comma-separated list of the variable names. For example

```
int x, y;
```

declares two variables, both of type **int**. We can even assign values to the variables, as in the following.

```
int minimumVotingAge = 18, minimumArmyAge = 16;
```

This shorthand is not as useful as one might think, because of course, we typically have a **comment** before each variable explaining what its meaning is. However, we can sometimes have one comment which describes a group of variables.

Here is the code for our age history program for dealing with two people using full dates.

```
001: // Print out an age history of two people.
002: // Arguments: present date, first birth date, second birth date.
003: // Each date is three numbers: day month year.
004: public class AgeHistory2
005: {
```

```
006:   // The present date, stored as three variables.
007:   private static int presentDay, presentMonth, presentYear;
008:
009:
010:   // Print the age history of one person, identified as personNumber.
011:   // The birth date must be less than the present date.
012:   private static void printAgeHistory
013:     (int personNumber, int birthDay, int birthMonth, int birthYear)
014:   {
015:     // Start by printing the event of birth.
016:     System.out.println("Pn " + personNumber + " was born on "
017:                          + birthDay + "/" + birthMonth + "/" + birthYear);
018:
019:     // Now we will go through the years since birth but before today.
020:     int someYear = birthYear + 1;
021:     int ageInSomeYear = 1;
022:     while (someYear < presentYear
023:             || someYear == presentYear && birthMonth < presentMonth
024:             || someYear == presentYear && birthMonth == presentMonth
025:               && birthDay < presentDay)
026:     {
027:       System.out.println("Pn " + personNumber + " was " + ageInSomeYear
028:                          + " on " + birthDay + "/" + birthMonth
029:                          + "/" + someYear);
030:       someYear++;
031:       ageInSomeYear++;
032:     } // while
033:
034:     // At this point birthDay/birthMonth/someYear
035:     // will be the next birthday, aged ageInSomeYear.
036:     // This will be greater than or equal to the present date.
037:     // If the person has not yet had their birthday this year
038:     // someYear equals presentYear,
039:     // otherwise someYear equals presentYear + 1.
040:
041:     if (birthMonth == presentMonth && birthDay == presentDay)
042:       // then someYear must equal presentYear.
043:       System.out.println("Pn " + personNumber + " is "
044:                          + ageInSomeYear + " today!");
045:     else
046:       System.out.println("Pn " + personNumber + " will be "
047:                          + ageInSomeYear + " on " + birthDay + "/"
048:                          + birthMonth + "/" + someYear);
049:   } // printAgeHistory
```

Coffee time: | 8.6.1 | In the code above, did you see how the **condition** of the **while loop** has exploded with complexity, compared with the previous versions of the program that merely had one **relational operator**, i.e. `while (someYear != presentYear)`? Did this surprise you?

```
052:   // The main method: get arguments and call printAgeHistory.
053:   public static void main(String[] args)
054:   {
055:     // The present date, stored in three class variables.
056:     presentDay = Integer.parseInt(args[0]);
057:     presentMonth = Integer.parseInt(args[1]);
058:     presentYear = Integer.parseInt(args[2]);
059:
```

```
060:      // The dates of birth: these must be less than the present date.
061:      int birthDay1 = Integer.parseInt(args[3]);
062:      int birthMonth1 = Integer.parseInt(args[4]);
063:      int birthYear1 = Integer.parseInt(args[5]);
064:
065:      int birthDay2 = Integer.parseInt(args[6]);
066:      int birthMonth2 = Integer.parseInt(args[7]);
067:      int birthYear2 = Integer.parseInt(args[8]);
068:
069:      // Now print the two age histories.
070:      printAgeHistory(1, birthDay1, birthMonth1, birthYear1);
071:      printAgeHistory(2, birthDay2, birthMonth2, birthYear2);
072:   } // main
073:
074: } // class AgeHistory2
```

Coffee time: Of the nine variable assignments above, why do three of them not start with the word **int**?

8.6.1 Trying it

After we have **compiled** the program, we can **run** it with various **command line arguments**. First we'll try someone born this day and month last year, and another the same day 19 years ago.

```
Console Input / Output

$ java AgeHistory2 30 03 2015 30 03 2014 30 03 1996
(Output shown using multiple columns to save space.)
Pn 1 was born on 30/3/2014    Pn 2 was 6 on 30/3/2002     Pn 2 was 14 on 30/3/2010
Pn 1 is 1 today!              Pn 2 was 7 on 30/3/2003     Pn 2 was 15 on 30/3/2011
Pn 2 was born on 30/3/1996    Pn 2 was 8 on 30/3/2004     Pn 2 was 16 on 30/3/2012
Pn 2 was 1 on 30/3/1997       Pn 2 was 9 on 30/3/2005     Pn 2 was 17 on 30/3/2013
Pn 2 was 2 on 30/3/1998       Pn 2 was 10 on 30/3/2006    Pn 2 was 18 on 30/3/2014
Pn 2 was 3 on 30/3/1999       Pn 2 was 11 on 30/3/2007    Pn 2 is 19 today!
Pn 2 was 4 on 30/3/2000       Pn 2 was 12 on 30/3/2008
Pn 2 was 5 on 30/3/2001       Pn 2 was 13 on 30/3/2009
$ _
```

Now someone born yesterday, and another the same day 19 years ago.

```
Console Input / Output

$ java AgeHistory2 30 03 2015 29 03 2015 29 03 1996
(Output shown using multiple columns to save space.)
Pn 1 was born on 29/3/2015    Pn 2 was 6 on 29/3/2002     Pn 2 was 14 on 29/3/2010
Pn 1 will be 1 on 29/3/2016   Pn 2 was 7 on 29/3/2003     Pn 2 was 15 on 29/3/2011
Pn 2 was born on 29/3/1996    Pn 2 was 8 on 29/3/2004     Pn 2 was 16 on 29/3/2012
Pn 2 was 1 on 29/3/1997       Pn 2 was 9 on 29/3/2005     Pn 2 was 17 on 29/3/2013
Pn 2 was 2 on 29/3/1998       Pn 2 was 10 on 29/3/2006    Pn 2 was 18 on 29/3/2014
Pn 2 was 3 on 29/3/1999       Pn 2 was 11 on 29/3/2007    Pn 2 was 19 on 29/3/2015
Pn 2 was 4 on 29/3/2000       Pn 2 was 12 on 29/3/2008    Pn 2 will be 20 on 29/3/2016
Pn 2 was 5 on 29/3/2001       Pn 2 was 13 on 29/3/2009
$ _
```

Now someone born a year ago tomorrow, and another the same day 19 years ago.

```
Console Input / Output

$ java AgeHistory2 30 03 2015 31 03 2014 31 03 1996
(Output shown using multiple columns to save space.)
Pn 1 was born on 31/3/2014    Pn 2 was 6 on 31/3/2002     Pn 2 was 14 on 31/3/2010
Pn 1 will be 1 on 31/3/2015   Pn 2 was 7 on 31/3/2003     Pn 2 was 15 on 31/3/2011
Pn 2 was born on 31/3/1996    Pn 2 was 8 on 31/3/2004     Pn 2 was 16 on 31/3/2012
Pn 2 was 1 on 31/3/1997       Pn 2 was 9 on 31/3/2005     Pn 2 was 17 on 31/3/2013
Pn 2 was 2 on 31/3/1998       Pn 2 was 10 on 31/3/2006    Pn 2 was 18 on 31/3/2014
Pn 2 was 3 on 31/3/1999       Pn 2 was 11 on 31/3/2007    Pn 2 will be 19 on 31/3/2015
Pn 2 was 4 on 31/3/2000       Pn 2 was 12 on 31/3/2008
Pn 2 was 5 on 31/3/2001       Pn 2 was 13 on 31/3/2009
$ _
```

And this day last month, with the same day 19 years ago. (Does this seem a bit odd?)

```
Console Input / Output

$ java AgeHistory2 30 03 2015 30 2 2015 30 2 1996
(Output shown using multiple columns to save space.)
Pn 1 was born on 30/2/2015    Pn 2 was 6 on 30/2/2002     Pn 2 was 14 on 30/2/2010
Pn 1 will be 1 on 30/2/2016   Pn 2 was 7 on 30/2/2003     Pn 2 was 15 on 30/2/2011
Pn 2 was born on 30/2/1996    Pn 2 was 8 on 30/2/2004     Pn 2 was 16 on 30/2/2012
Pn 2 was 1 on 30/2/1997       Pn 2 was 9 on 30/2/2005     Pn 2 was 17 on 30/2/2013
Pn 2 was 2 on 30/2/1998       Pn 2 was 10 on 30/2/2006    Pn 2 was 18 on 30/2/2014
Pn 2 was 3 on 30/2/1999       Pn 2 was 11 on 30/2/2007    Pn 2 was 19 on 30/2/2015
Pn 2 was 4 on 30/2/2000       Pn 2 was 12 on 30/2/2008    Pn 2 will be 20 on 30/2/2016
Pn 2 was 5 on 30/2/2001       Pn 2 was 13 on 30/2/2009
$ _
```

Finally, a year ago next month, and the same day 19 years ago.

Console Input / Output
`$ java AgeHistory2 30 03 2015 30 4 2014 30 4 1996` (Output shown using multiple columns to save space.)

```
Pn 1 was born on 30/4/2014    Pn 2 was 6 on 30/4/2002     Pn 2 was 14 on 30/4/2010
Pn 1 will be 1 on 30/4/2015   Pn 2 was 7 on 30/4/2003     Pn 2 was 15 on 30/4/2011
Pn 2 was born on 30/4/1996    Pn 2 was 8 on 30/4/2004     Pn 2 was 16 on 30/4/2012
Pn 2 was 1 on 30/4/1997       Pn 2 was 9 on 30/4/2005     Pn 2 was 17 on 30/4/2013
Pn 2 was 2 on 30/4/1998       Pn 2 was 10 on 30/4/2006    Pn 2 was 18 on 30/4/2014
Pn 2 was 3 on 30/4/1999       Pn 2 was 11 on 30/4/2007    Pn 2 will be 19 on 30/4/2015
Pn 2 was 4 on 30/4/2000       Pn 2 was 12 on 30/4/2008
Pn 2 was 5 on 30/4/2001       Pn 2 was 13 on 30/4/2009
$ _
```

There are more tests we could try too. (Like somebody who was born on the 29th of February?)

8.6.2 Coursework: Reasoning about conditions

Complete the following **truth table**, in your logbook, and thereby show that the **conditions**
c1 = !(a1 < a2 || a1 == a2 && h1 <= h2)
and
c2 = a1 > a2 || a1 == a2 && h1 > h2
are equivalent.

a1 < a2	a1 == a2	a1 > a2	h1 <= h2	h1 > h2	c1	c2
true	false	false	true	false		
true	false	false	false	true		
false	true	false	true	false		
false	true	false	false	true		
false	false	true	true	false		
false	false	true	false	true		

Optional extra: Try to show this by 'simplifying' from one condition to the other.

8.7 Example: Truth tables

AIM:
To introduce the **boolean type**, and reinforce **logical operator**s. We also meet the String type and see that a **for update** can have multiple **statements**.

Our next example is a program which prints out a **truth table** for two **hard coded propositional expression**s (true or false **expression**s), thus allowing us to verify that they are equivalent. The two propositional expressions are
p1 = a && (b || c) and p2 = a && b || a && c.

Here is the result of **run**ning the finished program, showing that p1 and p2 are equivalent.

Console Input / Output

```
$ java TruthTable

|   a   |   b   |   c   |  p1   |  p2   |
|_____|_____|_____|_____|_____|
| true  | true  | true  | true  | true  |
| true  | true  | false | true  | true  |
| true  | false | true  | true  | true  |
| true  | false | false | false | false |
| false | true  | true  | false | false |
| false | true  | false | false | false |
| false | false | true  | false | false |
| false | false | false | false | false |
|_____|_____|_____|_____|_____|
$ _
```

See that there are eight lines in the table, because each of the three **variable**s, a, b and c, have two possible values.

Coffee time: `8.7.1` Did you expect the two **propositional expression**s to be equivalent? You can see that they are, by agreeing that the p1 and p2 columns are the same.

To make the example more concrete, you could replace a with `isRaining`, b with `haveUmbrella` and c with `amWaterproof`, to get the propositional expressions

```
isRaining && (haveUmbrella || amWaterproof)
```

and

```
isRaining && haveUmbrella || isRaining && amWaterproof
```

which you might more intuitively feel have the same meaning. Some would say these propositional expressions capture the essence of being 'comfortable' in the city of Manchester!

Propositional expressions are also known as **boolean expression**s.

Concept **Type: `boolean`.** There is a **type** in Java called `boolean`, and this is the type of all **conditions** used in **if else statement**s and **loop**s. It is named after the English mathematician, George Boole whose work in 1847 established the basis of modern logic[12]. The type contains just two **boolean literal** values called **true** and **false**. For example, 5 <= 5 is a **boolean expression**, which, because it has no **variables** in it, always has the same value when **evaluate**d. Whereas the **expression** `age1 < age2 || age1 == age2 && height1 <= height2` has a value which depends on the values of the variables in it.

Coffee time: `8.7.2` What is the value of 5 <= 5? Is it **true** or **false**? What about 5 < 5 || 5 == 5?

Our program will require three **boolean variable**s, one for each of the values a, b and c.

Concept **Variable: `boolean` variable.** The `boolean` **type** can be used in much the same way as `int` and `double`, in the sense that we can have **boolean variables** and **methods** can have `boolean` as their **return type**.

For example, consider the following code.

```
if (age1 < age2 || age1 == age2 && height1 <= height2)
   System.out.println("You are in the correct order.");
else
   System.out.println("Please swap over.");
```

We could, if we wished, write it using a **boolean** variable.

```
boolean correctOrder = age1 < age2 || age1 == age2 && height1 <= height2;
if (correctOrder)
   System.out.println("You are in the correct order.");
else
   System.out.println("Please swap over.");
```

Some people would argue that this makes for more readable code, as in effect, we have named the **condition** in a helpful way. How appropriate that is would depend on how obvious the code is otherwise, which is context dependent and ultimately subjective. Of course, the motive for storing the condition value in a **variable** is less subjective if we wish to use it more than once.

```
boolean correctOrder = age1 < age2 || age1 == age2 && height1 <= height2;
if (correctOrder)
   System.out.println("You are in the correct order.");
else
   System.out.println("Please swap over.");
```

```
... Lots of stuff here.

if (!correctOrder)
   System.out.println("Don't forget to swap over!");
```

Many novice programmers, and even some so-called experts, when writing the code above may have actually written the following.

```
boolean correctOrder;
if (age1 < age2 || age1 == age2 && height1 <= height2)
   correctOrder = true;
else
   correctOrder = false;

if (correctOrder == true)
   System.out.println("You are in the correct order.");
else
   System.out.println("Please swap over.");

... Lots of stuff here.

if (correctOrder == false)
   System.out.println("Don't forget to swap over!");
```

There are three *terrible* things wrong with this code (two of them are the same really) – identify them, *and do not write code like that!*

Coffee time:
| 8.7.3 |

Assuming that be is some **boolean** expression and bv1 and bv2 are some **boolean** variables, why is it so terrible to write the following?

```
if (bv1 == true)
    if (be) bv2 = true;
    else    bv2 = false;
```

Here is our truth table printing program.

```
001: // Program to print out the truth table
002: // for two hard coded propositional expressions p1 and p2.
003: // The expressions have three boolean variables, a, b, and c.
004: // Each column of the table occupies 7 characters plus separator.
005: public class TruthTable
006: {
```

The two propositional expressions are hard coded as separate **methods** with a **return type** of **boolean**, and are given the three values for a, b and c as **method parameters**.

```
007:    // The first propositional expression, p1.
008:    private static boolean p1(boolean a, boolean b, boolean c)
009:    {
010:       return a && (b || c);
011:    } // p1
012:
013:
```

```
014:    // The second propositional expression, p2.
015:    private static boolean p2(boolean a, boolean b, boolean c)
016:    {
017:      return a && b || a && c;
018:    } // p2
019:
020:
021:    // Print a line of underscores as wide as the truth table.
022:    private static void printStraightLine()
023:    {
024:      System.out.println(" _____ ");
025:    } // printStraightLine
026:
027:
028:    // Print the headings for the truth table.
029:    private static void printHeadings()
030:    {
031:      System.out.println("|   a   |   b   |   c   |  p1   |  p2   |");
032:    } // printHeadings
033:
034:
035:    // Print a line of underscores
036:    // with vertical bars for the column separators.
037:    private static void printColumnsLine()
038:    {
039:      System.out.println("|_____|_____|_____|_____|_____|");
040:    } // printColumnsLine
041:
042:
043:    // To print a row, we use formatRowItem to make the
044:    // column entries have 7 characters.
045:    private static void printRow(boolean a, boolean b, boolean c)
046:    {
047:      System.out.println("|" + formatRowItem(a) + "|" + formatRowItem(b)
048:                        + "|" + formatRowItem(c)
049:                        + "|" + formatRowItem(p1(a, b, c))
050:                        + "|" + formatRowItem(p2(a, b, c)) + "|");
051:    } // printRow
```

We have used lots of **string literal**s in our programs up to now. Our next method is one which **return**s a string value as its result.

Concept **Type: String.** The **type** of **text data string**s, such as **string literal** values and **concatenation**s of such, is called String in Java.

The formatRowItem() method takes a **boolean** method parameter and returns a String comprising of seven **character**s, representing the given value. We want the result to always have the same length so that the table lines up nicely.

```
054:    // Take a boolean row item and return a string of 7 characters
055:    // to represent that item.
056:    private static String formatRowItem(boolean rowItem)
057:    {
```

```
058:      return rowItem ? " true  " : " false ";
059:    } // formatRowItem
```

Coffee time: [8.7.4]   Notice that we did *not* write rowItem == true before the ?. Such code is terrible – every time you are tempted to write it, you should chastise yourself!

The **main method** essentially consists of three **nested loops**, one for each of the variables a, b and c. Each of these **for loops executes** twice: once for its variable being **true** and once for **false**. We cannot use a **boolean variable** to control a for loop, because there are only two values – we would need a third one to indicate that we had processed both of the others. However, we can make sure our loops each execute twice using an **int variable**, and make our **boolean** variables swap from **true** to **false** at the end of the execution of the **loop body**.

Concept **Statement: for loop: multiple statements in for update.** Java **for loop**s are permitted to have more than one **statement** in their **for update**, that is, the part which is **executed** after the **loop body**. Rather than always being one statement, this part may be a list of statements with commas (,) between them.

One appropriate use for this feature is to have a for loop that executes twice, once each for the two possible values of a **boolean variable**.

For example, the following code prints out scenarios to help train people to live in the city of Manchester!

```
boolean haveUmbrella = true;
boolean isRaining = true;
for (int countU = 1; countU <= 2; countU++, haveUmbrella = !haveUmbrella)
  for (int countR = 1; countR <= 2; countR++, isRaining = !isRaining)
  {
    System.out.println("It is" + (isRaining ? "" : " not") + " raining.");
    System.out.println
      ("You have " + (haveUmbrella ? "an" : "no") + " umbrella.");
    if (isRaining && !haveUmbrella)
      System.out.println("You get wet!");
    else
      System.out.println("You stay dry.");
    System.out.println();
  } // for
```

Here is the main method of the TruthTable program.

```
062:    // The main method has nested loops to generate table rows.
063:    public static void main(String[] args)
064:    {
065:      printStraightLine();
066:      printHeadings();
067:      printColumnsLine();
068:
069:      // Start off with all three variables being true.
070:      boolean a = true, b = true, c = true;
071:
072:      // Execute twice for the 'a' variable,
073:      // and ensure 'a' goes from true to false.
074:      for (int aCount = 1; aCount <= 2; aCount++, a = !a)
075:        // Do the same for 'b', for each 'a' value.
```

```
076:        for (int bCount = 1; bCount <= 2; bCount++, b = !b)
077:            // Do the same for 'c', for each 'b' value.
078:            for (int cCount = 1; cCount <= 2; cCount++, c = !c)
079:                // Print a row for each a, b and c combination.
080:                printRow(a, b, c);
081:
082:        printColumnsLine();
083:    } // main
084:
085: } // class TruthTable
```

Coffee time: 8.7.5 In some programming languages, such as Perl[17], it is possible to treat **data** as program code at **run time**. But this is not so in Java (maybe that is a good thing?). How easy would it be to alter this program so that the propositional expressions are supplied as **command line argument**s rather than being hard coded?

8.7.1 Trying it

We have already seen the program **run** on page 132, so we don't need to show it again here.

8.7.2 Coursework: `TruthTable34`

In this task you will write another version of the **truth table** program, called `TruthTable34`, which shows a truth table for *three* **propositional expression**s which are **hard coded** as **method**s p1, p2 and p3 respectively, and which are expressions involving *four* propositional **variable**s, a, b, c and d. Your table will thus have 16 lines plus titles and box lines, and 7 columns.

The three propositional expressions to hard code in your program are as follows.

p1	(((a || b) && c) || ((b || c) && d)) && (a || d)
p2	a && c || b && d || c && d
p3	(b || c) && (c || d) && (a || d)

If you have studied discrete mathematics you should be able to spot the relationship between the first of these propositional expressions and the other two. What are those relationships?

Undertake the usual tasks of **design**ing the program, implementing and testing it, and finally recording your results.

8.8 Example: Producing a calendar

AIM: To reinforce much of the material presented in this chapter. We also revisit `System.out.printf()`.

To finish this chapter, let us now have a program which produces a calendar for a given month.

The program will be given the start day of the month, between 1 and 7 inclusive. These numbers represent Sunday to Saturday. It will also be given the number of days in the month, typically 28, 29, 30 or 31. For example, if given the values 3 and 28 our program will produce the following.

```
                    Console Input / Output
$ java Calendar 3 28

--------------------
|Su Mo Tu We Th Fr Sa|
|      01 02 03 04 05|
|06 07 08 09 10 11 12|
|13 14 15 16 17 18 19|
|20 21 22 23 24 25 26|
|27 28               |
|                    |
--------------------

$ _
```

Our **main method** will take the **command line arguments**, convert them to **integers** and then call the **method** `printMonth()` with those numbers. Just to be different, let us start the **class** with the main method. In fact, we declare each method after it is used, in this example.

```
001: // Program to print a calendar for a single given month.
002: // The first argument is the number of the start day, 1 to 7
003: // (Sunday = 1, Monday = 2, ..., Saturday = 7).
004: // The second argument is the last date in the month, e.g. 31.
005: public class Calendar
006: {
007:   public static void main(String[] args)
008:   {
009:     printMonth(Integer.parseInt(args[0]), Integer.parseInt(args[1]));
010:   } // main
```

To print a given month, we need the first day (Sunday to Saturday) of it and the last date in that month. We represent the days Sunday to Saturday as the numbers 1 to 7.

Our method uses a **nested loop** to print out the calendar for the month. It also has code to print day column headings, etc.. It calls the separate methods `printMonthLineOfHyphens()`, `printDayNames()`, `printDateSpace()`, and `printDate()` to assist in the process.

```
013: // Print the calendar for the month.
014: private static void printMonth(int monthStartDay, int lastDateInMonth)
015: {
016:   // Keep track of which day (1-7) is the next to be printed out.
017:   int nextDayColumnToUse = monthStartDay;
018:
019:   // Keep track of the next date to be printed out.
020:   int nextDateToPrint = 1;
021:
022:   // The top line of hyphens.
023:   printMonthLineOfHyphens();
024:   // The column headings.
025:   printDayNames();
026:
027:   // We always print out as many rows as we need,
028:   // but with a minimum of 6 to encourage consistent format.
029:   int noOfRows = 0;
030:   while (nextDateToPrint <= lastDateInMonth || noOfRows < 6)
031:   {
032:     // Print one row.
033:     System.out.print("|");
034:     for (int dayColumnNo = 1; dayColumnNo <= 7; dayColumnNo++)
035:     {
036:       // Print a space separator between day columns.
037:       if (dayColumnNo > 1)
038:         System.out.print(" ");
039:
040:       // We either print spaces or a date.
041:       if (dayColumnNo != nextDayColumnToUse
042:           || nextDateToPrint > lastDateInMonth)
043:         printDateSpace();
044:       else
```

```
045:        {
046:           printDate(nextDateToPrint);
047:           nextDayColumnToUse++;
048:           nextDateToPrint++;
049:        } // else
050:      } // for
051:
052:      // End the row.
053:      System.out.println("|");
054:      noOfRows++;
055:
056:      // Get ready for the next row.
057:      nextDayColumnToUse = 1;
058:    } // while
059:
060:    // The bottom line of hyphens.
061:    printMonthLineOfHyphens();
062:  } // printMonth
```

The method `printMonthLineOfHyphens()` simply prints out a line of hyphens the same width as a row of the printed calendar for a month. To achieve this, it calls a separate method `printDateHyphens()` which prints out a short line of hyphens the same width as used to print a single date in the calendar. This is a good idea as it means `printMonthLineOfHyphens()` would not need to be changed if it was ever decided to use more width to print out the dates.

```
065:  // Print a line of hyphens as wide as the table,
066:  // starting and ending with a space so the corners look right.
067:  private static void printMonthLineOfHyphens()
068:  {
069:    System.out.print(" ");
070:    for (int dayColumnNo = 1; dayColumnNo <= 7; dayColumnNo++)
071:    {
072:      if (dayColumnNo > 1)
073:        System.out.print("-");
074:      printDateHyphens();
075:    } // for
076:    System.out.println(" ");
077:  } // printMonthLineOfHyphens
```

The method `printDayNames()` prints the titles of the day columns on the calendar for a month. It calls the separate method `printDayName()` which prints the name of the given day (1-7) using the same width as used to print a single date in the calendar.

```
080:  // Print the day name headings.
081:  private static void printDayNames()
082:  {
083:    System.out.print("|");
084:    for (int dayColumnNo = 1; dayColumnNo <= 7; dayColumnNo++)
085:    {
086:      if (dayColumnNo > 1)
087:        System.out.print(" ");
088:      printDayName(dayColumnNo);
089:    } // for
090:    System.out.println("|");
091:  } // printDayNames
```

The method printDayName() takes an **int** and, if the value is in the range 1 to 7, prints out the name of the corresponding day using two **characters**. This is carefully chosen to be the same width as used to print a single date in the calendar.

```
094:    // Print the day name of the given day number, as two characters.
095:    private static void printDayName(int dayNo)
096:    {
097:       // Our days are numbered 1 - 7, from Sunday.
098:       switch (dayNo)
099:       {
100:         case 1: System.out.print("Su"); break;
101:         case 2: System.out.print("Mo"); break;
102:         case 3: System.out.print("Tu"); break;
103:         case 4: System.out.print("We"); break;
104:         case 5: System.out.print("Th"); break;
105:         case 6: System.out.print("Fr"); break;
106:         case 7: System.out.print("Sa"); break;
107:       } // switch
108:    } // printDayName
```

The method printDateSpace() prints out two spaces, which is the same width as used to print a single date in the calendar. This is used when printing a row of the calendar for a month in columns that have no date in that month (i.e. before the first or after the last date).

```
111:    // Print spaces as wide as a date, i.e. two spaces.
112:    private static void printDateSpace()
113:    {
114:       System.out.print("  ");
115:    } // printDateSpace
```

The method printDateHyphens() prints out two hyphens, which is the same width as used to print a single date in the calendar.

```
118:    // Print hyphens as wide as a date, i.e. two hyphens.
119:    private static void printDateHyphens()
120:    {
121:       System.out.print("--");
122:    } // printDateHyphens
```

The method printDate() takes a given **int** and, assuming it is a sensible date, prints it out with a width of two characters. For this program, we wish the number to be printed with **zero padding** rather than **space padding**.

Concept **Standard API: System: out.printf(): zero padding.** We can ask System.out.printf() for **zero padding** rather than **space padding** of a number by placing a leading zero on the desired minimum width in the **format specifier**.

The following code fragment contains an example which prints a string representation of 123, with leading zeroes so that the result is ten **characters** long.

```
System.out.println("1234567890");
System.out.printf("%010d%n", 123);
```

Here is the effect.

```
1234567890
0000000123
```

Similarly,

```
System.out.println("1234567890");
System.out.printf("%010.2f%n", 123.456);
```

produces the following.

```
1234567890
0000123.46
```

```
125:     // Print a date, using two characters, with a leading zero if required.
126:     private static void printDate(int date)
127:     {
128:         System.out.printf("%02d", date);
129:     } // printDate
130:
131: } // class Calendar
```

8.8.1 Trying it

After we have **compiled** the program, we can **run** it with various **command line arguments**.

Console Input / Output
$ **java Calendar 6 29; java Calendar 7 31; java Calendar 3 30**
(Output shown using multiple columns to save space.)
`--------------------   --------------------   --------------------` `|Su Mo Tu We Th Fr Sa|   |Su Mo Tu We Th Fr Sa|   |Su Mo Tu We Th Fr Sa|` `| 01 02|	01|	01 02 03 04 05|` `|03 04 05 06 07 08 09| |02 03 04 05 06 07 08| |06 07 08 09 10 11 12|` `|10 11 12 13 14 15 16| |09 10 11 12 13 14 15| |13 14 15 16 17 18 19|` `|17 18 19 20 21 22 23| |16 17 18 19 20 21 22| |20 21 22 23 24 25 26|` `|24 25 26 27 28 29	|23 24 25 26 27 28 29| |27 28 29 30 |` `|	|30 31		|` `-------------------- -------------------- --------------------` `$ _`

8.8.2 Coursework: `CalendarHighlight`

In this task you will write another version of the calendar program, called `CalendarHighlight`, which produces the calendar in a wider format and also takes a third **command line argument**, which is a day (1 to 31) that should be highlighted. The wider format is produced by using four **character**s per date instead of two. The desired date should be highlighted by placing a **greater than** sign (>) before it and a **less than** sign (<) after it. Here is an example **run** of the finished program.

Console Input / Output
$ **java CalendarHighlight 3 28 9**

`-------------------------------------`
`| Su   Mo   Tu   We   Th   Fr   Sa |`
`|           01   02   03   04   05 |`
`| 06   07   08  >09<  10   11   12 |`
`| 13   14   15   16   17   18   19 |`
`| 20   21   22   23   24   25   26 |`
`| 27   28                          |`
`|                                  |`
`-------------------------------------`
`$ _`

Undertake the usual tasks of planning **test data**, **design**ing the program, implementing and testing it, and finally recording your results.

8.9 Concepts covered in this chapter

Here is a list of the concepts that were covered in this chapter, each with a self-test question. You can use this to check you remember them being introduced, and perhaps re-read some of them before going on to the next chapter.

Expression	
– boolean: logical operators (p.128)	What are the values of the following expressions? 1. `3 < 4 && (7 > 10 || 19 == 20)` 2. `3 < 4 && (7 > 10 || 19 != 20)` 3. `3 < 4 || (7 > 10 && 19 == 20)` 4. `3 < 4 || (7 > 10 && 19 != 20)` 5. `3 < 4 && 7 > 10 || 19 == 20` 6. `3 < 4 && 7 > 10 || 19 != 20` 7. `3 < 4 || 7 > 10 && 19 == 20` 8. `3 < 4 || 7 > 10 && 19 != 20`

Method	
Method (p.118)	Why are these things called methods?
– private (p.118)	When should methods have private visibility?
– accepting parameters (p.118)	What two attributes does a method parameter have at compile time? How many parameters can a method have?
– calling a method (p.119)	What is the difference between method arguments and method parameters?
– void methods (p.120)	Can a void method have parameters? What (else) can it *not* have?
– returning a value (p.122)	What statement is used to produce the result from a method? How do we know what kind of result can be produced?
– changing parameters does not affect arguments (p.124)	What is the name for the mechanism for passing arguments to methods in Java? What is the significance of the approach?

Standard API	
– System: out.printf() (p.126)	How do we print an **int** value with space padding up to twelve characters?
– System: out.printf(): zero padding (p.140)	How do we get an **int** value printed with zero padding up to twelve characters?

Statement	

– for loop: multiple statements in for update (p.136)	What does the following code do?
	```int y = 100;```
	```for (int x = 0; x < y; x++, y--)```
	``` System.out.println(x + y);```

Type	
– boolean (p.133)	Why is this type called boolean?
– String (p.135)	Why do text data strings need to be members of a type?

Variable	
– local variables (p.124)	How do we stop two methods having variables of the same name? What other term is used for local variables?
– class variables (p.124)	What are the differences between class variables and local variables?

– a group of variables can be declared together (p.129)	What is wrong with the following?
	```int count = 10, isRaining = false,```
	``` retirementAge = 65;```

– boolean variable (p.133)	What is wrong with code like the following?
	```if (be == true) bv = true;```
	```else bv = false;```

Chapter 9

Consolidation of concepts so far

A good foundation
deserves a good home!

9.1   Chapter aims

This chapter serves one of two purposes, depending upon how much programming experience you have or had before starting to read this book.

If you had done little or no programming before starting and you have read through this far, then now is an ideal time for a quick consolidation of what we have covered. You should use this as confirmation of your understanding, or if there is anything you feel unsure about, you should go back to the appropriate page and reread it.

If you have done a significant amount of programming before picking up this book, but not in Java, then you may be able to skip the previous chapters and use this one just to see what you have missed. You may need to look back at some concepts you are not so sure about, and do some of the coursework.

The chapter is divided into two sections – the first covers Java concepts and the second looks at program **design** concepts. Some of the ideas in the second section were presented only by an 'osmosis effect' in the previous chapters – so please read that section carefully.

The chapter contains the following sections.

Section	Aims	Associated Coursework
9.2 Java concepts (p.144)	To consolidate and summarize the Java concepts introduced in the preceding chapters. We also introduce some more simple concepts which were not covered before, but which compliment those that were – such as the `float` **type**.	(None.)
9.3 Program design concepts (p.150)	To look more formally at the process of **design**ing an **algorithm** and writing a program. In particular, we look closely at **designing variables**.	(None.)

9.2 Java concepts

AIM:
To consolidate and summarize the Java concepts introduced in the preceding chapters. We also introduce some more simple concepts which were not covered before, but which compliment those that were – such as the `float type`.

We divide our discussion into subsections focusing on particular aspects of Java.

9.2.1 Java source code lexical details

A Java program consists of one or more **source code text file**s containing symbols separated by **white space** – spaces, tabs and **new line**s. The use of tabs is not recommended as it invariably leads to formatting problems at some point, typically when you want a hard copy in a hurry....

The types of symbol are as follows.

Symbol type	Examples	Description
Non-alphanumeric	`{ } ; + >=`	Used as **operator**s and general **syntax** punctuation.
Reserved word	`public while if`	Lower case letter special words used as part of the Java syntax.
Identifier	`HelloWorld println` `x2 madeFromWords`	Names of **class**es, **method**s and **variable**s. These must start with a letter, and can contain letters, digits and underscores, and cannot be the same as a **reserved word**. By convention, class names start with an upper case letter, whilst method and (most) variable names start with a lower case letter.

Literal values	`12345 123.45`
	`1.2345e3 1.2345E-3`
	`"Hello world!"`
		Fixed values of particular **type**s.

Comments	`// Rest of line.`	These help make the program human readable. They are ignored by the **compiler**.

Java distinguishes between upper and lower case letters, so `HelloWorld` is not the same as `Helloworld`.

All **string literal**s (p.18) must be ended on the line they are started on (p.21). We can put **escape sequence**s (p.49) into them to embed **character**s we cannot otherwise have. These include `\b, \t, \n, \f, \r, \", \'` and `\\`.

9.2.2 Classes, methods, types, variables and layout

Programs are divided into pieces called **class**es (p.16). This helps make programming manageable – a large program can be constructed as a number of small parts. It also allows for reuse – a class can be used in many programs if it is appropriate. If the class is called `MyClassName` then its **source code** is written, using a **text editor** (p.5), in a **text file** (p.5) called `MyClassName.java`. The **compiler**, `javac` (p.9), is then used to produce the **byte code** form (p.6), stored in a **binary file** (p.5) called `MyClassName.class`. This is then run by the **interpreter**, or **virtual machine**, `java` (p.9).

A class can contain **method**s and **class variable**s. A method contains the instructions to perform some task which is a part of the program (p.118). Class variables are available to be used in all the methods in the class (p.124). A method may define **local variable**s within itself, which can only be used in that method (p.124).

Class variables and methods can be defined to have **public** visibility, which means they can be accessed from other classes (p.17), or **private** visibility, which means they can only be used inside the class they are defined in (p.118). Both are declared with the **reserved word** `static`, which means they can be used in the **static context** (p.17) which already exists when the program starts to **run**.

Variables (p.36) are declared by giving their **type** (p.36) followed by their name (p.37). A **variable** can be given a value when it is declared (p.42).

Here is a list of types, of which we have met four so far.

Type	Example values	Description
`boolean` (p.133)	`true` `false`	True or false values.
`byte`	-128 up to 127	An **integer** occupying only one **byte** (8 **bit**s).
`short`	-32768 up to 32767	An integer occupying two bytes (16 bits).
`int` (p.36)	-2^{31} up to $2^{31}-1$, e.g. 32768	An integer occupying four bytes (32 bits).
`long`	-2^{63} up to $2^{63}-1$, e.g. 10L	An integer occupying eight bytes (64 bits).
`float`	`5.0f` `5.0F`	A **real** number stored using the **single precision** floating number technique, using four bytes.
`double` (p.54)	`5.0d` `5.0D` `5.0`	A real number stored using the **double precision** floating number technique, using eight bytes.
`char`	`'a'` `'A'` `'1'` `';'`	A single **character**, stored as a **Unicode** value, using two bytes.
`String` (p.135)	`"Hello world!"`	A string of characters.

Unicode[20] is a coding convention for the storage of characters that aims to encode every character in every human language. The first 128 codes are identical to the older **ASCII**[9] character set.

Here are the types we did not previously meet.

Concept **Type: `long`.** The **type `int`** allows for the storage of **integers** in the range -2^{31} through to $2^{31}-1$. This is because it uses four **byte**s, i.e. 32 **binary digit**s. $2^{31}-1$ is 2147483647. Although this is plenty for most purposes, we sometimes need whole numbers in a bigger range. The type **`long`** represents **long integers** and uses eight bytes, i.e. 64 **bit**s. A **`long` variable** can store numbers from -2^{63} through to $2^{63}-1$. The value of $2^{63}-1$ is 9223372036854775807.

A **long literal** is written with an `L` on the end, to distinguish it from an **int literal**, as in `-15L` and `2147483648L`.

Concept **Type: `short`.** The **type `short`** represents **short integers** using two **byte**s, i.e. 16 **binary digit**s. A **short variable** can store numbers from -2^{15} through to $2^{15}-1$. The value of $2^{15}-1$ is 32767. We would typically use this type when we have a huge number of **integer**s, which happen to lie in the restricted range, and we are concerned about the amount of memory (or **file** space) needed to store them.

Concept **Type: `byte`.** The **type `byte`** represents **integer**s using just one **byte**, i.e. 8 **binary digit**s. A **`byte` variable** can store numbers from -2^7 through to 2^7-1. The value of 2^7-1 is 127.

Concept **Type: `char`.** Characters in Java are represented by the **type `char`**. A **char variable** can store a single **character** at any time.

Concept **Type: `char`: literal.** A **character literal** can be written in our program by enclosing it in single quotes. For example `'J'` is a character literal.

Concept **Variable: `char` variable.** We can declare **char variable**s in Java, that is **variable**s which have the **type `char`**. For example the code

```
char firstLetter = 'J';
```

declares a variable of type **`char`**, with the name `firstLetter`. At **run time**, this variable is allowed to hold a **`char` data** item, that is a single **character**.

In fact, we can have variables of any type defined in a similar way (pp.37,54,133).

Concept **Type: `char`: literal: escape sequences.** When writing a **character literal** we can use the same **escape sequences** that are available within **string literals**. These include the following.

```
char backspace = '\b';          char tab = '\t';
char newline = '\n';            char formFeed = '\f';
char carriageReturn = '\r';     char doubleQuote = '\"';
char singleQuote = '\'';        char backslash = '\\';
```

Concept **Type: `float`.** The **type `float`** is for **real** (fractional decimal) numbers, using the **floating point representation** with a **single precision** storage. It uses only four **bytes** per number, compared with **`double`** which employs **double precision** storage and so is far more accurate, but needs eight bytes per number.

A **float literal** is written with an f or F on the end, as in `0.0F`, `-129.934F` or `98.2375f`.

Methods have a **return type** which is written in the heading (p.122), or the **reserved word `void`** if they do not **return** a value (p.120). They also take **method parameters** declared in brackets after the method name (p.118). Each parameter is given a type and a name by which it is referred to inside the method body. A program always starts running at a method called `main` (pp.17,17). This takes a **list** of `Strings` (written as `String[]`) as its single parameter, these strings being the **command line arguments** (pp.8,17) supplied by the end user when the program is run. The **main method** is always a **void method** (pp.17,18).

Program **comment**s are used in the source code to enhance readability. These start with `//` and continue until the end of the line (p.82). It is a good idea to mark the end of code structures using a comment (p.83). Good programs are laid out well (p.31) with **indentation** (p.32) and careful splitting of long lines (p.43).

A typical single class program looks like the following (p.16) (the line numbers are not part of the code).

```
001: // Comments here to say what the program does.
002: // This may take several lines.
003: public class ProgramName
004: {
005:   // Each class variable should have comments saying what it is used for.
006:   private static int someVariable;
007:
008:   // Variables can be initialized when they are declared.
009:   private static double someOtherVariable = someVariable * 100.0;
010:
011:
012:   // Each method should have comments saying what it does.
013:   // If it does not return a result, we write the word void.
014:   public static void someMethod(int aParameter)
015:   {
016:     // Local variables should also have a comment.
017:     int aLocalVariable;
018:
019:     ... Method instruction statements go here.
020:     // Comments are used to help make tricky code readable.
021:     ...
022:   } // someMethod
023:
024:
```

```
025:    // Methods which are only of use in this class/program should be private.
026:    // If it returns a result, we state the type in the heading.
027:    private static double someOtherMethod(boolean parameter1, int parameter2)
028:    {
029:      double aLocalVariable;
030:      ...
031:      return something;
032:    } // someOtherMethod
033:
034:
035:    // The program always starts its execution at the main method.
036:    // The parameters are the command line arguments of the program.
037:    public static void main(String[] args)
038:    {
039:      ...
040:    } // main
041:
042: } // class ProgramName
```

Did you spot the semi-colon after the class and local variables?

9.2.3   Statements

Java instructions that make the computer do something are called **statement**s (p.18). All simple statements must end with a semi-colon (p.18). Statements are **execute**d sequentially (p.23).

A **method call** is used to invoke the body of a method (p.119).

```
someMethod(189);
```

Values for the **method parameter**s are called **method argument**s. They are passed to the parameters when the method is called. Any change made to the parameter values inside the method has no affect outside the **method** (p.124).

The **assignment statement** (pp.37,37) comprises a **variable** name, an **equal sign** (=) and an **expression**. The expression is **evaluate**d, and the result placed in the variable (p.38).

```
myVariable = myOtherVariable * 100;
```

Assignment statements are often used to update the value of a variable (p.70) and thus a number of **shorthand operator**s are provided for this purpose, such as **postfix increment** (++), **postfix decrement** (--) and **compound assignment** (e.g. *=) (p.87).

```
myVariable++;
myOtherVariable *= 10;
```

There are three **conditional execution** (p.60) statements. The **if else statement** (p.60) comprises a **condition** in brackets, and two statements, one of which is executed.

```
if (myVariable < myOtherVariable)
  smallest = myVariable;
else
  smallest = myOtherVariable;
```

The **if statement** (p.64) has no **else** nor a second statement inside it.

The **switch statement** contains many lists of statements, typically one of which will be executed, depending on the value of an expression yielding a simple discrete value, such as `char`, `byte`, `short`, `int` – notably not `double`. (From Java 7.0, `String` values are allowed.) There are two styles, the most common has **break statements** (p.107).

```
switch(...)
{
  case v1: case v2: ...
    ... Statements.
    break;
  case v3: ...
    ... Statements.
    break;
  default:
    ... Statements.
    break;
} // switch
```

The other style does not have break statements (p.110). Although it is rarely appropriate, the styles can be mixed.

There are three **repeated execution** (p.70) statements. The **while loop** (p.71) comprises a **condition** in brackets, and one statement which is executed zero or more times.

```
while (myVariable < myOtherVariable)
  myVariable *= 2;
```

The **do while loop** (p.112) has its condition tested at the end, and so executes the statement at least once.

```
do
  myVariable *= 2;
while (myVariable < myOtherVariable);
```

The **for loop** has a **for initialization**, a continuation condition, and a **for update** to be executed after the **loop body** (p.77).

```
int sum1To10 = 0;
for (int count = 1; count <= 10; count++)
  sum1To10 += count;
```

The for update can actually be a list of statements separated by commas (,) (p.136).

The statements inside a conditional statement, or a **loop** are often a **compound statement** (p.66) , so that in effect more than one statement can be executed.

```
while (myVariable < myOtherVariable)
{
  myVariable *= 2;
  myOtherVariable--;
} // while
```

A variable may be defined inside a compound statement, in which case it can only be used inside that statement (p.92). Localizing variables in this way is a good idea when it is possible.

The statements inside a conditional statement, or a loop can be any statement, including other conditional statements and loops (p.92). We lay out **nested** if else statements in a particular way (p.62).

9.2.4   Expressions

An **expression** can contain the following items.

- **literal value**s, such as **boolean literal**s (true or false) (p.133), **integer literal**s (e.g. 123, 123L) (p.37), **floating point literal**s (e.g. 12.3, 12.3F) (p.54) and **string literal**s (e.g. "123") (p.18);

- **variables** (p.36);

- **operator**s, such as **arithmetic operator**s (p.38), **relational operator**s (p.60) and **logical operator**s (p.128);

- brackets and

- **method call**s (p.119) to **non-void method**s (p.122).

Operators include +, -, * and / for **addition**, **subtraction**, **multiplication** and **division** (p.38). Use of **integer division** truncates the result to yield an **integer** (pp.52,52). To get **double division** at least one **operand** must be a double (p.55). All these operators have **left associativity**.

Another operator we have not yet seen is the **remainder** or **modulo** operator.

Concept **Expression: arithmetic: remainder operator.** Another **arithmetic operator** in Java is the **remainder operator**, also known as the **modulo** operator, %. When used with two **integer operand**s, it yields the remainder obtained from dividing the first operand by the second. As an example, the following **method** determines whether a given int **method parameter** is an even number.

```
public static boolean isEven(int number)
{
  return number % 2 == 0;
} // isEven
```

The + operator is an **overloaded operator** as it is used for both **addition** and for string **concatenation** (p.26).

Values of **type int** are turned into their usual string representation automatically when used as an operand for string concatenation (p.38). For example, "Age next year is " + ageNextYear. The same is true for double values (p.55), as well as the other types.

If we need to turn a double into an int (by discarding any decimal places), we use a type **cast** (p.79).

Conditions are also known as **boolean expression**s (p.60), and simple ones can be built from the **relational operator**s <, >, <=, >=, != and == (p.60). The **logical operator**s &&, || and ! can be used to construct complex **condition**s (p.128).

Expressions which are not fully bracketed are disambiguated using **operator precedence** (p.45) and **operator associativity** (p.48).

The **conditional operator** (p.94) can be used sparingly to produce alternative results within expressions, e.g. max = x > y ? x : y.

The **command line argument**s, which is a **list** of Strings, can be accessed individually using an **index** written in square brackets (p.26). The index can be a literal, variable or an expression (p.79). These indices start at zero. We can also see the length of the list by appending .length to it (p.79).

```
for (int index = 0; index < args.length; index++)
  System.out.println(args[index]);
```

9.2.5 Errors

There are four kinds of error we can make in our programs: **syntactic error** when we break the **syntax** rules of the language (p.20), **semantic error** when what we have written does not make any sense (p.22), **run time error** when the program causes an **exception** during its execution (p.24), and **logical error** when everything seems to work fine, but the program produces the wrong result (p.29). Syntactic and semantic errors are collectively known as **compile time errors** (p.22).

9.2.6 Standard classes

Java comes with lots of **class**es ready to use in its **application program interface (API)**. We have met some of the features of a few so far.

The class System contains **method**s for printing results on **standard output** (p.7).

Name	Return	Parameter	Description	Page
System.out.println		String	Print the given string and a **new line** on the output.	(p.18)
System.out.println		(none)	Produce a new line on the output.	(p.98)
System.out.println		int	Print the decimal representation of the given **int** and a new line on the output.	(p.38)
System.out.print		String	Print the given string with no new line on the output.	(p.98)
System.out.printf		String, value	Prints a formatted representation of the given value, according to the given **format specifier** string (e.g. "%010.2f%n").	(p.126) (p.140)

In fact there is a version of System.out.print() and System.out.println() for all the **type**s we have met so far. System.out.println() produces a new line using the platform dependent **line separator**, which is a **new line character** on Linux and a **carriage return character** followed by a new line character on Microsoft Windows.

The classes Integer and Double contain methods to convert a given String into the number it represents.

Name	Return	Parameter	Description	Page
Integer.parseInt	int	String	Convert the given string into the **int** it represents, or cause an **exception** if it cannot.	(p.41)
Double.parseDouble	double	String	Convert the given string into the **double** it represents, or cause an exception if it cannot.	(p.54)

The class Math contains methods for various mathematical **function**s including the following.

Name	Return	Parameter	Description	Page
Math.pow	double	double, double	Returns the first parameter raised to the second.	(p.73)
Math.abs	double	double	Returns the **absolute value** of the parameter.	(p.87)
Math.sin	double	double	Returns the sin of the given value, which is expressed in radians.	
Math.toRadians	double	double	Returns the radians equivalent of the given degrees value.	

There is also the constant Math.PI (p.87).

9.3 Program design concepts

AIM:
To look more formally at the process of **design**ing an **algorithm** and writing a program. In particular, we look closely at **designing variables**.

We have seen lots of example programs in the previous chapters, and by a process of osmosis, especially if you have done the coursework too, you will have started to pick up the skill of programming. Now is a good time to try and formalize this a little – how do we write a program? More correctly at this stage, we really mean how do we write a **method**, e.g. the **main method**? Yet another way of saying this is, how do we write an **algorithm**?

Clearly if the program is very simple then you can just write it. But if it is not then you need a *process* of some sort. Here are some guidelines expressed as a number of steps.

1. Understand the problem – obviously you cannot possibly get the computer to solve it otherwise. (It is amazing how many people overlook this!)

2. Ask yourself how you would solve the problem if you were not going to program a computer. If you cannot answer this then almost certainly you will fail to get the computer to do it.

3. Consider whether the way you would do it is the way the computer should do it. Often it is, because we humans are actually very good at being lazy, and finding the best way to do something when we put our minds to it. On the other hand, sometimes the way a computer would do it is different because of the nature of computers compared with us – they are very quick at doing mindless things.

4. Decide how the computer should do it, i.e. what is the **basic method** your algorithm will use.

5. Design the **variable**s used in the algorithm, very carefully. We shall say more about this shortly.

6. Design the algorithm itself in **pseudo code** (p.73). If the previous step is done properly, this one will almost do itself.

7. Finally implement the algorithm in code – this should be the easiest part if the previous steps have been followed carefully.

9.3.1 Designing the variables

When first learning to program, it is too easy to have the view that a **variable** is just a named location where your code can stick a value of the appropriate **type** and change it from time to time. Whilst this view is correct, it is too computer centric to be of much help to us as program **design**ers. It does not encourage us to focus on the *meaning* of **data** while we are **designing variables**, and we should recognize that if we get this wrong, our programs will probably not work and/or will be badly written. A classic mistake of many programmers, even those who have been doing it a long time, is to recognize that a variable is needed of a certain type, and then, quickly decide what it should be called without carefully considering what the variable means – resulting in some cryptic names and **bug**gy code. In fairness, the language Java is almost inviting this attitude by asking you to present the type of a variable before its name. Whereas really, we should think about these the other way round.

Let us see an example of code that might have been written by such a programmer. Assume the method `getCurrentHumidity()` and the constant `PRECIPITATION_THRESHOLD` are available to us.

```
boolean b;
if (getCurrentHumidity() > PRECIPITATION_THRESHOLD)
  b = true;
else
  b = false;
```

Then later this variable is used to ensure we have an umbrella.

```
if (b == true)
  System.out.println("Take your umbrella!");
```

Does this code look okay? Well, yes, it looks like it might work. But do you recall reading that you should chastise yourself if you write code like this `if (b == true)`? Let us choose a better name for the **boolean variable**, by asking ourselves what it really means.

```
boolean rainIsLikely;
if (getCurrentHumidity() > PRECIPITATION_THRESHOLD)
   rainIsLikely = true;
else
   rainIsLikely = false;
```

Also.

```
if (rainIsLikely == true)
   System.out.println("Take your umbrella!");
```

Is the inappropriateness of this code more obvious now that we know what the variables means in relation to the problem? How often do you ask somebody "Do you think it will rain equals true?". So, let us write the code properly this time!

We do not need the **if else statement**.

```
boolean rainIsLikely
   = getCurrentHumidity() > PRECIPITATION_THRESHOLD;
```

And we do not need the `==` true.

```
if (rainIsLikely)
   System.out.println("Take your umbrella!");
```

So, there was an example of a poorly designed variable leading to poor *style*. How about an example where it leads to code that does not work?

Let us say we wish to count some items. Here is some pseudo code for an algorithm.

```
int i = 1
while there are more items
   get an item
   i++
end-while
output "There were " i " items"
```

> *Coffee time:* What is wrong with this design and how should it be fixed? There are two obvious ways to fix it. Which is best?
>
> 9.3.1

Better late than never, let us think carefully about what the variable really is. It is the number of items we have had so far. Let us call it `itemCountSoFar`.

```
int itemCountSoFar = 1
while there are more items
   get an item
   itemCountSoFar++
end-while
output "There were " itemCountSoFar " items"
```

Ah ha! The first line is a *lie* – that is where the error is.

Alternatively, we may have decided that the variable is the sequence number of the *next* item to be obtained, so we call it `nextItemNumber`.

```
int nextItemNumber = 1
while there are more items
   get an item
   nextItemNumber++
```

```
end-while
output "There were " nextItemNumber " items"
```

Now the last line is a lie – *that* is where the error is!

The real problem was that `i` was an ambiguous name, arising from a lack of design about what the variable really means, leading to it being treated with a different interpretation in two different parts of the design. Of the two alternative, designed, names, which is best, `itemCountSoFar` or `nextItemNumber`? This is subjective, but you might consider that there is always a count of the items seen so far, but there is not always a next item . . . .

So, variables are to be treated with some respect and designed carefully. They should represent identifiable entities in the problem being solved by the algorithm. If you cannot find a sentence that fully and precisely describes the meaning of a variable, then it is a bad variable! Think again, or you will regret it. Having found that sentence, you condense it into a few words to make the variable name. *Then* you can identify the type that the variable needs to have.

If you design your variables well then later when you design the algorithm, all you have to do is make sure the value of each variable always reflects its meaning – the code will almost write itself. Well designed and named variables will also help you debug your code if you make a mistake so that it does not work. And, your code is easier to read and so is more maintainable too!

9.3.2 Designing the algorithm

In the previous chapters, we have seen various examples of the the design process, where we expressed the algorithm at a high level of **abstraction** in pseudo code, and then systematically added more detail until the level of abstraction had been lowered to make the implementation in Java straightforward. For example, we first met pseudo code in Section 5.3 on page 73 with the `MinimumBitWidth` program. Here was our first version of the design.

```
get numberOfValues from command line
noOfBits = 0
while noOfBits is too small
  increment noOfBits
output noOfBits
```

After we were happy with that level of abstraction, we lowered it by filling in more detail for the most abstract parts.

```
numberOfValues = args[0]
noOfBits = 0
while 2^noOfBits < numberOfValues
  noOfBits++
s.o.p noOfBits
```

This level of abstraction is close enough to Java that we were able to implement the program.

Our next example was from Section 5.10 on page 86 for the `PiEstimation` program.

```
obtain tolerance from command line
set up previousEstimate as value from no terms
set up latestEstimate as value from one term
while previousEstimate is not within tolerance of latestEstimate
  previousEstimate = latestEstimate
  add next term to latestEstimate
end-while
print out latestEstimate
print out the number of terms used
print out the standard known value of Pi for comparison
```

We then lowered the level of abstraction.

```
double tolerance = args[0]
double previousEstimate = 0
double latestEstimate = 4
int termCount = 1
while previousEstimate is not within tolerance of latestEstimate
  previousEstimate = latestEstimate
  add next term to latestEstimate
  termCount++
end-while
s.o.p latestEstimate
s.o.p termCount
s.o.p the standard known value of Pi for comparison
```

And finally, we lowered it again.

```
double tolerance = args[0]
double previousEstimate = 0
double latestEstimate = 4
int termCount = 1
int nextDenominator = 3
int nextNumeratorSign = -1
while Math.abs(latestEstimate - previousEstimate) > tolerance
  previousEstimate = latestEstimate
  latestEstimate += nextNumeratorSign * 4 / nextDenominator
  termCount++
  nextNumeratorSign *= -1
  nextDenominator += 2
end-while
s.o.p latestEstimate
s.o.p termCount
s.o.p Math.PI
```

Another example, from Section 6.6 on page 101 was the TimesTable program. Our design started as follows.

```
print the box top line
print column headings
print headings underline
for row = 1 to 10
  print a row
print the box bottom line
```

Ultimately, in a later chapter in Section 8.5 on page 125, this program was implemented using separate methods to avoid repeated code and, more interestingly right now, to help keep the program manageable. The observation here is that steps we identify in our early, most abstract, versions of a design might end up being separate methods in the final program.

```
001: // Program to print out a neat multiplication table.
002: public class TimesTable
003: {
004:   // The size of the table -- the number of rows and columns.
005:   private static int tableSize = 12;
006:
007:
008:   // The main method implements the top level structure of the table.
009:   public static void main(String[] args)
```

```
010:    {
011:       // Top line.
012:       printLine();
013:
014:       // Column headings.
015:       printColumnHeadings();
016:
017:       // Underline headings.
018:       printLine();
019:
020:       // Now the rows.
021:       for (int row = 1; row <= tableSize; row++)
022:         printRow(row);
023:
024:       // Bottom line.
025:       printLine();
026:    } // main
...
076: } // class TimesTable
```

So, here is the generalization of the algorithm design process.

1. Identify the main steps of the algorithm.

2. Express the algorithm in terms of those main steps.

3. Then separately expand on each step using the same process, i.e., identify its main steps...

This process is sometimes called **top down stepwise refinement**.

9.4 Concepts covered in this chapter

This chapter has served mainly as a summary of the previous chapters, to act either as a consolidation for you, if you studied them, or as a potential entry point if you have programmed before. In either case, you should not continue to the next chapter until you are happy with all the concepts covered so far. Whichever applies to you, now is (another) good time to go through the end of chapter concept lists for all eight preceding chapters, plus the list below for those few concepts that were introduced here.

Concepts introduced in this chapter.

Chapter	Concept list
1	Page 13
2	Page 33
3	Page 57
4	Page 67
5	Page 90
6	Page 106
7	Page 114
8	Page 141

Expression	
– arithmetic: remainder operator (p.149)	Which of the following conditions are **true**? 1. 6 % 3 == 0 2. 8 % 4 == 2 3. 5 % 4 > 12 % 10 4. 8 % 4 < 16 % 12

Type	
– char (p.145)	What values are represented by this type?
– char: literal (p.145)	What is the difference between 'J' and "J"?
– char: literal: escape sequences (p.146)	What is an escape sequence? How do we have a character literal which is a single quote?

Type	
– long (p.145)	How many bits are used by values of this type?
– short (p.145)	How many bits are used by values of this type?
– byte (p.145)	How many bits are used by values of this type?
– float (p.146)	How many bits are used by values of this type?
Variable	
– char variable (p.145)	How many characters can a char variable store at any time?

Chapter 10

Separate classes

A collection of leaves, twigs and branches,
arranged in a certain way on a trunk,
is called a tree.

A collection of trees,
growing close together,
is called a wood.

These are abstractions, without which
we could never see the wood for the leaves.

10.1   Chapter aims

All of the programs we have seen up to now have been written in one **class**. In general, however, Java programs are divided into more than one class, and you may recall we have previously stated two reasons for this.

 Coffee time: `10.1.1`   Can you remember those two reasons? One of them is about size, and the other is relevant every time we use, say, System or Math.

In this chapter we introduce the idea of using a class as a template for the **construct**ion of **object**s, which can then be used by code in some other class. You will meet the essential Java technology for undertaking what is called **object oriented programming**, including **constructor method**s, **instance variable**s, and **instance method**s. These features significantly help us to reduce the inherent complexity of sophisticated programs. The chapter illustrates this benefit by revisiting the age history example.

The chapter contains the following sections.

Section	Aims	Associated Coursework
10.2 Age history with Date class (p.158)	To introduce the principle of using more than one **class** in a program, and in particular, the idea of using a class as a template for the **construct**ion of **ob**-**ject**s. We also introduce **instance variable**s, **con**-**structor method**s, creating **new** objects, the fact that a **class** is a **type** and the use of **reference**s.	Write a **class** to store quadratic polynomials, and a program that adds together two quadratic polynomials to form a third. (p.166)

Section	Aims	Associated Coursework
10.3 Improving the Date class: lessThan() and equals() methods (p.166)	To introduce the concept of **instance methods**. We also look at common misunderstandings about **variables** and **references**.	Extend a **class** that stores quadratic polynomials, and write a program that compares the 'size' of two quadratic polynomials. (p.171)
10.4 Improving the Date class: toString() method (p.172)	To reinforce the concept of **instance methods**. We also note that a **method** might have no **method parameters**.	Extend a **class** that stores quadratic polynomials, and modify programs that add together, and compare the 'size' of, two quadratic polynomials. (p.174)
10.5 Improving the Date class: addYear() method (p.174)	To further reinforce **instance methods**, meet Java's toString() convention and focus on the visibility of **instance variables**. We also see a **return type** which is a **class**.	Further extend a **class** that stores quadratic polynomials, and modify a program that adds together two quadratic polynomials. (p.179)
10.6 Alternative style (p.180)	To show an alternative way of talking about **instance variables** and **instance methods** from within the same **class**, using **this**.	(None.)

10.2 Example: Age history with **Date** class

AIM: To introduce the principle of using more than one **class** in a program, and in particular, the idea of using a class as a template for the **construction** of **objects**. We also introduce **instance variables**, **constructor methods**, creating **new** objects, the fact that a **class** is a **type** and the use of **references**.

In our latest version of the AgeHistory2 program from Section 8.6 on page 129, we needed to use three **variables** to store each date – one for the day, another for the month and a third for the year. In our minds we think of these as a single entity, a date, which has three parts. We would really like to have this idea reflected in our program.

Concept **Class: objects: contain a group of variables.** We can group a collection of **variables** into one entity by creating an **object**. For example, we might wish to represent a point in two dimensional space using an *x* and a *y* value to make up a coordinate. We would probably wish to combine our x and y variables into a single object, a Point.

10.2.1 The **Date** class

In order to combine three variables representing the components of a date into one **object**, we shall need to define a **class** telling Java how to make such objects. We have previously said that the purpose of classes is to break large programs into smaller pieces, and to enable such pieces to be reused in other programs (e.g. most programs use the System class). The third reason for having classes is so we can make objects.

Concept **Class: objects: are instances of a class.** Before we can make **objects**, we need to tell Java how the objects are to be **constructed**. For example, to make a Point object, we would need to tell Java that there are to be a pair of **variables** inside it, called x and y, and tell it what **types** these variables have, and how they get their values. We achieve this by writing a **class** which will act as a template for the creation of objects. We need to write such a template class for each kind of object we wish to have. For example, we would write a `Point` class describing how to make `Point` objects. If, on the other hand, we wanted to group together a load of variables describing attributes of wardrobes, so we could make objects each of which represents a single wardrobe, then we would probably call that class `Wardrobe`. Java lets us choose any name that we feel is appropriate, except **reserved word**s (although by convention we always start the name with a capital letter).

Once we have described the template, we can get Java to make objects of that class at **run time**. We say that these objects are **instance**s of the class. So, for example, particular `Point` objects would all be instances of the `Point` class. We can create as many different `Point` objects as we wish, each containing its own x and y variables, all from the one template, the `Point` class.

Concept **Variable: instance variables.** The **variable**s that we wish to have inside **object**s are called **instance variable**s because they belong to the **instance**s of a **class**. We declare them in much the same way as we declare **class variable**s, except without the **reserved word static**. For example, the following code is part of the definition of a `Point` class with two instance variables to be used to store the components of a `Point` object.

```
public class Point
{
  private double x;
  private double y;
  ...
} // class Point
```

Like class variables, instance variables have a visibility **modifier** – the above variables have both been declared as being **private**, which means they can only be accessed by code inside the class which has declared them.

Class variables belong to the class in which they are declared, and they are created at **run time** in the **static context** when the class is loaded into the **virtual machine**. There is only one copy of each class variable. By contrast, instance variables are created dynamically, in a **dynamic context**, when the object they are part of is created during the **run** of the program. There are as many copies of each instance variable as there are instances of the class: each object has its own set of instance variables.

For our improved `AgeHistory2` program, we are going to have a separate class called `Date` which will be used as a template for creating `Date` objects. This will be saved in the **file** `Date.java` and **compiled** separately. The class will have three **instance variable**s, one for each of the components of a date. We make these have **public** visibility so they can be accessed by our **main method**, which will live as usual in the `AgeHistory2` class.

```
001: // Representation of a date.
002: public class Date
003: {
004:   // The day, month and year of the date.
005:   public int day, month, year;
```

The code above has told Java that our `Date` objects will each have three instance variables. We next need to say how to **construct** a `Date` object, in particular, how Java will give the three variables their values.

Concept **Method: constructor methods.** A **class** which is to be used as a template for making **object**s should be given a **constructor method**. This is a special kind of **method** which contains instructions for the **construct**ion of objects that are **instance**s of the class. A constructor method always has the same name as the class it is defined in. It is usually declared as being **public**, but we do not specify a **return type** or write the **reserved word void**. Constructor methods can have **method parameter**s, and typically these are the initial values for some or all of the **instance variable**s.

For example, the following might be a constructor method for a `Point` class, which has two instance variables, x and y.

```
public Point (double requiredX, double requiredY)
{
  x = requiredX;
  y = requiredY;
} // Point
```

This says that in order to construct an object which is an instance of the class `Point`, we need to supply two **double** values, the first will be placed in the x instance variable, and the second in the y instance variable. Constructor methods are called in a similar way to any other **method**, except that we precede the **method call** with the **reserved word new**. For example, the following code would create a **new** object, which is an instance of the class `Point`, and in which the instance variables x and y have the values 7.4 and -19.9 respectively.

```
new Point (7.4, -19.9);
```

We can create as many `Point` objects as we wish, each of them having their own pair of instance variables, and so having possibly different values for x and y. These next four `Point` objects are the coordinates of a rectangle which is centred around the origin of a graph, point (0, 0).

```
new Point (-20, 40);
new Point (-20, -40);
new Point (20, 40);
new Point (20, -40);
```

This is illustrated in the following diagram.

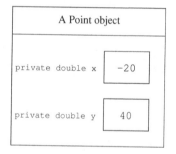

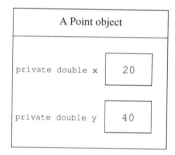

All four `Point` objects each have two instance variables, called x and y.

In our `Date` class, the constructor will be given three **int** values, which it will use to set the values of our three date component instance variables.

```
008:    // Construct a date -- given the required day, month and year.
009:    public Date(int requiredDay, int requiredMonth, int requiredYear)
010:    {
```

```
011:     day = requiredDay;
012:     month = requiredMonth;
013:     year = requiredYear;
014:   } // Date
015:
016: } // class Date
```

10.2.2 The full `Date` code

```
001: // Representation of a date.
002: public class Date
003: {
004:   // The day, month and year of the date.
005:   public int day, month, year;
006:
007:
008:   // Construct a date -- given the required day, month and year.
009:   public Date(int requiredDay, int requiredMonth, int requiredYear)
010:   {
011:     day = requiredDay;
012:     month = requiredMonth;
013:     year = requiredYear;
014:   } // Date
015:
016: } // class Date
```

We can **compile** the Date **class**, but we cannot **run** it – it is not a program, as it has no **main method**.

Console Input / Output
`$ javac Date.java`
`$ java Date`
`Exception in thread "main" java.lang.NoSuchMethodError: main`
`$ _`

10.2.3 The `AgeHistory2` class

The rest of our program code lives in the AgeHistory2 **class**, and is very similar to our previous version of the program, except that it will use our Date class to store dates, instead of three separate **variables** for each date.

Before we show the declaration of our **class variable** to store the present date, we need to observe that a class is a **type**, and thus we can have variables of a class type.

Concept **Class: is a type.** A **type** is essentially a **set** of values. The `int` type is all the whole numbers that can be represented using 32 **binary digit**s, the `double` type is all the **real** numbers that can be represented using the **double precision** technique and the `boolean` type contains the values `true` and `false`. A **class** can be used as a template for creating **objects**, and so is regarded in Java as a type: the set of all objects that can be created which are **instance**s of that class. For example, a Point class is a type which is the set of all Point objects that can be created. (Pedantically, we might instead say each class *has* an associated type of the same name.)

Concept **Variable: of a class type.** As a **class** is a **type**, we can use one in much the same way as we use the built-in types, such as `int`, `double` and `boolean`. This means we can declare a **variable** whose type is a class. For example, if we have a class Point then we can have variables of type Point.

```
Point p1;
Point p2;
```

161

The above defines two **local variable**s or **method variable**s of type `Point`. We also can have **class variable**s and even **instance variable**s whose type is a class.

Our program declares a class variable of type `Date`.

```
001: // Print out an age history of two people.
002: // Arguments: present date, first birth date, second birth date.
003: // Each date is three numbers: day month year.
004: public class AgeHistory2
005: {
006:    // The present date.
007:    private static Date presentDate;
```

This class variable will be used to store a **reference** to a newly created `Date` **object** containing the three date components supplied as **command line argument**s.

Concept **Variable: of a class type: stores a reference to an object.**   There is one important difference between a **variable** whose **type** is a built-in **primitive type**, such as `int` and one whose type is a **class**. With the former, Java knows from the type how much memory will be needed for the variable. For example, a **double variable** needs more memory than an **int variable**, but all variables of type `int` need the same amount of memory, as do those of type `double`. Java needs this information so that it knows how to allocate memory addresses for variables.

By contrast, it is not possible to calculate how much memory will be needed to store an **object**, because **instance**s of different classes will have different sizes, and in some cases it is possible for different instances of the same class to have different sizes! The only time the size of an object is reliably known is when it is created, at **run time**.

To deal with this situation in a systematic way, variables which are of a class type do not store an object, but instead store a **reference** to an object. A reference to an object is essentially the memory address at which the object resides in memory, and is only known at run time when the object is created. Because they are really just memory addresses, the size of all references is the same, and is fixed. So by using references in variables of a class type, rather than actually storing objects, Java knows how much memory to allocate for any such variable.

Strictly speaking then, the type associated with a class, is actually the **set** of possible *references* to instances of the class, rather than the set of actual instances themselves.

Concept **Type: primitive versus reference.**   Each **type** in Java is either a **primitive type** or a **reference type**. Values of primitive types have a size which is known at **compile time**. For example, every `int` value comprises four **byte**s. Types for which the size of an individual value is only known at **run time**, such as **class**es, are known as reference types because the values are always accessed via a **reference**.

Coffee time: `10.2.1`   Do you think `String` is a **reference type** or a **primitive type**? Hint: how long is a string?

Concept **Class: making instances with new.**   An **instance** of a **class** is created by calling the **constructor method** of the class, using the **reserved word** `new`, and supplying **method argument**s for the **method parameter**s. At **run time** when this code is **executed**, the Java **virtual machine**, with the help of the constructor method code, creates an **object** which is an instance of the class. Although it is not stated in its heading, a constructor method always **return**s a value, which is a **reference** to the **new**ly created object. This reference can then be stored in a **variable**, if we wish. For example, if we have a `Point` class, then we might have the following code.

```
Point topLeft     = new Point(-20, 40);
Point bottomLeft  = new Point(-20, -40);
Point topRight    = new Point(20, 40);
Point bottomRight = new Point(20, -40);
```

This declares four variables, of **type** Point and creates four instances of the class Point representing the four corners of a rectangle. The four variables each contain a reference to one of the points. This is illustrated in the following diagram.

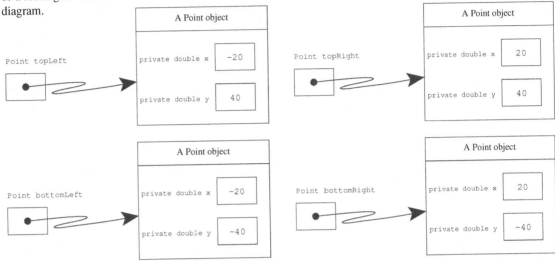

All four Point objects each have two **instance variables**, called x and y.

In our previous version of the AgeHistory2 program, our three class variables each held one **int** component of the present date. This can be illustrated by the following diagram.

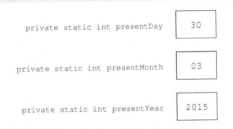

In our new version, we have one class variable which will contain a **reference** to a Date object, which in turn will contain the three components of the present date stored in **int instance variables**.

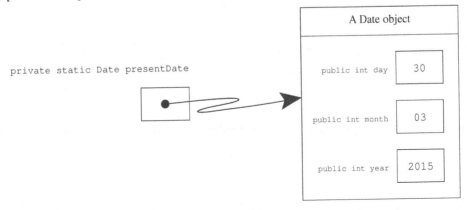

To make our discussion a little easier to follow, our latest version of the AgeHistory2 class has the **main method** appearing before the separate **method** to print out a single age history. Our main method parses the first three command line arguments, passes the resulting **int** values as **method argument**s to the Date **constructor method**, and stores the resulting reference in our presentDate variable.

```
010:    // The main method: get arguments and call printAgeHistory.
011:    public static void main(String[] args)
012:    {
013:        // The present date.
014:        presentDate = new Date(Integer.parseInt(args[0]),
015:                               Integer.parseInt(args[1]),
016:                               Integer.parseInt(args[2]));
```

Next, our main method has two **local variable**s in which it stores references to Date objects for the two birthdays. It then calls the printAgeHistory() method twice, passing the person number and the reference to the corresponding birthday.

```
018:    // The dates of birth: these must be less than the present date.
019:        Date birthDate1 = new Date(Integer.parseInt(args[3]),
020:                                   Integer.parseInt(args[4]),
021:                                   Integer.parseInt(args[5]));
022:
023:        Date birthDate2 = new Date(Integer.parseInt(args[6]),
024:                                   Integer.parseInt(args[7]),
025:                                   Integer.parseInt(args[8]));
026:
027:    // Now print the two age histories.
028:        printAgeHistory(1, birthDate1);
029:        printAgeHistory(2, birthDate2);
030:    } // main
```

As you can see, the use of a separate Date class has improved our main method, making it more succinct, by raising the level of **abstraction** with regard to the dates.

Next we look at the printAgeHistory() method. The first thing we should say is that this is now given a single Date argument for the birth date, instead of three separate date components.

Concept **Method: accepting parameters: of a class type.** The **method parameter**s of a **method** can be of any **type**, including **class**es. A parameter which is of a class type must be given a **method argument** value of that type when the method is invoked, for example a **reference** to an **object** which is an **instance** of the class named as the parameter type.

Our printAgeHistory() method will be given a person number and a reference to a Date object for the birth date.

```
033:    // Print the age history of one person, identified as personNumber.
034:    // The birth date must be less than the present date.
035:    private static void printAgeHistory(int personNumber, Date birthDate)
036:    {
```

Concept **Class: accessing instance variables.** The **instance variable**s of an **object** can be accessed by taking a **reference** to the object and appending a dot (.) and then the name of the **variable**. For example, if the variable p1 contains a reference to a Point object, and Point objects have an instance variable called x, then the code p1.x is the instance variable x, belonging to the Point referred to by p1.

Coffee time: 10.2.2   Where else have we seen a dot being used to address something?

Our `printAgeHistory()` method contains code to access the instance variables of the `Date` objects referred to by `birthDate` and `presentDate`.

```
037:    // Start by printing the event of birth.
038:    System.out.println("Pn " + personNumber + " was born on "
039:                    + birthDate.day + "/" + birthDate.month
040:                    + "/" + birthDate.year);
041:
042:    // Now we will go through the years since birth but before today.
043:    int someYear = birthDate.year + 1;
044:    int ageInSomeYear = 1;
045:    while (someYear < presentDate.year
046:            || someYear == presentDate.year
047:               && birthDate.month < presentDate.month
048:            || someYear == presentDate.year
049:               && birthDate.month == presentDate.month
050:               && birthDate.day < presentDate.day)
051:    {
052:      System.out.println("Pn " + personNumber + " was " + ageInSomeYear
053:                    + " on " + birthDate.day + "/" + birthDate.month
054:                    + "/" + someYear);
055:      someYear++;
056:      ageInSomeYear++;
057:    } // while
058:
059:    // At this point birthDate.day/birthDate.month/someYear
060:    // will be the next birthday, aged ageInSomeYear.
061:    // This will be greater than or equal to the present date.
062:    // If the person has not yet had their birthday this year
063:    // someYear equals presentDate.year,
064:    // otherwise someYear equals presentDate.year + 1.
065:
066:    if (birthDate.month == presentDate.month
067:        && birthDate.day == presentDate.day)
068:      // then someYear must equal presentDate.year.
069:      System.out.println("Pn " + personNumber + " is "
070:                    + ageInSomeYear + " today!");
071:    else
072:      System.out.println("Pn " + personNumber + " will be "
073:                    + ageInSomeYear + " on " + birthDate.day + "/"
074:                    + birthDate.month + "/" + someYear);
075:  } // printAgeHistory
076:
077: } // class AgeHistory2
```

Coffee time: 10.2.3   The introduction of a separate `Date` class helped improve part of the program, but has so far made other parts of the program worse than it was when we stored a date using three separate variables! Identify which parts were made better, and which worse.

10.2.4   Trying it

We can **run** the program with various **command line argument**s, obtaining the same results as we did from the previous version of the program in Section 8.6.1 on page 131.

10.2.5   Coursework: `AddQuadPoly`

In this task you will create a **class** called `QuadPoly` which will be used to represent quadratic polynomials, such as $6x^2 + 4x + 2$. Don't worry if Maths is not your favourite subject – you're not going to do anything too Mathematical. The class will have three **double instance variable**s, one for each of the three coefficients of a quadratic polynomial. These will be declared **public**. (If you have read ahead, then please do *not* yet make them **private**.) The class will also have a **constructor method**, which will be passed the three coefficient values as its **method parameters**. (The variable in these polynomials will always be x, and so its name need not be stored.)

You will also write a program called `AddQuadPoly`. This will take six **command line argument**s, these being two triples of coefficients, each triple being the coefficients of one quadratic polynomial. It will create an **instance** of `QuadPoly` for each of the two given quadratic polynomials. It will then create a third instance, representing the **addition** of the two given polynomials. Finally it will print out a report showing the addition. The following is an example **run**.

Console Input / Output
`$ java AddQuadPoly 6 4 2 3 2 1`
`Polynomial:      6.0x^2 + 4.0x + 2.0`
`added to:        3.0x^2 + 2.0x + 1.0`
`results in:      9.0x^2 + 6.0x + 3.0`
`$ _`

Note how the three polynomials are to be printed using ordinary text, with a `^` **character** before the power instead of attempting to raise the 2 into a superscript, such as in $6.0x^2$. Each polynomial is printed as follows, where the three question marks in the format are replaced by the values of the three coefficients.

```
?x^2 + ?x + ?
```

Your `System.out.println` calls should all be in your main method. If you are tempted to write the program without creating three instances of `QuadPoly` (because it would in fact be easier right now) then you are seriously missing the point!

Undertake the usual tasks of planning **test data**, **design**ing the classes, implementing them, testing the program, and finally recording your results.

Optional extra: Extend the program so that it can add together any number of polynomials listed as command line arguments, displaying the intermediate resulting polynomials as it goes along. Make it be able to handle the cases of there being no arguments $(0x^2 + 0x + 0)$, just one polynomial, and the erroneous cases of the number of arguments not being divisible by three!

10.3   Improving the `Date` class: `lessThan()` and `equals()` methods

AIM:
> To introduce the concept of **instance methods**. We also look at common misunderstandings about **variables** and **references**.

Our version of the `AgeHistory2` program from the previous section contains complex code to compare two dates in the **condition** of the **while loop** and in the **if else statement** following the while loop. In this section we shall see how to simplify this code, by moving the date comparison logic to the `Date` **class**, putting it inside **instance methods**.

Concept **Method: class versus instance methods.** When we define a **method**, we can write the **reserved word** `static` in its heading, meaning that it can be **executed** in the **static context**, that is, it can be used as soon as the **class** is loaded into the **virtual machine**. These are known as **class method**s, because they belong to the class. By contrast, if we omit the `static` **modifier** then the method is an **instance method**. This means it can only be run in a **dynamic context**, attached to a particular **instance** of the class.

166

This parallels the distinction between **class variable**s and **instance variable**s. There is one copy of a class variable, created when the class is loaded. There is one copy of an instance variable for every instance, created when the instance is created.

We can think of methods in the same way: class methods belong to the class they are defined in, and there is one copy of their code at **run time**, ready for use immediately. Instance methods belong to an instance, and there are as many copies of the code at run time as there are instances. Of course, the virtual machine does not really make copies of the code of instance methods, but it *behaves* as though it does, in the sense that when an instance method is executed, it runs in the context of the instance that it belongs to.

For example, suppose we have a `Point` class with instance variables x and y. We might wish to have an instance method which takes no **method parameters**, but **returns** the distance of a point from the origin. Pythagoras[18] tells us that this is $\sqrt{x^2 + y^2}$. (We can use the `sqrt()` method from the `Math` class.)

```
public double distanceFromOrigin()
{
  return Math.sqrt(x * x + y * y);
} // distanceFromOrigin
```

A class method can be accessed by taking the name of the class, and appending a dot (.) and then the name of the method. `Math.sqrt` is a handy example right now.

An instance method belonging to an **object** can be accessed by taking a **reference** to the *object* and appending a dot (.) and then the name of the method. For example, if the **variable** p1 contains a reference to a `Point` object, then the code p1.distanceFromOrigin() invokes the instance method distanceFromOrigin(), belonging to the `Point` referred to by p1.

The following code would print the numbers 5 and 75.

```
Point p1 = new Point(3, 4);
Point p2 = new Point(45, 60);

System.out.println(p1.distanceFromOrigin());
System.out.println(p2.distanceFromOrigin());
```

When the method is called via p1 it uses the instance variables of the object referred to by p1, that is the values 3 and 4 respectively. When the method is called via p2 it uses the values 45 and 60 instead.

For another example, we may wish to have a method which determines the distance between a point and a given other point.

```
public double distanceFromPoint(Point otherPoint)
{
  double xDistance = x - otherPoint.x;
  double yDistance = y - otherPoint.y;

  return Math.sqrt(xDistance * xDistance + yDistance * yDistance);
} // distanceFromPoint
```

The following code would print the number 70.0, twice.

```
System.out.println(p1.distanceFromPoint(p2));
System.out.println(p2.distanceFromPoint(p1));
```

10.3.1 The Date class

The first part of our improved Date class is the same as in the previous section.

```
001: // Representation of a date.
002: public class Date
003: {
004:   // The day, month and year of the date.
005:   public int day, month, year;
006:
007:
008:   // Construct a date -- given the required day, month and year.
009:   public Date(int requiredDay, int requiredMonth, int requiredYear)
010:   {
011:     day = requiredDay;
012:     month = requiredMonth;
013:     year = requiredYear;
014:   } // Date
```

However, it now also contains two new instance methods. One of them compares this Date **object** with a given other one, and **return**s **true** if they are **equivalent**, i.e. they represent the same date, or **false** otherwise. In order to represent the same date, all three **instance variable**s in this object must each have the same value in the other object.

```
017:   // Compare this date with a given other one, for equality.
018:   public boolean equals(Date other)
019:   {
020:     return day == other.day && month == other.month && year == other.year;
021:   } // equals
```

Our second instance method similarly compares this Date object with a given other one, but returns **true** if the date represented by this one is **less than** that represented by the other, **false** otherwise.

```
024:   // Compare this date with a given other one, for less than.
025:   public boolean lessThan(Date other)
026:   {
027:     return year < other.year
028:           || year == other.year
029:               && (month < other.month
030:                   || month == other.month && day < other.day);
031:   } // lessThan
032:
033: } // class Date
```

We can **compile** this new version of the Date **class**.

```
Console Input / Output
$ javac Date.java
$ _
```

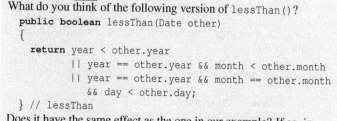

Coffee time: `10.3.1`
What do you think of the following version of lessThan()?
```
public boolean lessThan(Date other)
{
  return year < other.year
        || year == other.year && month < other.month
        || year == other.year && month == other.month
            && day < other.day;
} // lessThan
```
Does it have the same effect as the one in our example? If so, in what ways is it better or worse?

10.3.2 The AgeHistory2 class

As in the last section, the rest of our program code lives in the AgeHistory2 **class**. The first part of it is the same.

```
001: // Print out an age history of two people.
002: // Arguments: present date, first birth date, second birth date.
003: // Each date is three numbers: day month year.
```

```
004: public class AgeHistory2
005: {
006:    // The present date.
007:    private static Date presentDate;
008:
009:
010:    // The main method: get arguments and call printAgeHistory.
011:    public static void main(String[] args)
012:    {
013:       // The present date.
014:       presentDate = new Date(Integer.parseInt(args[0]),
015:                              Integer.parseInt(args[1]),
016:                              Integer.parseInt(args[2]));
017:
018:       // The dates of birth: these must be less than the present date.
019:       Date birthDate1 = new Date(Integer.parseInt(args[3]),
020:                                  Integer.parseInt(args[4]),
021:                                  Integer.parseInt(args[5]));
022:
023:       Date birthDate2 = new Date(Integer.parseInt(args[6]),
024:                                  Integer.parseInt(args[7]),
025:                                  Integer.parseInt(args[8]));
026:
027:       // Now print the two age histories.
028:       printAgeHistory(1, birthDate1);
029:       printAgeHistory(2, birthDate2);
030:    } // main
```

The changes all exist in the `printAgeHistory()` **class method**.

```
033:    // Print the age history of one person, identified as personNumber.
034:    // The birth date must be less than the present date.
035:    private static void printAgeHistory(int personNumber, Date birthDate)
036:    {
037:       // Start by printing the event of birth.
038:       System.out.println("Pn " + personNumber + " was born on "
039:                          + birthDate.day + "/" + birthDate.month
040:                          + "/" + birthDate.year);
```

We replace the **int variable** `someYear` with a `Date` **variable**, called `someBirthday`. This is so we can use the new `Date` comparison **instance methods** in the **while loop** and the **if else statement** that follows. We also rename the variable `ageInSomeYear` to `ageOnSomeBirthday`.

```
042:    // Now we will go through the years since birth but before today.
043:    // We keep track of the birthday we are considering.
044:    Date someBirthday
045:       = new Date(birthDate.day, birthDate.month, birthDate.year + 1);
046:    int ageOnSomeBirthday = 1;
```

The **condition** of the while loop is changed so that it uses the `lessThan()` instance method. This makes the code here *much* simpler than in the previous section.

```
047:    while (someBirthday.lessThan(presentDate))
048:    {
049:       System.out.println("Pn " + personNumber + " was " + ageOnSomeBirthday
050:                          + " on " + someBirthday.day + "/" + someBirthday.month
051:                          + "/" + someBirthday.year);
052:       someBirthday = new Date(someBirthday.day, someBirthday.month,
053:                               someBirthday.year + 1);
054:       ageOnSomeBirthday++;
055:    } // while
```

See how each time we go round the **loop**, the **reference** in the variable `someBirthday` is changed to refer to a **new** `Date` – one representing the next birthday.

Finally the **condition** of the if else statement following our while loop is changed to use the `equals()` instance method. This too makes the code here simpler than in the previous section.

```
057:    // Now deal with the next birthday.
058:    if (someBirthday.equals(presentDate))
059:       System.out.println("Pn " + personNumber + " is "
060:                          + ageOnSomeBirthday + " today!");
061:    else
062:       System.out.println("Pn " + personNumber + " will be "
063:                          + ageOnSomeBirthday + " on " + someBirthday.day
064:                          + "/" + someBirthday.month + "/" + someBirthday.year);
065:    } // printAgeHistory
066:
067: } // class AgeHistory2
```

Coffee time: `10.3.2` Java would have permitted us to write the condition of the if else statement as `someBirthday == presentDate`. Why would this not work?

Coffee time: `10.3.3` The introduction of instance methods has helped improve more of the program. What aspects still have room for improvement?

10.3.3 Trying it

We can **run** the program with various **command line argument**s, and still obtain the same results as we did in Section 8.6.1 on page 131.

10.3.4 Avoid misunderstanding references

Concept **Variable: of a class type: stores a reference to an object: avoid misunderstanding.** Students new to the idea of **reference**s often fail to appreciate their significance, and make one or sometimes both of the following two mistakes.

1. Misconception: A **variable** is an **object**.

2. Misconception: A variable contains an object.

Neither of these are true, as we have already said: variables (of a **class type**) can contain a *reference* to an object. A common question is "why do we have to write `Date` twice in the following?".

```
Date someBirthday
= new Date(birthDate.day, birthDate.month, birthDate.year + 1);
```

It is because we are doing three things.

1. We are declaring a variable.

2. We are **construct**ing an object.

3. We are storing a reference to that object in the variable.

So we can have a variable without an object.

```
Date someBirthday;
```

And we can have an object without a variable – could that be useful?

```
new Date(birthDate.day, birthDate.month, birthDate.year + 1);
```

Yes, it can be useful: for example, when we want to use objects just once, straight after constructing them.

```
System.out.println(new Point(3, 4).distanceFromPoint(new Point(45, 60)));
```

If we wish, we can have two variables referring to the same object.

```
Date theSameBirthday = someBirthday;
```

Also, we can change the value of a variable making it refer to a different object.

```
someBirthday = new Date(someBirthday.day, someBirthday.month,
                        someBirthday.year + 1);
```

This creates a **new** Date **object**, and stores the **reference** to it in someBirthday – overwriting the reference to the previous Date object. This is illustrated in the following diagram.

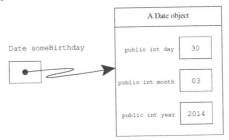

```
someBirthday = new Date(someBirthday.day, someBirthday.month, someBirthday.year + 1);
```

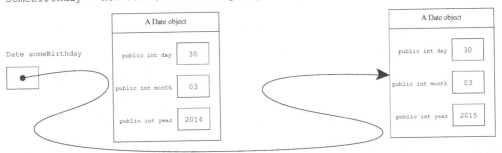

10.3.5 Coursework: CompareQuadPoly

In this task you will copy the QuadPoly **class** from the previous task and extend it, by adding two **instance methods**. The first one will compare the instance of QuadPoly it belongs to with another one given as a **method parameter**, and **return** **true** if and only if they are **equivalent**, i.e. they represent the same polynomial. The second instance method will also compare the QuadPoly **object** with another, but return **true** if and only if this one is **less than** the other one. For a quadratic polynomial, $a1x^2 + b1x + c1$ to be less than another, $a2x^2 + b2x + c2$ then $a1$ must be **less than** $a2$, or if they are **equal**, then $b1$ must be less than $b2$, or if they are also equal, then $c1$ must be less than $c2$. (If you have read ahead, then please do *not* yet add a toString() instance method.)

You will also write a program called CompareQuadPoly. This will take six **command line arguments**, this being two triples of coefficients, each triple being the coefficients of one quadratic polynomial. It will create an **instance** of QuadPoly for each of the two given quadratic polynomials. It will then use the two instance methods to compare them, to determine if they are equivalent, or the first one is less than, or **greater than** the second, and report the results. The following are some example **run**s.

```
            Console Input / Output
$ java CompareQuadPoly 1 2 3 2 3 1
The polynomial:          1.0x^2 + 2.0x + 3.0
is smaller than:         2.0x^2 + 3.0x + 1.0
$ _
```

```
            Console Input / Output
$ java CompareQuadPoly 3 2 1 3 2 1
The polynomial:          3.0x^2 + 2.0x + 1.0
is the same as:          3.0x^2 + 2.0x + 1.0
$ _
```

```
            Console Input / Output
$ java CompareQuadPoly 3 2 1 1 2 3
The polynomial:          3.0x^2 + 2.0x + 1.0
is greater than:         1.0x^2 + 2.0x + 3.0
$ _
```

Undertake the usual tasks of planning **test data**, **design**ing the classes, implementing them, testing the program, and finally recording your results.

Optional extra: Extend the program so that it can compare any number of polynomials listed as command line arguments, displaying the intermediate resulting polynomials as it compares each with the previous. At the end, it could report the smallest and largest polynomials encountered.

10.4 Improving the `Date` class: `toString()` method

AIM:
To reinforce the concept of **instance methods**. We also note that a **method** might have no **method parameters**.

Our version of the `AgeHistory2` program from the previous section is much improved, but contains several places where we print out a date. In this section, we are going to improve it further by introducing another **instance method**, one which will **return** a `String` representation of a `Date` **object**.

10.4.1 The `Date` class

The first part of our further improved `Date` **class** is the same as in the previous section.

```
001: // Representation of a date.
002: public class Date
003: {
004:    // The day, month and year of the date.
005:    public int day, month, year;
006:
007:
008:    // Construct a date -- given the required day, month and year.
009:    public Date(int requiredDay, int requiredMonth, int requiredYear)
010:    {
011:       day = requiredDay;
012:       month = requiredMonth;
013:       year = requiredYear;
014:    } // Date
015:
016:
017:    // Compare this date with a given other one, for equality.
018:    public boolean equals(Date other)
019:    {
020:       return day == other.day && month == other.month && year == other.year;
021:    } // equals
022:
023:
024:    // Compare this date with a given other one, for less than.
025:    public boolean lessThan(Date other)
026:    {
```

```
027:        return year < other.year
028:            || year == other.year
029:                && (month < other.month
030:                    || month == other.month && day < other.day);
031:    } // lessThan
```

We add another **instance method** to **return** the day/month/year `String` representation of a date. It takes no **method parameter**s.

> *Concept* **Method: a method may have no parameters.** The list of **method parameter**s given to a **method** may be empty. This is typical for methods which always have the same effect or **return** the same result, or their result depends solely on the value of **instance variable**s rather than some values in the context where the method is called.

A good name for our new instance method is `toString` as it 'converts' a date into its string representation.

```
034:    // Return the day/month/year representation of the date.
035:    public String toString()
036:    {
037:        return day + "/" + month + "/" + year;
038:    } // toString
039:
040: } // class Date
```

We can **compile** this new version of the Date class.

```
                          Console Input / Output
$ javac Date.java
$ _
```

10.4.2 The `AgeHistory2` class

Our improvements in this section centre around us using the `toString()` **instance method** of the Date **class** in the `printAgeHistory()` **class method**.

```
001: // Print out an age history of two people.
002: // Arguments: present date, first birth date, second birth date.
003: // Each date is three numbers: day month year.
004: public class AgeHistory2
005: {
006:    // The present date.
007:    private static Date presentDate;
008:
009:
010:    // The main method: get arguments and call printAgeHistory.
011:    public static void main(String[] args)
012:    {
013:        // The present date.
014:        presentDate = new Date(Integer.parseInt(args[0]),
015:                               Integer.parseInt(args[1]),
016:                               Integer.parseInt(args[2]));
017:
018:        // The dates of birth: these must be less than the present date.
019:        Date birthDate1 = new Date(Integer.parseInt(args[3]),
020:                                   Integer.parseInt(args[4]),
021:                                   Integer.parseInt(args[5]));
022:
023:        Date birthDate2 = new Date(Integer.parseInt(args[6]),
024:                                   Integer.parseInt(args[7]),
025:                                   Integer.parseInt(args[8]));
026:
027:        // Now print the two age histories.
028:        printAgeHistory(1, birthDate1);
029:        printAgeHistory(2, birthDate2);
030:    } // main
```

```
033:    // Print the age history of one person, identified as personNumber.
034:    // The birth date must be less than the present date.
035:    private static void printAgeHistory(int personNumber, Date birthDate)
036:    {
037:       // Start by printing the event of birth.
038:       System.out.println("Pn " + personNumber + " was born on "
039:                          + birthDate.toString());
040:
041:       // Now we will go through the years since birth but before today.
042:       // We keep track of the birthday we are considering.
043:       Date someBirthday
044:         = new Date(birthDate.day, birthDate.month, birthDate.year + 1);
045:       int ageOnSomeBirthday = 1;
046:       while (someBirthday.lessThan(presentDate))
047:       {
048:          System.out.println("Pn " + personNumber + " was " + ageOnSomeBirthday
049:                             + " on " + someBirthday.toString());
050:          someBirthday = new Date(someBirthday.day, someBirthday.month,
051:                                  someBirthday.year + 1);
052:          ageOnSomeBirthday++;
053:       } // while
054:
055:       // Now deal with the next birthday.
056:       if (someBirthday.equals(presentDate))
057:          System.out.println("Pn " + personNumber + " is "
058:                             + ageOnSomeBirthday + " today!");
059:       else
060:          System.out.println("Pn " + personNumber + " will be "
061:                             + ageOnSomeBirthday + " on "
062:                             + someBirthday.toString());
063:    } // printAgeHistory
064:
065: } // class AgeHistory2
```

10.4.3 Trying it

We can **run** the program with various **command line argument**s, and still obtain the same results as we did in Section 8.6.1 on page 131.

10.4.4 Coursework: `AddQuadPoly` and `CompareQuadPoly` with `toString()`

In this task you will copy the `QuadPoly` **class** from the previous task and further extend it, by adding an **instance method** called `toString`. This will **return** a `String` representing the polynomial in the format previously introduced.

You will also copy the programs `AddQuadPoly` and `CompareQuadPoly` from the previous tasks, and modify them to make appropriate use of the new instance method.

Undertake the usual tasks of planning **test data** (consider if it will be different to the previous version of each program), **design**ing the modifications, implementing them, testing the programs, and finally recording your results.

10.5 Improving the `Date` class: `addYear()` method

AIM:
To further reinforce **instance method**s, meet Java's `toString()` convention and focus on the visibility of **instance variable**s. We also see a **return type** which is a **class**.

In this section we will finish tinkering with the AgeHistory2 program, by completing our process of improvements. There are three things we shall do.

1. Introduce an **instance method** in the Date **class**, to create a **new** Date from an existing one, which represents the date that is one year later. Once we use this in the AgeHistory2 class, it will be the case that there is no longer any direct access to the **instance variable**s of the Date **object**s from outside the Date class.

2. Make the Date class safer by changing the visibility of its instance variables to **private**.

3. Use Java's toString() convention to implicitly call the toString() instance method of our Date objects.

10.5.1 The **Date** class

We make the Date class safer by changing the three **instance variables** to be **private**. This means other **classes**, such as AgeHistory2, will not be able to access them directly.

Concept **Variable: instance variables: should be private by default.** Java allows us to give **public** visibility to our **instance variable**s if we wish, but generally it is a good idea to define them as **private**. This permits us to alter the way we implement the **class**, without it affecting the code in other classes. For example, the programmer who has the job of maintaining a Point class with instance variables x and y, might decide it was better to re-implement the class to use instance variables that store the polar coordinate radius and angle instead. This might be because some new **methods** being added to the class would work much more easily in the polar coordinate system. Because the x and y instance variables had originally been made private, the programmer would know that there could not be any mention of them in other classes. So it would be safe to replace them with ones of a different name and which work differently. To make the points behave the same as before, the values given to the **constructor method** would be converted from *x* and *y* values to polar values, before being stored, and the toString() method could convert them back again.

The only reason we originally made the Date instance variables **public** was that we had not met **instance methods**, and so could not avoid the need to access them from the other class. Making them private is better. For example, if we so wished, at some time in the future we could safely alter the class so that it stores the date as just a number of days since some epoch day. You might well say "Why would we want to do that"? The point is that we do not know – **software** is a living thing. Programs need to be made maintainable so they can easily meet the changing world they serve. This includes building in flexibility by separating the way they work from what they do where possible.

```
001: // Representation of a date.
002: public class Date
003: {
004:   // The day, month and year of the date.
005:   private int day, month, year;
```

The next part of our further improved Date class is the same as in the previous section.

```
008:   // Construct a date -- given the required day, month and year.
009:   public Date(int requiredDay, int requiredMonth, int requiredYear)
010:   {
011:     day = requiredDay;
012:     month = requiredMonth;
013:     year = requiredYear;
014:   } // Date
015:
016:
017:   // Compare this date with a given other one, for equality.
018:   public boolean equals(Date other)
019:   {
020:     return day == other.day && month == other.month && year == other.year;
021:   } // equals
```

```
024:    // Compare this date with a given other one, for less than.
025:    public boolean lessThan(Date other)
026:    {
027:      return year < other.year
028:             || year == other.year
029:                && (month < other.month
030:                    || month == other.month && day < other.day);
031:    } // lessThan
032:
033:
034:    // Return the day/month/year representation of the date.
035:    public String toString()
036:    {
037:      return day + "/" + month + "/" + year;
038:    } // toString
```

Now we add the new instance method to create and **return** a Date which is one year later than this one. This will be used to **loop** through the birthdays in the AgeHistory2 class.

Concept **Method: returning a value: of a class type.** A **method** may **return** a result back to the code that called it, and this may be of any **type**, including a **class**. In such cases, the value returned will typically be a **reference** to an **object** which is an **instance** of the class named as the **return type**.

For example, in a Point class with **instance variable**s x and y, we might have an **instance method** to return a Point which is half way along a straight line between this Point and a given other Point.

```
public Point halfWayPoint(Point otherPoint)
{
  double newX = (x + otherPoint.x) / 2;
  double newY = (y + otherPoint.y) / 2;
  return new Point(newX, newY);
} // halfWayPoint
```

The method creates a **new object** and then returns a reference to it. This might be used as follows.

```
Point p1 = new Point(3, 4);
Point p2 = new Point(45, 60);

Point halfWayBetweenP1AndP2 = p1.halfWayPoint(p2);
```

The reference to the new Point returned by the instance method, is stored in the **variable** halfWayBetweenP1AndP2. It would, of course, be the point $(24, 32)$. This is illustrated in the following diagram.

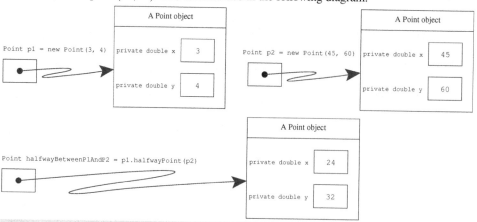

176

Coffee time: `10.5.1` Suppose the `Point` class in the concept above had an `equals()` instance method, defined as follows.

```
public boolean equals(Point other)
{
    return x == other.x && y == other.y;
} // equals
```

Explain why the values of `equalByReference` and `equalByMethod` are different after the following code is run.

```
Point halfWayBetweenP1AndP2 = p1.halfWayPoint(p2);
Point halfWayBetweenP2AndP1 = p2.halfWayPoint(p1);
boolean equalByReference
    = halfWayBetweenP1AndP2 == halfWayBetweenP2AndP1;
boolean equalByMethod
    = halfWayBetweenP1AndP2.equals(halfWayBetweenP2AndP1);
```

Coffee time: `10.5.2` What are the values of the same **variables** after the following *alternative* code is run?

```
Point halfWayBetweenP1AndP2 = p1.halfWayPoint(p2);
Point halfWayBetweenP2AndP1 = halfWayBetweenP1AndP2;
boolean equalByReference
    = halfWayBetweenP1AndP2 == halfWayBetweenP2AndP1;
boolean equalByMethod
    = halfWayBetweenP1AndP2.equals(halfWayBetweenP2AndP1);
```

Here is our instance method to return a `Date` which is one year later than this one.

```
041:  // Return a new Date which is one year later than this one.
042:  public Date addYear()
043:  {
044:      return new Date(day, month, year + 1);
045:  } // addYear
046:
047: } // class Date
```

We can **compile** this new version of the `Date` class.

Console Input / Output
`$ javac Date.java`
`$ _`

10.5.2 The `AgeHistory2` class

Our improvements in this section centre around us using the `addYear()` **instance method** of the `Date` **class** in the `printAgeHistory()` **class method**, and the Java convention of implicit calls to `toString()`.

Concept **Type: `String`: conversion: from object.** It is quite common for **class**es to have an **instance method** which is **design**ed to produce a `String` representation of an **object**. It is conventional in Java for such **method**s to be called `toString`. For example, a `Point` class with `x` and `y` **instance variable**s might have the following `toString()` method.

```
public String toString()
{
    return "(" + x + "," + y + ")";
} // toString
```

For convenience, whenever the Java **compiler** finds an **object reference** as an **operand** of the **concatenation operator** it assumes that the object's `toString()` method is to be invoked to produce the required `String`.

For example, consider the following code.

```
Point p1 = new Point(10, 40);
System.out.println("The point is " + p1.toString());
```

Thanks to the compiler's convenient implicit assumption about toString(), the above code could, and probably would, have been written as follows.

```
Point p1 = new Point(10, 40);
System.out.println("The point is " + p1);
```

For our further convenience, there is a separate version of System.out.println() that takes any single object rather than a string, and prints its toString(). Thus, the code

```
System.out.println(p1);
```

has the same effect as the following.

```
System.out.println("" + p1);
```

The first part of AgeHistory2 is the same as before.

```
001: // Print out an age history of two people.
002: // Arguments: present date, first birth date, second birth date.
003: // Each date is three numbers: day month year.
004: public class AgeHistory2
005: {
006:    // The present date.
007:    private static Date presentDate;
008:
009:
010:    // The main method: get arguments and call printAgeHistory.
011:    public static void main(String[] args)
012:    {
013:       // The present date.
014:       presentDate = new Date(Integer.parseInt(args[0]),
015:                              Integer.parseInt(args[1]),
016:                              Integer.parseInt(args[2]));
017:
018:       // The dates of birth: these must be less than the present date.
019:       Date birthDate1 = new Date(Integer.parseInt(args[3]),
020:                                  Integer.parseInt(args[4]),
021:                                  Integer.parseInt(args[5]));
022:
023:       Date birthDate2 = new Date(Integer.parseInt(args[6]),
024:                                  Integer.parseInt(args[7]),
025:                                  Integer.parseInt(args[8]));
026:
027:       // Now print the two age histories.
028:       printAgeHistory(1, birthDate1);
029:       printAgeHistory(2, birthDate2);
030:    } // main
```

In the printAgeHistory() class method, look out for places where we are implicitly calling toString() on Date **object**s, as well as the more obvious use of addYear().

```
033:    // Print the age history of one person, identified as personNumber.
034:    // The birth date must be less than the present date.
035:    private static void printAgeHistory(int personNumber, Date birthDate)
036:    {
037:       // Start by printing the event of birth.
038:       System.out.println("Pn " + personNumber + " was born on " + birthDate);
039:
040:       // Now we will go through the years since birth but before today.
041:       // We keep track of the birthday we are considering.
042:       Date someBirthday = birthDate.addYear();
```

```
043:    int ageOnSomeBirthday = 1;
044:    while (someBirthday.lessThan(presentDate))
045:    {
046:      System.out.println("Pn " + personNumber + " was " + ageOnSomeBirthday
047:                    + " on " + someBirthday);
048:      someBirthday = someBirthday.addYear();
049:      ageOnSomeBirthday++;
050:    } // while
051:
052:    // Now deal with the next birthday.
053:    if (someBirthday.equals(presentDate))
054:      System.out.println("Pn " + personNumber + " is "
055:                    + ageOnSomeBirthday + " today!");
056:    else
057:      System.out.println("Pn " + personNumber + " will be "
058:                    + ageOnSomeBirthday + " on " + someBirthday);
059:  } // printAgeHistory
060:
061: } // class AgeHistory2
```

Coffee time: What do you think would happen if we place, as an **operand** of **concatenation**, a **reference** to an object belonging to a class in which we have not defined a toString() instance method?

10.5.3

10.5.3 Trying it

We can **run** the program with various **command line argument**s, and still obtain the same results as we did in Section 8.6.1 on page 131.

10.5.4 Coursework: `QuadPoly` with an addition method

In this task you will copy the QuadPoly **class** from the previous task and make the **instance variable**s have **private** visibility. You will also further extend it, by adding an **instance method** which takes a given other **instance** of QuadPoly as a **method parameter** and **return**s a **new** QuadPoly **object**, being the result of adding this QuadPoly instance to the given other one.

You will also copy the program AddQuadPoly from the previous task, and modify it to make appropriate use of the new instance method.

Undertake the usual tasks of planning **test data** (consider if it will be different to the previous version of the program), **design**ing the modifications, implementing them, testing the program, and finally recording your results.

Optional extra: Add more instance methods to QuadPoly to subtract a given other polynomial, multiply this one by a constant and divide this one by a constant. Each of these will produce a new instance of QuadPoly. Then write a program called QuadPolyCalculator which permits arbitrary polynomial calculations. This will be based on the idea of an accumulator polynomial, which starts off as being $0x^2 + 0x + 0$. The **command line argument**s consist of a sequence of operation codes, each followed by an operand, which would either be a polynomial in the next three arguments, or a single number. For example, you might choose code 0 to represent addition, and this would be followed by three arguments representing a polynomial to be added to the accumulator. Code 2 might be multiplication, which would be followed by a single number to be multiplied by the accumulator. Each operation will produce output as it happens, and place its result back in the accumulator. At the end, the value of the accumulator will be reported. You could allow the **less than** operation to compare the accumulator with the following polynomial operand, and store whichever is the smallest in the accumulator. This would permit the program to be used to find the smallest of a sequence of polynomials, by preceding the first one with the addition operation code, and the subsequent ones with the less than operation code! You might add a **greater than** operation code too.

Hint: this would be a good use of a **switch statement**.

10.6 Alternative style

AIM:
To show an alternative way of talking about **instance variables** and **instance methods** from within the same **class**, using `this`.

If you look in other Java text books you may find code with a different style for the same Java technology you have met in this chapter, based on the use of the **this reference**.

Concept **Class: objects: this reference.** Sometimes, in **constructor methods** or in **instance methods** of a **class** we wish to refer to the **object** that the constructor is creating, or to which the instance method belongs. For this purpose, whenever the **reserved word this** is used in or as an **expression** it means a **reference** to the object that is being created by the constructor or that owns the instance method, etc.. We can only use the **this reference** in places where it makes sense, such as constructor methods, instance methods and **instance variable** initializations. So, `this` (when used in this way) behaves somewhat like an extra instance variable in each object, automatically set up to contain a reference to that object.

For example, in a `Point` class we may wish to have an instance method that yields a point which is half way between the origin and `this` point.

```
public Point halfThisPoint()
{
  return halfWayPoint(new Point(0, 0));
} // halfThisPoint
```

An alternative implementation would be as follows.

```
public Point halfThisPoint()
{
  return new Point(0, 0).halfWayPoint(this);
} // halfThisPoint
```

This author prefers to use the **this reference** only when needed, but some like a style where, for example, every access to an **instance variable** from within the same **class** is written using the **reserved word this** followed by a dot (.) followed by the name of the instance variable. To illustrate, here is the latest version of our `Date` class written in that style.

```
001: // Representation of a date.
002: public class Date
003: {
004:   // The day, month and year of the date.
005:   private int day, month, year;
006:
007:
008:   // Construct a date -- given the required day, month and year.
009:   public Date(int day, int month, int year)
010:   {
011:     this.day = day;
012:     this.month = month;
013:     this.year = year;
014:   } // Date
```

Notice that, unlike in the previous version, we have used the same names for the **method parameters** as we have for the instance variables. For example, `day` means the parameter, whereas as `this.day` means the instance variable.

```
017:   // Compare this date with a given other one, for equality.
018:   public boolean equals(Date other)
019:   {
020:     return this.day == other.day && this.month == other.month
021:             && this.year == other.year;
022:   } // equals
023:
024:
025:   // Compare this date with a given other one, for less than.
026:   public boolean lessThan(Date other)
027:   {
028:     return this.year < other.year
029:             || this.year == other.year
030:                && (this.month < other.month
031:                    || this.month == other.month && this.day < other.day);
032:   } // lessThan
033:
034:
035:   // Return the day/month/year representation of the date.
036:   public String toString()
037:   {
038:     return this.day + "/" + this.month + "/" + this.year;
039:   } // toString
040:
041:
042:   // Return a new Date which is one year later than this one.
043:   public Date addYear()
044:   {
045:     return new Date(this.day, this.month, this.year + 1);
046:   } // addYear
047:
048: } // class Date
```

As stated above, this author prefers not to use **this** unnecessarily.

10.7 Concepts covered in this chapter

Here is a list of the concepts that were covered in this chapter, each with a self-test question. You can use this to check you remember them being introduced, and perhaps re-read some of them before going on to the next chapter.

Class	
– objects: contain a group of variables (p.158)	Give two examples of kinds of objects which contain a group of associated variables.
– objects: are instances of a class (p.158)	In what sense is an object an instance of a class? Which class?
– objects: this reference (p.180)	What does **this** mean (when used as an expression)? Where can we use it?
– is a type (p.161)	What values are contained in the Date type?
– making instances with new (p.162)	What does a constructor method always do which, unlike other methods, is *not* stated in its heading?
– accessing instance variables (p.164)	What is the similarity in the notation for accessing class methods of a class and instance variables of an object?

Method	

– accepting parameters: of a class type (p.164)	Assuming the `Point` example from the chapter, is the following code legal, and if so, what will be output?
	
	``java
	if (new Point(10, 20)
	        .equals(new Point(10, 20)))
	    System.out.println
	      ("The two points are equivalent");
	else
	    System.out.println
	      ("The two points are not equivalent");
	``

– returning a value: of a class type (p.176)	Assuming the `Point` example from the chapter, is the following code legal, and if so, what will be output?
	
	``java
	System.out.println
	  (new Point(10, 10)
	      .halfWayPoint(new Point(20, 20)));
	``

– constructor methods (p.159)	How is the declaration of a constructor method distinguishable from other methods? How do we ensure that instance variables get a value which is appropriate to the object they belong to?
– class versus instance methods (p.166)	What are the differences between class methods and instance methods? How does an instance method know which instance variables to use for variable names without an object reference and a dot before them?
– a method may have no parameters (p.173)	In what sort of circumstances are we likely to want a method that has no parameters?

Type	
– `String`: conversion: from object (p.177)	What is the name of the instance method that allows us to have control of this conversion?
– primitive versus reference (p.162)	Which types, if any, are both primitive and reference? What about `String`?

Variable	
– instance variables (p.159)	What are the differences between a class variable and an instance variable, and how do we state which is which?
– instance variables: should be private by default (p.175)	What do we gain by making our instance variables private?
– of a class type (p.161)	How do we declare a variable of type `Date`?
– of a class type: stores a reference to an object (p.162)	What possible values can a variable of type `Date` hold?
– of a class type: stores a reference to an object: avoid misunderstanding (p.170)	What are the two common mistakes regarding variables, objects and references?

Chapter 11

Object oriented design

Inside every *complex* problem
is a *simple* view of it.

If you *start* with the *complex* problem,
you can *find* a *complex* solution.

If you *find* the *simple* view
you can *end* with a *simple* solution.

11.1   Chapter aims

In this chapter we take a second look at the technology introduced in the previous one, but this time consider how we approach the **design** of programs if we already know those ideas from the start. This is called **object oriented design**. First we revisit the AgeHistory2 program, adding in the extra feature of each person having a name as well as a birthday. For the sake of variety, we also give this version a **textual user interface** rather than rely on **command line arguments**. Our second example is a model of greedy children eating ice cream. This could form the basis of a simple computer game, but its particular interest here is that it has **mutable objects** – ones which can change their **object state**. This leads to us observing that some **instance methods** are **accessor methods**, and some are **mutator methods**.

The chapter contains the following sections.

Section	Aims	Associated Course-work
11.2 Age history revisited (p.184)	To introduce the principles of **object oriented design**. We also meet Scanner, **standard input**, Java's **package** structure and **import statement**, the **null reference**, **final variables**, multiple **return statements**, the **line separator system property**, and take a look at making **stubs** of classes and using **multi-line comments**.	Write a program to create and process two-dimensional shapes. (p.197)
11.3 Greedy children (p.201)	To reinforce **object oriented design**, particularly with **mutable objects**. We also meet multiple **constructor methods**, **class constants**, the **return statement** with no value, **accessor methods**, **mutator methods**, the dangers of **method parameters** which are **references**, converting the **null reference** to a string, and Math.random().	Write a program that simulates the behaviour of students using their mobile phones. (p.212)

Section	Aims	Associated Course-work
11.4 Greedy children gone wrong (p.215)	To look at the idea of an **object referenced by more than one variable** and the danger this presents when it is a **mutable object**.	(None.)

11.2 Example: Age history revisited

AIM:
To introduce the principles of **object oriented design**. We also meet `Scanner`, **standard input**, Java's **package** structure and **import statement**, the **null reference**, **final variable**s, multiple **return statements**, the **line separator system property**, and take a look at making **stub**s of **class**es and using **multi-line comment**s.

In the previous chapter we used the `AgeHistory2` program as a vehicle for introducing and motivating the Java concepts needed to support **object oriented programming**. Of course, we would not really develop a program in that manner, that is, by first writing it without using **object**s and gradually re-designing it until it uses them appropriately. We would instead get it right straight away! So in this section we revisit the program and use it this time as a vehicle to introduce the concept of **object oriented design**, showing how we would approach the development with the appropriate use of object orientation from the beginning.

Concept **Design: object oriented design.** When we are developing programs in an **object oriented programming** language, such as Java, we should use the principle of **object oriented design**. We start by identifying the **class**es we shall have in the program, by examining the **requirements statement** of the problem which the program is to solve. This is recognizing the idea that problems inherently involve interactions between 'real world' objects. These will be modelled in our program, by it creating **object**s which are **instance**s of the classes we identify.

In this view then, an object is an entity which has some kind of **object state** which might change over time, and some kind of **object behaviour** which might be based on its state.

From the requirements, we think carefully about the state and the behaviour of the objects in the problem. Then we decide how to model their behaviour using **instance method**s, and their state using **instance variable**s. There may, in general, be a need for **class variable**s and **class method**s too.

Coffee time: `11.2.1`   Why do you think the pieces of code making up a Java program are called **class**es?

The `AgeHistory` program in this section is a little different from the previous versions. Here is the **requirements statement** for it.

A program is required that will print out, on the **standard output**, the age history of any number of people. Each person has a name and a birth date. The age history of a person consists of a statement of their birth on their birth date, followed by a statement of their age on each of their birthdays which have occurred *before* the present date. Finally it ends with a statement saying what age they will be on their next birthday, including the present date, if their birthday is today. However, if the person has not yet been born, or is born on the present date then their age history consists merely of a statement stating or predicting their birth.

The program shall be **interactive** with a **textual user interface**. It shall prompt for the present date, to be entered by the user as three **integer**s in the order day, month then year. Then it shall prompt for the number of persons, which is to be entered as an integer. Then, for each person, it shall prompt for his or her name, to be entered as a string, and date of birth, to be entered as three integers in the order day, month then year. Then it shall produce the age history for that person.

The program is allowed to assume that the number of persons and components of dates are entered as strings representing legal integers. If the entered number of persons is **less than** one, the program will quietly do nothing more.

11.2.1 Identifying the classes

To help discover what classes we shall need in our program, we can use the technique of **noun identification**.

Concept **Design: object oriented design: noun identification.** One way to analyse the **requirements statement** in order to decide what **class**es to have in the program, is to simply go through the requirements and list all the nouns and noun phrases we can find. This is called **noun identification** and is useful because the objects inherent in the solution to most problems actually appear as nouns in the description of the problem. Some of the nouns will relate to **object**s that will exist at **run time**, and some will relate to classes in the program.

It is not the case that every noun found will be a class or an object, of course, and sometimes we need classes that do not appear as nouns in the requirements. However, the technique is usually a good way of starting the process.

Let us list the singular versions of the nouns (and noun phrases) found in our requirements (e.g. "people" is the plural of "person", and so we treat it as "person".) For each we analyse its use, and decide whether it will be a class, an object, or neither.

Noun	Usage in requirements	Class, object or how/what?
age	A number	`int`
age history	An effect on the output	A `String` with many lines
birth	An event to be reported	Part of age history
birth date	A date belonging to a person	An object, **instance variable** of a person
birthday	An event to be reported	Part of age history
component of date	Strings entered by the user	Become values of instance variables of `Date`
date of birth	Same as birth date	-
date	Used for present date, birth dates and birthdays	A class
day	Part of a date, a number	Instance variable in date objects
integer	Standard stuff	`int`
month	Part of a date, a number	Instance variable in date objects
name	A string belonging to a person	Instance variable of a person
number	Standard stuff	`int`
person	Many people inherent in problem	A class
present date	A date	An object
program	Standard stuff	A class to contain the main method
standard output	Standard stuff	Via `System.out.println()`
statement	An effect on the output	Via `System.out.println()`
string	Standard stuff	`String`
textual user interface	User interaction with program	**Via standard input**
today	Same as present date	-
user	The real person using the program	Via standard input and **standard output**
year	Part of a date, a number	Instance variable in date objects

So, we shall have three classes in our program: `AgeHistory`, `Date` and `Person`.

Class list for AgeHistory	
Class	**Description**
`AgeHistory`	The main class containing the **main method**. It will interact with the user and make instances of `Date` and `Person`.
`Date`	An instance of this will represent a date.
`Person`	An instance of this will represent a person.

11.2.2   Designing the class interfaces

Next we think about the three classes in our program, and how they interact. The **main method** will create a `Date` object for the present date, and this will need to be stored somewhere. As it is a date, the most appropriate place to put it is inside the `Date` class, **referenced** by a **class variable**. This follows a **design** principle prevalent in **object oriented programming**, that of **putting the logic where the data is**. The main method will then create a `Person` object for each person. This will require a `Date` object to be created for the person's birth date. Having created a `Person` object, the main method can obtain the age history of that person and print it out. It is appropriate to have an **instance method** in the `Person` class, which **return**s a `String` containing the age history of that person. This instance method will need to know the present date, which it can obtain from the `Date` class.

Public method interfaces for class **AgeHistory**.			
Method	**Return**	**Arguments**	**Description**
main	**void**	String[]	The main method for the program.

Public method interfaces for class **Date**.			
Method	**Return**	**Arguments**	**Description**
setPresentDate		Date	A **class method**: sets the present date to be the one given. This is ignored if the present date has already been been set.
getPresentDate	Date		A class method: returns the present date as set by `setPresentDate()`.
Constructor		int, int, int	Constructs a date representing the given day, month and then year values.
toString	String		Returns the day/month/year representation of the date.
equals	**boolean**	Date	Returns **true** if and only if this object represents the same date as the given other date.
lessThan	**boolean**	Date	Returns **true** if and only if this object represents a date earlier than that represented by the given other date.
addYear	Date		Returns a new date, one year on from this one.

Public method interfaces for class **Person**.			
Method	**Return**	**Arguments**	**Description**
Constructor		String, Date	Constructs a person with the given name and birth date.
ageHistory	String		Returns the age history of this person as a string with **new line**s in it.

We check our design so far, to ensure that we are happy that it has the appropriate **encapsulation** inherent in it.

Concept **Design: object oriented design: encapsulation.** An important principle in **object oriented design** is the idea of **encapsulation**. A well designed **class** encapsulates the behaviour of the **object**s that can be created from it, in such a way that in order to use the class, one only needs to know about its **public methods** (including **constructor methods**) and what they mean, rather than how they work and what **instance variable**s the class may have. To help achieve good encapsulation, we follow the principle of **putting the logic where the data is** – all the code pertaining to the behaviour of particular objects are included in their class, rather than sprinkled around the various different classes of the program.

Encapsulation is an instance of **abstraction**. Abstraction is the process of ignoring detail which is not necessary for us to know (at the moment). We can use a class without having to know how it works, for example, if it is written by somebody else. Or, we can **design** the details of one class at a time for our programs, without at that moment being concerned with the details of how the other classes work.

For an example which has little to do with Java, assume you have just bought a cheap DVD TV recorder from your local supermarket. Do you need to know how it works in order to use it? Do you need to remove the case lid in order to use it? No, you only need to know about the buttons on the *outside* of the case. That is, until it breaks (after all it was a cheap one). Only at that point do you, or perhaps better still a TV gadget engineer, need to remove the case and poke around inside.

Now that the interfaces have been identified, we can proceed with the development of each class.

11.2.3 The `AgeHistory` class

We have seen, and are about to see again, the idea of making **new instances** of **class**es we have written ourselves. It will come as no surprise that we can also make instances of many of the classes which come with Java in its **application program interface (API)**. In this program we are going to have a **textual user interface**, reading from the **standard input** using an instance of a class called `Scanner`.

Concept **Operating environment: standard input.** In addition to **standard output**, when programs **execute** they also have a **standard input** which allows text **data** to be entered into the program as it runs. If they are **run** from some kind of **command line interface**, such as a Unix **shell** or a Microsoft Windows **Command Prompt**, then this input is typically typed on the keyboard by the end user.

Concept **Standard API: `System: in`.** Inside the `System` **class**, in addition to the **class variable** called `out`, there is another called `in`. This contains a **reference** to an **object** which represents the **standard input** of the program.

Perhaps surprisingly, unlike the **standard output**, the standard input in Java is not easy to use as it is, and we typically access it via some other means, such as a `Scanner`.

In order for us to use `Scanner`, we need to know that the classes supplied as standard with Java are arranged into **packages**.

Concept **Package.** There are hundreds of **class**es that come with Java in its **application program interface (API)**, and even more that are available around the world for reusing in our programs if we wish. To help manage this huge number of classes, they are grouped into collections of related classes, called **packages**. But even this is not enough

---

to make things manageable, so packages are grouped into a hierarchy in a rather similar way to how a well organized **file system** is arranged into directories and sub-directories. For example, there is one group of standard packages called `java` and another called `javax`.

Concept **Package: `java.util`.** One of the standard Java **package**s in the package group `java` is called `util`. This means its full name is `java.util` – the package addressing mechanism uses a dot (`.`) in much the same way as Unix uses a slash, or Microsoft Windows uses a backslash, to separate directories in a filename path. `java.util` contains many generally useful utility **class**es. For example, there is a class called `Scanner` which lives there, so its **fully qualified name** is `java.util.Scanner`. This fully qualified name is unique: if someone else was to create a class called `Scanner` then it would not be in the same package, so the two would not be confused.

We can refer to a class using its fully qualified name, for example the following declares a **variable** of **type** `java.util.Scanner` and creates an **instance** of the class too.

```
java.util.Scanner inputScanner = new java.util.Scanner(System.in);
```

It would be very tiresome if every time we wanted to refer to a class in some **package** we had to use its **fully qualified name**, so Java permits us to **import** classes instead.

Concept **Class: importing classes.** At the start of the source **file** for a Java **class** we can write one or more **import statement**s. These start with the **reserved word `import`** and then give the **fully qualified name** of a class that lives in some **package** somewhere, followed by a semi-colon(`;`). An **import** for a class permits us to talk about it from then on, by using only its class name, rather than having to always write its fully qualified name. For example, importing `java.util.Scanner` would mean that every time we refer to `Scanner` the Java **compiler** knows we really mean `java.util.Scanner`.

```
import java.util.Scanner;
  ...
  Scanner inputScanner = new Scanner(System.in);
```

If we wish, we can import all the classes in a package using a * instead of a class name.

```
import java.util.*;
```

Many programmers consider this to be lazy, and it is better to import exactly what is needed, if only to help show precisely what is used by the class. There is also the issue of ambiguity: if two different packages have classes with the same name, but this class only needs one of them, then the lazy approach would cause an unnecessary problem.

However, every Java program has an automatic import for every class in the standard **package** `java.lang`, because these classes are used so regularly. That is why we can refer to `java.lang.System` and `java.lang.Integer`, etc. as just `System` and `Integer`, etc.. In other words, every class always implicitly includes the following import statement for convenience.

```
import java.lang.*;
```

In our age history program, we are going to use a `Scanner` working with `System.in` to get **data** from the user.

Concept **Standard API: `Scanner`.** Since the advent of Java 5.0 there is a standard **class** called `java.util.Scanner` which provides some simple features to read input **data**. In particular, it can be used to read `System.in` by passing that to its **constructor method** as follows.

```
import java.util.Scanner;
    ...
    Scanner inputScanner = new Scanner(System.in);
    ...
```

Each time we want a line of text we invoke the nextLine() **instance method**.

```
    String line = inputScanner.nextLine();
    ...
```

Or maybe we want to read an **integer** using nextInt().

```
    int aNumber = inputScanner.nextInt();
    // Skip past anything on the same line following the number.
    inputScanner.nextLine();
    ...
```

Essentially, System.in accesses the **standard input** as a stream of **byte**s of data. A Scanner turns these bytes into a stream of **characters** (i.e. **char** values) and offers a variety of instance methods to scan these into whole lines, or various tokens separated by **white space**, such as spaces, tabs and end of lines. Some of these instance methods are listed below.

Public method interfaces for class **Scanner** (some of them).			
Method	**Return**	**Arguments**	**Description**
nextLine	String		Returns all the text from the current point in the character stream up to the next end of line, as a String.
nextInt	int		Skips any spaces, tabs and end of lines and then reads characters which represent an integer, and **returns** that value as an **int**. It does not skip spaces, tabs or end of lines following those characters. The characters must represent an integer, or a **run time error** will occur.
nextBoolean	boolean		Similar to nextInt() except for a **boolean** value.
nextByte	byte		Similar to nextInt() except for a **byte** value.
nextDouble	double		Similar to nextInt() except for a **double** value.
nextFloat	float		Similar to nextInt() except for a **float** value.
nextLong	long		Similar to nextInt() except for a **long** value.
nextShort	short		Similar to nextInt() except for a **short** value.

There are very many more features in this class, including the ability to change what is considered to be characters that separate the various tokens.

So our program starts with an **import statement**.

```
001: import java.util.Scanner;
```

As usual, we have a **comment** at the start of our program about what it does and how it is used. In this case we can copy some of the text from the **requirements statement** and edit it. As this will span several lines, it is most convenient to use a **multi-line comment**.

Concept **Code clarity: comments: multi-line comments.** Another form of **comment** in Java allows us to have text which spans several lines. These start with the symbol /* and end with the symbol */, which typically will be several lines later in the code. These symbols, and all text between them, is ignored by the **compiler**.

Less usefully, we can have the start and end symbols on the same line, with program code on either side of the comment, if we wish.

Coffee time: One use of multi-line comments is to 'comment out' a section of code during development, perhaps because it is not completed yet. Do you think we can nest multi-line comments in Java, that is, have such a comment inside another one? Can we have single line comments inside a multi-line comment?

```
003: /* Program to print out the history of any number of named people's ages.
004:
005:     The age history of a person consists of a statement of their birth on their
006:     birth date, followed by a statement of their age on each of their birthdays
007:     which have occurred before the present date. Finally it ends with a
008:     statement saying what age they will be on their next birthday, including
009:     the present date, if their birthday is today. However, if the person has
010:     not yet been born, or is born on the present date then their age history
011:     consists merely of a statement stating or predicting their birth.
012:
013:     It first prompts for the present date, to be entered by the user as three
014:     integers in the order day, month then year. Then it prompts for the number
015:     of persons, which is to be entered as an integer. Then, for each person, it
016:     prompts for his or her name, to be entered as a string, and date of birth,
017:     to be entered as three integers in the order day, month then year. Then it
018:     produces the age history for that person.
019: */
020: public class AgeHistory
021: {
```

The **main method** creates a Scanner for System.in and uses it to interact with the user.

```
022:     public static void main(String[] args)
023:     {
024:         // For interaction with the user.
025:         Scanner inputScanner = new Scanner(System.in);
026:
027:         // The Date class needs to be told the present date.
028:         System.out.print("Enter today's date as three numbers, dd mm yyyy: ");
029:         int day = inputScanner.nextInt();
030:         int month = inputScanner.nextInt();
031:         int year = inputScanner.nextInt();
032:         Date.setPresentDate(new Date(day, month, year));
033:
034:         // Now find out how many people there are.
035:         System.out.print("Enter the number of people: ");
036:         int noOfPeople = inputScanner.nextInt();
037:         // Skip to the next line of input
038:         // or else first name will be blank!
039:         inputScanner.nextLine();
040:
041:         // For each person...
042:         for (int count = 1; count <= noOfPeople; count++)
043:         {
044:             // Obtain name and birthday.
```

```
045:        System.out.print("Enter the name of person " + count + ": ");
046:        String name = inputScanner.nextLine();
047:        System.out.print("Enter his/her birthday (dd mm yyyy): ");
048:        int birthDay = inputScanner.nextInt();
049:        int birthMonth = inputScanner.nextInt();
050:        int birthYear = inputScanner.nextInt();
051:        // Skip to next line, or else next name will be blank!
052:        inputScanner.nextLine();
053:
054:        Date birthDate = new Date(birthDay, birthMonth, birthYear);
055:        Person person = new Person(name, birthDate);
056:        System.out.println(person.ageHistory());
057:    } // for
058: } // main
059:
060: } // class AgeHistory
```

11.2.4 Stubbing Date and Person

Suppose we wanted to **compile** the AgeHistory **class** before we write the Date and Person classes. We would of course get **compile time errors**.

```
                    Console Input / Output
$ javac AgeHistory.java
AgeHistory.java:32: cannot find symbol
symbol  : class Date
location: class AgeHistory
        Date.setPresentDate(new Date(day, month, year));
                                     ^

AgeHistory.java:32: cannot find symbol
symbol  : variable Date
location: class AgeHistory
        Date.setPresentDate(new Date(day, month, year));
        ^

AgeHistory.java:54: cannot find symbol
symbol  : class Date
location: class AgeHistory
          Date birthDate = new Date(birthDay, birthMonth, birthYear);
                 ^

AgeHistory.java:54: cannot find symbol
symbol  : class Date
location: class AgeHistory
          Date birthDate = new Date(birthDay, birthMonth, birthYear);
                               ^

AgeHistory.java:55: cannot find symbol
symbol  : class Person
location: class AgeHistory
          Person person = new Person(name, birthDate);
                 ^

AgeHistory.java:55: cannot find symbol
symbol  : class Person
location: class AgeHistory
          Person person = new Person(name, birthDate);
                              ^

6 errors
$ _
```

However, if we want to *successfully* compile the program this early in the development, we can quickly create **stub**s for the other classes.

Concept **Class: stub.** During development of a program with several **class**es, we often produce a **stub** for the classes we have not yet implemented. This just contains some or all of the **public** items of the class, with empty, or almost empty, bodies for the **method**s. In other words, it is the bare minimum needed to allow the classes we have so far developed to be **compile**d.

Any **non-void method**s are written with a single **return statement** to yield some temporary value of the right **type**.

These stubs are then developed into the full class code at some later stage.

For example, stubs for the Person and Date classes could be as follows.

```
001: public class Person
002: {
003:   public Person(String s, Date d) {}
004:   public String ageHistory() { return "An age history"; }
005: } // class Person
```

```
001: public class Date
002: {
003:   public Date(int d, int m, int y) {}
004:   public static void setPresentDate(Date d) {}
005: } // class Date
```

Coffee time: 11.2.3 Are you surprised that Java lets us put the body of a **method** on the same line as its heading? That may be fine for stubs which will be thrown away shortly, but do you think it is appropriate for proper code? Ever?

With these stubs we can compile AgeHistory.java without getting any errors.

Console Input / Output
`$ javac AgeHistory.java`
`$ _`

We can even **run** the program!

Console Input / Output
`$ java AgeHistory`
`Enter today's date as three numbers, dd mm yyyy: 30 03 2015`
`Enter the number of people: 0`
`$ _`

Of course, if we run it with **test data** for more than zero persons, it will only print a single line per person, containing the text An age history.

Console Input / Output
`$ java AgeHistory`
`Enter today's date as three numbers, dd mm yyyy: 30 03 2015`
`Enter the number of people: 2`
`Enter the name of person 1: John`
`Enter his/her birthday (dd mm yyyy): 24 4 1959`
`An age history`
`Enter the name of person 2: Alison`
`Enter his/her birthday (dd mm yyyy): 27 11 1982`
`An age history`
`$ _`

Once we are satisfied that the AgeHistory code probably works, we can embark on the full development of the other classes.

11.2.5 The Date class

The Date **class** here is very similar to that in the previous chapter. The main difference is the **class variable** to store the present date, and the **class method**s to set and access it. This **variable** will refer to a Date **object** after the present date has been set, but to start off with it contains a **null reference**.

Concept **Variable: of a class type: null reference.** When an **object** is created, the **constructor method return**s a **reference** to it, which is then used for all accesses to the object. Typically, this reference is stored in a **variable**.

```
Point p1 = new Point(75, 150);
```

There is a special reference value, known as the **null reference**, which does not refer to an object. We can talk about it using the **reserved word null**. It is used, for example, as a value for a variable when we do not want it to refer to any object at this moment in time.

```
Point p2 = null;
```

So, in the example code here we have two Point variables, p1 and p2, but (at **run time**) only one Point object.

Suppose the Point **class** has **instance method**s getX() and getY() with their obvious implementations. Then obtaining the *x* value of the object referenced by p1 is fine; the following code would print 75.

```
System.out.println(p1.getX());
```

However, the similar code involving p2 would cause a **run time error** (an **exception** called NullPointerException).

```
System.out.println(p2.getX());
```

This is because there is no object referenced by p2, and so any attempt to access the referenced object must fail.

Here is the Date code.

```
001: // Representation of a date.
002: public class Date
003: {
004:   // Class variable to hold the present date.
005:   private static Date presentDate = null;
006:
007:
008:   // Class method to set the present date.
009:   // This does nothing if it has already been set.
010:   public static void setPresentDate(Date requiredPresentDate)
011:   {
012:     if (presentDate == null)
013:       presentDate = requiredPresentDate;
014:   } // setPresentDate
015:
016:
017:   // Class method to obtain the present date.
018:   public static Date getPresentDate()
019:   {
020:     return presentDate;
021:   } // getPresentDate
```

We intend, as was true in the previous versions of this program, that **instance**s of the Date class are **immutable objects**.

Concept **Class: objects: may be mutable or immutable.** Sometimes when we **design** a **class** we desire that the **instance**s of it are **immutable objects**. This means that once such an **object** has been **construct**ed, its **object state** cannot be changed. That is, there is no way for the values of the **instance variable**s to be altered after the object is constructed.

By contrast, objects which can be altered are known as **mutable object**s.

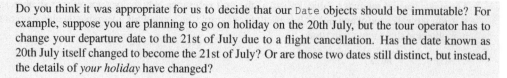

Coffee time: `11.2.4` Do you think it was appropriate for us to decide that our `Date` objects should be immutable? For example, suppose you are planning to go on holiday on the 20th July, but the tour operator has to change your departure date to the 21st of July due to a flight cancellation. Has the date known as 20th July itself changed to become the 21st of July? Or are those two dates still distinct, but instead, the details of *your holiday* have changed?

One way to ensure that our `Date` objects are immutable, is to declare all the **instance variable**s as being **final variable**s.

Concept **Variable: final variables.** When we declare a **variable** we can write the **reserved word final** as one of its **modifier**s before the **type** name. This means that once the variable has been given a value, that value cannot be altered.

If an **instance variable** is declared to be a **final variable** then it must be explicitly assigned a value by the time the **object** it belongs to has finished being **construct**ed. This would be done either by assigning a value in the **variable declaration**, or via an **assignment statement** inside the **constructor method**.

```
024:   // Instance variables: the day, month and year of a date.
025:   private final int day, month, year;
```

The rest of the class is the same as it was previously.

```
028:   // Construct a date -- given the required day, month and year.
029:   public Date(int requiredDay, int requiredMonth, int requiredYear)
030:   {
031:     day = requiredDay;
032:     month = requiredMonth;
033:     year = requiredYear;
034:   } // Date
035:
036:
037:   // Compare this date with a given other one, for equality.
038:   public boolean equals(Date other)
039:   {
040:     return day == other.day && month == other.month && year == other.year;
041:   } // equals
042:
043:
044:   // Compare this date with a given other one, for less than.
045:   public boolean lessThan(Date other)
046:   {
047:     return year < other.year
048:            || year == other.year
049:               && (month < other.month
050:                   || month == other.month && day < other.day);
051:   } // lessThan
052:
053:
054:   // Return the day/month/year representation of the date.
055:   public String toString()
056:   {
057:     return day + "/" + month + "/" + year;
058:   } // toString
059:
060:
061:   // Return a new Date which is one year later than this one.
062:   public Date addYear()
063:   {
064:     return new Date(day, month, year + 1);
065:   } // addYear
066:
067: } // class Date
```

11.2.6 The `Person` class

Now we create the **class** called `Person` that will hold a name, a date of birth and offer an `ageHistory()` **instance method**. We wish the **instance**s of this to be **immutable object**s.

```
001: // Representation of a person.
002: public class Person
003: {
004:   // The name and birthday of a person.
005:   private final String name;
006:   private final Date birthDate;
007:
008:
009:   // Construct a person -- given the required name and birthday.
010:   public Person(String requiredName, Date requiredBirthDate)
011:   {
012:     name = requiredName;
013:     birthDate = requiredBirthDate;
014:   } // Person
```

The result **return**ed by the `ageHistory()` instance method is a `String` which contains **new line**s inside it. Rather than just using a **new line character** to separate the lines, we shall use the platform dependent **line separator** so that our program is portable.

Concept **Standard API: System: getProperty().** When a program is **running**, various **system property** values hold information about such things as the Java version and platform being used, the home directory of the user, etc.. The **class method** `System.getProperty()` takes the name of such a property as its `String` **method parameter** and **return**s the corresponding `String` value.

Concept **Standard API: System: getProperty(): line.separator.** `System.getProperty()` maps the name `line.separator` onto the **system property** which is the **line separator** for the platform in use.

We shall store (a **reference** to) the line separator in a **variable**, with a conveniently short name, and use that where we might otherwise have written `"\n"`. (We also provide a way to change it so we can reuse the class in Section 13.13 on page 277 where the value *must* be `"\n"`!)

```
017:   // The correct line separator for this platform.
018:   private static String NLS = System.getProperty("line.separator");
019:
020:   // Override the default line separator.
021:   public static void setLineSeparator(String requiredLineSeparator)
022:   {
023:     NLS = requiredLineSeparator;
024:   } // setLineSeparator
025:
026:
027:   // Return the age history of this person.
028:   public String ageHistory()
029:   {
030:     Date presentDate = Date.getPresentDate();
031:
```

```
032:     // Deal with cases where the person has just been born
033:     // or is not yet born.
034:     if (presentDate.equals(birthDate))
035:       return name + " was, or will be, born today!";
036:     else if (presentDate.lessThan(birthDate))
037:       return name + " will be born on " + birthDate;
038:     else // The person was born before today.
039:     {
040:       // Start with the event of birth.
041:       String result = name + " was born on " + birthDate;
042:
043:       // Now we will go through the years since birth but before today.
044:       // We keep track of the birthday we are considering.
045:       Date someBirthday = birthDate.addYear();
046:       int ageOnSomeBirthday = 1;
047:       while (someBirthday.lessThan(presentDate))
048:       {
049:         result += NLS + name + " was " + ageOnSomeBirthday
050:                    + " on " + someBirthday;
051:         someBirthday = someBirthday.addYear();
052:         ageOnSomeBirthday++;
053:       } // while
054:
055:       // Now deal with the next birthday.
056:       if (someBirthday.equals(presentDate))
057:         result += NLS + name + " is " + ageOnSomeBirthday + " today!";
058:       else
059:         result += NLS + name + " will be " + ageOnSomeBirthday
060:                    + " on " + someBirthday;
061:
062:       return result;
063:     } // else
064:   } // ageHistory
065:
066: } // class Person
```

The generation of an age history is done in the `Person` class, because it is about persons, whereas the code to print an age history to **standard output** is in the `AgeHistory` class, because that is what *this* program needs to do. At some point in the future, we may require a program that, say, writes age histories to a **file**. Because we have followed the rule of **putting the logic where the data is** and achieved good **encapsulation**, we would be able to use the `Person` class in that program without needing to change it.

Notice the multiple occurrences of the **return statement** in the above code.

Concept **Method: returning a value: multiple returns.** The **return statement** is how we specify what value is to be **return**ed as the result of a **non-void method**. The **statement** causes the execution to end, and control to transfer back to the code that called the **method**. Typically, this is written as the last statement in the method, but we can actually write one or more anywhere in the method.

The Java **compiler** checks to make sure that we have been sensible, and that:

- There is no path through the method that does not end with a return statement.
- There is no code in the method that can never be reached due to an earlier occurring return statement.

 Coffee time: [11.2.5] Does the above `ageHistory()` instance method satisfy those rules?

11.2.7 Trying it

We can **run** the program with various inputs – this is nowhere near a full set of tests.

Console Input / Output

```
$ java AgeHistory
Enter today's date as three numbers, dd mm yyyy: 30 03 2015
Enter the number of people: 1
Enter the name of person 1: Joey
Enter his/her birthday (dd mm yyyy): 30 03 2015
Joey was, or will be, born today!
$ _
```

Console Input / Output

```
$ java AgeHistory
Enter today's date as three numbers, dd mm yyyy: 30 03 2015
Enter the number of people: 1
Enter the name of person 1: Abi
Enter his/her birthday (dd mm yyyy): 31 03 2015
Abi will be born on 31/3/2015
$ _
```

Console Input / Output

```
$ java AgeHistory
Enter today's date as three numbers, dd mm yyyy: 30 03 2015
Enter the number of people: 2
Enter the name of person 1: John
Enter his/her birthday (dd mm yyyy): 24 4 1959
John was born on 24/4/1959
John was 1 on 24/4/1960
John was 2 on 24/4/1961
(... lines removed to save space.)
John will be 56 on 24/4/2015
Enter the name of person 2: Alison
Enter his/her birthday (dd mm yyyy): 27 11 1982
Alison was born on 27/11/1982
Alison was 1 on 27/11/1983
Alison was 2 on 27/11/1984
(... lines removed to save space.)
Alison will be 33 on 27/11/2015
$ _
```

11.2.8 Coursework: `ShapeShift`

Here you will create a program called `ShapeShift` which does calculations and manipulations of simple shapes. The main class has been written for you – here it is.

```
001: import java.util.Scanner;
002:
003: /* This program performs simple calculations and manipulations of
004:    simple shapes expressed in two-dimensional coordinate geometry.
005:
006:    First it asks the user to choose a shape, from a choice of three.
007:    Then it prompts for details of the shape.
008:    *  A circle is specified by giving the X and then Y coordinate
009:       of its centre, followed by its radius.
010:    *  A Triangle is specified by giving the X and Y coordinates
011:       of each of its three corner points.
012:    *  A rectangle is specified by giving the X and Y coordinates
013:       of two of its diagonally opposite corner points.
014:
015:    Following this data, the user is prompted to specify an X offset
016:    and a Y offset.
017:
```

197

```
018:    The program creates the specified shape, and also a similar one,
019:    in which each point has been shifted by the X and Y offsets.
020:
021:    The program then reports the following on the standard output.
022:    *    The details of the original shape -- giving all the points
023:         (one, three, or four) and, for a circle, its radius.
024:    *    The area and perimeter of the shape.
025:    *    The details of the shifted shape.
026: */
027: public class ShapeShift
028: {
029:    // A scanner to interact with the user.
030:    private static Scanner inputScanner = new Scanner(System.in);
031:
032:
033:    // Helper method to read a point from the input.
034:    private static Point inputPoint(String prompt)
035:    {
036:      System.out.print(prompt);
037:      double x = inputScanner.nextDouble();
038:      double y = inputScanner.nextDouble();
039:      return new Point(x, y);
040:    } // inputPoint
041:
042:
043:    // The X and Y amount to shift the first shape to get the second.
044:    private static double xShift, yShift;
045:
046:
047:    // Helper method to read the X and Y shifts.
048:    private static void inputXYShifts()
049:    {
050:      System.out.print("Enter the offset as X Y: ");
051:      xShift = inputScanner.nextDouble();
052:      yShift = inputScanner.nextDouble();
053:    } // inputXYShifts
054:
055:
056:    // The main method.
057:    public static void main(String[] args)
058:    {
059:      // Obtain shape choice.
060:      System.out.print("Choose circle (1), triangle (2), rectangle (3): ");
061:      int shapeChoice = inputScanner.nextInt();
062:
063:      // Process the shape based on the choice.
064:      switch (shapeChoice)
065:      {
066:        // Circle.
067:        case 1:
068:          Point centre = inputPoint("Enter the centre as X Y: ");
069:          System.out.print("Enter the radius: ");
070:          double radius = inputScanner.nextDouble();
```

```
071:                Circle originalCircle = new Circle(centre, radius);
072:                inputXYShifts();
073:                Circle shiftedCircle = originalCircle.shift(xShift, yShift);
074:                System.out.println();
075:                System.out.println(originalCircle);
076:                System.out.println("has area " + originalCircle.area()
077:                                + ", perimeter " + originalCircle.perimeter());
078:                System.out.println("and when shifted by X offset " + xShift
079:                                + " and Y offset " + yShift + ", gives");
080:                System.out.println(shiftedCircle);
081:            break;
082:
083:         // Triangle.
084:         case 2:
085:             Point pointA = inputPoint("Enter point A as X Y: ");
086:             Point pointB = inputPoint("Enter point B as X Y: ");
087:             Point pointC = inputPoint("Enter point C as X Y: ");
088:             Triangle originalTriangle = new Triangle(pointA, pointB, pointC);
089:             inputXYShifts();
090:             Triangle shiftedTriangle = originalTriangle.shift(xShift, yShift);
091:             System.out.println();
092:             System.out.println(originalTriangle);
093:             System.out.println("has area " + originalTriangle.area()
094:                                + ", perimeter " + originalTriangle.perimeter());
095:             System.out.println("and when shifted by X offset " + xShift
096:                                + " and Y offset " + yShift + ", gives");
097:             System.out.println(shiftedTriangle);
098:            break;
099:
100:         // Rectangle.
101:         case 3:
102:             Point diag1End1 = inputPoint("Enter one corner as X Y: ");
103:             Point diag1End2 = inputPoint("Enter opposite corner as X Y: ");
104:             Rectangle originalRectangle = new Rectangle(diag1End1, diag1End2);
105:             inputXYShifts();
106:             Rectangle shiftedRectangle = originalRectangle.shift(xShift, yShift);
107:             System.out.println();
108:             System.out.println(originalRectangle);
109:             System.out.println("has area " + originalRectangle.area()
110:                                + ", perimeter " + originalRectangle.perimeter());
111:             System.out.println("and when shifted by X offset " + xShift
112:                                + " and Y offset " + yShift + ", gives");
113:             System.out.println(shiftedRectangle);
114:            break;
115:
116:         // Bad choice.
117:         default:
118:             System.out.println("That wasn't 1, 2 or 3!");
119:            break;
120:     } // switch
121:   } // main
122:
123: } // class ShapeShift
```

All you have to do is write the other classes.

The following are example **run**s of the program to help clarify the requirements.

```
Console Input / Output
$ java ShapeShift
Choose circle (1), triangle (2), rectangle (3): 1
Enter the centre as X Y: 0 0
Enter the radius: 1
Enter the offset as X Y: 2 2

Circle((0.0,0.0),1.0)
has area 3.141592653589793, perimeter 6.283185307179586
and when shifted by X offset 2.0 and Y offset 2.0, gives
Circle((2.0,2.0),1.0)
$ _
```

```
Console Input / Output
$ java ShapeShift
Choose circle (1), triangle (2), rectangle (3): 2
Enter point A as X Y: 0 0
Enter point B as X Y: 10 0
Enter point C as X Y: 0 20
Enter the offset as X Y: 5 10

Triangle((0.0,0.0),(10.0,0.0),(0.0,20.0))
has area 100.0, perimeter 52.3606797749979
and when shifted by X offset 5.0 and Y offset 10.0, gives
Triangle((5.0,10.0),(15.0,10.0),(5.0,30.0))
$ _
```

```
Console Input / Output
$ java ShapeShift
Choose circle (1), triangle (2), rectangle (3): 3
Enter one corner as X Y: 0 0
Enter opposite corner as X Y: 10 20
Enter the offset as X Y: 0 0

Rectangle((0.0,0.0),(10.0,0.0),(10.0,20.0),(0.0,20.0))
has area 200.0, perimeter 60.0
and when shifted by X offset 0.0 and Y offset 0.0, gives
Rectangle((0.0,0.0),(10.0,0.0),(10.0,20.0),(0.0,20.0))
$ _
```

Start by designing your **test data** in your logbook.

Your program will consist of five **class**es, Point, Circle, Triangle, Rectangle and the already given ShapeShift. Next identify and record the **public instance method**s and **class method**s for each of the four classes you will write. Endeavour to associate behaviour (i.e. **method**s) with the most appropriate classes. Here are some hints.

- Which classes should have a toString() instance method?

- Should shape classes have methods to find the area and perimeter of a shape?

- Should they additionally have a method to create a shifted shape from an existing one?

- Shifting shapes requires creating **new** points which are shifts of old ones. Where is that shifting best done?

- Perimeters of certain shapes are based on distances between points – does that suggest an instance method in the Point class?

- Are the points **mutable object**s or **immutable object**s? What about the shapes?

- All **instance variable**s should be **private**, so you may need some instance methods in some classes, to give read access to the instance variables. For example, Point might have getX() and getY().

Next you should write **stubs** for the three shape classes, so that you can **compile** and try out the main class.

Now **design** the implementations of your classes (at a level of **abstraction** that is appropriate to you) and then implement them. Do you want to think about the order of implementation so you can compile them as you proceed? Will you use a stub for `Point`?

Here are some implementation hints.

- To calculate the area of a triangle, you can use Hero's formula. Let a, b and c be the lengths of the sides of the triangle. Then the semi-perimeter, s is

$$s = (a+b+c)/2$$

and the *area* is

$$area = \sqrt{s(s-a)(s-b)(s-c)}$$

- Given two opposite corners of a rectangle, i.e. both ends of one diagonal, $(x1, y1)$ and $(x2, y2)$ the other two corners are found as $(x1, y2)$ and $(x2, y1)$.

Finally record your results. It may well be that during your implementation, you changed your plan of which class should have what method. This is okay, but you should record such changes, and the reason for them.

Optional extra: Dare you consider having another shape, which is an irregular four sided polygon? Assuming the points are given in a sensible order, then computing the perimeter would not be too hard, but how would you get the area?

11.3 Example: Greedy children

AIM: To reinforce **object oriented design**, particularly with **mutable objects**. We also meet multiple **constructor methods**, **class constants**, the **return statement** with no value, **accessor methods**, **mutator methods**, the dangers of **method parameters** which are references, converting the **null reference** to a string, and `Math.random()`.

The example in this section is a program which contains a tongue-in-cheek model of greedy children scoffing ice cream. This could, for example, be part of some computer game for youngsters. Here is the **requirements statement** for the program.

A program is required that will provide a very simple model of the behaviour of greedy children visiting ice cream parlours. Each greedy child has a name and a fixed capacity, which is an amount of ice cream he or she can hold. This capacity can either be specified, or be chosen as a random number up to some maximum. A child also has an amount of ice cream currently in the stomach. This starts off as being zero, but increases through eating, up to his or her capacity. Children can visit ice cream parlours and attempt to eat an amount of ice cream. Being greedy, they may well attempt to eat more than they have room left for, in which case they simply end up spilling the excess ice cream down their T-shirt! A child keeps track of how much ice cream he or she has spilt, which is initially zero.

Ice cream parlours have a name and an amount of ice cream, initially zero. They can accept deliveries of ice cream, which increases their stock level. They also can serve ice cream to greedy children, which reduces their stock level. Greedy children ask for an amount of ice cream, which they will attempt to eat, unless the parlour's stock level is **less than** that amount, in which case the children are served with as much ice cream as is left.

The program should demonstrate the simple model by creating some children and parlours, and have some deliveries made, and children served, etc.. As this is done, reports should be produced on the **standard output**, enabling the user of the program to follow the events. In this sense then, the main method of the program will tell a little story, and can be made to tell a different story by changing the code.

201

11.3.1 Identifying the classes

By analysing the requirements, we can decide to have three **class**es in our program: GreedyChildren, GreedyChild, and IceCreamParlour.

Class list for GreedyChildren	
Class	**Description**
GreedyChildren	The main class containing the **main method**. It will make instances of IceCreamParlour and GreedyChild.
IceCreamParlour	An instance of this will represent an ice cream parlour.
GreedyChild	An instance of this will represent a greedy child.

11.3.2 Designing the class interfaces

We identify the **public method**s in each class.

Public method interfaces for class GreedyChildren.			
Method	**Return**	**Arguments**	**Description**
main	**void**	String[]	The main method for the program.

Public method interfaces for class IceCreamParlour.			
Method	**Return**	**Arguments**	**Description**
Constructor		String	Construct an ice cream parlour with the given String name.
acceptDelivery		**double**	Accept an ice cream delivery of the given amount, which increases the stock level.
tryToServe	**double**	**double**	Attempt to serve the given amount of ice cream, and **return** the amount actually served. This is the amount asked for, or as much as the parlour can provide if the stock is too low. The stock level is reduced by the amount returned.
toString	String		Returns a representation of the ice cream parlour, showing name and stock level.

Public method interfaces for class GreedyChild.			
Method	**Return**	**Arguments**	**Description**
Constructor		String, **double**	Construct a greedy child with the given String name and **double** stomach capacity.
Constructor		String	Construct a greedy child with the given String name and a randomly chosen stomach capacity.
enterParlour		IceCreamParlour	This child enters the given parlour, implicitly leaving any parlour s/he is already in.
leaveParlour			This child leaves the parlour s/he is currently in, if any, so that s/he is not in any parlour afterwards.
Continued...	...	...	...

202

		...continued: **Public method interfaces for class `GreedyChild`.**	
Method	**Return**	**Arguments**	**Description**
eat		double	If this child is in a parlour, s/he attempts to eat ice cream, served by that parlour. The amount desired is the given **double**. The served amount adds to his/her stomach contents, with any excess being spilt once s/he is full. The method has no effect if s/he is not in a parlour.
toString	String		Returns a representation of the greedy child, showing name, capacity, contents, spillage and which parlour the child is currently in.

`GreedyChild` will also have a fixed maximum value for the randomly chosen stomach capacity.

You should have noticed that we plan to have two **constructor method**s for the `GreedyChild` class.

Concept **Method: constructor methods: more than one.** A **class** can have more than one **constructor method** as long as the number, order and/or **type**s of the **method parameter**s are different. This distinction is necessary so that the **compiler** can tell which constructor should be used when an **object** is being created.

Coffee time: 11.3.1 Look at the interface descriptions above and decide which classes will be used to make **mutable objects**.

Now that the interfaces have been identified, we can proceed with the development of each class.

11.3.3 The `IceCreamParlour` class

```
001: /* Ice cream parlours have a name and an amount of ice cream, initially zero.
002:    They can accept deliveries of ice cream, which increases their stock level.
003:    They also can serve ice cream to greedy children, which reduces their stock
004:    level. Greedy children ask for an amount of ice cream, which they will
005:    attempt to eat, unless the parlour's stock level is less than that amount,
006:    in which case the children are served with as much ice cream as is left.
007: */
008: public class IceCreamParlour
009: {
```

The **class** has two **instance variable**s.

```
010:    // The name of the parlour.
011:    private final String name;
012:
013:    // The amount of ice cream in stock.
014:    private double iceCreamInStock = 0;
```

Coffee time: 11.3.2 What is the significance of us making one of these instance variables be a **final variable**, but not the other? Are **instance**s of `IceCreamParlour` **mutable objects**?

The **constructor method** is given the name of the parlour.

```
017:    // Construct an ice cream parlour -- given the required name.
018:    public IceCreamParlour(String requiredName)
019:    {
020:      name = requiredName;
021:    } // IceCreamParlour
```

The parlour can accept a delivery of ice cream.

```
024:    // Accept delivery of ice cream.
025:    public void acceptDelivery(double amount)
026:    {
027:      iceCreamInStock += amount;
028:    } // acceptDelivery
```

When asked to serve an amount of ice cream, the parlour actually serves as much as it can, up to that amount.

```
031:    // Serve ice cream. Attempt to serve the amount desired
032:    // but as much as we can if stock is too low.
033:    // Return the amount served.
034:    public double tryToServe(double desiredAmount)
035:    {
036:      double amountServed = desiredAmount;
037:      if (amountServed > iceCreamInStock)
038:        amountServed = iceCreamInStock;
039:
040:      iceCreamInStock -= amountServed;
041:      return amountServed;
042:    } // tryToServe
```

Finally we have the toString() **instance method**.

```
045:    // Return a String giving the name and state.
046:    public String toString()
047:    {
048:      return name + " has " + iceCreamInStock + " in stock";
049:    } // toString
050:
051: } // class IceCreamParlour
```

11.3.4 The GreedyChild class

```
001: /* Each greedy child has a name and a fixed stomach size, which is an amount
002:    of ice cream he or she can hold. This capacity can either be specified, or
003:    be chosen as a random number up to some maximum. A child also has a current
004:    stomach contents which starts off as being zero, but increases, through
005:    eating, up to his or her stomach size. Children can visit ice cream
006:    parlours and attempt to eat an amount of ice cream. Being greedy, they may
007:    well attempt to eat more than they have room left for, in which case they
008:    simply end up spilling the excess ice cream down their T-shirt! A child
009:    keeps track of how much ice cream he or she has spilt, initially zero.
010: */
011: public class GreedyChild
012: {
```

The **class** has a **class constant** for the maximum randomly chosen stomach capacity.

Concept **Variable: final variables: class constant.** A **class variable** which is declared to be a **final variable** (i.e. its **modifier**s include the **reserved word**s `static` and `final`) is also known in Java as a **class constant**. An example of this is the **variable** in the **class** `java.lang.Math` called `PI`.

```
public static final double PI = 3.14159265358979323846;
```

By convention, class constants are usually named using only capital letters with the words separated by underscores (_).

```
013:   // When a GreedyChild is created with no given capacity
014:   // a random one is chosen up to this maximum.
015:   public static final double MAXIMUM_RANDOM_STOMACH_SIZE = 20.0;
```

The **class** has five **instance variable**s, of which only two are **final variable**s.

```
017:   // The name of the child.
018:   private final String name;
019:
020:   // The amount of ice cream the child can hold before being full.
021:   private final double stomachSize;
022:
023:   // The total amount of ice cream that the child has spilt by
024:   // attempting to eat after being full. Initially zero.
025:   private double tShirtStainSize = 0;
026:
027:   // The amount of ice cream currently in the child's stomach.
028:   // Initially zero.
029:   private double stomachContents = 0;
030:
031:   // The ice cream parlour the child is currently in,
032:   // or null if s/he is not in one.
033:   private IceCreamParlour currentParlour = null;
```

One **constructor method** is given the name and stomach size of the child.

```
036:   // Construct a greedy child  -- given the required name and size.
037:   public GreedyChild(String requiredName, double requiredStomachSize)
038:   {
039:     name = requiredName;
040:     stomachSize = requiredStomachSize;
041:   } // GreedyChild
```

The other constructor method is just given the name, and chooses the stomach size randomly.

Concept **Standard API: `Math`: `random()`.** The standard **class** `java.lang.Math` contains a **class method** called random. This takes no **method argument**s and **return**s some **double** value, r, such that $0.0 \le r < 1.0$ is true. The value is chosen in a pseudo random fashion, using an **algorithm** which exhibits the characteristics of an approximately uniform distribution of random numbers.

In order to obtain a random number which is on a scale from zero to `MAXIMUM_RANDOM_STOMACH_SIZE` we simply take the value from `Math.random()` and multiply it by our desired maximum.

```
044:    // Construct a greedy child  -- given the required name
045:    // with a randomly chosen size.
046:    public GreedyChild(String requiredName)
047:    {
048:      name = requiredName;
049:      stomachSize = Math.random() * MAXIMUM_RANDOM_STOMACH_SIZE;
050:    } // GreedyChild
```

The child can enter and leave parlours.

```
053:    // Enter an ice cream parlour.
054:    public void enterParlour(IceCreamParlour parlourEntered)
055:    {
056:      currentParlour = parlourEntered;
057:    } // enterParlour
058:
059:
060:    // Leave an ice cream parlour.
061:    public void leaveParlour()
062:    {
063:      currentParlour = null;
064:    } // leaveParlour
```

When in a parlour, the child can eat ice cream.

Concept **Method: return with no value.** A **void method** may contain **return statements** which do not have an associated **return** value – just the **reserved word return**. These cause the execution of the **method** to end, and control to transfer back to the code that called the method. Every void method behaves as though it has an implicit return statement at the end, unless it has one explicitly written.

The use of return statements throughout the body of a method permits us to design them using a **single entry, multiple exit** principle: every call of the method starts at the beginning, but depending on **conditions** the execution may exit at various points.

```
067:    // Attempt to eat a given amount of ice cream from the current parlour.
068:    // No effect if no parlour. Otherwise parlour attempts to serve that amount.
069:    // Excess is spilt once full.
070:    public void tryToEat(double amountDesired)
071:    {
072:      if (currentParlour == null)
073:        return;
074:
075:      double amountServed = currentParlour.tryToServe(amountDesired);
076:      double roomLeft = stomachSize - stomachContents;
077:      if (amountServed <= roomLeft)
078:        stomachContents += amountServed;
079:      else
080:      {
081:        stomachContents = stomachSize;
082:        tShirtStainSize += amountServed - roomLeft;
083:      } // if
084:    } // tryToEat
```

Finally we have the toString() **instance method**.

```
087:    // The correct line separator for this platform.
088:    private static final String NLS = System.getProperty("line.separator");
089:
090:
091:    // Return a String giving the name and state.
092:    public String toString()
093:    {
094:      return name + " is " + stomachContents + "/" + stomachSize + " full"
095:             + " and has spilt " + tShirtStainSize + NLS
096:             + "(currently in " + currentParlour + ")";
097:    } // toString
098:
099: } // class GreedyChild
```

Coffee time: 11.3.3 In toString() above, what do you think will happen when currentParlour contains the **null reference**, null?

Concept **Method: accessor methods.** A **public instance method** whose job it is to reveal all or some part of the **object state**, without changing it, is known as an **accessor method**. Perhaps the most obvious example of this is an instance method called getSomeVariable, where someVariable is the name of an **instance variable**. However, a well **designed class** with good **encapsulation** does not systematically reveal to its user what its instance variables are. Hence the more general idea of an accessor method: it exposes the value of some *feature*, which might or might not be directly implemented as a single instance variable.

Concept **Method: mutator methods.** A **public instance method** whose job it is to set or update all or some part of the **object state** is known as a **mutator method**. Perhaps the most obvious example of this is an instance method called setSomeVariable, where someVariable is the name of an **instance variable**. However, the more general idea of a mutator method is that it changes the value of some feature, which might or might not be directly implemented as a single instance variable.

Obviously, only **mutable objects** have mutator methods.

Coffee time: 11.3.4 Which instance methods in IceCreamParlour and GreedyChild are **accessor methods** and which are **mutator methods**?

11.3.5   The GreedyChildren class

The **class** GreedyChildren contains the **main method**.

```
001: /* This program demonstrates the simple model of greedy children eating at ice
002:    cream parlours. It creates some children and parlours, has deliveries made
003:    to the parlours, and children served at them. As this is done, it reports
004:    on the standard output, enabling the user of the program to follow the
005:    events. So the main method tells a story, and can easily be altered to tell
006:    a different one.
007: */
008: public class GreedyChildren
009: {
```

The class has two helper **methods** which make the main method easier. These make some change to the model and report it to **standard output**.

```
010:    // Private helper method to make a delivery and report it.
011:    private static void deliver(IceCreamParlour parlour, double amount)
012:    {
013:      System.out.println(parlour);
014:      System.out.println("accepts delivery of " + amount);
015:      parlour.acceptDelivery(amount);
016:      System.out.println("Result: " + parlour);
017:      System.out.println();
018:    } // deliver
```

Observe for the above **class method** that we supply a **reference** to an IceCreamParlour **object** as a **method argument**, and the corresponding object gets altered.

Concept **Method: changing parameters does not affect arguments: but referenced objects can be changed.** All **method parameter**s obtain their values from the corresponding **method argument** using the **call by value** principle. This means a **method** cannot have any effect on the calling environment via its method parameters if they are of a **primitive type**.

However, if a method parameter is of a **reference type** then there is nothing to stop the code in the method following the **reference** supplied as the argument, and altering the state of the **object** it refers to (if it is a **mutable object**). Indeed, such behaviour is often exactly what we want.

In the abstract example below, assume that changeState() is an **instance method** in the **class** SomeClass which alters the values of some of the **instance variable**s.

```
public static void changeSomething(SomeClass object, SomeType value)
{
  object.changeState(value); // This really changes the object referred to.
  object = null;             // This has no effect outside of this method.
  ...
} // changeSomething
  ...
  SomeClass variable = new SomeClass();
  changeSomething(variable, someValueOfSomeType);
```

At the end of the above code, the change caused by the first line of the method has had an impact outside of the method, whereas the second line has had no such effect.

Another helper method is used when children eat.

```
021:    // Private helper method to have a child eat at a parlour.
022:    private static void eat(GreedyChild child, double amount,
023:                            IceCreamParlour parlour)
024:    {
025:      System.out.println(child);
026:      System.out.println("is entering " + parlour);
027:      child.enterParlour(parlour);
028:      System.out.println(child);
029:      System.out.println("is eating " + amount);
030:      child.tryToEat(amount);
031:      System.out.println("Result: " + child);
032:      System.out.println();
033:    } // eat
```

Finally, we have the main method.

```
036:    // The main method tells the 'story'.
037:    public static void main(String[] args)
038:    {
039:      System.out.println("Greedy children:");
040:      GreedyChild child1 = new GreedyChild("Bloated Basil", 20);
041:      System.out.println(child1);
042:      System.out.println("Making child with random capacity less than "
043:                          + GreedyChild.MAXIMUM_RANDOM_STOMACH_SIZE);
044:      GreedyChild child2 = new GreedyChild("Cautious Cathy");
045:      System.out.println(child2);
046:      GreedyChild child3 = new GreedyChild("Lanky Larry", 4);
047:      System.out.println(child3);
048:      System.out.println();
049:
050:      System.out.println("Ice cream parlours:");
051:      IceCreamParlour parlour1 = new IceCreamParlour("Glacial Palacial");
052:      System.out.println(parlour1);
053:      IceCreamParlour parlour2 = new IceCreamParlour("Nice 'n' Icey");
054:      System.out.println(parlour2);
055:      IceCreamParlour parlour3 = new IceCreamParlour("Dreamy Creamy Cup");
056:      System.out.println(parlour3);
057:      System.out.println();
058:
059:      System.out.println("Deliveries:");
060:      System.out.println();
061:      deliver(parlour1, 50);
062:      deliver(parlour2, 10);
063:      deliver(parlour3, 30);
064:      System.out.println("Eating:");
065:      System.out.println();
066:      eat(child1, 15, parlour1);
067:      eat(child2, 1, parlour1);
068:      eat(child3, 2, parlour1);
069:      eat(child1, 8, parlour2);
070:      eat(child2, 1, parlour2);
071:      eat(child3, 2, parlour2);
072:      eat(child1, 10, parlour3);
073:      eat(child2, 1, parlour3);
074:      eat(child3, 2, parlour3);
075:    } // main
076:
077: } // class GreedyChildren
```

11.3.6   Trying it

You will notice when we **run** the program that the **null reference** is printed as null.

Console Input / Output

```
$ java GreedyChildren
Greedy children:
Bloated Basil is 0.0/20.0 full and has spilt 0.0
(currently in null)
Making child with random capacity less than 20.0
Cautious Cathy is 0.0/14.61935574753314 full and has spilt 0.0
(currently in null)
Lanky Larry is 0.0/4.0 full and has spilt 0.0
(currently in null)

Ice cream parlours:
Glacial Palacial has 0.0 in stock
Nice 'n' Icey has 0.0 in stock
Dreamy Creamy Cup has 0.0 in stock

Deliveries:

Glacial Palacial has 0.0 in stock
accepts delivery of 50.0
Result: Glacial Palacial has 50.0 in stock
```

(Continued ...)

```
                              (...cont.)
Nice 'n' Icey has 0.0 in stock
accepts delivery of 10.0
Result: Nice 'n' Icey has 10.0 in stock


Dreamy Creamy Cup has 0.0 in stock
accepts delivery of 30.0
Result: Dreamy Creamy Cup has 30.0 in stock


Eating:


Bloated Basil is 0.0/20.0 full and has spilt 0.0
(currently in null)
is entering Glacial Palacial has 50.0 in stock
Bloated Basil is 0.0/20.0 full and has spilt 0.0
(currently in Glacial Palacial has 50.0 in stock)
is eating 15.0
Result: Bloated Basil is 15.0/20.0 full and has spilt 0.0
(currently in Glacial Palacial has 35.0 in stock)


Cautious Cathy is 0.0/14.61935574753314 full and has spilt 0.0
(currently in null)
is entering Glacial Palacial has 35.0 in stock
Cautious Cathy is 0.0/14.61935574753314 full and has spilt 0.0
(currently in Glacial Palacial has 35.0 in stock)
is eating 1.0
Result: Cautious Cathy is 1.0/14.61935574753314 full and has spilt 0.0
(currently in Glacial Palacial has 34.0 in stock)


Lanky Larry is 0.0/4.0 full and has spilt 0.0
(currently in null)
is entering Glacial Palacial has 34.0 in stock
Lanky Larry is 0.0/4.0 full and has spilt 0.0
(currently in Glacial Palacial has 34.0 in stock)
is eating 2.0
Result: Lanky Larry is 2.0/4.0 full and has spilt 0.0
(currently in Glacial Palacial has 32.0 in stock)


Bloated Basil is 15.0/20.0 full and has spilt 0.0
(currently in Glacial Palacial has 32.0 in stock)
is entering Nice 'n' Icey has 10.0 in stock
Bloated Basil is 15.0/20.0 full and has spilt 0.0
(currently in Nice 'n' Icey has 10.0 in stock)
is eating 8.0
Result: Bloated Basil is 20.0/20.0 full and has spilt 3.0
(currently in Nice 'n' Icey has 2.0 in stock)


Cautious Cathy is 1.0/14.61935574753314 full and has spilt 0.0
(currently in Glacial Palacial has 32.0 in stock)
is entering Nice 'n' Icey has 2.0 in stock
Cautious Cathy is 1.0/14.61935574753314 full and has spilt 0.0
(currently in Nice 'n' Icey has 2.0 in stock)
is eating 1.0
Result: Cautious Cathy is 2.0/14.61935574753314 full and has spilt 0.0
(currently in Nice 'n' Icey has 1.0 in stock)
(Continued ...)
```

```
                              (...cont.)
Lanky Larry is 2.0/4.0 full and has spilt 0.0
(currently in Glacial Palacial has 32.0 in stock)
is entering Nice 'n' Icey has 1.0 in stock
Lanky Larry is 2.0/4.0 full and has spilt 0.0
(currently in Nice 'n' Icey has 1.0 in stock)
is eating 2.0
Result: Lanky Larry is 3.0/4.0 full and has spilt 0.0
(currently in Nice 'n' Icey has 0.0 in stock)

Bloated Basil is 20.0/20.0 full and has spilt 3.0
(currently in Nice 'n' Icey has 0.0 in stock)
is entering Dreamy Creamy Cup has 30.0 in stock
Bloated Basil is 20.0/20.0 full and has spilt 3.0
(currently in Dreamy Creamy Cup has 30.0 in stock)
is eating 10.0
Result: Bloated Basil is 20.0/20.0 full and has spilt 13.0
(currently in Dreamy Creamy Cup has 20.0 in stock)

Cautious Cathy is 2.0/14.61935574753314 full and has spilt 0.0
(currently in Nice 'n' Icey has 0.0 in stock)
is entering Dreamy Creamy Cup has 20.0 in stock
Cautious Cathy is 2.0/14.61935574753314 full and has spilt 0.0
(currently in Dreamy Creamy Cup has 20.0 in stock)
is eating 1.0
Result: Cautious Cathy is 3.0/14.61935574753314 full and has spilt 0.0
(currently in Dreamy Creamy Cup has 19.0 in stock)

Lanky Larry is 3.0/4.0 full and has spilt 0.0
(currently in Nice 'n' Icey has 0.0 in stock)
is entering Dreamy Creamy Cup has 19.0 in stock
Lanky Larry is 3.0/4.0 full and has spilt 0.0
(currently in Dreamy Creamy Cup has 19.0 in stock)
is eating 2.0
Result: Lanky Larry is 4.0/4.0 full and has spilt 1.0
(currently in Dreamy Creamy Cup has 17.0 in stock)

$ _
```

11.3.7 Representing `null` as a string

Concept **Type: `String`: conversion: from object: null reference.**   For convenience, whenever the Java **compiler** finds an **object reference** as an **operand** of the **concatenation operator** it assumes that the object's `toString()` **instance method** is to be invoked to produce the required `String`. However, the reference might be the **null reference** in which case there is no object on which to invoke `toString()`, so instead, the string `"null"` is used.

In fact, assuming `someString` is some `String` and `myVar` is a **variable** of a **reference type**, then the code:

```
someString + myVar
```

is actually treated as follows.

```
someString + (myVar == null
              ? "null"
              : (myVar.toString() == null ? "null" : myVar.toString()))
```

The same applies to the first operand of string concatenation if that is an object reference.

For this reason, most Java programmers prefer to use `"" + myVar` rather than `myVar.toString()` when they wish to convert the object referenced by `myVar` to a string, because it avoids the possibility of an **exception** if `myVar` contains the null reference.

Coffee time: [11.35] However, `"" + myVar` and `myVar.toString()` do not have the same effect if `myVar` is not **null** but `myVar.toString()` is. What is that difference?

11.3.8 Coursework: `StudentsCalling`

In this task you will create a program called `StudentsCalling` which simulates a simple scenario in which students purchase and use mobile phones.

- A student has a name which cannot be changed, and a mobile phone, although not to begin with.

- A phone has a name (i.e. make and model number) and an account, both of which are fixed. It also keeps track of the total number of seconds of phone calls made on it, starting with zero.

- An account has a provider (i.e. the name of the service provider) which is fixed and a balance, in whole *pence*, which starts off as zero.

- A student may purchase a mobile phone, in which case they discard their previous one if they have previously purchased one.

- A student may top up their phone with a whole number of *pounds*. If they have no phone, then an attempt to top up their phone is ignored!

- A student may make a call of desired duration, in seconds, on their phone. If they have no phone, then an attempt to make a call is ignored!

- A phone may be topped up with a whole number of *pounds*, which simply causes its account to be topped up with that same amount.

- A phone can have a call made on it, of a desired duration, which causes it to request that call on its account. The account **return**s the actual duration of the call, which may be **less than** that desired (i.e. when there is not enough balance to pay for it). The phone keeps track of the total actual duration of all the calls made on it.

- An account may be topped up with a whole number of *pounds*. This adds to the current balance.

- An account may have a call requested on it for a desired duration. In this wonderful world, all account providers charge only one penny per second for any call! The actual call duration will be limited to the current balance on the account. The balance is reduced by the actual duration. The actual duration is also returned as the result of the call request.

- The main program will create some students, create some phones with accounts, which the students purchase, and cause the students to make calls. At each stage the behaviour of the program will be reported to the **standard output**.

The following is an example **run** of the program to help clarify the requirements.

```
                            Console Input / Output
$ java StudentsCalling
Creating student Chatty Charlie
Result:
Student(Chatty Charlie,null)

Creating student Norman No Friends
Result:
Student(Norman No Friends,null)

Creating student Popular Penny
Result:
Student(Popular Penny,null)

This next call has no effect, as has no phone!
Student(Chatty Charlie,null)
is making a call for desired 300 seconds
Result:
Student(Chatty Charlie,null)

This next top up has no effect, as has no phone!
Student(Norman No Friends,null)
is topping up by 20
Result:
Student(Norman No Friends,null)

Student(Chatty Charlie,null)
is buying phone Snotia BIFR
with account World@1
Result:
Student(Chatty Charlie,Phone(Snotia BIFR,0,Account(World@1,0)))

Student(Norman No Friends,null)
is buying phone Cyoo L8TRON
with account 4FRN Touch
Result:
Student(Norman No Friends,Phone(Cyoo L8TRON,0,Account(4FRN Touch,0)))

Student(Popular Penny,null)
is buying phone Tisonly 14U
with account Foney Friends
Result:
Student(Popular Penny,Phone(Tisonly 14U,0,Account(Foney Friends,0)))

Student(Chatty Charlie,Phone(Snotia BIFR,0,Account(World@1,0)))
is topping up by 10
Result:
Student(Chatty Charlie,Phone(Snotia BIFR,0,Account(World@1,1000)))

Student(Norman No Friends,Phone(Cyoo L8TRON,0,Account(4FRN Touch,0)))
is topping up by 20
Result:
Student(Norman No Friends,Phone(Cyoo L8TRON,0,Account(4FRN Touch,2000)))

(Continued ...)
```

```
                                   (...cont.)
Student(Popular Penny,Phone(Tisonly 14U,0,Account(Foney Friends,0)))
is topping up by 30
Result:
Student(Popular Penny,Phone(Tisonly 14U,0,Account(Foney Friends,3000)))

Student(Chatty Charlie,Phone(Snotia BIFR,0,Account(World@1,1000)))
is making a call for desired 300 seconds
Result:
Student(Chatty Charlie,Phone(Snotia BIFR,300,Account(World@1,700)))

This next call should be truncated to 700 seconds.
Student(Chatty Charlie,Phone(Snotia BIFR,300,Account(World@1,700)))
is making a call for desired 1200 seconds
Result:
Student(Chatty Charlie,Phone(Snotia BIFR,1000,Account(World@1,0)))

Student(Chatty Charlie,Phone(Snotia BIFR,1000,Account(World@1,0)))
is making a call for desired 10 seconds
Result:
Student(Chatty Charlie,Phone(Snotia BIFR,1000,Account(World@1,0)))

Student(Norman No Friends,Phone(Cyoo L8TRON,0,Account(4FRN Touch,2000)))
is making a call for desired 10 seconds
Result:
Student(Norman No Friends,Phone(Cyoo L8TRON,10,Account(4FRN Touch,1990)))

Student(Popular Penny,Phone(Tisonly 14U,0,Account(Foney Friends,3000)))
is making a call for desired 65 seconds
Result:
Student(Popular Penny,Phone(Tisonly 14U,65,Account(Foney Friends,2935)))

Student(Popular Penny,Phone(Tisonly 14U,65,Account(Foney Friends,2935)))
is making a call for desired 115 seconds
Result:
Student(Popular Penny,Phone(Tisonly 14U,180,Account(Foney Friends,2820)))

Student(Popular Penny,Phone(Tisonly 14U,180,Account(Foney Friends,2820)))
is making a call for desired 488 seconds
Result:
Student(Popular Penny,Phone(Tisonly 14U,668,Account(Foney Friends,2332)))

Student(Popular Penny,Phone(Tisonly 14U,668,Account(Foney Friends,2332)))
is making a call for desired 302 seconds
Result:
Student(Popular Penny,Phone(Tisonly 14U,970,Account(Foney Friends,2030)))

Student(Popular Penny,Phone(Tisonly 14U,970,Account(Foney Friends,2030)))
is making a call for desired 510 seconds
Result:
Student(Popular Penny,Phone(Tisonly 14U,1480,Account(Foney Friends,1520)))

(Continued ...)
```

```
                         (...cont.)
Student(Popular Penny,Phone(Tisonly 14U,1480,Account(Foney Friends,1520)'))
is making a call for desired 250 seconds
Result:
Student(Popular Penny,Phone(Tisonly 14U,1730,Account(Foney Friends,1270)))

Now let us discard a phone.
Student(Popular Penny,Phone(Tisonly 14U,1730,Account(Foney Friends,1270)))
is buying phone Simm UL8R
with account VerTuleTyat
Result:
Student(Popular Penny,Phone(Simm UL8R,0,Account(VerTuleTyat,0)))

$ _
```

Your program will consist of four **classes**, Student, Phone, Account and StudentsCalling. The latter will contain the **main method**. Start by **design**ing these classes in your logbook, identifying the **public instance method**s and **class method**s for each of them. Endeavour to associate behaviour (i.e. **method**s) with the most appropriate classes.

Next you should design your 'story', that is, the sequence of operations you wish the simulation to undertake. You should make your 'story' significantly different to the example one above! That is, have different student names, phone names, account names, different number of students, different order and number of calls, etc..

Next design the implementations of your classes (at a level of **abstraction** that is appropriate to you). Note that all calls to System.out.println() should be inside StudentsCalling: the others are model classes. Then implement your classes. Do you want to think about the order of implementation so you can **compile** them as you proceed? Will you use **stub**s?

Here are some implementation hints.
- You can use the **null reference**, null, as the value for a student's phone to begin with.
- The toString() method of Student can rely on the toString() method of Phone which in turn can use the toString() method of Account.
- Use **private** helper methods in the StudentsCalling class, to save you repeating code that prints out what is happening at each stage.

After implementation you should record your results. It may well be that during your implementation, you changed your plan of which class should have what method. This is okay, but you should record such changes, and the reason for them, in your logbook.

Optional extra: You can think of ways to make the simulation more realistic. For example:
- Suddenly there is a period of inflation again, and account providers have to charge more than one penny per second. Change your program so that an account has a rate, expressed in pence per minute.
- Perhaps rates vary depending on what time of day the call is made?
- Accounts ought to have a unique account number, assigned when they are created.
- Consider having a Provider class, so an account has a provider. Perhaps all the accounts for a particular provider have the same rate, but different providers have different rates.
- Now the providers are in competition again, perhaps it should be possible to change the account on an existing phone?

11.4   Example: Greedy children gone wrong

AIM: To look at the idea of an **object referenced by more than one variable** and the danger this presents when it is a **mutable object**.

To finish this chapter, we use the example from the previous section to explore the relationship between **variable**s, **reference**s and **mutable object**s. We have a cut-down version of the program which has a 'bug' in it caused by us 'accidentally' having an **object referenced by more than one variable**.

Concept **Variable: of a class type: holding the same reference as some other variable.** A **variable** which is of a **class type** can hold a **reference** to any **instance** of that class (plus the **null reference**). There is nothing to stop two (or more) variables having the same reference value. For example, the following code creates one `Point` **object** and has it referred to by two variables.

```
Point p1 = new Point(10, 30);

Point p2 = p1;
```

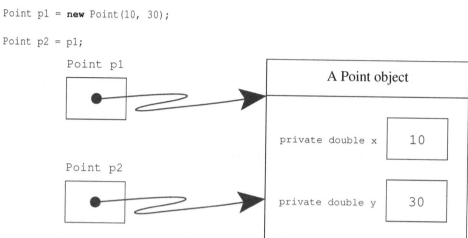

This reminds us that a variable is *not* itself an object, but merely a holder for a reference to an object.

Having two or more **variable**s refer to the same **object** can cause us no problems if it is an **immutable object** because we cannot change the object's state no matter which variable we use to access it. So, in effect, the object(s) referred to by the two variables behave the same as they would if they were two different objects. The following code has the same *effect* as the above fragment, almost no matter what we do with p1 and p2 subsequently.

```
Point p1 = new Point(10, 30);

Point p2 = new Point(10, 30);
```

The only behavioural difference between the two fragments is the **condition**s p1 == p2 and p1 != p2 which are **true** and **false** respectively for the first code fragment, and the other way round for the second one.

If, on the other hand, an **object referenced by more than one variable** is a **mutable object** we have to be careful because any change made via any one of the variables causes the change to occur in the (same) object referred to by the other variables. This may be, and often is, exactly what we want, or it may be a problem if our **design** is poor or if we have made a mistake in our code and the variables were not meant to share the object.

Consider the following simple example.

```
public class Employee
{
  private final String name;
  private int salary;

  public Employee(String requiredName, int initialSalary)
  {
    name = requiredName;
    salary = initialSalary;
  } // Employee
```

```
public String getName()
{
  return name;
} // getName

public void setSalary(int newSalary)
{
  salary = newSalary;
} // setSalary

public int getSalary()
{
  return salary;
} // getSalary

} // class Employee

...

Employee debora = new Employee("Debs", 50000);
Employee sharmane = new Employee("Shaz", 40000);

...

Employee worstEmployee = debora;
Employee bestEmployee = sharmane;

...
```

Now let us have an accidental piece of code.

```
worstEmployee = bestEmployee;
```

Then we carry on with intentional code.

```
...

bestEmployee.setSalary(55000);
worstEmployee.setSalary(0);

System.out.println("Our best employee, " + bestEmployee.getName()
                  + ", is paid " + bestEmployee.getSalary());
System.out.println("Our worst employee, " + worstEmployee.getName()
                  + ", is paid " + worstEmployee.getSalary());
```

The effect of the accidental sharing is to give Sharmane, who is our best employee, a pay increase to 55,000 immediately followed by a pay cut to zero because worstEmployee and bestEmployee are both referring to the same object, the one which is also referred to by sharmane. Meanwhile our worst employee, Debora, gets to keep her 50,000! Further more, the report only actually talks about Sharmane in both contexts!

```
Our best employee, Shaz, is paid 0
Our worst employee, Shaz, is paid 0
```

Here is our revisit to the `GreedyChildren` program. The `IceCreamParlour` and `GreedyChild` **class**es are the same as in the last section. The `GreedyChildren` program has been cut down, as follows.

```
001: public class GreedyChildren
002: {
003:   // Private helper method to make a delivery and report it.
004:   private static void deliver(IceCreamParlour parlour, double amount)
005:   {
006:     System.out.println(parlour);
007:     System.out.println("accepts delivery of " + amount);
008:     parlour.acceptDelivery(amount);
009:     System.out.println("Result: " + parlour);
010:     System.out.println();
011:   } // deliver
```

Our simplified **main method** makes only some **instance**s of `IceCreamParlour`.

```
014:   public static void main(String[] args)
015:   {
016:     IceCreamParlour parlour1 = new IceCreamParlour("Glacial Palacial");
017:     System.out.println(parlour1);
018:     IceCreamParlour parlour2 = new IceCreamParlour("Nice 'n' Icey");
019:     System.out.println(parlour2);
020:     IceCreamParlour parlour3 = new IceCreamParlour("Dreamy Creamy Cup");
021:     System.out.println(parlour3);
022:     System.out.println();
```

Now, let us have the 'accidental' piece of code.

```
023:     parlour3 = parlour1;
```

Then we just have a delivery to each parlour and print out a report.

```
025:     System.out.println("Deliveries:");
026:     System.out.println();
027:     deliver(parlour1, 50);
028:     deliver(parlour2, 10);
029:     deliver(parlour3, 30);
030:
031:     System.out.println("Total ice cream delivered was " + (50 + 10 + 30));
032:     System.out.println("which is waiting in parlours as follows.");
033:     System.out.println(parlour1);
034:     System.out.println(parlour2);
035:     System.out.println(parlour3);
036:   } // main
037:
038: } // class GreedyChildren
```

Coffee time: `11.4.1`   Before reading on, predict what the output of the program will be.

11.4.1 Trying it

Now let's see if your prediction was right.

```
                    Console Input / Output
$ java GreedyChildren
Glacial Palacial has 0.0 in stock
Nice 'n' Icey has 0.0 in stock
Dreamy Creamy Cup has 0.0 in stock

Deliveries:

Glacial Palacial has 0.0 in stock
accepts delivery of 50.0
Result: Glacial Palacial has 50.0 in stock

Nice 'n' Icey has 0.0 in stock
accepts delivery of 10.0
Result: Nice 'n' Icey has 10.0 in stock

Glacial Palacial has 50.0 in stock
accepts delivery of 30.0
Result: Glacial Palacial has 80.0 in stock

Total ice cream delivered was 90
which is waiting in parlours as follows.
Glacial Palacial has 80.0 in stock
Nice 'n' Icey has 10.0 in stock
Glacial Palacial has 80.0 in stock
$ _
```

Coffee time:
Was your prediction (more or less) correct? How much ice cream was really delivered – 90 or 170? How much did the Dreamy Creamy Cup get?

11.5 Concepts covered in this chapter

Here is a list of the concepts that were covered in this chapter, each with a self-test question. You can use this to check you remember them being introduced, and perhaps re-read some of them before going on to the next chapter.

Class	
– objects: may be mutable or immutable (p.193)	What is the difference between a mutable and an immutable object?
– importing classes (p.188)	What does import do for us? Which package has all its classes imported automatically?
– stub (p.191)	What are stubs used for?
Code clarity	
– comments: multi-line comments (p.189)	What symbols are used to start and end a multi-line comment?
Design	
– object oriented design (p.184)	In object oriented design, in what sense is the design oriented around objects?
– object oriented design: noun identification (p.185)	What two interesting things might nouns that appear in the requirements statements relate to?
– object oriented design: encapsulation (p.187)	How does the idea of encapsulation relate to the default of making our instance variables private? What principle do we follow when deciding in which class our code should reside?

Method	
– changing parameters does not affect arguments: but referenced objects can be changed (p.208)	What is the name of the mechanism for passing arguments to methods in Java? What is the significance of the approach for arguments of a primitive type and those of a reference type?
– constructor methods: more than one (p.203)	In what way must each constructor be distinguished from the others?
– returning a value: multiple returns (p.196)	What two things are checked by the compiler in this context?
– return with no value (p.206)	What do we mean by the phrase 'single entry, multiple exit'?
– accessor methods (p.207)	Which of the following method headings suggest they are accessor methods? `private void` updateFeature() `public void` updateFeature() `private int` getFeature() `public int` getFeature() `private static int` getFeature() `public static int` getFeature() `private void` setFeature(`int` f) `public void` setFeature(`int` f)
– mutator methods (p.207)	What kind of objects never have mutator methods?
Operating environment	
– standard input (p.187)	What is the standard input used for?
Package	
Package (p.187)	What is a package?
– java.util (p.188)	What is a fully qualified name?
Standard API	
– Math: random() (p.205)	What is the range of the result? Exactly?
– System: getProperty() (p.195)	What kinds of information does this give us? What is the return type?
– System: getProperty(): line.separator (p.195)	Exactly how do we obtain the line separator?
– System: in (p.187)	What kind of Java variable is System.in?
– Scanner (p.188)	What method is used to read lines of text? And what is used to read **int** values?
Type	
– String: conversion: from object: null reference (p.211)	How does Java ensure the implicit toString() convention does not fail with null references?
Variable	
– final variables (p.194)	What must be done to a final instance variable, by what stage, and what cannot be done later?
– final variables: class constant (p.205)	A class constant is another name for what?
– of a class type: null reference (p.192)	Which object does **null** refer to?
– of a class type: holding the same reference as some other variable (p.216)	Is it mutable or immutable objects for which having more than one variable holding its reference is particularly an issue, and why?

Chapter 12

Software reuse and the standard Java API

> A rose by any other name
> would smell as sweet.
>
> A wheel by any other name
> would need reinventing as little!

12.1 Chapter aims

In the previous chapter we looked at the principle of **object oriented design**, focusing on the the use of **class**es to help us produce a well structured program. Here we shift focus to looking at the use of classes as a means of obtaining **software reuse**, that is the ability to have code which can be used in more than one program.

We start by revisiting our Date class, looking at ways to make it more generally usable by extending it with more features. We also use this as a vehicle for exploring a related topic: how do we provide documentation about the way a class should be used, so that a programmer who wishes to use it can do so without having to look at the actual code? This is answered by Java's **doc comment** mechanism.

We then take a brief look at the standard Java **application program interface** (**API**), that is the huge number of already written classes that come with Java, complete with their user documentation, ready for us to reuse in our programs. This is followed by us observing that the **type** String is in fact such a standard class, and we take a look at some of its **instance methods**.

We finish the chapter with an example that performs manipulations on String **object**s and **char** values.

The chapter contains the following sections.

Section	Aims	Associated Coursework
12.2 A reusable Date class, with doc comments (p.222)	To explore the notion of **software reuse** and introduce **doc comments**. We also introduce the convention of having a compareTo() **instance method**.	Add **doc comments** to an existing **class**. (p.232)
12.3 The standard Java API (p.233)	To take a brief look at the standard Java **application program interface** (**API**).	(None.)
12.4 The String class (p.233)	To take a closer look at String.	(None.)

Section	Aims	Associated Coursework
12.5 Simple Encryption (p.235)	To take a look at String manipulation, such as extracting individual **char** values from a String. We also look at how comparisons between two **char** values can be achieved, and the way we can **cast** between **char** and **int** values, and meet **overloaded methods**.	Write a **class** that allows for the conversion between decimal and Roman numbers. (p.240)

12.2   Example: A reusable Date class, with doc comments

AIM:
To explore the notion of **software reuse** and introduce **doc comments**. We also introduce the convention of having a compareTo() **instance method**.

The Date **class** we used in the AgeHistory program in Section 11.2.5 on page 193 was written specifically for that program. We can imagine, however, that there are lots of programs which need to manipulate dates, all having a mixture of similar and different requirements of the Date class. We have already stated that one of the benefits of classes in Java is the opportunity for **software reuse** – a class can be used in many programs.

When we are writing a class which is *intended* for use in *many* programs we approach it a little differently from when we are writing one for a particular program. Instead of being driven by specific requirements, we try to imagine the features that are generally useful. For example, a more widely usable Date class would have a greaterThan() **instance method** as well as lessThan(). In fact, it would probably also use the Java convention of having a compareTo() instance method.

Concept **Class: objects: compareTo().** It is quite common to require the ability to compare an **object** with another from the same **class**, based on some **total order**, that is, a notion of **less than**, **greater than** and **equivalence**. A Java convention for this is to have an **instance method** called compareTo which takes (a **reference** to) another object as its **method parameter**, and **return**s an **int**. A result of 0 indicates the two objects are **equivalent**, a negative value indicates this object is less than the other, and a positive value indicates this object is greater than the other.

```
Date husbandsBirthday = ...
Date wifesBirthday = ...

if (husbandsBirthday.compareTo(wifesBirthday) > 0)
  System.out.println("The husband is older than the wife");
else if (husbandsBirthday.compareTo(wifesBirthday) == 0)
  System.out.println("The husband is the same age as the wife");
else
  System.out.println("The husband is younger than the wife");
```

A more reusable Date class would have addDay() and addMonth() instance methods as well as addYear(). The former would need to calculate whether the year is a leap year, in order to determine how many days there are in February. It would probably also support instance methods for subtracting a day, month and year. Another feature that might be of general use is an instance method to calculate how many days exist between a Date and a given other one. The list is endless – the more useful features we add to the class, the more reusable it becomes.

Another issue to consider when writing reusable classes is user documentation. A class is not used directly by an end user, but instead by another programmer who wishes to use it in his or her programs. Java has a mechanism to help with the production of **class user documentation**, called **doc comments**.

Concept **Java tools: javadoc.** A **class** which is intended to be reusable in many programs should have user documentation to enable another programmer to use it without having to look at the implementation code. In Java this is achieved by the implementer of the class writing **doc comment**s in the code, and then processing them with the javadoc program. This tool produces a web page which describes the class from the information in the doc comments and from the structure of the class itself, and this page is linked to the pages for other classes as appropriate. For example, the heading of each **public method** is documented on the web page, with the description of the method being taken by javadoc from the doc comment which the implementer supplied for the method.

The resulting user documentation produced by javadoc can be placed anywhere we wish – on a web server for example. Meanwhile the *source* of that documentation is kept with the **source code** for the class, indeed it is inside the same **file**. This excellent idea makes it easy for the programmer to maintain information on how to use the class as he or she alters the code, but without restricting where the final documentation can be put.

A doc comment starts with the symbol /** and ends with */. These are written in certain places as follows.

- A comment before the start of the class (after any **import statement**s) describing its purpose.

- A comment before each public **variable** describing the meaning of that variable.

- A comment before each public method describing what it does, its **method parameter**s and **return** value.

- Optionally, a comment before each **private** variable and method. This is less useful than documentation for public items as normal users of the class do not have access to the private ones. So, many programmers do not write doc comments for these (although of course they do write ordinary **comment**s!). On the other hand, some take the view that anybody who needs to *maintain* the class is, in effect, a user of both the public *and* private parts, and so user documentation of the whole class is of benefit.

The implementer writes user documentation text as appropriate inside the doc comments. The emphasis is on how to use the features, not on how they are implemented. He or she also includes various **doc comment tag**s to help the javadoc program process the text properly. Here are some of the most commonly used tags.

Tag	Meaning	Where used
@author author name(s)	State the author of the code.	Before the class starts.
@param parameter description	Describe a method parameter.	Before a method.
@return description	Describe a method result.	Before a method.

Most doc comments use more than one line, and it is conventional (but not essential) to start continuation lines with an asterisk (*) neatly lined up with the first asterisk in the opening comment symbol. The first sentence should be a summary of the whole thing being documented – these are copied to a summary area of the final documentation.

For a doc comment tag to be recognized by javadoc, it must be the first word on a line of the comment, preceded only by **white space**, or an asterisk.

Doc comments are sometimes (but wrongly) called **javadoc comment**s.

Here is the code of a (more) reusable Date class, including doc comments. The class starts with a brief description, including the author's name.

```
001: /**
002:  * This class represents calendar dates and provides certain
003:  * manipulations of them.
004:  *
005:  * @author John Latham
006:  */
```

We have chosen for this example to provide *user* documentation by writing **doc comment**s for the **public** components (only) of the class.

```
007: public class Date
008: {
009:   // Class variable to hold the present date.
010:   private static Date presentDate = null;
```

For the **class method** setPresentDate() we write a doc comment saying what it does, and in particular what is the meaning of its **method parameter**. Notice that the first sentence summarizes the behaviour and the second one elaborates upon it.

```
013:  /**
014:   * Set the present date.
015:   * This is ignored if the date has already been set.
016:   *
017:   * @param requiredPresentDate The required date for the present day.
018:   */
019:  public static void setPresentDate(Date requiredPresentDate)
020:  {
021:    if (presentDate == null)
022:      presentDate = requiredPresentDate;
023:  } // setPresentDate
```

The following abstract web browser window shows a fragment of the resulting web page produced by the javadoc program, containing the documentation for setPresentDate().

Web Browser Window
....
setPresentDate
public static void **setPresentDate**(Date requiredPresentDate)
Set the present date. This is ignored if the date has already been set.
Parameters:
requiredPresentDate - The required date for the present day.
....

The getPresentDate() class method is similarly documented.

```
026:  /**
027:   * Get the present date.
028:   *
029:   * @return The present date, or null if it has not been set.
030:   */
031:  public static Date getPresentDate()
032:  {
033:    return presentDate;
034:  } // getPresentDate
```

Next we define the **instance variable**s for which we shall not write doc comments, as they are **private** and we are providing only *user* documentation in this example.

```
037:   // Instance variables: the day, month and year of a date.
038:  private final int day, month, year;
```

In this, more robust, version of the class, the **constructor method** will undertake checks that the given date component values are legal, and quietly adjust them if they are not. This makes use of a private helper **instance method** daysInMonth().

```
041:  /**
042:   * Construct a date. If the day and/or month components are zero
043:   * or negative, they are treated as being 1; if they are too
044:   * large, they are treated as being the largest value allowed.
045:   *
046:   * @param requiredDay The required day.
047:   * @param requiredMonth The required month.
048:   * @param requiredYear The required year.
049:   */
050:  public Date(int requiredDay, int requiredMonth, int requiredYear)
051:  {
052:    year = requiredYear;
053:
054:    if       (requiredMonth < 1)  month = 1;
055:    else if (requiredMonth > 12) month = 12;
056:    else                         month = requiredMonth;
057:
058:    if       (requiredDay < 1)             day = 1;
059:    else if (requiredDay > daysInMonth()) day = daysInMonth();
060:    else                                  day = requiredDay;
061:  } // Date
```

This is what the generated documentation for the constructor method looks like.

Web Browser Window

....

Date

```
public Date(int requiredDay,
            int requiredMonth,
            int requiredYear)
```

Construct a date. If the day and/or month components are zero or negative, they are treated as being 1; if they are too large, they are treated as being the largest value allowed.

Parameters:
    requiredDay - The required day.
    requiredMonth - The required month.
    requiredYear - The required year.

....

Next we have an **accessor method** for each of the date components.

```
064:  /**
065:   * Yields the day component of this date.
066:   *
067:   * @return The day of this date.
068:   */
069:  public int getDay()
070:  {
071:    return day;
072:  } // getDay
073:
074:
```

```
075:   /**
076:    * Yields the month component of this date.
077:    *
078:    * @return The month of this date.
079:    */
080:   public int getMonth()
081:   {
082:     return month;
083:   } // getMonth
084:
085:
086:   /**
087:    * Yields the year component of this date.
088:    *
089:    * @return The year of this date.
090:    */
091:   public int getYear()
092:   {
093:     return year;
094:   } // getYear
```

> *Coffee time:* 12.2.1
> What is the value of new Date(32, 1, 2015).getDay()?
> What alternative strategy might we have chosen for turning
> such an illegal date into a legal one?

The toString() instance method implementation is the same as we have seen in the previous version of the class.

```
097:   /**
098:    * Provides the day/month/year representation of this date.
099:    *
100:    * @return A String day/month/year representation of this date.
101:    */
102:   public String toString()
103:   {
104:     return day + "/" + month + "/" + year;
105:   } // toString
```

Next we have the compareTo() instance method we talked about above.

```
108:   /**
109:    * Compare this date with a given other one.
110:    *
111:    * @param other The other date to compare with.
112:    *
113:    * @return The value 0 if the other date represents the same date
114:    * as this one; a value less than 0 if this date is less than the
115:    * other; and a value greater than 0 if this date is greater than
116:    * the other.
117:    */
118:   public int compareTo(Date other)
119:   {
120:     if (year != other.year)          return year - other.year;
121:     else if (month != other.month)   return month - other.month;
122:     else                             return day - other.day;
123:   } // compareTo
```

> *Coffee time:* 12.2.2
> Are you
> convinced the
> compareTo()
> instance method
> will work for all
> dates?

226

Here is the documentation generated for compareTo().

Web Browser Window

compareTo

public int **compareTo**(Date other)

Compare this date with a given other one.

Parameters:
other - The other date to compare with.

Returns:
The value 0 if the other date represents the same date as this one; a value less than 0 if this date is less than the other; and a value greater than 0 if this date is greater than the other.

Next we have three specific comparisons corresponding to the three possible results from compareTo().

```
126:  /**
127:   * Compare this date with a given other one, for equality.
128:   *
129:   * @param other The other date to compare with.
130:   *
131:   * @return true if and only if they represent the same date.
132:   */
133:  public boolean equals(Date other)
134:  {
135:    return compareTo(other) == 0;
136:  } // equals
137:
138:
139:  /**
140:   * Compare this date with a given other one, for less than.
141:   *
142:   * @param other The other date to compare with.
143:   *
144:   * @return true if and only if this date is less than the other.
145:   */
146:  public boolean lessThan(Date other)
147:  {
148:    return compareTo(other) < 0;
149:  } // lessThan
150:
151:
152:  /**
153:   * Compare this date with a given other one, for greater than.
154:   *
155:   * @param other The other date to compare with.
156:   *
157:   * @return true if and only if this date is greater than the other.
158:   */
159:  public boolean greaterThan(Date other)
160:  {
161:    return compareTo(other) > 0;
162:  } // greaterThan
```

227

Coffee time: 12.2.3 Now that `lessThan()` is implemented differently from the previous version of this class, will we need to alter the `AgeHistory` program that uses it? Will we even need to recompile `AgeHistory.java`?

Making a date which is one day later is trickier than making one that is one year later. We use the private helper **instance method** `daysInMonth()` to determine whether the month must be changed.

```
165:  /**
166:   * Construct a new date which is one day later than this one.
167:   *
168:   * @return A new date which is one day later than this one.
169:   */
170:  public Date addDay()
171:  {
172:    int newDay = day + 1;
173:    int newMonth = month;
174:    int newYear = year;
175:    if (newDay > daysInMonth())
176:    {
177:      newDay = 1;
178:      newMonth++;
179:      if (newMonth > 12)
180:      {
181:        newMonth = 1;
182:        newYear++;
183:      } // if
184:    } // if
185:    return new Date(newDay, newMonth, newYear);
186:  } // addDay
```

Making a date which is one month later is slightly easier.

```
189:  /**
190:   * Construct a new date which is one month later than this one.
191:   * If the day is too large for that month, it is truncated to
192:   * the number of days in that month.
193:   *
194:   * @return A new date which is one month later than this one.
195:   */
196:  public Date addMonth()
197:  {
198:    int newMonth = month + 1;
199:    int newYear = year;
200:    if (newMonth > 12)
201:    {
202:      newMonth = 1;
203:      newYear++;
204:    } // if
205:    // Day will be corrected in constructor if too high.
206:    return new Date(day, newMonth, newYear);
207:  } // addMonth
```

Coffee time: 12.2.4 What is the value of `new Date(31, 1, 2015).addMonth().getDay()`?

Adding a year is trivial!

```
210:    /**
211:     * Construct a new date which is one year later than this one.
212:     * If this date is a leap day, it returns 28th February of the next year.
213:     *
214:     * @return A new date which is one year later than this one.
215:     */
216:    public Date addYear()
217:    {
218:        // Day will be corrected in constructor for 29th February.
219:        return new Date(day, month, year + 1);
220:    } // addYear
```

> **Coffee time:** What is the value of `new Date(29, 2, 2016).addYear().getDay()`?
> _12.2.5_

Next we have three instance methods that produce a date which is earlier than this one.

```
223:    /**
224:     * Construct a new date which is one day earlier than this one.
225:     *
226:     * @return A new date which is one day earlier than this one.
227:     */
228:    public Date subtractDay()
229:    {
230:        int newDay = day - 1;
231:        int newMonth = month;
232:        int newYear = year;
233:        if (newDay < 1)
234:        {
235:            newDay = 31; // Will be corrected in constructor if too high.
236:            newMonth--;
237:            if (newMonth < 1)
238:            {
239:                newMonth = 12;
240:                newYear--;
241:            } // if
242:        } // if
243:        return new Date(newDay, newMonth, newYear);
244:    } // subtractDay
245:
246:
247:    /**
248:     * Construct a new date which is one month earlier than this one.
249:     * If the day is too large for that month, it is truncated to
250:     * the number of days in that month.
251:     *
252:     * @return A new date which is one month earlier than this one.
253:     */
254:    public Date subtractMonth()
255:    {
256:        int newMonth = month - 1;
257:        int newYear = year;
258:        if (newMonth < 1)
259:        {
260:            newMonth = 12;
261:            newYear--;
262:        } // if
```

```
263:    // Day will be corrected in constructor if too high.
264:    return new Date(day, newMonth, newYear);
265: } // subtractMonth
266:
267:
268: /**
269:  * Construct a new date which is one year earlier than this one.
270:  * If this date is a leap day, it returns 28th February of the previous year.
271:  *
272:  * @return A new date which is one year earlier than this one.
273:  */
274: public Date subtractYear()
275: {
276:    // Day will be corrected in constructor for 29th February.
277:    return new Date(day, month, year - 1);
278: } // subtractYear
```

Finally, for the public features, we have an instance method that works out the number of days between this date and another.

```
281: /**
282:  * Calculate how many days this date is from a given other.
283:  * If the other date is less than this one, then the distance
284:  * is negative. It is non-negative otherwise (including zero
285:  * if they represent the same date).
286:  *
287:  * @param other The other date.
288:  *
289:  * @return The distance in days.
290:  */
291: public int daysFrom(Date other)
292: {
293:    // The code here is a prototype
294:    // -- the result should be computed more efficiently than this!
295:    if (equals(other))
296:      return 0;
297:    else if (lessThan(other))
298:    {
299:      Date someDate = addDay();
300:      int noOfDaysDistance = 1;
301:      while (someDate.lessThan(other))
302:      {
303:        someDate = someDate.addDay();
304:        noOfDaysDistance++;
305:      } // while
306:      return noOfDaysDistance;
307:    } // else if
308:    else
309:    {
310:      Date someDate = subtractDay();
311:      int noOfDaysDistance = -1;
312:      while (someDate.greaterThan(other))
313:      {
314:        someDate = someDate.subtractDay();
```

```
315:        noOfDaysDistance--;
316:      } // while
317:      return noOfDaysDistance;
318:    } // else
319:  } // daysFrom
```

Coffee time: 12.2.6 How could we go about making a more efficient version of `daysFrom()`?

All that remains now are the two private helper **instance method**s. The first determines how many days there are in the month of this date. For February, it uses the second instance method to work out whether the year of this date is a leap year.

```
322:  // Calculate the number of days in the month.
323:  private int daysInMonth()
324:  {
325:    switch (month)
326:    {
327:      case  1: return 31;
328:      case  2: if (isLeapYear()) return 29;
329:               else              return 28;
330:      case  3: return 31;
331:      case  4: return 30;
332:      case  5: return 31;
333:      case  6: return 30;
334:      case  7: return 31;
335:      case  8: return 31;
336:      case  9: return 30;
337:      case 10: return 31;
338:      case 11: return 30;
339:      case 12: return 31;
340:      default: return 0;
341:    } // switch
342:  } // daysInMonth
```

For `isLeapYear()`, we use the **remainder operator** (see page 149) in a single **return statement**.

```
345:  // Return true if and only if year is a leap year.
346:  // (Ignoring the pre Gregorian Reformation complication -- for now.)
347:  // Year is a leap year if it is divisible by 4
348:  //                 and is not divisible by 100
349:  //                 or is divisible by 400.
350:  private boolean isLeapYear()
351:  {
352:    return year % 4 == 0
353:           && (year % 100 != 0 || year % 400 == 0);
354:  } // isLeapYear
355:
356: } // class Date
```

Coffee time: 12.2.7 Check you agree that this code will **return** the right answer for each of the years 1900 (not a leap year), 2000 (a leap year), 2001 (not a leap year), 2008 (a leap year) and 2100 (not a leap year).

12.2.1 Trying it

We can **compile** the class.

Console Input / Output
`$ javac Date.java`
`$ _`

Coffee time: 12.2.8 What would be a good way to test it?

231

Once we have removed any errors, we can process the class with the javadoc program. The -author option makes it take note of the @author tag(s) – they are ignored otherwise.

```
                    Console Input / Output
$ javadoc -author Date.java
Loading source file Date.java...
Constructing Javadoc information...
Standard Doclet version 1.6.0_22
Building tree for all the packages and classes...
Generating Date.html...
Generating package-frame.html...
Generating package-summary.html...
Generating package-tree.html...
Generating constant-values.html...
Building index for all the packages and classes...
Generating overview-tree.html...
Generating index-all.html...
Generating deprecated-list.html...
Building index for all classes...
Generating allclasses-frame.html...
Generating allclasses-noframe.html...
Generating index.html...
Generating help-doc.html...
Generating stylesheet.css...
$ _
```

This has produced the following **files**.

```
                              Console Input / Output
$ ls *.html *.css
Date.html                  help-doc.html         package-summary.html
allclasses-frame.html      index-all.html        package-tree.html
allclasses-noframe.html    index.html            stylesheet.css
constant-values.html       overview-tree.html
deprecated-list.html       package-frame.html
$ _
```

We can view the documentation by running a web browser on the file index.html.

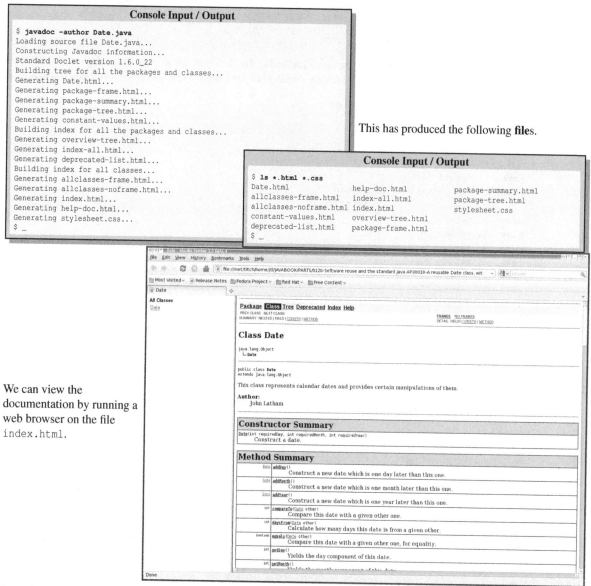

Java **class**es which are designed for **software reuse** need user documentation, and hopefully the introduction here has shown you that **doc comment**s make it easy to provide that support.

12.2.2 Coursework: StudentsCalling with doc comments

Copy your **class**es from the coursework in Section 11.3.8 on page 212 and add **doc comment**s to the **public** items in them. Then run the javadoc program and examine the results. In particular, look at the summary sections and note how the first sentence of each doc comment has been used there.

12.3 The standard Java API

AIM: To take a brief look at the standard Java **application program interface** (API).

The most obvious example of **software reuse** in Java is the standard **class**es that come with a Java installation. We have already seen and used snippets of several, including System, Math, Integer, Double and of course Scanner. There are hundreds more of them, all documented from **doc comment**s inside their implementation code. This describes an **application program interface** (API) for each class.

> *Coffee time:* Find the local copy of the **API** on-line documentation for the standard classes that come with your
> *12.3.1* Java installation. Or, if you do not have a copy, search on the Internet to find it at the Oracle website.[16] Bookmark these pages for future use. Now browse through the classes. Unfortunately, the documentation is not really aimed at novice Java programmers, so please do not let yourself be intimidated by the amount of detail, or by concepts that you have not yet met. However if you persist you will be able to find it useful. As an example, find the documentation for Math.pow() to remind you which order the two **method argument**s need to be given in.

Another of the standard classes is one called Date – you should not be surprised to find that date manipulation is provided already. In the interests of your learning, we did reinvent a wheel after all![1]

As we have said previously, the standard classes are grouped into **package**s, such as java.lang and java.util. Package java.lang is special, because the classes in there can be referred to without us needing to use their **fully qualified name**. For example, java.lang.System can simply be called System. Classes in other packages, such as java.util.Scanner, can only be used without full qualification if we have inserted an **import statement** for them at the start of our class.

12.4 The String class

AIM: To take a closer look at String.

Since very early on in in this book we have been using strings and it is now time to look at them in more detail.

> *Concept* **Standard API: String.** Strings in Java are **object**s of the standard **class** java.lang.String. This class is defined in the same way as any other, but the Java language also knows about **string literal**s and the string **concatenation operator**. So, strings are semi-built-in to Java. All the other built-in types are **primitive type**s, but String is a **reference type**.
>
> When we write
>
> ```
> String name = "Java";
> ```
>
> we are asking for an object of **type** String to be created, containing the text Java, and for a **reference** to that object to be placed in the **variable** called name. So, even though we do not use the special word **new**, whenever we write a string literal in our code, we are asking for a **new** String object to be created.

---

[1]The main difference between the standard Date class and ours here is that standard Date **object**s are **mutable object**s – a design decision that some programmers feel is inappropriate for a model of fixed entities.

String name

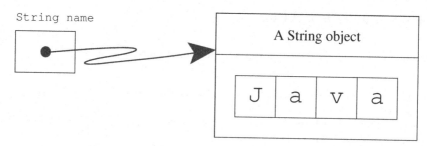

The text of a String is stored as a sequence of **character**s, each of these is a member of the **char** type. This text cannot be changed: Strings are **immutable object**s.

The **type char** was introduced in Section 9.2.2 on page 145.

Coffee time: 12.4.1
Is **char** a **primitive type** or a **reference type**?

Concept **Standard API: String: some instance methods.** Strings have **instance method**s, some of which are listed below.

Public method interfaces for class **String** (some of them).			
Method	**Return**	**Arguments**	**Description**
charAt	**char**	int	This **return**s the **character** at the specified **string index**. The characters are indexed from zero upwards.
compareTo	**int**	String	Compares the text of this with the given other, using **lexicographic order**ing (alphabetic/dictionary order). Returns 0 if they are equal, a negative **int** if this is **less than** the other, a positive **int** otherwise.
endsWith	**boolean**	String	Returns **true** if and only if the text of this string ends with that of the given other.
equals	**boolean**	String	Returns **true** if and only if this string contains the same text as the given other.
indexOf	**int**	String	Returns the index within this string of the first occurrence of the given other string, or -1 if it does not occur.
length	**int**		Returns the length of this string.
startsWith	**boolean**	String	Returns **true** if and only if the text of this string starts with that of the given other.
substring	String	**int**	Returns a **new** string that is a substring of this string. The substring begins with the character at the given index and extends to the end of this string.
substring	String	**int, int**	Returns a new string that is a substring of this string. The substring begins at the first given index and extends to the character at the second index minus one.
toLowerCase	String		Returns a new string which is the same as this one except that all upper case letters are replaced with their corresponding lower case letter.
toUpperCase	String		Returns a new string which is the same as this one except that all lower case letters are replaced with their corresponding upper case letter.

In the next section we shall use some of these **instance method**s in a program that manipulates string values.

Coffee time:
`12.4.2`

Did you notice the `equals()` instance method listed in the table above? Why in general can we not use the `==` **operator** to compare whether two strings have the same value? For example, what are the values of `equalByReference` and `equalByMethod` in the code below?

```
String s1 = "Java"; String s2 = "Java Fun".substring(0, 4);
boolean equalByReference = s1 == s2;
boolean equalByMethod = s1.equals(s2);
```

Coffee time: `12.4.3`

Take a look at the **API** on-line documentation for the `String` **class**, to see what other **methods** are available.

Coffee time:
`12.4.4`

If a `String` is an **immutable object**, how come we can write code like the following? Isn't the `String` which is contained in `result` being changed?

```
String result = "1";
for (int count = 2; count <= 10; count++)
  result += " " + count;
```

Coffee time:
`12.4.5`

Find out about the `StringBuffer` class that supports sequences of **characters** which are **mutable objects**. Under what circumstances would it really be better to use a `StringBuffer` instead of a `String`? And vice versa? Flick back through this book and try to find places where we might have appropriately used `StringBuffer`.

12.5 Example: Simple Encryption

AIM: To take a look at `String` manipulation, such as extracting individual **char** values from a `String`. We also look at how comparisons between two **char** values can be achieved, and the way we can **cast** between **char** and **int** values, and meet **overloaded methods**.

The example in this section performs a simple encode and decode operation for secret agents. It is based on one of the simplest forms of encoding, known as a **Caesar cipher**[11], which is not especially secure, but nevertheless we shall use it because of its simplicity. A Caesar cipher is a shifting of the letters of the alphabet by a fixed amount. For example, a shift of one would turn all occurrences of the letter A into B, B into C, and so on, and Z into A.

B	E	W	A	R	E		T	H	E		L	A	D	Y		K	I	L	L	E	R
C	F	X	B	S	F		U	I	F		M	B	E	Z		L	J	M	M	F	S

A shift of minus one would have the opposite effect, as would a shift of 25. Either of these values could thus be used to decode a message encoded using a shift of one.

Our program has two **class**es in it.

Class list for Crypt	
Class	**Description**
`Crypt`	The main class containing the **main method**. It will make two **instances** of `CaesarCipher`, one for encoding by a given shift and the other for decoding.
`CaesarCipher`	An instance of this will provide a cipher that shifts by a fixed amount.

235

12.5.1   The `CaesarCipher` class

We implement the `CaesarCipher` **class** with the intention that it can be reused in other programs and so we write **doc comment**s for the **public** items.

```
001: /**
002:  * This class implements a Caesar cipher with a fixed shift
003:  * specified per object at construction time. Cipher objects can
004:  * then translate a String or a single character as required.
005:  *
006:  * @author John Latham
007:  */
008: public class CaesarCipher
009: {
010:   // The shift value for the cipher. This must be 0..25.
011:   private final int cipherShift;
012:
013:
014:   /**
015:    * Construct a cipher with the given shift.
016:    * Any value outside the range 0 to 25 is converted using modulo 26.
017:    *
018:    * @param requiredCipherShift The shift to be used for this cipher.
019:    */
020:   public CaesarCipher(int requiredCipherShift)
021:   {
022:     // We store only the modulo 26 of the shift,
023:     // as we only shift the 26 letters.
024:     // The following converts negative numbers into the equivalent
025:     // non-negative one, e.g. -1 becomes 25.
026:     cipherShift = (requiredCipherShift % 26 + 26) % 26;
027:   } // CaesarCipher
```

> *Coffee time:* Convince yourself that the above code works, for example that the following are all **equivalent**.
> `12.5.1`
> `new CaesarCipher(54);` `new CaesarCipher(28);`
> `new CaesarCipher(-50);` `new CaesarCipher(-24);`
> `new CaesarCipher(2);`

```
030:   /**
031:    * Yields the cipher shift of this cipher.
032:    *
033:    * @return The shift used for this cipher.
034:    */
035:   public int getCipherShift()
036:   {
037:     return cipherShift;
038:   } // getCipherShift
```

It might be handy to have **instance method**s to create `CaesarCipher`s which are based on this one.

```
041:   /**
042:    * Constructs a new CaesarCipher with a cipher shift which is one
043:    * greater (modulo 26) than that used for this cipher.
044:    *
```

```
045:     * @return The new CaesarCipher.
046:     */
047:    public CaesarCipher incrementShift()
048:    {
049:      return new CaesarCipher(cipherShift + 1);
050:    } // incrementShift
051:
052:
053:    /**
054:     * Constructs a new CaesarCipher with a cipher shift which is one
055:     * less (modulo 26) than that used for this cipher.
056:     *
057:     * @return The new CaesarCipher.
058:     */
059:    public CaesarCipher decrementShift()
060:    {
061:      return new CaesarCipher(cipherShift - 1);
062:    } // decrementShift
```

We have two `translate()` **instance method**s, one to translate a `String` and the other to translate a single **char**.

Concept **Method: overloaded methods.** The **method signature** of a method is its name and list of **types** of its **method parameters**. Java permits us to have **overloaded methods**, that is, more than one **method** with the same name within one **class**, as long as they have different signatures. E.g. they may have a different number of parameters, different types, the same types but in a different order, etc.. If two methods had the same signature then the **compiler** could never know which one was intended by a **method call** with **method arguments** matching both of them.

For example, the method `System.out.println()` can be used with no arguments, with a single `String` as an argument, or with an argument of some other type, such as **int** or any **object**. These are in fact different methods with the same name!

Here is our `translate()` instance method which takes a `String` **method parameter**. It calls the other `translate()` instance method, which works on a single **char** for each **character** in the string.

```
065:    /**
066:     * Translate a string.
067:     *
068:     * @param message The string to be translated.
069:     * @return The translated message.
070:     */
071:    public String translate(String message)
072:    {
073:      String result = "";
074:      for (int index = 0; index < message.length(); index++)
075:        result += translate(message.charAt(index));
076:      return result;
077:    } // translate
```

 Coffee time: 12.5.2 Assuming you did look up the `StringBuffer` class, are you tempted to want to rewrite the above instance method?

237

To translate a single character, we need to check that it is a letter, as other characters are to remain unchanged. We do this using the comparisons on **char** values.

Concept **Type: char: comparisons.** Values of **type char** may be compared using the usual <, <=, ==, !=, >= and > **relational operators**. Characters are stored in the computer using numeric **character codes** – each one has a unique number – and when two **characters** are compared, the result is formed from the same comparison on the two numbers.

Generally speaking we do not need to know the actual numbers used for specific characters. However, there are certain properties that are useful to know, such as that the number for 'A' is one **less than** that for 'B', which is one less than the number used for 'C', and so on. In other words, the upper case alphabetic letters have contiguous character codes. The same is true of the lower case alphabet, and also the digit characters '0' through to '9'. The character codes for the digits are all less than those for the upper case letters, which are all less than those for the lower case letters.

For example, the following **method** checks whether a given character is a lower case alphabetic character.

```
public static boolean isLowerCase(char aChar)
{
  return aChar >= 'a' && aChar <= 'z';
} // isLowerCase
```

A method similar to this is provided in the standard **class** java.lang.Character. That one also works for **locale**s (i.e. languages) other than English.

Another property worth remembering is that, for the English characters, the code for each upper case letter is 32 less than the code for the corresponding lower case letter.

Having determined that the given **char** value is a letter, our translate() instance method will then exploit the ordering property of the **character codes**, by converting characters to and from those **integer** values.

Concept **Type: char: casting to and from int.** The numeric **character code** used to store a **character** may be obtained by **casting** a **char** value to an **int**. We can achieve this by writing (int) in front of it. For example, (int)'A' is the numeric code used to store a capital A.

We can also convert in the opposite direction, by casting an **int** to a **char**. For example, at the end of the following fragment of code, the **variable** letterB will contain an upper case B character.[2]

```
int codeForA = (int)'A';
char letterB = (char) (codeForA + 1);
```

The following **method returns** the upper case equivalent of a given character, if it is a lower case letter, or the original character if not. It assumes availability of the method isLowerCase().

```
public static char toUpperCase(char aChar)
{
  if (isLowerCase(aChar))
    return (char) ((int)aChar - (int)'a' + (int)'A');
  else
    return aChar;
} // toUpperCase
```

---

[2]Actually, the cast in the first line from **char** to **int** would be implicit, but it is good style to write it anyway. In the second line, the cast from **int** to **char** is required.

A method similar to this is provided in the standard **class** java.lang.Character. That one also works for **locale**s (i.e. languages) other than English.

Here is the second translate() instance method.

```
080:    /**
081:     * Translate a single character.
082:     * If it is a letter it is shifted within its alphabet
083:     * (i.e. upper or lower case).
084:     * If it is not a letter, it is returned unchanged.
085:     *
086:     * @param message The character to be translated.
087:     * @return The translated character.
088:     */
089:    public char translate(char aChar)
090:    {
091:      if (aChar >= 'A' && aChar <= 'Z')
092:      {
093:        int letterNo = (int)aChar - (int)'A';
094:        letterNo = (letterNo + cipherShift) % 26;
095:        return (char) (letterNo + (int)'A');
096:      } // if
097:      else if (aChar >= 'a' && aChar <= 'z')
098:      {
099:        int letterNo = (int)aChar - (int)'a';
100:        letterNo = (letterNo + cipherShift) % 26;
101:        return (char) (letterNo + (int)'a');
102:      } // else if
103:      else
104:        return aChar;
105:    } // translate
106:
107: } // class CaesarCipher
```

12.5.2   The Crypt class

The Crypt **class** simply contains the **main method** of the program. It creates two **instance**s of CaesarCipher, one for encoding and the other for decoding.

```
001: /* Program to encode / decode a message using a Caesar cipher.
002:
003:    The shift for the cipher is given as the first command line argument. The
004:    message is given as the second command line argument.
005:
006:    The message is translated by two ciphers, one with the given shift and the
007:    other with the negation of the given shift. The first is thus an encoding
008:    of the message, the second is a decoding. Both messages are printed on the
009:    standard output.
010: */
011: public class Crypt
012: {
```

```
013:    public static void main(String[] args)
014:    {
015:       int shift = Integer.parseInt(args[0]);
016:       String message = args[1];
017:       CaesarCipher encoder = new CaesarCipher(shift);
018:       CaesarCipher decoder = new CaesarCipher(-shift);
019:
020:       System.out.println(encoder.translate(message));
021:       System.out.println(decoder.translate(message));
022:    } // main
023:
024: } // class Crypt
```

12.5.3 Trying it

To encode a message we **run** the program with the required shift value and the message, and take the *first* line of the output.

```
                  Console Input / Output
$ java Crypt 5 "The truth is out there..."
Ymj ywzym nx tzy ymjwj...
Ocz ompoc dn jpo oczmz...
$ _
```

To decode the message, we enter the same shift value with the encoded string and take the *second* line of the output.

```
                  Console Input / Output
$ java Crypt 5 "Ymj ywzym nx tzy ymjwj..."
Dro dbedr sc yed drobo...
The truth is out there...
$ _
```

12.5.4 Coursework: `RomanNumber`

In this task you will create a reusable **class** called `RomanNumber` which can be used to convert between Roman Numbers and decimal numbers.

You will provide *two* **constructor method**s for this class. One will take an **int** and build a `RomanNumber` corresponding to that number. The other will take a `String` of Roman digits and build a `RomanNumber` corresponding to that number.

The class will also provide two **instance method**s. One will **return** an **int**, being the decimal number corresponding to the `RomanNumber` **instance**. The other instance method will return a `String`, which is the Roman number representation of the `RomanNumber` instance.

For the purposes of this exercise, you may assume your constructors will never be given a non-positive number, or a `String` which is not a legal Roman number.

This class can be used to convert an **integer** to its Roman equivalent string by **construct**ing an instance of `RomanNumber` from the integer, and then accessing the string value of it. To convert the other way, one could create an instance of `RomanNumber` from a string of Roman digits, and then access the integer value of it.

The rules of Roman numbers are explained below.

To help you choose names for the two instance methods, you should look at the **API** documentation of the `Integer` class. That class can be used to convert between **int** values and `String` representations in decimal, so it would be sensible to be consistent in style of names in your class.

In order to test your class, write a program called `RomanNumberTest`. This will accept a Roman number string from the first **command line argument**, convert it to an integer and then using a **loop**, print that number and the next 19 numbers, each with its Roman number equivalent, on the **standard output**. The program may assume that the argument is a legal Roman Number.

Here is an example **run**.

Console Input / Output
`$ java RomanNumberTest MMXV`

<small>(Output shown using multiple columns to save space.)</small>

Roman for 2015 is MMXV	Roman for 2025 is MMXXV
Roman for 2016 is MMXVI	Roman for 2026 is MMXXVI
Roman for 2017 is MMXVII	Roman for 2027 is MMXXVII
Roman for 2018 is MMXVIII	Roman for 2028 is MMXXVIII
Roman for 2019 is MMXIX	Roman for 2029 is MMXXIX
Roman for 2020 is MMXX	Roman for 2030 is MMXXX
Roman for 2021 is MMXXI	Roman for 2031 is MMXXXI
Roman for 2022 is MMXXII	Roman for 2032 is MMXXXII
Roman for 2023 is MMXXIII	Roman for 2033 is MMXXXIII
Roman for 2024 is MMXXIV	Roman for 2034 is MMXXXIV
`$ _`	

The Roman number system

In Roman numbers, there is no zero, nor any negative number. There are 7 digits and 6 pairs of digits, with values as follows.

Digit	Value
M	1000
D	500
C	100
L	50
X	10
V	5
I	1

Digit pair	Value
CM	900
CD	400
XC	90
XL	40
IX	9
IV	4

These are placed next to each other, with largest values on the left, and smallest on the right. The number represented is simply the sum of the values of the digits and digit pairs. The sample output from the test program (above) shows examples. Notice how each digit pair consists of a digit followed by a greater valued digit, and that the value is the value of the greater minus the value of the lesser. E.g. the value of "CM" is 1000 − 100. Perhaps contrary to your intuition, the Romans did not have other pairs than these 6. One cannot write "MIM" to mean 1999, instead it is written as "MCMXCIX": 1000 plus 900 plus 90 plus 9.

How to convert to and from Roman numbers

To convert a Roman number into an integer, we can scan the **character**s in the String from left to right and add the values of the characters to the **int** number being thus accumulated. So we start this accumulation with the value zero. However, if the value of any character is **greater than** that of the previous one, then we have just had the second character of a digit pair. In this case we subtract the value previously added, twice, and then add the value of this character. You may wish to treat the first character of the Roman number String differently from the others, as it has no previous one. For all the other characters, we shall compare the value with the value of the previous character. Some examples follow.

Roman							Decimal
XIV	X 10	I +1	V -2 +5				14
CDXLIV	C 100	D -200 +500	X +10	L -20 + 50	I +1	V -2 +5	444
CMXCIX	C 100	M -200 +1000	X +10	C -20 +100	I +1	X -2 +10	999
MIM	M 1000	I +1	M -2 +1000				1999

Notice that the last line is an illegal Roman number string, yet the **algorithm** suggested will still produce a result, and effectively behaves as though "IM" actually is a legal digit pair with the value 999.

As said above, you may assume your constructors are not given illegal strings, so there is no need for you to write code that checks legality.

Converting an integer into a Roman number is a little easier. We accumulate the sequence of Roman digits in a result String, starting with an empty string, as follows. While the number is **greater than or equal** to 1000, subtract a 1000 from it and append "M" to the result. Now do this for 900 with "CM", 500 with "D", 400 with "CD" and so on.

Implementation tips

You may find it easiest to have two **instance variable**s, one an **int** and the other a String. Each constructor simply copies its given argument to one of the instance variables, and then calculates the value of the other. You should consider having **private method**s to assist in the conversions, and perhaps reduce the amount of repeated code.

Deliverables

First design your **test data** in your logbook, then **design pseudo code** for your two conversion algorithms, before implementing the classes. During implementation you should document your RomanNumber class with **doc comments**. After completing the test program, you should run the javadoc program and browse the resulting index.html **file**.

12.6 Concepts covered in this chapter

Here is a list of the concepts that were covered in this chapter, each with a self-test question. You can use this to check you remember them being introduced, and perhaps re-read some of them before going on to the next chapter.

Class	
– objects: compareTo() (p.222)	What three (ranges of) values are returned by a compareTo method, and what does each mean?

Java tools	
– javadoc (p.223)	What tags do we use to specify a method interface?

Method	

– overloaded methods (p.237)	What is the maximum number of the 12 following methods that we could have legally in the same class?
	
	 `public Cooks burn(char coal, int oven){...}`
	 `private Cooks burn(char grilled, int fire){...}`
	 `public static Cooks burn(char mingly, int ime) {...}`
	 `private static Cooks burn(char treuse, int glass) {...}`
	
	 `public static void burn(char treuse, int glass) {...}`
	 `private static void burn(char mingly, int ime) {...}`
	 `public void burn(char grilled, int fire) {...}`
	 `private void burn(char coal, int oven) {...}`
	
	 `public double burn(char coal, int gasBbq) {...}`
	 `public static double burn(char coal, int fixedGasBbq) {...}`
	 `private double burn(char coal, int secretHotSpot) {...}`
	 `private static double burn(char jes, int rest) {...}`

Standard API	
– String (p.233)	Is String a built-in type or a reference type? Is it a primitive type?
– String: some instance methods (p.234)	Name six String instance methods (two may have the same name!).

Type	
– char: comparisons (p.238)	What is the value of each of the following conditions? 1. `'A' < 'B'` 2. `'A' < 'a'` 3. `'Z' < 'a'` 4. `'0' < '1'` 5. `'0' < 'A'` 6. `'0' < 'a'`

– char: casting to and from int (p.238)	What is the value of the following expression?
	 `"" + (char) ((int)'J' - 2)`
	 `   + (char) ((int)'c' + 2)`
	 `   + (char) ((int)'n' - 2)`
	 `   + (char) ((int)'j' + 2)`
	 `   + (char) ((int)'q' - 2)`

Chapter 13

Graphical user interfaces

The GUI is the dashboard of modern programs –
bringing complex applications
to the Sunday software driver.

13.1 Chapter aims

In this chapter we explore the Java technology required to make programs that have a **graphical user interface** (**GUI**). We introduce a significant number of **class**es, from the Java **application program interface** (**API**), which are dedicated to providing parts of GUIs or supporting them. We also include a discussion of **event driven programming**, which in Java relies on the notion that the **virtual machine** uses **thread**s to achieve parallel execution.

If desired, the chapter can be skipped or delayed without significant impact on later chapters.

The chapter contains the following sections.

Section	Aims	Associated Coursework
13.2 Hello world with a GUI (p.244)	To give a first introduction to Java **graphical user interface** (**GUI**) programs, in particular, the **class**es JFrame, Container and JLabel, together with the java.awt and javax.swing **package**s they belong to. We also talk about the idea of a class **extend**ing another class.	Write a **GUI** program to greet the world, in French. (p.249)
13.3 Hello solar system with a GUI (p.249)	To introduce the notion of **layout manager** and, in particular, FlowLayout.	Write a **GUI** program to greet your family. (p.250)
13.4 Hello solar system with a GridLayout (p.251)	To introduce the **layout manager** called GridLayout.	Write a **GUI** program to greet your family, using a GridLayout. (p.252)
13.5 Adding JLabels in a loop (p.252)	To illustrate the idea of creating **graphical user interface** (**GUI**) components in a **loop**.	Write a program to display a times table, using a **GUI** with JLabel **object**s. (p.253)

Section	Aims	Associated Coursework
13.6 Tossing a coin (p.253)	To introduce the Java **listener** model together with JButton, ActionEvent and ActionListener. This requires some discussion of the notion of **thread**s and **event driven programming**, as well as **interface**s. We also revisit JLabel.	(None.)
13.7 Stop clock (p.260)	To reinforce the Java **listener** model together with JButton, ActionEvent and ActionListener. We also introduce the idea of having the ActionListener **object** be the JFrame itself, and meet System.currentTimeMillis().	Modify a stop clock program so that it has a split time button. (p.263)
13.8 GCD with a GUI (p.264)	To introduce JTextField.	Modify a GCD program that has a **GUI**, so that it finds the GCD of three numbers. (p.266)
13.9 Enabling and disabling components (p.266)	To explore the principle of enabling and disabling **graphical user interface (GUI)** components, and revisit JButton and JTextField.	Modify a stop clock program so that the split time button is disabled when the clock is not running. (p.267)
13.10 Single times table with a GUI (p.267)	To introduce JTextArea and the **layout manager** called BorderLayout.	(None.)
13.11 GCD-with Panels (p.270)	To introduce the idea of using JPanel **object**s to make a more sophisticated interface.	(None.)
13.12 Single times table with a ScrollPane (p.273)	To introduce the use of JScrollPane and revisit JTextField.	Write a **GUI** version of the program to show the weights that are obtainable on a balance scale using three weights. (p.276)
13.13 Age history with a GUI (p.277)	To reinforce the **graphical user interface (GUI)** concepts with an example having two JButtons and many JFrames, for which we revisit FlowLayout and ActionEvent.	(None.)

13.2 Example: Hello world with a GUI

AIM:
To give a first introduction to Java **graphical user interface (GUI)** programs, in particular, the **class**es JFrame, Container and JLabel, together with the java.awt and javax.swing **package**s they belong to. We also talk about the idea of a class **extend**ing another class.

Up to this point, the **user interface** to all our programs has been via **command line argument**s and **standard output**, or via an **interactive textual user interface** through the use of Scanner on **standard input**. The **command line** may be the most appropriate interface for certain applications, particularly for more expert users. However most modern **application program**s are aimed at users who expect to interact with them via a **graphical user interface** or **GUI**.

Our first program with a GUI is one which displays a single message in a new window on the screen. This simple example serves as a vehicle for introducing many of the concepts that we need to employ in more sophisticated GUI programs.

Programs with a graphical user interface in Java use the **Java Swing** system, which is built on top of the older **Abstract Windowing Toolkit**. These consist of a number of standard **class**es offering GUI features, from which we make **instance**s and plug them together to make GUIs for our programs. These standard classes are grouped into **package**s.

Concept **Package: `java.awt` and `javax.swing`.** Inside the group of **packages** known as java, there is one called awt, so the the full name of the package is java.awt. It contains the **classes** that make up the original Java **graphical user interface** system known as the **Abstract Windowing Toolkit** (AWT). For example, there is a class that lives inside java.awt called Container, and so its **fully qualified name** is java.awt.Container.

Another group, javax contains a package called swing and this is the set of classes which make up the more modern **Java Swing** system, which is built on top of AWT. For example, there is a class that lives inside javax.swing called JFrame, and so its fully qualified name is javax.swing.JFrame.

Java programs that provide a **GUI** typically need to use classes from both these packages.

The HelloWorld program will use three classes from these two packages, namely javax.swing.JFrame, javax.swing.JLabel and java.awt.Container. Rather than write the **fully qualified name**s of these classes in the main code of our program, we will **import** them using three **import statement**s.

```
001: import java.awt.Container;
002: import javax.swing.JFrame;
003: import javax.swing.JLabel;
```

The window that our program will make appear, will be an instance of the class javax.swing.JFrame, or just JFrame as we can now call it.

Concept **GUI API: `JFrame`.** Each **instance** of the **class** javax.swing.JFrame corresponds to a window that appears on the screen.

The JFrame class represents basic empty windows. Our program will have some additional logic in it to make a window which is not empty and behaves in the way we would like it to do. To achieve this, we create a class which is an **extension** of JFrame.

Concept **Class: extending another class.** A **class** may be declared to say that it **extend**s another class, using the **reserved word `extends`**. For example, the following says that the class HelloWorld extends the class javax.swing.JFrame.

```
import javax.swing.JFrame;
public class HelloWorld extends JFrame
```

This means that all **instance**s of HelloWorld have the properties that any instance of JFrame would have, but also have all the properties that we additionally define in the HelloWorld class. It is a way of adding properties to a class without actually changing the class – the new class is an **extension** of the other one.

```
005: // Program to display a Hello World greeting in a window.
006: public class HelloWorld extends JFrame
007: {
```

In the **constructor method** for our HelloWorld class, we first set the title of the window, as follows.

Concept **GUI API: JFrame: setTitle().** The **class** javax.swing.JFrame has an **instance method** called setTitle which takes a String to be used as the title of the window. This string typically appears in the title bar of the window, depending upon what window manager the user is using (in Unix worlds there is a massive variety of window managers to choose from).

Because our class HelloWorld is an extension of JFrame, it automatically contains the setTitle() instance method defined in JFrame, so we can use it here without any prefix.

```
008:   // Constructor.
009:   public HelloWorld()
010:   {
011:     setTitle("Hello World");
```

Next we want to add a GUI component to the window. In order to do this, we need to access the **content pane** of the window.

Concept **GUI API: JFrame: getContentPane().** The **class** javax.swing.JFrame has an **instance method** called getContentPane which **returns** the **content pane** of the JFrame. This is the part of the JFrame that holds the **graphical user interface (GUI)** components of the window. It is an **instance** of java.awt.Container.

Concept **GUI API: Container.** The **class** java.awt.Container implements part of a **graphical user interface (GUI)**. An **instance** of the class is a component that is allowed to contain other components.

Thanks to our import statements, we can refer to java.awt.Container as just Container. Also, we can use the **instance method** getContentPane() of the JFrame class without any prefix, because it is automatically part of this extension to JFrame.

```
012:     Container contents = getContentPane();
```

For this program we want to add a single GUI component to the content pane, this being an instance of a javax.swing.JLabel or just JLabel.

Concept **GUI API: JLabel.** The **class** javax.swing.JLabel implements a particular part of a **graphical user interface (GUI)** which simply displays a small piece of text, that is, a label. The label text is specified as a String **method argument** to one of the JLabel **constructor methods**.

We shall create a **new** JLabel and add it to the content pane, via its add() instance method.

Concept **GUI API: Container: add().** The **class** java.awt.Container has an **instance method** called add which takes a **graphical user interface (GUI)** component and includes it in the collection of components to be displayed within the container.

Let us choose a message for this program that is more elaborate, and more 'cheesy', than the boring "Hello World!" message.

```
013:     contents.add(new JLabel("Greetings to all who dwell on Planet Earth!"));
```

Next we will specify what we would like to happen when a user of the program presses the close button on the title bar of the JFrame window.

Concept **GUI API: JFrame: setDefaultCloseOperation().** The **class** javax.swing.JFrame has an **instance method** called setDefaultCloseOperation which takes a **method parameter** that specifies what the JFrame should do when the end user presses the close button on the title bar of the window. There are four possible settings as follows.

- **Do nothing on close** – Don't do anything.

- **Hide on close** – Hide the window, so that it is no longer visible, but do not destroy it.

- **Dispose on close** – Destroy the window.

- **Exit on close** – Exit the whole program.

The parameter is actually an **int**, but we do not need to know what exact value to give as a **method argument**, because there are four **class constant**s defined in JFrame which have the right values.

```
public static final int DO_NOTHING_ON_CLOSE = ?;
public static final int HIDE_ON_CLOSE = ?;
public static final int DISPOSE_ON_CLOSE = ?;
public static final int EXIT_ON_CLOSE = ?;
```

We simply use whichever class constant suits us, as in the following example.

```
setDefaultCloseOperation(DISPOSE_ON_CLOSE);
```

In our HelloWorld program, we would like the Java **virtual machine** to exit when the user presses the close button.

```
014:    setDefaultCloseOperation(EXIT_ON_CLOSE);
```

The final thing we need to do in the constructor method, is to make this JFrame arrange itself ready for being displayed. This is known as **pack**ing.

Concept **GUI API: JFrame: pack().** The **class** javax.swing.JFrame has an **instance method** called pack. This makes the JFrame arrange itself ready for being shown on the screen. It works out the sizes and positions of all its components, and (in general) the size of the window itself. Typically pack() is called after all the **graphical user interface (GUI)** components have been added to the JFrame.

```
015:    pack();
016: } // HelloWorld
```

Next we have a **main method** which creates an instance of HelloWorld.

```
019:    // Create a HelloWorld and make it appear on screen.
020:    public static void main(String[] args)
021:    {
022:        HelloWorld theHelloWorld = new HelloWorld();
```

The final step for the program is to make the HelloWorld instance show itself on the physical screen, as follows.

247

> *Concept* **GUI API: JFrame: setVisible().** The **class** `javax.swing.JFrame` has an **instance method** called
> `setVisible`. This takes a **boolean method parameter**, and if this value is **true** then it makes the `JFrame` **object**
> cause the window it represents to appear on the physical screen, or disappear otherwise.

```
023:     theHelloWorld.setVisible(true);
024:   } // main
025:
026: } // class HelloWorld
```

13.2.1 The full `HelloWorld` code

```
001: import java.awt.Container;
002: import javax.swing.JFrame;
003: import javax.swing.JLabel;
004:
005: // Program to display a Hello World greeting in a window.
006: public class HelloWorld extends JFrame
007: {
008:   // Constructor.
009:   public HelloWorld()
010:   {
011:     setTitle("Hello World");
012:     Container contents = getContentPane();
013:     contents.add(new JLabel("Greetings to all who dwell on Planet Earth!"));
014:     setDefaultCloseOperation(EXIT_ON_CLOSE);
015:     pack();
016:   } // HelloWorld
017:
018:
019:   // Create a HelloWorld and make it appear on screen.
020:   public static void main(String[] args)
021:   {
022:     HelloWorld theHelloWorld = new HelloWorld();
023:     theHelloWorld.setVisible(true);
024:   } // main
025:
026: } // class HelloWorld
```

13.2.2 Trying it

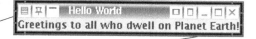

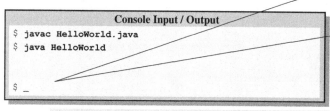

```
                 Console Input / Output
$ javac HelloWorld.java
$ java HelloWorld



$ _
```

The GUI appears, and then when we press the close
button on the window frame, the program ends.

 Coffee   Suppose we wanted the program to display *two* windows giving the greeting, instead of one.
time: `13.2.1` What changes would we need to make?

13.2.3 Coursework: `HelloWorld` GUI in French

In this task, you will take the `HelloWorld` **GUI** example and change it to greet the world in French (or some other language).

Optional extra: Make two greeting windows appear (with the same greeting).

13.3 Example: Hello solar system with a GUI

AIM: To introduce the notion of **layout manager** and, in particular, `FlowLayout`.

This program is a **graphical user interface (GUI)** version of `HelloSolarSystem` which says hello or goodbye to all nine planets. The essential difference between this and the example in the previous section, is that it will have nine `JLabel` **object**s instead of just one. However, this leads to us being concerned about how these nine items should be laid out.

```
001: import java.awt.Container;
002: import java.awt.FlowLayout;
003: import javax.swing.JFrame;
004: import javax.swing.JLabel;
005:
006: // Program to display a greeting to all nine planets, in a window.
007: public class HelloSolarSystem extends JFrame
008: {
009:   // Constructor.
010:   public HelloSolarSystem()
011:   {
012:     setTitle("Hello Solar System");
013:     Container contents = getContentPane();
```

When we intend to place more than one component into a `Container` we need to be concerned about how we wish those components to be arranged, or laid out. The easiest way to achieve this is to choose a **layout manager**.

Concept **GUI API: `LayoutManager`.** A **layout manager** is a **class** which contains the logic for laying out **graphical user interface (GUI)** components within an **instance** of `java.awt.Container` in some set pattern. There are various types of layout manager, including the following most common ones.

- `java.awt.FlowLayout` – arrange the components in a horizontal line.

- `java.awt.GridLayout` – arrange the components in a grid.

- `java.awt.BorderLayout` – arrange the components with one at the centre, and one at each of the four sides.

For our first version of the program, we shall choose a `FlowLayout`.

Concept **GUI API: `LayoutManager`: `FlowLayout`.** The **class** `java.awt.FlowLayout` is a **layout manager** which positions all the components within an **instance** of `java.awt.Container` in a horizontal row. The components appear in the order they were added to the container.

To use a layout manager, we make an **instance** of whichever type we desire to have, and then tell the `Container` that we wish it to use that layout manager, via its `setLayout()` **instance method**.

Concept **GUI API: Container: setLayout().** The **class** `java.awt.Container` has an **instance method** called `setLayout` which takes an **instance** of one of the **layout manager** classes, and uses that to lay out its **graphical user interface (GUI)** components each time a lay out is needed, for example, when the window it is part of is **pack**ed.

```
015:    // We want the planet names to appear in one line.
016:    contents.setLayout(new FlowLayout());
```

Now we add nine `JLabel` objects, and we know that these will appear in the final window, in a single row, in the order we add them.

```
018:    contents.add(new JLabel("Hello Mercury!"));
019:    contents.add(new JLabel("Hello Venus!"));
020:    contents.add(new JLabel("Hello Earth!"));
021:    contents.add(new JLabel("Hello Mars!"));
022:    contents.add(new JLabel("Hello Jupiter!"));
023:    contents.add(new JLabel("Hello Saturn!"));
024:    contents.add(new JLabel("Hello Uranus!"));
025:    contents.add(new JLabel("Hello Neptune!"));
026:    contents.add(new JLabel("Goodbye Pluto!"));
027:
028:    setDefaultCloseOperation(EXIT_ON_CLOSE);
029:    pack();
030: } // HelloSolarSystem
```

Finally we have the **main method**, which simply creates an instance and makes it visible.

```
033:    // Create a HelloSolarSystem and make it appear on screen.
034:    public static void main(String[] args)
035:    {
036:      HelloSolarSystem theHelloSolarSystem = new HelloSolarSystem();
037:      theHelloSolarSystem.setVisible(true);
038:    } // main
039:
040: } // class HelloSolarSystem
```

13.3.1   Trying it

13.3.2   Coursework: `HelloFamily` GUI

The coursework in Section 2.5.2 on page 24, asked you to produce a program called `HelloFamily` which greeted a number of your relatives. In this task you will write a version of that program which produces a window and greets the same relatives using labels. Each greeting should use a separate label. Use a `FlowLayout` **object** to manage the layout of the components in the window.

13.4 Example: Hello solar system with a `GridLayout`

AIM: To introduce the **layout manager** called `GridLayout`.

A `FlowLayout` is perfect for some jobs, but not all. An alternative **layout manager** which is perhaps better for the `HelloSolarSystem` program is a `GridLayout`.

Concept **GUI API: LayoutManager: GridLayout.** The **class** `java.awt.GridLayout` is a **layout manager** which positions all the components within an **instance** of `java.awt.Container` in a rectangular grid. The container is divided into equal-sized rectangles, and one component is placed in each rectangle. The components appear in the order they were added to the container, filling up one row at a time.

When we create a `GridLayout` **object**, we provide a pair of **int method argument**s to the **constructor method**, the first specifies the number of rows, and the second the number of columns. One of these values should be zero. For example, the following **constructs** a `GridLayout` which has three rows, and as many columns as are needed depending upon the number of components being laid out.

```
new GridLayout(3, 0);
```

This next example constructs a `GridLayout` which has two columns, and as many rows as are needed depending upon the number of components being laid out.

```
new GridLayout(0, 2);
```

If both the rows and columns arguments are non-zero, then *the columns argument is totally ignored*! Neither values may be negative, and at least one of them must be non-zero, otherwise we get a **run time error**.

We can also specify the horizontal and vertical gaps that we wish to have between items in the grid. These can be given via a constructor method that takes four arguments.

```
new GridLayout(0, 5, 10, 20);
```

The above example creates a `GridLayout` that has five columns, with a horizontal gap of 10 pixels between each column, and a vertical gap of 20 pixels between each row. A pixel is the smallest unit of display position. Its exact size will depend on the resolution and physical size of the computer monitor.

```
001: import java.awt.Container;
002: import java.awt.GridLayout;
003: import javax.swing.JFrame;
004: import javax.swing.JLabel;
005:
006: // Program to display a greeting to all nine planets, in a window.
007: public class HelloSolarSystem extends JFrame
008: {
009:   // Constructor.
010:   public HelloSolarSystem()
011:   {
012:     setTitle("Hello Solar System");
013:     Container contents = getContentPane();
```

As there are (or were) nine planets, the obvious nice layout is a three by three grid. We can achieve this either by `new GridLayout(0, 3)` or by `new GridLayout(3, 0)` – the effect would be the same. We shall opt for a gap of 10 pixels between the rows and 20 between the columns.

```
015:     // Set layout to be a grid of 3 columns.
016:     // This will also give 3 rows, as there are 9 items.
017:     contents.setLayout(new GridLayout(0, 3, 20, 10));
```

The rest of the program is the same as previously.

```
019:     contents.add(new JLabel("Hello Mercury!"));
020:     contents.add(new JLabel("Hello Venus!"));
021:     contents.add(new JLabel("Hello Earth!"));
022:     contents.add(new JLabel("Hello Mars!"));
023:     contents.add(new JLabel("Hello Jupiter!"));
024:     contents.add(new JLabel("Hello Saturn!"));
025:     contents.add(new JLabel("Hello Uranus!"));
026:     contents.add(new JLabel("Hello Neptune!"));
027:     contents.add(new JLabel("Goodbye Pluto!"));
028:
029:     setDefaultCloseOperation(EXIT_ON_CLOSE);
030:     pack();
031:   } // HelloSolarSystem
```

Finally we have the **main method**, which simply creates an **instance** and makes it visible.

```
034:   // Create a HelloSolarSystem and make it appear on screen.
035:   public static void main(String[] args)
036:   {
037:     HelloSolarSystem theHelloSolarSystem = new HelloSolarSystem();
038:     theHelloSolarSystem.setVisible(true);
039:   } // main
040:
041: } // class HelloSolarSystem
```

13.4.1 Trying it

13.4.2 Coursework: `HelloFamily` GUI with `GridLayout`

In this task, you will copy and change your HelloFamily program to use a GridLayout. Experiment with different values for the row and column **method parameter**s in order to see how these effect the layout.

In order to make it easier to try out different values for the parameters, **design** the code so that the program takes two **integer command line argument**s – the values for the number of rows and number of columns. These will then be passed to the **constructor method** and used by it to create an appropriate GridLayout **object**.

Optional extra: Make your program produce 10 windows, each having a different gap between the components. The row gaps should range from 2 to 20 in steps of 2 pixels and the column gaps from 4 to 40 insteps of 4.

13.5 Adding `JLabel`s in a loop

AIM:
To illustrate the idea of creating **graphical user interface (GUI)** components in a **loop**.

There is no example here, just a piece of coursework, and also the observation that a **graphical user interface (GUI)** can have a variable number of components in it, with these components being created and added inside a **loop**.

13.5.1   Coursework: `TimesTable` using `JLabels`

In this task you will write a program, called `TimesTable`, which takes two **integer command line arguments**, *m* and *n*. It displays an *m*-times table with *n* entries, in a window. You can assume that *m* and *n* will be integers, and that *n* is non-negative. Choose better names for your **variables** than *m* and *n*! Use `JLabel` **objects** to display the numbers and symbols and a `GridLayout` object to manage the layout. Choose horizontal and vertical gaps so that the window is laid out nicely.

For example, when given the arguments 3 and 10, we should see something like the following.

(Hint: `""` + x produces a `String` from the number x.)

Optional extra: Find out how to set the colour of components, and choose a different colour to be used for alternating rows.

		Times Table			
1	X	3	=	3
2	X	3	=	6
3	X	3	=	9
4	X	3	=	12
5	X	3	=	15
6	X	3	=	18
7	X	3	=	21
8	X	3	=	24
9	X	3	=	27
10	X	3	=	30

13.6   Example: Tossing a coin

AIM: To introduce the Java **listener** model together with `JButton`, `ActionEvent` and `ActionListener`. This requires some discussion of the notion of **thread**s and **event driven programming**, as well as **interface**s. We also revisit `JLabel`.

This next example is a program to provide a very simple coin tossing facility. It will have a single button that can be pressed by the user (that is, clicked using the mouse). Whenever this happens, the 'coin' will be tossed, with the resulting 'heads' or 'tails' being displayed in a label.

In order for you to properly understand how **interactive graphical user interface** (**GUI**) programs work, it is necessary to have an appreciation of Java **thread**s.

Concept **Execution: parallel execution – threads.** Computers appear to be able to perform more than one task at the same time. For example, we can run several programs at once and they run in parallel. At the **operating system** level, each program runs in a separate **process**, and the computer shares its **central processing unit** time fairly between the current processes.

The Java **virtual machine** has a built-in notion of processes, called **thread**s, which allows for a single program to be doing more than one thing at a time. When a Java program is started, the virtual machine creates one thread, called the **main thread**, which is set off to **run** the body of the **main method**. This **executes** the **statements** in the main method, including the statements of any **method call**s it finds. Upon reaching the end of the main method, this thread terminates, which causes the virtual machine to exit if that was the only thread existing at the time. If, however there are any other threads which have not yet terminated, then the virtual machine continues to run them. It exits the program only when all the threads have ended. (Actually, we can also get it to exit by calling `System.exit()`.)

All of the Java program examples before this chapter used only the **main thread** and so the program ended when the **main method** had finished being **executed**. However, the story gets a little more complicated when we have GUIs appearing on the screen.

Concept **Execution: parallel execution – threads: the GUI event thread.** When we have a program that places a **graphical user interface** (**GUI**) window on the screen, the Java **virtual machine** creates another **thread**, which we shall call the **GUI event thread**. This is created when the first window of the program is shown. As a result of this, the program does *not* end when the **main thread** reaches the end of the **main method** – this is of course what we want for a program with a GUI.

(In reality, the virtual machine creates several GUI event threads, but it suffices to think of there being just the one.)

The GUI event thread spends most of its life asleep – quietly doing nothing. When the end user of the program does something that might be of interest to the program, the **operating system** informs the virtual machine, which in turn wakes up the GUI event thread. Such interesting things include moving the mouse into, out of, or within a window belonging to the program, pressing a mouse key while the mouse is over such a window, typing a keyboard key while a window of the program has keyboard focus, etc.. These things are collectively known as **event**s.

When it is woken up, the GUI event thread looks to see what might have changed as a result of the end user's action. For example, he or she may have pressed a GUI button belonging to the program. For each event which is definitely interesting, the GUI event thread **execute**s some code which is designed to process that event. Then it goes back to sleep again.

Concept **Execution: event driven programming.** A large part of writing programs with **graphical user interface**s (**GUIs**) is about constructing the code which will process the **event**s associated with the end user's actions. This is known as **event driven programming**. Essentially, the **main method** sets up the GUI of the program via **method call**s, and then it ends. From then on, the code associated with processing GUI events does all the work – when the end user does things which cause such events to happen. That is, the program becomes driven by the events.

Our `CoinTosser` will use an **event driven process** – each time the button is pressed the coin will be tossed. To link our own **event** processing code to the button we shall need to use the Java **listener** model.

Concept **GUI API: Listeners.** Java uses a **listener** model for the processing of **graphical user interface** (**GUI**) **event**s. When something happens that needs dealing with, such as the end user pressing a GUI button, the **GUI event thread** creates an **object** representing the event before doing any processing that may be required. The event has an **event source**, which is some Java GUI object associated with the cause of the event. For example, an event created because the end user has pressed a button will have that button as its source. Each possible event source keeps a set of **listener** objects that have been registered as wishing to be 'told' if an event is created from that source. The GUI event thread processes the event by simply calling a particular **instance method** belonging to each of these listeners.

Let us consider an *abstract* example. Suppose we have some object that can be an event source, for example it might be a button. To keep it an abstract example, let us say it is an **instance** of `SomeKindOfEventSource`.

```
SomeKindOfEventSource source = new SomeKindOfEventSource(...);
```

Suppose also we wish events from that source to be processed by some code that we write. Let us put that in a **class** called `SomeKindOfEventListener` for this abstract example.

```
public class SomeKindOfEventListener
{
  public void processSomeKindOfEvent(SomeKindOfEvent e)
  {
    ... Code that deals with the event.
  } // processSomeKindOfEvent
} // class SomeKindOfEventListener
```

To link our code to the event source, we would make an instance of `SomeKindOfEventListener` and register it with the event source as a listener.

```
SomeKindOfEventListener listener = new SomeKindOfEventListener(...);

source.addSomeKindOfListener(listener);
```

The above code (or rather a concrete version of it) would typically be run in the **main thread** during the set up of the GUI. The following diagram illustrates the finished relationship between the source and listener objects.

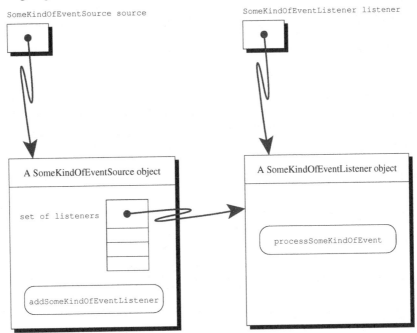

Now when an event happens, the GUI event thread can look at the set of listeners in the source object, and call the `processSomeKindOfEvent()` instance method belonging to each of them. So, when our `source` object generates an event, the `processSomeKindOfEvent()` instance method in our `listener` object is called.

Java Swing actually has several different kinds of listener for supporting different kinds of event. The above example is just an **abstraction** of this idea, so do *not* take the names `SomeKindOfEventSource`, `SomeKindOfEventListener`, `processSomeKindOfEvent` and `addSomeKindOfListener` literally – each type of event has corresponding names that are appropriate to it. For example, events generated by GUI buttons are known as `ActionEvents` and are processed by `ActionListener` objects which have an `actionPerformed()` instance method and are linked to the event source by an `addActionListener()` instance method.

13.6.1 The `CoinTosser` class

Our `CoinTosser` class **import**s a number of standard **class**es, one of which is new to this example and will be explained shortly.

```
001: import java.awt.Container;
002: import java.awt.GridLayout;
```

```
003: import javax.swing.JButton;
004: import javax.swing.JFrame;
005: import javax.swing.JLabel;
006:
007: // A simple coin tossing program. The button tosses the coin.
008: // The label shows how many tosses there have been
009: // and whether the latest one was heads or tails.
010: public class CoinTosser extends JFrame
011: {
```

The **constructor method** creates a JLabel and a JButton which it adds to the **content pane** with a single column GridLayout.

Concept **GUI API: JButton.** The **class** javax.swing.JButton implements a particular part of a **graphical user interface (GUI)** which offers a button for the end user to 'press' using the mouse. The text to be displayed on the button is specified as a String **method argument** to the JButton **constructor method**.

```
012:    // Constructor.
013:    public CoinTosser()
014:    {
015:      setTitle("Coin Tosser");
016:      Container contents = getContentPane();
017:      // Use a grid layout with one column.
018:      contents.setLayout(new GridLayout(0, 1));
019:
020:      JLabel headsOrTailsJLabel = new JLabel("Not yet tossed");
021:      contents.add(headsOrTailsJLabel);
022:
023:      JButton tossCoinJButton = new JButton("Toss the Coin");
024:      contents.add(tossCoinJButton);
```

The code which will be **run** when the JButton is pressed will reside in a separate class called TossCoinActionListener – this will be a **listener** which is capable of listening to the JButton. In order for this to work, when we write TossCoinActionListener, we shall ensure it is an ActionListener – the particular kind of listener that can be linked to a JButton.

Meanwhile, here we simply create an **instance** of TossCoinActionListener and register it as an ActionListener for the button.

Concept **GUI API: JButton: addActionListener().** The **class** javax.swing.JButton has an **instance method** called addActionListener. This takes as its **method parameter** an ActionListener **object**, and remembers it as being a **listener** interested in processing the **event** caused by an end-user pressing this button.

```
    public void addActionListener(ActionListener listener)
    {
      ... Remember that listener wants to be informed of action events.
    } // addActionListener
```

```
026:    // The action listener for the button needs to update the heads/tails
027:    // JLabel, so we pass that reference to its constructor.
028:    TossCoinActionListener listener
029:      = new TossCoinActionListener(headsOrTailsJLabel);
030:    tossCoinJButton.addActionListener(listener);
031:
032:    setDefaultCloseOperation(EXIT_ON_CLOSE);
033:    pack();
034:  } // CoinTosser
```

Finally, we have a **main method** which creates an instance of CoinTosser and makes it visible.

```
037:    // Create a CoinTosser and make it appear on screen.
038:    public static void main(String[] args)
039:    {
040:      CoinTosser theCoinTosser = new CoinTosser();
041:      theCoinTosser.setVisible(true);
042:    } // main
043:
044: } // class CoinTosser
```

13.6.2 The `TossCoinActionListener` class

The kind of **event** that is generated when a button is pressed is called an ActionEvent, and any **class** that wants its **instance**s to be a **listener** for these must **implement** the ActionListener **interface**.

Concept **Interface.** An **interface** is like a **class**, except all the **instance method**s in it must have no bodies. It is used as the basis of a kind of contract, in the sense that it may be declared that some class **implements** an interface. This means that it supplies full definitions for all the body-less instance methods listed in the interface. For example, the following code

```
public class MyClass implements SomeInterface
{
  ...
} // MyClass
```

says that the class being defined, MyClass, provides full definitions for all the instance methods listed in the interface SomeInterface. So, for example, if a **method** somewhere has a **method parameter** of **type** SomeInterface, then an **instance** of MyClass could be supplied as a corresponding **method argument**, as it satisfies the requirements of being of type SomeInterface.

Concept **GUI API: Listeners: `ActionListener` interface.** The standard **interface** called java.awt.event.ActionListener contains a body-less **instance method** which is called actionPerformed. The intention is that a full implementation of this instance method will contain code to process an **event** caused by the user doing something like pressing a **graphical user interface (GUI)** button.

We declare that the class TossCoinActionListener implements ActionListener and then a little later provide an implementation of the **instance method** listed in ActionListener.

```
001: import java.awt.event.ActionEvent;
002: import java.awt.event.ActionListener;
003: import javax.swing.JLabel;
```

```
004:
005: // The ActionListener for CoinTosser's TossCoin JButton. Each time
006: // actionPerformed is called, we count the number of tosses, and update the
007: // given JLabel with that count, plus either "Heads" or "Tails".
008: public class TossCoinActionListener implements ActionListener
009: {
010:   // The JLabel that needs to be updated.
011:   private final JLabel headsOrTailsJLabel;
012:
013:   // We count the tosses, so it is clear when we have a new toss.
014:   private int noOfTosses = 0;
015:
016:
017:   // Constructor.
018:   public TossCoinActionListener(JLabel requiredHeadsOrTailsJLabel)
019:   {
020:     headsOrTailsJLabel = requiredHeadsOrTailsJLabel;
021:   } // TossCoinActionListener
```

Next we have our implementation of the actionPerformed() instance method, which will be called when the end user presses the button in a CoinTosser.

Concept **GUI API: ActionEvent.** When the **GUI event thread** detects that the end user has performed an 'action', such as pressing a button, it creates an **instance** of the **class** java.awt.event.ActionEvent in which it stores information about the **event**. For example, it stores a **reference** to the **event source object**, such as the button that was pressed.

Concept **GUI API: Listeners: ActionListener interface: actionPerformed().** After creating an **instance** of java.awt.event.ActionEvent when the end user has performed an 'action' such as pressing a button, the **GUI event thread** finds out from that **event source** which ActionListener **objects** have registered with it as wanting to be told about the **event**. The GUI event thread then invokes the **instance method** called actionPerformed belonging to each of those registered ActionListeners, passing the ActionEvent object as a **method argument**.

So, the heading of the actionPerformed() instance method is as follows.

```
public void actionPerformed(ActionEvent event)
```

Each implementation of the method will perform whatever task is appropriate as a response to the particular action in a particular program.

In this program, we do not need to look at the ActionEvent **method parameter** supplied to actionPerformed() because we only have one button that we are listening to. If we had more than one, we could find out which one had caused the **event** by getting the **event source** from the ActionEvent.

Our code will want to change the text of the JLabel to show the number of tosses and which side of the coin has been chosen.

Concept **GUI API: JLabel: setText().** The **class** javax.swing.JLabel has an **instance method** called setText which takes a String **method argument** and changes the text of the label to it.

We use `Math.random()` to decide whether the coin should show heads or tails.

```
024:    // Action performed: update noOfTosses and headsOrTailsJLabel.
025:    public void actionPerformed(ActionEvent event)
026:    {
027:       noOfTosses++;
028:       if (Math.random() >= 0.5)
029:          headsOrTailsJLabel.setText("Toss " + noOfTosses + ": Heads");
030:       else
031:          headsOrTailsJLabel.setText("Toss " + noOfTosses + ": Tails");
032:    } // actionPerformed
033:
034: } // class TossCoinActionListener
```

The following diagram helps illustrate the **event driven process**. First the **main thread** sets up the **graphical user interface** (**GUI**), and then ends. Then, whenever the user presses the button, the **GUI event thread** wakes up and processes the event.

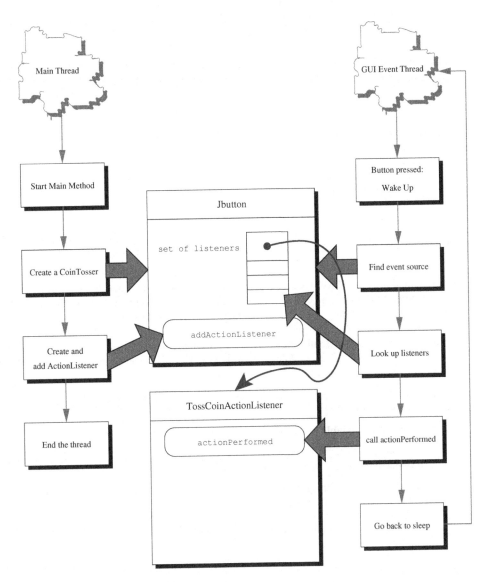

13.6.3 Trying it

The following screen dumps show a sample of what the **GUI** looks like before the button is pressed, and again after each of three presses. One should expect a different sequence of results each time the program is **run**.

13.7 Example: Stop clock

AIM:
To reinforce the Java **listener** model together with JButton, ActionEvent and ActionListener. We also introduce the idea of having the ActionListener **object** be the JFrame itself, and meet System.currentTimeMillis().

In this section we have a program to provide a very simple stop clock facility. It will have a single button that can be pressed by the user, which toggles the state of the clock between running and stopped. When it is started, it displays that fact, and when it is stopped it shows this new state and also the number of seconds elapsed between the two times.

Our StopClock class **import**s a number of standard **class**es.

```
001: import java.awt.Container;
002: import java.awt.GridLayout;
003: import java.awt.event.ActionEvent;
004: import java.awt.event.ActionListener;
005: import javax.swing.JButton;
006: import javax.swing.JFrame;
007: import javax.swing.JLabel;
008:
009: // A simple stop clock program. The button stops and starts the clock.
010: // The clock records start time, stop time and shows elapsed time.
```

Our **graphical user interface (GUI)** will have a start/stop button on it which will be pressed by the end user, and we shall want the program to run some code when this happens. As in the previous example, we will need an ActionListener to process the corresponding ActionEvent **object**s from this **event source**. However, unlike in the previous example, our plan is to have the StopClock object *itself* be the ActionListener, rather than have a separate object. Thus, we declare that the class StopClock **extends** JFrame and *also* **implements** ActionListener. This means, in effect, that it is both a JFrame and an ActionListener, although it still has to provide its own implementation of the **instance method** listed in ActionListener.

```
011: public class StopClock extends JFrame implements ActionListener
012: {
```

We have an **instance variable** to record whether or not the clock is running.

```
013:    // True if and only if the clock is running.
014:    private boolean isRunning = false;
```

In common with some **operating system**s, Java represents the current time as the number of milliseconds since midnight, January 1, 1970. This value is a **long**.

Coffee time: [13.7.1] Find out, for example by searching on the Internet, what is the significance of midnight at the start of January 1st 1970.

```
016:    // The time when the clock is started
017:    // as milliseconds since midnight, January 1, 1970.
018:    private long startTime = 0;
019:
020:    // The time when the clock is stopped
021:    // as milliseconds since midnight, January 1, 1970.
022:    private long stopTime = 0;
```

We create a number of JLabel **object**s and add them to the window. Some of these will contain a fixed piece of text that does not change, and the others will have their text changed during the **run**ning of the program. We declare instance variables to store **reference**s to those that will be changed, so that the code which makes the changes will be able to gain access to them.

```
024:    // A label for showing the start time.
025:    private final JLabel startTimeJLabel = new JLabel("Not started");
026:
027:    // A label for showing the stop time.
028:    private final JLabel stopTimeJLabel = new JLabel("Not started");
029:
030:    // A label for showing the elapsed time.
031:    private final JLabel elapsedTimeJLabel = new JLabel("Not started");
```

 Coffee time: 13.7.2 Declaring the above instance variables as **final variable**s means their value cannot be changed. Why will that not stop us from changing the value (i.e. the text) of JLabels **reference**d by them?

```
034:    // Constructor.
035:    public StopClock()
036:    {
037:      setTitle("Stop Clock");
038:
039:      Container contents = getContentPane();
040:      // Use a grid layout with one column.
041:      contents.setLayout(new GridLayout(0, 1));
042:
043:      contents.add(new JLabel("Started at:"));
044:      contents.add(startTimeJLabel);
045:
046:      contents.add(new JLabel("Stopped at:"));
047:      contents.add(stopTimeJLabel);
048:
049:      contents.add(new JLabel("Elapsed time (seconds):"));
050:      contents.add(elapsedTimeJLabel);
```

The button enabling the end user to start and stop the clock will be an **instance** of JButton.

```
052:      JButton startStopJButton = new JButton("Start / Stop");
```

In order for this instance of StopClock to be able to process **event**s caused by an end-user pressing the button, it will need to register *itself* as an ActionListener for the button. You may recall the **this reference, this** from Section 10.6 on page 180. We can use it here to tell the JButton object that this instance of StopClock wants to be informed when the button is pressed. That is, this object wants to be an ActionListener for the button.

```
053:      startStopJButton.addActionListener(this);
```

Then we add the button and complete the **constructor method** as usual.

```
054:     contents.add(startStopJButton);
055:
056:     setDefaultCloseOperation(EXIT_ON_CLOSE);
057:     pack();
058:   } // StopClock
```

Coffee time: Before continuing, make a sketch of what you think the StopClock GUI will look like. *13.7.3*

Next we have our implementation of the actionPerformed() instance method, which will be called when the end user presses the button. Once again we do not need to look at the ActionEvent **method parameter** supplied to actionPerformed() because we only have one button that we are listening to.

```
061:   // Perform action when the button is pressed.
062:   public void actionPerformed(ActionEvent event)
063:   {
064:     if (!isRunning)
065:     {
066:       // Start the clock.
```

We shall use the the **class method** currentTimeMillis() from the System class to obtain the current time when the clock is started and stopped.

> *Concept* **Standard API: System: currentTimeMillis().** The **class** java.lang.System contains a **class method** called currentTimeMillis which **returns** the current date and time expressed as the number of milliseconds since midnight, January 1, 1970. This value is a **long**.

JLabel does not have a version of setText() that takes an **int** so when we need to set the text to a number we use **concatenation** with "" to turn the **method argument** into a String.

```
067:       startTime = System.currentTimeMillis();
068:       startTimeJLabel.setText("" + startTime);
069:       stopTimeJLabel.setText("Running...");
070:       elapsedTimeJLabel.setText("Running...");
071:       isRunning = true;
072:     } //if
073:     else // isRunning
074:     {
075:       // Stop the clock and show the updated times.
076:       stopTime = System.currentTimeMillis();
077:       stopTimeJLabel.setText("" + stopTime);
078:       long elapsedMilliSeconds = stopTime - startTime;
079:       elapsedTimeJLabel.setText("" + elapsedMilliSeconds / 1000.0);
080:       isRunning = false;
081:     } // else
082:     // It is a good idea to pack again
083:     // because the size of the labels may have changed.
084:     pack();
085:   } // actionPerformed
```

Coffee time: Why do we divide the elapsed time by 1000? *13.7.4*

The **main method** simply creates an instance of StopClock and makes it visible.

```
088:   // Create a StopClock and make it appear on screen.
089:   public static void main(String[] args)
090:   {
091:     StopClock theStopClock = new StopClock();
```

```
092:      theStopClock.setVisible(true);
093:    } // main
094:
095: } // class StopClock
```

13.7.1 Trying it

These screen dumps show what the **GUI** looks like before the button is pressed, after it is pressed once and finally after a second press.

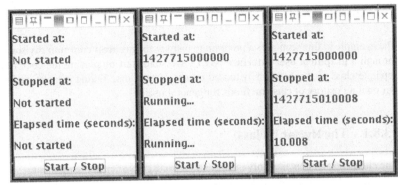

Coffee time: [13.7.5] Showing the start and stop time as milliseconds is, perhaps, interesting for someone new to that idea, but not really so for anyone who actually wants to use the program. Think about changing the **design** so that the GUI does not show the start and stop times, but just shows the running status (not-started, running or stopped) instead.

13.7.2 Coursework: `StopClock` with split time

In this task you will take the `StopClock` program and change it to add a split time button. Your program should still be called `StopClock`, and behave as follows.

- The **GUI** has two buttons: `Start/Stop` and `Split`.

- It has four output displays: the start time, stopped time, split time and elapsed time. Each of these is a `JLabel` and each also has a fixed `JLabel` to explain it.

- The clock starts when the `Start/Stop` button is pressed. The current time is shown as the start time.

- If the `Split` button is pressed while the clock is running, the clock will show the elapsed time as the split time.

- If the `Split` button is pressed again while the clock is running, the split time will be updated.

- The clock is stopped by pressing the `Start/Stop` button, at which point it will display the current time as the stopped time, and calculate, and display the elapsed time. The split time will be unchanged.

- If the `Split` button is pressed while the clock is not running, nothing happens.

In order to implement this program, you will need to make use of the `getSource()` **instance method** of `ActionEvent`. This takes no **method arguments** and **returns** a **reference** to the **object** which was responsible for causing the **event**. So, for example, you may have code like the following.

```
if (event.getSource() == startStopJButton)
   ...
```

You will need to turn the **method variable** `startStopJButton` into an **instance variable**. Why is that?

Optional extra: Improve the GUI, from an end user's point of view, by removing the start and stop times: show just the status instead.

Optional extra: Extend the program to allow the recording of several split times, with a button for each split time.

Optional extra: Also, why not add a facility to pause and resume the clock?

13.8 Example: GCD with a GUI

AIM:
To introduce `JTextField`.

The example in this section is a program to display the **greatest common divisor** of two numbers supplied by the end user through a **graphical user interface (GUI)**. We shall start by placing the code to compute the GCD of two numbers in a separate **class** so it can be easily reused in many programs. Taking inspiration from the standard `Math` class, let us create our own repository of **class method**s for general use.

13.8.1 The MyMath class

The **class** `MyMath` contains only `greatestCommonDivisor()` at the moment.

As it is intended for **software reuse** we write **doc comment**s for it. We do not need to present the code here because you have seen it before, and in any case it is sufficient to read the **API** documentation in order to use it!

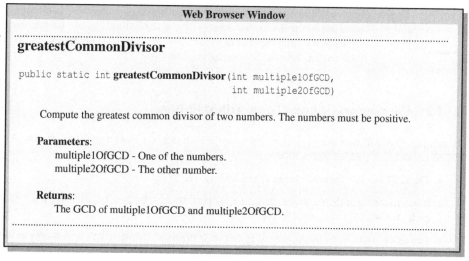

Web Browser Window

greatestCommonDivisor

```
public static int greatestCommonDivisor(int multiple1OfGCD,
                                        int multiple2OfGCD)
```

Compute the greatest common divisor of two numbers. The numbers must be positive.

Parameters:
multiple1OfGCD - One of the numbers.
multiple2OfGCD - The other number.

Returns:
The GCD of multiple1OfGCD and multiple2OfGCD.

13.8.2 The GCD class

The `GCD` class will provide a GUI for the program, and also its **main method**. We shall meet one new class in this code, called `javax.swing.JTextField`.

```
001: import java.awt.Container;
002: import java.awt.GridLayout;
003: import java.awt.event.ActionEvent;
004: import java.awt.event.ActionListener;
005: import javax.swing.JButton;
006: import javax.swing.JFrame;
007: import javax.swing.JLabel;
008: import javax.swing.JTextField;
009:
010: // Calculates the GCD of two integers.
011: public class GCD extends JFrame implements ActionListener
012: {
```

The most appropriate way for the user to enter the numbers is through **instance**s of the class `javax.swing.JTextField`.

Concept **GUI API: `JTextField`.** The **class** `javax.swing.JTextField` implements a particular part of a **graphical user interface (GUI)** which allows a user to enter a small piece of text. One of the **constructor methods** of the class takes a single `int` **method parameter**. This is the minimum number of **character**s of text we would like the field to be wide enough to display.

We can also use a `JTextField` to display a small piece of text generated from within the program.

```
013:    // A JTextField for each number.
014:    private final JTextField number1JTextField = new JTextField(20);
015:    private final JTextField number2JTextField = new JTextField(20);
016:
017:    // A JTextField for the result.
018:    private final JTextField resultJTextField = new JTextField(20);
```

As usual, the **constructor method** creates the GUI components and adds them to the `JFrame`. It also uses the **this reference** to link this **object** as the `ActionListener` for the `JButton`.

```
021:    // Constructor.
022:    public GCD()
023:    {
024:        setTitle("GCD");
025:
026:        Container contents = getContentPane();
027:        contents.setLayout(new GridLayout(0, 1));
028:
029:        contents.add(new JLabel("Number 1"));
030:        contents.add(number1JTextField);
031:        contents.add(new JLabel("Number 2"));
032:        contents.add(number2JTextField);
033:
034:        JButton computeJButton = new JButton("Compute");
035:        contents.add(computeJButton);
036:        computeJButton.addActionListener(this);
037:
038:        contents.add(new JLabel("GCD of Number 1 and Number 2"));
039:        contents.add(resultJTextField);
040:
041:        setDefaultCloseOperation(EXIT_ON_CLOSE);
042:        pack();
043:    } // GCD
```

Coffee time: 13.8.1 Before continuing, make a sketch of what you think the GCD GUI will look like.

The `actionPerformed()` **instance method** will obtain **data** from the input text fields, perform the calculation and present the result in the output text field.

Concept **GUI API: `JTextField`: `getText()`.** The **class** `javax.swing.JTextField` has an **instance method** called `getText` which takes no **method arguments** and **returns** the text contents of the text field, as a `String`.

Concept **GUI API: `JTextField`: `setText()`.** The **class** `javax.swing.JTextField` has an **instance method** called `setText` which takes a `String` as its **method argument** and changes the text of the text field to the given value.

```
046:    // Act upon the button being pressed.
047:    public void actionPerformed(ActionEvent event)
048:    {
049:      int number1 = Integer.parseInt(number1JTextField.getText());
050:      int number2 = Integer.parseInt(number2JTextField.getText());
051:      int theGCD = MyMath.greatestCommonDivisor(number1, number2);
052:      resultJTextField.setText("" + theGCD);
053:    } // actionPerformed
```

Coffee time: [13.8.2]
Is there anything to stop the user
from changing the result, by
typing directly into its text field?

The **main method** simply creates an **instance** of GCD and makes it appear on the screen.

```
056:    // Create a GCD and make it appear on screen.
057:    public static void main(String[] args)
058:    {
059:      GCD theGCD = new GCD();
060:      theGCD.setVisible(true);
061:    } // main
062:
063: } // class GCD
```

Coffee time: [13.8.3] Do we need the **local variable** theGCD in the main
method? What if the body was simply the following?
new GCD().setVisible(true);
Would that work?

13.8.3 Trying it

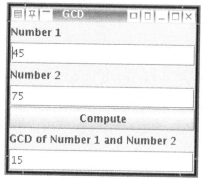

13.8.4 Coursework: GCD GUI for three numbers

In this task you will produce a version of the GCD program with a **GUI**, that
calculates the GCD of *three* numbers rather than two. This will require you to
add an additional field to the interface, and alter the code of the **class** so that it
calculates the appropriate value. As with the example in the section, the code for
obtaining the GCD should reside in a separate MyMath class.

Optional extra: The GCD program requires that the user enters **integer** values.
What happens if he or she supplies values that are not integers? How might you
go about addressing this issue?

13.9 Enabling and disabling components

AIM:
To explore the principle of enabling and disabling **graphical user interface (GUI)**
components, and revisit JButton and JTextField.

There is no example here, just a few concepts and a piece of coursework.

Concept **GUI API: JButton: setEnabled().** The **class** javax.swing.JButton has an **instance method** called
setEnabled, which takes a **boolean method parameter**. If it is given the value **false**, the button becomes disabled,
that is any attempt to press it has no effect. If instead the parameter is **true**, the button becomes enabled. When in
the disabled state, the button will typically look 'greyed out'.

Concept **GUI API: JTextField: setEnabled().** The **class** javax.swing.JTextField has an **instance method** called setEnabled, which takes a **boolean method parameter**. If it is given the value **false**, the text field becomes disabled, that is any attempt to type into it has no effect. If instead the parameter is **true**, the text field becomes enabled. When in the disabled state, the text field will typically look 'greyed out'.

Concept **GUI API: JButton: setText().** The **class** javax.swing.JButton has an **instance method** called setText which takes a String and changes the text label displayed on the button, to the given **method argument**.

13.9.1 Coursework: StopClock using a text field and disabled split button

In this task you will change your StopClock program as follows.

- Have the start/stop button labelled Start when the clock is not running, and Stop when it is.
- Disable the split button when the clock is not running, enable it when the clock is running.
- Use JTextField **objects** rather than JLabel objects to display the times. Make it so that the end user cannot edit the text showing in these text fields.

Optional extra: Make the stop clock more pretty by using colours appropriately.

13.10 Example: Single times table with a GUI

AIM: To introduce JTextArea and the **layout manager** called BorderLayout.

The example in this section is a version of the program which prints a single times table. The user will enter the multiplier in a JTextField and then press a JButton to make the program display its resulting table in a JTextArea.

Concept **GUI API: JTextArea.** The **class** javax.swing.JTextArea implements a particular part of a **graphical user interface** (GUI) which displays a larger piece of text, consisting of multiple lines. The size of the text area can be specified as **method argument**s to the **constructor method**, as the number of rows (lines) and the number of columns (characters per line).

To arrange the components of the **graphical user interface** (GUI) in this program, we shall use a BorderLayout.

Concept **GUI API: LayoutManager: BorderLayout.** The **class** java.awt.BorderLayout is a **layout manager** which has slots for five components, one at the centre, and one at each of the four sides around the centre. The names of these positions are modelled using five **class constant**s called BorderLayout.CENTER, BorderLayout.NORTH, BorderLayout.SOUTH, BorderLayout.WEST. and BorderLayout.EAST.

A BorderLayout is designed to be used when there is one **graphical user interface** (GUI) component which is in some sense the main component, for example a JTextArea which contains some result of the program. We can put this in the BorderLayout.CENTER position and some other component above in the BorderLayout.NORTH position, and/or below in the BorderLayout.SOUTH position, and/or to the left in the BorderLayout.WEST position and/or to the right in the BorderLayout.EAST position.

This is shown in the following diagram.

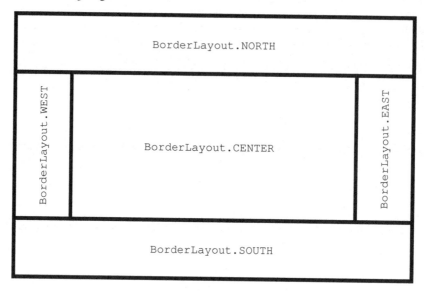

We shall use only three of the five positions: the multiplier text field will go at BorderLayout.NORTH, the result text area at BorderLayout.CENTER, and the button to make the table be generated will be placed at BorderLayout.SOUTH.

```
001: import java.awt.BorderLayout;
002: import java.awt.Container;
003: import java.awt.event.ActionEvent;
004: import java.awt.event.ActionListener;
005: import javax.swing.JButton;
006: import javax.swing.JFrame;
007: import javax.swing.JTextArea;
008: import javax.swing.JTextField;
009:
010: // Program to show a times table for a multiplier chosen by the user.
011: public class TimesTable extends JFrame implements ActionListener
012: {
013:   // A text field for the user to enter the multiplier.
014:   private final JTextField multiplierJTextField = new JTextField(5);
015:
016:   // A text area for the resulting times table, 15 lines of 20 characters.
017:   private final JTextArea displayJTextArea = new JTextArea(15, 20);
```

The **constructor method** will set up the GUI as usual, except that when we come to add the components, we specify the position for each one.

Concept **GUI API: Container: add(): adding with a position constraint.** The **class** java.awt.Container has another **instance method** called add which takes a **graphical user interface (GUI)** component and some other **object** constraining how the component should be positioned. This is intended for use with **layout managers** that use position constraints, such as java.awt.BorderLayout. For example, the following code makes the JLabel appear in the north position of myContainer.

```
        myContainer.setLayout(new BorderLayout());
        myContainer.add(new JLabel("This is in the north"), BorderLayout.NORTH);
```

```
020:   // Constructor.
021:   public TimesTable()
022:   {
023:     setTitle("Times Table");
024:
025:     Container contents = getContentPane();
026:     contents.setLayout(new BorderLayout());
027:
028:     contents.add(multiplierJTextField, BorderLayout.NORTH);
029:     contents.add(displayJTextArea, BorderLayout.CENTER);
030:
031:     JButton displayJButton = new JButton("Display");
032:     contents.add(displayJButton, BorderLayout.SOUTH);
033:     displayJButton.addActionListener(this);
034:
035:     setDefaultCloseOperation(EXIT_ON_CLOSE);
036:     pack();
037:   } // TimesTable
```

Coffee time: `13.10.1` If we wanted to stop the user from typing directly into the text area, what do you imagine we would need to do?

Coffee time: `13.10.2` Before continuing, make a sketch of what you think the TimesTable GUI will look like.

The `actionPerformed()` **instance method** generates the result text and places it in the `JTextArea`.

Concept **GUI API: JTextArea: setText().** The **class** `javax.swing.JTextArea` has an **instance method** called `setText` which takes a `String` as a **method argument** and changes the text of the text area to the given value. This `String` may contain **new line character**s in it, and the text area will display the text appropriately as separate lines.

Concept **GUI API: JTextArea: append().** The **class** `javax.swing.JTextArea` has an **instance method** called `append` which takes a `String` and appends it onto the end of the text already in the text area. Any required line breaks must be made by including explicit **new line character**s.

```
040:   // Act upon the button being pressed.
041:   public void actionPerformed(ActionEvent event)
042:   {
043:     // Empty the text area to remove any previous result.
044:     displayJTextArea.setText("");
045:
046:     int multiplier = Integer.parseInt(multiplierJTextField.getText());
047:
048:     displayJTextArea.append("--------------------------------\n");
049:     displayJTextArea.append("| Times table for " + multiplier + "\n");
050:     displayJTextArea.append("--------------------------------\n");
051:     for (int thisNumber = 1; thisNumber <= 10; thisNumber++)
052:       displayJTextArea.append("| " + thisNumber + " x " + multiplier
053:                               + " = " + thisNumber * multiplier + "\n");
054:     displayJTextArea.append("--------------------------------\n");
055:   } // actionPerformed
```

Coffee time: `13.10.3` What would be the consequence if we missed out the bit that sets the text to empty, given that `JTextArea` **object**s start with no text anyway?

269

In our **main method**, we simply create an **instance** of TimesTable and make it visible. As we do not wish to do anything else with that instance, we do not actually need to store a **reference** to it in a **variable**.

```
058:   // Create a TimesTable and make it appear on the screen.
059:   public static void main(String[] args)
060:   {
061:     new TimesTable().setVisible(true);
062:   } // main
063:
064: } // class TimesTable
```

13.10.1   Trying it

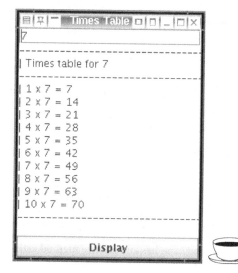

Coffee time: 13.10.4
Look back at the main methods of the previous examples in this chapter. For which ones could we have decided *not* to store the reference to the instance of the GUI in a variable? Given that these variables are **method variables** and so are 'destroyed' when the main method ends, does it actually make any difference to the Java **virtual machine** whether or not we use them to temporarily store a reference to the GUI?

13.11   Example: GCD-with Panels

AIM:
To introduce the idea of using JPanel **objects** to make a more sophisticated interface.

In this example, we are going to re-implement the GCD program from Section 13.8.2 on page 264 to have a nicer interface. We shall use JPanel **objects** to enable us to have more control over the layout.

Concept **GUI API: JPanel.** The **class** javax.swing.JPanel is an **extension** of the older java.awt.Container, which means that it is a component that is allowed to contain other components, and it has add() **instance methods** allowing us to add components to it. JPanel is designed to work well with the rest of the **Java Swing package**, and is the recommended kind of container to use when we wish to group a collection of components so that they are treated as one for layout purposes.

Here is a plan of our improved **graphical user interface** (GUI). It will use a GridLayout to obtain a two by one layout. Each of these two components will be a JPanel object. The top one will be a JPanel with a two by two GridLayout, and the bottom one will be a JPanel with a one by two GridLayout. The right component of this latter one will itself be another JPanel with a two by one GridLayout.

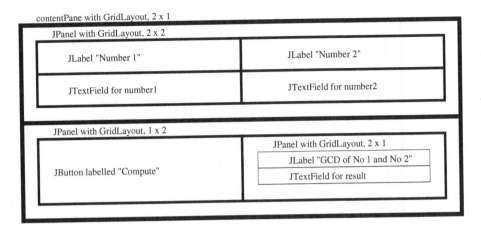

Here is the code.

```
001: import java.awt.Container;
002: import java.awt.GridLayout;
003: import java.awt.event.ActionEvent;
004: import java.awt.event.ActionListener;
005: import javax.swing.JButton;
006: import javax.swing.JFrame;
007: import javax.swing.JLabel;
008: import javax.swing.JPanel;
009: import javax.swing.JTextField;
010:
011: // Calculates the GCD of two integers.
012: public class GCD extends JFrame implements ActionListener
013: {
014:    // A JTextField for each number.
015:    private final JTextField number1JTextField = new JTextField(20);
016:    private final JTextField number2JTextField = new JTextField(20);
017:
018:    // A JTextField for the result.
019:    private final JTextField resultJTextField = new JTextField(20);
```

The **constructor method** builds the GUI according to our plan.

```
022:    // Constructor.
023:    public GCD()
024:    {
025:       setTitle("GCD");
026:
027:       Container contents = getContentPane();
028:       // Main layout will be 2 by 1.
029:       contents.setLayout(new GridLayout(0, 1));
030:
031:       // A JPanel for the top half of the main grid.
032:       // This will have a layout of 2 by 2.
033:       // It will contain two labels, and two text fields for input.
034:       JPanel numberFieldsJPanel = new JPanel();
035:       contents.add(numberFieldsJPanel);
036:       numberFieldsJPanel.setLayout(new GridLayout(0, 2));
037:
038:       // A JPanel for the bottom half of the main grid.
039:       // This will have a layout of 1 by 2.
040:       // It will contain the button and JPanel for the result.
041:       JPanel buttonAndResultJPanel = new JPanel();
042:       contents.add(buttonAndResultJPanel);
043:       buttonAndResultJPanel.setLayout(new GridLayout(0, 2));
```

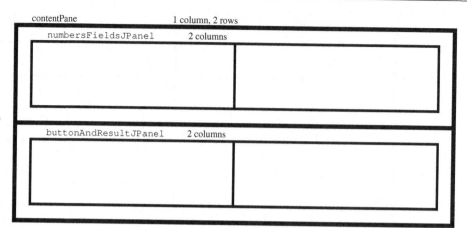

The following sketch shows what we have so far.

```
045:    // Two labels and two text fields for the top JPanel.
046:    numberFieldsJPanel.add(new JLabel("Number 1"));
047:    numberFieldsJPanel.add(new JLabel("Number 2"));
048:    numberFieldsJPanel.add(number1JTextField);
049:    numberFieldsJPanel.add(number2JTextField);
```

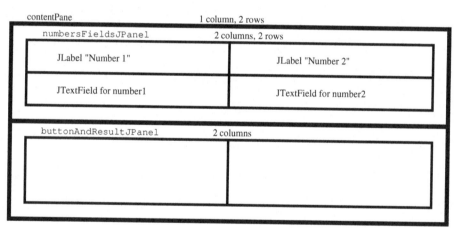

Adding those four components to the top JPanel will make it use two rows.

```
051:    // The compute button will live in the left of the bottom JPanel.
052:    JButton computeJButton = new JButton("Compute");
053:    buttonAndResultJPanel.add(computeJButton);
054:    computeJButton.addActionListener(this);
055:
056:    // A JPanel for the right of the bottom half of the main grid.
057:    // This will have a layout of 2 by 1.
058:    // It will contain a label and a text field for the result.
059:    JPanel resultJPanel = new JPanel();
060:    buttonAndResultJPanel.add(resultJPanel);
061:    resultJPanel.setLayout(new GridLayout(0, 1));
```

The GUI is nearly complete, with the following structure.

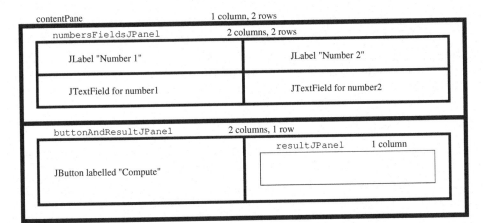

Finally we add two components into this bottom right JPanel which will make it have two rows in the one column, as per our plan on page 270.

```
063:    // A label and a text field for the bottom right JPanel.
064:    resultJPanel.add(new JLabel("GCD of Number 1 and Number 2"));
065:    resultJPanel.add(resultJTextField);
066:
067:    setDefaultCloseOperation(EXIT_ON_CLOSE);
068:    pack();
069: } // GCD
070:
071:
072:    // Act upon the button being pressed.
073:    public void actionPerformed(ActionEvent event)
074:    {
075:      int number1 = Integer.parseInt(number1JTextField.getText());
076:      int number2 = Integer.parseInt(number2JTextField.getText());
077:      int theGCD = MyMath.greatestCommonDivisor(number1, number2);
078:      resultJTextField.setText("" + theGCD);
079:    } // actionPerformed
080:
081:
082:    // Create a GCD and make it appear on screen.
083:    public static void main(String[] args)
084:    {
085:      new GCD().setVisible(true);
086:    } // main
087:
088: } // class GCD
```

Coffee time: `13.11.1` Convince yourself that the above code will result in a GUI that is laid out as we planned.

13.11.1 Trying it

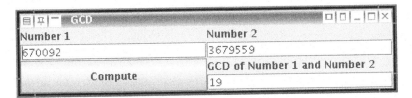

Coffee time: `13.11.2`
Can you think of other ways that we could have obtained the same layout?

13.12 Example: Single times table with a **ScrollPane**

AIM: To introduce the use of JScrollPane and revisit JTextField.

In this section we revisit the `TimesTable` program from Section 13.10 on page 268. We shall make it a little more flexible by adding a second `JTextField` enabling the user to choose how many rows of the **multiplication** table should be displayed.

This leads to a situation in which the number of lines of text being displayed in the `JTextArea` could exceed the size we have set for it, and so we would want the text to be scrollable by the user. Perhaps surprisingly, `JTextArea` **object**s do not provide scrolling features by default. Instead, we make use of a separate **graphical user interface** (**GUI**) **class** called `JScrollPane`.

> *Concept* **GUI API: JScrollPane.** The **class** `javax.swing.JScrollPane` implements a particular part of a **graphical user interface** (**GUI**) which provides a scrolling facility over another component.
>
> The simplest way to use it is to invoke the **constructor method** which takes a GUI component as a **method parameter**. This creates a `JScrollPane` **object** which provides a scrollable view of the given component.
>
> As an example, consider the following code which adds a `JTextArea` to the **content pane** of a `JFrame`.
>
> ```
> Container contents = getContentPane();
> contents.add(new JTextArea(15, 20));
> ```
>
> To make the `JTextArea` scrollable, we would replace the above with the following code instead.
>
> ```
> Container contents = getContentPane();
> contents.add(new JScrollPane(new JTextArea(15, 20)));
> ```

```
001: import java.awt.BorderLayout;
002: import java.awt.Container;
003: import java.awt.GridLayout;
004: import java.awt.event.ActionEvent;
005: import java.awt.event.ActionListener;
006: import javax.swing.JButton;
007: import javax.swing.JFrame;
008: import javax.swing.JLabel;
009: import javax.swing.JPanel;
010: import javax.swing.JTextArea;
011: import javax.swing.JTextField;
012: import javax.swing.JScrollPane;
013:
014: // Program to show a times table for a multiplier chosen by the user.
015: // The user also chooses the size of the table.
016: public class TimesTable extends JFrame implements ActionListener
017: {
```

We will have a `JTextField` for the multiplier and for the table size. The latter will have an initial value thus providing a default table size.

> *Concept* **GUI API: JTextField: initial value.** The **class** `javax.swing.JTextField` has a **constructor method** which takes a `String` **method parameter** to be used as the initial value for the text inside the text field.
>
> ```
> JTextField nameJTextField = new JTextField("Type your name here.");
> ```

```
018:     // A text field for the user to enter the multiplier.
019:     private final JTextField multiplierJTextField = new JTextField(5);
020:
```

```
021:    // A text field for the user to enter the table size, initial value 10.
022:    private final JTextField tableSizeJTextField = new JTextField("10");
023:
024:    // A text area for the resulting times table, 15 lines of 20 characters.
025:    private final JTextArea displayJTextArea = new JTextArea(15, 20);
```

The **constructor method** uses a JPanel to group together the two JTextFields, each with a JLabel.

```
028:    // Constructor.
029:    public TimesTable()
030:    {
031:      setTitle("Times Table");
032:
033:      Container contents = getContentPane();
034:      contents.setLayout(new BorderLayout());
035:
036:      // A JPanel for the two text fields.
037:      // It will be a GridLayout of two times two,
038:      // at the top of the JFrame contents.
039:      JPanel numbersPanel = new JPanel(new GridLayout(2, 0));
040:      contents.add(numbersPanel, BorderLayout.NORTH);
041:
042:      // Add two JLabels, and two JTextFields to the numbersPanel.
043:      numbersPanel.add(new JLabel("Multiplier:"));
044:      numbersPanel.add(multiplierJTextField);
045:      numbersPanel.add(new JLabel("Table size:"));
046:      numbersPanel.add(tableSizeJTextField);
047:
048:      // The result JScrollPane/JTextArea goes in the centre.
049:      contents.add(new JScrollPane(displayJTextArea), BorderLayout.CENTER);
050:
051:      // The JButton goes at the bottom.
052:      JButton displayJButton = new JButton("Display");
053:      contents.add(displayJButton, BorderLayout.SOUTH);
054:      displayJButton.addActionListener(this);
055:
056:      setDefaultCloseOperation(EXIT_ON_CLOSE);
057:      pack();
058:    } // TimesTable
```

The `actionPerformed()` **instance method** is similar to the one in the previous version of the program, but different in the obvious way.

```
061:    // Act upon the button being pressed.
062:    public void actionPerformed(ActionEvent event)
063:    {
064:      // Empty the text area to remove any previous result.
065:      displayJTextArea.setText("");
066:
067:      int multiplier = Integer.parseInt(multiplierJTextField.getText());
068:      int tableSize = Integer.parseInt(tableSizeJTextField.getText());
069:
070:      displayJTextArea.append("------------------------------\n");
071:      displayJTextArea.append("| Times table for " + multiplier + "\n");
072:      displayJTextArea.append("------------------------------\n");
073:      for (int thisNumber = 1; thisNumber <= tableSize; thisNumber++)
074:        displayJTextArea.append("| " + thisNumber + " x " + multiplier
075:                        + " = " + thisNumber * multiplier + "\n");
076:      displayJTextArea.append("------------------------------\n");
077:    } // actionPerformed
```

Finally we have the **main method**.

```
080:   // Create a TimesTable and make it appear on the screen.
081:   public static void main(String[] args)
082:   {
083:     new TimesTable().setVisible(true);
084:   } // main
085:
086: } // class TimesTable
```

13.12.1   Trying it

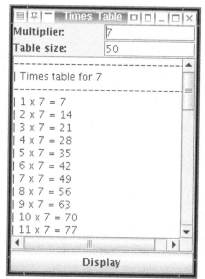

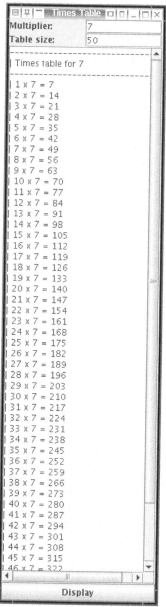

One of the nicest things about **layout managers** is their ability to rearrange the **GUI** when the end user alters the size or shape of the window. For example, this second screen dump (which has been scaled down) shows what happens to the TimesTable program if the user tall maximizes[a] the window. The TextArea, in the centre of the BorderLayout is stretched to use the new space, while the components at the north are left at their normal sizes.

---

[a]Tall maximizing is the process of making a window have a height the same as that of the screen, but without changing the width. Some window managers aimed at clever users offer a button to achieve the effect – it is the one which is fourth from the right in the screen dumps shown here. This is very convenient for applications which are essentially a portrait oriented page, and is better than full screen maximizing as the user can have more than one window visible side by side at the same time.

13.12.2   Coursework: ThreeWeights GUI

In this task you will write a **GUI** version of the ThreeWeights coursework example from Section 3.7.3 on page 50. The program should offer the same functionality as the original one, that is, the user provides three weights and is then shown the possible values that can be weighed using them.

The user input should be through the use of text fields, and the results should be displayed in a scrollable text area.

Rather than have 27 System.out.println() calls as in the previous version of the exercise, a simpler way to compute the results is to use three **nested loops**, one for each weight. Each **loop variable** will be a multiplier for the corresponding weight, going through the values -1, 0 and 1. -1 represents placing that weight in the same pan as the gold, 0 represents not using that weight, and 1 represents placing that weight in the pan opposite the gold.

276

13.13 Example: Age history with a GUI

AIM: To reinforce the **graphical user interface (GUI)** concepts with an example having two JButtons and many JFrames, for which we revisit FlowLayout and ActionEvent.

We finish this chapter with a **graphical user interface (GUI)** version of the AgeHistory program. We reuse the Person **class** from the previous version of the program in Section 11.2.6 on page 195, together with our improved reusable Date class from Section 12.2 on page 224. All we need to do is write a GUI version of the main class.

The GUI allows the end user to set the current date, a name and a birthday in text fields, and then obtain the age history in a text area. If the details of another person are required, the user can either replace the name and birthday information in the current window, or obtain an entirely separate copy of the window so as to have both displayed on the screen at the same time. In fact, there can be any number of copies of the window at the same time.

```
001: import java.awt.BorderLayout;
002: import java.awt.Container;
003: import java.awt.FlowLayout;
004: import java.awt.GridLayout;
005: import java.awt.event.ActionEvent;
006: import java.awt.event.ActionListener;
007: import javax.swing.JButton;
008: import javax.swing.JFrame;
009: import javax.swing.JLabel;
010: import javax.swing.JPanel;
011: import javax.swing.JScrollPane;
012: import javax.swing.JTextArea;
013: import javax.swing.JTextField;
014:
015: /* Report the age history of a person.
016:    Current date and person details are entered through text fields.
017:    The result is displayed in a text area.
018:    A ``new'' button enables multiple displays.
019: */
020: public class AgeHistory extends JFrame implements ActionListener
021: {
```

The class has eight **instance variable**s for collecting input in text fields and displaying the result in a text area.

```
022:    // JTextFields for the present date.
023:    private final JTextField presentDayJTextField = new JTextField(2);
024:    private final JTextField presentMonthJTextField = new JTextField(2);
025:    private final JTextField presentYearJTextField = new JTextField(4);
026:
027:    // JTextFields for the name and birthday.
028:    private final JTextField nameJTextField = new JTextField(15);
029:    private final JTextField birthDayJTextField = new JTextField(2);
030:    private final JTextField birthMonthJTextField = new JTextField(2);
031:    private final JTextField birthYearJTextField = new JTextField(4);
032:
033:    // JTextArea for the result.
034:    private final JTextArea ageHistoryJTextArea = new JTextArea(15, 20);
```

We will have *two* JButtons, one to produce the resulting age history, and the other to create a **new** window, as follows.

```
036:    // The age history display button.
037:    private final JButton displayJButton = new JButton("Display");
038:
039:    // The new window button.
040:    private final JButton newJButton = new JButton("New");
```

Thanks to the New button, we might have several **instances** of AgeHistory windows. It is nice to keep a count of them and make the titles of each one contain its number as an identifier. So the first one created will be called Age History (1) and the second will be called Age History (2), and so on. To help achieve this, we have a **class variable** that is incremented each time we make a new instance.

```
041:    // Each instance has its count in the title.
042:    private static int instanceCount = 0;
043:
044:
045:    // Constructor.
046:    public AgeHistory()
047:    {
048:        instanceCount++;
049:        setTitle("Age History (" + instanceCount + ")");
```

Coffee time: What would happen if we omitted the **reserved word static** from the declaration of instanceCount?

13.13.1

We again here use JPanels to group together the components within a BorderLayout.

```
050:        Container contents = getContentPane();
051:        contents.setLayout(new BorderLayout());
052:
053:        // The top panel is for the inputs.
054:        // It will be a grid of 3 by 2.
055:        JPanel inputDataJPanel = new JPanel();
056:        contents.add(inputDataJPanel, BorderLayout.NORTH);
057:        inputDataJPanel.setLayout(new GridLayout(0, 2));
058:
059:        // Top left of inputDataJPanel.
060:        inputDataJPanel.add(new JLabel("Present date"));
```

The next item to be added, which will go at the top right, will itself be another JPanel. This will hold the three components of the present date, separated by two "/" labels, all laid out with a FlowLayout having a left alignment.

Concept **GUI API: LayoutManager: FlowLayout: alignment.** The **class** java.awt.FlowLayout can be given an alignment mode, passed as a **method argument** to one of its **constructor methods**. It affects the behaviour of the layout in cases when the component is larger than is needed to hold the components that are in it.

The argument is an **int** value, and should be an appropriate **class constant**, including the following.

- FlowLayout.CENTER – the laid out items are centred in the container.

- FlowLayout.LEFT – the laid out items are on the left of the container, with unused space on the right.

- FlowLayout.RIGHT – the laid out items are on the right of the container, with unused space on the left.

If we do not specify an alignment then centred alignment is used.

```
062:        // Top right of inputDataJPanel.
063:        // A JPanel with left aligned FlowLayout,
064:        // For today's date components.
```

```
065:     JPanel presentDayJPanel = new JPanel();
066:     inputDataJPanel.add(presentDayJPanel);
067:     presentDayJPanel.setLayout(new FlowLayout(FlowLayout.LEFT));
068:
069:     // JTextFields for present date components, with JLabels.
070:     presentDayJPanel.add(presentDayJTextField);
071:     presentDayJPanel.add(new JLabel("/"));
072:     presentDayJPanel.add(presentMonthJTextField);
073:     presentDayJPanel.add(new JLabel("/"));
074:     presentDayJPanel.add(presentYearJTextField);
```

The name of the person needs a label and a text field.

```
076:     // Middle left of inputDataJPanel.
077:     inputDataJPanel.add(new JLabel("Person name"));
078:
079:     // Middle right of inputDataJPanel.
080:     // Use a JPanel so that alignment matches rows above and below.
081:     JPanel nameJPanel = new JPanel();
082:     inputDataJPanel.add(nameJPanel);
083:     nameJPanel.setLayout(new FlowLayout(FlowLayout.LEFT));
084:     nameJPanel.add(nameJTextField);
085:
086:     // Bottom left of inputDataJPanel.
087:     inputDataJPanel.add(new JLabel("Birthday"));
```

We have a similar structure for the birth date as we had for the present date.

```
089:     // Bottom right of inputDataJPanel.
090:     // A JPanel with left aligned FlowLayout,
091:     // For birthday components.
092:     JPanel birthdayJPanel = new JPanel();
093:     inputDataJPanel.add(birthdayJPanel);
094:     birthdayJPanel.setLayout(new FlowLayout(FlowLayout.LEFT));
095:
096:     // JTextFields for birthday components, with JLabels.
097:     birthdayJPanel.add(birthDayJTextField);
098:     birthdayJPanel.add(new JLabel("/"));
099:     birthdayJPanel.add(birthMonthJTextField);
100:     birthdayJPanel.add(new JLabel("/"));
101:     birthdayJPanel.add(birthYearJTextField);
```

Our code continues, putting the result text area in the centre, and buttons in a panel at the end.

```
103:     // The result JTextArea goes in the centre.
104:     contents.add(new JScrollPane(ageHistoryJTextArea), BorderLayout.CENTER);
105:
106:     // The buttons go at the bottom, in a JPanel with a FlowLayout.
107:     JPanel buttonJPanel = new JPanel();
108:     contents.add(buttonJPanel, BorderLayout.SOUTH);
109:     buttonJPanel.setLayout(new FlowLayout());
110:     buttonJPanel.add(displayJButton);
111:     displayJButton.addActionListener(this);
112:     buttonJPanel.add(newJButton);
113:     newJButton.addActionListener(this);
```

If this **object** is not the first to be created, then it might be that the end user has already set the present date via another window. In this case we want to copy the values into the text fields and disable them, because, as you will recall, in our Date class one can set the present date only once.

```
115:      // Allow for the possibility that the present date has already been set.
116:      Date presentDate = Date.getPresentDate();
117:      if (presentDate != null)
118:      {
119:        presentDayJTextField.setText("" + presentDate.getDay());
120:        presentMonthJTextField.setText("" + presentDate.getMonth());
121:        presentYearJTextField.setText("" + presentDate.getYear());
122:        presentDayJTextField.setEnabled(false);
123:        presentMonthJTextField.setEnabled(false);
124:        presentYearJTextField.setEnabled(false);
125:      } // if
```

When the user presses the close button of one window, we do not want it to end the program unless that was the last window. So we use DISPOSE_ON_CLOSE rather than EXIT_ON_CLOSE. Since Java 1.4, this should cause the program to exit when the last window is closed.

```
127:      setDefaultCloseOperation(DISPOSE_ON_CLOSE);
128:      pack();
129:    } // AgeHistory
```

Coffee time: Before continuing, make a sketch of what you think the AgeHistory GUI will look like. `13.13.2`

The actionPerformed() **instance method** needs to determine which one of the two JButtons has been pressed. It will access this information from the given ActionEvent.

Concept **GUI API: ActionEvent: getSource().** The **class** java.awt.event.ActionEvent has an **instance method** called getSource which **returns** a **reference** to the **object** that caused the **event**.

```
132:    // Act upon the button being pressed.
133:    public void actionPerformed(ActionEvent event)
134:    {
135:      if (event.getSource() == newJButton)
136:        new AgeHistory().setVisible(true);
137:
138:      else if (event.getSource() == displayJButton)
139:      {
140:        // Set the present date only if it has not already been set.
141:        if (Date.getPresentDate() == null)
142:        {
143:          Date presentDay
144:            = new Date(Integer.parseInt(presentDayJTextField.getText()),
145:                       Integer.parseInt(presentMonthJTextField.getText()),
146:                       Integer.parseInt(presentYearJTextField.getText())
147:                      );
148:          Date.setPresentDate(presentDay);
149:          // Disable these now.
150:          presentDayJTextField.setEnabled(false);
151:          presentMonthJTextField.setEnabled(false);
152:          presentYearJTextField.setEnabled(false);
153:        } // if
```

```
154:        // Compute and display the age history.
155:        String name = nameJTextField.getText();
156:        Date birthday
157:            = new Date(Integer.parseInt(birthDayJTextField.getText()),
158:                       Integer.parseInt(birthMonthJTextField.getText()),
159:                       Integer.parseInt(birthYearJTextField.getText())
160:                      );
161:        Person person = new Person(name, birthday);
162:        ageHistoryJTextArea.setText(person.ageHistory());
163:      } // else if
164:    } // actionPerformed
```

In our **main method**, we simply create an **instance** of AgeHistory and make it visible.

```
167:    // Create an AgeHistory and make it appear on screen.
168:    public static void main(String[] args)
169:    {
170:      // Ensure we use just \n for age history line separator on all platforms.
171:      Person.setLineSeparator("\n");
172:      new AgeHistory().setVisible(true);
173:    } // main
174:
175: } // class AgeHistory
```

13.13.1 Trying it

This is what one window looks like.

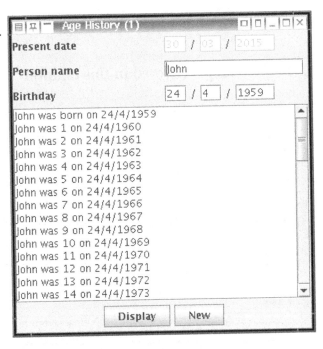

Now let us see the effect of the end user pressing the New button twice.

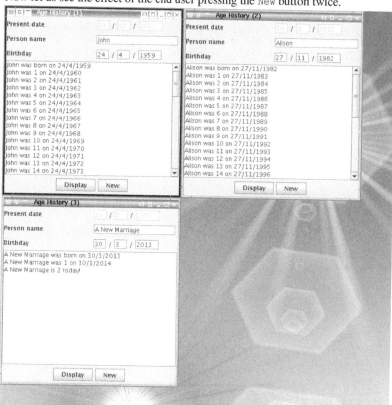

Coffee time:
Our example here has a subtle **design bug**. Figure out how we can end up with a date being shown in the text fields for the present date which is not the value that is actually being used for the present date! (Hint: what if the New button is pressed before the Display button?) What is a simple fix for this problem?

13.14 Concepts covered in this chapter

Here is a list of the concepts that were covered in this chapter, each with a self-test question. You can use this to check you remember them being introduced, and perhaps re-read some of them before going on to the next chapter.

Class	
– extending another class (p.245)	If A extends B, do instances of A have the properties of those of B, plus more, or vice versa?
Execution	
– parallel execution – threads (p.253)	When does the main thread end? When does the virtual machine exit?
– parallel execution – threads: the GUI event thread (p.254)	What does the GUI event thread (usually) spend most of its time doing?
– event driven programming (p.254)	How does event driven programming differ from the style used in the main method?
GUI API	
– ActionEvent (p.258)	What sort of information is held in these objects?
– ActionEvent: getSource() (p.280)	What is returned by this?
– Container (p.246)	What is the purpose of this class?

GUI API	
– `Container: add()` (p.246)	What argument is given to this method?
– `Container: add()`: adding with a position constraint (p.268)	How do we specify the constraint?
– `Container: setLayout()` (p.250)	What kind of argument does this method have?
– `JButton` (p.256)	How do we specify the label when we create one of these?
– `JButton: addActionListener()` (p.256)	What type is the parameter to this method?
– `JButton: setEnabled()` (p.266)	What type is the method argument?
– `JButton: setText()` (p.267)	What type is the method argument?
– `JFrame` (p.245)	What part of a GUI does `javax.swing.JFrame` correspond to?
– `JFrame: setTitle()` (p.246)	Where does the given title typically appear?
– `JFrame: getContentPane()` (p.246)	What is the return type of this method?
– `JFrame: setDefaultCloseOperation()` (p.247)	What four choices do we have as arguments to this method?
– `JFrame: pack()` (p.247)	When should this method be called and what does it do?
– `JFrame: setVisible()` (p.248)	What type of argument is this method given?
– `JLabel` (p.246)	What is the purpose of this class?
– `JLabel: setText()` (p.258)	What type is the method parameter?
– `JTextArea` (p.267)	What arguments can we give to the constructor?
– `JTextArea: setText()` (p.269)	What happens if the given `String` contains new line characters?
– `JTextArea: append()` (p.269)	What is the difference between this and `setText()`?
– `JTextField` (p.265)	What does `20` mean in `new JTextField(20)`?
– `JTextField: getText()` (p.265)	What method arguments does this have?
– `JTextField: setText()` (p.265)	What type is the method argument?
– `JTextField: setEnabled()` (p.267)	What type is the method argument?
– `JTextField`: initial value (p.274)	How do we specify the initial value?
– `LayoutManager` (p.249)	What does a layout manager do to what things within what other thing?
– `LayoutManager: FlowLayout` (p.249)	In what pattern does this make the components appear, and in what order?
– `LayoutManager: FlowLayout`: alignment (p.278)	Name three alignment modes for `FlowLayout`.
– `LayoutManager: GridLayout` (p.251)	In what pattern does this make the components appear, and in what order?
– `LayoutManager: BorderLayout` (p.267)	How many positions does this have, and what are their names?
– Listeners (p.254)	How do we link a listener object to an event source object?
– Listeners: `ActionListener` interface (p.257)	How many method bodies are contained in this interface?
– Listeners: `ActionListener` interface: `actionPerformed()` (p.258)	What type of method parameter does this take?
– `JPanel` (p.270)	What do these contain?
– `JScrollPane` (p.274)	How do we use this class?

283

Interface	
Interface (p.257)	If A implements B, does A have definitions of the methods in B, or vice versa?
Package	
– java.awt and javax.swing (p.245)	What does AWT stand for? Which is newer AWT or Swing?
Standard API	
– System: currentTimeMillis() (p.262)	What is the return type of this method?

Chapter 14

Arrays

Ten green bottles standing on a wall
– an array of empties, not an empty array.
And if one green bottle should accidentally fall
there'd be a free place for another to stay!

14.1   Chapter aims

An **array** is a **list** of items, allowing us to store a number of values in one place, with either an arbitrary order or a chosen one. This chapter explores the definition and use of arrays from simple **array creation** and **array element access**, through **sorting** items, to **partially filled arrays** with **array extension**, and finally to **two-dimensional arrays**. At an appropriate point, we reinforce the understanding of **reference**s by having several arrays containing references to the same **object**s.

The chapter contains the following sections.

Section	Aims	Associated Coursework
14.2 Salary analysis (p.286)	To introduce the basic concepts of **arrays**, including **array type**, **array variable**s, **array creation**, **array element access**, **array length** and **empty arrays**. We also meet `Math.round()` and revisit `System.out.printf()` and **division** by zero.	Write a program that analyses student coursework marks. (p.292)
14.3 Sorted salary analysis (p.293)	To reinforce **arrays** and introduce the idea of **sorting**, together with one simple sorting **algorithm**. We also introduce the **for-each loop**, and have an array as a **method parameter** to a **method**.	Write a program that analyses student coursework marks, and presents the results in a **sort**ed order. (p.298)
14.4 Get a good job (p.299)	To examine **arrays** in which the **array element**s are **references** to **object**s. In particular, we see how this impacts on **sorting** with the use of a `compareTo()` **instance method**. We also revisit `System.out.printf()` and meet `String.format()`.	Write a program that analyses named student coursework marks, and presents the results in a **sort**ed order. (p.305)
14.5 Sort out a job share? (p.305)	To introduce **partially filled arrays** with **array extension**, **array copying** to make a **shallow copy** and **returning** an **array** from a **method**. We also look at **object sharing** as we have three arrays containing **references** to the same **object**s. Along the way we meet the use of a `Scanner` on a **file**, **enum type**s and `split()` on a `String`.	Write a random order text line **sort**ing puzzle program. (p.317)

Section	Aims	Associated Coursework
14.6 Diet monitoring (p.319)	To reinforce ideas met so far, and introduce **array initializer** and **array search**ing, for which we revisit the **logical operators**.	Write a program to allow the user to view certain phone call details. (p.325)
14.7 A weekly diet (p.328)	To introduce **two-dimensional array**s.	Write a program that finds the shortest path through a maze. (p.332)

14.2 Example: Salary analysis

AIM:
To introduce the basic concepts of **arrays**, including **array type**, **array variables**, **array creation**, **array element access**, **array length** and **empty arrays**. We also meet `Math.round()` and revisit `System.out.printf()` and **division** by zero.

The program in this first section is one which performs simple analysis of a **list** of salaries presented on the **standard input**. We use a `Scanner` to provide a **textual user interface**.

```
001: import java.util.Scanner;
002:
003: /* This program analyses integer salaries entered by the user.
004:    It outputs each salary together with its difference from the
005:    mean of the salaries. There must be at least one salary.
006: */
007: public class SalaryAnalysis
008: {
```

As our program is small, we shall write all the code in its **main method**. First we prompt the user to tell us how many salaries will be input.

```
009:    public static void main(String[] args)
010:    {
011:        // A Scanner for getting data from the user.
012:        Scanner salariesScanner = new Scanner(System.in);
013:
014:        System.out.print("Enter the number of salaries: ");
015:        int numberOfSalaries = salariesScanner.nextInt();
```

We shall store the salaries as a list of numbers before processing them, and to achieve this, we shall use an **array**.

Concept **Array.** An **array** is a fixed size, ordered collection (**list**) of items of some particular **type**. The items are stored next to each other in **computer memory** at **run time**. As an example, the following is a representation of an array of 8 **int** values, which happen to be the first 8 **prime numbers** (excluding 1).

2	3	5	7	11	13	17	19

Each box, or **array element**, contains a value, which can be changed if desired. In other words, each element is a separate **variable**. At the same time, the array as a whole is a single entity. This is rather similar to the idea of an **object** having **instance variable**s, except that the elements of an array must all be of the same type.

Indeed, arrays in Java *are* **object**s.

Concept **Type: array type.** Whilst it is true that **arrays** in Java are **objects**, they are treated somewhat differently from **instances** of **classes**. To obtain an **array type**, we do not write a class and then use its name. Instead we simply write the **type** of the **array elements** followed by a left and then a right square bracket ([]). The type of the elements is known as the **array base type**.

For example, int[] is the type of arrays with **int** as the base type, that is ones which contain elements that are **int** values. String[] is the type of arrays which contain elements that are **references** to String objects.

Coffee time: 14.2.1 You have actually met arrays before in this book, in fact we have been using them frequently since the very beginning! Where, and what for?

Concept **Variable: of an array type.** We can declare **variables** of an **array type** rather like we can of any other **type**. For example, here is a variable of type int[].

    int[] salaries;

As **arrays** are **objects**, they are accessed via **references**. So an **array variable** at **run time** holds either a *reference* to an array or the **null reference**. The following diagram shows the above variable referring to an array of **int** values.

int[] salaries

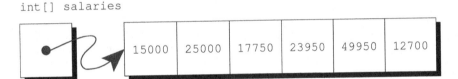

Our SalaryAnalysis main method will have a **method variable** which will hold a **reference** to an array containing the **int** salaries. We need to make a **new** array of the correct size.

Concept **Array: array creation.** We can create an **array** in Java using the **reserved word new**, like we do with other **objects**. However, instead of following this with the name of a **class**, we can state the **array base type** and then, in square brackets, the size of the array. For example, the following creates an array of ten **double** values.

    new double[10]

At **run time**, this code yields a **reference** to the **new**ly created array, which we typically would want to store in a **variable**.

    double[] myFingerLengths = new double[10];

Thanks to the use of references, the size of an array does not need to be known at **compile time**, because the **compiler** does not need to allocate memory for it. This means at **run time** we can create an array which is the right size for the actual **data** being processed.

    int noOfEmployees = Integer.parseInt(args[0]);

    String[] employeeNames = new String[noOfEmployees];

287

In our `SalaryAnalysis` program, the size of the array is supplied by the user at **run time** – it is the same as the number of salaries, which our program has already obtained from the input.

```
017:      // Salaries are ints, stored in an array.
018:      int[] salaries = new int[numberOfSalaries];
```

The newly created array will need to have values placed into the **array element**s, and so we shall access each one using an **array index**.

Concept **Array: element access.** The **array element**s in an **array** can be accessed individually via an **array index**. This is a whole number **greater than or equal** to zero. The first element in an array is indexed by zero, the second by one, and so on. To access an element, we write a **reference** to the array, followed by the index within left and right square brackets.

For example, assuming we have the array

```
double[] myFingerLengths = new double[10];
```

and somehow we have placed the lengths of my fingers and thumbs into the ten elements of `myFingerLengths`, then the following code would compute the total length of my fingers and thumbs.

```
double myTotalFingerLength = 0;
for (int index = 0; index < 10; index++)
  myTotalFingerLength += myFingerLengths[index];
```

So, arrays are a bit like ordinary **object**s with the array elements being **instance variable**s, except that the number of instance variables is chosen when the array is created, they are all the same **type**, they are 'named' by indices rather than names, and they are accessed using a different **syntax**.

The salaries are given by the user so we simply obtain them one at a time using a **for loop**.

```
020:      // Obtain the salaries from the input.
021:      for (int index = 0; index < numberOfSalaries; index++)
022:      {
023:        System.out.print("Enter salary # " + (index + 1) + ": " );
024:        salaries[index] = salariesScanner.nextInt();
025:      } // for
```

Next we **loop** through the `salaries` array to find the sum of them.

```
027:      // Now compute the sum of the salaries.
028:      int sumOfSalaries = 0;
029:      for (int index = 0; index < numberOfSalaries; index++)
030:        sumOfSalaries += salaries[index];
```

 Coffee time: [14.2.2] Could we have combined the above two for loops into one? Would that make the program clearer? Faster?

We wish the program to report the mean average salary, rounded to the nearest pound.

Concept **Standard API: Math: round().** The standard **class** java.lang.Math contains a **class method** called round. This takes a **double method argument** and **return**s a **long** value which is the nearest whole number to the given one. If we wish to turn that result into an **int** then we would of course **cast** it, as in the following example.

```
int myPennies = ... Obtain this somehow.
int myNearlyPounds = (int) Math.round(myPennies / 100.0);
```

Back in our salary analysis program, we compute the mean salary and display the results.

```
032:    // Compute the mean, which is a double, not an integer.
033:    double meanSalary = sumOfSalaries / (double)numberOfSalaries;
034:
035:    // But we also want to round it to simplify the results.
036:    int meanSalaryRounded = (int) Math.round(meanSalary);
037:
038:    // Produce the results.
039:    System.out.println();
040:    System.out.println("The mean salary is:\t" + meanSalary);
041:    System.out.println("which rounds to:\t" + meanSalaryRounded);
042:    System.out.println();
```

We shall use System.out.printf() to produce formatted results.

Concept **Standard API: System: out.printf(): string item.** We can ask System.out.printf() to print a String item by using s as the conversion **character** in the **format specifier**. For example,

```
System.out.println("123456789012345");
System.out.printf("%15s%n", "Hello World");
```

has this effect.

```
123456789012345
    Hello World
```

If the item following the format specifier string is not itself a string, but some other **object** then its toString() is used. For example, assuming a Point **class** is defined as expected, then the code

```
System.out.println("123456789012345");
System.out.printf("%15s%n", new Point(3, 4));
```

produces the following.

```
123456789012345
      (3.0,4.0)
```

Concept **Standard API: System: out.printf(): fixed text and many items.** We can give System.out.printf() a format string with more than one **format specifier** in it, together with more than one value to be printed. What is more, any text in the format string which is not part of a format specifier is simply printed as it appears. Also, if no width is given for a format specifier then its natural width is used.

For example,

```
Point p1 = new Point(3, 4);
Point p2 = new Point(45, 60);
```

289

```
System.out.printf("The distance between %s and %s is %1.2f.%n",
                  p1, p2, p1.distanceFromPoint(p2));
```

produces the following output.

```
The distance between (3.0,4.0) and (45.0,60.0) is 70.00.
```

Here is the rest of our `SalaryAnalysis` code.

```
044:     for (int index = 0; index < numberOfSalaries; index++)
045:     {
046:       int differenceFromMean = salaries[index] - meanSalaryRounded;
047:       String comparisonToMean = differenceFromMean == 0
048:                            ? "zero difference from"
049:                            : (differenceFromMean < 0
050:                               ? "less than" : "greater than");
051:       System.out.printf("Person %2d earns %5d, which is %5d %s the mean%n",
052:                         (index + 1), salaries[index],
053:                         Math.abs(differenceFromMean), comparisonToMean);
054:     } // for
055:   } // main
056:
057: } // class SalaryAnalysis
```

Coffee time: 14.2.3   Notice the **nested conditional expression**s in the code above. Do you think that is an acceptable style, or is it pushing the boundaries of code clarity?

 Coffee time: 14.2.4   Before reading on, predict what the results will look like for the following input salaries.
15049, 49959, 25750, 24627, 12523, 19852

14.2.1   Trying it

To start with, let us try the program with several salaries. Notice that we have carefully ensured that one of them is exactly **equal** to the rounded mean.

```
                    Console Input / Output
$ java SalaryAnalysis
Enter the number of salaries: 6
Enter salary # 1: 15049
Enter salary # 2: 49959
Enter salary # 3: 25750
Enter salary # 4: 24627
Enter salary # 5: 12523
Enter salary # 6: 19852

The mean salary is:    24626.666666666668
which rounds to:       24627

Person 1 earns 15049, which is  9578 less than the mean
Person 2 earns 49959, which is 25332 greater than the mean
Person 3 earns 25750, which is  1123 greater than the mean
Person 4 earns 24627, which is     0 zero difference from the mean
Person 5 earns 12523, which is 12104 less than the mean
Person 6 earns 19852, which is  4775 less than the mean
$ _
```

Next we try just two salaries.

```
                        Console Input / Output
$ java SalaryAnalysis
Enter the number of salaries: 2
Enter salary # 1: 15000
Enter salary # 2: 25000

The mean salary is:     20000.0
which rounds to:        20000

Person  1 earns 15000, which is  5000 less than the mean
Person  2 earns 25000, which is  5000 greater than the mean
$ _
```

It may seem a bit strange, but we can have just one salary.

```
                        Console Input / Output
$ java SalaryAnalysis
Enter the number of salaries: 1
Enter salary # 1: 15000

The mean salary is:     15000.0
which rounds to:        15000

Person  1 earns 15000, which is     0 zero difference from the mean
$ _
```

What if we **run** the program with no salaries?

```
            Console Input / Output
$ java SalaryAnalysis
Enter the number of salaries: 0

The mean salary is:     NaN
which rounds to:        0

$ _
```

In this case, the sum of the salaries is zero, as is their count, and so the program has **evaluate**d the **expression** 0 / (double) 0 which, perhaps surprisingly, does *not* produce an **exception**.

14.2.2 Double division by zero: not a number

Concept **Expression: arithmetic: `double` division: by zero.** When using the **double division** operation in Java, if the numerator is not zero but the denominator is zero, the result we get is a model of **infinity**. This is represented, for example by `System.out.println()`, as Infinity.

However, if both the numerator and the denominator are zero, we instead get a model of the concept **not a number**, which is represented as NaN.

This behaviour of double division is in contrast to **integer division**, which produces an **exception** if the denominator is zero.

Coffee time: 14.2.5 By looking at the **API** on-line documentation of the `Math.round()` **class method**, figure out why NaN gets 'rounded' to 0 in the SalaryAnalysis program when it is given no salaries.

14.2.3 An empty array is still an array!

Running the `SalaryAnalysis` program with no salaries showed us that we are allowed to have an **array** of no elements. Such an **empty array** simply has an **array length** of zero.

Concept **Array: length.** Every **array** in Java has a **public instance variable** called `length`, of **type int**, which contains the **array length** or size of the array. It is, of course, a **final variable**, so we cannot change its value.

```
int[] myArray = new int[25];
int myArrayLength = myArray.length;
```

In the above code fragment, the **variable** `myArrayLength` will have the value `25`.

Concept **Array: empty array.** When we create an **array** we say how many **array element**s it should have, and this number can be zero. Although such an **empty array** may not seem of much use, it still exists – we can access its **array length** for example.

```
int[] myEmptyArray = new int[0];
System.out.println(myEmptyArray.length);
```

The above code will output zero, whereas the following code will cause a **run time error** (in fact a `NullPointerException`), because there is no array so we cannot ask for its length.

```
int[] myNonArray = null;
System.out.println(myNonArray.length);
```

14.2.4 Coursework: Mark analysis

Write a program, called `MarkAnalysis`, that takes a **list** of student coursework marks and produces a report. The scores are entered by the user, after he or she has been prompted to say how many there are. Each score is a whole number **greater than or equal** to 0. The program should output the mean average, minimum and maximum of the scores, and a list of the scores, each along with their difference from the mean average score, shown to two decimal places (using `System.out.printf()`).

In your **main method**, you should first read the scores into an **int array** using one **loop**, before finding the minimum, maximum and mean using a second, and then printing the results using a third. (You could combine the first two loops into one, but perhaps that would be less clear?)

You may assume that any input values are valid. However, if the number of scores is not at least one, your program should display a suitable message and exit.

Here is an example **run** of the program.

```
                    Console Input / Output
$ java MarkAnalysis
Enter the number of marks: 6
Enter mark # 1: 8
Enter mark # 2: 6
Enter mark # 3: 9
Enter mark # 4: 8
Enter mark # 5: 5
Enter mark # 6: 4

The mean mark is:       6.666666666666667
The minimum mark is:    4
The maximum mark is:    9

Person | Score | difference from mean
     1 |     8 |   1.33
     2 |     6 |  -0.67
     3 |     9 |   2.33
     4 |     8 |   1.33
     5 |     5 |  -1.67
     6 |     4 |  -2.67
$ _
```

Hint: Use the following **format specifier** string. `"%6d | %5d | %6.2f%n"`

292

14.3   Example: Sorted salary analysis

AIM: To reinforce **arrays** and introduce the idea of **sort**ing, together with one simple sorting **algorithm**. We also introduce the **for-each loop**, and have an array as a **method parameter** to a **method**.

In this section we alter the program from the previous one – this time the output is presented in ascending order of salary.

Most of the program is the same as before, except that we call a separate **class method** to **sort** the **array** into ascending order before producing the results. We also use a **for-each loop** to replace one of the **for loops**.

The first part of the program is the same as previously.

```
001: import java.util.Scanner;
002:
003: /* This program analyses integer salaries entered by the user.
004:    It outputs each salary together with its difference from the
005:    mean of the salaries. There must be at least one salary.
006:    The salaries are output in ascending order.
007: */
008: public class SalaryAnalysis
009: {
010:   public static void main(String[] args)
011:   {
012:     // A Scanner for getting data from the user.
013:     Scanner salariesScanner = new Scanner(System.in);
014:
015:     System.out.print("Enter the number of salaries: ");
016:     int numberOfSalaries = salariesScanner.nextInt();
017:
018:     // Salaries are ints, stored in an array.
019:     int[] salaries = new int[numberOfSalaries];
020:
021:     // Obtain the salaries from the input.
022:     for (int index = 0; index < numberOfSalaries; index++)
023:     {
024:       System.out.print("Enter salary # " + (index + 1) + ": " );
025:       salaries[index] = salariesScanner.nextInt();
026:     } // for
```

The next part of the code calculates the sum of the salaries, a process which is not dependent on the *positions* of the salaries in the **list**, only on the actual values of them. For this reason, it is better expressed using a **for-each loop**.

Concept **Statement: for-each loop: on arrays.**   Java 5.0 introduced a new **statement** called the **enhanced for statement**, more commonly known as the **for-each loop**.[1]

It is best explained by example. Suppose we have the following.

```
double[] myFingerLengths = new double[10];
```

```
... Code here to assign values to the array elements.
```

Then we can find the sum of the **array element**s with the following for-each loop.

```
double myTotalFingerLength = 0;
for (double fingerLength : myFingerLengths)
  myTotalFingerLength += fingerLength;
```

---

[1]The popular name for this loop may seem odd, because the word each is not used in it, but the meaning of the statement is similar to a concept in languages such as Perl[17], which does use the phrase for each. And we actually say 'for each' when we read out the Java statement.

This is saying that we want to **loop** over all the elements in the **array** which is **referenced** by myFingerLengths, storing each element in turn in the variable fingerLength, and adding it to the value of myTotalFingerLength. In other words 'for each fingerLength in myFingerLengths, add fingerLength to myTotalFingerLength'.

The above for-each loop is actually a shorthand for the following **for loop**.

```
double myTotalFingerLength = 0;
for (int index = 0; index < myFingerLengths.length; index++)
{
  double fingerLength = myFingerLengths[index];
  myTotalFingerLength += fingerLength;
} // for
```

Here is the general case of the for-each loop when used with arrays, where anArray is a variable referring to some array with **array base type** SomeType and elementName is any suitable **variable** name.

```
for (SomeType elementName : anArray)
  ... Statement using elementName.
```

This general case is simply a shorthand for the following.

```
for (int index = 0; index < anArray.length; index++)
{
  SomeType elementName = anArray[index];
  ... Statement using elementName.
} // for
```

A for-each loop can and should be used instead of a for loop in places where we wish to loop over all the elements of a single array, and the **array index** is *only* used to access (not change) the elements of that array. In other words, for processing where the element values matter, but their position in the array is not directly used, and there is only one array. So, for example, the following code cannot be replaced with a for-each loop.

```
int weightedSum = 0;
for (int index = 0; index < numbers.length; index++)
  weightedSum += numbers[index] * index;
```

Neither can this.

```
for (int index = 0; index < numbers.length; index++)
  otherNumbers[index] = numbers[index];
```

Finally, a common error (even in some Java text books!) is to think that a for-each loop can be used to *change* the array elements. For example, the following code **compile**s without errors, but it does not do what you might expect!

```
int[] numbers = new int[100];
for (int number : numbers)
  number = 10;
```

The for-each loop above is a shorthand for the following, which you can see achieves nothing.

```
for (int index = 0; index < numbers.length; index++)
{
  int number = numbers[index];
  number = 10;
} // for
```

Back to our SalaryAnalysis program, here is the code to compute the sum of the salaries.

```
028:     // Now compute the sum of the salaries.
029:     int sumOfSalaries = 0;
030:     for (int salary : salaries)
031:         sumOfSalaries += salary;
```

Then we compute the mean, sort the array using our class method we have not yet written, and output the results as previously.

```
033:     // Compute the mean, which is a double, not an integer.
034:     double meanSalary = sumOfSalaries / (double)numberOfSalaries;
035:
036:     // But we also want to round it to simplify the results.
037:     int meanSalaryRounded = (int) Math.round(meanSalary);
038:
039:     // Sort the salaries into ascending order.
040:     sort(salaries);
041:
042:     // Produce the results.
043:     System.out.println();
044:     System.out.println("The mean salary is:\t" + meanSalary);
045:     System.out.println("which rounds to:\t" + meanSalaryRounded);
046:     System.out.println();
047:
048:     for (int index = 0; index < numberOfSalaries; index++)
049:     {
050:         int differenceFromMean = salaries[index] - meanSalaryRounded;
051:         String comparisonToMean = differenceFromMean == 0
052:                                 ? "zero difference from"
053:                                 : (differenceFromMean < 0
054:                                     ? "less than" : "greater than");
055:         System.out.printf("Person %2d earns %5d, which is %5d %s the mean%n",
056:                         (index + 1), salaries[index],
057:                         Math.abs(differenceFromMean), comparisonToMean);
058:     } // for
059: } // main
```

Coffee time:

14.3.1

Why did we not replace the other two for loops with a for-each loop? What do you think of the following code as an alternative to the first for loop?

```
int salaryNo = 1;
for (int salary : salaries)
{
    System.out.print("Enter salary # " + salaryNo + ": ");
    salary = salariesScanner.nextInt();
    salaryNo++;
} // for
```

The next part of our program is for sorting the array.

Concept **Design: Sorting a list.** A **list** of items, such as an **array**, contains those items in some, perhaps arbitrary, order. We often want to rearrange them into a *specific* order, without losing or gaining any. This is known as **sort**ing. For example, a list of numbers may be sorted into ascending or descending numerical order, a list of names may be sorted alphabetically, etc..

There are many different **algorithm**s for sorting lists, including **bubble sort, insertion sort, selection sort, quick sort, merge sort, tree sort** ....

We shall use **bubble sort** in our SalaryAnalysis program.

Concept **Design: Sorting a list: bubble sort.** One **algorithm** for **sort**ing is known as **bubble sort**. This works by passing through the **list** looking at adjacent items, and swapping them over if they are in the wrong order. One pass through is not enough to ensure the list gets completely sorted, so more passes must be made until it is. However, after the first pass, the 'highest' item, that is, the one that should end up being furthest from the start of the list, must actually be at the end of the list.

For example suppose we start with the following list and wish to sort it into ascending order.

45	78	12	79	60	17

On the first pass, we compare 45 with 78, which are in order, and then 78 with 12 which need swapping. Next we compare 78 with 79, and so on. Eventually we end up with 79 being at the end of the list.

Start		45	78	12	79	60	17
45 <= 78	okay	45 <=	78	12	79	60	17
78 > 12	swap	45	12 <=	78	79	60	17
78 <= 79	okay	45	12	78 <=	79	60	17
79 > 60	swap	45	12	78	60 <=	79	17
79 > 17	swap	45	12	78	60	17 <=	79

The highest number, 79, is in place, but the preceding items are not yet sorted.

After the second pass, the second highest item must be at the penultimate place in the list, and so on. It follows that, if there are N items in the list, then $N-1$ passes are enough to guarantee the whole list is sorted. Furthermore, the first pass needs to look at $N-1$ adjacent pairs, but the next pass can look at one less, because we know the highest item is in the right place at the end. The very last pass only needs to look at one pair, as all the other items must be in place by then.

Going back to our example, here are the results at the end of the next passes.

Pass						
2	12	45	60	17	78	79
3	12	45	17	60	78	79
4	12	17	45	60	78	79
5	12	17	45	60	78	79

Notice that pass 5 was actually unnecessary as the **array** became sorted after pass 4.

Here is some **pseudo code** for sorting anArray using bubble sort.

```
for passCount = 1 to anArray length - 1
  for pairLeftIndex = 0 to anArray length - 1 - passCount
    if items in anArray at pairLeftIndex and pairLeftIndex + 1
                     are out of order
      swap them over
```

This can be improved by observing that the list may get sorted before the maximum number of passes needed to guarantee it. For example it could be sorted to start with! Here is an alternative **design**.

```
int unsortedLength = anArray length
boolean changedOnThisPass
do
  changedOnThisPass = false
  for pairLeftIndex = 0 to unsortedLength - 2
    if items in anArray at pairLeftIndex and pairLeftIndex + 1
                     are out of order
      swap them over
```

```
        changedOnThisPass = true
      end-if
    end-for
    unsortedLength--
  while changedOnThisPass
```

Coffee time: [14.3.2]   Use the bubble sort **algorithm** (on paper) to sort the following numbers into *descending* order rather than ascending order which has already been explored.

| 45 | 78 | 12 | 79 | 60 | 17 |

The code to sort the array in our `SalaryAnalysis` program is to be written in a separate class method which will be passed a **reference** to the array as a **method parameter**.

Concept **Method: accepting parameters: of an array type.** The **method parameters** of a **method** can be of any **type**, including **arrays**. A parameter which is of an **array type** must be given a **method argument** value of that type when the method is invoked. This value will of course be a **reference** to an array which has **array elements** of the **array base type**, or the **null reference**.

The most obvious example of this is the `String[]` **command line argument** array, which is passed to the **main method** by the Java **virtual machine**.

Here is our code to sort the array.

```
062:   // Sort a given array of int into ascending order.
063:   private static void sort(int[] anArray)
064:   {
065:     // Each pass of the sort reduces unsortedLength by one.
066:     int unsortedLength = anArray.length;
067:     boolean changedOnThisPass;
068:     do
069:     {
070:       changedOnThisPass = false;
071:       for (int pairLeftIndex = 0;
072:            pairLeftIndex < unsortedLength - 1; pairLeftIndex++)
073:       if (anArray[pairLeftIndex] > anArray[pairLeftIndex + 1])
074:       {
075:         int thatWasAtPairLeftIndex = anArray[pairLeftIndex];
076:         anArray[pairLeftIndex] = anArray[pairLeftIndex + 1];
077:         anArray[pairLeftIndex + 1] = thatWasAtPairLeftIndex;
078:         changedOnThisPass = true;
079:       } // if
080:       unsortedLength--;
081:     } while (changedOnThisPass);
082:   } // sort
083:
084: } // class SalaryAnalysis
```

Coffee time: [14.3.3]   Suppose we decided we wanted the output to be sorted in *descending* order of salary. What change would we need to make to our program?

Coffee time: [14.3.4]   Sorting an array is quite a common thing we wish to do in our programs. Clearly it is good for you to see how we can write our own code for sorting, but do you think it is likely that there is in fact some code in a standard **class** somewhere? See if you can find it! Does it allow us to choose which order to sort into?

14.3.1 Trying it

Let us try the program with some of the same **test data** as last time, to check the output is **sort**ed by salary.

```
                        Console Input / Output
$ java SalaryAnalysis
Enter the number of salaries: 6
Enter salary # 1: 15049
Enter salary # 2: 49959
Enter salary # 3: 25750
Enter salary # 4: 24627
Enter salary # 5: 12523
Enter salary # 6: 19852

The mean salary is:     24626.666666666668
which rounds to:        24627

Person  1 earns 12523, which is 12104 less than the mean
Person  2 earns 15049, which is  9578 less than the mean
Person  3 earns 19852, which is  4775 less than the mean
Person  4 earns 24627, which is     0 zero difference from the mean
Person  5 earns 25750, which is  1123 greater than the mean
Person  6 earns 49959, which is 25332 greater than the mean
$ _
```

Coffee time: ⟨14.3.5⟩
Does the output still make sense?
For example, what is the meaning
of `Person 1`? While they are only
numbers, perhaps it does not matter
that the output numbers bear no
correspondence to the input ones.
Or perhaps it should! How could
we modify our program so that the
person numbers produced in the
output were the position of that
salary in the input **list**?

14.3.2 Coursework: Mark analysis with sorting

Modify your program from the last
task so that it presents the results in
ascending order of mark. Use your
own sort method, which can be based
on the code in the example for this
section. (Could this change the way
you find your maximum and
minimum?)

Here is an example **run** of the
program.

```
                    Console Input / Output
$ java MarkAnalysis
Enter the number of marks: 6
Enter mark # 1: 8
Enter mark # 2: 6
Enter mark # 3: 9
Enter mark # 4: 8
Enter mark # 5: 5
Enter mark # 6: 4

The mean mark is:       6.666666666666667
The minimum mark is:    4
The maximum mark is:    9

Person | Score | difference from mean
     1 |     4 |  -2.67
     2 |     5 |  -1.67
     3 |     6 |  -0.67
     4 |     8 |   1.33
     5 |     8 |   1.33
     6 |     9 |   2.33
$ _
```

14.4 Example: Get a good job

AIM: To examine **arrays** in which the **array element**s are **references** to **objects**. In particular, we see how this impacts on **sort**ing with the use of a `compareTo()` **instance method**. We also revisit `System.out.printf()` and meet `String.format()`.

Assume you are thinking of one day having a job. Perhaps one of the factors in helping you choose who you would like to work for is how much they are prepared to pay you! In this section we have a program which is a variation of the previous. Its input **data** is a **list** of pairs, each consisting of the name of a firm that employs computer programmers, followed by their typical starting salary for such a post. The program works out the mean salary as before, and presents the list **sort**ed in ascending order of salary. What makes this program a bit trickier than the previous is that we have to keep the name of the firm and their typical salary together while we sort the list.

We divide the program into two **class**es.

Class list for JobAnalysis	
Class	**Description**
JobAnalysis	The main class containing the **main method**. It will read the input data, and make **instance**s of Job.
Job	An instance of this will represent a firm's name together with their typical salary.

Public method interfaces for class `JobAnalysis`.			
Method	**Return**	**Arguments**	**Description**
main	**void**	String[]	The main method for the program.

We shall also have a **private class method** to **sort** the Jobs in the JobAnalysis class.

Public method interfaces for class `Job`.			
Method	**Return**	**Arguments**	**Description**
Constructor		String, int	Constructs a job with the given employer and salary.
getEmployer	String		Gives the employer.
getSalary	int		Gives the salary.
compareTo	int	Job	Compare this job with the given other, to support ordering by ascending salary.
toString	String		Returns a string representation of the job.

14.4.1 The Job class

The Job **class** allows us to make **object**s which pair together a firm's name with their salary, using **instance variable**s.

```
001: // A class for representing a Job,
002: // comprising a firm's name and their typical salary.
003: public class Job
004: {
005:   // The name of the firm for this instance.
006:   private final String employer;
```

```
008:   // Their typical salary.
009:   private final int salary;
```

The **constructor method** sets the instance variables.

```
012:   // The constructor method.
013:   public Job(String requiredEmployer, int requiredSalary)
014:   {
015:     employer = requiredEmployer;
016:     salary = requiredSalary;
017:   } // Job
```

We have an **accessor method** for each instance variable.

```
020:   // Get the employer.
021:   public String getEmployer()
022:   {
023:     return employer;
024:   } // getEmployer
025:
026:
027:   // Get the salary.
028:   public int getSalary()
029:   {
030:     return salary;
031:   } // getSalary
```

We have a compareTo() **instance method** for comparing this job against a given other one with the usual **int** result which is negative, zero or positive. This provides an ordering based on ascending salary. However, if the salaries are the same, then we compare the employers instead, and you will recall from Section 12.4 on page 234 that String has a compareTo() instance method.

```
034:   // Compare this Job with a given other,
035:   // basing the comparison on the salaries, then the employers.
036:   // Returns -ve(<), 0(=) or +ve(>) int. -ve means this one is the smallest.
037:   public int compareTo(Job other)
038:   {
039:     if (salary == other.salary)
040:       return employer.compareTo(other.employer);
041:     else
042:       return salary - other.salary;
043:   } // compareTo
```

Finally, toString() provides a representation of the job, showing the firm's name and their salary.

Concept **Standard API: System: out.printf(): left justification.**
    If we wish an item printed by System.out.printf() to be left justified, rather than right justified, then we can place a hyphen in front of the width in the **format specifier**. For example,

```
System.out.println("123456789012345X");
System.out.printf("%-15sX%n", "Hello World");
```

produces the following.

```
123456789012345X
Hello World    X
```

Concept **Standard API: String: format().** The standard **class** java.lang.String has a **class method** to produce formatted String representations of values. It is called format and was introduced in Java 5.0. It works with a **format specifier** string in precisely the same way as System.out.printf() except that the result is **return**ed rather than printed.

For example, the code

```
System.out.println(String.format("The distance between %s and %s is %1.2f.",
                          p1, p2, p1.distanceFromPoint(p2)));
```

has precisely the same effect as the following. (Observe the %n.)

```
System.out.printf("The distance between %s and %s is %1.2f.%n",
                          p1, p2, p1.distanceFromPoint(p2));
```

```
046:    // Return a string representation.
047:    public String toString()
048:    {
049:      return String.format("%-15s pays %5d", employer, salary);
050:    } // toString
051:
052: } // class Job
```

14.4.2 The JobAnalysis class

The **main method** lives in the **class** JobAnalysis. It will work by taking the input **data** in pairs, creating Job **object**s and storing them in an **array**. This array will then be **sort**ed by a separate **class method**, before the results are output.

Concept **Array: of objects.**
An **array** can contain values of any **type**, including **object**s. Of course, as with any other kind of **variable**, the **array element**s of an array with an **array base type** which is a **class**, actually contain **reference**s to the objects.

The most obvious example of an array of objects, is the **command line argument**s passed to the **main method**.

```
public static void main(String[] args)
```

The following diagram shows the above **method parameter** referring to an array, with the array elements themselves referring to String objects.

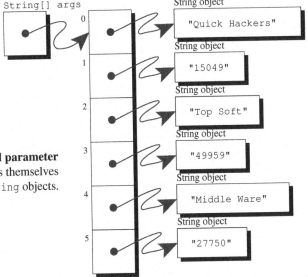

The example in the above concept shows `args` referring to an array of `String` **references**, and would be how our **command line arguments** might look for this program, if we used that technique rather than having a `Scanner` with **standard input**.

Here is our program code.

```
001: import java.util.Scanner;
002:
003: /* Program to analyse Job information supplied by the user. Each Job comprises
004:    a firm name and their typical salary. Output is mean salary and ascending
005:    sorted list of jobs. There must be at least one job.
006: */
007: public class JobAnalysis
008: {
009:   public static void main(String[] args)
010:   {
```

To obtain the input data, we make a `Scanner` for the standard input. Then we prompt the user to tell us how many jobs there are, and create an array of that size.

```
011:   // A Scanner for getting data from the user.
012:   Scanner inputScanner = new Scanner(System.in);
013:
014:   System.out.print("Enter the number of jobs: ");
015:   int noOfJobs = inputScanner.nextInt();
016:   // Skip past the end of that line.
017:   inputScanner.nextLine();
018:
019:   // We keep the jobs in an array.
020:   Job[] jobs = new Job[noOfJobs];
```

Next we have a **for loop** in which we ask the user to supply the name of an employer, followed by the corresponding salary, so we can **construct** a `Job` **object** and store a reference to it in our array.

```
022:   // Read the data in pairs,
023:   // build Job objects and store them in jobs array.
024:   for (int jobCount = 1; jobCount <= noOfJobs; jobCount++)
025:   {
026:     System.out.print("Enter the name of employer " + jobCount + ": ");
027:     String employer = inputScanner.nextLine();
028:     System.out.print("Enter the salary for '" + employer + "': ");
029:     int salary = inputScanner.nextInt();
030:     // Skip past the end of that line.
031:     inputScanner.nextLine();
032:     jobs[jobCount - 1] = new Job(employer, salary);
033:   } // for
```

The following diagram illustrates the situation at this point in the program, assuming there are 3 jobs.

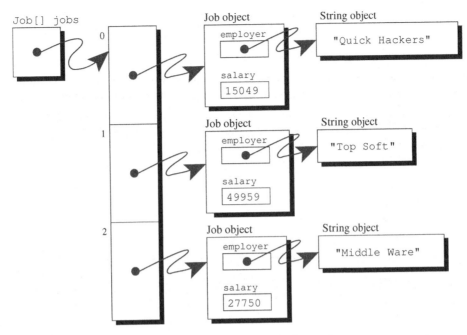

We compute the sum of the salaries in a similar way to how we did in the previous program, except we now must use the **accessor method** to obtain the salary from each `Job` object.

```
035:     // Now compute the sum of the salaries.
036:     int sumOfSalaries = 0;
037:     for (Job job : jobs)
038:        sumOfSalaries += job.getSalary();
```

Finally, for the main method, we compute the mean, sort the array and output the results.

```
040:     // Compute the mean, which is a double, not an integer.
041:     double meanSalary = sumOfSalaries / (double)noOfJobs;
042:
043:     // But we also want to round it to simplify the results.
044:     int meanSalaryRounded = (int) Math.round(meanSalary);
045:
046:     // Sort the jobs by salary into ascending order.
047:     sort(jobs);
048:
049:     // Produce the results.
050:     System.out.println();
051:     System.out.println("The mean salary is:\t" + meanSalary);
052:     System.out.println("which rounds to:\t" + meanSalaryRounded);
053:     System.out.println();
```

Because we no longer need the **array index** to appear in the output, we can use a **for-each loop** to go through the array. Also note the use of the **accessor method** to obtain the salary.

```
055:     // Output each job.
056:     for (Job job : jobs)
057:     {
058:        int differenceFromMean = job.getSalary() - meanSalaryRounded;
059:        String comparisonToMean = differenceFromMean == 0
060:                            ? "zero difference from"
061:                            : (differenceFromMean < 0
062:                                ? "less than" : "greater than");
```

303

```
063:        System.out.printf("%s, which is %5d %s the mean%n",
064:                          job, Math.abs(differenceFromMean), comparisonToMean);
065:      } // for
066:    } // main
```

The class method to sort the array is also very similar to the one in the previous program. The main difference is that we use the `compareTo()` **instance method** from the Job objects rather than the **greater than operator** to determine whether an adjacent pair of items is in the wrong order.

```
069:    // Sort the given array of Jobs using compareTo on the Job objects.
070:    private static void sort(Job[] anArray)
071:    {
072:      // Each pass of the sort reduces unsortedLength by one.
073:      int unsortedLength = anArray.length;
074:      boolean changedOnThisPass;
075:      do
076:      {
077:        changedOnThisPass = false;
078:        for (int pairLeftIndex = 0;
079:             pairLeftIndex < unsortedLength - 1; pairLeftIndex++)
080:          if (anArray[pairLeftIndex].compareTo(anArray[pairLeftIndex + 1]) > 0)
081:          {
082:            Job thatWasAtPairLeftIndex = anArray[pairLeftIndex];
083:            anArray[pairLeftIndex] = anArray[pairLeftIndex + 1];
084:            anArray[pairLeftIndex + 1] = thatWasAtPairLeftIndex;
085:            changedOnThisPass = true;
086:          } // if
087:        unsortedLength--;
088:      } while (changedOnThisPass);
089:    } // sort
090:
091: } // class JobAnalysis
```

14.4.3 Trying it

Let us try the program with 6 jobs.

```
                          Console Input / Output
$ java JobAnalysis
Enter the number of jobs: 6
Enter the name of employer 1: Quick Hackers
Enter the salary for 'Quick Hackers': 15049
Enter the name of employer 2: Top Soft
Enter the salary for 'Top Soft': 49959
Enter the name of employer 3: Middle Ware
Enter the salary for 'Middle Ware': 25750
Enter the name of employer 4: Mean Media
Enter the salary for 'Mean Media': 24627
Enter the name of employer 5: OK Coral
Enter the salary for 'OK Coral': 12523
Enter the name of employer 6: Cheaper Cheers
Enter the salary for 'Cheaper Cheers': 19852

The mean salary is:    24626.666666666668
which rounds to:       24627

OK Coral        pays 12523, which is 12104 less than the mean
Quick Hackers   pays 15049, which is  9578 less than the mean
Cheaper Cheers  pays 19852, which is  4775 less than the mean
Mean Media      pays 24627, which is     0 zero difference from the mean
Middle Ware     pays 25750, which is  1123 greater than the mean
Top Soft        pays 49959, which is 25332 greater than the mean
$ _
```

We would test it with more examples, but do not show that here.

14.4.4 Coursework: Mark analysis with student names and sorting

Modify your program from the last task so that each mark has an associated named student. You will need to create a **class** called `Student` with two **instance variables**, one for the name of a student and the other for his or her mark. This should provide a `compareTo()` **instance method** which you will use in your **sort** code, and a `toString()` to help produce the report.

Here is an example **run** of the program.

```
                    Console Input / Output
$ java MarkAnalysis
Enter the number of students: 6
Enter the name of student 1: Helen
Enter the mark for 'Helen': 8
Enter the name of student 2: Andy
Enter the mark for 'Andy': 6
Enter the name of student 3: John
Enter the mark for 'John': 9
Enter the name of student 4: Karen
Enter the mark for 'Karen': 8
Enter the name of student 5: Sanjay
Enter the mark for 'Sanjay': 5
Enter the name of student 6: George
Enter the mark for 'George': 4

The mean mark is:      6.666666666666667
The minimum mark is:   4
The maximum mark is:   9

Person and Score  | difference from mean
George      got   4 |  -2.67
Sanjay      got   5 |  -1.67
Andy        got   6 |  -0.67
Helen       got   8 |   1.33
Karen       got   8 |   1.33
John        got   9 |   2.33
$ _
```

You should make appropriate use of **for-each** loops. Hint: Use the following **format specifier** string. `"%-10s got %3d"`

14.5 Example: Sort out a job share?

AIM: To introduce **partially filled arrays** with **array extension**, **array copying** to make a **shallow copy** and **return**ing an **array** from a **method**. We also look at **object sharing** as we have three arrays containing **reference**s to the same **object**s. Along the way we meet the use of a `Scanner` on a **file**, **enum type**s and `split()` on a `String`.

The program in this section is an elaboration of the previous one. Each **command line argument** is the name of a **text file** containing **data** about jobs for a certain kind of job, stating which employers pay what salary. This data is read and processed, and presented twice: first **sort**ed by name of employer and then again by amount of salary.

We divide the program into three **classes**.

Class list for JobSurvey	
Class	**Description**
JobSurvey	The main class containing the **main method**. It will make an **instance** of JobList for each command line argument.
JobList	This holds a collection of Jobs, one for each data pair in the associated data **file**.
Job	An instance of this will represent a firm's name together with their typical salary.

305

Public method interfaces for class `JobSurvey`.			
Method	**Return**	**Arguments**	**Description**
main	**void**	String[]	The main method for the program.

Public method interfaces for class `JobList`.			
Method	**Return**	**Arguments**	**Description**
Constructor		Scanner	Constructs a job list, reading the information from the given Scanner.
toString	String		Returns a string representation of the job list including the jobs sorted by employer and again by salary.

Public method interfaces for class `Job`.			
Method	**Return**	**Arguments**	**Description**
Constructor		String, **int**	Constructs a job with the given employer and salary.
getEmployer	String		Gives the employer.
getSalary	**int**		Gives the salary.
compareTo	**int**	Job, SortOrder	Compare this job with the given other, to support ordering by employer or salary, as specified by the second argument.
toString	String		Returns a string representation of the job.

14.5.1   The `JobSurvey` class

`JobSurvey` contains the **main method** of the program. Its task is to make an **instance** of `JobList` for each **data text file** named as a **command line argument**. It does this by creating a `Scanner` which has access to the contents of the text file, and passing it to the **constructor method** of `JobList`.

Concept **Standard API: `Scanner`: for a file.**   The standard **class** `java.util.Scanner` can be used to read the contents of a **file**, such as `my-data.txt`, as follows.

```
import java.io.File;
import java.util.Scanner;
    ...
    Scanner input = new Scanner(new File("my-data.txt"));
```

`java.io.File` is a standard class used to represent file names.

Having obtained a `Scanner` for the file, we can then use its various **instance methods**, such as `nextLine()`, to read the **data**.

If we desire to read every line of the file, we might also use the `hasNextLine()` instance method – this **returns true** or **false** depending on whether there are more lines in the file.

```
    while (input.hasNextLine())
    {
      String line = input.nextLine();
      ...
    } // while
```

The creation of a `Scanner` for a file may cause a **run time error**, or **exception**, of a more serious kind than we have so far lived with in this book, and Java insists we deal with this in some way or other. As it happens, handling exceptions is the subject of the next chapter, so for now we shall simply add the words `throws Exception` to the heading of the main method. This is a way of telling everyone that during a **method call** to this **method**, an exception might happen which is not dealt with by it.

Here is the code of our main class. Note the use of a **for-each loop** to process the command line arguments.

```
001: import java.io.File;
002: import java.util.Scanner;
003:
004: /* Program to report jobs and their salaries.
005:    Each command line argument is the name of a text file containing:
006:       The first line is a name or description of the jobs.
007:       Subsequent lines describe one job, in the format:
008:          Employer (including spaces but not tabs) <TAB> salary
009:    Output is a report for each file containing:
010:       Name or description of the jobs, average salary
011:       Job details in name order and again in salary order.
012: */
013: public class JobSurvey
014: {
015:   public static void main(String[] args) throws Exception
016:   {
017:     for (String fileName : args)
018:     {
019:       JobList jobList = new JobList(new Scanner(new File(fileName)));
020:       System.out.println(jobList);
021:       System.out.println();
022:     } // for
023:   } // main
024:
025: } // class JobSurvey
```

14.5.2 The Job class

The first part of the **class** is the same as in the previous example.

```
001: // A class for representing a Job,
002: // comprising a firm's name and their typical salary.
003: public class Job
004: {
005:   // The name of the firm for this instance.
006:   private final String employer;
007:
008:   // Their typical salary.
009:   private final int salary;
010:
011:
012:   // The constructor method.
013:   public Job(String requiredEmployer, int requiredSalary)
014:   {
015:     employer = requiredEmployer;
016:     salary = requiredSalary;
017:   } // Job
018:
```

307

```
019:
020:    // Get the employer.
021:    public String getEmployer()
022:    {
023:      return employer;
024:    } // getEmployer
025:
026:
027:    // Get the salary.
028:    public int getSalary()
029:    {
030:      return salary;
031:    } // getSalary
```

As the program presents the jobs **sort**ed by employer and again by salary, the `compareTo()` **instance method** needs to be able to order by either ordering as required. This choice could be made via the use of two **class constant**s, one of which must be passed as a **method argument** to `compareTo()`.

Concept **Variable: final variables: class constant: a set of choices.**   One use of **class constant**s is to define a set of options for the users of a **class**, without them having to know what values have been chosen to model each option – they instead use the name of one or more class constants to represent their choices.

For example, the following could be possible directions available in a class that is part of a game that permits simple movement of some game entity.

```
public static final int UP = 0;
public static final int DOWN = 1;
public static final int LEFT = 2;
public static final int RIGHT = 3;
```

Apart from leading to more readable code, this technique gives us more flexibility: the maintainer of the **source code** might decide for some reason to change the values (but not the names) of the four constants. This should not cause any code outside of the class to need rewriting.

So, using this technique we would have two class constants as follows.

```
public static final int SORT_BY_EMPLOYER = 1;
public static final int SORT_BY_SALARY = 2;
```

We would then write `compareTo()` so that it takes an **int method parameter**.

```
public int compareTo(Job other, int sortOrder)
{
  switch (sortOrder)
  {
    case SORT_BY_EMPLOYER: ...
    case SORT_BY_SALARY:   ...
    default:               ...
  } // switch
} // compareTo
```

Whilst this approach works, it is a bit dangerous.

Concept **Variable: final variables: class constant: a set of choices: dangerous.**   The use of **int class constant**s to model a small set of options does have two dangers.

- The constants could be used for other purposes – e.g. they could be used inappropriately in some **arithmetic expression**.

- Someone may accidentally use another `int` value which is not one of the constants in places where a constant should be used. The **compiler** would accept it because it is an `int`.

Since Java 5.0 there has been a more robust way of specifying a set of choices.

Concept **Type: enum type.** An **enum type** is a feature which arrived in Java 5.0 that allows us to identify a **type** with an enumeration of named values. For example, we might have four possible directions in some game involving movement.

```
private enum Direction { UP, DOWN, LEFT, RIGHT }
```

This behaves rather like we have defined a **class** called `Direction`, and four **variable**s, each referring to a unique **instance** of `Direction`. So, for example, we can have the following.

```
private Direction currentDirection = Direction.UP;
private Direction nextDirection = null;
```

If we wanted the type to be available in other classes, then we would declare it as **public**.

Enum types can also be used in **switch statement**s.

```
switch (currentDirection)
{
  case UP:     ...
  case DOWN:   ...
  case LEFT:   ...
  case RIGHT:  ...
  default:     ...
} // switch
```

So we shall use an **enum type** for the two possible sort orders.

```
034:   // These are the possible sort orders.
035:   // If more are required, then add here and update compareTo.
036:   public enum SortOrder { BY_EMPLOYER, BY_SALARY }
```

Our `compareTo()` instance method takes a method parameter which is of the enum type and compares by employer or salary as required. It uses the `equals()` and `compareTo()` instance methods of the `String` class to compare the two employer names.

```
039:   // Compare this Job with a given other,
040:   // basing the comparison on the given sort order.
041:   // Returns -ve(<), 0(=) or +ve(>) int. -ve means this one is the smallest.
042:   public int compareTo(Job other, SortOrder sortOrder)
043:   {
044:     switch (sortOrder)
045:     {
046:       case BY_EMPLOYER: if (employer.equals(other.employer))
047:                           return salary - other.salary;
048:                         else
049:                           return employer.compareTo(other.employer);
```

```
050:      case BY_SALARY:    if (salary == other.salary)
051:                             return employer.compareTo(other.employer);
052:                         else
053:                             return salary - other.salary;
054:      default:           return 0;
055:   } // switch
056: } // compareTo
```

Notice that, in order for every path through the **method** to end in a **return statement**, we need to have a default entry, even though both enumeration values have been covered by the other entries. One reason is that sortOrder could be **null**, and another reason is more subtle.

Coffee time: [14.5.1] Imagine that the enum type is defined in one class, and the **switch statement** appears in another. What would happen if a third value was added to the enum type, without the second class being re**compiled**?

Coffee time: [14.5.2] If we wished to alter the sorting by salary so that it was descending, instead of ascending, what change would we need to make to compareTo()?

Finally, toString() is the same as before.

```
059:   // Return a string representation.
060:   public String toString()
061:   {
062:      return String.format("%-15s pays %5d", employer, salary);
063:   } // toString
064:
065: } // class Job
```

14.5.3 The JobList class

An **instance** of JobList is supplied with a Scanner from which it reads the **data** for the **list** of Jobs. The first line of this text is used as the description of the JobList itself – e.g. it might be the name of a particular kind of job.

```
001: import java.util.Scanner;
002:
003: /* A JobList holds a list of Job objects, the data for which is read from a
004:    Scanner passed to the constructor. It sorts these by employer and by
005:    salary. The toString method returns a String showing both lists.
006: */
007: public class JobList
008: {
009:   // The description of this JobList.
010:   private final String description;
```

For the convenience of whomever places the Job data in the **text file** for us to process, we do not require that the number of jobs is stated up front, we shall instead count them as we read and store them. But how big should the **array** be? Too big and we waste memory space, too small and we might not have enough elements for all the jobs. To get round this problem we shall use a **partially filled array** together with **array extension**.

Concept **Array: partially filled array.** An **array** has a fixed size, specified when it is created. A **partially filled array** is one in which not all of the **array elements** are used, only a leading portion of them. The size of this portion is typically stored in a separate **variable**.

For example, suppose we have an array of 100 elements, of which initially none are in use.

```
private final int MAX_NO_OF_ITEMS = 100;
private int noOfItemsInArray = 0;
private SomeType[] anArray = new SomeType[MAX_NO_OF_ITEMS];
```

We can add another item into the array, or do nothing if it is full, as follows.

```
if (noOfItemsInArray < MAX_NO_OF_ITEMS)
{
  anArray[noOfItemsInArray] = aNewItem;
  noOfItemsInArray++;
} // if
```

Concept **Array: array extension.** If we are using a **partially filled array** then we may need to worry about the problem of it becoming full when we still wish to add more items into it. The principle of **array extension** deals with this by making a **new**, bigger **array** and copying items from the original into it.

We start by making an array of a certain size, with no items in it.

```
private static final int INITIAL_ARRAY_SIZE = 100;
private static final int ARRAY_RESIZE_FACTOR = 2;
private int noOfItemsInArray = 0;
private SomeType[] anArray = new SomeType[INITIAL_ARRAY_SIZE];
```

When we come to add an item, we make a bigger array if required.

```
if (noOfItemsInArray == anArray.length)
{
  SomeType[] biggerArray
    = new SomeType[anArray.length * ARRAY_RESIZE_FACTOR];
  for (int index = 0; index < noOfItemsInArray; index++)
    biggerArray[index] = anArray[index];
  anArray = biggerArray;
} // if

anArray[noOfItemsInArray] = aNewItem;
noOfItemsInArray++;
```

The new array does not need to be twice as big as the original, just at least one element bigger. However, increasing the size by only one at a time would be slow due to the need for copying the existing elements across.

So, we have two **instance variable**s, an **int** for the number of jobs, and an **array** which we make sure is at least as big as the number of jobs.

```
012:   // The number of Jobs.
013:   private int noOfJobs;
014:
015:   // The jobs in original order.
016:   // Only the first 0 to noOfJobs - 1 indices are used.
017:   private Job[] jobsInOriginalOrder;
```

Our other instance variables include an array for the jobs **sort**ed by employer name, another for them sorted by salary, and the mean and rounded mean salaries.

```
019:   // The jobs in ascending order by employer name.
020:   private final Job[] jobsSortedByEmployer;
```

```
021:
022:    // The jobs in ascending order by salary.
023:    private final Job[] jobsSortedBySalary;
024:
025:    // The mean and rounded mean salary.
026:    private final double meanSalary;
027:    private final int meanSalaryRounded;
```

The **constructor method** is given a Scanner, from which it reads the first line as the description of the JobList, and then the job data.

```
030:    // The constructor is given a Scanner from which to read
031:    //     the description of the JobList
032:    //     and then the job data.
033:    public JobList(Scanner scanner)
034:    {
035:       description = scanner.nextLine();
036:       readJobsInOriginalOrder(scanner);
```

After that, a **private** helper **instance method** is used to copy the elements of this array into a **newly** created one which is just big enough. We use it twice, once for each of the other two **array variables**.

Concept **Method: returning a value: of an array type.** A **method** may **return** a result back to the code that called it. This result may be of any **type**, including an **array type**. This value will of course be a **reference** to an **array** which contains **array elements** of the appropriate type as stated in the **return type** (or the **null reference**).

```
038:       // Copy the jobs into two arrays.
039:       jobsSortedByEmployer = copyJobArray(jobsInOriginalOrder, noOfJobs);
040:       jobsSortedBySalary = copyJobArray(jobsInOriginalOrder, noOfJobs);
```

Another private helper instance method is used to sort each of these arrays. This will be passed two **method arguments**: a (**reference** to) the array to be sorted, and a value specifying the sort order.

Concept **Type: enum type: access from another class.** If we declare a **public enum type**, then it can be used in other **class**es. We access it using dots (.) rather like we do for other kinds of access from another class.

For example, if the enum type Direction is defined in the class Movement, then we could refer to it, and one of its values as follows.

```
      Movement.Direction requestedDirection = Movement.Direction.UP;
```

```
042:       // Sort each array into its correct order.
043:       sort(jobsSortedByEmployer, Job.SortOrder.BY_EMPLOYER);
044:       sort(jobsSortedBySalary, Job.SortOrder.BY_SALARY);
```

Then the mean salary is computed in a similar way to previous programs.

```
046:       // Now compute the sum of the salaries.
047:       int sumOfSalaries = 0;
048:       for (Job job : jobsSortedBySalary)
049:          sumOfSalaries += job.getSalary();
050:
```

```
051:     // Compute the mean, which is a double, not an integer.
052:     meanSalary = sumOfSalaries / (double)noOfJobs;
053:
054:     // But we also want to round it to simplify the results.
055:     meanSalaryRounded = (int) Math.round(meanSalary);
056:   } // JobList
```

Our instance method to read the job data first creates an array of a certain initial size. Should this array need extending, a new one is created with a size which is a multiple of the current one. To aid testing of the program, we set these values small so that we don't need to have too much data before the array extensions occur.

```
059:   // Initial size of the jobsInOriginalOrder array.
060:   private static final int INITIAL_ARRAY_SIZE = 2;
061:
062:   // When jobsInOriginalOrder is full, we extend it by this factor.
063:   private static final int ARRAY_RESIZE_FACTOR = 2;
```

The data in the Scanner contains one job description per line. We use another helper instance method to read one line from this data and create a corresponding instance of Job.

```
066:   // Read job data from the given Scanner, count them using noOfJobs,
067:   // and store in jobsInOriginalOrder -- extending as required.
068:   private void readJobsInOriginalOrder(Scanner scanner)
069:   {
070:     jobsInOriginalOrder = new Job[INITIAL_ARRAY_SIZE];
071:     noOfJobs = 0;
072:     while (scanner.hasNextLine())
073:     {
074:       // Obtain the next Job.
075:       Job currentJob = readOneJob(scanner);
076:       // Extend the array if it is too small.
077:       if (noOfJobs == jobsInOriginalOrder.length)
078:       {
079:         Job[] biggerArray
080:           = new Job[jobsInOriginalOrder.length * ARRAY_RESIZE_FACTOR];
081:         for (int index = 0; index < jobsInOriginalOrder.length; index++)
082:           biggerArray[index] = jobsInOriginalOrder[index];
083:         jobsInOriginalOrder = biggerArray;
084:       } // if
085:       // Finally store the Job and update noOfJobs.
086:       jobsInOriginalOrder[noOfJobs] = currentJob;
087:       noOfJobs++;
088:     } // while
089:   } // readJobsInOriginalOrder
```

Coffee time: Why did we not declare noOfJobs and jobsInOriginalOrder as being **final** variables?

Our instance method to create a Job obtains the next line from the Scanner and splits it into two parts – the name of the employer and the salary. There is a handy instance method in the String **class** for this.

Concept **Standard API: String: split().**
One of the many **instance methods** in the standard **class** java.lang.String is called split. It **returns** an **array** of Strings in which each **array element** is a portion of the String to which the instance method belongs. How the string is split into portions depends on the **method argument** given to split(). This argument is another String containing a **regular expression** describing what separates the portions.

Here are some examples.

String and regular expression	Resulting array
`"The-cat-sat-on-the-mat".split("-")`	`{ "The", "cat", "sat", "on", "the", "mat" }`
`"The--cat--sat--on--the--mat".split("-")`	`{ "The", "", "cat", "", "sat", "", "on", "", "the", "", "mat" }`
`"The--cat--sat--on--the--mat".split("-+")`	`{ "The", "cat", "sat", "on", "the", "mat" }`
`"The-cat--sat---on----the--mat".split("-+")`	`{ "The", "cat", "sat", "on", "the", "mat" }`

In the last two examples, the regular expression `"-+"` means "one or more hyphens".

Coffee time: [14.5.4]   Read the Java **API** on-line documentation to find out more about **regular expressions**.

Back in our `JobList` class, the two items in each line of data are separated by a **tab character**.

```
092:   // Read one line of text from the Scanner,
093:   // split it into employer name <TAB> salary,
094:   // create a corresponding Job and return it.
095:   private Job readOneJob(Scanner scanner)
096:   {
097:     String[] jobData = scanner.nextLine().split("\t");
098:     return new Job(jobData[0], Integer.parseInt(jobData[1]));
099:   } // readOneJob
```

Next we have an instance method to make a copy of the original array into the two other arrays (by being called twice from the constructor method). This makes a **shallow copy** of the array given as its first **method argument**, but only copies a leading portion. The length of this portion is given as its second method argument.

Concept **Array: shallow copy.** When we copy an **array** containing **references** to **objects**, we can either make a **shallow copy** or a **deep copy**. A shallow copy contains the same references, so the objects end up being shared between the two arrays. A deep copy contains references to *copies* of the original objects.

```
102:   // Return a shallow copy of given source,
103:   // but only the first dataLength elements.
104:   private Job[] copyJobArray(Job[] source, int dataLength)
105:   {
106:     Job[] result = new Job[dataLength];
107:     for (int index = 0; index < dataLength; index++)
108:       result[index] = source[index];
109:     return result;
110:   } // copyJobArray
```

Coffee time: [14.5.5]   Why can we not use a **for-each loop** in the above code?

The following diagram illustrates the sharing of Job **object**s between the arrays. It shows the jobsInOriginalOrder and jobsSortedBySalary arrays, after the constructor method code has completed. (The jobsSortedByEmployer array is not shown.) The data consisted of six salaries input to the program (along with employer names) in the order 15049, 49959, 25750, 24627, 12523 and then 19852. The instance variable jobsInOriginalOrder contains a reference to an array containing references to six Job objects. These references are stored in the array in the order they were input. Note also the two unused positions of that array – it has been extended, twice, to a size of eight. The array variable jobsSortedBySalary contains a reference to an array containing references to the same six objects, but this time in an order which is ascending by the values of the salary instance variables.

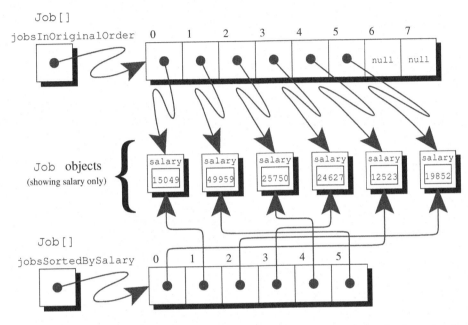

The code to sort an array is much the same as in the previous example, except we here take the sort order as a **method parameter** which we pass on to the compareTo() instance method of the Jobs.

```
113:  // Sort the given array of Jobs
114:  // using compareTo on the Job objects with the given sortOrder.
115:  private void sort(Job[] anArray, Job.SortOrder sortOrder)
116:  {
117:    // Each pass of the sort reduces unsortedLength by one.
118:    int unsortedLength = anArray.length;
119:    boolean changedOnThisPass;
120:    do
121:    {
122:      changedOnThisPass = false;
123:      for (int pairLeftIndex = 0;
124:           pairLeftIndex < unsortedLength - 1; pairLeftIndex++)
125:        if (anArray[pairLeftIndex]
126:            .compareTo(anArray[pairLeftIndex + 1], sortOrder) > 0)
127:        {
128:          Job thatWasAtPairLeftIndex = anArray[pairLeftIndex];
129:          anArray[pairLeftIndex] = anArray[pairLeftIndex + 1];
130:          anArray[pairLeftIndex + 1] = thatWasAtPairLeftIndex;
131:          changedOnThisPass = true;
132:        } // if
133:      unsortedLength--;
134:    } while (changedOnThisPass);
135:  } // sort
```

Finally, `toString()` produces a report containing both sorted lists of job details. Notice our use of `%n` with `String.format()` to get the correct **line separator**, so that our code is portable.

```
138:    // Return job details sorted by employer name and then salary.
139:    public String toString()
140:    {
141:        return String.format("Job list: %s\tAverage: %f%n%n"
142:                            + "Sorted by employer%s%n%nSorted by salary%s",
143:                            description, meanSalary,
144:                            listOneJobArray(jobsSortedByEmployer),
145:                            listOneJobArray(jobsSortedBySalary));
146:    } // toString
147:
148:
149:    // Helper method for toString.
150:    private String listOneJobArray(Job[] jobArray)
151:    {
152:        String result = "";
153:        for (Job job : jobArray)
154:        {
155:            int differenceFromMean = job.getSalary() - meanSalaryRounded;
156:            String comparisonToMean = differenceFromMean == 0
157:                            ? "zero difference from"
158:                            : (differenceFromMean < 0
159:                                ? "less than" : "greater than");
160:            result +=
161:                String.format("%n%s, which is %5d %s the mean",
162:                            job, Math.abs(differenceFromMean), comparisonToMean);
163:        } // for
164:        return result;
165:    } // listOneJobArray
166:
167: } // class JobList
```

 Coffee time: [14.5.6] In a previous coffee time you were invited to find out about `StringBuffer`. Do you think the `toString()` instance method above would be a good place to use one?

14.5.4 Trying it

We'll try our program with two **files**: one for programmer jobs and the other for tester jobs.

To list a **text file** on Unix we can use the `cat` command (on Microsoft Windows we use `type`).

Console Input / Output
`$ cat programmers.txt`
Programmers
Quick Hackers   15049
Top Soft   49959
Middle Ware   25750
Mean Media   24627
OK Coral   12523
Cheaper Cheers   19852
`$ _`

Console Input / Output
`$ cat testers.txt`
Testers
Quick Hackers   13999
Top Soft   49059
Middle Ware   24049
Mean Media   23316
OK Coral   10999
Cheaper Cheers   18474
`$ _`

```
                        Console Input / Output
$ java JobSurvey programmers.txt testers.txt
Job list: Programmers   Average: 24626.666667

Sorted by employer
Cheaper Cheers   pays 19852, which is   4775 less than the mean
Mean Media       pays 24627, which is      0 zero difference from the mean
Middle Ware      pays 25750, which is   1123 greater than the mean
OK Coral         pays 12523, which is  12104 less than the mean
Quick Hackers    pays 15049, which is   9578 less than the mean
Top Soft         pays 49959, which is  25332 greater than the mean

Sorted by salary
OK Coral         pays 12523, which is  12104 less than the mean
Quick Hackers    pays 15049, which is   9578 less than the mean
Cheaper Cheers   pays 19852, which is   4775 less than the mean
Mean Media       pays 24627, which is      0 zero difference from the mean
Middle Ware      pays 25750, which is   1123 greater than the mean
Top Soft         pays 49959, which is  25332 greater than the mean


Job list: Testers      Average: 23316.000000

Sorted by employer
Cheaper Cheers   pays 18474, which is   4842 less than the mean
Mean Media       pays 23316, which is      0 zero difference from the mean
Middle Ware      pays 24049, which is    733 greater than the mean
OK Coral         pays 10999, which is  12317 less than the mean
Quick Hackers    pays 13999, which is   9317 less than the mean
Top Soft         pays 49059, which is  25743 greater than the mean

Sorted by salary
OK Coral         pays 10999, which is  12317 less than the mean
Quick Hackers    pays 13999, which is   9317 less than the mean
Cheaper Cheers   pays 18474, which is   4842 less than the mean
Mean Media       pays 23316, which is      0 zero difference from the mean
Middle Ware      pays 24049, which is    733 greater than the mean
Top Soft         pays 49059, which is  25743 greater than the mean

$ _
```

Coffee time: [14.5.7]
So, is it true – do testers get paid less than programmers? Should they?

Coffee time: [14.5.8]   Did you notice a %f without a precision (number of decimal places) in the **format specifier** string in our toString()? Can you guess what the default number of decimal places is?

14.5.5 Coursework: Random order text puzzle

In this coursework you will write a program that sets an **interactive** puzzle for the user to solve. The program is **run** with a **command line argument** which is the name of a **file** containing a few lines of text. These are read in and presented in a random order to the user, who is invited to pick one line to be swapped with the last one, repeatedly, until they are back in their original order.

The text might be part of the lyrics of a song, or a poem, or a quote, etc., or may have some other quality about it that gives a clue for working out the correct order.

Here is an example run of the program.

```
                   Console Input / Output
$ java RandomOrderPuzzle test-data.txt
0       are sorted as they started off,
1       it obvious
2       what the correct
3       Is
4       should be now that they
5       i.e. in order of increasing word count?
6       order of these lines

Enter a line number to swap with the last one: 3
0       are sorted as they started off,
1       it obvious
2       what the correct
3       order of these lines
4       should be now that they
5       i.e. in order of increasing word count?
6       Is

Enter a line number to swap with the last one: 0
0       Is
1       it obvious
2       what the correct
3       order of these lines
4       should be now that they
5       i.e. in order of increasing word count?
6       are sorted as they started off,

Enter a line number to swap with the last one: 5
0       Is
1       it obvious
2       what the correct
3       order of these lines
4       should be now that they
5       are sorted as they started off,
6       i.e. in order of increasing word count?

Game over in 3 moves.
$ _
```

Write your solution in a **class** called RandomOrderPuzzle. The **main method** will create a Scanner for the file, and pass it to the **constructor method** to make an **instance** of RandomOrderPuzzle. Then it will make another Scanner for the **textual user interface**.

The constructor method will read in the text, and store it in an **array** of Strings, using **array extension** as required. Then it will make a copy of this array into a second array, and randomize the order of this copy.

The class will also provide three **instance methods** for use in the main method. One will swap a given line of the copied array with its last line. Another will check to see whether the lines of the copy array are (now) in the same order as the original one. The third is a toString() which list the lines from the randomized copy in their current order.

Here is the main method, and a **private** instance method to randomize the order of a given array.

```
...
011:    public static void main(String[] args) throws Exception
012:    {
013:        Scanner fileScanner = new Scanner(new File(args[0]));
014:        RandomOrderPuzzle puzzle = new RandomOrderPuzzle(fileScanner);
015:
016:        Scanner inputScanner = new Scanner(System.in);
017:        System.out.println(puzzle);
018:        int moveCount = 0;
019:        while (! puzzle.isSorted())
020:        {
021:            System.out.print("Enter a line number to swap with the last one: ");
022:            puzzle.swapLine(inputScanner.nextInt());
023:            System.out.println(puzzle);
```

```
024:        moveCount++;
025:     } // while
026:     System.out.println("Game over in " + moveCount + " moves.");
027:   } // main
...
084:   private void randomizeStringArrayOrder(String[] anArray)
085:   {
086:     for (int itemsRemaining = anArray.length;
087:          itemsRemaining > 0; itemsRemaining--)
088:     {
089:       int anIndex = (int) (Math.random() * itemsRemaining);
090:       String itemAtAnIndex = anArray[anIndex];
091:       anArray[anIndex] = anArray[anArray.length - 1];
092:       anArray[anArray.length - 1] = itemAtAnIndex;
093:     } // for
094:   } // randomizeStringArrayOrder
...
```

14.6   Example: Diet monitoring

AIM: To reinforce ideas met so far, and introduce **array initializer** and **array search**ing, for which we revisit the **logical operator**s.

In this section we develop a simple program to aid people who are monitoring their diet. Each time the user eats, he or she records the food name (e.g. "pizza") together with how many grams have been eaten. This is written as a line, with (possibly multiple) **tab character**s separating the two fields, in a **text file** called diet-diary.txt.

Here is an example.

Console Input / Output	
$ **cat diet-diary.txt**	
pizza	400
garlic bread	200
cheesecake	260
burger	200
fries	180
milkshake	400
fried chicken	360
wedges	270
$ _	

The job of the program is to produce a summary table showing how much of each nutritional component, such as protein, carbohydrate, etc. has been eaten. To do this, it has access to a text file of **data** about lots of named foods. Here is a sample – the first line of the text file contains just titles to remind the user which columns refer to what nutritional component. The amounts are recorded in grams per *kilogram* of the food.

Console Input / Output					
$ **cat food-details.txt**					
Food	Protein	Carb	Fat	Fibre	Sodium
burger	150	200	100	25	12
cheesecake	50	300	200	6	5
fried chicken	225	115	190	15	10
fries	35	400	150	50	12
garlic bread	130	420	95	25	5
milkshake	28	202	32	1	2
pizza	140	300	119	25	8
wedges	210	390	99	41	12
$ _					

319

The program is divided into three **class**es.

Class list for Diet	
Class	**Description**
Diet	The **main method** makes an **instance** of FoodList from food-details.txt. It then accumulates nutritional components from food items listed in diet-diary.txt, and outputs those totals.
FoodList	This will make an **instance** of Food for each item specified in the text file, and store them in an **array**.
Food	An instance of this will store a food name together with its nutritional data.

Public method interfaces for class **Diet**.			
Method	**Return**	**Arguments**	**Description**
main	**void**	String[]	The main method for the program.

Public method interfaces for class **FoodList**.			
Method	**Return**	**Arguments**	**Description**
Constructor		Scanner	Constructs a food list, reading from the given Scanner.
findFood	Food	String	Return (a **reference** to) the Food **object** corresponding to the food named by the given String, or **null** if it is not recognized.

Public method interfaces for class **Food**.			
Method	**Return**	**Arguments**	**Description**
Constructor		String	Constructs a Food with the details specified by the given String. This will be a line of text from the food-details.txt data text file.
getName	String		Returns the food name.
componentMilliGramsForWeight	**int**[]	**int**	Produces an array of nutritional component amounts corresponding to a given number of grams of the food being consumed.

14.6.1 The Food class

The first thing we define in the Food **class** is a **class constant array** of nutritional component names. This both provides the spelling of those components and the order in which nutritional data must be provided in the food-details.txt **text file**.

Concept **Array: array creation: initializer.** When we declare an **array variable** we can at the same time create the actual array by listing the **array element**s which are to be placed in it, using an **array initializer**. This is *instead* of saying how big the array is. Java counts this **list**, creates an array that big, and assigns the elements in the order listed. For example, the following code declares an **array variable** which refers to an array containing the first eight **prime number**s (excluding 1).

```
int[] smallPrimes = {2, 3, 5, 7, 11, 13, 17, 19};
```

This is just a shorthand for the following.

```
int[] smallPrimes = new int[8];
...
smallPrimes[0]=2;   smallPrimes[1]=3;   smallPrimes[2]=5;
smallPrimes[3]=7;   smallPrimes[4]=11;  smallPrimes[5]=13;
smallPrimes[6]=17;  smallPrimes[7]=19;
```

```
001: // Representation of a food, as a name
002: // together with nutritional data in grams per kilogram.
003: public class Food
004: {
005:    // This defines the spelling and order of nutritional components.
006:    public static final String[] NUTRITIONAL_COMPONENTS
007:      = { "Protein", "Carb", "Fat", "Fibre", "Sodium" };
```

Each **instance** of Food has a name and nutritional component data, the latter being stored in an `int` array with the data in the same order as in NUTRITIONAL_COMPONENTS.

```
009:    // The name of this food.
010:    private final String name;
011:
012:    // Nutritional data in the same order as NUTRITIONAL_COMPONENTS.
013:    private final int[] nutrientGramsPerKilogram
014:      = new int[NUTRITIONAL_COMPONENTS.length];
```

The **constructor method** is given a `String` containing the name and then the nutritional data as whole grams per kilogram. These fields are separated by one or more tabs – multiple tabs are permitted to help line up the columns in food-details.txt as the food names may vary considerably in length. We use `split()` with a delimiter pattern of "\t+", which means one or more tabs.

```
017:    // Constructor is given name and data as tab separated parts of a string.
018:    public Food(String details)
019:    {
020:      String[] detailParts = details.split("\t+");
021:      name = detailParts[0];
022:      for (int index = 0; index < NUTRITIONAL_COMPONENTS.length; index++)
023:        nutrientGramsPerKilogram[index]
024:          = Integer.parseInt(detailParts[index + 1]);
025:    } // Food
```

We have an **accessor method** for the name of the food.

```
028:    // Accessor for name.
029:    public String getName()
030:    {
031:      return name;
032:    } // getName
```

Finally we have an **instance method** that takes a given amount of food, and **return**s an array of nutritional data for that given amount, with nutritional components in the same order as in NUTRITIONAL_COMPONENTS. To achieve accuracy, without having to use **double**s, the data is returned as *milligrams* of each nutritional component – we multiply the number of *grams* by the amount per *kilogram*. For example, if sweetcorn contains 250 grams of carbohydrate per kilogram, and 50 grams is eaten, then that is $50/1000 \times 250$ grams of carbohydrate, or just 50×250 milligrams.

```
035:    // Returns the number of milligrams of each component
036:    // for the given number of grams consumed.
037:    public int[] componentMilliGramsForWeight(int grams)
038:    {
039:      int[] result = new int[NUTRITIONAL_COMPONENTS.length];
040:      for (int index = 0; index < NUTRITIONAL_COMPONENTS.length; index++)
041:        result[index] = nutrientGramsPerKilogram[index] * grams;
042:      return result;
043:    } // componentMilliGramsForWeight
044:
045: } // class Food
```

Coffee time: `14.6.1` By declaring the array NUTRITIONAL_COMPONENTS as a **final variable**, have we made it impossible for code (inside or outside of this class) to alter the order or spellings of the components?

14.6.2 The `FoodList` class

The job of the `FoodList` **class** is to build an **array** of `Food` **object**s from the **text file** and provide a search facility to find the `Food` object for a given food name.

The first part of the code is self explanatory – watch for the use of a **partially filled array** with **array extension**.

```
001: import java.util.Scanner;
002:
003: // Keeps a list of food items, and provides a search facility.
004: public class FoodList
005: {
006:    // For array extension of foodList.
007:    private static final int INITIAL_ARRAY_SIZE = 100, ARRAY_RESIZE_FACTOR = 2;
008:
009:    // The food details are stored in a partially filled array
010:    // with an associated count.
011:    private int noOfFoodItems;
012:    private Food[] foodList;
013:
014:
015:    // The constructor reads the food details from the given scanner
016:    // and stores them in foodList, extending as necessary.
017:    public FoodList(Scanner scanner)
018:    {
019:      foodList = new Food[INITIAL_ARRAY_SIZE];
020:      // The first line is just titles.
021:      scanner.nextLine();
022:      noOfFoodItems = 0;
023:      while (scanner.hasNextLine())
024:      {
025:        // Food constructor parses the whole line.
026:        Food latestFood = new Food(scanner.nextLine());
027:        // Extend the array if it is full.
028:        if (noOfFoodItems == foodList.length)
029:        {
030:          Food[] biggerArray = new Food[foodList.length * ARRAY_RESIZE_FACTOR];
031:          for (int index = 0; index < foodList.length; index++)
032:            biggerArray[index] = foodList[index];
033:          foodList = biggerArray;
034:        } // if
```

```
035:      // Store the new item and count it.
036:      foodList[noOfFoodItems] = latestFood;
037:      noOfFoodItems++;
038:    } // while
039:  } // FoodList
```

To search for a `Food` object given the name of the food, we move an **array index** from the beginning of the array through each element until we either find the one we want, or we have looked at every element. We shall write code that exploits the fact that `&&` is conditional.

Concept **Expression: boolean: logical operators: conditional.** The **logical operator**s `&&` and `||` in Java are called **conditional and** and **conditional or** because they have an important property, which distinguishes them from their classical logic counterparts. They are lazy. This means that if they can determine their result after evaluating their left **operand**, they will not **evaluate** their right one. That is, if the first **disjunct** of `||` evaluates to `true` it will not evaluate the second; and if the first **conjunct** of `&&` evaluates to `false` it will not evaluate the second. This allows us to safely write **condition**s such as the following. `data == null || data.length == 0`

Concept **Design: Searching a list: linear search.** The simplest way to find an item in a **list** of items, such as an **array**, is to perform a **linear search** – starting at the front and looking at each item in turn. For example, the following **array search method** finds the position of a given `int` in a given **array**, or **return**s -1 if the number is not found.

```
private int posOfInt(int[] anArray, int toFind)
{
  int searchPos = 0;
  while (searchPos < anArray.length && anArray[searchPos] != toFind)
    searchPos++;
  if (searchPos == anArray.length) return -1;
  else                             return searchPos;
} // posOfInt
```

If the value of `toFind` is not in the array, then eventually the value of `searchPos` will reach `anArray.length`. At that point the first **conjunct** of the **while loop condition**, `searchPos < anArray.length` becomes `false` and hence so does the **conjunction** itself, without it evaluating the second conjunct, `anArray[searchPos] != toFind`. If on the other hand we swapped over the two conjuncts, when `searchPos` reaches that same value the (now) first conjunct would cause an `ArrayIndexOutOfBoundsException`.

```
// Definitely silly code.
while (anArray[searchPos] != toFind && searchPos < anArray.length)
  searchPos++;
```

Coffee time: As an aside, can you think of a single **return statement** to replace the **if else statement** after the loop in the example above? (Hint: add one to `searchPos`, use the **remainder operator** and subtract one again.) Which is better style? [14.6.2]

Here is our **instance method** to find the required `Food` object using a **linear search**.

```
042:  // Find the Food object corresponding to foodName
043:  // or return null if not found.
044:  public Food findFood(String foodName)
045:  {
046:    int foodIndex = 0;
047:    while (foodIndex < noOfFoodItems
048:           && ! foodList[foodIndex].getName().equals(foodName))
049:      foodIndex++;
```

```
050:     if (foodIndex == noOfFoodItems) return null;
051:     else                            return foodList[foodIndex];
052:   } // findFood
053:
054: } // class FoodList
```

14.6.3   The Diet class

The **main method** creates a FoodList from food-details.txt, then reads diet-diary.txt accumulating the nutritional component amounts as it goes, and finally it prints out the totals in a table.

```
001: import java.io.File;
002: import java.util.Scanner;
003:
004: /* This program reads food information from food-details.txt
005:    and diet information from diet-diary.txt
006:    and produces a table of how much nutritional component was eaten.
007: */
008: public class Diet
009: {
010:   // The FoodList to be obtained from food-details.txt.
011:   private static FoodList foodList;
012:
013:
014:   // The main method.
015:   public static void main(String[] args) throws Exception
016:   {
017:     foodList = new FoodList(new Scanner(new File("food-details.txt")));
018:     readDietDiary(new Scanner(new File("diet-diary.txt")));
019:     printDietTable();
020:   } // main
```

We accumulate the amounts of each nutritional component in an **array**, storing the items in the same order as in Food.NUTRITIONAL_COMPONENTS.

```
023:   // An array of total nutritional component amounts:
024:   // Index is [component number]
025:   // and data is accumulated as number of milligrams of that component.
026:   private static int[] dietTable = new int[Food.NUTRITIONAL_COMPONENTS.length];
```

Reading the diet diary is just a job of taking each line, splitting it into food name and amount, finding that food, getting the nutritional components for that amount and accumulating them in dietTable.

```
029:   // Read the diet information from the given Scanner
030:   // accumulating nutritional components in dietTable.
031:   private static void readDietDiary(Scanner scanner)
032:   {
033:     // First initialize the amounts to zero.
034:     for (int componentIndex = 0;
035:          componentIndex < Food.NUTRITIONAL_COMPONENTS.length; componentIndex++)
036:       dietTable[componentIndex] = 0;
037:     // Now read each line.
038:     while (scanner.hasNextLine())
039:     {
```

```
040:        String[] portionDetails = scanner.nextLine().split("\t+");
041:        // Food name is the first item.
042:        Food food = foodList.findFood(portionDetails[0]);
043:        if (food == null)
044:          System.out.println("Unrecognized food name: " + portionDetails[0]);
045:        else
046:        {
047:          // Food amount is the second item.
048:          int amount = Integer.parseInt(portionDetails[1]);
049:          // Obtain nutritional components from that amount.
050:          int[] foodComponents = food.componentMilliGramsForWeight(amount);
051:          // And accumulate them in dietTable.
052:          for (int componentIndex = 0;
053:               componentIndex < Food.NUTRITIONAL_COMPONENTS.length;
054:               componentIndex++)
055:            dietTable[componentIndex] += foodComponents[componentIndex];
056:        } // else
057:      } // while
058:    } // readDietDiary
```

When we print the table we remember to divide by 1000 to convert from milligrams to grams.

```
061:    // Print the dietTable as grams (so divide by 1000).
062:    private static void printDietTable()
063:    {
064:      for (int componentIndex = 0;
065:           componentIndex < Food.NUTRITIONAL_COMPONENTS.length; componentIndex++)
066:        System.out.println(Food.NUTRITIONAL_COMPONENTS[componentIndex] + "\t"
067:                        + Math.round(dietTable[componentIndex] / 1000));
068:    } // printDietTable
069:
070: } // class Diet
```

14.6.4 Trying it

Let us try the program with the **test data** we saw earlier.

Console Input / Output
$ **java Diet**
Protein 280
Carb   621
Fat   273
Fibre   47
Sodium 17
$ _

Coffee time: `14.6.3`
Find out about `equalsIgnoreCase()` from the `String` **class**, and propose a change so that the user would not need to have consistent capitalization in the names of the food items.

Coffee time: `14.6.4`
Suppose you wish to delete an element from an arbitrarily ordered **partially filled array**. How can you, using only one assignment and one decrement?

Coffee time: `14.6.5`
How could we add saturated fat to the program? What extra issue would we have for Kcals?

14.6.5 Coursework: Viewing phone call details

Here you will write a program that reads in a **file** of phone call details, and allows the user to see some of those calls with a total cost and duration. The first **command line argument** is the name of a **text file** containing the details of one phone call per line, comprising the phone number, including spaces at the appropriate places, the duration of the call, in the format hh:mm:ss, and the cost of the call, in pounds, as a decimal number. These three items are separated by single **tab characters**.

Here is some sample **data**.

```
Console Input / Output
$ cat test-phone-calls.txt
07571 78764      00:00:16       0.120
01537 82608      00:00:04       0.070
01492 88229      01:02:58       0.860
08479 88844      00:03:56       0.070
08901 24241      00:00:33       0.060
07546 88323      00:02:40       0.250
07571 78764      00:07:12       0.910
08474 02751      00:05:37       0.150
0161 296 410     00:03:02       0.190
0161 296 682     00:00:57       0.090
01537 82608      00:00:20       0.070
01537 82608      00:30:10       0.450
08479 77777      00:02:50       0.070
07571 78764      00:06:23       0.800
07728 50344      00:04:20       0.380
0161 296 682     00:00:06       0.070
07571 78764      00:44:28       2.930
0161 803 487     00:15:59       0.260
0161 297 617     00:13:24       0.530
08476 05080      00:00:14       0.060
08476 05080      00:04:09       0.130
07571 78764      00:00:03       0.120
0161 803 487     00:00:48       0.070
08479 88844      00:01:05       0.060
08901 27274      00:02:30       0.090
07571 78764      00:08:18       0.630
0161 297 629     00:01:05       0.120
07936 84350      00:11:13       1.330
07936 84350      00:01:59       0.270
0161 297 629     00:00:01       0.090
07571 78764      00:46:27       3.060
08479 77777      00:03:17       0.070
07955 65414      00:20:41       1.400
01492 88229      01:24:12       0.850
$ _
```

The user selects a subset of the calls by entering a prefix of the phone numbers he or she wishes to view. Here is an example **run**.

```
Console Input / Output
$ java PhoneCalls test-phone-calls.txt
Enter phone number prefix, or Q to quit: 075
07571 78764      00:00:16       0.12
07546 88323      00:02:40       0.25
07571 78764      00:07:12       0.91
07571 78764      00:06:23       0.80
07571 78764      00:44:28       2.93
07571 78764      00:00:03       0.12
07571 78764      00:08:18       0.63
07571 78764      00:46:27       3.06

Calls matched:  8
Total duration: 01:55:47
Total cost:     8.82


Enter phone number prefix, or Q to quit: 0161 2
0161 296 410     00:03:02       0.19
0161 296 682     00:00:57       0.09
0161 296 682     00:00:06       0.07
0161 297 617     00:13:24       0.53
0161 297 629     00:01:05       0.12
0161 297 629     00:00:01       0.09

Calls matched:  6
Total duration: 00:18:35
Total cost:     1.09

Enter phone number prefix, or Q to quit: 0161 8
0161 803 487     00:15:59       0.26
0161 803 487     00:00:48       0.07

Calls matched:  2
Total duration: 00:16:47
Total cost:     0.33

Enter phone number prefix, or Q to quit: Q
$ _
```

You should create four **class**es.

Class list for PhoneBook	
Class	**Description**
PhoneCalls	The main class containing the **main method**. It will make an **instance** of PhoneCallList and then prompt the user for input.
PhoneCallList	An instance of this will represent the **list** of phone calls and will contain instances of PhoneCall.
PhoneCall	An instance of this will represent a single phone call comprising phone number, duration and cost.
Duration	An instance of this represents a period of time which can be seen in hh:mm:ss format, and which can be added to another duration to yield a **new** one.

Here is the main method to get you started.

```
...
016:    public static void main(String[] args) throws Exception
017:    {
018:      callList = new PhoneCallList(new Scanner(new File(args[0])));
019:      Scanner inputScanner = new Scanner(System.in);
020:      String userInput;
021:      do
022:      {
023:        System.out.print("Enter phone number prefix, or Q to quit: ");
024:        userInput = inputScanner.nextLine();
025:        if (! userInput.equals("Q"))
026:          System.out.println(callList.matchingCallsReport(userInput));
027:      } while (! userInput.equals("Q"));
028:    } // main
...
```

You should think carefully where the logic to decide whether a particular phone call matches the user's input should go: is it to reside in `PhoneCallList` or `PhoneCall`? (Hint: is it about a phone call, or about a list?) Either way, you can use the `startsWith()` **instance method** of the `String` class.

To help you further, here is the code for the `Duration` class.

```
001: // Representation of a time duration.
002: public class Duration
003: {
004:   // Represented as a hh:mm:ss string and as total seconds.
005:   private final String stringRep;
006:   private final int totalSeconds;
007:
008:
009:   // Constructs from a hh:mm:ss string.
010:   public Duration(String requiredStringRep)
011:   {
012:     stringRep = requiredStringRep;
013:     String[] parts = requiredStringRep.split(":");
014:     int hours = Integer.parseInt(parts[0]);
015:     int minutes = Integer.parseInt(parts[1]);
016:     int seconds = Integer.parseInt(parts[2]);
017:     totalSeconds = (hours * 60 + minutes) * 60 + seconds;
018:   } // Duration
019:
020:
021:   // Constructs from a total number of seconds.
022:   public Duration(int requiredNoOfSeconds)
023:   {
024:     totalSeconds = requiredNoOfSeconds;
025:     int hours = totalSeconds / 3600;
026:     int minutes = (totalSeconds % 3600) / 60;
027:     int seconds = totalSeconds % 60;
028:     stringRep = String.format("%02d:%02d:%02d", hours, minutes, seconds);
029:   } // Duration
030:
031:
```

```
032:   // Returns the hh:mm:ss representation.
033:   public String toString()
034:   {
035:     return stringRep;
036:   } // toString
037:
038:
039:   // Adds this to another to create a new.
040:   public Duration add(Duration other)
041:   {
042:     return new Duration(totalSeconds + other.totalSeconds);
043:   } // add
044:
045: } // class Duration
```

Optional extra: Instead of merely a leading prefix of phone numbers, why not allow the user to enter any pattern? (Hint: look at the `matches()` instance method of the `String` class.)

Optional extra: Add the date and time of calls to the program (and its data).

14.7   Example: A weekly diet

AIM: To introduce **two-dimensional arrays**.

The program in this section is an elaboration of the previous one, enabling users to monitor their diet for each day of a week.

As before, when the user eats, a record is made of the food and the amount, but also, in front of that data, the day of the week is recorded.

The program will produce a table of nutritional component amounts, with a row for each day of the week.

The food details stored in `food-details.txt` is the same as in the previous section. In fact much of the program is also the same – the **class** Food and FoodList are identical. Then, instead of Diet we have WeeklyDiet.

Console Input / Output

```
$ cat diet-diary.txt
Mon     pizza          400
Mon     garlic bread   200
Mon     cheesecake     260
Tue     burger         200
Tue     fries          180
Tue     milkshake      400
Wed     fried chicken  360
Wed     wedges         270
Thu     pizza          650
Fri     burger         400
Fri     fries          360
Sat     fried chicken  360
Sat     wedges         540
Sun     garlic bread   800
Sun     cheesecake     260
$ _
```

14.7.1   The `WeeklyDiet` class

The first part of the **class** is the same as Diet was before.

```
001: import java.io.File;
002: import java.util.Scanner;
003:
004: /* This program reads food information from food-details.txt
005:    and diet information from diet-diary.txt
006:    and produces a table of how much nutritional component was eaten
007:    on each day of the week.
008: */
009: public class WeeklyDiet
010: {
011:   // The FoodList to be obtained from food-details.txt.
012:   private static FoodList foodList;
013:
014:
015:   // The main method.
016:   public static void main(String[] args) throws Exception
017:   {
018:     foodList = new FoodList(new Scanner(new File("food-details.txt")));
019:     readDietDiary(new Scanner(new File("diet-diary.txt")));
020:     printDietTable();
021:   } // main
```

328

We have an **array** in which we store the names of the week days. This allows us to recognize them in `diet-diary.txt`, and turn them into an **array index**. For example, when we see `Wed` in that **data** we can search the array and turn it into the day index 2. We also use this array for the titles on the output table.

```
024:    // Days of the week -- this defines spelling for use in diet-diary.txt
025:    // and their order in dietTable.
026:    private static final String[] DAY_NAMES
027:       = { "Mon", "Tue", "Wed", "Thu", "Fri", "Sat", "Sun" };
```

We have a **private** helper **instance method** to do an **array search** on DAY_NAMES.

```
030:    // Find the day index for the given day name, or -1 if not found.
031:    private static int findDayIndex(String dayName)
032:    {
033:       int dayIndex = 0;
034:       while (dayIndex < DAY_NAMES.length
035:              && ! DAY_NAMES[dayIndex].equals(dayName))
036:         dayIndex++;
037:       if (dayIndex == DAY_NAMES.length)
038:       {
039:         System.out.println("Unrecognized day name: " + dayName);
040:         return -1;
041:       } // if
042:       return dayIndex;
043:    } // findDayIndex
```

The nutritional component amounts are accumulated in an array as before, except that this time we have a **two-dimensional array**.

Concept **Array: array of arrays.** The **array elements** of an **array** may be of any **type**, including arrays. This means the elements of the array are **references** to other arrays. For example, the following diagram shows an **array variable** which contains a reference to an array of arrays of **int** values.

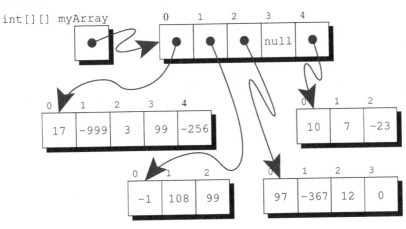

The type of the variable is `int[][]`, that is **int** array, array. The variable references an array of 5 values, the first of which is a reference to an array of 5 numbers, the second a reference to an array of 3 numbers, the third is a reference to an array of 4 numbers, the fourth is the **null reference** and the final element is a reference to an array of 3 numbers.

These arrays could be created, ready for the numbers to be put in them, as follows.

```
int[][] myArray = new int[5][];
myArray[0] = new int[5];   myArray[1] = new int[3];   myArray[2] = new int[4];
myArray[3] = null;         myArray[4] = new int[3];
```

329

Concept **Array: array of arrays: two-dimensional arrays.**

A very common situation when we have an **array** of arrays, is that none of the **array element**s are the **null reference** and all of the arrays they **reference** are the same length. This is known as a **two-dimensional array**, and is essentially a model of a rectangular grid.

For example, the following diagram shows a **variable** which contains a reference to a two-dimensional array of **int** values.

This two-dimensional array could be created (without the numbers being assigned into it yet) by the following code.

```
int[][] my2DArray = new int[5][];
my2DArray[0] = new int[4];
my2DArray[1] = new int[4];
my2DArray[2] = new int[4];
my2DArray[3] = new int[4];
my2DArray[4] = new int[4];
```

Two-dimensional arrays are so common, that Java provides a shorthand notation for defining them. The shorthand for the above example is as follows.

```
int[][] my2DArray = new int[5][4];
```

The code `new int[5][4]` makes an array of length 5 get created at **run time**, and also 5 arrays of length 4, which are capable of holding **int** values, with these latter 5 arrays being referenced by the 5 elements in the first array.

In our program we want a two-dimensional array of **int** values where the first **array index** is the day of the week, 0 to 6; and the second index is the nutritional component, 0 to `Food.NUTRITIONAL_COMPONENTS.length - 1`. So, in the previous program we had an array of amounts, indexed by nutritional component. Now we have seven of those arrays, one for each day of the week, that is, an array of seven items, each of which is an array of nutritional component amounts.

```
046:    // A two dimensional array of nutritional component amounts:
047:    // Index is [day number][component number]
048:    // and data is accumulated as number of milligrams of that component
049:    // eaten on that day.
050:    private static int[][] dietTable
051:       = new int[DAY_NAMES.length][Food.NUTRITIONAL_COMPONENTS.length];
```

Reading the diet information is similar to before. However, when we initialize the array to zero, we need two **nested loop**s, one for each dimension of the array.

Concept **Array: element access: in two-dimensional arrays.**   Each grid element in a **two-dimensional array** is indexed by two indices – the first **array index** accesses the row **array**, and the second accesses the **array element** within that row. For example, given the code

```
int[][] my2DArray = new int[5][4];
```

then `my2DArray[0]` is a **reference** to the first row, and so `my2DArray[0][0]` is the first element in the first row. Similarly, `my2DArray[4][3]` is the last element in the last row.

```
054:    // Read the diet information from the given Scanner
055:    // accumulating nutritional components in dietTable.
056:    private static void readDietDiary(Scanner scanner)
057:    {
058:        // First initialize the amounts to zero.
059:        for (int dayIndex = 0 ; dayIndex < DAY_NAMES.length; dayIndex++)
060:            for (int componentIndex = 0;
061:                 componentIndex < Food.NUTRITIONAL_COMPONENTS.length;
062:                 componentIndex++)
063:                dietTable[dayIndex][componentIndex] = 0;
```

When we read data from the `Scanner`, the first item in each line is the day name.

```
064:        // Now read each line.
065:        while (scanner.hasNextLine())
066:        {
067:            String[] portionDetails = scanner.nextLine().split("\t+");
068:            // Day name is the first item.
069:            int dayIndex = findDayIndex(portionDetails[0]);
070:            // Food name is the second item.
071:            Food food = foodList.findFood(portionDetails[1]);
072:            if (food == null)
073:                System.out.println("Unrecognized food name: " + portionDetails[1]);
074:            if (dayIndex != -1 && food != null)
075:            {
076:                // Food amount is the third item.
077:                int amount = Integer.parseInt(portionDetails[2]);
078:                // Obtain nutritional components from that amount.
079:                int[] foodComponents = food.componentMilliGramsForWeight(amount);
```

Having obtained the nutritional components for that amount of food, we add them to the totals for the specific `dayIndex`.

```
080:                // And accumulate them in dietTable.
081:                for (int componentIndex = 0;
082:                     componentIndex < Food.NUTRITIONAL_COMPONENTS.length;
083:                     componentIndex++)
084:                    dietTable[dayIndex][componentIndex]
085:                        += foodComponents[componentIndex];
086:            } // if
087:        } // while
088:    } // readDietDiary
```

The result table requires headings for the columns.

```
091:    // Print the dietTable as grams (so divide by 1000).
092:    private static void printDietTable()
093:    {
094:        // First print the column headings.
095:        for (String componentName : Food.NUTRITIONAL_COMPONENTS)
096:            System.out.print("\t" + componentName);
097:        System.out.println();
```

And then we use two nested loops, one for the rows and the inner one for the columns. This inner **for-each loop** reminds us that a **two-dimensional array** is just an array of arrays.

```
099:        // Now print the rows, one for each day of the week.
100:        for (int dayIndex = 0; dayIndex < DAY_NAMES.length; dayIndex++)
101:        {
102:            System.out.print(DAY_NAMES[dayIndex]);
103:            for (int amountOfComponentEaten : dietTable[dayIndex])
104:                System.out.print(
105:                    "\t" + Math.round(amountOfComponentEaten / 1000));
```

331

```
106:        System.out.println();
107:      } // for
108:    } // printDietTable
109:
110: } // class WeeklyDiet
```

Console Input / Output					
$ **java WeeklyDiet**					
	Protein	Carb	Fat	Fibre	Sodium
Mon	95	282	118	16	5
Tue	47	192	59	14	5
Wed	137	146	95	16	6
Thu	91	195	77	16	5
Fri	72	224	94	28	9
Sat	194	252	121	27	10
Sun	117	414	128	21	5
$ _					

14.7.2 Trying it

Let us try it with the **test data** we saw earlier.

Coffee time: [14.7.1]

What would happen if we declared DAY_NAMES as follows?

private static final String[] DAY_NAMES
= { "Sun", "Mon", "Tue", "Wed", "Thu", "Fri", "Sat" };

14.7.3 Coursework: Maze solver

The program you are going to write here will read in textual representations of mazes and solve them. Mazes consist of a matrix of cells, each of which can be an entrance, an exit, a hedge, or a space. Each maze must have at least one entry point, at least one exit point, and at least one path of space cells between some entrance and exit. Paths can only turn 90 degrees, that is, there is no use of diagonal movement. The job of the program is to print out each maze showing the *shortest* path from any entrance to its nearest exit.

Here is sample **data**, showing three very similar mazes, each stored in a **text file**. A hedge cell is represented by a #, an entrance by a ?, an exit by a ! and a space by a space.

Console Input / Output
$ **cat test-maze-1.txt test-maze-2.txt test-maze-3.txt**

```
(Output shown using multiple columns to save space.)

#?################    #?################    #?################
#                 #    #                 #    #                 #
# ############### #    # ############### #    # ############### #
# #           #  # #   # #           #  # #   # #           #  # #
# # #### #    #  ##    # # #### #    #  ##    # # #### #    #  ##
#   #     ####### ##   # # #     ####### ##   # # #     ####### ##
# # #     #      #    # # #     #      #    # # #     # ### #####
#   # ##          #    #   # ##          #    #   # ##          #
################!#    ################!#    ################!#
$ _
```

And here is the result of **run**ning the program on that data, where the shortest path is shown using dot (.) **character**s.

Console Input / Output
$ **java MazeSolver test-maze-1.txt test-maze-2.txt test-maze-3.txt**

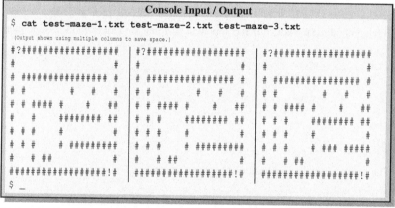

```
(Output shown using multiple columns to save space.)

#?################    #?################    #?################
#.                #    #.                #    #.................#
#.############### #    #.############### #    # ###############.#
#.#......  #    # #   #.#......  #    # #   # #           #  #..#
#.#.####.#    #  ##   #.#.####.#    #  ##   # # #### #    #  .##
#...#   .####### ##   #.#.#   .####### ##   # # #     #######.##
# # #   .#      #    #.#.#   .#      #    # # #     #    ....  #
# # #   .# #########   #.#.#   .# #########   # # #   # ###.#####
#   # ##...........#   #...# ##...........#   #   # ##      .....#
################!#    ################!#    ################!#
$ _
```

How will it work?

The solution is based on repeatedly making moves from entrances, fanning outwards in all possible directions, until we reach an exit. We start the search at every entrance simultaneously. In move one we fan out to every cell accessible from each entrance. In move two we further fan out to every (new) cell accessible from each cell we accessed in move one, and so on. In order to know which cells we have accessed in which move, we set up a **two-dimensional array** of numbers, the same dimensions as the maze, and store the move count at each cell as we reach it. So, the entrances have a move count of zero, those next to the entrances contain the number one, the neighbours of those contain a two, and so on.

The following diagram shows this process for the first example maze above.

And this one shows it for the third example maze.

Note that, depending on the maze, it might be that not every space cell gets visited before an exit is found.

Having reached an exit, we stop fanning out and instead work backwards along the shortest path to mark it.

Here is **pseudo code** for the **algorithm**.

```
move-count = 0
found-exit = false
while !found-exit
  consider every cell in turn
    if the cell value == move-count
      consider each of its four neighbours in turn or until found exit
        if the neighbour cell is an exit
          found-exit = true
```

```
           mark the path back to the start from this cell
         else if the neighbour cell is an unreached space
            neighbour cell value = move-count + 1
   move-count++
end-while
```

To mark the path back from the neighbour of the exit which has been reached, you do something like the following.

```
path position is given as row and column of the exit's neighbour
move-count = the value at this path position
while moveCount != 0
  mark this path position as part of the path
  move-count--
  find the neighbour which holds the value move-count
    path position = that neighbour's row and column
```

Implementation help

You will find the following code useful to help you **loop** through the four neighbours of each cell. (You may recall the **remainder operator**, %, from Section 9.2.4 on page 149.)

```
private int[] neighbourOffsets = {-1, 0, 1, 0};
...

for (int neighbour = 0; !foundAnExit && neighbour <= 3; neighbour++)
{
  int neighbourColumn = column + neighbourOffsets[neighbour];
  int neighbourRow = row + neighbourOffsets[(neighbour + 1) % 4];
  ...
} // for
```

Here is some of the solution to get you started.

```
001: import java.io.File;
002: import java.util.Scanner;
003:
004: /* Reads a maze representation from each file given as an argument
005:    and prints it out showing the shortest route from any entrance to an exit.
006: */
007: public class MazeSolver
008: {
009:   public static void main(String[] args) throws Exception
010:   {
011:     for (String filename : args)
012:       System.out.print(new MazeSolver(new Scanner(new File(filename))));
013:   } // main
014:
015:
016:   // The dimensions of the maze are fixed.
017:   private static final int HEIGHT = 10;
018:   private static final int WIDTH = 20;
019:
020:   // The values for cells in the maze model.
021:   // Start: this must be zero because you get there in zero steps.
022:   private static final int START = 0;
```

```
023:
024:    // Space, hedge, path and end: must all be negative
025:    // so they are not ambiguous with a move count.
026:    private static final int SPACE = -1;
027:    private static final int HEDGE = -2;
028:    private static final int PATH = -3;
029:    private static final int END = -4;
030:
031:    // The characters used in the file and output to represent the maze.
032:    private static final char SPACE_REP = ' ';
033:    private static final char HEDGE_REP = '#';
034:    private static final char START_REP = '?';
035:    private static final char END_REP = '!';
036:    private static final char PATH_REP = '.';
037:
038:    // The maze model. It is two bigger in each dimension so we can have an
039:    // extra hedge around the whole maze. This means every real cell has 4
040:    // neighbours, so we don't need to check edges of the array.
041:    private final int[][] maze = new int[HEIGHT + 2][WIDTH+ 2];
042:
043:
044:    // Construct a MazeSolver from the given scanner for a file
045:    // which must contain HEIGHT lines each of WIDTH characters.
046:    public MazeSolver(Scanner input)
047:    {
048:      // First we place a surround of HEDGE cells.
049:      for (int row = 0; row < HEIGHT + 2; row++)
050:        maze[row][0] = maze[row][WIDTH + 1] = HEDGE;
051:      for (int column = 0; column < WIDTH + 2; column++)
052:        maze[0][column] = maze[HEIGHT + 1][column] = HEDGE;
053:
054:      // Next we read the maze, assuming the file is valid.
055:      // This goes in to positions 1 to HEIGHT and 1 to WIDTH
056:      // leaving the surrounding hedge unchanged.
057:      for (int row = 1; row <= HEIGHT; row++)
058:      {
059:        String mazeLine = input.nextLine();
060:        for (int column = 1; column <= WIDTH; column++)
061:        {
062:          char inputChar = mazeLine.charAt(column - 1);
063:          switch (inputChar)
064:          {
065:            case SPACE_REP: maze[row][column] = SPACE; break;
066:            case HEDGE_REP: maze[row][column] = HEDGE; break;
067:            case START_REP: maze[row][column] = START; break;
068:            case END_REP:   maze[row][column] = END;   break;
069:          } // switch
070:        } // for
071:      } // for
072:
073:      // Then we solve it.
074:      solve();
075:    } // MazeSolver
```

335

```
076:
077:
078:    // Each cell has four neighbours: these offsets help us find them.
079:    private int[] neighbourOffsets = {-1, 0, 1, 0};
080:
081:
082:    // Find the shortest path from any START to any END.
083:    // There must exist such a path or else....
084:    private void solve()
085:    {
...
112:    } // solve
113:
114:
115:    // Mark the path backwards from row, column.
116:    private void markPathBackFrom(int row, int column)
117:    {
...
138:    } // markPathBackFrom
139:
140:
141:    // The correct line separator for this platform.
142:    private static final String NLS = System.getProperty("line.separator");
143:
144:
145:    // Return a text representation of the maze.
146:    public String toString()
147:    {
148:      String result = "";
149:      for (int row = 1; row <= HEIGHT; row++)
150:      {
151:        for (int column = 1; column <= WIDTH; column++)
152:          switch (maze[row][column])
153:          {
154:            case HEDGE: result += HEDGE_REP; break;
155:            case START: result += START_REP; break;
156:            case END:   result += END_REP;   break;
157:            case PATH:  result += PATH_REP;  break;
158:            // Anything else will be a space which is not part of the path.
159:            default:    result += SPACE_REP;
160:          } // switch
161:        result += NLS;
162:      } // for
163:      return result;
164:    } // toString
165:
166: } // class MazeSolver
```

Note: your solution will probably have a different line count.

Coffee time: What happens if the program is run on a maze that does not have a path from an entrance to an exit?

`14.7.2`

Optional extra: Improve your program so that it deals sensibly with bad mazes.

Optional extra: Perhaps using **int** values for the cells is not a good **object oriented design** approach. So, posh up your program by making it have a Cell **class**, which contains an **instance variable** for the cell type and a separate move count if it is a space cell. You could take this further, e.g. each cell could also contain its row and column **array index**, and an **array** of **references** to the four neighbouring cells to make looping through them even easier.

14.8 Concepts covered in this chapter

Here is a list of the concepts that were covered in this chapter, each with a self-test question. You can use this to check you remember them being introduced, and perhaps re-read some of them before going on to the next chapter.

Array	
Array (p.286)	Does an array object have a variable or fixed size?
– array creation (p.287)	Do we need to change the program source code in order to change the size of an array used by a program?

– array creation: initializer (p.320)	Which of the following variable declarations are legal?
	
	1. `int {} smallPrimes`
	   `= {2, 3, 5, 7, 11, 13, 17, 19};`
	2. `int[] smallPrimes`
	   `= [2, 3, 5, 7, 11, 13, 17, 19];`
	3. `int[] smallPrimes`
	   `= {2, 3, 5, 7, 11, 13, 17, 19};`
	4. `int {} smallPrimes`
	   `= [2, 3, 5, 7, 11, 13, 17, 19];`

– array of arrays (p.329)	How many `int` variables are created by the following code?
	`int[][] anArray = new int[4][];`
	`for (int index = 0;`
	`     index < anArray.length;`
	`     index++)`
	`  anArray[index] = new int[index];`

– array of arrays: two-dimensional arrays (p.330)	How many references are involved in the following? `int[][] my2DArray = new int[5][4];`
– element access (p.288)	What set of indices does an array of ten elements have?
– element access: in two-dimensional arrays (p.330)	Consider the following. `int[][] my2DArray = new int[5][4];` Which element is accessed by `my2DArray[4][1]`? 1. The first element in the last row. 2. The second element in the last row. 3. The first element in the penultimate row. 4. The fourth element in the first row. 5. The third element in the first row.
– length (p.292)	How do we find the length of an array?
– empty array (p.292)	What is the difference between an array variable containing **null**, and an one containing a reference to an empty array?
– of objects (p.301)	What does an 'array of objects' contain?
– partially filled array (p.310)	What other variable do we need to support a partially filled array?
– array extension (p.311)	What is the minimum size increase? What is a good size increase?
– shallow copy (p.314)	What is the difference between shallow and deep copies?
Design	
– Searching a list: linear search (p.323)	How does this approach work?
– Sorting a list (p.295)	Give three examples of a sort order on simple data, such as numbers or names.

Design	
– Sorting a list: bubble sort (p.296)	For an array of length *n*, how many pair comparisons are needed worst case? (I.e. how many passes, and how many pairs on each pass?)

Expression	
– arithmetic: `double` division: by zero (p.291)	What is the essential difference between double division by zero and that of integer division?
– boolean: logical operators: conditional (p.323)	Which of the following expressions could produce an exception, where `size` and `sum` are **int** variables? 1. `size == 0 || sum / size >= 10` 2. `sum / size < 10 && size != 0`

Method	
– accepting parameters: of an array type (p.297)	What is the most obvious example of this?
– returning a value: of an array type (p.312)	In what sense does a method never return an array?

Standard API	
– `Math: round()` (p.289)	What is the return type of this method?
– `Scanner`: for a file (p.306)	How do we use `Scanner` to read every line of a file?
– `String: format()` (p.301)	What is the difference between this and `System.out.printf()`?
– `String: split()` (p.313)	What does this do?
– `System: out.printf()`: string item (p.289)	What happens if the item matching `"%s"` is not a string?
– `System: out.printf()`: fixed text and many items (p.289)	What is output by the following? ```\nSystem.out.printf(\n "From %s to %s is %1.2f miles.%n",\n "here", "eternity", 1.0/0);\n```
– `System: out.printf()`: left justification (p.300)	What is the difference between right and left justification, and how do we obtain each one?

Statement	
– for-each loop: on arrays (p.293)	When should we use a for-each loop? In particular, what can it not do?

Type	
– enum type (p.309)	What are these used for?
– enum type: access from another class (p.312)	How do we use an enum type defined in another class?
– array type (p.287)	How do we write the type of an array which has a `String` base type?

Variable	
– final variables: class constant: a set of choices (p.308)	What benefits does this approach have, compared with using the integer values directly?
– final variables: class constant: a set of choices: dangerous (p.308)	What are the dangers of this approach?
– of an array type (p.287)	In what sense does an array type variable never contain an array?

Chapter 15

Exceptions

> Without exception, catching
> run time errors will keep your holiday so nice.
>
> Without exception catching,
> run time errors will keep your holidays on ice!

15.1 Chapter aims

So far in the development of most of our programs, we have made unreasonable assumptions about the reliability of the end user. As a result, the programs contain little or no code to guard against erroneous input. It is time to address this issue. We start by taking a closer look at **exception**s and how we might avoid them – but explain why we do not do so! Then we examine Java's **exception catching** mechanism with which we permit exceptions to happen, but recover from them. This leads us on to observing that there are many kinds of exception which we might want to treat differently. We also see how we can **throw** exceptions in our own code when abnormal situations arise.

The chapter contains the following sections.

Section	Aims	Associated Coursework
15.2 Age next year revisited (p.340)	To take a closer look at **run time error**s, or as Java calls them, **exception**s.	Take a program you have seen before and analyse where it can go wrong. (p.341)
15.3 Age next year with exception avoidance (p.342)	To show how we can avoid **exception**s using **conditional execution**. We also meet the `Character` **class**.	Take a program you have seen before and make it avoid **exception**s. (p.343)
15.4 Age next year with exception catching (p.344)	To introduce **exception catching** using the **try statement**. We also take a look at **standard error**.	Take a program you have seen before and make it **catch exception**s. (p.346)
15.5 Age next year with multiple exception catching (p.347)	To observe that there are many kinds of **exception** and introduce the idea of multiple **exception catching** by having a **try statement** with many **catch clause**s.	Take a program you have seen before and make it **catch** multiple **exception**s. (p.349)
15.6 Age next year throwing an exception (p.350)	To introduce the idea of creating an **exception** and **throw**ing an exception when we have detected a problem, using the **throw statement**.	Take a program you have seen before and make it **throw** its own **exception**s and **catch** them. (p.351)

Section	Aims	Associated Coursework
15.7 Single times table with exception catching (p.352)	To illustrate the use of **exception catching** in **graphical user interface** (**GUI**) programs.	Take a program with a **GUI**, that you have seen before, and make it **catch exceptions**. (p.353)
15.8 A reusable `Date` class with exceptions (p.354)	To introduce the **throws clause** together with its associated **doc comment tag**. We also look at supplying an **exception cause** when we create an **exception**, and discuss the use of `RuntimeExceptions`.	Modify a **class** so that it uses **nested try statements**. (p.366)
15.9 Date difference with command line arguments (p.366)	To further illustrate the use of **exceptions** and introduce the `getCause()` **instance method** in the `Exception` **class**.	(None.)
15.10 Date difference with standard input (p.368)	To introduce the idea of obtaining possibly erroneous information from the end user on **standard input**, detecting problems with it, and requesting it again until it is acceptable.	(None.)

15.2 Example: Age next year revisited

AIM:
To take a closer look at **run time errors**, or as Java calls them, **exceptions**.

In this section, we revisit one of the early programs, from Section 3.4 on page 41, in order to examine what happens when the user **run**s it without the right input.

```
001: // Gets current age from first argument, and reports age next year.
002: public class AgeNextYear
003: {
004:   public static void main(String[] args)
005:   {
006:     int ageNow = Integer.parseInt(args[0]);
007:     int ageNextYear = ageNow + 1;
008:
009:     System.out.println("Your age now is " + ageNow);
010:     System.out.println("Your age next year will be " + ageNextYear);
011:   } // main
012: } // class AgeNextYear
```

There are two ways that the user can make this program fail. First, they might run it without a **command line argument**, and so it will have a problem when trying to access `args[0]`. Second, they may supply an argument which is not the string representation of a whole number (or one outside the range of **int**), and so `Integer.parseInt()` will not be able to interpret the value as an **int**.

When an **exceptional** circumstance occurs, an **instance** of the **class** `Exception` is created.

Concept **Exception.** A **run time error** is called an **exception** in Java. There is a standard **class** called `java.lang.Exception` which is used to record and handle exceptions. When an exceptional situation happens, an **instance** of this class is created, containing information about the error, stored in its **instance variable**s. In particular, it includes a **stack trace** containing the source line number, **method** name and class name at which the error occurred. This stack also contains the same information for the method that called the one that failed, and so on, right back up to the main method (for an error occurring in the **main thread**).

Let us run the AgeNextYear program with erroneous input in order to analyse the exceptions produced.

15.2.1 Trying it

One possible **exception** we can get from the program occurs when the user supplies no **command line argument**s.

Console Input / Output
| ```
$ java AgeNextYear
Exception in thread "main" java.lang.ArrayIndexOutOfBoundsException: 0
        at AgeNextYear.main(AgeNextYear.java:6)
$ _
``` |

In this case, the kind of exception generated is an ArrayIndexOutOfBoundsException when args[0] fails. As the error is detected directly in the **main method**, the **stack trace** contains only one entry. Whenever an exception occurs in the **main thread**, the default action of the Java **virtual machine** is to print out the details of the associated Exception **object**, and then end the **thread**. This will cause the program to terminate, unless there is another thread still running (such as the **GUI event thread**).

The second possible exception for our program is caused by the user supplying a string which does not represent an **int** value.

Console Input / Output
| ```
$ java AgeNextYear ""
Exception in thread "main" java.lang.NumberFormatException: For input string: ""
        at java.lang.NumberFormatException.forInputString(NumberFormatException.
java:48)
        at java.lang.Integer.parseInt(Integer.java:470)
        at java.lang.Integer.parseInt(Integer.java:499)
        at AgeNextYear.main(AgeNextYear.java:6)
$ java AgeNextYear 25.25
Exception in thread "main" java.lang.NumberFormatException: For input string: "2
5.25"
        at java.lang.NumberFormatException.forInputString(NumberFormatException.
java:48)
        at java.lang.Integer.parseInt(Integer.java:458)
        at java.lang.Integer.parseInt(Integer.java:499)
        at AgeNextYear.main(AgeNextYear.java:6)
$ _
``` |

In these cases we get another kind of exception called NumberFormatException. The error is detected within Integer.parseInt(), which itself was called from our **main method**.

There are also two other possible conditions which are not appropriate, but which will not cause the program to produce an exception. One is that the user might supply the representation of a negative number.

Console Input / Output
| ```
$ java AgeNextYear -25
Your age now is -25
Your age next year will be -24
$ _
``` |

The other inappropriate situation that does not lead to an exception is when the user supplies more than one argument.

Console Input / Output
| ```
$ java AgeNextYear 55 25
Your age now is 55
Your age next year will be 56
$ _
``` |

Over the next few sections we shall evolve the AgeNextYear program until it is suitably robust against all these user errors.

15.2.2 Coursework: FishTankVolume robustness analysis

Take another look at the FishTankVolume program from Section 3.5 on page 42. Make a list of all the circumstances that can cause an **exception** and another list of circumstances which merely produce inappropriate results.

15.3 Example: Age next year with exception avoidance

AIM:
To show how we can avoid **exceptions** using **conditional execution**. We also meet the
`Character` **class**.

In order to avoid the two possible **exceptions** discussed in the previous section, we could add some code to the `AgeNextYear`
program which checks the validity of the user's input.

First, we add a **method** to check that a `String` contains only digits, and is not empty. This uses the `isDigit()` method
from the `Character` **class**.

Concept **Standard API: `Character`.** The standard **class** `java.lang.Character` contains many **class method**s to
help with manipulation of **characters**, including the following.

Method	Return	Arguments	Description
Public method interfaces for class `Character` (some of them).			
`isWhitespace`	`boolean`	`char`	Returns **true** if the given **char** is a **white space** character, (e.g. **space character**, **tab character**, **new line character**), or **false** otherwise.
`isDigit`	`boolean`	`char`	Returns **true** if the given **char** is a digit (e.g. `'0'`, `'8'`), or **false** otherwise.
`isLetter`	`boolean`	`char`	Returns **true** if the given **char** is a letter (e.g. `'A'`, `'a'`), or **false** otherwise.
`isLetterOrDigit`	`boolean`	`char`	Returns **true** if the given **char** is a letter or a digit, or **false** otherwise.
`isLowerCase`	`boolean`	`char`	Returns **true** if the given **char** is a lower case letter, or **false** otherwise.
`isUpperCase`	`boolean`	`char`	Returns **true** if the given **char** is an upper case letter, or **false** otherwise.
`toLowerCase`	`char`	`char`	Returns the lower case equivalent of the given **char** if it is an upper case letter, or the given **char** if it is not.[1]
`toUpperCase`	`char`	`char`	Returns the upper case equivalent of the given **char** if it is a lower case letter, or the given **char** if it is not.[1]

```
001: // Gets current age from first argument, and reports age next year.
002: // Gives an error message if age is not a valid number.
003: public class AgeNextYear
004: {
005:   // Returns true if and only if given string is all digits and not empty.
006:   private static boolean isNonEmptyDigits(String shouldBeDigits)
007:   {
008:     boolean okaySoFar = shouldBeDigits.length() != 0;
009:     int index = 0;
010:     while (okaySoFar && index < shouldBeDigits.length())
011:     {
012:       okaySoFar = Character.isDigit(shouldBeDigits.charAt(index));
013:       index++;
014:     } // while
015:     return okaySoFar;
016:   } // isNonEmptyDigits
```

[1]For maximum portability of code to different regions of the world, it is better to use the `String` versions of these methods.

We place an **if else statement** around the code we had in the previous version of the program, with a **condition** that checks the **command line argument**s: the first one must exist and be a non-empty string of digits.

```
019:   // Check argument and compute result or report error.
020:   public static void main(String[] args)
021:   {
022:     if (args.length > 0 && isNonEmptyDigits(args[0]))
023:     {
024:       int ageNow = Integer.parseInt(args[0]);
025:       int ageNextYear = ageNow + 1;
026:
027:       System.out.println("Your age now is " + ageNow);
028:       System.out.println("Your age next year will be " + ageNextYear);
029:     } // if
030:     else
031:       System.out.println("Please supply your age, as a whole number.");
032:   } // main
033:
034: } // class AgeNextYear
```

Coffee time: What would happen if we swapped the order of the **conjunct**s in the if else statement condition above?

15.3.1

15.3.1 Trying it

Let us try the program with no **command line arguments**.

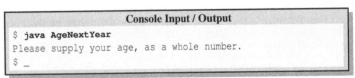

Console Input / Output
$ **java AgeNextYear**
Please supply your age, as a whole number.
$ _

And now an argument which is not a whole number.

Console Input / Output
$ **java AgeNextYear ""**
Please supply your age, as a whole number.
$ **java AgeNextYear 25.25**
Please supply your age, as a whole number.
$ _

Whilst it is true that we *think* we have made the program robust against **exception**s, we should not be satisfied with this approach. First, it was rather a lot of work – the program has doubled in size. Second, the checks that our new parts of the code make are also being made by the parts of the program that caused the exceptions in the first place. That is, when the **expression** args[0] is **evaluate**d, a check is made that the length of args is at least one, and an Exception is created if it is not. Also, the code inside Integer.parseInt() is surely checking that each **character** of the **method argument** is a digit.

Coffee time: Worse still, we haven't even avoided all possible exceptions – what command line argument could we present that passes our test and yet still causes Integer.parseInt() to **throw** a NumberFormatException?

15.3.2

15.3.2 Coursework: `FishTankVolume` exception avoidance

Despite what we have just said about not being satisfied with the approach, you are here going to try it. Write a version of the FishTankVolume program from Section 3.5 on page 42 which avoids **exception**s.

15.4 Example: Age next year with exception catching

AIM:
To introduce **exception catching** using the **try statement**. We also take a look at **standard error**.

In many cases, a better approach than writing code to avoid **exceptions** is to allow them to happen, but **catch** them afterwards. This can lead to simpler code with less duplication of checks on **data**. In this section we alter our `AgeNextYear` program so that it uses this better approach, and also we make it print some of its error messages to **standard error** instead of sending it all to **standard output**.

Concept **Operating environment: standard error.** When programs **execute**, in addition to **standard output** and **standard input**, they also have another facility called **standard error**. This is intended to be used for output about errors and exceptional circumstances, rather than program results. In some **operating environments** there might be no difference between **standard output** and **standard error** in practice, but their separation at the program level enables them to be handled differently where that is permitted. For example, on Unix systems, the end user can redirect the standard output into a **file**, whilst leaving the standard error to appear on the screen, or vice versa, etc. as desired. Nowadays, this is also true of Microsoft Windows.

Concept **Standard API: System: err.println().** Inside the `java.lang.System` **class**, in addition to **class variables** called `out` and `in` there is another called `err`. This contains a **reference** to an **object** which represents the **standard error** of the program. Via this object we have the **methods** `System.err.println()`, `System.err.print()` and `System.err.printf()`. These cause their given **method arguments** to be displayed on the standard error.

In this version of the program we shall use **exception catching** with the help of a **try statement**.

Concept **Statement: try statement.** The **try statement** is used to implement **exception catching** in Java. It uses the **reserved words** `try` and `catch`, as follows.

```
try
{
  ... Code here that might cause an exception to happen.
} // try
catch (Exception exception)
{
  ... Code here to deal with the exception.
} // catch
```

The **statement** consists of two parts, the **try block** and the **catch clause**. When the try statement is **executed**, the code inside the try block is obeyed as usual. However, if at some point during this execution an **exception** occurs, an **instance** of `java.lang.Exception` is created, and then control immediately transfers to the catch clause. The newly created `Exception` **object** is available to the code in the catch clause, as an **exception parameter**, which is a bit like a **method parameter**. For this reason, we must declare a name (and **type**) for the exception in the round brackets following the reserved word `catch`.

For example, the following **method** computes the mean average of an **array** of `int` values, dealing with the possibility of the **reference** being the **null reference** or the array being an **empty array**, by **catch**ing the exception and **return**ing zero instead.

```
private double average(int[] anArray)
{
  try
  {
    int total = anArray[0];
    for (int i = 1; i < anArray.length; i++)
      total += anArray[i];
    return total / (double) anArray.length;
  } // try
  catch (Exception exception)
  {
    // Report the exception and carry on.
    System.err.println(exception);
    return 0;
  } // catch
} // average
```

Note: unlike most Java **statement**s that may contain other statements, the two parts of the try statement must both be **compound statement**s, even if they only contain one statement!

Concept **Exception: getMessage().** When an **instance** of java.lang.Exception is created, it may be given a text message helping to describe the reason for the error. This may be retrieved from an Exception **object** via its getMessage() **instance method**.

Here is our new version of the AgeNextYear program. You will see that we have decided to report our own error message, together with the message from inside the exception, to standard output, whilst also reporting the (toString() of the) exception itself to standard error.

```
001: // Gets current age from first argument, and reports age next year.
002: // Gives an error message if age is not a valid number.
003: public class AgeNextYear
004: {
005:   public static void main(String[] args)
006:   {
007:     try
008:     {
009:       int ageNow = Integer.parseInt(args[0]);
010:       int ageNextYear = ageNow + 1;
011:
012:       System.out.println("Your age now is " + ageNow);
013:       System.out.println("Your age next year will be " + ageNextYear);
014:     } // try
015:     catch (Exception exception)
016:     {
017:       System.out.println("Please supply your age, as a whole number.");
018:       System.out.println("Exception message was: '"
019:                           + exception.getMessage() + "'");
020:       System.err.println(exception);
021:     } // catch
022:   } // main
023:
024: } // class AgeNextYear
```

15.4.1 Trying it

Let us try the program with the same erroneous **test data** as last time.

```
                   Console Input / Output
$ java AgeNextYear
Please supply your age, as a whole number.
Exception message was: '0'
java.lang.ArrayIndexOutOfBoundsException: 0
$ java AgeNextYear ""
Please supply your age, as a whole number.
Exception message was: 'For input string: ""'
java.lang.NumberFormatException: For input string: ""
$ java AgeNextYear 25.25
Please supply your age, as a whole number.
Exception message was: 'For input string: "25.25"'
java.lang.NumberFormatException: For input string: "25.25"
$ _
```

Now let us try those again, this time redirecting **standard output** to /dev/null – the Unix concept of nowhere. It is a **file** that is never full when you are writing to it, and always empty when you are reading from it! On Microsoft Windows, this same idea is just called nul.[2] On both systems, output redirection is specified using >.

```
                   Console Input / Output
$ java AgeNextYear > /dev/null
java.lang.ArrayIndexOutOfBoundsException: 0
$ java AgeNextYear "" > /dev/null
java.lang.NumberFormatException: For input string: ""
$ java AgeNextYear 25.25 > /dev/null
java.lang.NumberFormatException: For input string: "25.25"
$ _
```

And once more, this time redirecting **standard error** to /dev/null. The code 2> is used instead of just > to redirect standard error rather than standard output. This works on Microsoft Windows too (except use nul instead of /dev/null).

```
                   Console Input / Output
$ java AgeNextYear 2> /dev/null
Please supply your age, as a whole number.
Exception message was: '0'
$ java AgeNextYear "" 2> /dev/null
Please supply your age, as a whole number.
Exception message was: 'For input string: ""'
$ java AgeNextYear 25.25 2> /dev/null
Please supply your age, as a whole number.
Exception message was: 'For input string: "25.25"'
$ _
```

Whilst we did include our own message to the user, we have to admit that the overall error message the user is receiving on standard output is not really very good. Ideally, we would like to give our own different error messages for the different kinds of error.

15.4.2 Coursework: `FishTankVolume` exception catching

Write another version of the `FishTankVolume` program from Section 3.5 on page 42. This should not avoid **exceptions**, but instead **catch** them in a single **catch clause**. (In the next task you can improve it by having multiple catch clauses.)

---

[2]Curiously, this means you cannot have a normal file called nul.

15.5 Example: Age next year with multiple exception catching

AIM: To observe that there are many kinds of **exception** and introduce the idea of multiple **exception catching** by having a **try statement** with many **catch clause**s.

The `AgeNextYear` program we have developed so far can be improved further by giving the user different error messages for the two different causes of an **exception**. We start by formalizing an observation which we have already implicitly made, that Java has many kinds of exception.

Concept **Exception: there are many types of exception.** The **class** `java.lang.Exception` is a general model of **exception**s. Java also has many classes for modelling exceptions which are more specific to a particular kind of error. Here are a few of the ones from the `java.lang` **package**, each listed with an example error situation which causes an **instance** of the exception class to be created.

Exception class	Example use
ArrayIndexOutOfBoundsException	When some code tries to access an **array element** using an **array index** which is not in the range of the **array** being indexed.
IllegalArgumentException	When a **method** is passed a **method argument** which is inappropriate in some way.
NumberFormatException	In the `parseInt()` method of the `java.lang.Integer` class when it is asked to interpret an invalid `String` method argument as an **int**. (Actually, `NumberFormatException` is a particular kind of the more general `IllegalArgumentException`.)
ArithmeticException	When an **integer division** has a denominator which is zero.
NullPointerException	When we have code that tries to access the **object referenced** by a **variable**, but the variable actually contains the **null reference**.

In order to make our program behave differently for the different kinds of exception that can arise, we can use a **try statement** which has multiple **catch clause**s.

Concept **Statement: try statement: with multiple catch clauses.** The **try statement** may have more than one **catch clause**, each of which is designed to **catch** a different kind of **exception**. When an exception occurs in the **try block**, the execution control transfers to the first matching catch clause, if there is one, or continues to propagate out of the try statement if there is not.

For example, consider the following **method** which finds the largest of some numbers stored in an **array** of `String` **object**s.

```java
private int maximum(String[] anArray)
{
  try
  {
    int maximumSoFar = Integer.parseInt(anArray[0]);
    for (int i = 1; i < anArray.length; i++)
    {
      int thisNumber = Integer.parseInt(anArray[i]);
      if (thisNumber > maximumSoFar)
        maximumSoFar = thisNumber;
    } // for
    return maximumSoFar;
```

```
        } // try
      catch(NumberFormatException exception)
      {
        System.err.println("Cannot parse item as an int: "
                              + exception.getMessage());
        return 0;
      } // catch
      catch(ArrayIndexOutOfBoundsException exception)
      {
        System.err.println("There is no maximum, as there are no numbers!");
        return 0;
      } // catch
    } // maximum
```

If the array **referenced** by the **method parameter** is an **empty array**, that is, it has no elements, then an ArrayIndexOutOfBoundsException object will be created when the code tries to access the first **array element**. This will be caught by the second catch clause. If, on the other hand, one of the strings in the array does not represent an **int** then a NumberFormatException object will be created inside the parseInt() method, and this will be caught by the first catch clause.

However, if the given **method argument** was actually the **null reference**, that is, there is no array at all – not even an empty one, then a NullPointerException object is created when the code tries to follow the array reference to access element zero of it.

```
    int maximumSoFar = Integer.parseInt(anArray[0]);
```

The code anArray[0] means "follow the reference in the **variable** anArray to the array referenced by it, and then get the value stored at **array index** 0 in that array." In this example there is no catch clause matching a NullPointerException, so the execution control transfers out of the try statement altogether, and out of the method. If the **method call** was itself inside the following try statement, then the NullPointerException would get caught there.

```
    try
    {
      int max = maximum(null);
      ...
    } // try
    catch (NullPointerException exception)
    {
      System.err.println("Silly me!");
    } // catch
```

Our new version of the AgeNextYear program shall have a catch clause for each of the particular exceptions we expect to get, but also a general one to **catch** any other exceptions that might arise. This makes our program robust against us having overlooked any other possible source of errors.

```
001: // Gets current age from first argument, and reports age next year.
002: // Gives an error message if age is not a valid number.
003: public class AgeNextYear
004: {
005:   public static void main(String[] args)
006:   {
007:     try
008:     {
009:       int ageNow = Integer.parseInt(args[0]);
010:       int ageNextYear = ageNow + 1;
011:
```

```
012:       System.out.println("Your age now is " + ageNow);
013:       System.out.println("Your age next year will be " + ageNextYear);
014:     } // try
015:     catch (ArrayIndexOutOfBoundsException exception)
016:     {
017:       System.out.println("Please supply your age.");
018:       System.err.println(exception);
019:     } // catch
020:     catch (NumberFormatException exception)
021:     {
022:       System.out.println("Your age must be a whole number!");
023:       System.out.println("Exception message was: `"
024:                          + exception.getMessage() + "'");
025:       System.err.println(exception);
026:     } // catch
027:     // Other exceptions should not happen,
028:     // but we catch anything else, lest we have overlooked something.
029:     catch (Exception exception)
030:     {
031:       System.out.println("Something unforeseen has happened. :-(");
032:       System.out.println("Exception message was: `"
033:                          + exception.getMessage() + "'");
034:       System.err.println(exception);
035:     } // catch
036:   } // main
037:
038: } // class AgeNextYear
```

Coffee time: 15.5.1   How can we test the third catch clause in the code above? For example, could we create a `NullPointerException` somehow? Would that need us to alter the code of the program, just for that test, or is there a way we could test the code without altering it? (Hint: think how you could get the **main method** to be given the **null reference** as its **method argument**, using a different **class**.)

15.5.1   Trying it

Let us try the program with the same erroneous **test data** as last time.

```
Console Input / Output

$ java AgeNextYear
Please supply your age.
java.lang.ArrayIndexOutOfBoundsException: 0
$ java AgeNextYear ""
Your age must be a whole number!
Exception message was: `For input string: ""'
java.lang.NumberFormatException: For input string: ""
$ java AgeNextYear 25.25
Your age must be a whole number!
Exception message was: `For input string: "25.25"'
java.lang.NumberFormatException: For input string: "25.25"
$ _
```

15.5.2   Coursework: `FishTankVolume` multiple exception catching

Write yet another version of the `FishTankVolume` program from Section 3.5 on page 42. This time it should **catch exceptions** in appropriate multiple **catch clauses**.

15.6 Example: Age next year throwing an exception

AIM:
To introduce the idea of creating an **exception** and **throwing** an exception when we have detected a problem, using the **throw statement**.

The AgeNextYear program we have developed so far can be improved further by us writing some code to deal with the other erroneous conditions, namely the user entering a negative age or more than one **command line argument**. These situations lead to inappropriate behaviour of the program, rather than to **exceptions**. In order to deal with them in the same way as the others, we shall create **instances** of Exception for them.

Concept **Exception: creating exceptions.** The standard **class** java.lang.Exception has a number of **constructor methods** enabling us to create **instances** of it. One of these takes no **method arguments**, and creates an Exception that has no message associated with it. A second constructor method takes a String which is to be used as the message. The other kinds of **exception**, such as ArrayIndexOutOfBoundsException, IllegalArgumentException, NumberFormatException, ArithmeticException and NullPointerException also have these two constructor methods.

Having created an Exception, we then need to **throw** it so it can be caught in one of our **catch clauses** later in the code.

Concept **Statement: throw statement.** The **throw statement** is used when we wish our code to trigger the **exception** mechanism of Java. It consists of the **reserved word throw**, followed by a **reference** to an Exception **object**. When the **statement** is **executed**, the Java **virtual machine** finds the closest **try statement** that is currently being executed, which has a **catch clause** that matches the kind of exception being thrown, and transfers execution control to that catch clause. If there is no matching catch clause to be found, then the exception is reported and the **thread** is terminated.

For example, here we **throw** an **instance** of the general java.lang.Exception **class** without a specific message.

```
throw new Exception();
```

This next one has a message.

```
throw new Exception("This is the message associated with the exception");
```

And finally, this example is throwing an instance of java.lang.NumberFormatException with a message.

```
NumberFormatException exception
  = new NumberFormatException("Only digits please");
throw exception;
```

Our new version of AgeNextYear shall throw an ArrayIndexOutOfBoundsException if there are too many arguments, or a NumberFormatException if the age is negative. Each of these is caught by the corresponding **catch clause**.

```
001: // Gets current age from first argument, and reports age next year.
002: // Gives an error message if age is not a valid number.
003: public class AgeNextYear
004: {
005:   public static void main(String[] args)
006:   {
007:     try
008:     {
009:       int ageNow = Integer.parseInt(args[0]);
```

```
010:     if (args.length > 1)
011:       throw new ArrayIndexOutOfBoundsException
012:                  ("You have supplied " + args.length + " arguments!");
013:     if (ageNow < 0)
014:       throw new NumberFormatException
015:                  ("Your age of " + ageNow + " is negative!");
016:
017:     int ageNextYear = ageNow + 1;
018:     System.out.println("Your age now is " + ageNow);
019:     System.out.println("Your age next year will be " + ageNextYear);
020:   } // try
021:   catch (ArrayIndexOutOfBoundsException exception)
022:   {
023:     System.out.println("Please supply your age, and nothing else.");
024:     System.out.println("Exception message was: '"
025:                        + exception.getMessage() + "'");
026:     System.err.println(exception);
027:   } // catch
028:   catch (NumberFormatException exception)
029:   {
030:     System.out.println("Your age must be a non-negative whole number!");
031:     System.out.println("Exception message was: '"
032:                        + exception.getMessage() + "'");
033:     System.err.println(exception);
034:   } // catch
035:   // Other exceptions should not happen,
036:   // but we catch anything else, lest we have overlooked something.
037:   catch (Exception exception)
038:   {
039:     System.out.println("Something unforeseen has happened. :-(");
040:     System.out.println("Exception message was: '"
041:                        + exception.getMessage() + "'");
042:     System.err.println(exception);
043:   } // catch
044:   } // main
045:
046: } // class AgeNextYear
```

15.6.1   Trying it

Let us try the program with two **command line arguments**.

```
                        Console Input / Output
$ java AgeNextYear 55 25
Please supply your age, and nothing else.
Exception message was: 'You have supplied 2 arguments!'
java.lang.ArrayIndexOutOfBoundsException: You have supplied 2 arguments!
$ _
```

And now one which is negative.

```
                        Console Input / Output
$ java AgeNextYear -25
Your age must be a non-negative whole number!
Exception message was: 'Your age of -25 is negative!'
java.lang.NumberFormatException: Your age of -25 is negative!
$ _
```

15.6.2   Coursework: `FishTankVolume` throwing exceptions

Write one more version of the `FishTankVolume` program from Section 3.5 on page 42. This will **throw exceptions** for inappropriate inputs which would otherwise not cause an exception, and **catch** all the exceptions in appropriate multiple **catch clauses**.

15.7 Example: Single times table with exception catching

AIM:
To illustrate the use of **exception catching** in **graphical user interface (GUI)** programs.

In this section we revisit the `TimesTable` program with a **graphical user interface (GUI)**, from Section 13.10 on page 268, and make it robust against the user entering a multiplier that is not the representation of an **int**. If you did not study the GUI chapter then please feel free to skip to Section 15.8 on page 354.

The previous version of the program will **throw** an **exception** in the `parseInt()` **method** of the `Integer` **class**, during the execution of the `actionPerformed()` method. This will be caught by the **GUI event thread**, which will simply report it on the **standard error** of the program, and then go back to sleep to wait for more GUI **event**s.

It is much better for us to **catch** the exception within the `actionPerformed()` method and report an error message in the `JTextArea` which is normally used to display the resulting times table.

The first part of the program is the same as before.

```
001: import java.awt.BorderLayout;
002: import java.awt.Container;
003: import java.awt.event.ActionEvent;
004: import java.awt.event.ActionListener;
005: import javax.swing.JButton;
006: import javax.swing.JFrame;
007: import javax.swing.JTextArea;
008: import javax.swing.JTextField;
009:
010: // Program to show a times table for a multiplier chosen by the user.
011: public class TimesTable extends JFrame implements ActionListener
012: {
013:   // A text field for the user to enter the multiplier.
014:   private final JTextField multiplierJTextField = new JTextField(5);
015:
016:   // A text area for the resulting times table, 15 lines of 20 characters.
017:   private final JTextArea displayJTextArea = new JTextArea(15, 20);
018:
019:
020:   // Constructor.
021:   public TimesTable()
022:   {
023:     setTitle("Times Table");
024:
025:     Container contents = getContentPane();
026:     contents.setLayout(new BorderLayout());
027:
028:     contents.add(multiplierJTextField, BorderLayout.NORTH);
029:     contents.add(displayJTextArea, BorderLayout.CENTER);
030:
031:     JButton displayJButton = new JButton("Display");
032:     contents.add(displayJButton, BorderLayout.SOUTH);
033:     displayJButton.addActionListener(this);
034:
035:     setDefaultCloseOperation(EXIT_ON_CLOSE);
036:     pack();
037:   } // TimesTable
```

The change exists in the `actionPerformed()` method, where we now catch the exception.

```
040:   // Act upon the button being pressed.
041:   public void actionPerformed(ActionEvent event)
042:   {
043:     try
044:     {
045:       // Empty the text area to remove any previous result.
046:       displayJTextArea.setText("");
```

```
047:
048:        int multiplier = Integer.parseInt(multiplierJTextField.getText());
049:
050:        displayJTextArea.append("-------------------------------\n");
051:        displayJTextArea.append("| Times table for " + multiplier + "\n");
052:        displayJTextArea.append("-------------------------------\n");
053:        for (int thisNumber = 1; thisNumber <= 10; thisNumber++)
054:          displayJTextArea.append("| " + thisNumber + " x " + multiplier
055:                                  + " = " + thisNumber * multiplier + "\n");
056:        displayJTextArea.append("-------------------------------\n");
057:      } // try
058:      catch (NumberFormatException exception)
059:      {
060:        displayJTextArea.setText("Error parsing multiplier '"
061:                                  + multiplierJTextField.getText() + "'");
062:      } // catch
063:    } // actionPerformed
```

The **main method** is the same as in the previous version.

```
066:    // Create a TimesTable and make it appear on the screen.
067:    public static void main(String[] args)
068:    {
069:      TimesTable theTimesTable = new TimesTable();
070:      theTimesTable.setVisible(true);
071:    } // main
072:
073: } // class TimesTable
```

15.7.1 Trying it

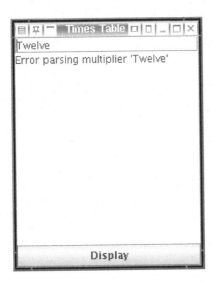

Coffee time:

15.7.1

What would we do if there was no handy place in our **GUI** to display our error message? How easy would it be for us to make a separate window appear in which we display the error?

15.7.2 Coursework: `TimesTable` with a `ScrollPane` catching exceptions

Write a version of the `TimesTable` with a `ScrollPane` program from Section 13.12 on page 274 that **catch**es the **exception** caused by the user entering **data** which is not a valid representation of an **int**.

15.8 Example: A reusable `Date` class with exceptions

AIM:
To introduce the **throws clause** together with its associated **doc comment tag**. We also look at supplying an **exception cause** when we create an **exception**, and discuss the use of `RuntimeExceptions`.

In the light of what we now know about **exception**s, we here improve the `Date` example from Section 12.2 on page 224. This is still not our final version: that is discussed in Section 17.3 on page 435 after we have gained even more wisdom.

The **class** starts off the same as it did before.

```
001: /**
002:  * This class represents calendar dates and provides certain
003:  * manipulations of them.
004:  *
005:  * @author John Latham
006:  */
007: public class Date
008: {
009:   // Class variable to hold the present date.
010:   private static Date presentDate = null;
```

The **class method** `setPresentDate()`, which is designed to be called only once, previously just ignored any subsequent calls. The one here will instead **throw** an exception if it is called more than once.

Concept **Method: that throws an exception.** A **method** has a body of code which is **execute**d when a **method call** invokes it. If it is possible for that code to cause an **exception** to be **thrown**, either directly or indirectly, which is not caught by it, then the method must have a **throws clause** stating this in its heading. We do this by writing the **reserved word `throws`** followed by the kind(s) of exception, after the **method parameter** list. For example, the `charAt()` **instance method** of the `java.lang.String` **class throws** an exception if the given **string index** is not in range.

```
public char charAt(int index) throws IndexOutOfBoundsException
{
  ...
} // charAt
```

As another example, suppose in some program we have a **class** which provides **mutable object**s representing customer details. An **instance** of the class is allowed to have the customer name changed, but the new name is not allowed to be empty.

```
public class Customer
{
  private String familyName, firstNames;
  ...
  public void setName(String requiredFamilyName, String requiredFirstNames)
            throws IllegalArgumentException
  {
    if (requiredFamilyName == null || requiredFirstNames == null
        || requiredFamilyName.equals("") || requiredFirstNames.equals(""))
      throw new IllegalArgumentException("Name cannot be null or empty");

    familyName = requiredFamilyName;
    firstNames = requiredFirstNames;
  } // setName
  ...
} // class Customer
```

When we write **doc comment**s for a **method** we include documentation for any exceptions it **throws**.

Concept **Java tools: javadoc: throws tag.** There is another **doc comment tag** which is used to describe the **exception**s that a **method throws**.

Tag	Meaning	Where used
@throws exception name and description	Describes the circumstances leading to an exception.	Before a method.

Here is our new version of the setPresentDate() class method.

```
013:   /**
014:    * Set the present date.
015:    * The date must not have already been set.
016:    *
017:    * @param requiredPresentDate The required date for the present day.
018:    *
019:    * @throws Exception if present date has already been set
020:    *                   or if given date is null.
021:    */
022:   public static void setPresentDate(Date requiredPresentDate) throws Exception
023:   {
024:     if (requiredPresentDate == null)
025:       throw new Exception("Present date cannot be set to null");
026:     if (presentDate != null)
027:       throw new Exception("Present date has already been set");
028:     presentDate = requiredPresentDate;
029:   } // setPresentDate
```

This is what the **application program interface (API)** documentation looks like.

Web Browser Window

setPresentDate

```
public static void setPresentDate(Date requiredPresentDate)
                        throws java.lang.Exception
```

Set the present date. The date must not have already been set.

Parameters:
    requiredPresentDate - The required date for the present day.

Throws:
    java.lang.Exception - if present date has already been set or if given date is null.

Similarly, getPresentDate() now throws an exception if the present date has *not* been set.

```
032:   /**
033:    * Get the present date.
034:    *
035:    * @return The present date.
036:    *
037:    * @throws Exception if present date has not been set.
038:    */
```

```
039:   public static Date getPresentDate() throws Exception
040:   {
041:     if (presentDate == null)
042:       throw new Exception("Present date has not been set");
043:     return presentDate;
044:   } // getPresentDate
```

The class has the same **instance variable**s as before.

```
047:   // Instance variables: the day, month and year of a date.
048:   private final int day, month, year;
```

In the previous version, if the **constructor method** was given three date components (day, month, and year) that did not make a legal date, then it 'corrected' the values. For example, if the day was zero or negative, it was set to one instead. Here we will instead throw an exception for such illegal dates.

In addition, the way we calculate whether a year is a leap year will only work properly for dates since the Gregorian Reformation[13]. Prior to this, people thought that *every* fourth year was a leap year leading to there being too many leap days. Pope Gregory arranged for a correction to be made – essentially changing the rules to what we have encoded in this class, but also eliminating in one go all the days that had been wrongly accumulated since 0AD. (Interestingly many uneducated people at the time believed their life had been shortened by those days being skipped!) By the end of 1752, many countries in the world had adopted the Gregorian Reformation. So, our improved implementation only permits dates from 1753 onwards.

```
051:   /**
052:    * Construct a date, given the three int components.
053:    *
054:    * @param requiredDay The required day.
055:    * @param requiredMonth The required month.
056:    * @param requiredYear The required year.
057:    *
058:    * @throws Exception if the date components do not form a legal date since
059:    *                   the start of 1753 (post Gregorian Reformation).
060:    */
061:   public Date(int requiredDay, int requiredMonth, int requiredYear)
062:         throws Exception
063:   {
064:     year = requiredYear;
065:     month = requiredMonth;
066:     day = requiredDay;
067:     // Now check these components are legal, throw exception if not.
068:     checkDateIsLegal();
069:   } // Date
```

The **private instance method** checkDateIsLegal() has the job of checking the legality of the date. It simply throws an Exception if the date is not legal, otherwise it does nothing. It uses the daysInMonth() instance method which is presented shortly.

```
072:   // Check legality of date components and throw exception if illegal.
073:   private void checkDateIsLegal() throws Exception
074:   {
075:     if (year < 1753)
076:       throw new Exception("Year " + year + " must be >= 1753");
077:
078:     if (month < 1 || month > 12)
079:       throw new Exception("Month " + month + " must be from 1 to 12");
080:
```

```
081:    if (day < 1 || day > daysInMonth())
082:      throw new Exception("Day " + day + " must be from 1 to " + daysInMonth()
083:                              + " for " + month + "/" + year);
084:  } // checkDateIsLegal
```

Notice that if an exception is thrown by `checkDateIsLegal()`, it will continue to be thrown by the constructor, because the latter does not **catch** it.

Our new version of `Date` also has a second constructor, one that takes a `String` representation of a date, such as `"30/03/2015"`. We will first split the string in to three **int** values, using the `split()` instance method from the `String` class, and then check the legality of the date.

However, this splitting up may fail, for example there may be **less than** three values, or one of them might not be the representation of an **int**. These would result in an `ArrayIndexOutOfBoundsException` or a `NumberFormatException` respectively. In such cases we wish to catch these 'low level' exceptions and throw a **new** Exception which is more meaningful, with a message about the date being in the wrong format. This new `Exception` is, in effect, caused by the one we caught. For situations like this, `Exception` **objects** have a facility to keep track of the one that caused them.

Concept **Exception: creating exceptions: with a cause.** The standard **class** `java.lang.Exception` also has two more **constructor methods** enabling us to create **instances** which know about another **exception** that caused this one to be created. One of these takes the message and the **exception cause**, the other just takes the cause (and hence has no message). Whenever we **throw** a **new** exception inside a **catch clause**, it is good practice to include the caught exception as the cause of the new one.

Many of the other kinds of exception also have these two constructor methods.

Here is the code for our extra `Date` constructor method.

```
087:  /**
088:   * Construct a date, given a String holding the
089:   * day/month/year representation of the date.
090:   *
091:   * @param dateString The required date as day/month/year.
092:   *
093:   * @throws Exception if dateString is not legal.
094:   */
095:  public Date(String dateString) throws Exception
096:  {
097:    try
098:    {
099:      String[] dateElements = dateString.split("/");
100:      if (dateElements.length > 3)
101:        throw new Exception("Too many date elements");
102:        // This exception will be caught below.
103:      day = Integer.parseInt(dateElements[0]);
104:      month = Integer.parseInt(dateElements[1]);
105:      year = Integer.parseInt(dateElements[2]);
106:    } // try
107:    catch (Exception exception)
108:      { throw new Exception("Date '" + dateString
109:                            + "' is not in day/month/year format",
110:                          exception); }
```

```
111:    // If we get to here, we just check the date components are legal.
112:    checkDateIsLegal();
113: } // Date
```

Coffee time: 15.8.1 What if the **method argument** passed to this new constructor method is the **null reference**? Have we overlooked that scenario?

The next part of the class is the same as before.

```
116: /**
117:  * Yields the day component of this date.
118:  *
119:  * @return The day of this date.
120:  */
121: public int getDay()
122: {
123:    return day;
124: } // getDay
125:
126:
127: /**
128:  * Yields the month component of this date.
129:  *
130:  * @return The month of this date.
131:  */
132: public int getMonth()
133: {
134:    return month;
135: } // getMonth
136:
137:
138: /**
139:  * Yields the year component of this date.
140:  *
141:  * @return The year of this date.
142:  */
143: public int getYear()
144: {
145:    return year;
146: } // getYear
147:
148:
149: /**
150:  * Provides the day/month/year representation of this date.
151:  *
152:  * @return A String day/month/year representation of this date.
153:  */
154: public String toString()
155: {
156:    return day + "/" + month + "/" + year;
157: } // toString
```

If the instance methods for comparing a date with another one are given a **method argument** which is the **null reference** instead of a **reference** to a Date, then when the code tries to access the instance variables of the other date a NullPointerException will be produced. NullPointerException is a particular kind of the more general RuntimeException which Java treats a little differently from how it treats other kinds of Exception.

Concept **Method: that throws an exception: RuntimeException.** Generally, every **exception** that *possibly* can be **thrown** by a **method**, either directly by a **throw statement** or indirectly via another method, etc., must either be caught by the method, or it must say in its **throws clause** that it **throws** the exception. However, Java relaxes this rule for certain kinds of exception known as RuntimeException. These represent common erroneous situations which are usually avoidable and for which we typically write code to ensure they do not happen.

The `java.lang.RuntimeException` **class** is a kind of `Exception`, and examples of more specific classes which are kinds of `RuntimeException` include `ArrayIndexOutOfBoundsException`, `IllegalArgumentException`, `NumberFormatException`, `ArithmeticException` and `NullPointerException` (all from the `java.lang` **package**).

It would be a major inconvenience to *have* to always declare that these common cases might happen, or to explicitly **catch** them, in situations where we know they will not be **thrown** due to the way we have written the code. So, for these kinds of exception, Java leaves it as an option for us to declare whether they might be thrown by a method. For example, in the following method there is an **array reference**, and also an (implicit) **array element** access. These could in principle result in a `NullPointerException` and an `ArrayIndexOutOfBoundsException` respectively. The Java **compiler** is not clever enough to be able to reason whether such an exception can actually occur, whereas we know they cannot because of the way our code works.

```java
public int sum(int[] array)
{
  if (array == null)
    return 0;

  int sum = 0;
  for (int element : array)
    sum += element;
  return sum;
} // sum
```

On the other hand, the following method *can* cause some kinds of `RuntimeException` – if given a **null reference** or an **empty array**. Java still cannot know this without us declaring it in the heading.

```java
public double mean(int[] array)
              throws NullPointerException, ArrayIndexOutOfBoundsException
{
  int sum = array[0];
  for (int index = 1; index < array.length; index++)
    sum += array[index];
  return (double)sum / array.length;
} // sum
```

For code which is intended for **software reuse**, it is a good idea for us to be disciplined about this relaxation of the normal rule. If we write a method that can throw some exception which is a `RuntimeException`, because we have not written the code in a way which always avoids the possibility, or indeed we explicitly throw such an exception, then we should still declare it in the method heading, even though we are not forced to.

Exceptions for which we must either have a **catch clause** or list in a **throws clause** are known as **checked exception**s, and those for which the rule is relaxed, that is `RuntimeException` and its specific kinds, are known as **unchecked exception**s.

Coffee time: **Why** have we been able to get so far through this book without needing to write the **reserved word** `throws` in our programs (except when using a `Scanner` on a **file**)? Now that you know about it, can you think of places where we might include it if we were writing all those programs again?

Even though Java does not force us to, we declare that each date comparison instance method might throw a `NullPointerException`, because we have not written code to ensure it does not.

```
160:    /**
161:     * Compare this date with a given other one.
162:     *
163:     * @param other The other date to compare with.
164:     *
165:     * @return The value 0 if the other date represents the same date
166:     * as this one; a value less than 0 if this date is less than the
167:     * other; and a value greater than 0 if this date is greater than
168:     * the other.
169:     *
170:     * @throws NullPointerException if other is null.
171:     */
172:    public int compareTo(Date other) throws NullPointerException
173:    {
174:      if (year != other.year)       return year - other.year;
175:      else if (month != other.month) return month - other.month;
176:      else                          return day - other.day;
177:    } // compareTo
```

Web Browser Window

....

compareTo

```
public int compareTo(Date other)
             throws java.lang.NullPointerException
```

Compare this date with a given other one.

Parameters:
    other - The other date to compare with.

Returns:
    The value 0 if the other date represents the same date as this one; a value less than 0 if this date is less than the other; and a value greater than 0 if this date is greater than the other.

Throws:
    java.lang.NullPointerException - if other is null.

....

```
180:    /**
181:     * Compare this date with a given other one, for equality.
182:     *
183:     * @param other The other date to compare with.
184:     *
185:     * @return true if and only if they represent the same date.
186:     *
187:     * @throws NullPointerException if other is null.
188:     */
189:    public boolean equals(Date other) throws NullPointerException
190:    {
191:      return compareTo(other) == 0;
192:    } // equals
193:
194:
```

```
195:   /**
196:    * Compare this date with a given other one, for less than.
197:    *
198:    * @param other The other date to compare with.
199:    *
200:    * @return true if and only if this date is less than the other.
201:    *
202:    * @throws NullPointerException if other is null.
203:    */
204:   public boolean lessThan(Date other) throws NullPointerException
205:   {
206:     return compareTo(other) < 0;
207:   } // lessThan
208:
209:
210:   /**
211:    * Compare this date with a given other one, for greater than.
212:    *
213:    * @param other The other date to compare with.
214:    *
215:    * @return true if and only if this date is greater than the other.
216:    *
217:    * @throws NullPointerException if other is null.
218:    */
219:   public boolean greaterThan(Date other) throws NullPointerException
220:   {
221:     return compareTo(other) > 0;
222:   } // greaterThan
```

The instance method addDay() involves an interesting twist, due to the addition of exceptions. The method creates a new Date, and the constructor for Date can throw an exception. This means the addDay() method *must* either catch this exception, or throw it. However, we know that the newly created Date cannot be erroneous due to the checks made in the code, and so the exception will not get thrown. Nevertheless, we still need to explicitly catch the exception in order to avoid being forced to state that the method might throw one.

```
225:   /**
226:    * Construct a new date which is one day later than this one.
227:    *
228:    * @return A new date which is one day later than this one.
229:    */
230:   public Date addDay()
231:   {
232:     int newDay = day + 1;
233:     int newMonth = month;
234:     int newYear = year;
235:     if (newDay > daysInMonth())
236:     {
237:       newDay = 1;
238:       newMonth++;
239:       if (newMonth > 12)
240:       {
241:         newMonth = 1;
242:         newYear++;
243:       } // if
244:     } // if
245:     // This cannot cause an exception, but Java does not know that.
246:     try { return new Date(newDay, newMonth, newYear); }
247:     catch (Exception exception) { return null; }
248:   } // addDay
```

Coffee time: 15.8.3   What if we had decided that the constructor should throw a RuntimeException rather than an Exception. Would that have made a difference to us here?

<table>
<tr><td>

Coffee
time:

`15.8.4`

</td><td>

As you might have guessed, we can, if we wish, nest a **try statement** inside the **try block** or **catch clause** of another. What do you think of the following alternative implementation of addDay()? Does it work? Is it a nice style? Is it more efficient – in most cases? In the worst case?

</td></tr>
</table>

```
public Date addDay()
{
   // First try the obvious.
   try { return new Date(day + 1, month, year); }
   catch (Exception exception1)
   {
      // Okay, so day must have been the last in the month.
      // Now try the first of the next month.
      try { return new Date(1, month + 1, year); }
      catch (Exception exception2)
      {
         // Okay, so month must have been 12.
         // Now try the first of the next year.
         // This cannot cause an exception.
         try { return new Date(1, 1, year + 1); }
         catch (Exception exception3) { return null; }
      } // catch
   } // catch
} // addDay
```

The previous version of the addMonth() method relied on the constructor to limit the day of the month to its maximum value for the new month. Here we have to do that work in addMonth() so that we avoid an exception from the constructor. It uses the daysInMonth() class method which is presented shortly.

```
251: /**
252:  * Construct a new date which is one month later than this one.
253:  * If the day is too large for that month, it is truncated to
254:  * the number of days in that month.
255:  *
256:  * @return A new date which is one month later than this one.
257:  */
258: public Date addMonth()
259: {
260:    int newDay = day;
261:    int newMonth = month + 1;
262:    int newYear = year;
263:    if (newMonth > 12)
264:    {
265:       newMonth = 1;
266:       newYear++;
267:    } // if
268:    if (newDay > daysInMonth(newMonth, newYear))
269:       newDay = daysInMonth(newMonth, newYear);
270:    // This cannot cause an exception, but Java does not know that.
271:    try { return new Date(newDay, newMonth, newYear); }
272:    catch (Exception exception) { return null; }
273: } // addMonth
```

At first glance, we might have expected that the implementation of addYear() is simply a case of making a new date with the same day and month, with a year increased by one. However, there is one day and month combination which would cause failure because it does not exist in the following year.

```
276: /**
277:  * Construct a new date which is one year later than this one.
278:  * If this date is a leap day, it returns 28th February of the next year.
279:  *
```

```
280:    * @return A new date which is one year later than this one.
281:    */
282:   public Date addYear()
283:   {
284:     // This cannot cause an exception, but Java does not know that.
285:     try
286:     {
287:       if (day == 29 && month == 2)
288:         return new Date(28, month, year + 1);
289:       else
290:         return new Date(day, month, year + 1);
291:     } // try
292:     catch (Exception exception) { return null; }
293:   } // addYear
```

The instance methods which subtract a day, or month, or year, can throw an exception, because the new Date could be **less than** the start of 1753.

As with addDay(), subtractDay() avoids inappropriate exceptions from the constructor by carefully choosing the new values. However, the **construct**ion of the resulting Date is not wrapped in a try statement, so that a pre-1753 exception can escape.

```
296:   /**
297:    * Construct a new date which is one day earlier than this one.
298:    * This can throw an exception
299:    * if the new date is earlier than the start of 1753.
300:    *
301:    * @return A new date which is one day earlier than this one.
302:    *
303:    * @throws Exception if the new date is earlier than the start of 1753.
304:    */
305:   public Date subtractDay() throws Exception
306:   {
307:     int newDay = day - 1;
308:     int newMonth = month;
309:     int newYear = year;
310:     if (newDay < 1)
311:     {
312:       newMonth--;
313:       if (newMonth < 1)
314:       {
315:         newMonth = 12;
316:         newYear--;
317:       } // if
318:       newDay = daysInMonth(newMonth, newYear);
319:     } // if
320:     return new Date(newDay, newMonth, newYear);
321:   } // subtractDay
```

The implementation of subtractMonth() is similarly different from that of addMonth().

```
324:   /**
325:    * Construct a new date which is one month earlier than this one.
326:    * This can throw an exception
327:    * if the new date is earlier than the start of 1753.
328:    * If the day is too large for that month, it is truncated to
329:    * the number of days in that month.
330:    *
331:    * @return A new date which is one month earlier than this one.
332:    *
333:    * @throws Exception if the new date is earlier than the start of 1753.
334:    */
```

```
335:   public Date subtractMonth() throws Exception
336:   {
337:     int newDay = day;
338:     int newMonth = month - 1;
339:     int newYear = year;
340:     if (newMonth < 1)
341:     {
342:       newMonth = 12;
343:       newYear--;
344:     } // if
345:     if (newDay > daysInMonth(newMonth, newYear))
346:       newDay = daysInMonth(newMonth, newYear);
347:     return new Date(newDay, newMonth, newYear);
348:   } // subtractMonth
```

And finally, subtractYear() is to be compared with addYear().

```
351:   /**
352:    * Construct a new date which is one year earlier than this one.
353:    * This can throw an exception
354:    * if the new date is earlier than the start of 1753.
355:    * If this date is a leap day, it returns 28th February of the previous year.
356:    *
357:    * @return A new date which is one year earlier than this one.
358:    *
359:    * @throws Exception if the new date is earlier than the start of 1753.
360:    */
361:   public Date subtractYear() throws Exception
362:   {
363:     if (day == 29 && month == 2)
364:       return new Date(28, month, year - 1);
365:     else
366:       return new Date(day, month, year - 1);
367:   } // subtractYear
```

The daysFrom() method is essentially the same as before, except that we need to catch the impossible exception from subtractDay().

```
370:   /**
371:    * Calculate how many days this date is from a given other.
372:    * If the other date is less than this one, then the distance
373:    * is negative. It is non-negative otherwise (including zero
374:    * if they represent the same date).
375:    *
376:    * @param other The other date.
377:    *
378:    * @return The distance in days.
379:    *
380:    * @throws NullPointerException if other is null.
381:    */
382:   public int daysFrom(Date other) throws NullPointerException
383:   {
384:     // The code here is a prototype
385:     // -- the result should be computed more efficiently than this!
386:     if (equals(other))
387:       return 0;
388:     else if (lessThan(other))
389:     {
390:       Date someDate = addDay();
391:       int noOfDaysDistance = 1;
392:       while (someDate.lessThan(other))
393:       {
394:         someDate = someDate.addDay();
```

```
395:        noOfDaysDistance++;
396:      } // while
397:      return noOfDaysDistance;
398:    } // else if
399:    else
400:      try // We should not get an exception from subtractDay,
401:          //  because target date is legal. But Java does not know this.
402:      {
403:        Date someDate = subtractDay();
404:        int noOfDaysDistance = -1;
405:        while (someDate.greaterThan(other))
406:        {
407:          someDate = someDate.subtractDay();
408:          noOfDaysDistance--;
409:        } // while
410:        return noOfDaysDistance;
411:      } // try
412:      // Java does not know we cannot get an exception.
413:      catch (Exception e){ return 0; }
414:  } // daysFrom
```

All that remains to implement from the previous version is the **private** instance method to find the number of days in the month, and its helper instance method to determine whether this is a leap year. Now that we sometimes check the validity of the day and month *before* we create a Date, as well as from within the constructor, we implement daysInMonth() as both an instance method and a class method, the former calling the latter, and the latter taking a month and year as **method parameters**.

```
417:  // Calculate the number of days in the month.
418:  private int daysInMonth()
419:  {
420:    return daysInMonth(month, year);
421:  } // daysInMonth
```

Partly for the sake of being different, we use **arrays** here to look up the number of days in a month, rather than have them coded into a **switch statement** as we did before. Notice how we choose to ignore the first element in the arrays, instead of having to subtract one from the month.

```
424:  // Number of days in each month for normal and leap years.
425:  // The first index (0) is not used.
426:  private static final int[]
427:    DAYS_PER_MONTH_NON_LEAP_YEAR
428:        //  Jan Feb Mar Apr May Jun Jul Aug Sep Oct Nov Dec
429:        = {0, 31, 28, 31, 30, 31, 30, 31, 31, 30, 31, 30, 31},
430:    DAYS_PER_MONTH_LEAP_YEAR
431:        = {0, 31, 29, 31, 30, 31, 30, 31, 31, 30, 31, 30, 31};
432:
433:
434:  // Calculate the number of days in a given month for a given year.
435:  // This will never be called with a month out of range 1 to 12.
436:  private static int daysInMonth(int month, int year)
437:  {
438:    if (isLeapYear(year)) return DAYS_PER_MONTH_LEAP_YEAR[month];
439:    else                  return DAYS_PER_MONTH_NON_LEAP_YEAR[month];
440:  } // daysInMonth
```

The helper method isLeapYear() is now a class method rather than an instance method – it has to be because it is called from a class method.

```
443:    // Return true if and only if year is a leap year.
444:    // (We can ignore pre Gregorian Reformation years.)
445:    // Year is a leap year if it is divisible by 4
446:    //                and is not divisible by 100
447:    //                or is divisible by 400.
448:    private static boolean isLeapYear(int year)
449:    {
450:      return year % 4 == 0
451:           && (year % 100 != 0 || year % 400 == 0);
452:    } // isLeapYear
453:
454: } // class Date
```

Coffee time: | 15.8.5 | In this exploration of the Date example, we added code to **throw** exceptions which are Exception objects. We might instead have chosen to use RuntimeException objects. What difference would that make? Which would really be the most appropriate?

15.8.1 Trying it

For brevity, we do not show tests for our new Date **class** here. However, we shall use it in the next two sections for a program that finds the difference between two given dates.

15.8.2 Coursework: Date class with nested try statements

Recall the *alternative* addDay() **instance method** from a coffee time on page 362. Modify the Date **class** from this section to make it use that alternative **nested try statement**s approach for *all* instance methods which create a **new** Date.

Write a program called TestRelativeDates to test your implementation. This should contain a **main method** with hard-coded **test data**. One simple approach would be to create a 'reference' date, and then have a **loop** which takes it forwards one day at a time, over a, say, two year period (including a leap year). Inside the loop you print out the reference date together with five dates **construct**ed relatively from it.

15.9 Example: Date difference with command line arguments

AIM: To further illustrate the use of **exceptions** and introduce the getCause() **instance method** in the Exception **class**.

In this section we show a simple program that uses our Date **class**. It is given two dates as **command line argument**s and outputs the number of days between them. In the next section we present a variation of the program which takes its **data** from the **standard input** using a Scanner. Of particular interest is how our approach to **exception** handling differs between the two programs.

We also include code to show the causes of **exceptions**.

Concept **Exception: getCause().** The **exception cause** stored inside an Exception may be retrieved via its getCause() **instance method**. This will **return** the **null reference** if no cause was given.

Here is the command line argument version of the program.

```
001: // Obtain two dates in day/month/year format from first and second arguments.
002: // Report how many days there are from first to second,
003: // which is negative if first date is the earliest one.
004: public class DateDifference
005: {
006:   public static void main(String[] args)
007:   {
008:     try
009:     {
010:       // The two dates come from args 0 and 1.
011:       Date date1 = new Date(args[0]);
012:       Date date2 = new Date(args[1]);
013:       if (args.length > 2)
014:         throw new ArrayIndexOutOfBoundsException(args.length + " is > 2");
015:       System.out.println("From " + date1 + " to " + date2 + " is "
016:                         + date1.daysFrom(date2) + " days");
017:     } // try
018:     catch (ArrayIndexOutOfBoundsException exception)
019:     {
020:       System.out.println("Please supply exactly two dates");
021:       System.err.println(exception);
022:       if (exception.getCause() != null)
023:         System.err.println("Caused by: " + exception.getCause());
024:     } // catch
025:     catch (Exception exception)
026:     {
027:       System.out.println(exception.getMessage());
028:       System.err.println(exception);
029:       if (exception.getCause() != null)
030:         System.err.println("Caused by: " + exception.getCause());
031:     } // catch
032:   } // main
033:
034: } // class DateDifference
```

15.9.1 Trying it

First we try the program with two legal dates.

```
                        Console Input / Output
$ java DateDifference 30/03/2014 30/03/2015
From 30/3/2014 to 30/3/2015 is 365 days
$ java DateDifference 30/03/2015 30/03/2014
From 30/3/2015 to 30/3/2014 is -365 days
$ _
```

Next we test the
ArrayIndexOutOfBoundsException
exceptions.

```
                        Console Input / Output
$ java DateDifference
Please supply exactly two dates
java.lang.ArrayIndexOutOfBoundsException: 0
$ java DateDifference 30/03/2014
Please supply exactly two dates
java.lang.ArrayIndexOutOfBoundsException: 1
$ java DateDifference 30/03/2014 30/03/2015 ExtraArgument
Please supply exactly two dates
java.lang.ArrayIndexOutOfBoundsException: 3 is > 2
$ _
```

Then we test the invalid date format exceptions.

```
                          Console Input / Output
$ java DateDifference 30/03/2015 "Hello mum"
Date 'Hello mum' is not in day/month/year format
java.lang.Exception: Date 'Hello mum' is not in day/month/year format
Caused by: java.lang.NumberFormatException: For input string: "Hello mum"
$ java DateDifference 30/03 "Hello mum"
Date '30/03' is not in day/month/year format
java.lang.Exception: Date '30/03' is not in day/month/year format
Caused by: java.lang.ArrayIndexOutOfBoundsException: 2
$ _
```

And finally we test illegal date exceptions.

```
                          Console Input / Output
$ java DateDifference 30/03/2015 03/30/2015
Month 30 must be from 1 to 12
java.lang.Exception: Month 30 must be from 1 to 12
$ java DateDifference 30/03/2015 2015/03/30
Year 30 must be >= 1753
java.lang.Exception: Year 30 must be >= 1753
$ java DateDifference 30/03/2015 30/2/2015
Day 30 must be from 1 to 28 for 2/2015
java.lang.Exception: Day 30 must be from 1 to 28 for 2/2015
$ _
```

15.10 Example: Date difference with standard input

AIM:
To introduce the idea of obtaining possibly erroneous information from the end user on **standard input**, detecting problems with it, and requesting it again until it is acceptable.

To finish this chapter, we present our second version of the DateDifference program, one that obtains its input from the user via the **standard input** using a Scanner.

```
001: import java.util.Scanner;
002:
003: // Obtain two dates in day/month/year format from the user.
004: // Report how many days there are from first to second,
005: // which is negative if first date is earliest one.
006: public class DateDifference
007: {
008:   public static void main(String[] args)
009:   {
010:     // A scanner for reading from standard input.
011:     Scanner input = new Scanner(System.in);
```

We shall have a separate **method** to obtain a single date from the user, and call it twice. This will be given the Scanner for the input, and a String indicating which date we are reading. The method will persist in getting the user to enter a legal date, which it will **return** as an **instance** of Date.

```
012:     // The two dates are obtained from the user.
013:     Date date1 = inputDate(input, "first");
014:     Date date2 = inputDate(input, "second");
015:
```

```
016:      System.out.println();
017:      System.out.println("From " + date1 + " to " + date2 + " is "
018:                          + date1.daysFrom(date2) + " days");
019:    } // main
```

Next we have our separate method to obtain a date from the user. The basic approach is to read a line of text, try to interpret it as a legal date, complain if that fails, and continually read another line of text until finally the user enters a date which is valid.

```
022:    // Obtain a date from the user via the given Scanner.
023:    // The second argument is part of the prompt.
024:    // Keep repeating until user has entered a valid date.
025:    private static Date inputDate(Scanner input, String whichDate)
026:    {
027:      // Result will eventually refer to a legal date.
028:      Date result = null;
029:      System.out.print("Please type the " + whichDate + " date: ");
030:      // Keep trying until we get a legal date.
031:      boolean inputValidYet = false;
032:      do
033:      {
034:        try
035:        {
036:          result = new Date(input.nextLine());
037:          // If we get here then date was valid.
038:          inputValidYet = true;
039:        } // try
040:        catch (Exception exception)
041:        {
042:          System.out.println(exception.getMessage());
043:          System.out.print("Please re-type the " + whichDate + " date: ");
044:        } // catch
045:      } while (!inputValidYet);
046:      // When we get here the result must be a valid date.
047:      return result;
048:    } // inputDate
049:
050: } // class DateDifference
```

15.10.1 Trying it

Let us start with an example of when the user gets it right first time.

```
┌─────────────────────────────────────────┐
│          Console Input / Output          │
├─────────────────────────────────────────┤
│ $ java DateDifference                    │
│ Please type the first date: 30/03/2015   │
│ Please type the second date: 30/03/2016  │
│                                          │
│ From 30/3/2015 to 30/3/2016 is 366 days  │
│ $ _                                      │
└─────────────────────────────────────────┘
```

Now let's see what happens with a truly dumb-user!

```
┌──────────────────────────────────────────────────────┐
│                Console Input / Output                 │
├──────────────────────────────────────────────────────┤
│ $ java DateDifference                                 │
│ Please type the first date: Umm, err...               │
│ Date 'Umm, err...' is not in day/month/year format    │
│ Please re-type the first date: Oh, a date!            │
│ Date 'Oh, a date!' is not in day/month/year format    │
│ Please re-type the first date: 30/03/2015             │
│ Please type the second date: Another one?             │
│ Date 'Another one?' is not in day/month/year format   │
│ Please re-type the second date: 30/03/2016            │
│                                                       │
│ From 30/3/2015 to 30/3/2016 is 366 days               │
│ $ _                                                   │
└──────────────────────────────────────────────────────┘
```

369

15.11   Concepts covered in this chapter

Here is a list of the concepts that were covered in this chapter, each with a self-test question. You can use this to check you remember them being introduced, and perhaps re-read some of them before going on to the next chapter.

Exception	
Exception (p.340)	What information is contained in an Exception object?
– creating exceptions (p.350)	What is the difference between the following? 1. `public Exception(){ ... }` 2. `public Exception(String m){ ... }`
– creating exceptions: with a cause (p.357)	When does an Exception have a cause?
– getMessage() (p.345)	What does this return?
– there are many types of exception (p.347)	Name five types of exception.
– getCause() (p.366)	What is the cause of an exception?

Java tools	
– javadoc: throws tag (p.355)	Where do we use this?

Method	
– that throws an exception (p.354)	How do we specify the kind of exceptions a method might throw?
– that throws an exception: RuntimeException (p.358)	What is different about this kind of exception, compared with other kinds?

Operating environment	
– standard error (p.344)	What is the difference between this and standard output?

Standard API	
– System: err.println() (p.344)	What kind of Java item is System.err? (E.g. is it an instance variable?)
– Character (p.342)	What class features does this class provide?

Statement	
– try statement (p.344)	What parts does a try statement have?
– try statement: with multiple catch clauses (p.347)	What happens if two catch clauses match an exception?
– throw statement (p.350)	Where does control transfer to when this statement is executed?

Chapter 16

Inheritance

The wisdom we fail to inherit
we are condemned to recreate.

16.1 Chapter aims

One of the core principles of **object oriented programming** is the idea that a **class** might **inherit** some of its properties from another. We have already met this implicitly in the context of **graphical user interfaces** (if you studied that chapter) – for example `HelloWorld` inherited properties from `JFrame`. This made `HelloWorld` a particular kind of `JFrame`. We also met the idea, even more implicitly, with **exception**s – when we talked about there being different kinds of, say, `RuntimeException`. The main aim of this chapter is to properly introduce **inheritance** and explore various aspects of it.

As usual, the new concepts are motivated by being used in program examples. However, unlike the previous chapters which each used several examples, we here have a single program which we develop throughout the chapter. The finished program is larger than previous ones, consisting of over 3000 lines of code, divided into nearly 40 **class**es. Thus, a secondary aim of the chapter is to illustrate how we can develop and test a larger program incrementally. The development is divided into phases, which are subdivided into sections, each being the implementation and testing of one or more classes. We do not cover the whole program, only the parts which act as a vehicle for discussing inheritance.

The chapter contains the following sections.

Section	Aims	Associated Coursework
16.2 The Notional Lottery game (p.372)	To introduce the example program used throughout this chapter.	(None.)
16.3 The `Person` class (p.373)	To introduce the ideas of **superclass, subclass, inheritance**, and **is a** relationships.	Write a **class** that can be used to keep track of stock items, and test it. (p.376)
16.4 The `AudienceMember` class (p.378)	To finish introducing **superclass, subclass** and **inheritance**, and briefly meet **UML**. Also, to introduce the principles of invoking the **constructor method** of the superclass, and having **instance method**s that **override** one from the superclass.	Write a **subclass** which **override**s some **instance method**s. (p.382)
16.5 The `Punter` class (p.382)	To reinforce the ideas of **superclass, subclass, inheritance**, invoking the superclass **constructor method**, and **instance method**s that **override** another.	Write another **subclass** which **override**s some **instance method**s. (p.384)

Section	Aims	Associated Coursework
16.6 The `Person` abstract class (p.384)	To introduce the concepts of **abstract class** and **abstract method**.	Make a **class** into an **abstract class**. (p.387)
16.7 The remaining simple subclasses of `Person` (p.388)	To reinforce the concepts covered in the chapter so far, and introduce the ideas of **polymorphism** and **dynamic method binding**. We also meet **final classes** and **final method**s.	Make some more **subclass**es and explore **polymorphism** and **dynamic method binding**. (p.392)
16.8 The `MoodyPerson` classes (p.392)	To introduce the ideas of adding more **object state** and **instance method**s in a subclass, testing for an **instance** of a particular **class**, and **cast**ing to a subclass. We also see how a **constructor method** can invoke another from the same class.	Have additional state in some **subclasses**. (p.399)
16.9 The `Ball` class (p.399)	This section is mainly for progressing the development of the program, however the `java.awt.Color` **class** is introduced.	(None.)
16.10 The `BallContainer` classes (p.401)	To show another example of **inheritance**. We also see how to delete an **array element** from a **partially filled array**.	(None.)
16.11 The `Game` class (p.406)	To illustrate the difference between **is a** and **has a** relationships.	Write a **class** each **instance** of which **has a** number of instances of another class stored in it. (p.408)
16.12 The `Worker` classes (p.410)	To show an example of a **superclass** which is (appropriately) not an **abstract class**. We also show how we can use an **instance method** defined in the superclass, from a **subclass** which **overrides** it.	To write a non-**abstract class** which has a **subclass**, and use an **instance method** defined in the **superclass** from a subclass which **overrides** it. (p.416)
16.13 The `CleverPunter` class (p.416)	To reinforce **inheritance** concepts, and complete the model **class**es of the Notional Lottery program.	Add more complexity to an **inheritance hierarchy** at appropriate places. (p.421)
16.14 The GUI classes (p.421)	To characterize the rest of the Notional Lottery program development.	(None.)
16.15 The `Object` class and constructor chaining (p.422)	To introduce the **class** `Object` and the fact that the **constructor method** of the **superclass** is invoked implicitly by default. We also take a more thorough look at **constructor chaining**.	Add tracing to existing **constructor method**s in order to explore **constructor chaining**. (p.426)
16.16 Overloaded methods versus override (p.426)	To take a closer look at **overloaded method**s and in particular how an intended **override** can accidentally become an overload. We revisit the overloaded methods `System.out.println()`, and look at `toString()` from the `Object` **class**.	Add to your **instance method**s that **override** another, an **annotation** which helps protect against errors. (p.430)

16.2 The Notional Lottery game

AIM:
To introduce the example program used throughout this chapter.

The example program developed during this chapter is a game for children, called the Notional Lottery. It is not intended to promote gambling, but rather, through play, to equip the young players with an intuitive understanding of realistic probabilities, and so counter the enchantment of institutionalized gambling advertisements. However, any specific similarity to any real life lottery is unintentional.

When embarking on the development of any program, we typically start by identifying its detailed requirements. But such doesn't make good reading, particularly as the program is quite complex. So, in order to keep the coverage interesting in this chapter, we here present just an overview of the requirements and only give more details on demand as we proceed through the development.

The game comprises models of people who are in some way connected with the lottery, and also models of lottery games. The latter consist of a machine containing balls and a landing rack into which some of the balls are ejected from the machine. The end user can choose which people he or she would like to have, and the sizes of the lottery games. Some of the chosen people play the lottery, and it is hoped that the child will quickly realize that these people very rarely win unless the lottery games are kept much smaller than real life ones.

The development of the program is divided into two phases. First we create the underlying model of the program, that is people and lottery games. Then we develop the **graphical user interface** to the program. This chapter covers the first phase only, and we say just a little about the second phase at the end.

16.3 The `Person` class

AIM: To introduce the ideas of **superclass**, **subclass**, **inheritance**, and **is a** relationships.

There are several kinds of person which the end user can choose to see in his or her **run** of the program. For example, there are audience members, TV hosts, psychics, etc.. The child can make the people speak, and they all say different things depending on what kind of person they are. For example, audience members always say "Oooooh!", TV hosts always say "Welcome suckers!" and psychics always say "I can see someone very happy!". Some kinds of people always smile, some always frown, and some can change their mood.

Each kind of person will be modelled by a separate **class**, from which the program can make **instance**s at **run time**. However, as well as these being kept separate, we wish to model the reality that they are all kinds of the same thing, with some properties in common. So, we will have a general class called `Person` from which the more specific kinds of person get some of their properties via **inheritance**.

Concept **Inheritance.** A **class** can be used to model a category of **object**s with certain characteristics that exist in some way in the requirements of the program. However, sometimes the requirements exhibit sub-categories of objects. For example, a program which is designed to simulate traffic movement to help with road planning would probably have a class called `Vehicle`, representing the category of all road vehicles. This would contain properties which are common to all vehicles, such as average speed, and the relationship between their position and traffic lights, etc.. Sub-categories of vehicle might be bicycle, private car, taxi, bus, lorry etc.. These all have different specific properties – for example bicycles can be secured to many suitable fixed objects, such as railings and of course bicycle stands, whereas cars need car parks and metered side streets, etc.. Lorries need specific access and unloading points at specific places, such as shops that require regular deliveries. The road simulation would probably want to model people wishing to move about on the roads, and in this respect, bicycles, private cars, taxis and buses have a current and maximum number of passengers. Lorries might instead have a current and maximum load capacity. The behaviour of taxis and buses respectively link to the properties of taxi ranks and bus stops. And so on.

We would want to model these sub-categories as separate classes, each with whatever properties they specifically need, and yet still model the idea that they are all vehicles with the general properties. In **object oriented programming** we signify this relationship by having **superclass**es and **subclass**es. A superclass is something which models the general category of certain objects, and a subclass models a sub-category of those objects. So, we might decide that `Vehicle` is the superclass of all road vehicles, and that the class `Bicycle` models the sub-category of bicycles, and have the classes `PrivateCar`, `Taxi`, `Bus`, `Lorry`, etc. for the other specific sub-categories.

By saying that a class is a subclass of another, its superclass, we are modelling the **is a** relationship. So, in the above example, a bicycle **is a** vehicle, that is, an **instance** of `Bicycle` is also an instance of `Vehicle`.

The relationship between superclasses and their subclasses is known as **inheritance** because the subclasses **inherit** the general properties from the superclass, as well as adding any specific properties of their own.

Back in our Notional Lottery program, the class `AudienceMember` will be a **subclass** of `Person`. This is modelling the idea that an audience member **is a** person. We shall have other subclasses for the other kinds of person.

In this section we develop the `Person` class, and in order to test it, we also develop a `TestPerson` program.

16.3.1 The `Person` class

A `Person` **object** has two **instance variables**, one to store the name of the person, and the other to store the phrase which the person has said most recently. The former is a **final variable** because the name cannot be changed once the person is **construct**ed.

```
001: // Representation of a person involved somehow in the lottery.
002: public class Person
003: {
004:   // The name of the person.
005:   private final String personName;
006:
007:   // The Person's latest saying.
008:   private String latestSaying;
```

The **constructor method** is given the name of the person, which it stores. It also sets the latest saying to be a phrase which is the person introducing him or herself.

```
011:   // Constructor is given the person's name.
012:   public Person(String requiredPersonName)
013:   {
014:     personName = requiredPersonName;
015:     latestSaying = "I am " + personName;
016:   } // Person
```

Next we have an **accessor method** for the person's name. This will be used mostly by the **GUI** part of the program, to display the name of the person along with a simple picture which represents them.

```
019:   // Returns the Person's name.
020:   public String getPersonName()
021:   {
022:     return personName;
023:   } // getPersonName
```

Similarly, we also have an accessor method for the person's latest saying. This text will be shown by the GUI inside a speech bubble coming out of the person's mouth.

```
026:   // Returns the Person's latest saying.
027:   public String getLatestSaying()
028:   {
029:     return latestSaying;
030:   } // getLatestSaying
```

The GUI will also want to show a textual description of the kind of the person next to its image, and it will obtain this via the `getPersonType()` **instance method**. Each of the subclasses will have a different description, for example, an `AudienceMember` object will return the `String` `"Audience Member"`. One way to achieve this is to define the instance method here in the **superclass**, and have each subclass redefine it to return the appropriate result for that kind of person.

```
033:    // Returns the name of the type of Person.
034:    public String getPersonType()
035:    {
036:      return "Person";
037:    } // getPersonType
```

A person can either be happy, or unhappy. The GUI will draw the person's face with a smile or a frown, depending on the result of the instance method `isHappy()`. In the Notional Lottery program, most kinds of person are always happy, and so the best definition to place here is one that **returns true**. The classes which represent those kinds of people that are unhappy will redefine this instance method.

```
040:    // Returns whether or not the Person is happy.
041:    public boolean isHappy()
042:    {
043:      return true;
044:    } // isHappy
```

The main feature that all the kinds of person have in common, is the ability to speak. When the `speak()` instance method is invoked by the end user, via the GUI, the person's latest saying is replaced by their current saying. (This will then appear in the speech bubble, via the GUI calling the `getLatestSaying()` instance method.) The current saying of a person depends on the kind of person. We can achieve this by having the instance method `getCurrentSaying()` defined here, but redefined in each of the subclasses. The instance method `speak()` simply copies this phrase into the `latestSaying`.

```
047:    // Returns the Person's current saying.
048:    public String getCurrentSaying()
049:    {
050:      return "I have nothing to say";
051:    } // getCurrentSaying
052:
053:
054:    // Causes the person to speak by updating their latest saying from
055:    // their current saying.
056:    public void speak()
057:    {
058:      latestSaying = getCurrentSaying();
059:    } // speak
```

Finally, we have a `toString()` instance method. This will be used to help with testing during development.

```
062:    // Mainly for testing.
063:    public String toString()
064:    {
065:      return getPersonType() + " " + getPersonName()
066:              + " " + isHappy() + " " + getLatestSaying();
067:    } // toString
068:
069: } // class Person
```

16.3.2 The `TestPerson` class

Rather than wait until the whole program is completed before trying any of it, we will test each section of the incremental development as we go along. To test the `Person` **class**, we simply create an **instance** of it, output the result of the `toString()` **method**, invoke the `speak()` and then output it again.

```
001: // Create a Person and make them speak.
002: public class TestPerson
003: {
004:   public static void main(String[] args)
005:   {
006:     Person person = new Person("Ivana Vinnit");
007:     System.out.println(person);
008:     person.speak();
009:     System.out.println(person);
010:   } // main
011:
012: } // class TestPerson
```

16.3.3 Trying it

Console Input / Output
`$ java TestPerson`
Person Ivana Vinnit true I am Ivana Vinnit
Person Ivana Vinnit true I have nothing to say
`$ _`

16.3.4 Coursework: Stock control system

Imagine you are setting up a computer parts shop, and will need **software** to keep track of stock and prices. You will have various kinds of stock item, but to start with you will implement a **class** called `StockItem` with the following properties. In later coursework tasks you will make various **subclass**es of this. An **instance** of `StockItem` represents a particular thing which the shop sells, with a fixed stock code, variable quantity in stock and variable price.

Public method interfaces for class `StockItem`.			
Method	**Return**	**Arguments**	**Description**
Constructor		`int, int`	Create a `StockItem` with the given **int** price (in whole pence) and **int** initial quantity in stock. The price is exclusive of VAT (sales tax). Each `StockItem` object is allocated a unique fixed **int** stock code.
`getStockCode`	`int`		Returns the stock code for this stock item.
`getStockType`	`String`		Returns the string `"Stock item type"`. This will be redefined in subclasses.
`getDescription`	`String`		Returns the string `"A description of the stock item"`. This will be redefined in subclasses.
`getQuantityInStock`	**int**		Returns the quantity in stock of this stock item.
`increaseStock`	**void**	`int`	Increases the stock level by the given amount. If it is **less than** one, an `IllegalArgumentException` is **thrown** with a suitable message.
Continued...	...	...	...

			...continued: **Public method interfaces for class StockItem.**
Method	**Return**	**Arguments**	**Description**
sellStock	**boolean**	**int**	Attempts to reduce the stock level by the given amount. If it is less than one, an IllegalArgumentException is thrown with a suitable message. If the amount is otherwise **less than or equal** to the stock level, then the reduction is successful and **true** is **return**ed. Else there is no effect, but **false** is returned.
setPriceExVat	**void**	**int**	Set the price of this item to the given **int**. This is the price before VAT.
getPriceExVat	**int**		Returns the price before VAT.
getVatRate	**double**		Returns the standard percentage VAT rate, which is currently 20.0. This may be redefined in some subclasses.
getPriceIncVat	**int**		Returns the price including VAT (as specified by getVatRate()) rounded to the nearest penny.
toString	String		Returns a string giving the stock code, the stock type, the description, the quantity in stock, the price excluding VAT and the price including VAT. It uses the appropriate **method**s above to obtain the stock type, description, quantity and prices.

To allocate a unique fixed stock code to each StockItem **object** you might have the following code.

```
...
007:    // The number of stock items created so far.
008:    private static int noOfStockItemsCreated = 0;
009:
010:    // The fixed stock code of this item.
011:    private final int stockCode;
...
021:    public StockItem(int initialPriceExVat, int initialQuantityInStock)
022:    {
023:       noOfStockItemsCreated++;
024:       stockCode = noOfStockItemsCreated;
...
027:    } // StockItem
...
```

You will test this with a program called TestStockItem. This will make some instances of StockItem, increase stock, sell some stock and change the price, whilst printing out the items in between.

An example **run** might be as follows.

```
                         Console Input / Output
$ java TestStockItem
Creating a keyboard stock item, 10 in stock @ 499.
SC1: Stock item type, A description of the stock item (10 @ 499p/599p)
Creating a monitor stock item, 20 in stock @ 9999.
SC2: Stock item type, A description of the stock item (20 @ 9999p/11999p)
Obtain 10 more keyboards.
SC1: Stock item type, A description of the stock item (20 @ 499p/599p)
Obtain 20 more monitors.
SC2: Stock item type, A description of the stock item (40 @ 9999p/11999p)
Sell 5 keyboards.
SC1: Stock item type, A description of the stock item (15 @ 499p/599p)
Sell 10 monitors.
SC2: Stock item type, A description of the stock item (30 @ 9999p/11999p)
Change keyboard price to 399.
SC1: Stock item type, A description of the stock item (15 @ 399p/479p)
Change monitor price to 7999.
SC2: Stock item type, A description of the stock item (30 @ 7999p/9599p)
$ _
```

16.4 The AudienceMember class

AIM:
To finish introducing **superclass**, **subclass** and **inheritance**, and briefly meet **UML**. Also, to introduce the principles of invoking the **constructor method** of the superclass, and having **instance methods** that **override** one from the superclass.

In this section we shall develop the model for one of the kinds of person, namely the AudienceMember **class**. We also write a TestAudienceMember program to test it.

16.4.1 The AudienceMember class

The AudienceMember class is a **subclass** of the Person class. We can state this by declaring that it **extends** Person.

Concept **Inheritance: a subclass extends its superclass.** A **subclass** is said to be an **extension** of its **superclass**, because, in addition to **inherit**ing the properties of the superclass, it may have more properties that the superclass does not have. We state the relationship by declaring in the heading for the subclass that it **extends** the superclass. For example, in a program to simulate traffic flow we might have the following.

```
public class Bicycle extends Vehicle
{
  ...
  public void chainToRailings(Railings railings)
  {
    ...
  } // chainToRailings
  ...
} // class Bicycle
```

So a Bicycle **object** has all the properties of a Vehicle, but also has the feature of being able to be chained to railings.

As well as being used to represent **is a** relationships between the model **class**es of our programs, subclasses are commonly used in the **graphical user interface** parts of our programs. For example, the following says that the HelloWorld class is a subclass of the javax.swing.JFrame class. This means HelloWorld is an extension of JFrame, that is, an **instance** of HelloWorld is a JFrame **object** too, but with extra properties that a plain JFrame object does not have.

```
import javax.swing.JFrame;
public class HelloWorld extends JFrame
{
  ... Code to add a JLabel with the text "Hello World!" in it.
} // class HelloWorld
```

In our Notional Lottery program, every **instance** of AudienceMember **is a** Person **object** too.

```
001: // Representation of an audience member watching the lottery.
002: public class AudienceMember extends Person
003: {
```

The **constructor method** is given the name of the person, which we pass on to the constructor method of the **superclass**, Person, using the **reserved word super**.

Concept **Inheritance: invoking the superclass constructor.** In the body of the **constructor method** of a **subclass** we typically start by invoking a constructor method of its **superclass**. This is done by writing the **reserved word super** followed by the appropriate **method argument**s in brackets. Such a **superclass constructor call** must be the first **statement** in the body of the constructor method, and furthermore, the superclass must have a constructor method which matches the supplied arguments.

For example, in a traffic flow simulation program, when a vehicle is added to the simulation it probably would always be given a position, direction and current speed.

```
public class Vehicle
{
  ...
  public Vehicle(Position requiredPosition,
                 Direction requiredDirection, Speed requiredSpeed)
  {
    ... Code that does something with requiredPosition,
    ... requiredDirection and requiredSpeed.
  } // Vehicle
  ...
} // class Vehicle
```

Instead of creating plain `Vehicle` **object**s we would make **instance**s of a subclass, such as `Bicycle`. We would still supply the position, direction and current speed information to the constructor method of `Bicycle`, and it would most likely simply pass it on to the constructor method of `Vehicle`.

```
public class Bicycle extends Vehicle
{
  ...
  public Bicycle(Position position, Direction direction, Speed speed)
  {
    super(position, direction, speed);
    ... Code specific to making a Bicycle, if any, goes here.
  } // Bicycle
  ...
} // class Bicycle
```

In our Notional Lottery program, the superclass of `AudienceMember` is `Person`. This means the reserved word **super** below refers to the constructor method of `Person`.

```
004:   // Constructor is given the person's name.
005:   public AudienceMember(String name)
006:   {
007:     super(name);
008:   } // AudienceMember
```

So, the name passed to the constructor method of `AudienceMember` is passed on to the constructor method of `Person`, which places it in the **instance variable** `personName`. That code also initializes the `latestSaying` instance variable. For an `AudienceMember`, that is all we wish the constructor method to do.

The `Person` class has lots of **instance method**s which the `AudienceMember` class **inherit**s, such as `getPersonName()`, `getLatestSaying()` and `getPersonType()`, etc.. For the latter, the definition which is inherited is not suitable in this subclass – it **return**s the `String` `"Person"` whereas for an `AudienceMember`, we require `getPersonType()` to return

"Audience Member". To change this behaviour we write a replacement definition for the instance method – we **override** the inherited definition.

Concept **Inheritance: overriding a method.** The **instance method**s of a **superclass** are **inherit**ed by its **subclass**es. Sometimes, the definition of an instance method needs to be changed in a subclass, in which case the subclass simply redefines it. The subclass version **override**s the inherited definition. To override an instance method, the redefinition must have the same name and **types** of **method parameter**s otherwise it is a definition of a different **method**! It must also still be an instance method, and have the same **return type**. (Actually, the return type of the new instance method can be a subclass of the return type of the one in the superclass.)

For example, in a traffic flow simulation program, most kinds of vehicle probably perform an emergency stop in much the same way. However, a bicycle probably does it differently to most.

```
public class Vehicle
{
  ...
  public void emergencyStop()
  {
    ... General code for most vehicles.
  } // emergencyStop
  ...
} // class Vehicle

public class Bicycle extends Vehicle
{
  ...
  public void emergencyStop()
  {
    ... Specific code for bicycles.
  } // emergencyStop
  ...
} // class Bicycle
```

Coffee time: `16.4.1` Why can we not override a **class method**? Hint: instance methods are accessed via (a **reference** to) an object. How are class methods accessed?

In our Notional Lottery program, `AudienceMember` has its own specific definition of the `getPersonType()` instance method.

```
011:  // Returns the name of the type of Person.
012:  public String getPersonType()
013:  {
014:    return "Audience Member";
015:  } // getPersonType
```

Coffee time: `16.4.2` What would happen if we accidentally mistyped the name of this instance method, as say, `getPersontype`? What would happen if instead we got the name right, but declared it here to be a **void method**?

Finally, we similarly override the `getCurrentSaying()` instance method from the superclass with one which returns the current saying of an audience member.

```
018:  // Returns the Person's current saying.
019:  public String getCurrentSaying()
020:  {
021:    return "Oooooh!";
022:  } // getCurrentSaying
023:
024: } // class AudienceMember
```

We can represent our **inheritance hierarchy** so far with the following **UML class diagram**.

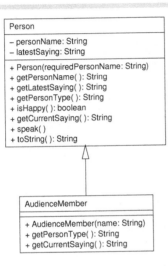

This diagram shows us that `Person` objects have seven instance methods, and so do `AudienceMember` objects. However, the latter have different definitions for two of them.

Coffee time: 16.4.3
How many **instance variable**s does an `AudienceMember` object have? Hint: an `AudienceMember` object is also a `Person` object.

16.4.2 The full `AudienceMember` code

```
001: // Representation of an audience member watching the lottery.
002: public class AudienceMember extends Person
003: {
004:    // Constructor is given the person's name.
005:    public AudienceMember(String name)
006:    {
007:      super(name);
008:    } // AudienceMember
009:
010:
011:    // Returns the name of the type of Person.
012:    public String getPersonType()
013:    {
014:      return "Audience Member";
015:    } // getPersonType
016:
017:
018:    // Returns the Person's current saying.
019:    public String getCurrentSaying()
020:    {
021:      return "Oooooh!";
022:    } // getCurrentSaying
023:
024: } // class AudienceMember
```

16.4.3 The `TestAudienceMember` class

We can test our `AudienceMember` **class** in the same way as we tested the `Person` class. The `toString()` **method**, which we implicitly use here, is **inherit**ed from `Person`. That method invokes four other methods, namely `getPersonType()`, `getPersonName()`, `isHappy()` and `getLatestSaying()`. The `AudienceMember` class **overrides** the first of these, whereas the other three have been inherited as is. We also use the `speak()` method, which is inherited as is from `Person`. However, that calls the method `getCurrentSaying()` which the `AudienceMember` class overrides.

```
001: // Create an AudienceMember and make them speak.
002: public class TestAudienceMember
003: {
004:   public static void main(String[] args)
005:   {
006:     AudienceMember audienceMember = new AudienceMember("Ivana Di Yowt");
007:     System.out.println(audienceMember);
008:     audienceMember.speak();
009:     System.out.println(audienceMember);
010:   } // main
011:
012: } // class TestAudienceMember
```

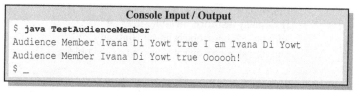 *Coffee time:* *16.4.4* Before looking at the test results in the next section, figure out what the output of the `TestAudienceMember` program should be.

16.4.4 Trying it

```
Console Input / Output
$ java TestAudienceMember
Audience Member Ivana Di Yowt true I am Ivana Di Yowt
Audience Member Ivana Di Yowt true Oooooh!
$ _
```

Notice that this shows the `speak()` **instance method** from `Person` has correctly used `getCurrentSaying()` from `AudienceMember` rather than the one defined in `Person`.

16.4.5 Coursework: Your first stock item!

Your new computer parts shop has obtained a load of very cheap mouse mats, which are going to be your first item on sale. Create a **class** `MouseMat` which is a **subclass** of `StockItem`. This will **override** the **instance methods** `getStockType()` and `getDescription()` with ones that **return** `"Mouse mat"` and `"Plain blue cloth, foam backed"` respectively.

Test this with a program called `TestMouseMat` which makes an **instance** of `MouseMat` (you would probably not want more than one instance), increasing and then selling some stock and changing the price, whilst printing out the item in between.

16.5 The `Punter` class

AIM:
To reinforce the ideas of **superclass**, **subclass**, **inheritance**, invoking the superclass **constructor method**, and **instance methods** that **override** another.

In this section we shall develop the model for another of the kinds of person, namely the `Punter` **class**. We also write a `TestPunter` program.

A punter **is a** person who dreams of winning the lottery, but is not clever enough to actually play it! As you might expect, this sort of person is never happy. (Later we shall meet clever punters, who are clever enough to play the lottery, but not clever enough to know better than to play it!)

16.5.1   The `Punter` class

The implementation of the `Punter` class is very similar to that of `AudienceMember`. The principle difference is that people who are punters are always unhappy instead of being always happy.

```
001: // Representation of a person playing the lottery.
002: public class Punter extends Person
003: {
004:    // Constructor is given the person's name.
005:    public Punter(String name)
006:    {
007:       super(name);
008:    } // Punter
009:
010:
011:    // Returns the name of the type of Person.
012:    public String getPersonType()
013:    {
014:       return "Punter";
015:    } // getPersonType
```

`Punter` additionally **overrides** the `isHappy()` **instance method**.

```
018:    // Returns whether or not the Person is happy.
019:    public boolean isHappy()
020:    {
021:       return false;
022:    } // isHappy
```

Like `AudienceMembers`, `Punters` have their own `getCurrentSaying()`.

```
025:    // Returns the Person's current saying.
026:    public String getCurrentSaying()
027:    {
028:       return "Make me happy: give me lots of money";
029:    } // getCurrentSaying
030:
031: } // class Punter
```

We can represent our **inheritance hierarchy** so far with the following **UML class diagram**.

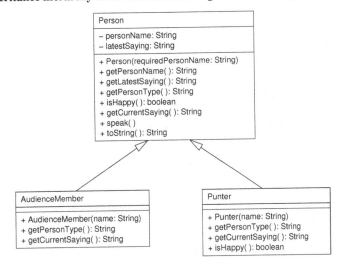

383

16.5.2 The `TestPunter` class

We can test our `Punter` **class** in the same way as we tested `AudienceMember`.

```
001: // Create a Punter and make them speak.
002: public class TestPunter
003: {
004:   public static void main(String[] args)
005:   {
006:     Punter punter = new Punter("Ian Arushfa Rishly Ving");
007:     System.out.println(punter);
008:     punter.speak();
009:     System.out.println(punter);
010:   } // main
011:
012: } // class TestPunter
```

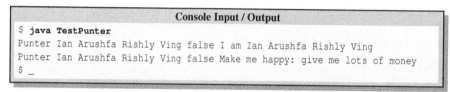

Coffee time: Before looking at the test results in the next section, figure out what the output of the `TestPunter` program should be.

16.5.1

16.5.3 Trying it

```
                          Console Input / Output
$ java TestPunter
Punter Ian Arushfa Rishly Ving false I am Ian Arushfa Rishly Ving
Punter Ian Arushfa Rishly Ving false Make me happy: give me lots of money
$ _
```

Notice that the results correctly show that the person is not happy.

16.5.4 Coursework: Your catalogue

Your mouse mats are selling like hot cakes and you dream of the days soon to come when you will sell other things too. In fact, you decide it is time to have a catalogue!

Create a **class** `Catalogue` which is a **subclass** of `StockItem`. This will **override** the **instance methods** `getStockType()` and `getDescription()` with ones that **return** `"Catalogue"` and `"List of all items and prices"` respectively.

Your new class will also override `getVatRate()` with one that **return**s zero, because books do not have VAT charged on them.

Test this with a program called `TestCatalogue` which makes an **instance** of `Catalogue` (you would probably not want more than one instance) increasing and then selling some stock and changing the price, whilst printing out the item in between.

16.6 The `Person` abstract class

AIM:
To introduce the concepts of **abstract class** and **abstract method**.

So far we have developed the `Person` **class** with two **subclass**es, `AudienceMember` and `Punter`. However, there are some things which are unsatisfactory about our implementation of `Person`. Firstly, we intend that the program should not make any **instance**s of `Person` directly, only subclasses of `Person`. We would like a way of having that enforced for us by Java, in case we or programmers modifying the program in the future, make a mistake. Relatedly, we have supplied an implementation for the **instance method**s `getPersonType()` and `getCurrentSaying()` despite the fact that *all* the subclasses of `Person` will **override** them both. We would like to be able to declare that a `Person` **object** has these instance methods, but without having to supply a **method implementation** which is never used.

In this section we present an improved version of Person which deals with these issues.

16.6.1 The `Person` class

We intend that no direct instances of the Person class shall be made, and so we declare it to be an **abstract class**.

Concept **Inheritance: abstract class.** If we wish that no **instances** of a particular **class** should be made, we can declare it as an **abstract class**. This is done by including the **reserved word abstract** before the word **class** in its heading. The **compiler** will produce an error if any code attempts to create a direct instance of an abstract class.

For example, in a program that simulates traffic flow, it is likely that we do not wish any direct instances of the class Vehicle to be made, only **subclass**es of it.

```
public abstract class Vehicle
{
  ...
} // class Vehicle

public class Bicycle extends Vehicle
{
  ...
} // class Bicycle
```

The following code would produce an error message from the compiler.

```
Vehicle v = new Vehicle(...);
```

Whereas this code would be allowed.

```
Bicycle b = new Bicycle(...);
```

Coffee time: What about the following?
```
Vehicle v = new Bicycle(...);
```
16.6.1

We insert the **reserved word abstract** into the Person class heading.

```
001: // Representation of a person involved somehow in the lottery.
002: public abstract class Person
003: {
```

The next part of the class remains unchanged from our first implementation of it.

```
004:   // The name of the person.
005:   private final String personName;
006:
007:   // The Person's latest saying.
008:   private String latestSaying;
009:
010:
011:   // Constructor is given the person's name.
012:   public Person(String requiredPersonName)
013:   {
014:     personName = requiredPersonName;
015:     latestSaying = "I am " + personName;
016:   } // Person
017:
018:
019:   // Returns the Person's name.
020:   public String getPersonName()
021:   {
022:     return personName;
023:   } // getPersonName
024:
```

```
025:
026:    // Returns the Person's latest saying.
027:    public String getLatestSaying()
028:    {
029:      return latestSaying;
030:    } // getLatestSaying
```

Previously, we supplied a full definition for the instance method `getPersonType()`, even though we intended that every subclass of `Person` would **override** it. The second, and perhaps most valuable, advantage of an **abstract class** is that it can contain **abstract method**s.

Concept **Inheritance: abstract method.** An **abstract class** is permitted to have **abstract methods** declared in it. These are **instance methods** which have **modifiers** (such as **public** – but not **static**), **return type**, name and **method parameters** as usual, but also include the **reserved word abstract** and instead of a body defined within braces, the heading is followed by a semi-colon (`;`). This declares only the **method interface**, i.e. the **method signature** and **return type**, and not the **method implementation**.

For example, in a traffic flow simulation program, the abstract class `Vehicle` might have an abstract method that decides whether the vehicle can pass down a particular route. It may well be that each kind of vehicle needs to implement this in a different way.

```
public abstract class Vehicle
{
  ...
  public abstract boolean canPassDown(Route r);
  ...
} // class Vehicle
```

All **subclass**es of the abstract class must either provide a method implementation of all the abstract methods, or themselves be abstract classes. When we write an abstract method, we are saying that all (non-abstract) subclasses of the abstract class contain an instance method with the given method interface (name, method parameters and return type), but the implementations of the instance method are provided by the subclasses, rather than one being defined here. This saves us having to provide an implementation that is never used, in cases where *every* subclass would **override** it with their own version.

```
public class Bicycle extends Vehicle
{
  ...
  public boolean canPassDown(Route r)
  {
    ... Code for deciding if this bicycle can pass down the route.
  } // canPassDown
  ...
} // class Bicycle
```

When a subclass defines a non-abstract instance method which is also defined in its **superclass**, we say that it **override**s the one from the superclass. When it defines an instance method which is declared as an abstract method in its superclass, we say it provides a **method implementation**. We can think of an override as *replacing* the method implementation from the superclass.

In our new version of the `Person` class, we declare `getPersonType()` to be an **abstract method**.

```
033:    // Returns the name of the type of Person.
034:    public abstract String getPersonType();
```

In contrast to the `getPersonType()` instance method, we do not make `isHappy()` abstract, because we know that most subclasses of `Person` are always happy. Thus we provide a **default implementation** in this **superclass** which can be **inherit**ed as is by those subclasses that are always happy, and the ones that require a different behaviour can override it.

```
037:    // Returns whether or not the Person is happy.
038:    public boolean isHappy()
039:    {
040:      return true;
041:    } // isHappy
```

The current saying of a person is *always* specific to the kind of person, so we declare `getCurrentSaying()` as an abstract method.

```
044:    // Returns the Person's current saying.
045:    public abstract String getCurrentSaying();
```

Finally, the rest of the class is the same as in the previous version.

```
048:    // Causes the person to speak by updating their latest saying from
049:    // their current saying.
050:    public void speak()
051:    {
052:      latestSaying = getCurrentSaying();
053:    } // speak
054:
055:
056:    // Mainly for testing.
057:    public String toString()
058:    {
059:      return getPersonType() + " " + getPersonName()
060:            + " " + isHappy() + " " + getLatestSaying();
061:    } // toString
062:
063: } // class Person
```

16.6.2   The `AudienceMember` and `Punter` classes

The changes we have made to the `Person` class require no changes to be made to the previously developed `AudienceMember` and `Punter` classes. The only comment worth making is that now, strictly speaking, `AudienceMember` and `Punter` do not **override** the instance methods `getPersonType()` and `getCurrentSaying()`, instead they just have **method implementations** of them. However, `Punter` still overrides `isHappy()`.

16.6.3   Trying it

To show that we cannot now make a direct **instance** of `Person`, we shall attempt to **recompile** the `TestPerson` **class**, listed in Section 16.3.2 on page 376.

```
                        Console Input / Output
$ javac TestPerson.java
TestPerson.java:6: Person is abstract; cannot be instantiated
    Person person = new Person("Ivana Vinnit");
                    ^
1 error
$ _
```

16.6.4   Coursework: An abstract stock item

Alter your **class** called `StockItem` so that it becomes an **abstract class**. There are two **instance methods** which you should change to become **abstract methods**.

Confirm that you cannot make **instances** of `StockItem` by attempting to **compile** `TestStockItem`. Check that your other test programs **run** the same as they did before.

16.7 The remaining simple subclasses of `Person`

AIM:
To reinforce the concepts covered in the chapter so far, and introduce the ideas of **polymorphism** and **dynamic method binding**. We also meet **final classes** and **final methods**.

In this section we develop the remaining 'simple' **subclass**es of Person required in the Notional Lottery program. These are the **class**es Director, Psychic and TVHost. We then go on to create the program TestPersonSubclasses which tests all the subclasses of Person developed so far.

16.7.1 The `Director` class

This class represents a person who is a director of the company that runs the lottery. It is similar to AudienceMember.

```
001: // Representation of a director of the lottery company.
002: public class Director extends Person
003: {
004:     // Constructor is given the person's name.
005:     public Director(String name)
006:     {
007:         super(name);
008:     } // Director
```

The class has **method implementation**s for the **abstract method**s getPersonType() and getCurrentSaying().

```
011:     // Returns the name of the type of Person.
012:     public String getPersonType()
013:     {
014:         return "Director";
015:     } // getPersonType
016:
017:
018:     // Returns the Person's current saying.
019:     public String getCurrentSaying()
020:     {
021:         return "This business is MY pleasure";
022:     } // getCurrentSaying
023:
024: } // class Director
```

Coffee time:
[16.7.1]
Are directors happy or unhappy? (Daft question?)

16.7.2 The `Psychic` class

The **class** Psychic is used to represent a person who is employed by the lottery company to make 'amusing' predictions about the jackpot winners. It is similar to Director.

```
001: // Representation of a psychic entertainer for the lottery.
002: public class Psychic extends Person
003: {
004:     // Constructor is given the person's name.
005:     public Psychic(String name)
006:     {
007:         super(name);
008:     } // Psychic
009:
```

```
010:
011:    // Returns the name of the type of Person.
012:    public String getPersonType()
013:    {
014:      return "Psychic";
015:    } // getPersonType
016:
017:
018:    // Returns the Person's current saying.
019:    public String getCurrentSaying()
020:    {
021:      return "I can see someone very happy!";
022:    } // getCurrentSaying
023:
024: } // class Psychic
```

16.7.3 The TVHost class

The **class** TVHost is used to represent a person who is employed by the lottery company to be cheerful and make lottery players feel special. It is similar to Psychic.

```
001: // Representation of a TV Host fronting the lottery TV programme.
002: public class TVHost extends Person
003: {
004:    // Constructor is given the person's name.
005:    public TVHost(String name)
006:    {
007:      super(name);
008:    } // TVHost
009:
010:
011:    // Returns the name of the type of Person.
012:    public String getPersonType()
013:    {
014:      return "TV Host";
015:    } // getPersonType
016:
017:
018:    // Returns the Person's current saying.
019:    public String getCurrentSaying()
020:    {
021:      return "Welcome, suckers!";
022:    } // getCurrentSaying
023:
024: } // class TVHost
```

We can represent our **inheritance hierarchy** so far with the following **UML class diagram**.

16.7.4 The `TestPersonSubclasses` class

The tests needed for each **subclass** of Person are essentially the same: create an **instance**, print it out, make it speak, and print it out again. Rather than have a separate program to test each subclass it is more convenient to have one program to test them all.

The approach we will take is this: define an **array** of Person, containing one instance of each subclass of Person. Then **loop** through this array testing each of them one at a time.

```
001: // Create one of each type of person, and make them speak.
002: public class TestPersonSubclasses
003: {
004:   public static void main(String[] args)
005:   {
006:     Person[] persons =
007:       {
008:         new AudienceMember("Ivana Di Yowt"),
009:         new Director("Sir Lance Earl Otto"),
010:         new Psychic("Miss T. Peg de Gowt"),
011:         new Punter("Ian Arushfa Rishly Ving"),
012:         new TVHost("Terry Bill Woah B'Gorne")
013:       };
```

The above code declares an array of **type** Person, containing one instance of each of the subclasses defined so far. This reminds us that an instance of a subclass is also an instance of its **superclass**. For example, the first **array element** is both an AudienceMember and a Person. This multiplicity of type is known as **polymorphism** – the **object**s are **polymorphic**.

> *Concept* **Inheritance: polymorphism.** An **instance** of a **subclass** is also an instance of its **superclass**. For example, in a traffic flow simulation program, if the **class** Bicycle is a subclass of Vehicle, then an instance of Bicycle **is a** Bicycle and also it **is a** Vehicle. It may be treated as a Bicycle, because that is its **type**. However, it also may be treated as a Vehicle because that is also its type. It has *both* these forms. We say that it is **polymorphic**, which means 'has many forms'. Java supports **polymorphism** via the use of **inheritance**.

Next, our code loops through the array, passing each element to the testPerson() **method**. Again, this is fine because each object **is an** instance of Person.

```
015:     for (Person person : persons)
016:       testPerson(person);
017:   } // main
018:
019:
020:   // Make the given person speak, reporting the before and after toString.
021:   private static void testPerson(Person person)
022:   {
023:     System.out.println("----------------------------------------------------");
024:     System.out.println(person);
025:     person.speak();
026:     System.out.println(person);
027:   } // testPerson
028:
029: } // class TestPersonSubclasses
```

In the `testPerson()` method, two of the **method parameter**'s **instance methods** are called, namely `toString()` and `speak()`. The first of these itself calls the methods `getPersonType()`, `getPersonName()`, `isHappy()` and `getLatestSaying()`. Some of those have been **inherit**ed by the subclass, some have **method implementation**s in the subclass, and one, `isHappy()`, has an **override** in `Punter`. Similarly, `speak()` calls `getCurrentSaying()`, which is implemented in the subclasses. As a result of this, the **compiler** when compiling the `Person` **class** cannot know which actual method will be used when the program is **run**ning. Indeed, we know that different versions of the methods will be used at different moments for the same **method calls**! It is only at **run time** that the **virtual machine** can decide which method to actually use for these method calls. This is known as **dynamic method binding**.

Concept **Inheritance: polymorphism: dynamic method binding.** In general, a **class** might have a **subclass**, which might **override** some of its **instance methods**. Also, **abstract methods** are designed to have different **method implementation**s in different subclasses. Thus, when the **compiler** produces the **byte code** for a **method call** on an instance method, it does not know which actual **method implementation** will get used – the same call could invoke different versions of the method at different moments, depending on the value of the **object reference** at **run time**.

For example, assume we have the class `Vehicle` with the instance method `emergencyStop()`, and subclass `PoshCar` that does not override it, and another subclass `Bicycle` that does. Which version of the method is called by the second line in the following code?

```
Vehicle funRide = Math.random() < 0.5 ? new PoshCar(...) : new Bicycle(...);
funRide.emergencyStop();
```

Only at run time can the answer be determined: the reference stored in `funRide` refers either to a `PoshCar` object, in which case the version from `Vehicle` is used, or a `Bicycle` object, in which case the version from `Bicycle` is used. The process of determining at run time which actual method to invoke is known as **dynamic method binding**.

As a programmer, we have to be aware of this principle, because it means that our code might not behave as we expected it to in some subclass where some of our instance methods have been replaced with ones that do something different to what we were expecting. Instance methods which are declared as **private** are safe – they cannot be overridden because they are not even visible in any subclass.

Concept **Inheritance: final methods and classes.** If we wish that no **subclass** may **override** a particular **public instance method**, we can declare it as a **final method** by including the **reserved word** `final` in its heading. This should be used with care – it may be that future requirements dictate that a subclass which has not yet been written needs its own version of the instance method, but it would not be able to have one without us removing the **final modifier** in the **superclass**.

Similarly, we can state that a **class** is a **final class** and cannot have any subclasses at all, by including `final` in the class heading.

Coffee time: Look at the instance methods of the `Person` class and decide which might appropriately be declared as **final methods**. For example, will any subclass need to have its own version of `toString()`?

16.7.2

16.7.5 Trying it

```
                        Console Input / Output
$ java TestPersonSubclasses
---------------------------------------------------
Audience Member Ivana Di Yowt true I am Ivana Di Yowt
Audience Member Ivana Di Yowt true Oooooh!
---------------------------------------------------
Director Sir Lance Earl Otto true I am Sir Lance Earl Otto
Director Sir Lance Earl Otto true This business is MY pleasure
---------------------------------------------------
Psychic Miss T. Peg de Gowt true I am Miss T. Peg de Gowt
Psychic Miss T. Peg de Gowt true I can see someone very happy!
---------------------------------------------------
Punter Ian Arushfa Rishly Ving false I am Ian Arushfa Rishly Ving
Punter Ian Arushfa Rishly Ving false Make me happy: give me lots of money
---------------------------------------------------
TV Host Terry Bill Woah B'Gorne true I am Terry Bill Woah B'Gorne
TV Host Terry Bill Woah B'Gorne true Welcome, suckers!
$ _
```

The results are as we expected – each person has a different person type and says a different phrase. All are happy except the punter.

16.7.6 Coursework: More stock items

You have obtained a big box of CPUs, a bin bag full of keyboards and a crate of hard discs.

Create the **classes** CPU, Keyboard and HardDisc, **return**ing the following values from getStockType() and getDescription().

Class	**Result from** getStockType()	**Result from** getDescription()
CPU	"CPU"	"Really fast"
Keyboard	"Keyboard"	"Cream, non-click"
HardDisc	"Hard disc"	"Lots of space"

Write a program called TestStockItemSubclasses which has a **class method** to test just one **instance** of a StockItem given to it as a **method parameter**. This will increase the stock, sell some stock and change the price, printing out the item in between.

The class will also have a **main method** which builds an **array** containing one instance of each **subclass** of StockItem you have written so far, and then, in a **loop**, calls the class method to test each one.

16.8 The MoodyPerson classes

AIM:
To introduce the ideas of adding more **object state** and **instance methods** in a **subclass**, testing for an **instance** of a particular **class**, and **cast**ing to a subclass. We also see how a **constructor method** can invoke another from the same class.

The remaining **subclass**es of Person are less simple than those we have seen so far. Coming up, we have the following.

Name	Brief description
Teenager	Just for fun – a person that can be made to be happy or unhappy at will.
CleverPunter	Someone who actually plays the lottery.
Worker	Someone who makes balls and fills up a lottery machine.
TraineeWorker	A worker who gets the ball numbers wrong sometimes.

All of these kinds of person have one thing in common – they are neither always happy, nor always unhappy; their mood can be changed. This suggests that we could benefit from another subclass of Person, called MoodyPerson, a kind of person whose happiness state can change. Then, the above listed kinds of person can be subclasses of MoodyPerson, so they all **inherit** the mood changing properties. This shows us that a subclass can itself have a subclass.

In this section, we develop the MoodyPerson and Teenager classes, leaving the other subclasses of MoodyPerson until after lottery games have been developed, because those sorts of people interact with that part of the program. We also add more code to the TestPersonSubclasses program in this section, to enable it to test **instance**s of MoodyPerson.

16.8.1   The **MoodyPerson** class

The MoodyPerson **class** will be defined as an **abstract class** because we do not want to have any direct instances of it.

```
001: // Representation of a person involved in the lottery
002: // who can change their happiness state.
003: public abstract class MoodyPerson extends Person
004: {
```

In order to record whether the moody person is currently happy or not, we shall need an extra **instance variable**. We are adding more **object state** in this subclass.

> *Concept* **Inheritance: adding more object state.**   A **subclass** is said to be an **extension** of its **superclass**, because in general it may add more properties that the superclass does not have. One way of **extend**ing is to add more **object state**, that is, additional **instance variables**.

```
005:   // The state of the Person's happiness.
006:   private boolean isHappyNow;
```

The **constructor method** of MoodyPerson takes *two* **method parameters**: one is the name of the person as before, and the second is an initial value for the new instance variable. It passes the name on to the constructor method of Person, and stores the initial happiness in isHappyNow. Recall that the **superclass constructor call** *must* be the first **statement** in the constructor method.

```
009:   // Constructor is given the person's name and initial happiness.
010:   public MoodyPerson(String name, boolean initialHappiness)
011:   {
012:     super(name);
013:     isHappyNow = initialHappiness;
014:   }  // MoodyPerson
```

> *Coffee time:* Why must the call to **super** be the first statement?
>
> *16.8.1*

For convenience in those subclasses of MoodyPerson which always start off being happy, we shall also supply a second constructor method which only takes the person's name. This will assume the person is initially happy.

> *Concept* **Method: constructor methods: more than one: using this.**   Typically, the **method parameters** to **constructor methods** are values for **instance variables**, and in **class**es where there are several instance variables it can be convenient to have multiple constructor methods, some of which assume sensible default values for some instance variables.
>
> For example, in a Point class, it might quite reasonably be decided that for convenience, we can easily obtain a representation of the origin by **constructing** a Point using no **method arguments**.

```
public class Point
{
  private final double x, y;

  public Point(double requiredX, double requiredY)
  {
    x = requiredX;
    y = requiredY;
  } // Point

  public Point()
  {
    x = 0;
    y = 0;
  } // Point


  ...
} // class Point
```

In effect, the second constructor method above is rather like a wrapper around the first one, and we can make this relationship explicit by actually calling the first constructor method from the second. We do this using the **reserved word this**, and passing the desired arguments in brackets. So, another way of writing the second constructor above is as follows.

```
public Point()
{
  this(0, 0);
} // Point
```

Such an **alternative constructor call** must be the first **statement** in the body of the constructor method, and, of course, the class must have another constructor method which matches the supplied arguments.

Our second constructor method in the MoodyPerson class takes only the name of the person. It passes this to the first constructor method along with an assumed initial happiness.

```
017:    // Alternative constructor is given the person's name
018:    // and initial happiness is assumed to be true.
019:    public MoodyPerson(String name)
020:    {
021:      this(name, true);
022:    }  // MoodyPerson
```

We **override** the isHappy() **instance method** of the Person class with one that **returns true** or **false** depending on the mood.

```
025:    // Returns whether or not the Person is happy.
026:    public boolean isHappy()
027:    {
028:      return isHappyNow;
029:    } // isHappy
```

Finally, we need a method to set the state of happiness. So, we also add another instance method in this subclass.

Concept **Inheritance: adding more instance methods.** Another way of **extend**ing the **superclass** in a **subclass** is to add more **instance methods**. This is especially likely to be desired if the subclass also has additional **instance variable**s.

```
032:   // Sets the happiness of the person to the given state.
033:   public void setHappy(boolean newHappiness)
034:   {
035:     isHappyNow = newHappiness;
036:   } // setHappy
037:
038: } // class MoodyPerson
```

16.8.2 The Teenager class

The Teenager **class** does not really have anything to do with the Notional Lottery game, it is there just for extra fun for the end users. They will be invited to create a teenager that models their big sister or brother, and set the mood through the **GUI**, to match that of their sibling.

The code is similar to that of TVHost, except it is a **subclass** of MoodyPerson rather than Person.

```
001: // Representation of a teenager.
002: public class Teenager extends MoodyPerson
003: {
```

Teenagers always start off being unhappy, so the **constructor method** just takes the name of the person. It passes this String along with the **method argument false** to the first constructor method of the MoodyPerson class. This in turn passes the name on to the constructor method of the Person class.

```
004:   // Constructor is given the person's name.
005:   public Teenager(String name)
006:   {
007:     super(name, false);
008:   } // Teenager
```

We provide **method implementation**s for the **abstract methods** getPersonType() and getCurrentSaying(). Note that the **method interface**s to these **methods** are **inherit**ed from MoodyPerson which inherited them from Person without implementing them.

```
011:   // Returns the name of the type of Person.
012:   public String getPersonType()
013:   {
014:     return "Teenager";
015:   } // getPersonType
```

The current saying of a teenager depends on whether he or she is happy.

```
018:   // Returns the Person's current saying.
019:   public String getCurrentSaying()
020:   {
021:     if (isHappy())
022:       return "Isn't life wonderful?";
023:     else
024:       return "It's not fair!";
025:   } // getCurrentSaying
026:
027: } // class Teenager
```

We can represent our **inheritance hierarchy** so far with the following **UML class diagram**.

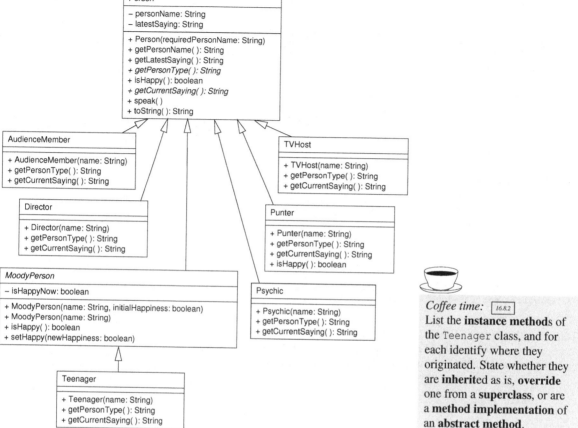

Coffee time: 16.8.2
List the **instance methods** of
the Teenager class, and for
each identify where they
originated. State whether they
are **inherit**ed as is, **override**
one from a **superclass**, or are
a **method implementation** of
an **abstract method**.

16.8.3 The `TestPersonSubclasses` class

We modify our TestPersonSubclasses program so that if the Person in the **array is a** MoodyPerson we do an extra set
of tests. We make the moody person change his or her happiness, speak, then print out the person, and then repeat these
three steps.

Our **array** has a Teenager added to it.

```
001: // Create one of each type of person, and make them speak.
002: public class TestPersonSubclasses
003: {
004:   public static void main(String[] args)
005:   {
006:     Person[] persons =
007:       {
008:         new AudienceMember("Ivana Di Yowt"),
009:         new Director("Sir Lance Earl Otto"),
010:         new Psychic("Miss T. Peg de Gowt"),
011:         new Punter("Ian Arushfa Rishly Ving"),
012:         new Teenager("Homer Nalzone"),
013:         new TVHost("Terry Bill Woah B'Gorne")
014:       };
```

```
015:
016:    for (Person person : persons)
017:      testPerson(person);
018:  } // main
```

We alter the `testPerson()` **method** so that if the `Person` **method parameter** is also a `MoodyPerson`, then it calls the new method `testMoodyPerson()`, which performs the new tests. We use the **`instanceof` operator** to determine whether the `Person` **object** is also an **instance** of `MoodyPerson`.

Concept **Inheritance: testing for an instance of a class.** The **reserved word `instanceof`** is a **binary infix operator** which takes an **object reference** as its left **operand**, and a **class** name as its right operand. It yields **`true`** if the reference refers to an object which **is an instance** of the named class (including being an instance of a **subclass** of the named class), **`false`** otherwise.

For example, in a traffic flow simulation program, if the class `Tandem` is a subclass of `Bicycle` which is a subclass of `Vehicle`, then the following code might be found.

```
Vehicle vehicle = new Tandem(...);
... Code that might change what vehicle refers to.
if (vehicle instanceof Bicycle)
   ... Code that is only run if vehicle is still referring to a Bicycle,
   ... perhaps still the original Tandem.
```

The `testMoodyPerson()` method takes a `MoodyPerson` as a parameter, rather than any other kind of `Person`. This means we need to **cast** the `Person` object to a `MoodyPerson`.

Concept **Inheritance: casting to a subclass.** An **instance** of a **subclass is an** instance of its **superclass** too. This means something which is of the subclass **type** can always be used wherever the superclass type is required. For example, in a traffic flow simulation program, if `Bicycle` is a subclass of `Vehicle`, then the following would be permitted.

```
Vehicle vehicle1 = new Bicycle(...);
```

However, obviously not every instance of a superclass is also an instance of a particular one of its subclasses, and so something of the superclass type cannot automatically be used where something of a subclass type is required.

For example, the following is not permitted.

```
Vehicle vehicle1 = new Bicycle(...);
...
Bicycle bicycle1 = vehicle1;
```

The problem is in the last line – `vehicle1` is definitely of type `Vehicle`, but as far as Java is concerned, its value might not be of type `Bicycle`, and so a **compile time error** will result.

If we are convinced that it is safe to treat something of the superclass type as though it is of a particular subclass type, then we can **cast** the value to that subclass, by preceding the value with the name of the subclass in brackets. For example, the following is appropriate if we are sure that after the code represented as ... has been **execute**d, the value of the **variable** `vehicle1` is still a **reference** to a `Bicycle` **object**.

```
Vehicle vehicle1 = new Bicycle(...);
...
Bicycle bicycle1 = (Bicycle)vehicle1;
```

The **compiler** will accept this on face value, but the type cast is checked at **run time**. If it turns out that the value being cast to a subtype is not a reference to an object of that type, then a `ClassCastException` object is **thrown**.

A common misunderstanding is that a **class** cast somehow changes the object that is being cast. Rather, it merely *checks* that the object is already of the stated type. This is in contrast to a **primitive type** cast, such as converting a **double** into an **int**, which really does create a new value from the old one.

Here is the modified `testPerson()` method and the `testMoodyPerson()` method.

```
021:    // Make the given person speak, reporting the before and after toString.
022:    private static void testPerson(Person person)
023:    {
024:      System.out.println("-------------------------------------------------");
025:      System.out.println(person);
026:      person.speak();
027:      System.out.println(person);
028:      if (person instanceof MoodyPerson)
029:        testMoodyPerson((MoodyPerson)person);
030:    } // testPerson
031:
032:
033:    // Make the given moody person change happiness then speak,
034:    // reporting the after toString; all twice.
035:    private static void testMoodyPerson(MoodyPerson moodyPerson)
036:    {
037:      for (int count = 1; count <= 2; count++)
038:      {
039:        moodyPerson.setHappy(! moodyPerson.isHappy());
040:        moodyPerson.speak();
041:        System.out.println(moodyPerson);
042:      } // for
043:    } // testMoodyPerson
044:
045:  } // class TestPersonSubclasses
```

Coffee time: 16.8.3 In the code above, what would happen if we did not cast `person` to `MoodyPerson` when passing its value to `testMoodyPerson()`? What if that method parameter was declared to be of **type** `Person`?

16.8.4 Trying it

We **run** the `TestPersonSubclasses` program again, and note that the `Teenager` correctly gets treated as a `MoodyPerson`, and has the extra tests done on it.

```
Console Input / Output
$ java TestPersonSubclasses
-------------------------------------------------
Audience Member Ivana Di Yowt true I am Ivana Di Yowt
Audience Member Ivana Di Yowt true Oooooh!
-------------------------------------------------
Director Sir Lance Earl Otto true I am Sir Lance Earl Otto
Director Sir Lance Earl Otto true This business is MY pleasure
-------------------------------------------------
Psychic Miss T. Peg de Gowt true I am Miss T. Peg de Gowt
Psychic Miss T. Peg de Gowt true I can see someone very happy!
-------------------------------------------------
Punter Ian Arushfa Rishly Ving false I am Ian Arushfa Rishly Ving
Punter Ian Arushfa Rishly Ving false Make me happy: give me lots of money
-------------------------------------------------
Teenager Homer Nalzone false I am Homer Nalzone
Teenager Homer Nalzone false It's not fair!
Teenager Homer Nalzone true Isn't life wonderful?
Teenager Homer Nalzone false It's not fair!
-------------------------------------------------
TV Host Terry Bill Woah B'Gorne true I am Terry Bill Woah B'Gorne
TV Host Terry Bill Woah B'Gorne true Welcome, suckers!
$ _
```

16.8.5 Coursework: Lots of different mouse mats!

Your shop is really beginning to take off – you now have several kinds of mouse mat! This causes you to think again about your MouseMat **class**. Only your first ones fit the description which you previously **hard coded**, and so you decide that a description suitable to particular mouse mats should be given when an **instance** of MouseMat is created. You realize that there may be other kinds of stock item that have similar simple variations in their descriptions, and so you decide to create another **abstract class** which is a **subclass** of StockItem, called TextDescriptionStockItem, and have MouseMat be a subclass of that. An **instance** of TextDescriptionStockItem will be given its description when it is created. Also, because you anticipate that descriptions might be refined due to customer feedback, they can be changed later.

Public method interfaces for class **TextDescriptionStockItem**.			
Method	**Return**	**Arguments**	**Description**
Constructor		String, int, int	Creates an instance of TextDescriptionStockItem with the given textual description, **int** initial price (in whole pence) and **int** initial quantity. The price is exclusive of VAT (sales tax).
getDescription	String		Returns the description that was given to the **constructor method**.
setDescription	**void**	String	Sets the description to the given string.

Read the rest of this task, and then draw a **UML class diagram** showing the full **inheritance hierarchy**, from StockItem downwards, as it will be when you have finished the task.

After drawing your diagram, implement the TextDescriptionStockItem class.

Now change MouseMat so that it is a **subclass** of TextDescriptionStockItem and remove getDescription() from it.

Alter TestStockItemSubclasses so that it makes two instances of MouseMat with different descriptions and prices. Add an extra **class method** that tests a TextDescriptionStockItem by making some change to its description (e.g. adding some text to it). Alter the existing class method that tests a StockItem so that, if the StockItem is also an instance of TextDescriptionStockItem, it will call your new class method to perform those additional tests.

You have also obtained various books about building computers that you would like to sell. Create the class Book which is another subclass of TextDescriptionStockItem. Remember that books are zero rated for VAT. Get rid of your Catalogue class – you have decided that your catalogue is better off being an instance of Book. Alter your test program so that it also creates some instances of Book – including one for your catalogue.

16.9 The Ball class

AIM: This section is mainly for progressing the development of the program, however the java.awt.Color **class** is introduced.

We now change our focus away from **subclass**es of Person for a while, to develop the lottery game side of the program model. In this section we present the **class** used to represent lottery balls.

Each ball has an **integer** number, and a colour. The simplest way to represent a colour is to use the class java.awt.Color, which is one of the **graphical user interface** classes. This is especially true in this program as images of balls of the appropriate colour will eventually be used in the **GUI** part of the program.

Concept **GUI API: Color.** The **class** java.awt.Color implements colours to be used in **graphical user interface**s. Each Color **object** comprises four values in the range 0 to 255, one for each of the primary colours red, green and blue, and a fourth component (alpha) for opacity.

For convenience, the class includes a number of **class constant**s containing **reference**s to Color objects which represent some common colours.

```
public static final Color black     = new Color(0,     0,    0, 255);
public static final Color white     = new Color(255, 255, 255, 255);
public static final Color red       = new Color(255,   0,    0, 255);
public static final Color green     = new Color(0,    255,   0, 255);
public static final Color blue      = new Color(0,      0,  255, 255);

public static final Color lightGray = new Color(192, 192, 192, 255);
public static final Color gray      = new Color(128, 128, 128, 255);
public static final Color darkGray  = new Color(64,   64,   64, 255);

public static final Color pink      = new Color(255, 175, 175, 255);
public static final Color orange    = new Color(255, 200,   0, 255);
public static final Color yellow    = new Color(255, 255,   0, 255);
public static final Color magenta   = new Color(255,   0, 255, 255);
public static final Color cyan      = new Color(0,    255, 255, 255);
```

Coffee time: 16.9.1
From these examples, suggest what may be the heading of the **constructor method** for Color.

Among many other features, there is an **instance method** getRGB() which **return**s a unique **int** for each **equivalent** colour, based on the four component values.

The Ball class is fairly straightforward.

```
001: import java.awt.Color;
002:
003: // Representation of a lottery ball, comprising colour and value.
004: public class Ball
005: {
006:    // The numeric value of the ball.
007:    private final int value;
008:
009:    // The colour of the ball.
010:    private final Color colour;
011:
012:
013:    // A ball is constructed by giving a number and a colour.
014:    public Ball(int requiredValue, Color requiredColour)
015:    {
016:      value = requiredValue;
017:      colour = requiredColour;
018:    } // Ball
019:
020:
021:    // Returns the numeric value of the ball.
022:    public int getValue()
023:    {
024:      return value;
025:    } // getValue
```

```
028:    // Returns the colour of the ball.
029:    public Color getColour()
030:    {
031:      return colour;
032:    } // getColour
```

```
035:     // Compares this ball's value with another, returning
036:     // < 0 if this ball's value is smaller than the other's,
037:     // > 0 if it is greater, or if the values are equal then
038:     //                          compare the RGB numbers of the colours instead.
039:     public int compareTo(Ball other)
040:     {
041:       if (value == other.value)
042:         return colour.getRGB() - other.colour.getRGB();
043:       else
044:         return value - other.value;
045:     } // compareTo
046:
047:
048:     // Mainly for testing.
049:     public String toString()
050:     {
051:       return "Ball " + value + " " + colour;
052:     } // toString
053:
054: } // class Ball
```

Coffee time:	Is an **instance** of Ball a **mutable object** or an **immutable object**?
	16.9.2

16.10 The `BallContainer` classes

AIM: To show another example of **inheritance**. We also see how to delete an **array element** from a **partially filled array**.

Lottery games consist of a machine, containing balls, and a landing rack, also containing balls. These two kinds of **object** have some features in common, and some features specific to each of them. This suggests the use of a **superclass** for the common features, which we shall call `BallContainer` and two **subclass**es each adding the specific features, which we shall call `Machine` and `Rack`. We also create the **class** `TestBallContainers` to test these, but for brevity we do not show the testing here.

We can represent this **inheritance hierarchy** with the following **UML class diagram**.

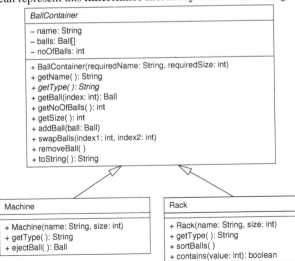

There are several places in these three classes at which we might sensibly **throw exceptions**, but instead we deliberately keep the code simple here. In the next chapter, which is a revisit to the topic of exceptions, we take another look at these classes in that light.

16.10.1   The `BallContainer` class

The **abstract class** `BallContainer` is the **superclass** of `Machine` and `Rack`. A `BallContainer` has a name and a collection of `Ball`s stored in a **partially filled array**.

```
001: // Representation of a container of balls for the lottery,
002: // with a fixed size and zero or more balls in a certain order.
003: public abstract class BallContainer
004: {
005:    // The name of the BallContainer.
006:    private final String name;
007:
008:    // The balls contained in the BallContainer.
009:    private final Ball[] balls;
010:
011:    // The number of balls contained in the BallContainer.
012:    // These are stored in balls, indexes 0 to noOfBalls - 1.
013:    private int noOfBalls;
```

When a `BallContainer` is created, we supply its name and its size, which is the maximum number of balls it can contain.

```
016:    // Constructor is given the name and size.
017:    public BallContainer(String requiredName, int requiredSize)
018:    {
019:       name = requiredName;
020:       balls = new Ball[requiredSize];
021:       noOfBalls = 0;
022:    } // BallContainer
```

We have various **accessor methods** for retrieving information from the `BallContainer`.

```
025:    // Returns the BallContainer's name.
026:    public String getName()
027:    {
028:       return name;
029:    } // getName
030:
031:
032:    // Returns the name of the type of BallContainer.
033:    public abstract String getType();
034:
035:
036:    // Returns the Ball at the given index in the BallContainer,
037:    // or null if that index is not in the range 0 to noOfBalls - 1.
038:    public Ball getBall(int index)
039:    {
040:       if (index >= 0 && index < noOfBalls)
041:          return balls[index];
042:       else
043:          return null;
044:    } // getBall;
045:
046:
047:    // Returns the number of balls in the BallContainer.
048:    public int getNoOfBalls()
```

```
049:    {
050:       return noOfBalls;
051:    } // getNoOfBalls
052:
053:
054:    // Returns the size of the BallContainer.
055:    public int getSize()
056:    {
057:       return balls.length;
058:    } // getSize
```

And some **mutator methods** to change the BallContainer.

```
061:    // Adds the given ball into the BallContainer, at the next highest unused
062:    // index position. Has no effect if the BallContainer is full.
063:    public void addBall(Ball ball)
064:    {
065:       if (noOfBalls < balls.length)
066:       {
067:          balls[noOfBalls] = ball;
068:          noOfBalls++;
069:       } // if
070:    } // addBall
071:
072:
073:    // Swaps the balls at the two given index positions.
074:    // Has no effect if either index is not in the range 0 to noOfBalls - 1.
075:    public void swapBalls(int index1, int index2)
076:    {
077:       if (index1 >= 0 && index1 < noOfBalls
078:             && index2 >=0 && index2 < noOfBalls)
079:       {
080:          Ball thatWasAtIndex1 = balls[index1];
081:          balls[index1] = balls[index2];
082:          balls[index2] = thatWasAtIndex1;
083:       } // if
084:    } // swapBalls;
085:
086:
087:    // Removes the Ball at the highest used index position.
088:    // Has no effect if the BallContainer is empty.
089:    public void removeBall()
090:    {
091:       if (noOfBalls > 0)
092:          noOfBalls--;
093:    } // removeBall
```

Finally, we have toString() to help with testing.

```
096:    // Mainly for testing.
097:    public String toString()
098:    {
099:       String result = getType() + " " + name + "(<=" + balls.length + ")";
100:       for (int index = 0; index < noOfBalls; index++)
101:          result += String.format("%n%d %s", index, balls[index]);
```

403

```
102:      return result;
103:   } // toString
104:
105: } // class BallContainer
```

16.10.2 The Machine class

A Machine **is a** BallContainer with the ability to eject a Ball at random.

```
001: // Representation of a lottery machine,
002: // with the facility for a randomly chosen ball to be ejected.
003: public class Machine extends BallContainer
004: {
005:    // Constructor is given the name and size.
006:    public Machine(String name, int size)
007:    {
008:       super(name, size);
009:    } // Machine
```

We have a **method implementation** for the **abstract method** getType().

```
012:    // Returns the name of the type of BallContainer.
013:    public String getType()
014:    {
015:       return "Lottery machine";
016:    } // getType
```

We add an **instance method** to eject a ball at random.

> *Concept* **Array: partially filled array: deleting an element.** The simplest way to delete an **array element** from a **partially filled array** with an arbitrary order, is to replace the unwanted item with the one at the end of the used portion and decrement the count of items.
>
> ```
> int indexToBeDeleted = ...
> noOfItemsInArray--;
> anArray[indexToBeDeleted] = anArray[noOfItemsInArray];
> ```

In the case here, we can achieve that effect by using swapBalls() and removeBall().

```
019:    // Randomly chooses a ball in the machine, and ejects it.
020:    // The ejected ball is returned. If the machine is empty then
021:    // it has no effect, and returns null.
022:    public Ball ejectBall()
023:    {
024:       if (getNoOfBalls() <= 0)
025:          return null;
026:       else
027:       {
028:          // Math.random() * getNoOfBalls yields a number
029:          // which is >= 0 and < number of balls.
030:          int ejectedBallIndex = (int) (Math.random() * getNoOfBalls());
031:
032:          Ball ejectedBall = getBall(ejectedBallIndex);
```

```
033:
034:          swapBalls(ejectedBallIndex, getNoOfBalls() - 1);
035:          removeBall();
036:
037:          return ejectedBall;
038:       } // else
039:    } // ejectBall
040:
041: } // class Machine
```

16.10.3   The Rack class

A Rack **is a** BallContainer with the ability to **sort** its Ball **object**s, and test if it contains a Ball with the given value. It is otherwise comparable with Machine.

```
001: // Representation of a landing rack of balls for the lottery,
002: // with the facility for them to be sorted into order,
003: // and another to determine if it contains a ball of a given value.
004: public class Rack extends BallContainer
005: {
006:    // Constructor is given the name and size.
007:    public Rack(String name, int size)
008:    {
009:       super(name, size);
010:    } // Rack
```

We have a **method implementation** for the **abstract method** getType().

```
013:    // Returns the name of the type of BallContainer.
014:    public String getType()
015:    {
016:       return "Landing rack";
017:    } // getType
```

We add an **instance method** to sort the balls using **bubble sort** which is similar to that seen previously (e.g. in Section 14.4.2 on page 304).

```
020:    // Sorts the balls in the Rack into ascending order,
021:    // using their compareTo() methods.
022:    public void sortBalls()
023:    {
024:       // Each pass of the sort reduces unsortedLength by one.
025:       int unsortedLength = getNoOfBalls();
026:       boolean changedOnThisPass;
027:       do
028:       {
029:          changedOnThisPass = false;
030:          for (int pairLeftIndex = 0;
031:               pairLeftIndex < unsortedLength - 1; pairLeftIndex++)
032:             if (getBall(pairLeftIndex).compareTo(getBall(pairLeftIndex + 1)) > 0)
033:             {
034:                swapBalls(pairLeftIndex, pairLeftIndex + 1);
035:                changedOnThisPass = true;
036:             } // if
037:          unsortedLength--;
038:       } while (changedOnThisPass);
039:    } // sortBalls
```

We also add an instance method to say whether the rack contains a ball with a given value. This involves an **array search** (via getBall()) for which we use the **linear search algorithm**.

```
042:   // Return true if and only if the rack contains
043:   // a Ball with the given number.
044:   public boolean contains(int value)
045:   {
046:     boolean found = false;
047:     int index = 0;
048:     while (!found && index < getNoOfBalls())
049:     {
050:       found = getBall(index).getValue() == value;
051:       index++;
052:     } // while
053:     return found;
054:   } // contains
055:
056: } // class Rack
```

16.11   The Game class

AIM:
To illustrate the difference between **is a** and **has a** relationships.

In this section we develop the **class** to model a lottery game, which essentially consists of a machine and rack combined. We also create the TestGame program to test it, but for brevity we do not show that here.

An **instance** of Game **has a** Machine, and also **has a** Rack. An instance of Machine **is a** BallContainer, as is an instance of Rack.

> *Concept* **Inheritance: is a versus has a.**   When a **class**, A, is a **subclass** of another class, B, we say that an **object** of type A **is a** B.
>
> If, on the other hand, a class, C, has an **instance variable** of type D, we say that an object of type C **has a** D.

```
001: // Representation of a lottery game, comprising a machine and a rack.
002: public class Game
003: {
004:   // The machine for the game.
005:   private final Machine machine;
006:
007:   // The rack for the game.
008:   private final Rack rack;
```

When a game is created, the names and sizes of the machine and rack are specified.

```
011:   // Constructor takes name and size of the machine, and the rack.
012:   public Game(String machineName, int machineSize,
013:                 String rackName, int rackSize)
014:   {
015:     machine = new Machine(machineName, machineSize);
016:     rack = new Rack(rackName, rackSize);
017:   } // Game
```

We have a number of **accessor method**s to obtain information about the machine and the rack.

```
020:    // Return the size of the machine.
021:    public int getMachineSize()
022:    {
023:      return machine.getSize();
024:    } // getMachineSize
025:
026:
027:    // Return the size of the rack.
028:    public int getRackSize()
029:    {
030:      return rack.getSize();
031:    } // getRackSize
032:
033:
034:    // Return the number of balls in the rack.
035:    public int getRackNoOfBalls()
036:    {
037:      return rack.getNoOfBalls();
038:    } // getRackNoOfBalls
```

Adding a ball into the game causes it to be added into the machine.

```
041:    // Add a ball into the machine
042:    public void machineAddBall(Ball ball)
043:    {
044:      machine.addBall(ball);
045:    } // machineAddBall
```

Ejecting a ball causes one to be removed from the machine and inserted into the rack. A **reference** to the ejected ball is also **return**ed.

```
048:    // Eject a ball from the machine into the rack.
049:    // Also return the rejected Ball.
050:    public Ball ejectBall()
051:    {
052:      if (machine.getNoOfBalls() > 0
053:          && rack.getNoOfBalls() < rack.getSize())
054:      {
055:        Ball ejectedBall = machine.ejectBall();
056:        rack.addBall(ejectedBall);
057:        return ejectedBall;
058:      } // if
059:      else
060:        return null;
061:    } // ejectBall
```

CleverPunter **object**s will need to know if the rack in the game contains the numbers they have chosen.

```
064:    // Returns true if and only if the rack contains
065:    // a Ball with the given number.
066:    public boolean rackContains(int value)
067:    {
068:      return rack.contains(value);
069:    } // rackContains
```

The end user can have the balls in the rack **sort**ed whenever they desire to.

```
072:    // Sorts the balls in the Rack into ascending order.
073:    public void rackSortBalls()
074:    {
075:       rack.sortBalls();
076:    } // rackSortBalls
```

Finally, to help with testing we have `toString()`.

```
079:    // Mainly for testing.
080:    public String toString()
081:    {
082:       return String.format("%s%n%s", machine, rack);
083:    } // toString
084:
085: } // class Game
```

16.11.1   Coursework: Shopping baskets

As always, read the whole of this task and then plan in your logbook what classes you need, including what **method**s they will have, before starting your implementation.

Your computer parts shop has so many customers now that you wish to computerize the selling of your products. Write a **class** called `StockItemPurchaseRequest` which **has a** `StockItem` and an **int** quantity of that stock item required by a customer.

Write another class called `ShoppingBasket` which can contain any number of stock item purchase requests, using **array extension**. This should have an `add()` **instance method** which takes (a **reference** to) a `StockItem` and an **int** required quantity, and adds a corresponding `StockItemPurchaseRequest` to the shopping basket.

It will also have a `toString()` giving the contained stock item purchase requests, one per line.

And finally, it will have another instance method called `checkout`. This will go through the stock item purchase requests and sell them (reducing the stock quantities), if there are enough quantity in stock, or not otherwise. The successful purchase requests will be removed from the shopping basket, leaving only those that were not purchased. The result will be a `String` indicating for each purchase request whether it was purchased or not, along with the details of it, all followed by the total price with and without VAT. Test this with a program called `TestShoppingBasket`. Here is a sample implementation for that – feel free to alter it if you wish.

```
001: public class TestShoppingBasket
002: {
003:    public static void main(String[] args)
004:    {
005:       StockItem[] stockItems =
006:       {
007:          /* 0 */ new MouseMat("Plain blue cloth, foam backed", 150, 10),
008:          /* 1 */ new MouseMat("Pink vinyl with fluffy trim", 350, 10),
009:          /* 2 */ new Book("List of all items and prices", 150, 10),
010:          /* 3 */ new Book("Build a gaming monster", 1799, 0),
011:          /* 4 */ new CPU(1500, 10),
012:          /* 5 */ new HardDisc(5500, 10),
013:          /* 6 */ new Keyboard(200, 10)
014:       };
015:
```

```
016:      System.out.println("Stock before purchase:");
017:      for (StockItem stockItem : stockItems)
018:        System.out.println(stockItem);
019:      System.out.println();
020:
021:      ShoppingBasket shoppingBasket = new ShoppingBasket();
022:      shoppingBasket.add(stockItems[0], 2);
023:      shoppingBasket.add(stockItems[2], 1);
024:      shoppingBasket.add(stockItems[4], 8);
025:      shoppingBasket.add(stockItems[5], 9);
026:      shoppingBasket.add(stockItems[4], 3);
027:      shoppingBasket.add(stockItems[6], 8);
028:      shoppingBasket.add(stockItems[3], 1);
029:
030:      System.out.println("Shopping basket filled up:");
031:      System.out.println(shoppingBasket);
032:      System.out.println();
033:
034:      System.out.println("Performing Checkout:");
035:      System.out.println(shoppingBasket.checkout());
036:      System.out.println();
037:
038:      System.out.println("Shopping basket after checkout:");
039:      System.out.println(shoppingBasket);
040:      System.out.println();
041:
042:      System.out.println("Stock after checkout:");
043:      for (StockItem stockItem : stockItems)
044:        System.out.println(stockItem);
045:    } // main
046:
047: } // class TestShoppingBasket
```

Here is a sample **run** of the above code.

```
                      Console Input / Output
$ java TestShoppingBasket
Stock before purchase:
SC1: Mouse mat, Plain blue cloth, foam backed (10 @ 150p/176p)
SC2: Mouse mat, Pink vinyl with fluffy trim (10 @ 350p/411p)
SC3: Book, List of all items and prices (10 @ 150p/150p)
SC4: Book, Build a gaming monster (0 @ 1799p/1799p)
SC5: CPU, Really fast (10 @ 1500p/1763p)
SC6: Hard disc, Lots of space (10 @ 5500p/6463p)
SC7: Keyboard, Cream, non-click (10 @ 200p/235p)


Shopping basket filled up:
Shopping basket:
2 of SC1: Mouse mat, Plain blue cloth, foam backed (10 @ 150p/176p)
1 of SC3: Book, List of all items and prices (10 @ 150p/150p)
8 of SC5: CPU, Really fast (10 @ 1500p/1763p)
9 of SC6: Hard disc, Lots of space (10 @ 5500p/6463p)
3 of SC5: CPU, Really fast (10 @ 1500p/1763p)
8 of SC7: Keyboard, Cream, non-click (10 @ 200p/235p)
1 of SC4: Book, Build a gaming monster (0 @ 1799p/1799p)

(Continued ...)
```

```
                              (...cont.)
Performing Checkout:
Checkout report:
Purchased 2 of SC1: Mouse mat, Plain blue cloth, foam backed (8 @ 150p/176p)
Purchased 1 of SC3: Book, List of all items and prices (9 @ 150p/150p)
Purchased 8 of SC5: CPU, Really fast (2 @ 1500p/1763p)
Purchased 9 of SC6: Hard disc, Lots of space (1 @ 5500p/6463p)
Not purchased 3 of SC5: CPU, Really fast (2 @ 1500p/1763p)
Purchased 8 of SC7: Keyboard, Cream, non-click (2 @ 200p/235p)
Not purchased 1 of SC4: Book, Build a gaming monster (0 @ 1799p/1799p)
Total price ex vat: 63550p
Total price inc vat: 74653p

Shopping basket after checkout:
Shopping basket:
3 of SC5: CPU, Really fast (2 @ 1500p/1763p)
1 of SC4: Book, Build a gaming monster (0 @ 1799p/1799p)

Stock after checkout:
SC1: Mouse mat, Plain blue cloth, foam backed (8 @ 150p/176p)
SC2: Mouse mat, Pink vinyl with fluffy trim (10 @ 350p/411p)
SC3: Book, List of all items and prices (9 @ 150p/150p)
SC4: Book, Build a gaming monster (0 @ 1799p/1799p)
SC5: CPU, Really fast (2 @ 1500p/1763p)
SC6: Hard disc, Lots of space (1 @ 5500p/6463p)
SC7: Keyboard, Cream, non-click (2 @ 200p/235p)
$ _
```

Hint: in order to delete successfully purchased items from the ShoppingBasket, checkout() might create another (empty) ShoppingBasket into which it adds the StockItem and required quantity of *unsuccessful* requests. At the end it can copy the **instance variable**s of this temporary ShoppingBasket to replace those of the original one.

As usual, record in your logbook any changes you needed to make to your plan.

16.12   The Worker classes

AIM:
To show an example of a **superclass** which is (appropriately) not an **abstract class**. We also show how we can use an **instance method** defined in the superclass, from a **subclass** which **overrides** it.

In this section we develop the **class** Worker, which models the kind of person that creates balls and fills up lottery games with them. For extra fun, we also have the class TraineeWorker that is a kind of worker who is still learning to count – he or she has an efficiency rating which is the probability of getting a number right when creating the balls!

A TraineeWorker **is a** Worker. We can include these two new classes in our **UML class diagram** representing the Person **inheritance hierarchy**.

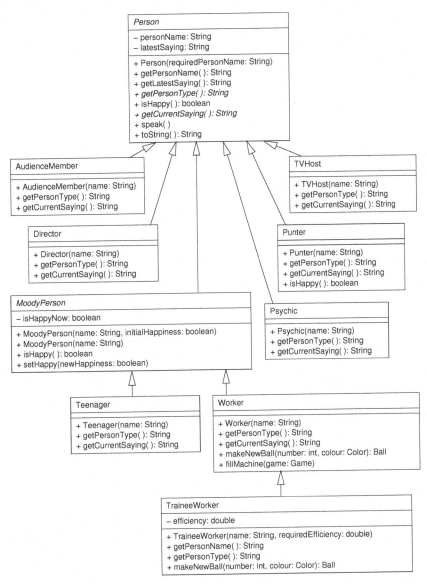

Both `Worker` and `TraineeWorker` are **subclass**es of `MoodyPerson`, so we can test the general moody person properties by simply adding a `Worker` and a `TraineeWorker` to the existing `TestPersonSubclasses` program. For brevity, we do not show that test here. To test the new properties we will develop the program `TestWorkers`, which we do include in this section.

16.12.1 The `Worker` class

Except for the new features, this is comparable with `Teenager`, a fellow **subclass** of `MoodyPerson`.

```
001: import java.awt.Color;
002:
```

```
003: // Representation of a worker making balls
004: // and filling up machines in the lottery.
005: public class Worker extends MoodyPerson
006: {
007:    // Constructor is given the person's name.
008:    public Worker(String name)
009:    {
010:       super(name);
011:    } // Worker
```

We have **method implementations** for the **abstract methods** getPersonType() and getCurrentSaying().

```
014:    // Returns the name of the type of Person.
015:    public String getPersonType()
016:    {
017:       return "Worker";
018:    } // getPersonType
019:
020:
021:    // Returns the Person's current saying.
022:    public String getCurrentSaying()
023:    {
024:       if (isHappy())
025:          return "Time for tea, I think";
026:       else
027:          return "Puff, pant, puff, pant";
028:    } // getCurrentSaying
```

The main extra feature of a Worker is that he or she can be asked to fill up a Game with **new**ly created balls. This essentially involves a **loop** that **construct**s a ball of the right colour and number, and inserts it into the game. We have a separate **instance method** to create a single ball, so that the TraineeWorker subclass can **override** it with one that sometimes gets the number wrong.

```
031:    // Returns a newly created Ball with the given number and colour.
032:    public Ball makeNewBall(int number, Color colour)
033:    {
034:       return new Ball(number, colour);
035:    } // makeNewBall
```

A worker knows that the colours of the balls are (similar to) the seven colours of the rainbow, approximately evenly spread through the balls in ascending numeric order. The numbers of the balls are always 1 up to the size of the machine in the game.

```
038:    // Makes this Worker fill the machine of the given Game.
039:    // The Balls are created as they are inserted into the Machine.
040:    public void fillMachine(Game game)
041:    {
042:       // Colours of balls are evenly spread between these colours,
043:       // in ascending order.
044:       Color[] colourGroupColours
045:          = new Color[] { Color.red, Color.orange, Color.yellow, Color.green,
046:                          Color.blue, Color.pink, Color.magenta };
047:       // This happiness change will show up when the GUI is added.
048:       setHappy(false);
049:       speak();
050:
051:       int noOfBalls = game.getMachineSize();
```

```
052:       for (int count = 1; count <= noOfBalls; count++)
053:       {
054:         // The colour group is a number from 0
055:         // to the number of colour groups - 1.
056:         // For the nth ball, we take the fraction
057:         // (n - 1) divided by the number of balls
058:         // and multiply that by the number of groups.
059:         int colourGroup = (int) ((count - 1.0) / (double)noOfBalls
060:                                 * (double) colourGroupColours.length);
061:         Color ballColour = colourGroupColours[colourGroup];
062:         game.machineAddBall(makeNewBall(count, ballColour));
063:       } // for
064:       setHappy(true);
065:       speak();
066:    } // fillMachine
067:
068: } // class Worker
```

16.12.2 The `TraineeWorker` class

`TraineeWorker` is a **subclass** of `Worker`. Note that the previous examples of **superclass**es were also **abstract class**es, whereas `Worker` is not. This is because we wish to have **instances** of `Worker` as well as `TraineeWorker`.

A `TraineeWorker` has both a name and an efficiency rating, which is a number between 0.0 and 1.0. The rating is the probability that he or she is concentrating hard when making balls. A value of 0.0 means the trainee worker is never concentrating, whereas a rating of 1.0 means he or she always is. If when making a ball the trainee is not concentrating, then the number will either be one less or one greater than the number desired.

```
001: import java.awt.Color;
002:
003: // Representation of a trainee lottery worker,
004: // who has an efficiency rating effecting accuracy of ball numbering.
005: public class TraineeWorker extends Worker
006: {
007:    // The efficiency of the TraineeWorker.
008:    private final double efficiency;
```

The **constructor method** takes the name of the person which its passes on to the superclass, and the efficiency rating which it stores in the `efficiency` **instance variable**.

```
011:    // Constructor is given the person's name and the required efficiency.
012:    public TraineeWorker(String name, double requiredEfficiency)
013:    {
014:       super(name);
015:       efficiency = requiredEfficiency;
016:    } // TraineeWorker
```

The `getPersonName()` **instance method** is used by the **GUI** part of the program to show the person's name. For a trainee worker we would like the efficiency to be shown too, so we **override** `getPersonName()` with one that takes the result from the superclass version of the **method** and appends the efficiency. This requires us to access the overridden method from the body of the method which is overriding it!

413

Concept **Inheritance: using an overridden method.** A **subclass** can **override** an **instance method** defined in a **superclass**, but sometimes the behaviour of the new version is based on that of the one it is overriding. This means we need to have a **method call** to the *superclass* version, which we can do by prepending the instance method name with the **reserved word super** and a dot.

For example, in a traffic flow simulation program where most kinds of vehicle probably perform an emergency stop in much the same way, perhaps a bicycle's behaviour is based on the more general one.

```
public class Vehicle
{
  ...
  public void emergencyStop()
  {
    ... General code for most vehicles.
  } // emergencyStop
  ...
} // class Vehicle

public class Bicycle extends Vehicle
{
  ...
  public void emergencyStop()
  {
    ... Specific code for bicycles.
    super.emergencyStop();
    ... More specific code for bicycles.
  } // emergencyStop
  ...
} // class Bicycle
```

This `super.` notation can be used in any instance method of the subclass, not just in the overriding method.

Here is the version of `getPersonName()` for the `TraineeWorker` **class**.

```
019:  // Returns the Person's name with the efficiency added in brackets.
020:  public String getPersonName()
021:  {
022:    return super.getPersonName() + " (" + efficiency + " efficiency)";
023:  } // getPersonName
```

Coffee Was `getPersonName()` one of the instance methods which you decided ought to be declared as
time: [16.12.1] a **final method** in Section 16.7.4 on page 391? Oops?

We **override** the method `getPersonType()`, defined in the `Worker` class, with one that prepends the string `"Trainee "` on the result.

```
026:  // Returns the name of the type of Person.
027:  public String getPersonType()
028:  {
029:    return "Trainee " + super.getPersonType();
030:  } // getPersonType
```

Finally, we override the `makeNewBall()` method with one that sometimes gets the number wrong.

```
033:  // Returns a newly created Ball with the given number and colour.
034:  // The ball's number may be wrong depending on the efficiency.
```

```
035:   public Ball makeNewBall(int number, Color colour)
036:   {
037:     if (Math.random() >= efficiency)
038:       if (Math.random() < 0.5)
039:         number--;
040:       else
041:         number++;
042:     return new Ball(number, colour);
043:   } // makeNewBall
044:
045: } // class TraineeWorker
```

16.12.3 The `TestWorkers` class

To test the features of the worker **class**es, we create an **instance** of each kind of worker, and a Game for them to fill with balls. (This is just a sample test, rather than a thorough one.)

```
001: // Create one of each type of worker,
002: // and get them to fill the machine of a game.
003: public class TestWorkers
004: {
005:   public static void main(String[] args)
006:   {
007:     testWorker(new Worker("May Kit Dewitt"),
008:                new Game("Lott O'Luck Larry", 3, "Slippery's Mile", 2));
009:     testWorker(new TraineeWorker("Darwin Marbest", 0.75),
010:                new Game("13th Time Lucky", 5, "Oooz OK Lose", 2));
011:   } // main
012:
013:
014:   // Make the given worker fill the given game,
015:   // reporting values before and after.
016:   private static void testWorker(Worker worker, Game game)
017:   {
018:     System.out.println("------------------------------------");
019:     System.out.println("Start with");
020:     System.out.println(game);
021:
022:     System.out.println("Balls added by");
023:     System.out.println(worker);
024:
025:     worker.fillMachine(game);
026:     System.out.println(game);
027:     System.out.println(worker);
028:   } // testWorker
029:
030: } // class TestWorkers
```

16.12.4 Trying it

Console Input / Output
`$ java TestWorkers`

Start with
Lottery machine Lott O'Luck Larry(<=3)
Landing rack Slippery's Mile(<=2)
Balls added by
Worker May Kit Dewitt true I am May Kit Dewitt
Lottery machine Lott O'Luck Larry(<=3)
0 Ball 1 java.awt.Color[r=255,g=0,b=0]
1 Ball 2 java.awt.Color[r=255,g=255,b=0]
2 Ball 3 java.awt.Color[r=0,g=0,b=255]
Landing rack Slippery's Mile(<=2)
Worker May Kit Dewitt true Time for tea, I think
(Continued ...)

```
                              (...cont.)
--------------------------------------------
Start with
Lottery machine 13th Time Lucky(<=5)
Landing rack Oooz OK Lose(<=2)
Balls added by
Trainee Worker Darwin Marbest (0.75 efficiency) true I am Darwin Marbest
Lottery machine 13th Time Lucky(<=5)
0 Ball 1 java.awt.Color[r=255,g=0,b=0]
1 Ball 3 java.awt.Color[r=255,g=200,b=0]
2 Ball 3 java.awt.Color[r=255,g=255,b=0]
3 Ball 3 java.awt.Color[r=0,g=0,b=255]
4 Ball 5 java.awt.Color[r=255,g=175,b=175]
Landing rack Oooz OK Lose(<=2)
Trainee Worker Darwin Marbest (0.75 efficiency) true Time for tea, I think
$ _
```

As you can see, the `TraineeWorker` has got some ball numbers wrong.

16.12.5   Coursework: Loads of disc space

Read the whole of this task, and then draw a **UML class diagram** showing the full **inheritance hierarchy**, from `StockItem` downwards, as it will be when you have finished the task.

Your shop just keeps getting better – now you have a whole variety of different sizes of hard disc on offer. Alter your `HardDisc` **class** so that the **constructor method** takes an additional **method parameter** which is the size of the disc in gigabytes. Alter the `getDescription()` **instance method** so that it **return**s, for example, `"1000GB of space"` – the actual number being the given size, of course.

And then you get a delivery of an amazing new kind of hard disc that is so reliable it is guaranteed to keep **data** safe from disc crash for a specified number of years. Write a **subclass** of `HardDisc` called `ReliableHardDisc`. Its constructor method takes one extra parameter which is the guarantee period. It **override**s `getDescription()` with one that appends, for example, `", guaranteed 20 years"` to the string obtained by the same instance method in the **superclass** – the actual number being the given guarantee period, of course.

Alter your `TestStockItemSubclasses` class to include the size for the `HardDisc`s and also add at least one `ReliableHardDisc`.

16.13   The `CleverPunter` class

AIM:
To reinforce **inheritance** concepts, and complete the model **classes** of the Notional Lottery program.

The final **class** in the model phase of the Notional Lottery program is `CleverPunter`. This is a **subclass** of `MoodyPerson`, and models the kind of person that plays a lottery game.

We develop the class in this section, together with its test program `TestCleverPunter`. (We also add a `CleverPunter` to the existing `TestPersonSubclasses` program, but do not show that here.) Let us start by completing our **UML class diagram** representing the `Person` **inheritance hierarchy**.

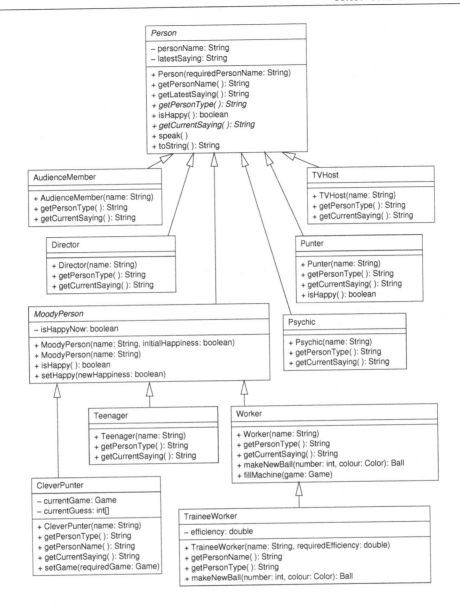

16.13.1 The `CleverPunter` class

A `CleverPunter` has two extra **instance variables**, the game he or she is currently playing, and his or her guess for that game. The code is comparable with `Worker` – a fellow **subclass** of `MoodyPerson`, but it has significant extra sophistication.

```
001: // Representation of a clever person playing the lottery who actually knows
002: // enough to make some guesses and score them against a game.
003: public class CleverPunter extends MoodyPerson
004: {
005:    // The game which is currently being played.
006:    private Game currentGame = null;
007:
```

```
008:   // The guess of what balls will come out.
009:   private int[] currentGuess = null;
```

The **constructor method** passes the given person name to that of the **superclass**.

```
012:   // Constructor is given the person's name.
013:   public CleverPunter(String name)
014:   {
015:     super(name);
016:   } // CleverPunter
```

We have a **method implementation** for the **abstract method** getPersonType().

```
019:   // Returns the name of the type of Person.
020:   public String getPersonType()
021:   {
022:     return "Clever Punter";
023:   } // getPersonType
```

We **override** the **instance method** getPersonName() with one that appends on the current guess, if the clever punter has one.

```
026:   // Returns the Person's name, with the current guess included.
027:   public String getPersonName()
028:   {
029:     String result = super.getPersonName();
030:     if (currentGuess != null && currentGuess.length != 0)
031:     {
032:       result += "(guess " + currentGuess[0];
033:       for (int index = 1; index < currentGuess.length; index++)
034:         result += "," + currentGuess[index];
035:       result += ")";
036:     } // if
037:     return result;
038:   } // getPersonName
```

Our **method implementation** for the abstract method getCurrentSaying() says a different phrase depending on the state of the guess and the game, and sets the happiness of the person accordingly. This uses a **private** instance method, getNoOfMatches(), to determine how many of the player's guesses match the landing rack in the game.

```
041:   // Returns the Person's current saying.
042:   public String getCurrentSaying()
043:   {
044:     if (currentGame == null)
045:     {
046:       setHappy(false);
047:       return "I need a game to play!";
048:     } // if
049:     else
050:     {
051:       int noOfMatches = getNoOfMatches();
052:       int noOfNonMatches = currentGame.getRackNoOfBalls() - noOfMatches;
053:       // Is happy if and only if there are no non-matches.
054:       setHappy(noOfNonMatches == 0);
055:       if (noOfMatches == currentGame.getRackSize())
056:         return "Yippee!! I've won the jackpot!";
057:       else if (noOfNonMatches != 0)
058:         return "Doh! " + noOfNonMatches + " not matched";
```

```
059:        else if (noOfMatches == 0) // I.e. the rack is still empty.
060:          return "I'm excited!";
061:        else
062:          return noOfMatches + " matched so far!";
063:      } // else
064:    } // getCurrentSaying
065:
066:
067:    // Helper method to find out how many of the guesses currently match the
068:    // game rack. Note: this does not get called if currentGuess is null.
069:    private int getNoOfMatches()
070:    {
071:      int noMatchedSoFar = 0;
072:      for (int oneNumber : currentGuess)
073:        if (currentGame.rackContains(oneNumber))
074:          noMatchedSoFar++;
075:      return noMatchedSoFar;
076:    } // getNoOfMatches
```

Finally, we have a new instance method to set the game to be played, and which causes a new guess to be made. A simple way to obtain a guess is to play a mock game – an example of **software reuse**!

```
079:    // Set the game being currently played.
080:    public void setGame(Game requiredGame)
081:    {
082:      currentGame = requiredGame;
083:      currentGuess = new int[currentGame.getRackSize()];
084:      // An easy way to obtain a guess is to play a mock game!
085:      Game mockGame = new Game("", currentGame.getMachineSize(),
086:                               "", currentGame.getRackSize());
087:      Worker mockWorker = new Worker("");
088:      mockWorker.fillMachine(mockGame);
089:      for (int index = 0; index < currentGame.getRackSize(); index++)
090:        currentGuess[index] = mockGame.ejectBall().getValue();
091:    } // setGame
092:
093: } // class CleverPunter
```

16.13.2 The `TestCleverPunter` class

The program `TestCleverPunter` takes **command line argument**s enabling us to try out various machine and rack sizes. We create a game of the given sizes, get a `Worker` to fill it up, then eject the right number of balls, getting a `CleverPunter` who is playing the game to speak at each stage.

```
001: // Given a machine size and a rack size from the first two arguments,
002: // create a game and a clever punter to play it,
003: // reporting result as eject each ball.
004: public class TestCleverPunter
005: {
006:   public static void main(String[] args)
007:   {
008:     int machineSize = Integer.parseInt(args[0]);
009:     int rackSize = Integer.parseInt(args[1]);
010:
```

```
011:      Game game = new Game("Lott O'Luck Larry", machineSize,
012:                           "Slippery's Mile", rackSize);
013:      Worker worker = new Worker("May Kit Dewitt");
014:      worker.fillMachine(game);
015:
016:      CleverPunter cleverPunter = new CleverPunter("Wendy Athinkile-Win");
017:      System.out.println(cleverPunter);
018:      cleverPunter.speak();
019:      System.out.println(cleverPunter);
020:
021:      cleverPunter.setGame(game);
022:      cleverPunter.speak();
023:      System.out.println(cleverPunter);
024:      for (int count = 1; count <= game.getRackSize(); count++)
025:      {
026:        System.out.println("Ejected: " + game.ejectBall().getValue());
027:        cleverPunter.speak();
028:        System.out.println(cleverPunter.isHappy()
029:                           + " " + cleverPunter.getLatestSaying());
030:      } // for
031:   } // main
032:
033: } // class TestCleverPunter
```

16.13.3 Trying it

```
Console Input / Output

$ java TestCleverPunter 10 5
Clever Punter Wendy Athinkile-Win true I am Wendy Athinkile-Win
Clever Punter Wendy Athinkile-Win false I need a game to play!
Clever Punter Wendy Athinkile-Win(guess 8,3,6,4,7) true I'm excited!
Ejected: 4
true 1 matched so far!
Ejected: 10
false Doh! 1 not matched
Ejected: 8
false Doh! 1 not matched
Ejected: 7
false Doh! 1 not matched
Ejected: 6
false Doh! 1 not matched
$ _
```

```
Console Input / Output

$ java TestCleverPunter 7 7
Clever Punter Wendy Athinkile-Win true I am Wendy Athinkile-Win
Clever Punter Wendy Athinkile-Win false I need a game to play!
Clever Punter Wendy Athinkile-Win(guess 6,2,4,3,7,1,5) true I'm excited!
Ejected: 7
true 1 matched so far!
Ejected: 6
true 2 matched so far!
Ejected: 5
true 3 matched so far!
Ejected: 2
true 4 matched so far!
Ejected: 1
true 5 matched so far!
Ejected: 3
true 6 matched so far!
Ejected: 4
true Yippee!! I've won the jackpot!
$ _
```

```
                          Console Input / Output
$ java TestCleverPunter 49 7
Clever Punter Wendy Athinkile-Win true I am Wendy Athinkile-Win
Clever Punter Wendy Athinkile-Win false I need a game to play!
Clever Punter Wendy Athinkile-Win(guess 36,12,30,26,27,15,17) true I'm excited!
Ejected: 49
false Doh! 1 not matched
Ejected: 43
false Doh! 2 not matched
Ejected: 45
false Doh! 3 not matched
Ejected: 13
false Doh! 4 not matched
Ejected: 6
false Doh! 5 not matched
Ejected: 7
false Doh! 6 not matched
Ejected: 1
false Doh! 7 not matched
$ _
```

16.13.4 Coursework: Making it more realistic

The computer parts shop example has been a little over simplified so far. In this task you will add more complexity to make it all a bit more realistic. You can add what you like, but here are some suggestions.

- CPUs have a vendor, architecture and speed.

- Hard discs have a physical size, vendor, rotational speed and cache/buffer size.

- Keyboards have colour, vendor, number of keys, and possible special features description.

- Perhaps every stock item could have a changeable part of its description, rather than just the TextDescriptionStockItem **class**.

Think of more ideas. Then identify the most appropriate place in the **inheritance hierarchy** to add each complexity, and implement them. You will add more **instance variables**, **instance methods** and alter existing instance methods as required. For example, getDescription() should perhaps incorporate the additional instance variables in its result.

16.14 The GUI classes

AIM: To characterize the rest of the Notional Lottery program development.

The second phase of development for the Notional Lottery game concerns the **graphical user interface class**es. However, the details of these would just be a distraction right now, so we will merely characterize this aspect of the resulting finished program.

- We have the class LotteryGUI to provide a graphical user interface.

- There are classes to provide images for model objects. We have PersonImage and BallImage, for providing images of people and balls respectively. Additionally, we have BallContainerImage which has two **subclass**es, MachineImage and RackImage.

- The Person class is modified so that each **instance** of it **has a** corresponding instance of PersonImage. This is created by the **constructor method** of Person, and stored in a new **instance variable**.

- Similarly, Ball, Machine and Rack **object**s each have a corresponding BallImage, MachineImage and RackImage object respectively.

- PersonImage objects have an update() **instance method** which ensures that the image appearing on the screen reflects the state of the Person object in the model. The Person class is modified to invoke this instance method whenever any changes are made to the state of a Person object. For example, in MoodyPerson, the setHappy() instance method becomes as follows.

```
...
032:    // Sets the happiness of the person to the given state.
033:    public void setHappy(boolean newHappiness)
034:    {
035:      isHappyNow = newHappiness;
036:      getImage().update();
037:    } // setHappy
...
```

- A similar relationship exists for the other model classes which have a corresponding image class.

- We have the classes SpeedController and SpeedControllerGUI to control the speed of the game.

- The Person and Ball classes have a flash() instance method added to them, which causes their image objects to flash on the screen. These are invoked at various points in the model, for example just before a ball is ejected from a machine.

- Each kind of Person has a different coloured face in their image, so a getColour() instance method is added to Person.

 Coffee time: 16.14.1 How would we add getColour() to the Person model classes, so that each type of person has a different colour?

16.15   The Object class and constructor chaining

AIM:
To introduce the **class** Object and the fact that the **constructor method** of the **super-class** is invoked implicitly by default. We also take a more thorough look at **constructor chaining**.

Having now mainly completed our coverage of **inheritance**, we should consolidate our understanding with four more concepts. Firstly, we have the **class** Object.

Concept **Standard API: Object.** All **object**s in Java are also **instance**s of the standard **class** called java.lang.Object. Unless a class is explicitly declared to **extend** some other class, then it implicitly extends Object directly. This means all classes in Java reside in a single **inheritance hierarchy**, which is a tree structure with the class Object at its root. Every class has a **superclass**, except for the class Object.

The Object class has one **constructor method** and it takes no **method arguments**.

```
public class Object
{
   ...
```

```
    public Object()
    {
      ... Code here to actually create an object,
      ... allocating memory for it, etc..
    } // Object
    ...
  } // class Object
```

You will recall that the **constructor method**s in the **subclass**es of the Notional Lottery program typically invoked the constructor method of their **superclass** as their first **statement**. What about those classes that did not **extend** another explicitly?

Concept **Inheritance: invoking the superclass constructor: implicitly.** In the body of a **constructor method**, if the first **statement** is not a **superclass constructor call** (using **super**), nor is it an **alternative constructor call** (using **this**), then a call to the constructor method of the **superclass** which has no **method arguments**, is assumed. This is because the first work which is done by a constructor method must be to actually create the **object**, that is, allocate memory for it, and this is done inside the constructor method of the java.lang.Object **class**.

For example, in the Person class, the constructor method we saw previously was as follows.

```
...
012:   public Person(String requiredPersonName)
013:   {
014:     personName = requiredPersonName;
015:     latestSaying = "I am " + personName;
016:   } // Person
...
```

This is treated exactly as though it has a call to the constructor method of the superclass of Person, which is the class Object.

```
...
012:   public Person(String requiredPersonName)
013:   {
014:     super();
015:     personName = requiredPersonName;
016:     latestSaying = "I am " + personName;
017:   } // Person
...
```

One way of looking at this is to say that, in order to create a Person **object**, we must first create an **instance** of Object. The principle of constructor methods calling a constructor method of the superclass is called **constructor chaining**.

Concept **Inheritance: constructor chaining.** Whenever a **constructor method** is invoked, the first thing done is either a call to another constructor method in the same **class**, or to a constructor method in the **superclass**. This in turn does the same, all the way up the **inheritance hierarchy** until eventually the constructor method of the java.lang.Object class is called. This process is known as **constructor chaining**.

Such chaining must always be possible for every class we write, or else we would not be able to have **object**s created at **run time** – it is the constructor method of Object that actually creates an object. So, one rule is that at least one constructor method of every class must *not* start with a call to another constructor method of the same class!

We can illustrate constructor chaining by examining what happens when a `TraineeWorker` object is created. Let us say we start with this code.

```
Person person = new TraineeWorker("Justin de Neaushob", 0.0);
```

This calls the constructor method of `TraineeWorker`.

```
...
012:    public TraineeWorker(String name, double requiredEfficiency)
013:    {
014:      super(name);
015:      efficiency = requiredEfficiency;
016:    } // TraineeWorker
...
```

The first line calls the constructor method of `Worker`.

```
...
008:    public Worker(String name)
009:    {
010:      super(name);
011:    } // Worker
...
```

This calls the second constructor method of `MoodyPerson`, the first line of which calls the first constructor method.

```
...
010:    public MoodyPerson(String name, boolean initialHappiness)
011:    {
012:      super(name);
013:      isHappyNow = initialHappiness;
014:    } // MoodyPerson
...
019:    public MoodyPerson(String name)
020:    {
021:      this(name, true);
022:    } // MoodyPerson
...
```

And the first line of that first `MoodyPerson` constructor method calls the constructor method of `Person`.

```
...
012:    public Person(String requiredPersonName)
013:    {
014:      personName = requiredPersonName;
015:      latestSaying = "I am " + personName;
016:    } // Person
...
```

Finally, this implicitly calls the constructor method of `Object`, in which the object is actually created! Then all the constructor method calls unstack as each one finishes and control is **return**ed to the one that called it.

Coffee time: 16.15.1 Suppose a (non-abstract) class does not have a constructor method defined by the programmer. Can it still be instantiated? How does this fit in with constructor chaining?

Concept **Method: constructor methods: default.** If we write a **class** and do not include a **constructor method** in it, then Java implicitly treats it as though we have defined a **public** empty one, which takes no **method arguments**. For example, for a class called FabulousThing, this would be as follows.

```
public FabulousThing()
{
} // FabulousThing
```

This is called a **default constructor** and is of course the same as one which simply invokes the constructor method of the **superclass**.

```
public FabulousThing()
{
  super();
} // FabulousThing
```

The default constructor is only assumed for classes that do not explicitly define a constructor method, which means that not every class actually has a constructor method which takes no arguments. For example, the class VeryFabulousThing, partially defined below, does not have such a constructor method.

```
public class VeryFabulousThing
{
  ... Some code, but no more constructor methods.
  public VeryFabulousThing(String name)
  {
    ...
  } // VeryFabulousThing
  ... Some code, but no more constructor methods.
} // class VeryFabulousThing
```

As a result, the following is illegal.

```
public class TheMostFabulousThingInTheUniverse extends VeryFabulousThing
{
  ... Code here, but no constructor method.
} // class TheMostFabulousThingInTheUniverse
```

This is because the class TheMostFabulousThingInTheUniverse cannot have a default constructor because its superclass does not have a constructor method that takes no arguments.

In practice, default constructors are not often what we want anyway. This author recommends that you *always* explicitly write at least one constructor method for every class which you intend there to be **instances** of, even when that constructor method is empty. This shows to anybody reading your code that it is deliberately empty, rather than has been omitted by mistake.

16.15.1 Trying it

```
                          Console Input / Output
$ javac TheMostFabulousThingInTheUniverse.java
TheMostFabulousThingInTheUniverse.java:1: cannot find symbol
symbol  : constructor VeryFabulousThing()
location: class VeryFabulousThing
public class TheMostFabulousThingInTheUniverse extends VeryFabulousThing
                                                       ^
1 error
$ _
```

16.15.2   Coursework: Exploring constructor chaining

Add `System.out.println()` calls to the **constructor method** of each `StockItem` **class** printing the name of the class. Add each call at the earliest point in the body of the constructor method that the **compiler** will let you. Once you have successfully **compile**d the classes, predict what the additional output will be from your `TestStockItemSubclasses` program *before* you **run** it. Then run it and see if you were right.

16.16   Overloaded methods versus override

AIM:
To take a closer look at **overloaded method**s and in particular how an intended **override** can accidentally become an overload. We revisit the overloaded methods `System.out.println()`, and look at `toString()` from the `Object` **class**.

As we have already said, Java permits us to have **overloaded method**s, that is, more than one **method** with the same name in the same **class** – including those **inherit**ed from the **superclass**. This can sometimes be confused with **instance method**s that **override** another, and so in this final section we take a closer look.

16.16.1   Does an `int` match a `double`?

Let's start by exploring **overloaded method**s through a contrived example.

```
001: public class WhoAmI
002: {
003:    public static void identify(int arg)
004:    {
005:       System.out.println("I am an int: " + arg);
006:    } // identify
007:
008:    public static void identify(double arg)
009:    {
010:       System.out.println("I am a double: " + arg);
011:    } // identify
012:
013:    public static void identifyToo(double arg)
014:    {
015:       System.out.println("I too am a double: " + arg);
016:    } // identifyToo
017:
018:    public static void main(String[] args)
019:    {
020:       identify(10);        // An int argument is surely an int.
021:       identify(20.0);      // A double argument is surely a double.
022:       identifyToo(30);     // An int argument is surely an int.
023:    } // main
024:
025: } // class WhoAmI
```

When we **run** the program, you might be slightly puzzled by the results.

```
                        Console Input / Output
$ java WhoAmI
I am an int: 10
I am a double: 20.0
I too am a double: 30.0
$ _
```

426

In the first **method call**, the **method argument** is an `int` and so there are two **methods** that match, both called `identify`. This is because an `int` method argument can match a `double` **method parameter**. Given such a choice, the **compiler** picks the one which is most specific, in this case the one which takes an `int`.

There is only one method that matches the second method call – an `int` method argument can match a `double` **method parameter**, but not vice-versa.

The third method call also has only one matching method. The `int` method argument is automatically **cast** into a `double`, that is, the compiler plants **byte code** as though we had written `(double)` in front of 30.

Coffee time: 16.16.1   What if we had two overloaded methods, one taking an `int` and a `double`, and the other taking the opposite – could we have a method call that would be ambiguous?

16.16.2   `System.out.println()` and inheritance

Perhaps the most obvious examples of **overloaded methods** are `System.out.println()` and `System.out.print()`.

Concept **Standard API: `System: out.println()`: with any argument.** The **class** `java.lang.System` has an **overloaded method** version of `out.println()` and `out.print()` for every **primitive type** of **method argument**, as well as `java.lang.Object`. Each treats its argument, `(arg)`, as `("" + arg)`. So, an `int` is output in decimal representation, and a non-null **object reference** has its `toString()` **instance method** used, etc..

Also, there is a version of `System.out.println()` and `System.out.print()` that take a **character array**, `char[]`, and print the characters in it.

What about **objects** from **class**es in which we did not write a `toString()`?

Concept **Standard API: `Object: toString()`.** The **class** `java.lang.Object` has a `toString()` **instance method**. This produces a `String` consisting of (a representation of) the **type** of the **object** followed by a `'@'` and a **hexadecimal** (i.e. base 16) number which is (by default) unique to the object. Classes which do not provide their own version **inherit** this default one.

We have previously said that **arrays** are objects: in fact the **superclass** of every array **type** is `java.lang.Object`. This means they have a `toString()` – they **inherit** the default one. So, what will be the result of **run**ning the following code?

```
001: public class PrintlnOverloadDemo
002: {
003:   private static char[] vowels = {'a', 'e', 'i', 'o', 'u'};
004:
005:   public static void main(String[] args)
006:   {
007:     System.out.println("Printing vowels as a char[]");
008:     System.out.println(vowels);
009:     System.out.println();
010:     System.out.println("Printing vowels as an Object");
011:     System.out.println((Object)vowels);
012:   } // main
013:
014: } // class PrintlnOverloadDemo
```

Coffee time: 16.16.2   Are you surprised that we can explicitly **cast** to a **superclass**? Could this ever cause a `ClassCastException` to be **thrown**?

427

The first time the array is printed there is a choice of two `System.out.println()` **methods**: the one that takes a `char[]` and, because an array is an object, the one that takes an `Object`. The former is chosen by the **compiler** because it is the most specific, and so the vowels are printed as a string of **characters**.

However, for the second print of the array we have told the compiler, via a **cast**, to treat it as an `Object`, thus we get the version of `System.out.println()` that takes an `Object`. This uses the `toString()` of the array, which produces the characters `[C` to represent `char[]` followed by `@` and the **hexadecimal** unique number of the array.

```
                    Console Input / Output
$ java PrintlnOverloadDemo
Printing vowels as a char[]
aeiou

Printing vowels as an Object
[C@1a46e30
$ _
```

16.16.3 Accidental overload

The **compiler** produces **byte code** to call a **method** with a particular **method interface** based on the **type**s of the **method arguments**. Where there is a choice of matching methods it will choose the most specific one – this decision is made at **compile time**. We also have **dynamic method binding**, thanks to the potential for **instance methods** to **override** others. This means at **run time** the correct **method implementation** is chosen for the method interface which was fixed at compile time.

Here we have a simple (but contrived) example to illustrate a common mistake in which an intended **override** results in an **overloaded method**. A police inspector **has a** name. He or she can interrogate another inspector, and when interrogated just gives his or her title and name.

```
001: public class Inspector
002: {
003:   private final String name;
004:
005:   public Inspector(String requiredName)
006:   {
007:     name = requiredName;
008:   } // Inspector
009:
010:   public String getName()
011:   {
012:     return name;
013:   } // getName
014:
015:   public void interrogate(Inspector suspect)
016:   {
017:     System.out.println("I am Inspector " + getName()
018:                         + ", who are you? " + suspect);
019:   } // interrogate
020:
021:   public String toString()
022:   {
023:     return "I am Inspector " + getName() + "!";
024:   } // toString
```

Finally, we have a **class method** to arrange an inspection between an inspecting officer and a suspect, both of whom are police inspectors!

```
026:   public static void makeInspection(Inspector inspectingOfficer,
027:                                      Inspector suspect)
028:   {
029:     inspectingOfficer.interrogate(suspect);
030:   } // makeInspection
031:
032: } // class Inspector
```

A chief inspector **is a** special case of an inspector, with a posher title.

```
001: public class ChiefInspector extends Inspector
002: {
003:   public ChiefInspector(String name)
004:   {
005:     super(name);
006:   } // ChiefInspector
007:
008:   public void interrogate(ChiefInspector suspect)
009:   {
010:     System.out.println("I am Chief Inspector " + getName()
011:                        + ", who are you? " + suspect);
012:   } // interrogate
013:
014:   public String toString()
015:   {
016:     return "I am Chief Inspector " + getName() + "!";
017:   } // toString
```

Now, let us make three inspections, first via the **class method** and then again directly using the **instance method**.

```
019:   public static void main(String[] args)
020:   {
021:     Inspector clouseau = new Inspector("Clouseau");
022:     ChiefInspector dreyfus = new ChiefInspector("Dreyfus");
023:
024:     Inspector.makeInspection(clouseau, dreyfus);
025:     Inspector.makeInspection(dreyfus, clouseau);
026:     Inspector.makeInspection(dreyfus, dreyfus);
027:     System.out.println();
028:     clouseau.interrogate(dreyfus);
029:     dreyfus.interrogate(clouseau);
030:     dreyfus.interrogate(dreyfus);
031:   } // main
032:
033: } // class ChiefInspector
```

Coffee time: ⸢16.16.3⸣ Before reading on, predict what the output will be. In particular, do you expect the results of the first three interrogations to be the same as the second three?

Are you ready for us to try it?...

```
                         Console Input / Output
$ java ChiefInspector
I am Inspector Clouseau, who are you? I am Chief Inspector Dreyfus!
I am Inspector Dreyfus, who are you? I am Inspector Clouseau!
I am Inspector Dreyfus, who are you? I am Chief Inspector Dreyfus!

I am Inspector Clouseau, who are you? I am Chief Inspector Dreyfus!
I am Inspector Dreyfus, who are you? I am Inspector Clouseau!
I am Chief Inspector Dreyfus, who are you? I am Chief Inspector Dreyfus!
$ _
```

In some of these outputs Chief Inspector Dreyfus is wrongly titled Inspector. Can you explain why? Look carefully at the ChiefInspector code, and you will see an instance method that was intended to **override** one from Inspector, but instead it is an **overloaded method**.

The fact that the **method parameter** is a **subclass** of the one in the **superclass** does not make it the same **method interface**. ChiefInspector thus has two different instance methods with the same name, one **inherit**ed and one added.

Mistakes like that are so common that in Java 5.0 a new feature was introduced to protect against them.

Concept **Inheritance: overriding a method: @Override annotation.** Java 5.0 introduced an idea called **annotation**s. These allow us to provide additional information to the **compiler** which can then be used to help in various ways. In particular, the **override annotation**, @Override, can be written immediately before the heading of an **instance method** that we believe **override**s one from the **superclass**, or is a **method implementation** of an **abstract method** in the superclass. The compiler will complain if this is not the case, thus protecting us from accidentally getting the **method signature** wrong – perhaps misspelling the method name or differently ordering the **method parameter type**s, etc. – thus creating an **overloaded method**.

Let us make a copy of ChiefInspector calling it SafeChiefInspector and add the **override annotation**.

```
001: public class SafeChiefInspector extends Inspector
002: {
...
008:   @Override
009:   public void interrogate(SafeChiefInspector suspect)
010:   {
011:     System.out.println("I am Chief Inspector " + getName()
012:                        + ", who are you? " + suspect);
013:   } // interrogate
...
```

```
                         Console Input / Output
$ javac SafeChiefInspector.java
SafeChiefInspector.java:8: method does not override or implement a method from a
  supertype
  @Override
  ^
1 error
$ _
```

16.16.4   Coursework: Using the @Override annotation

Go through your solutions to the tasks in this chapter and add the @Override **override annotation** to all **instance method**s which **override** another.

Also identify all the places where we should have put it in the example code.

16.17 Concepts covered in this chapter

Here is a list of the concepts that were covered in this chapter, each with a self-test question. You can use this to check you remember them being introduced, and perhaps re-read some of them before going on to the next chapter.

Array	
– partially filled array: deleting an element (p.404)	What two steps are needed to achieve this?

Design	
– UML (p.381)	What is UML short for?
– UML: class diagram (p.381)	In the representation of a class, how are public items distinguished from private ones?

GUI API	
– Color (p.400)	What four values are used to generate a colour?

Inheritance	
Inheritance (p.373)	If the relationship 'A is a B' is modelled by two classes A and B, which is the superclass and which is the subclass?
– invoking the superclass constructor (p.379)	How do we invoke the constructor of the superclass, and when?
– invoking the superclass constructor: implicitly (p.423)	When is this done?
– overriding a method (p.380)	What kinds of method can be overridden? Can the new version have a different body? Different parameters? Different name?
– overriding a method: @Override annotation (p.430)	What simple errors does this protect us from?
– polymorphism (p.390)	If an object is polymorphic, what does that mean? And how do we achieve it?
– polymorphism: dynamic method binding (p.391)	In what sense might a method be dynamically bound? Which types of method have this feature?
– a subclass extends its superclass (p.378)	In what way does a subclass extend its superclass ?
– abstract class (p.385)	How do we make a class abstract, and what can we not do with it when we have?
– abstract method (p.386)	How do we define an abstract method, and when do we? In what sense do we not override an abstract method?
– final methods and classes (p.391)	What does it mean to make a method final, and how do we achieve it? What kinds of method can be made final? What about a final class?
– adding more object state (p.393)	How do we create an extension of a class which has more state?
– adding more instance methods (p.395)	How is this idea related to adding more object state?
– testing for an instance of a class (p.397)	How do we determine if an object is an instance of a particular class?
– casting to a subclass (p.397)	What is the essential difference between a class cast and a primitive type cast?

– is a versus has a (p.406)	Which of the following models 'is a' and which models 'has a'?
	1. `public class DieselTrain extends Train`
	`{ ... }`
	2. `public class Train`
	`{ private Carriage[] carriages; ... }`

Inheritance	
– using an overridden method (p.414)	When might we want to use an overridden method, and how do we?
– constructor chaining (p.423)	What is the purpose of constructor chaining?

Method	
– constructor methods: more than one: using this (p.393)	When do we invoke another constructor from the same class, and how?
– constructor methods: default (p.425)	What exactly is a default constructor, and when do we get one?

Standard API	
– Object (p.422)	All classes, except Object, have something. What is that thing?
– Object: toString() (p.427)	What does this default toString() produce?
– System: out.println(): with any argument (p.427)	Assuming a Point class defined as one might expect, what is the effect of the following code? `System.out.println(new Point(10, 20));`

Chapter 17

Making our own exceptions

Exceptional behaviour
deserves exceptional distinction.

17.1　Chapter aims

The standard **exception class**es are sometimes not quite specific enough to model the exact nature of the exceptions we want to generate, so Java permits us to create our own. This chapter starts by looking at how an **inheritance hierarchy** is used to obtain the many different kinds of exception, before exploring how we can have our own.

The chapter contains the following sections.

Section	Aims	Associated Coursework
17.2 The exception inheritance hierarchy (p.433)	To explain how Java implements the idea of having lots of different kinds of **exception**.	(None.)
17.3 The Date class with its own exceptions (p.435)	To introduce the idea of making our own **exception**s.	Add your own **exception**s to the GreedyChildren example. (p.439)
17.4 The Notional Lottery with exceptions (p.439)	To reinforce the idea of defining our own **exception**s, and further it by having two of our own exception **class**es, where one is a **subclass** of the other.	Add a **subclass** of your own **exception** to the GreedyChildren example. (p.447)

17.2　The exception inheritance hierarchy

AIM: To explain how Java implements the idea of having lots of different kinds of **exception**.

We have already seen that there are many kinds of **exception** that can be created and **thrown**.

Coffee time: ⟨17.2.1⟩
How do you think that Java implements the idea of having many kinds of exception?

433

Concept **Exception: inheritance hierarchy.** All **exception**s in Java are modelled as **instance**s of **class**es. For example, the class `java.lang.Exception` models a very general idea of exception, and `java.lang.ArrayIndexOutOfBoundsException` a much more specific kind. The different kinds of exception are arranged in an **inheritance hierarchy**, with those classes near the top being models of quite general exceptions, and those at the bottom being very specific. An instance of `ArrayIndexOutOfBoundsException` is created when an **array index** is out of the legal range for the **array**. This class is a **subclass** of the more general `java.lang.IndexOutOfBoundsException`. A different subclass of `IndexOutOfBoundsException` is called `java.lang.StringIndexOutOfBoundsException`. Instances of this are created in circumstances such as supplying an illegal **method argument** to the `charAt()` **instance method** of a `String`. The class `IndexOutOfBoundsException` is itself a subclass of `java.lang.RuntimeException`, the kind of exception that Java does not *require* us to **catch**, although we sometimes do, and this class is a subclass of `Exception`.

We can show this relationship in a **UML class diagram**, including the **constructor method**s and some of the **public** instance methods.

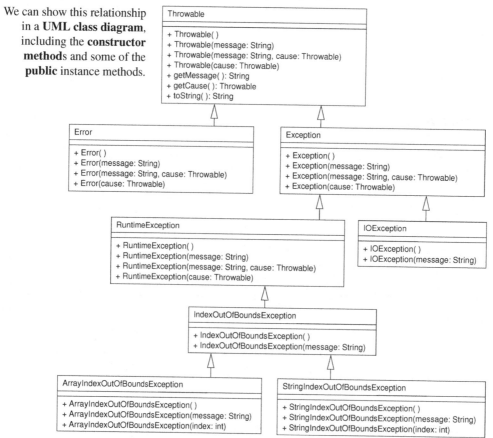

You can see that `Exception` is itself a subclass of something even more general called `java.lang.Throwable`, and there is a separate subclass of `Throwable` called `java.lang.Error`. The class `Throwable` is the **type** of all **object**s that can be **thrown** and handled by catches of a **try statement**. `Error` is the type of `Throwable`s which represent such serious conditions, that most programs do not bother trying to catch them. For example, `java.lang.OutOfMemoryError` is a subclass of `Error`, and an instance of it is thrown when the **virtual machine** has run out of memory to create any more objects. Catching this kind of condition is unlikely to be helpful in most situations, and so Java does not force us to. They are examples of **unchecked exception**s. However, ultimately the programmer knows best, so `Error`s *can* be caught if desired.

Exception is the type of Throwable which represents conditions that should typically be caught at some point. If a **method** contains code that could cause an Exception, or one of its subclasses, to be thrown, then the **compiler** forces the exception to either be caught within the method, or declared in the **throws clause** of the method – they are **checked exception**s.

However, the RuntimeException class (and its subclasses) represents the kind of possible exception which programmers usually avoid in the first place. For example, when **loop**ing an array index over an array, the code would probably be written to use the correct values, and so avoid an ArrayIndexOutOfBoundsException exception. It would be highly inconvenient to *have* to write a **catch clause** or a throws clause even though we know the exceptions are avoided, and so Java relaxes the rule for this subclass – they too are **unchecked exception**s. Of course, this means we must discipline ourselves: especially in code intended for **software reuse**, we *should* write catch or throws clauses if we have not eliminated the possibility of these exceptions!

The diagram above is only a sample. There are over 70 direct subclasses of Exception in the standard classes in Java 7.0, including java.io.IOException – instances of that can be thrown when processing **file**s. There are almost 50 direct subclasses of RuntimeException.

One advantage of this **inheritance hierarchy** is that when we catch exceptions, we can decide how general or specific we need to be. For example, the following fragment of code could cause an ArrayIndexOutOfBoundsException to be thrown in some circumstances, and in other cases a StringIndexOutOfBoundsException.

```
int arrayIndex, stringIndex;
String[] listOfStrings;

... Code here to populate the above array,
... and set arrayIndex and stringIndex.

char c = listOfStrings[arrayIndex].charAt(stringIndex)
```

We can catch any exceptions of type ArrayIndexOutOfBoundsException, caused by arrayIndex having a bad value. Alternatively we can catch exceptions caused by the value of stringIndex being unsuitable, that is StringIndexOutOfBoundsException exceptions. If we wish, we can have two **catch clause**s, one for each. However, the exception inheritance hierarchy allows us the option of having one catch clause to deal with both, if that is appropriate, by catching IndexOutOfBoundsException.

Coffee time: 17.2.2   Where does IllegalArgumentException fit into the **inheritance hierarchy**? How many **constructor method**s does it have? Find out by looking at the **API** on-line documentation.

17.3   Example: The **Date** class with its own exceptions

AIM: To introduce the idea of making our own **exceptions**.

In this section we revisit briefly the Date class from Section 15.8 starting on page 354 and improve it by creating and using our own **exception class**.

Concept **Exception: making our own exception classes.** Another advantage of **exceptions** being arranged in an **inheritance hierarchy** is that we can easily make our own exception **classes**. Sometimes, the leaf classes at the bottom of the standard exception inheritance hierarchy tree are not quite specific enough to suit the errors that can occur in our own code. They are, obviously, **design**ed to be appropriate to the standard classes. So, whenever we wish to **throw** an exception, we should ask ourselves whether there is a standard exception that nicely captures the meaning of the error, and if not, we should make our own exception class that does.

Making a new exception class is very easy. All we need to do is choose one of the standard classes which is closest to characterizing what we want, and make a **subclass** of it. Often this standard class will be either `java.lang.Exception` itself or `java.lang.RuntimeException`. We would choose the former if we want ours to be **checked exception**s, or the latter if we want them to be **unchecked exception**s because we believe the circumstances leading to them can be and typically should be avoided.

Most often, our own exception classes contain nothing but four **constructor method**s, one with no **method parameter**s, one which takes a `String` for the message associated with the exception, one which has both a message and a `Throwable` **exception cause**, and one which has only a cause. These simply invoke the corresponding constructor method from the **superclass**.

We present the `DateException` class here, describe the changes we need to make to the `Date` class and develop a modified version of the `DateDifference` program that **catch**es our new exceptions.

17.3.1 The `DateException` class

To make our own `DateException` class, we will **extend** `RuntimeException`. So **instance**s of `DateException` will also be instances of `RuntimeException`, and thus be **unchecked exception**s – programmers will not be forced to **catch** them. We have chosen this because we believe that all the erroneous conditions are avoidable and typically will be avoided.

```
001: // Exceptions to be used with the Date class.
002: public class DateException extends RuntimeException
003: {
004:   // Create DateException with no message and no cause.
005:   public DateException()
006:   {
007:     super();
008:   } // DateException
009:
010:
011:   // Create DateException with message but no cause.
012:   public DateException(String message)
013:   {
014:     super(message);
015:   } // DateException
016:
017:
018:   // Create DateException with message and cause.
019:   public DateException(String message, Throwable cause)
020:   {
021:     super(message, cause);
022:   } // DateException
023:
024:
025:   // Create DateException with no message but with cause.
026:   public DateException(Throwable cause)
027:   {
028:     super(cause);
029:   } // DateException
030:
031: } // class DateException
```

Coffee time: [17.3.1]
As an aside, think about programs which read and/or write **files**. Can errors occur in those scenarios which cannot be avoided by the programmer? Should the **exceptions** thus thrown be **checked exceptions** or unchecked? (Hint: look at the **UML class diagram**!)

Coffee time: [17.3.2]
Why do we have to write these **constructor method**s? Do `DateException` **object**s have any **instance method**s?

17.3.2 The `Date` class

Our new version of the `Date` **class** is the same as the one from Section 15.8 starting on page 354, except that most occurrences of `Exception` are changed to `DateException`. It is otherwise so similar that we do not list it here.

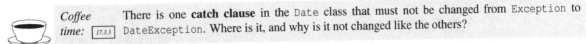

Coffee time: 17.3.3 There is one **catch clause** in the `Date` class that must not be changed from `Exception` to `DateException`. Where is it, and why is it not changed like the others?

Coffee time: 17.3.4 There were some places in the `Date` class from Section 15.8 where we had to catch an `Exception`, even though we knew that one would never be **thrown**. Is this still necessary with our new version?

Coffee time: 17.3.5 Some `Date` instance methods, such as `daysFrom()`, throw a `NullPointerException` when their `Date` **method argument** is the **null reference**. Should these be caught and turned into `DateExceptions`, or left as `NullPointerExceptions`?

17.3.3 The `DateDifference` class

Our new version of the `DateDifference` program is similar to the one found in Section 15.9 on page 367. As well as changing it to use `DateException` we have structured it differently, with **nested try statements**, so that the code to report to **standard error** occurs only once.

```
001: // Obtain two dates in day/month/year format from first and second arguments.
002: // Report how many days there are from first to second,
003: // which is negative if first date is earliest one.
004: public class DateDifference
005: {
006:   public static void main(String[] args)
007:   {
008:     try
009:     {
010:       try
011:       {
012:         Date date1 = new Date(args[0]);
013:         Date date2 = new Date(args[1]);
014:         if (args.length > 2)
015:           throw new ArrayIndexOutOfBoundsException(args.length + " is > 2");
016:         System.out.println("From " + date1 + " to " + date2 + " is "
017:                            + date1.daysFrom(date2) + " days");
018:       } // try
019:       catch (ArrayIndexOutOfBoundsException exception)
020:       {
021:         System.out.println("Please supply exactly two dates");
022:         throw exception;
023:       } // catch
024:       catch (DateException exception)
025:       {
026:         System.out.println("One of your dates has a problem.");
027:         System.out.println(exception.getMessage());
028:         throw exception;
029:       } // catch
030:       catch (Exception exception)
031:       {
032:         System.out.println("Something unforeseen has happened!");
033:         System.out.println(exception.getMessage());
034:         throw exception;
```

```
035:        } // catch
036:    } // try
037:    catch (Exception exception)
038:    {
039:        // All exceptions have been already reported to System.out.
040:        System.err.println(exception);
041:        if (exception.getCause() != null)
042:          System.err.println("Caused by: " + exception.getCause());
043:    } // catch
044:  } // main
045:
046: } // class DateDifference
```

Coffee time: Notwithstanding that it sounds like a contradiction in terms, can you foresee what could be an unforeseen **exception**?!

17.3.6

17.3.4 Trying it

Let us test the new `DateDifference` program in the same way as we did before. You can compare the output here with that from Section 15.9.1 on page 367.

Console Input / Output
```
$ java DateDifference 30/03/2014 30/03/2015
From 30/3/2014 to 30/3/2015 is 365 days
$ java DateDifference 30/03/2015 30/03/2014
From 30/3/2015 to 30/3/2014 is -365 days
$ _
```

Console Input / Output
```
$ java DateDifference
Please supply exactly two dates
java.lang.ArrayIndexOutOfBoundsException: 0
$ java DateDifference 30/03/2014
Please supply exactly two dates
java.lang.ArrayIndexOutOfBoundsException: 1
$ java DateDifference 30/03/2014 30/03/2015 ExtraArgument
Please supply exactly two dates
java.lang.ArrayIndexOutOfBoundsException: 3 is > 2
$ java DateDifference 30/03/2015 "Hello mum"
One of your dates has a problem.
Date 'Hello mum' is not in day/month/year format
DateException: Date 'Hello mum' is not in day/month/year format
Caused by: java.lang.NumberFormatException: For input string: "Hello mum"
$ java DateDifference 30/03 "Hello mum"
One of your dates has a problem.
Date '30/03' is not in day/month/year format
DateException: Date '30/03' is not in day/month/year format
Caused by: java.lang.ArrayIndexOutOfBoundsException: 2
$ java DateDifference 30/03/2015 03/30/2015
One of your dates has a problem.
Month 30 must be from 1 to 12
DateException: Month 30 must be from 1 to 12
$ _
```

Console Input / Output
```
$ java DateDifference 30/03/2015 2015/03/30
One of your dates has a problem.
Year 30 must be >= 1753
DateException: Year 30 must be >= 1753
$ _
```

Console Input / Output
```
$ java DateDifference 30/03/2015 30/2/2015
One of your dates has a problem.
Day 30 must be from 1 to 28 for 2/2015
DateException: Day 30 must be from 1 to 28 for 2/2015
$ _
```

17.3.5   A sneaky test?

And finally, what do you think of this sneaky test?

```
001: // Test DateDifference with a null arguments array!
002: public class DateDifferenceUnforeseenTest
003: {
004:    public static void main(String[] args)
005:    {
006:       DateDifference.main(null);
007:    } // main
008:
009: } // class DateDifferenceUnforeseenTest
```

Console Input / Output
$ **java DateDifferenceUnforeseenTest**
Something unforeseen has happened!
null
java.lang.NullPointerException
$ _

17.3.6   Coursework: `GreedyChildren` with exceptions

Copy the **class**es `GreedyChild` and `IceCreamParlour` from the example in Section 11.3 starting on page 201. Add two new classes `GreedyChildException` and `IceCreamParlourException`, both **subclass**es of `RuntimeException`. These should be able to handle causes, even though you might not need to use them at this stage.

Identify all the places in `GreedyChild` and `IceCreamParlour` where the **method**s might be given bad **method argument**s, and make them **throw** appropriate **exception**s. (Hint: bear in mind that some of these arguments are **reference**s.) Recall that Java does not force you to have **throws clause**s for **unchecked exception**s, but you nevertheless should do so for this task when such are possible.

Test the new features of each class using dedicated programs called `TestGreedyChildExceptions` and `TestIceCreamParlourExceptions` respectively. These should contain separate **try statement**s for each possible exceptional situation.

17.4   Example: The Notional Lottery with exceptions

AIM: To reinforce the idea of defining our own **exception**s, and further it by having two of our own exception **class**es, where one is a **subclass** of the other.

In this section we revisit the Notional Lottery example, with **exception**s in mind. Previously the program was used as a vehicle to explore **inheritance**, but we might well have chosen to use exceptions throughout it. For example, when the **graphical user interface** is developed, it will accept input from the end user, and the program will have to make checks that such input is valid. One way of doing this would be to write the checking code in the graphical user interface **class**es, but perhaps a better way will be to have the model classes check the validity and **throw** exceptions which the graphical user interface classes will **catch**.

Here we shall focus only on `BallContainer` and one of its **subclass**es, `Machine`. First we develop the classes `BallContainerException` and `MachineException`. Then we alter the classes `BallContainer` and `Machine`, so that they use these exceptions. Finally, we present a test program, `TestMachineExceptions`.

17.4.1   The `BallContainerException` class

The `BallContainerException` class is a subclass of `Exception` and thus **instance**s of it are **checked exception**s. An instance will be **thrown** when an invalid operation is performed on a `BallContainer` **object**, such as attempting to remove a ball when the container is empty.

The code is much the same as that for `DateException` from Section 17.3.1 on page 436, except that it is called `BallContainerException`! Also, it is a **subclass** of `Exception` rather than `RuntimeException`.

```
001: // Exceptions to be used with the BallContainer class.
002: public class BallContainerException extends Exception
003: {
004:     // Create BallContainerException with no message and no cause.
005:     public BallContainerException()
006:     {
007:       super();
008:     } // BallContainerException
009:
010:
011:     // Create BallContainerException with message but no cause.
012:     public BallContainerException(String message)
013:     {
014:       super(message);
015:     } // BallContainerException
016:
017:
018:     // Create BallContainerException with message and cause.
019:     public BallContainerException(String message, Throwable cause)
020:     {
021:       super(message, cause);
022:     } // BallContainerException
023:
024:
025:     // Create BallContainerException with no message but with cause.
026:     public BallContainerException(Throwable cause)
027:     {
028:       super(cause);
029:     } // BallContainerException
030:
031: } // class BallContainerException
```

17.4.2 The `MachineException` class

The `MachineException` **class** is a **subclass** of `BallContainerException`. An **instance** of this will be thrown when an invalid operation which is specific to machine-like behaviour, is performed on a `Machine` **object**. For example, attempting to *eject* a ball when the machine is empty. Recall that `ejectBall()` is an **instance method** of `Machine`, but not `BallContainer`.

`BallContainerExceptions` will be thrown by code inside the `BallContainer` class whereas `MachineExceptions` will be thrown by code inside the `Machine` class. As a `Machine` also **is a** `BallContainer`, this means that a `Machine` **object** will be able to **throw** both kinds of **exception** in different circumstances.

The code is much the same as that for `BallContainerException` from page 440 except that it is called `MachineException`, and it is not a direct subclass of `Exception`.

```
001: // Exceptions to be used with the Machine class.
002: public class MachineException extends BallContainerException
003: {
004:     // Create MachineException with no message and no cause.
005:     public MachineException()
006:     {
007:       super();
008:     } // MachineException
009:
010:
011:     // Create MachineException with message but no cause.
012:     public MachineException(String message)
013:     {
014:       super(message);
015:     } // MachineException
016:
017:
018:     // Create MachineException with message and cause.
019:     public MachineException(String message, Throwable cause)
020:     {
021:       super(message, cause);
022:     } // MachineException
023:
024:
025:     // Create MachineException with no message but with cause.
026:     public MachineException(Throwable cause)
027:     {
028:       super(cause);
029:     } // MachineException
030:
031: } // class MachineException
```

17.4.3 The `BallContainer` class

The first part of the new version of `BallContainer` is the same as the previous.

```
001: // Representation of a container of balls for the lottery,
002: // with a fixed size and zero or more balls in a certain order.
003: public abstract class BallContainer
004: {
005:   // The name of the BallContainer.
006:   private final String name;
007:
008:   // The balls contained in the BallContainer.
009:   private final Ball[] balls;
010:
011:   // The number of balls contained in the BallContainer.
012:   // These are stored in balls, indexes 0 to noOfBalls - 1.
013:   private int noOfBalls;
```

When a `BallContainer` is **construct**ed, we check that the given size is sensible. It must not be negative, indeed it only makes sense to have room for at least one ball. For example, the end user may well wish to have a game in which only one ball is ejected, which means the `Rack` would have a size of one. Any number **less than** one is silly, and so we get the **constructor method** to **throw** a `BallContainerException` if it is.

```
016:   // Constructor is given the name and size.
017:   public BallContainer(String requiredName, int requiredSize)
018:          throws BallContainerException
019:   {
020:     if (requiredSize < 1)
021:       throw new BallContainerException("Size must be at least 1");
022:     name = requiredName;
023:     balls = new Ball[requiredSize];
024:     noOfBalls = 0;
025:   } // BallContainer
```

The **instance method**s `getName()` and `getType()` are the same as before.

```
028:   // Returns the BallContainer's name.
029:   public String getName()
030:   {
031:     return name;
032:   } // getName
033:
034:
035:   // Returns the name of the type of BallContainer.
036:   public abstract String getType();
```

Previously, for `getBall()`, if the given **index** was not in range, the instance method **return**ed the **null reference**. The version here **throws** an **exception** instead.

```
039:   // Returns the Ball at the given index in the BallContainer.
040:   // Throws exception if that index is not in the range 0 to noOfBalls - 1.
041:   public Ball getBall(int index) throws BallContainerException
042:   {
043:     if (noOfBalls == 0)
044:       throw new BallContainerException("Cannot get ball: is empty");
045:
046:     if (index < 0 || index >= noOfBalls)
047:       throw new BallContainerException
048:                   ("Get ball at " + index + ": not in range 0.."
049:                    + (noOfBalls - 1));
050:     return balls[index];
051:   } // getBall;
```

The **instance methods** getNoOfBalls() and getSize() are the same as before.

```
054:   // Returns the number of balls in the BallContainer.
055:   public int getNoOfBalls()
056:   {
057:     return noOfBalls;
058:   } // getNoOfBalls
059:
060:
061:   // Returns the size of the BallContainer.
062:   public int getSize()
063:   {
064:     return balls.length;
065:   } // getSize
```

Previously, for addBall(), if the container was full we simply ignored the request.

```
068:   // Adds the given ball into the BallContainer, at the next highest unused
069:   // index position. Throws exception if the BallContainer is full.
070:   public void addBall(Ball ball) throws BallContainerException
071:   {
072:     if (noOfBalls == balls.length)
073:       throw new BallContainerException("Cannot add ball: is full");
074:     balls[noOfBalls] = ball;
075:     noOfBalls++;
076:   } // addBall
```

Similarly, swapBalls() did nothing if the two indices were not valid.

```
079:   // Swaps the balls at the two given index positions.
080:   // Throws exception if either index is not in the range 0 to noOfBalls - 1.
081:   public void swapBalls(int index1, int index2) throws BallContainerException
082:   {
083:     if (noOfBalls == 0)
084:       throw new BallContainerException("Cannot swap balls: is empty");
085:
086:     if (index1 < 0 || index1 >= noOfBalls)
087:       throw new BallContainerException
088:               ("Swap ball at " + index1 + ": not in range 0.."
089:               + (noOfBalls - 1));
090:
091:     if (index2 < 0 || index2 >= noOfBalls)
092:       throw new BallContainerException
093:               ("Swap ball at " + index2 + ": not in range 0.."
094:               + (noOfBalls - 1));
095:
096:     Ball thatWasAtIndex1 = balls[index1];
097:     balls[index1] = balls[index2];
098:     balls[index2] = thatWasAtIndex1;
099:   } // swapBalls;
```

Also, removeBall() previously had no effect if the container was already empty.

```
102:   // Removes the Ball at the highest used index position.
103:   // Throws exception if the BallContainer is empty.
104:   public void removeBall() throws BallContainerException
105:   {
106:     if (noOfBalls <= 0)
107:       throw new BallContainerException("Cannot remove ball: is empty");
108:     noOfBalls--;
109:   } // removeBall
```

Finally, `toString()` is the same as before (except that in Section 16.16.3 on page 430 we learnt that we ought to use the **override annotation**).

```
112:    // Mainly for testing.
113:    @Override
114:    public String toString()
115:    {
116:       String result = getType() + " " + name + "(<=" + balls.length + ")";
117:       for (int index = 0; index < noOfBalls; index++)
118:         result += String.format("%n%d %s", index, balls[index]);
119:       return result;
120:    } // toString
121:
122: } // class BallContainer
```

17.4.4 The `Machine` class

The `Machine` **class** has validity checks that are specific to machines. To start with, it would not make sense to have a machine with a size **less than** two!

```
001: // Representation of a lottery machine,
002: // with the facility for a randomly chosen ball to be ejected.
003: public class Machine extends BallContainer
004: {
005:    // Constructor is given the name and size.
006:    public Machine(String name, int size) throws BallContainerException
007:    {
008:      super(name, size);
009:      if (size < 2)
010:        throw new MachineException("Size must be at least 2");
011:    } // Machine
```

Coffee time: `17.4.1`
What would be the result of the code `new Machine("Empty", 0)`? What would be the result of `new Machine("Single", 1)`? What if we were to swap the two **statements** in the constructor method?

Coffee time: `17.4.2`
Why did we declare that the **constructor method throws** `BallContainerException` rather than `MachineException`? What would happen if we accidentally said it throws `MachineException`? What if `BallContainerException` was a **subclass** of `RuntimeException` rather than `Exception`?

The **instance method** `getType()` is the same as before.

```
014:    // Returns the name of the type of BallContainer.
015:    public String getType()
016:    {
017:      return "Lottery machine";
018:    } // getType
```

Previously, `ejectBall()` **return**ed the **null reference** if the machine was empty. Here instead, we **catch** the `BallContainerException` thrown by `getBall()`, and **throw** a `MachineException`, passing the `BallContainerException` as the cause of the `MachineException`.

```
021:    // Randomly chooses a ball in the machine, and ejects it.
022:    // The ejected ball is returned. If the machine is empty then
023:    // it throws an exception.
024:    public Ball ejectBall() throws MachineException
025:    {
026:      try
027:      {
028:        // Math.random() * getNoOfBalls yields a number
029:        // which is >= 0 and < number of balls.
030:        int ejectedBallIndex = (int) (Math.random() * getNoOfBalls());
031:
032:        Ball ejectedBall = getBall(ejectedBallIndex);
033:
```

443

```
034:          swapBalls(ejectedBallIndex, getNoOfBalls() - 1);
035:          removeBall();
036:
037:          return ejectedBall;
038:       } // try
039:       catch (BallContainerException exception)
040:       {
041:          throw new MachineException("Cannot eject ball: is empty", exception);
042:       } // catch
043:    } // ejectBall
044:
045: } // class Machine
```

17.4.5 The `TestMachineExceptions` class

To make testing easy, our `TestMachineExceptions` program is carefully **design**ed to take a number of **command line arguments** and go through a number of stages.

```
001: import java.awt.Color;
002:
003: /* For testing BallContainer and Machine with BallContainerException and
004:    MachineException. Depending on the values given, it will produce exceptions
005:    at different points, which we catch and print out. By running it with
006:    different values, we are able to test every possible throw statement in
007:    BallContainer and Machine.
008: */
009: public class TestMachineExceptions
010: {
011:    public static void main(String[] args)
012:    {
013:       int machineSize = Integer.parseInt(args[0]);
014:       int fillCount = Integer.parseInt(args[1]);
015:       int findIndex = Integer.parseInt(args[2]);
016:       int removeCount1 = Integer.parseInt(args[3]);
017:       int swapIndex1 = Integer.parseInt(args[4]);
018:       int swapIndex2 = Integer.parseInt(args[5]);
019:       int removeCount2 = Integer.parseInt(args[6]);
020:       int ejectCount = Integer.parseInt(args[7]);
021:
022:       try
023:       {
024:          System.out.println("Creating machine sized " + machineSize);
025:          Machine machine = new Machine("Test4U", machineSize);
026:
027:          System.out.println("Filling with " + fillCount + " balls");
028:          for (int i = 1; i <= fillCount; i++)
029:             machine.addBall(new Ball(i, Color.red));
030:
031:          System.out.println("Finding ball at " + findIndex);
032:          machine.getBall(findIndex);
033:
034:          System.out.println("Adding another ball");
035:          machine.addBall(new Ball(fillCount + 1, Color.red));
036:
```

```
037:        System.out.println("Removing " + removeCount1 + " balls");
038:        for (int i = 1; i <= removeCount1; i++)
039:          machine.removeBall();
040:
041:        System.out.println("Swapping balls at " + swapIndex1
042:                           + " and " + swapIndex2);
043:        machine.swapBalls(swapIndex1, swapIndex2);
044:
045:        System.out.println("Removing " + removeCount2 + " balls");
046:        for (int i = 1; i <= removeCount2; i++)
047:          machine.removeBall();
048:
049:        System.out.println("Ejecting " + ejectCount + " balls");
050:        for (int i = 1; i <= ejectCount; i++)
051:          machine.ejectBall();
052:
053:      } // try
054:      catch (Exception exception)
055:      {
056:        System.out.println("Got exception " + exception);
057:        if (exception.getCause() != null)
058:          System.out.println("Caused by: " + exception.getCause());
059:      } // catch
060:    } // main
061:
062: } // class TestMachineExceptions
```

17.4.6 Trying it

In the table below we have planned **test data** for 10 tests. Each has a value for the various **command line argument**s of TestMachineExceptions. The number -1 is given for values that will not be used by the program because it will **throw** an **exception** before that point. We also state the expected results, within which BCE and ME are short for BallContainerException and MachineException respectively.

No	Size	Fill	Find	Rem	Swap	Rem	Eject	Expected result
1	0	-1	-1	-1	-1, -1	-1	-1	BCE: Size must be at least 1
2	1	-1	-1	-1	-1, -1	-1	-1	ME: Size must be at least 2
3	5	0	1	-1	-1, -1	-1	-1	BCE: Cannot get ball: is empty
4	5	5	5	-1	-1, -1	-1	-1	BCE: Get ball at 5: not in range 0..4
5	5	5	4	-1	-1, -1	-1	-1	BCE: Cannot add ball: is full
6	5	1	0	2	0, 0	-1	-1	BCE: Cannot swap balls: is empty
7	5	4	3	0	-1, 0	-1	-1	BCE: Swap ball at -1: not in range 0..4
8	5	4	3	0	0, 5	-1	-1	BCE: Swap ball at 5: not in range 0..4
9	5	3	2	0	0, 1	5	-1	BCE: Cannot remove ball: is empty
10	5	3	2	0	0, 1	0	5	ME: Cannot eject ball: is empty

For the first test, we should get a BallContainerException, with the message "Size must be at least 1".

```
                    Console Input / Output
$ java TestMachineExceptions 0 -1 -1 -1 -1 -1 -1 -1
Creating machine sized 0
Got exception BallContainerException: Size must be at least 1
$ _
```

For the second test, we should get a MachineException, with the message "Size must be at least 2".

```
Console Input / Output
$ java TestMachineExceptions 1 -1 -1 -1 -1 -1 -1 -1
Creating machine sized 1
Got exception MachineException: Size must be at least 2
$ _
```

For the third test, we should get a BallContainerException, with the message "Cannot get ball: is empty".

```
Console Input / Output
$ java TestMachineExceptions 5 0 1 -1 -1 -1 -1 -1
Creating machine sized 5
Filling with 0 balls
Finding ball at 1
Got exception BallContainerException: Cannot get ball: is empty
$ _
```

For the fourth test, we should get a BallContainerException, with the message "Get ball at 5: not in range 0..4".

```
Console Input / Output
$ java TestMachineExceptions 5 5 5 -1 -1 -1 -1 -1
Creating machine sized 5
Filling with 5 balls
Finding ball at 5
Got exception BallContainerException: Get ball at 5: not in range 0..4
$ _
```

For the fifth test, we should get a BallContainerException, with the message "Cannot add ball: is full".

```
Console Input / Output
$ java TestMachineExceptions 5 5 4 -1 -1 -1 -1 -1
Creating machine sized 5
Filling with 5 balls
Finding ball at 4
Adding another ball
Got exception BallContainerException: Cannot add ball: is full
$ _
```

For the sixth test, we should get a BallContainerException, with the message "Cannot swap balls: is empty".

```
Console Input / Output
$ java TestMachineExceptions 5 1 0 2 0 0 -1 -1
Creating machine sized 5
Filling with 1 balls
Finding ball at 0
Adding another ball
Removing 2 balls
Swapping balls at 0 and 0
Got exception BallContainerException: Cannot swap balls: is empty
$ _
```

For the seventh test, we should get a BallContainerException, with the message "Swap ball at -1: not in range 0..4".

```
Console Input / Output
$ java TestMachineExceptions 5 4 3 0 -1 0 -1 -1
Creating machine sized 5
Filling with 4 balls
Finding ball at 3
Adding another ball
Removing 0 balls
Swapping balls at -1 and 0
Got exception BallContainerException: Swap ball at -1: not in range 0..4
$ _
```

For the eighth test, we should get a BallContainerException, with the message "Swap ball at 5: not in range 0..4".

```
Console Input / Output
$ java TestMachineExceptions 5 4 3 0 0 5 -1 -1
Creating machine sized 5
Filling with 4 balls
Finding ball at 3
Adding another ball
Removing 0 balls
Swapping balls at 0 and 5
Got exception BallContainerException: Swap ball at 5: not in range 0..4
$ _
```

For the ninth test, we should get a BallContainerException, with the message "Cannot remove ball: is empty".

```
Console Input / Output
$ java TestMachineExceptions 5 3 2 0 0 1 5 -1
Creating machine sized 5
Filling with 3 balls
Finding ball at 2
Adding another ball
Removing 0 balls
Swapping balls at 0 and 1
Removing 5 balls
Got exception BallContainerException: Cannot remove ball: is empty
$ _
```

For the tenth test, we should get a MachineException, with the message "Cannot eject ball: is empty". This one also has a cause.

```
Console Input / Output
$ java TestMachineExceptions 5 3 2 0 0 1 0 5
Creating machine sized 5
Filling with 3 balls
Finding ball at 2
Adding another ball
Removing 0 balls
Swapping balls at 0 and 1
Removing 0 balls
Ejecting 5 balls
Got exception MachineException: Cannot eject ball: is empty
Caused by: BallContainerException: Cannot get ball: is empty
$ _
```

Coffee time: 17.4.3
Explain why this tenth test result has a cause.

Coffee time: 17.4.4
To the outside world, it may seem a bit odd that attempting to construct a Machine of size zero yields a BallContainerException, whereas for size one we get a MachineException. How could we fix this so that both cases yield a MachineException with an appropriate message? (Hint: try.)

17.4.7 Coursework: MobileIceCreamParlour with exceptions

Now we have a **subclass** of IceCreamParlour representing what is, in effect, an ice cream van!

```
001: // An IceCreamParlour with the additional feature of needing to use fuel.
002: public class MobileIceCreamParlour extends IceCreamParlour
003: {
004:    // The amount of fuel left in the tank.
005:    private double fuelLeft = 0;
006:
```

447

```
007:
008:     // Construct a mobile ice cream parlour -- given the required name.
009:     public MobileIceCreamParlour(String name)
010:     {
011:       super(name);
012:     } // MobileIceCreamParlour
013:
014:
015:     // Put fuel in the tank.
016:     public void obtainFuel(double amount)
017:     {
018:       fuelLeft += amount;
019:     } // obtainFuel
020:
021:
022:     // Use some fuel by driving.
023:     public void drive(double desiredFuelUsed)
024:     {
025:       double fuelUsed = desiredFuelUsed <= fuelLeft ? desiredFuelUsed : fuelLeft;
026:       fuelLeft -= fuelUsed;
027:     } // drive
028:
029:
030:     // Return a String giving the name and state.
031:     @Override
032:     public String toString()
033:     {
034:       return super.toString() + "[fuel " + fuelLeft +"]";
035:     } // toString
036:
037: } // class MobileIceCreamParlour
```

Create a subclass of `IceCreamParlourException` called `MobileIceCreamParlourException`. Implement the above `MobileIceCreamParlour` **class**, but make it **throw** suitable **exception**s. Test this using a program called `TestMobileIceCreamParlourExceptions`.

17.5 Concepts covered in this chapter

Here is a list of the concepts that were covered in this chapter, each with a self-test question. You can use this to check you remember them being introduced, and perhaps re-read some of them before going on to the next chapter.

Exception	
– inheritance hierarchy (p.434)	What is the superclass of `Exception`? Which other class shares this parent? What is special about `RuntimeException`?
– making our own exception classes (p.435)	How many constructors do our own exception classes typically have, and what are they?

Chapter 18

Files

18.1 Chapter aims

In Section 11.2.3 on page 188 we met the **class** Scanner, which can be used to read input **data**. Scanner can be simple and convenient at times, and at some point you should get to know more about it by reading its **application program interface** (**API**) documentation. However, in this chapter we shall study the more fundamental aspects of **files**, upon which Scanner builds its behaviour. In particular, we look at reading **byte**s, **character**s and lines from **text file**s, writing the same, and also reading from and writing to **binary file**s.

The chapter contains the following sections.

Section	Aims	Associated Coursework
18.2 Counting bytes from standard input (p.450)	To introduce the principle of reading **byte**s from **standard input** using InputStream, meet the **try finally statement** and see that an **assignment statement** is actually an **expression** – and can be used as such *when appropriate*. We also meet IOException and briefly talk about initial values of **variable**s.	Write a program to produce a **check sum** of the **standard input**. (p.454)
18.3 Counting characters from standard input (p.456)	To introduce the principle of reading **character**s, instead of **byte**s, from **standard input**, using InputStreamReader.	Write a program to count the number of **words** in its **standard input**. (p.458)
18.4 Numbering lines from standard input (p.459)	To introduce the principle of reading lines from **standard input**, using BufferedReader.	Write a program to delete a field in tab separated text from the **standard input**. (p.460)
18.5 Numbering lines from text file to text file (p.461)	To introduce the principle of reading from a **text file** and writing to another, using BufferedReader with FileReader and PrintWriter with FileWriter. We also meet FileInputStream, OutputStream, FileOutputStream and OutputStreamWriter.	Write a program to delete a field in tab separated text from a **file**, with the results in another file. (p.467)

Section	Aims	Associated Coursework
18.6 Numbering lines from and to anywhere (p.467)	To illustrate that reading from **text files** and from **standard input** is essentially the same thing, as is writing to **text files** and to **standard output**. We also look at testing for the existence of a **file** using the File **class**, and revisit PrintWriter and PrintStream.	Write a program to delete a field in tab separated text either from **standard input** or a **file**, with the results going to either **standard output** or another file. (p.471)
18.7 Text photographs (p.471)	To see an example of reading **binary files**, where we did not choose the **file format**. This includes the process of turning **bytes** into **ints**, using a **shift operator** and an **integer bitwise operator**.	Write a program to encode a **binary file** as an **ASCII text file**, so that it can be sent in an email. (p.477)
18.8 Contour points (p.479)	To show an example of writing and reading **binary files** where we choose the **data** format, using DataOutputStream and DataInputStream **classes**.	Add features to some existing model **class**es so they can be written and read back from **binary files**. (p.483)

18.2 Example: Counting bytes from standard input

AIM:
To introduce the principle of reading **bytes** from **standard input** using InputStream, meet the **try finally statement** and see that an **assignment statement** is actually an **expression** – and can be used as such *when appropriate*. We also meet IOException and briefly talk about initial values of **variable**s.

We begin with a program that reads the **standard input** until it is finished, and then reports how many **bytes** it contained, and how many of each byte value, for those that appeared at least once. This feature could be useful in an **operating environment** in which the user can redirect standard input, so that it comes from a **file**, or from the output of a **run**ning program, and so see the profile of the bytes in that file or output.

We start by observing that file operations are prone to all sorts of **exception**al circumstances.

Concept **File IO API: IOException.** When processing **files**, there is much potential for things to go wrong. For example, attempting to read a file that does not exist, or the end user running out of file space while writing a file, or the **operating system** experiencing a disk or network filestore problem, and so on. As a result, most of the operations we can perform on files in Java are capable of **throw**ing an **exception**, of the **type** java.io.IOException. As you might expect, there are many **subclass**es of IOException, including java.io.FileNotFoundException.

IOException is itself a direct **subclass** of java.lang.Exception, rather than java.lang.RuntimeException and thus **instance**s of it are **checked exception**s, that is, we must write **catch clause**s or **throws clause**s for them. This is because the errors which cause them are not generally avoidable by writing code.

Our program will read the **data** from the standard input, byte by byte, and process them. This will require the use of an InputStream, and the typical way we use it appropriately exploits the fact that an **assignment statement** is an **expression**.

Concept **Statement: assignment statement: is an expression.** In Java, the **assignment statement** is actually an **expression**. The = symbol is an **operator**, which takes a **variable** as its left **operand**, and an expression as its right operand. It evaluates the expression, assigns it to the variable, *and then* yields the value of the expression as its result.

This allows us to write *horrible* code, such as the following.

```
int x = 10, y = 20, z;
int result = (z = x * y) + (y = z * 2);
```

This is an example of the more general idea of **side effect expression**s – expressions that change the value of some variables while they are being **evaluate**d. Generally speaking, side effect expressions are dangerous, as their use may lead to code that is difficult to understand and hence maintain – as the above example illustrates!

However, there are a few appropriate uses of treating assignment statements as expressions. One is when we wish to assign the same value to a number of variables in one go.

```
x = y = z = 10;
```

Unlike most operators, = has **right associativity**, which means the above example is the same as

```
x = (y = (z = 10));
```

and so makes sense. However, situations where we wish to give several variables the same value at once are not actually very common.

Coffee time: 18.2.1   What is the value of `result` in the example from the above concept?

There is a new piece of Java language that we need to know about before we look at `InputStream`.

Concept **Statement: try statement: with finally.** The **try statement** may optionally be given a **finally block**, which is a piece of code that will be **execute**d at the end of the whole try statement, regardless of whether the **try block** successfully completes, or if a **catch clause** is executed, or if control is being **thrown** out of the try statement.

The general form of a **try finally statement** is as follows.

```
try
{
    ... Code here that might cause an exception to happen.
} // try
catch (SomeException exception)
{
    ... Code here to deal with SomeException types of exception.
} // catch
catch (AnotherException exception)
{
    ... Code here to deal with AnotherException types of exception.
} // catch
... more catch clauses as required.
finally
{
    ... Code here that will be run, no matter what,
    ... as the last thing the statement does.
} // finally
```

Concept **File IO API: `InputStream`.** The basic building block for reading **data** in Java, is the **class** `java.io.InputStream`. This provides a view of the data as a **byte stream** – a continuous sequence of **byte**s.

The simplest way to access these bytes, one by one, is via the `read()` **instance method**. This takes no **method arguments** and **return**s the next byte from the stream. However, if there are no more bytes, because all of them

451

have been read (or there was none in the first place), then it returns the number −1 instead. If something goes wrong during the read, then an IOException is **thrown**.

The value returned by read() must be able to distinguish −1 from the byte value 255, which is the same as −1 in 8-bit number representation. For this reason, the result is actually an **int** in the range −1 to 255, rather than a **byte**.

As an example, here is possible skeleton code to process all the data in an InputStream. This is another appropriate use of treating an **assignment statement** as an **expression**: we have a **loop** which terminates when the result of some expression is a certain value, and we also want to use that result inside the body of the loop. Notice that we need to put brackets around the assignment statement; this is because = has a lower **operator precedence** than the != **operator**.

```java
InputStream inputData = null;
try
{
    inputData = ... Code to set up inputData.
    int currentByte;
    while ((currentByte = inputData.read()) != -1)
    {
        ... Code to do something with currentByte.
    } // while
} // try
catch (IOException exception)
{
    System.err.println("Ooops -- that didn't work! " + exception.getMessage());
} // catch
finally
{
    try { if (inputData != null) inputData.close(); }
    catch (IOException exception)
        { System.err.println("Could not close input " + exception); }
} // finally
```

Notice how we have used a **try finally statement** to make sure that there is an attempt to **close** the InputStream even if something else goes wrong.[1] It is a good idea to ensure we close input and/or output streams when we have finished with them. For example, on some **operating system**s that do not separate the notions of **file** name from file contents, a file cannot be deleted or renamed if a program has it open for reading or writing. Additionally, if we do not close output streams then the data might never get written to its destination!

The InputStream we want to process in this program is, of course, System.in.

> *Concept* **Standard API: System: in: is an InputStream.** The **class variable** called in, inside the
> java.lang.System **class** (i.e. System.in) holds a **reference** to an **object** which is an **instance** of
> java.io.InputStream. This enables our programs to access the **byte**s of their **standard input**.

Our ByteCount program has an **array** of 256 **int** values in which the occurrence count for each possible byte is accumulated in the **array element** at the **array index** which is **equal** to that byte. These counts need to start off with the value zero, and have one added to them each time an occurrence of the corresponding byte is read. On this occasion, we shall rely on the default initial values of the array elements, rather than write a **loop** to set them to zero.

---

[1] Java 7.0 introduced the **try with resources statement** which offers an alternative way of handling this scenario.

Concept **Variable: initial value.** When **class variables**, **instance variables**, and **array elements** are created, they are given a default initial value by the **virtual machine** (unless they are also final variables). In contrast, the **compiler** forces **local variables** (**method variables**) and **final variables** to be initialized by our code.

It is dangerous to *quietly* rely on default values when they happen to be the initial values we desire, mainly because anyone looking at our code (including ourselves) cannot tell the difference between us doing that and having forgotten to initialize! Another reason is that sometimes you, or a reader of your program, may misremember what initial value there is for a **variable** of a particular **type**. So, one rule of thumb is to always perform our own initialization to make it clear we have not overlooked it. However, where that is non-trivial (e.g. for array elements), we instead write a clear **comment** stating that we are happy the default value is what we want, and what that value is.

Here is the code for our `ByteCount` program.

```
001: import java.io.IOException;
002:
003: // Program to count the number of bytes on the standard input
004: // and report it on the standard output.
005: // Each byte that occurs at least once is listed with its own count.
006: public class ByteCount
007: {
008:   public static void main(String[] args)
009:   {
010:     // There are only 256 different byte values.
011:     // Default initial values will be zero, which is what we want.
012:     int[] byteCount = new int[256];
013:
014:     // The total number of bytes found so far.
015:     int allBytesCount = 0;
016:     try
017:     {
018:       int currentByte;
019:       while ((currentByte = System.in.read()) != -1)
020:       {
021:         allBytesCount++;
022:         byteCount[currentByte]++;
023:       } // while
024:     } // try
025:     catch (IOException exception)
026:     {
027:       System.err.println(exception);
028:     } // catch
029:     finally
030:     {
031:       try { System.in.close(); }
032:       catch (IOException exception)
033:         { System.err.println("Could not close input " + exception); }
034:     } // finally
035:
036:     // Report results.
037:     System.out.println("The number of bytes read was " + allBytesCount);
038:     for (int byteValue = 0; byteValue <= 255; byteValue++)
039:       if (byteCount[byteValue] != 0)
040:         System.out.println("Byte value " + byteValue + " occurred "
041:                            + byteCount[byteValue] + " times");
```

```
042:   } // main
043:
044: } // class ByteCount
```

Some readers might find it odd that we are closing `System.in`. The reasoning is that this particular program might well be used with **standard input** being redirected from a **file**. If it is not, then closing the input will do no harm, but if it is then the **close** will mean the file is released as soon as we do not need it any more.

Coffee time: 18.2.2
Why did we not have to write an **import statement** for `java.io.InputStream`, even though we are using it?

Coffee time: 18.2.3
Could we have used a **for-each loop** to print out the byte counts?

18.2.1 Trying it

Let us try it first with no input. On Unix, this means the user types ^D (i.e. hold down the `<Control>` key whilst typing D) straight away to mark the end of the input. On Microsoft Windows the equivalent is ^Z followed by the return key, ⏎ .

```
                Console Input / Output
$ java ByteCount
^D
The number of bytes read was 0
$ _
```

Now we try another example.

```
                Console Input / Output
$ java ByteCount
The cat
sat on
the mat
^D
The number of bytes read was 23
Byte value 10 occurred 3 times
Byte value 32 occurred 3 times
Byte value 84 occurred 1 times
Byte value 97 occurred 3 times
Byte value 99 occurred 1 times
Byte value 101 occurred 2 times
Byte value 104 occurred 2 times
Byte value 109 occurred 1 times
Byte value 110 occurred 1 times
Byte value 111 occurred 1 times
Byte value 115 occurred 1 times
Byte value 116 occurred 4 times
$ _
```

Coffee time: 18.2.4
Is the above result correct? My example was being **run** under Linux. Would you expect to get the same result under Microsoft Windows? (Hint: do they have the same **line separator**?)

18.2.2 Coursework: A check sum program

The problem of being able to detect whether a **file** of **data** has changed since a previous version has many applications in computing. For example, if you download a file from the Internet, how can you be sure that your copy of it is correct and has not been corrupted? Or, imagine a program, **run** every night, that generates individual timetables for students, compares each of them with the timetable from the day before, and emails the latest copy if it has changed.

You might expect that the only way to see if a file has changed is to compare it **byte** by byte with the original, but this is not so. An alternative is to calculate some kind of **check sum** of the file and compare it with the number obtained from the original file. A check sum is a number that is a **function** of the file contents, computed in such a way that even a tiny change in the file causes a difference to the number. Perhaps the website could tell you what the number should be (as long as you use the same check sum **algorithm**). Similarly, the timetable program need remember only the check sum for each student from the night before.

In this task you will write a program called CheckSum which reads all the bytes from **standard input** and outputs a single number on **standard output**. You should handle **exception**s in the same way as we did for the example in this section. You will use the **BSD check sum**[10] algorithm which has been around for many years. There are more sophisticated and complex alternatives available nowadays, however this simple one is still fairly good.

For each **byte** in the input, the check sum computed so far is subjected to a **rotate right**, and then that byte is added to it. A rotate right means each **bit** of the number moves one place to the right, with the rightmost bit rotating to the leftmost place. For example, the 16-bit number 1100110011001100 becomes 0110011001100110, and 0011001100110011 becomes 1001100110011001.

The BSD algorithm computes a 16-bit check sum, which you will store in a 32-bit **int**. So you need to take care that the rotation is done on only the lower 16 bits and the upper 16 always remain zero. Here is the **algorithm** expressed in **pseudo code**.

```
int checkSum = 0
for every byte from the input
  rotate checkSum right by one bit, treating it as a 16 bit number.
  checkSum += byte
  restrict checkSum to 16 bits.
end-for
output checkSum
```

To rotate checkSum right by one bit, whilst treating it as a 16 bit number, you can use the following pseudo code. (Note that 32768 is 2^{15}.)

```
if checkSum is even
  checkSum /= 2
else
  checkSum /= 2
  checkSum += 32768
```

You may prefer to express 32768 in your Java code as a **hexadecimal integer literal**, in the form 0x8000. (Also, you may prefer to find out about the bit **shift operator**s and use one of those instead of **division**).

To restrict checkSum to 16 bits you can use the following code, which works because you have just added a value **less than** 256 to a value that was less than 65536 (which is 2^{16}).

```
if checkSum >= 65536
  checkSum -= 65536
```

You may prefer to express 65536 as 0x10000. (Also, you may prefer to find out about the **integer bitwise operator**s and use one of those instead of an **if statement**.)

To perform a check sum of the data in a file, rather than input typed at the keyboard, you can redirect **standard input** to come from that file, using < on the **command line**. If you are using a Unix environment, you can probably test your program by comparing its output with that obtained from the sum command (which also outputs the size of the file as a number of one kilobyte blocks). Otherwise the book website has some example files for you to try, along with their correct check sums.

```
Console Input / Output
$ java CheckSum < CheckSum.java
51871
$ sum CheckSum.java
51871    2
$ _
```

(The check sum for *your* program code will probably not be the same as the one shown here.)

18.3 Example: Counting characters from standard input

AIM:
To introduce the principle of reading **characters**, instead of **bytes**, from **standard input**, using InputStreamReader.

If we really wanted a program to determine the size and profile of the **standard input**, there is a good chance we would be interested in the **character**s rather than the **byte**s. In many situations, this would be the same. When a Java program **run**s, it does so with knowledge of the **locale** in use on the **operating system**. A locale is a collection of information about a part of the world, for example the **file encoding** for characters, the currency symbol, etc.. In many situations the default locale has a character encoding in **text file**s such that each normal text character occupies one byte. Or it might be that some characters require more than one byte to represent them. This is especially likely to be the case in say, China, and the Middle East, but in any part of the world we may possibly be using a locale where some characters use more than one byte.

So, if we expect our programs to be portable, then we must treat **data** as characters rather than bytes, when it is characters we are concerned about.

The program in this section will read the data from the standard input, character by character, and process it. To achieve this, we shall wrap System.in with an InputStreamReader.

Concept **File IO API: InputStreamReader.** If we wish to treat an InputStream as a sequence of **characters**, rather than a sequence of **bytes**, we can wrap it up in an **instance** of the **class** java.io.InputStreamReader. This provides an **instance method** called read, which **return**s the next *character* from the wrapped up InputStream, or −1 if there are no more to be read. To achieve this, the instance method reads one or more bytes from the underlying InputStream for each character.

InputStreamReader has two **constructor method**s, one takes just an InputStream which it wraps up. It will (usually) use the the default **file encoding** in operation on the computer where the program is **run**. The second constructor method takes both an InputStream and the character encoding which is to be used – permitting us to read character streams that were generated under a different **locale**.

Here is the code for our CharacterCount program. It is similar to ByteCount, except for the appropriate renaming of **variable**s and rewording of **comment**s, etc..

```
001: import java.io.InputStreamReader;
002: import java.io.IOException;
003:
004: // Program to count the number of characters on the standard input
005: // and report it on the standard output.
006: // Each character that occurs at least once is listed with its own count.
007: public class CharacterCount
008: {
009:   public static void main(String[] args)
010:   {
011:     // There are 65536 different character values (two bytes).
012:     // Default initial values will be zero, which is what we want.
013:     int[] characterCount = new int[65536];
014:
015:     // We will read the input as characters.
016:     InputStreamReader input = new InputStreamReader(System.in);
017:
018:     // The total number of characters found so far.
019:     int allCharactersCount = 0;
```

```
020:    try
021:    {
022:      int currentCharacter;
023:      while ((currentCharacter = input.read()) != -1)
024:      {
025:        allCharactersCount++;
026:        characterCount[currentCharacter]++;
027:      } // while
028:    } // try
029:    catch (IOException exception)
030:    {
031:      System.err.println(exception);
032:    } // catch
033:    finally
034:    {
035:      try { input.close(); }
036:      catch (IOException exception)
037:        { System.err.println("Could not close input " + exception); }
038:    } // finally
039:
040:    // Report results.
041:    System.out.println("The number of characters read was "
042:                    + allCharactersCount);
043:    for (int characterValue = 0; characterValue <= 65535; characterValue++)
044:      if (characterCount[characterValue] != 0)
045:        System.out.println("Character value " + characterValue + " occurred "
046:                        + characterCount[characterValue] + " times");
047:  } // main
048:
049: } // class CharacterCount
```

18.3.1 Trying it

First we'll try it with an empty input.

```
Console Input / Output
$ java CharacterCount
^D
The number of characters read was 0
$ _
```

And now with the same input that we tried with the ByteCount program.

```
Console Input / Output
$ java CharacterCount
The cat
sat on
the mat
^D
The number of characters read was 23
Character value 10 occurred 3 times
Character value 32 occurred 3 times
Character value 84 occurred 1 times
Character value 97 occurred 3 times
Character value 99 occurred 1 times
Character value 101 occurred 2 times
Character value 104 occurred 2 times
Character value 109 occurred 1 times
Character value 110 occurred 1 times
Character value 111 occurred 1 times
Character value 115 occurred 1 times
Character value 116 occurred 4 times
$ _
```

Coffee time: [18.3.1] Did the last two tests produce the same results as obtained from the ByteCount program in Section 18.2.1 on page 454?

Now let's try **run**ning it with text from a **text file** containing a popular Chinese New Year greeting.

The **file** HappyNewYear-GBK.txt contains four Chinese **character**s encoded using the GBK encoding commonly used in China, plus a **new line character**. This is a total size of 9 **byte**s.

```
Console Input / Output
$ ls -l HappyNewYear-GBK.txt
-rw------- 1 jtl jtl 9 Mar 30 12:30 HappyNewYear-GBK.txt
$ _
```

Here is a screen dump of a simple Java program with a **graphical user interface**, which has read the text from the file and is displaying it (using a JLabel).

We will run our ByteCount and CharacterCount programs with **standard input** redirected from HappyNewYear-GBK.txt, using <. However, we also need to tell the **virtual machine** to use the GBK encoding, rather than the default one for the current **locale**, so that it will convert the bytes in the file into the proper characters. We can do that with the **command line argument**, -Dfile.encoding=GBK.

```
                    Console Input / Output
$ java -Dfile.encoding=GBK ByteCount < HappyNewYear-GBK.txt
The number of bytes read was 9
Byte value 10 occurred 1 times
Byte value 191 occurred 1 times
Byte value 192 occurred 1 times
Byte value 194 occurred 1 times
Byte value 196 occurred 1 times
Byte value 208 occurred 1 times
Byte value 214 occurred 1 times
Byte value 234 occurred 1 times
Byte value 236 occurred 1 times
$ _
```

And now we process the same file using our CharacterCount program.

```
                    Console Input / Output
$ java -Dfile.encoding=GBK CharacterCount < HappyNewYear-GBK.txt
The number of characters read was 5
Character value 10 occurred 1 times
Character value 20048 occurred 1 times
Character value 24180 occurred 1 times
Character value 24555 occurred 1 times
Character value 26032 occurred 1 times
$ _
```

Notice that the number of **bytes** is more than the number of characters – each character in that file, apart from the new line character, uses two bytes.

18.3.2 Coursework: Counting words

Write a program, WordCount which reads the **characters** from its **standard input**, counting how many words that contains, and reports the number on its **standard output**. You should handle **exceptions** in the same way as we did for the example in this section.

A character is either a **white space** character, such as **space character**, **tab character**, or **new line character**; or it is part of a word. To determine whether a **char** c is white space, you can use Character.isWhitespace(c).

A word is a non-empty sequence of any non-white space characters, preceded either by the beginning of the **file**, or a white space character, and followed either by the end of the file, or a white space character. There may be more than one white space character before and/or after a word, including before the first word, and after the last one.

Hint: the start of a word is at a character which is itself not white space, and which is either the first character in the input, or was preceded by a white space character.

Alternatively, think of the input as being:

- A possibly empty sequence of white space characters.

- A possibly empty sequence of words, each being:

    – A non-empty sequence of non-white space characters.

    – A possibly empty sequence of white space characters.

As usual, design **test data** in advance of **design**ing your program.

18.4 Example: Numbering lines from standard input

AIM: To introduce the principle of reading lines from **standard input**, using BufferedReader.

In this section, we develop a program to read from **standard input** and copy each line to **standard output**, with its line number prepended. We use a BufferedReader to enable us to read the input a line at a time.

Concept **File IO API: BufferedReader.** Whilst the **class** java.io.InputStreamReader converts **byte**s into **character**s, it does not provide an **instance method** to read a whole line of characters in one go. Instead, this functionality is provided by java.io.BufferedReader. This class wraps up an InputStreamReader **object** and provides the instance method readLine(), as well as read() for a single character (and other **method**s). We can create a BufferedReader object by providing the **constructor method** with an **instance** of InputStreamReader, which we wish it to wrap up.

The instance method readLine() takes no **method argument**s and **return**s a String, containing the next line of the input from the underlying InputStreamReader; or the **null reference** if there are no more lines to be read.

Here is the code for our LineNumber program.

```
001: import java.io.BufferedReader;
002: import java.io.InputStreamReader;
003: import java.io.IOException;
004:
005: // Program to add a line number to the lines from the standard input
006: // and show the result on the standard output.
007: public class LineNumber
008: {
009:   // The minimum number of digits in a line number.
010:   private static final int MINIMUM_LINE_NUMBER_DIGITS = 5;
011:
012:   // The format to use with printf for the line number and line.
013:   private static final String LINE_FORMAT
014:     = "%0" + MINIMUM_LINE_NUMBER_DIGITS + "d %s%n";
015:
016:
017:   // Read each line from input, and copy to output with a count.
018:   public static void main(String[] args)
019:   {
020:     BufferedReader input
021:       = new BufferedReader(new InputStreamReader(System.in));
```

```
022:    try
023:    {
024:      // Now copy input to output, adding line numbers.
025:      int noOfLinesReadSoFar = 0;
026:      String currentLine;
027:      while ((currentLine = input.readLine()) != null)
028:      {
029:        noOfLinesReadSoFar++;
030:        System.out.printf(LINE_FORMAT, noOfLinesReadSoFar, currentLine);
031:      } // while
032:    } // try
033:    catch (IOException exception)
034:    {
035:      System.err.println(exception);
036:    } // catch
037:    finally
038:    {
039:      try { input.close(); }
040:      catch (IOException exception)
041:        { System.err.println("Could not close input " + exception); }
042:    } // finally
043:  } // main
044:
045: } // class LineNumber
```

18.4.1 Trying it

First let us try the program with empty input.

Console Input / Output
$ `java LineNumber`
^D
$ _

And now, three lines of text.

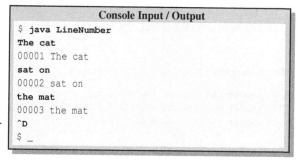

Console Input / Output
$ `java LineNumber`
The cat
00001 The cat
sat on
00002 sat on
the mat
00003 the mat
^D
$ _

18.4.2 Coursework: Deleting a field

Write a program called `DeleteField` which copies its **standard input** to its **standard output**, line by line, except that it deletes one of the fields on each line. The fields are separated by a single **tab character**, and are numbered from one upwards. The number of the field to be deleted is given as a **command line argument**.

Here is an example **run**.

Console Input / Output			
$ `java DeleteField 2`			
Name	**Coursework**	**Exam**	**Total**
Name	Exam	Total	
Fred Bloggs	**55**	**65**	**60**
Fred Bloggs	65	60	
Susan Smart	**100**	**90**	**95**
Susan Smart	90	95	
^D			

(Of course, in practice the program would be most useful if the input was being redirected from a **file**, rather than literally being typed in line by line – the above is really just for testing.)

460

You might find the following code helpful.

```
...
024:        // Divide the line into fields using tab as a delimiter.
025:        String[] fields = inputLine.split("\t");
026:        String editedLine = "";
027:        if (fields.length < fieldToDelete)
028:          editedLine = inputLine;
029:        else
030:        {
031:          // We build the new line in parts.
032:          // Add the fields before the one to be deleted.
033:          for (int index = 0; index < fieldToDelete - 1; index++)
034:            if (editedLine.equals("")) editedLine = fields[index];
035:            else                       editedLine += "\t" + fields[index];
036:          // Add the fields after the one to be deleted.
037:          for (int index = fieldToDelete; index < fields.length; index++)
038:            if (editedLine.equals("")) editedLine = fields[index];
039:            else                       editedLine += "\t" + fields[index];
040:        } // else
...
```

You should handle **exceptions** in the same way as we did for the example in this section (except you will need to consider problems relating to the command line argument).

If you wanted to delete two fields, and also your **data** was in a **text file**, then you could redirect the standard input to come from it, and pipe the **standard output** into the input of another run of your program.

Console Input / Output
| ```
$ cat input.txt
Name      Coursework       Exam      Total
Fred Bloggs        55       65        60
Susan Smart        100      90        95
$ java DeleteField 3 < input.txt | java DeleteField 2
Name      Total
Fred Bloggs       60
Susan Smart       95
$ _
``` |

The above should also work on Microsoft Windows (except use type rather than cat if you want to list the original text file).

18.5   Example: Numbering lines from text file to text file

AIM: To introduce the principle of reading from a **text file** and writing to another, using BufferedReader with FileReader and PrintWriter with FileWriter. We also meet FileInputStream, OutputStream, FileOutputStream and OutputStreamWriter.

In this section, we develop a version of the LineNumber program which reads its data from a **text file** and writes its result to another one. The names of these **files** are supplied as the first and second **command line argument**s respectively. For variety, and to continue experimenting with different **exception catching** styles, we also develop and use a LineNumberException **class**. However we do not need to show that class here as it is so similar to others we have seen.

Coffee time: 18.5.1   Write the LineNumberException class.

461
```

We use a FileReader to access the input text file.

Concept **File IO API: FileInputStream.** To read **bytes** from a **file**, we use an **instance** of the **class** java.io.FileInputStream. This is a **subclass** of java.io.InputStream which reads its input bytes from a file.

```
myDataAsBytes = new FileInputStream("my-binary-data");
```

Concept **File IO API: FileReader.** To read **characters** instead of **bytes** from a **file**, we can wrap a FileInputStream in an InputStreamReader. For convenience we can instead create an **instance** of java.io.FileReader, which then creates the required FileInputStream and InputStreamReader internally for us. FileReader is a **subclass** of java.io.InputStreamReader, and so has a read() **instance method** to read a **character**, and can be wrapped inside a BufferedReader to obtain a readLine() instance method. One of the **constructor methods** of FileReader takes the name of the file to be accessed.

Here is a possible skeleton use of FileReader.

```
FileReader fileReader = null;
try
{
   fileReader = new FileReader("my-data.txt");
   int currentCharacter;
   while ((currentCharacter = fileReader.read()) != -1)
   {
      ... do something with currentCharacter.
   } //while
} //try
catch (IOException exception)
{
   System.err.println(exception.getMessage());
} // catch
finally
{
   try { if (fileReader != null) fileReader.close(); }
   catch (IOException exception)
      { System.err.println("Could not close input file " + exception); }
} // finally
```

To enable us to read a line at a time, we wrap the FileReader inside a BufferedReader in our program.

To write **data** we need to use an OutputStream.

Concept **File IO API: OutputStream.** The basic building block for writing **data** in Java, is the **class** java.io.OutputStream. Like java.io.InputStream, this provides a view of the data as a **byte stream**. OutputStream has, amongst others, an **instance method** write() to write a single **byte**.

In this program we wish to write **characters** rather than **bytes** to the file.

Concept **File IO API: OutputStreamWriter.** If we wish to treat an OutputStream as a sequence of **characters**, rather than a sequence of **bytes**, we can wrap it up in an **instance** of the **class** java.io.OutputStreamWriter. This is analogous to java.io.InputStreamReader for InputStream **objects**. OutputStreamWriter has, amongst others, an **instance method** write() to write a single character.

To make the output go to a file, we shall in fact use a `FileWriter`.

Concept **File IO API: `FileOutputStream`.** To write **bytes** to a **file**, we use an **instance** of the **class** `java.io.FileOutputStream`. This is a **subclass** of `java.io.OutputStream` which writes its output bytes to a file.

Concept **File IO API: `FileWriter`.** To write **characters** instead of **bytes** to a **file**, we can wrap a `FileOutputStream` in an `OutputStreamWriter`. For convenience we can instead create an **instance** of `java.io.FileWriter`, which then creates the required `FileOutputStream` and `OutputStreamWriter` internally for us. `FileWriter` is a **subclass** of `java.io.OutputStreamWriter`, and so has a `write()` **instance method** to write a character. One of the **constructor methods** of `FileWriter` takes the name of the file to be written to.

Here is a possible skeleton use of `FileWriter`. Notice the call to the `close()` instance method in the **finally block** – it is a good idea to **close** files, especially for output files, when we have finished with them. If we do not, then it is possible that **data** written into the `FileWriter` might still be waiting in memory buffers, and never get written into the physical file.

```java
FileWriter fileWriter = null;
try
{
  fileWriter = new FileWriter("my-results.txt");
  boolean iFeelLikeIt = ...
  while (iFeelLikeIt)
  {
    int currentCharacter = ...
    fileWriter.write(currentCharacter);

    ...
    iFeelLikeIt = ...
  } // while
} // try
catch (IOException exception)
{
  System.err.println(exception.getMessage());
} // catch
finally
{
  try { if (fileWriter != null) fileWriter.close(); }
  catch (IOException exception)
    { System.err.println("Could not close output file " + exception); }
} // finally
```

Notice that the **variable** to hold each character is an **int**. Only the lowest 16 **bits**, which is the size of **char**, are used by `write()`. This avoids the need for us to **cast** the value to a **char** if we have in fact just obtained it from `read()` of an `InputStream`.

To enable us to write a line at a time, we wrap the `FileWriter` inside a `PrintWriter`.

Concept **File IO API: `PrintWriter`.** Whilst the **class** `java.io.OutputStreamWriter` (and its **subclass** `java.io.FileWriter`) converts **characters** into **bytes**, it does not provide **instance methods** to print whole lines of text, or decimal representations of numbers, etc.. Instead, this functionality is provided by `java.io.PrintWriter`. This class wraps up an `OutputStreamWriter` **object** and provides instance methods `println()`, and `print()` for a range of possible **method arguments**. Since Java 5.0 it also has printf(). We can create a PrintWriter object by providing the **constructor method** with an **instance** of OutputStreamWriter, which we wish it to wrap up.

The following diagram helps to show the interaction between the classes that process the data in our new LineNumber program.

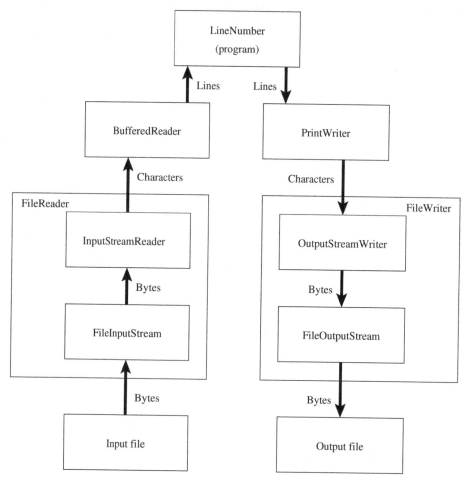

Concept **File IO API: PrintWriter: checkError().** Curiously, the **instance method**s of the java.io.PrintWriter **class** never **throw** any **exceptions**! (However, some of its **constructor method**s do.) So, to find out whether something has gone wrong with the printing, we can use its checkError() instance method. This **returns** a **boolean** which is **true** if there has been an error, **false** otherwise.

Hence, a typical use of PrintWriter might be as follows.

```
PrintWriter printWriter = null;
try
{
  printWriter = ...
```

```
     while (...)
     {
       ...
       printWriter.write(...);
       ...
     } // while
   } // try
   catch (IOException exception)
   {
     System.err.println(exception.getMessage());
   } // catch
   finally
   {
     if (printWriter != null)
     {
       // printWriter.close() does not throw an exception.
       printWriter.close();
       if (printWriter.checkError())
         System.err.println("Something went wrong with the output");
     } // if
   } // finally
```

Here is the code for the program. Note the need to set input and output to the **null reference** when we declare them. This is because we could end up in the **finally block** without having created the BufferedReader or PrintWriter **object**s if such **construc**tion **throw**s an **exception**, at which point those **variable**s would have no value.

```
001: import java.io.BufferedReader;
002: import java.io.FileReader;
003: import java.io.FileWriter;
004: import java.io.IOException;
005: import java.io.PrintWriter;
006:
007: // Program to add a line number to the lines from an input file
008: // and produce the result in an output file.
009: // The two file names are given as command line arguments.
010: public class LineNumber
011: {
012:   // The minimum number of digits in a line number.
013:   private static final int MINIMUM_LINE_NUMBER_DIGITS = 5;
014:
015:   // The format to use with printf for the line number and line.
016:   private static final String LINE_FORMAT
017:     = "%0" + MINIMUM_LINE_NUMBER_DIGITS + "d %s%n";
018:
019:
020:   // Read each line from input, and copy to output with a count.
021:   public static void main(String[] args)
022:   {
023:     BufferedReader input = null;
024:     PrintWriter output = null;
025:     try
026:     {
027:       if (args.length != 2)
028:         throw new LineNumberException
029:                     ("There must be exactly two arguments: infile outfile");
030:
```

```
031:        input = new BufferedReader(new FileReader(args[0]));
032:        output = new PrintWriter(new FileWriter(args[1]));
033:
034:        // Now copy input to output, adding line numbers.
035:        int noOfLinesReadSoFar = 0;
036:        String currentLine;
037:        while ((currentLine = input.readLine()) != null)
038:        {
039:          noOfLinesReadSoFar++;
040:          output.printf(LINE_FORMAT, noOfLinesReadSoFar, currentLine);
041:        } // while
042:      } // try
043:      catch (LineNumberException exception)
044:      {
045:        // We report LineNumberExceptions to standard output.
046:        System.out.println(exception.getMessage());
047:      } // catch
048:      catch (IOException exception)
049:      {
050:        // Other exceptions go to standard error.
051:        System.err.println(exception);
052:      } // catch
053:      finally
054:      {
055:        try { if (input != null) input.close(); }
056:        catch (IOException exception)
057:          { System.err.println("Could not close input " + exception); }
058:        if (output != null)
059:        {
060:          output.close();
061:          if (output.checkError())
062:            System.err.println("Something went wrong with the output");
063:        } // if
064:      } // finally
065:    } // main
066:
067: } // class LineNumber
```

18.5.1 Trying it

First let us try the program with the wrong number of **command line arguments**.

Console Input / Output
`$ java LineNumber`
`There must be exactly two arguments: infile outfile`
`$ java LineNumber input.txt`
`There must be exactly two arguments: infile outfile`
`$ java LineNumber input.txt result.txt extra-argument`
`There must be exactly two arguments: infile outfile`
`$ _`

We can use the **file** /dev/null (just nul on Microsoft Windows) to test our program with an **empty file** as input. Then we can use cat (type on Windows) to check the contents of our output file.

Console Input / Output
`$ java LineNumber /dev/null result.txt`
`$ cat result.txt`
`$ _`

Let us number the lines in a piece of Shakespeare[8].

```
         Console Input / Output
$ cat RomeoAndJuliet.txt
'Tis but thy name that is my enemy:
Thou art thyself, though not a Montague.
What's Montague? It is nor hand, nor foot
Nor arm nor face nor any other part
Belonging to a man. O be some other name.
What's in a name? That which we call a rose
By any other name would smell as sweet;
So Romeo would, were he not Romeo call'd,
Retain that dear perfection which he owes
Without that title. Romeo, doff thy name,
And for thy name, which is no part of thee,
Take all myself.
$ _
```

```
                    Console Input / Output
$ java LineNumber RomeoAndJuliet.txt result.txt
$ cat result.txt
00001 'Tis but thy name that is my enemy:
00002 Thou art thyself, though not a Montague.
00003 What's Montague? It is nor hand, nor foot
00004 Nor arm nor face nor any other part
00005 Belonging to a man. O be some other name.
00006 What's in a name? That which we call a rose
00007 By any other name would smell as sweet;
00008 So Romeo would, were he not Romeo call'd,
00009 Retain that dear perfection which he owes
00010 Without that title. Romeo, doff thy name,
00011 And for thy name, which is no part of thee,
00012 Take all myself.
$ _
```

The file pandoras-box.txt does not exist (so we cannot open it!).

```
                         Console Input / Output
$ java LineNumber pandoras-box.txt result.txt
java.io.FileNotFoundException: pandoras-box.txt (No such file or directory)
$ _
```

The directory CaveOfWonders does not exist (so we cannot create a file in it).

```
                         Console Input / Output
$ java LineNumber RomeoAndJuliet.txt CaveOfWonders/lamp.txt
java.io.FileNotFoundException: CaveOfWonders/lamp.txt (No such file or directory
)
$ _
```

Coffee time: [18.5.2] Observe the above **exception** – is it a surprise that an attempt to create a new file results in a complaint about it not being found?

18.5.2 Coursework: Deleting a field, from file to file

Write a version of your DeleteField program from Section 18.4.2 on page 460, that takes its input from a named **file** and puts its output in another named file. You should handle **exception**s in the same way as we did for the example in this section.

18.6 Example: Numbering lines from and to anywhere

AIM: To illustrate that reading from **text file**s and from **standard input** is essentially the same thing, as is writing to **text file**s and to **standard output**. We also look at testing for the existence of a **file** using the File **class**, and revisit PrintWriter and PrintStream.

In this section, we develop another version of the LineNumber program which reads its **data** from either **standard input** or a **text file** and writes its result to either **standard output** or another text file.

467

The names of the input and output **files** are supplied as the first and second **command line arguments** respectively. However, if the first argument is missing, or is just -, then the standard input is used, and if the second argument is missing or -, then the standard output is used.

To do this without significant code repetition, we wish to be able to treat standard output in the same way as we do a file. That is, we would like to get a `PrintWriter` that is set up to send its output either to the file, or to standard output, depending on the user's wishes.

Concept **Standard API: `System: out: is an OutputStream`.** The **class variable** called `out`, inside the `java.lang.System` **class** (i.e. `System.out`) holds a **reference** to an **object** which is an **instance** of `java.io.OutputStream`. This enables our programs to produce **bytes** on their **standard output**.

More precisely, `System.out` is an instance of `java.io.PrintStream`, which is a **subclass** of `OutputStream`. Unlike basic `OutputStream` objects, a `PrintStream` object also has **instance methods** `print()`, `println()` and (since Java 5.0) `printf()`, which take various **method arguments** and write their **character** representations as bytes.

Concept **Standard API: `System: err: is an OutputStream`.** The **class variable** called `err`, inside the `java.lang.System` **class** (i.e. `System.err`) holds a **reference** to an **object** which is an **instance** of `java.io.PrintStream`, a **subclass** of `java.io.OutputStream`. This enables our programs to produce **bytes** on their **standard error**.

Concept **File IO API: `PrintWriter: versus PrintStream`.** An often asked question is, what is the difference between `java.io.PrintStream` and `java.io.PrintWriter`? `PrintStream` is a **subclass** of `OutputStream`, and so has `write()` **instance methods** for writing **bytes**, but also has `print()`, `println()` and `printf()` instance methods for printing representations of things as **characters**, (e.g. decimal representations of **int**s, `String`s as lines, etc.). A `PrintWriter` is a wrapper around an **instance** of `java.io.OutputStreamWriter` and provides `print()`, `println()` and `printf()` instance methods for printing representations as characters via that `OutputStreamWriter`. It does not have any way to write bytes.

The desire to write a *mixture* of bytes and characters to the same stream is highly unusual – we nearly always want either all bytes or all characters, the latter sometimes with the ability to print representations. `PrintStream` primarily exists for `System.out` and `System.err`, so that the **standard output** and the **standard error** are each available as a stream of bytes, but can also be conveniently treated as 'printable' – e.g. for error messages, debugging messages, or very simple programs.

Programs that need to produce representations as a stream of characters should use `PrintWriter` rather than `PrintStream`, *because* `PrintWriter` does not have instance methods to write bytes; we cannot accidentally use them. (And programs that wish to produce a stream of bytes should not use `PrintStream` so we cannot accidentally use the printing methods.)

Concept **File IO API: `PrintWriter: can also wrap an OutputStream`.** `System.out` is an `OutputStream` (actually its **subclass**, `PrintStream`). If we wish to treat it as a `PrintWriter`, then we can wrap it up inside an `OutputStreamWriter` and then inside a `PrintWriter`.

```
PrintWriter systemOut = new PrintWriter(new OutputStreamWriter(System.out));
```

However, for convenience one of the **constructor methods** of `PrintWriter` can take an `OutputStream` directly, and **construct** the intermediate `OutputStreamWriter` internally for us.

```
PrintWriter systemOut = new PrintWriter(System.out);
```

All **instances** of output **classes** which act as wrappers around some other output class **object** may typically store their output in an internal buffer before sending it to the wrapped up object, in an effort to speed up overall operation of our programs. Such buffers are **flushed** by calls to the `flush()` **instance method**, or when the output is **closed**, via the `close()` **instance method**. For a `PrintWriter` which is wrapping up `System.out`, it is likely we would want to enable **automatic flushing**. This ensures that **data** is sent all the way through to appearing at the final destination (e.g. the screen) whenever one of the `println()` or `printf()` instance methods has finished producing its result (but not `print()`). Automatic flushing can be enabled by using a separate constructor method which takes an additional **boolean method argument**.

```
PrintWriter systemOut = new PrintWriter(System.out, true);
```

To make the program a little more interesting, we shall also have it check that the output file does not already exist, rather than overwrite some existing data.

Concept **File IO API: `File`.** The **class** `java.io.File` allows us to examine properties of **file**s. Although the class is called `File`, it is really all about file *names*, and properties of any files of those names. One **constructor method** of the `File` class takes the path name of a file as its single **method argument**. There are a number of **instance method**s, including `exists()` which **return**s a **boolean** indicating whether or not the `File` **object** represents a file that actually exists. In other words, whether or not the path name given to the constructor method is the name of a file that currently exists.

Coffee time: Find out about the other features of the `File` **class** by looking at the **API** on-line documentation. [18.6.1]

Here is the code for our latest `LineNumber` program.

```
001: import java.io.BufferedReader;
002: import java.io.File;
003: import java.io.FileReader;
004: import java.io.FileWriter;
005: import java.io.InputStreamReader;
006: import java.io.IOException;
007: import java.io.PrintWriter;
008:
009: // Program to add a line number to the lines from an input file
010: // and produce the result in an output file.
011: // The two file names are given as command line arguments.
012: // If a filename is missing, or is "-", then standard input/output is used.
013: public class LineNumber
014: {
015:   // The minimum number of digits in a line number.
016:   private static final int MINIMUM_LINE_NUMBER_DIGITS = 5;
017:
018:   // The format to use with printf for the line number and line.
019:   private static final String LINE_FORMAT
020:     = "%0" + MINIMUM_LINE_NUMBER_DIGITS + "d %s%n";
021:
022:
023:   // Read each line from input, and copy to output with a count.
024:   public static void main(String[] args)
025:   {
026:     BufferedReader input = null;
027:     PrintWriter output = null;
028:     try
029:     {
030:       // Check for too many args before opening files, in case wrong names.
031:       if (args.length > 2)
032:         throw new LineNumberException("Too many arguments");
033:
```

```
034:      if (args.length < 1 || args[0].equals("-"))
035:          input = new BufferedReader(new InputStreamReader(System.in));
036:      else
037:          input = new BufferedReader(new FileReader(args[0]));
038:
039:      if (args.length < 2 || args[1].equals("-"))
040:          output = new PrintWriter(System.out, true);
041:      else
042:      {
043:          if (new File(args[1]).exists())
044:            throw new LineNumberException("Output file "
045:                                          + args[1] + " already exists");
046:
047:          output = new PrintWriter(new FileWriter(args[1]));
048:      } // else
049:
050:      // Now copy input to output, adding line numbers.
051:      int noOfLinesReadSoFar = 0;
052:      String currentLine;
053:      while ((currentLine = input.readLine()) != null)
054:      {
055:        noOfLinesReadSoFar++;
056:        output.printf(LINE_FORMAT, noOfLinesReadSoFar, currentLine);
057:      } // while
058:    } // try
059:    catch (LineNumberException exception)
060:    {
061:      // We report LineNumberExceptions to standard output.
062:      System.out.println(exception.getMessage());
063:    } // catch
064:    catch (IOException exception)
065:    {
066:      // Other exceptions go to standard error.
067:      System.err.println(exception);
068:    } // catch
069:    finally
070:    {
071:      try { if (input != null) input.close(); }
072:      catch (IOException exception)
073:        { System.err.println("Could not close input " + exception); }
074:      if (output != null)
075:      {
076:        output.close();
077:        if (output.checkError())
078:          System.err.println("Something went wrong with the output");
079:      } // if
080:    } // finally
081:  } // main
082:
083: } // class LineNumber
```

18.6.1   Trying it

We test the program, first with too many **command line arguments**.

Console Input / Output
$ **java LineNumber input.txt result.txt extra-argument**
Too many arguments
$ _

Next we try two named **files**.

Console Input / Output
$ **cat input.txt**
Big
Cheese
$ **java LineNumber input.txt result.txt**
$ **cat result.txt**
00001 Big
00002 Cheese
$ _

470

This test has a named file for input, but uses **standard output** for the result.

```
Console Input / Output
$ java LineNumber input.txt -
00001 Big
00002 Cheese
$ _
```

The next test has a named output file, but uses **standard input**. However, we deliberately try to use the same file for output as before, which of course, already exists.

```
Console Input / Output
$ java LineNumber - result.txt
Output file result.txt already exists
$ cat result.txt
00001 Big
00002 Cheese
$ _
```

```
Console Input / Output
$ rm result.txt
$ java LineNumber - result.txt
Hello
Mum
^D
$ cat result.txt
00001 Hello
00002 Mum
$ _
```

Okay, so let us remove that file (using the rm command, or del on Microsoft Windows) and try again.

Finally, the remaining three tests all get their **test data** from standard input and produce results on standard output.

Console Input / Output	Console Input / Output	Console Input / Output
$ java LineNumber - -	$ java LineNumber -	$ java LineNumber
Hello	Hello	Hello
00001 Hello	00001 Hello	00001 Hello
Mum	Mum	Mum
00002 Mum	00002 Mum	00002 Mum
^D	^D	^D
$ _	$ _	$ _

18.6.2 Coursework: Deleting a field, from anywhere to anywhere

Write a version of your DeleteField program from Section 18.5.2 on page 467, that takes its input from **standard input** or a named **file**, and puts its output on **standard output** or in another named file. You should handle **exceptions** in the same way as we did for the example in this section.

18.7 Example: Text photographs

AIM: To see an example of reading **binary files**, where we did not choose the **file format**. This includes the process of turning **bytes** into **ints**, using a **shift operator** and an **integer bitwise operator**.

The program in this section is one which produces an 'ASCII art' impressionist text version of a given digital photograph, on the **standard output**. The user chooses the width and height of the output text image, that is, the number of **characters** per line, and the number of lines. The darkest regions of the original image are represented in the output using dark characters, such as ' # ', and lighter regions as, say, ' * ' and ' . ', with the lightest being shown as a space. Compared with the original picture, the output obviously contains much less information, and yet, it can be remarkably recognizable, especially if it is a portrait of somebody you know. For best effect, you can print it on a large piece of paper and stand well back!

471

For example, here is a picture of Lizzy (from a few years ago), followed by what she looks like after being run through our program.

The original image must be a 24 **bit** per pixel .bmp **file**[7]. Images in this format are easy to produce and are (usually) not compressed, and so are fairly easy to read as **data**. Our program reads the image data as a stream of **byte**s using a FileInputStream. Much of the program is about making sense of the bytes in the file, as they are presented in a specific **file format** which we didn't choose. For example, the width and height of the image are stored at a certain point, as a sequence of bytes in a particular order.

```
┌─────────────────────────────────────────────┐
│              Console Input / Output           │
├─────────────────────────────────────────────┤
│ $ java Bmp2Txt 75 50 lizzy.bmp                │
│ [ASCII art representation of the image]       │
│ $ _                                           │
└─────────────────────────────────────────────┘
```

```java
001: import java.io.FileInputStream;
002: import java.io.FileNotFoundException;
003: import java.io.IOException;
004:
005: // Simple program to produce a text version of a 24 bit BMP format image file.
006: // The first argument is the desired text width, the second is the height.
007: // The third argument is the name of BMP file.
008: // The text image is produced on the standard output.
009: public class Bmp2Txt
010: {
011:   // The characters used for the text image.
012:   // The first is used for the darkest pixels,
013:   // the second for the next lightest, and so on.
014:   // A good choice will depend on the font in use on the output.
015:   // (We should reverse the order when using white print on black.)
016:   private static final String SHADES_STRING = "#@*+. ";
```

```
017:
018:    // The above is for convenient editing if we want to alter the
019:    // characters used. This next array is actually used to
020:    // map a scaled brightness on to a text character.
021:    private static final char[] SHADE_CHARS = SHADES_STRING.toCharArray();
022:
023:    // The bytes from the input image.
024:    private static FileInputStream inputImage;
025:
026:    // The width and height of the input image.
027:    private static int inputHeight, inputWidth;
028:
029:    // The width and height of the desired text image.
030:    private static int outputWidth, outputHeight;
031:
032:    // Our output image will be stored in this 2D array.
033:    // Position 0,0 is bottom left.
034:    // Each pixel records the monochrome brightness level.
035:    private static int[][] outputImage;
```

We would like to do some simple checking to ensure that the file is in the expected format. So, every time we read a byte, we check that we have not reached the end of the file. For convenience we have a separate method that performs this check and **throws** an IOException if it fails, or **returns** the next byte otherwise.

```
038:    // Read a single byte from the input image file
039:    // and throw an exception if there is none left!
040:    private static int readByte() throws IOException
041:    {
042:      int result = inputImage.read();
043:      if (result == -1)
044:        throw new IOException("Unexpected end of file");
045:      return result;
046:    } // readByte
```

Certain parts of the file contain information that is not relevant to this program, so we wish to skip over those bytes.

```
049:    // Skip irrelevant bytes from the input image file.
050:    private static void skipIrrelvantBytes(int skipCount) throws IOException
051:    {
052:      for (int count = 1; count <= skipCount; count++)
053:        readByte();
054:    } // skipIrrelvantBytes
```

The height and width of the input image are stored at a certain point in the file using four consecutive bytes each. We shall need to read these four bytes, and turn them into the **integer** they represent. To help do that, we can use a **shift operator**, and also an **integer bitwise operator**.

Concept **Expression: arithmetic: shift operators.** Some more **arithmetic operator**s in Java are the **shift operator**s, <<, >> and >>>. The **left shift operator**, <<, yields the number obtained by shifting the first **operand** left by the number of **bit**s given in the second operand, placing zeroes in that many rightmost places. The **unsigned right shift** operator, >>>, similarly shifts rightwards, placing zeroes on the left. The **signed right shift** operator, >>, is the same, except it places ones on the left if the number being shifted is negative.

For example, 1000 is 0001111101000 in **binary**.

4096	2048	1024	512	256	128	64	32	16	8	4	2	1
0	0	0	1	1	1	1	1	0	1	0	0	0
0+	0+	0+	512+	256+	128+	64+	32+	0+	8+	0+	0+	0 = 1000

When this is shifted left by three places, 1000 << 3, we get the result 8000 which is 1111101000000 in binary.

4096	2048	1024	512	256	128	64	32	16	8	4	2	1
1	1	1	1	1	0	1	0	0	0	0	0	0
4096+	2048+	1024+	512+	256+	0+	64+	0+	0+	0+	0+	0+	0 = 8000

Whereas, 1000 >> 3 and 1000 >>> 3 both yield 0000001111101 in binary, which is 125.

4096	2048	1024	512	256	128	64	32	16	8	4	2	1
0	0	0	0	0	0	1	1	1	1	1	0	1
0+	0+	0+	0+	0+	0+	64+	32+	16+	8+	4+	0+	1 = 125

Shifting left by n bits, has the same effect as **multiplication** by 2^n and discarding any overflow. Signed shifting right by n bits has the same effect as **division** by 2^n and discarding any remainder.

Concept **Expression: arithmetic: integer bitwise operators.** The operators |, &, and ^, when applied to numeric **operand**s, have the effect of an **integer bitwise or**, **integer bitwise and** and **integer bitwise exclusive or**, respectively. The result is obtained by pairing the corresponding **bit**s of each operand according to the following table.

bit n of op1	bit n of op2	bit n of op1 | op2	bit n of op1 & op2	bit n of op1 ^ op2
0	0	0	0	0
0	1	1	0	1
1	0	1	0	1
1	1	1	1	0

For example, the value 1000 which is 1111101000 in **binary**, when anded with the value 23 which is 0000010111 in binary, yields 0000000000 – because they have no corresponding bit values in common. When they are instead or-ed together, we get 1111111111 in binary, which is 1023. This happens to be the same as 1000 + 23, but **integer bitwise or** is the same as **addition** only when the two numbers have no corresponding bits with the same value.

In our input image file, of the four bytes representing the width or height, the least significant byte comes first, then the next least significant, and so on. So to turn these four separate bytes into a single 32 bit number, we must **left shift** the second byte by 8, the third by 16 and the fourth by 24, and then combine all four together using **integer bitwise or**.

```
057:    // Read an int from the next four bytes in the input image file.
058:    // Least significant byte is first.
059:    private static int readInt() throws IOException
060:    {
061:      return readByte() | readByte() << 8 | readByte() << 16 | readByte() << 24;
062:    } // readInt
```

Coffee time: [18.7.1] How could we have used **multiplication** and **addition** to achieve the same result as the **left shift** and **integer bitwise or** above?

Each pixel of the input image is represented using three bytes, one each for the red, green and then blue components of the colour at that point. We wish to convert this colour into a monochrome brightness, taking account of the fact that green is perceived by most people to be brighter than red, and red to be brighter than blue. A commonly used ratio for measuring perceived brightness is 299 : 587 : 114 for *red* : *green* : *blue*.

```
065:    // Read a pixel value from the input file and return its brightness.
066:    // The pixel is stored as 3 bytes for RGB.
067:    // Compute the brightness as (R*299 + G*587 + B*114)/1000.
068:    private static int readPixelBrightness() throws IOException
069:    {
070:      int red = readByte();
071:      int green = readByte();
072:      int blue = readByte();
073:      return (red * 299 + green * 587 + blue * 114) / 1000;
074:    } // readPixelBrightness
```

At the right point in the input file, the image itself is stored as height number of rows, each containing width number of pixels. The first row corresponds to the bottom of the image. The first pixel in each row corresponds to the left of the image. We wish to read these pixel values, and store each one in its corresponding scaled pixel of our output image. The output image will (typically) contain many fewer pixels than the input image.

```
077:    // Read the image from the input file and scale into the output array.
078:    private static void readImage() throws IOException
079:    {
080:      // The first row of input pixels is the bottom of the image.
081:      // I.e., in a BMP file, position 0,0 is bottom left.
082:      for (int inputY = 0; inputY < inputHeight; inputY++)
083:      {
084:        for (int inputX = 0; inputX < inputWidth; inputX++)
085:        {
086:          int pixelValue = readPixelBrightness();
087:          // This pixel address needs to be scaled to fit output image.
088:          int outputX = inputX * outputWidth / inputWidth;
089:          int outputY = inputY * outputHeight / inputHeight;
090:          // Add the input pixel value to the output pixel,
091:          outputImage[outputX][outputY] += pixelValue;
092:        } // for
093:        // Each row of the input image is zero padded to a multiple of 4 bytes.
094:        skipIrrelvantBytes(inputWidth % 4);
095:      } // for
096:    } // readImage
```

We need to find the brightness of the brightest pixel in the output image, so that when we come to write it as text, we can scale each value to the range of output characters chosen. A brightness of zero will be mapped onto the darkest character, the maximum brightness will be mapped onto the lightest character, and all other values will be linearly mapped between.

```
099:    // Find the highest valued pixel in the output image.
100:    private static int maxOutputBrightness()
101:    {
102:      int maxBrightnessSoFar = 0;
103:      for (int y = 0; y < outputHeight; y++)
104:        for (int x = 0; x < outputWidth; x++)
105:          if (outputImage[x][y] > maxBrightnessSoFar)
106:            maxBrightnessSoFar = outputImage[x][y];
107:      return maxBrightnessSoFar;
108:    } // maxOutputBrightness
```

Writing the output image involves **loop**ing through the outputImage **array** and printing out the appropriate text character representing the brightness of each pixel.

```
111:   // Write the text image to standard output.
112:   private static void writeTextImage()
113:   {
114:     int maxBrightness = maxOutputBrightness();
115:     // Scale each pixel brightness to one of the SHADE_CHARS.
116:     for (int y = outputHeight - 1; y >= 0; y--)
117:     {
118:       for (int x = 0; x < outputWidth; x++)
119:         System.out.print(SHADE_CHARS[outputImage[x][y] * SHADE_CHARS.length
120:                                                  / (maxBrightness + 1)]);
121:       System.out.println();
122:     } // for
123:   } // writeTextImage
```

Finally, we have our **main method**. This consists of calling the **method**s written above, with that code wrapped in a **try statement** which has a **catch clause** for the various things that can go wrong.

```
126:   // The main method gets arguments and parses the image file at the top level.
127:   public static void main(String[] args)
128:   {
129:     // The name of the input image file, which must be in 24 bit BMP format.
130:     String filename = null;
131:     try
132:     {
133:       // Check we have three arguments.
134:       if (args.length != 3)
135:         throw new ArrayIndexOutOfBoundsException(); // Caught below.
136:
137:       // The first two command line arguments
138:       // are the required width and height of the text image.
139:       outputWidth = Integer.parseInt(args[0]);
140:       outputHeight = Integer.parseInt(args[1]);
141:       outputImage = new int[outputWidth][outputHeight];
142:
143:       // The third argument is the original BMP image file name.
144:       filename = args[2];
145:       inputImage = new FileInputStream(filename);
146:
147:       skipIrrelvantBytes(18);
148:       inputWidth = readInt();
149:       inputHeight = readInt();
150:       skipIrrelvantBytes(28);
151:       readImage();
152:
153:       // Check end of file.
154:       if (inputImage.read() != -1)
155:         throw new IOException("Data after end of image");
156:
157:       writeTextImage();
158:     } // try
159:     catch (ArrayIndexOutOfBoundsException exception)
160:     {
161:       System.err.println("Please (only) supply: width height filename");
162:     } // catch
```

```
163:    catch (NumberFormatException exception)
164:    {
165:      System.err.println("Supplied dimension is not a number: "
166:                              + exception.getMessage());
167:    } // catch
168:    catch (FileNotFoundException exception)
169:    {
170:      System.err.println("Cannot open image file " + filename);
171:    } // catch
172:    catch (IOException exception)
173:    {
174:      System.err.println("Problem reading image file: "
175:                              + exception.getMessage());
176:    } // catch
177:    finally
178:    {
179:      try { if (inputImage != null) inputImage.close(); }
180:      catch (IOException exception)
181:        { System.err.println("Could not close image file " + exception); }
182:    } // finally
183:  } // main
184:
185: } // class Bmp2Txt
```

18.7.1 Trying it

Let us try the program
with another photograph
(taken *more* than a few
years ago!).

```
Console Input / Output

$ java Bmp2Txt 50 25 me.bmp
###########@**@@@@#@@@@@@##########@@@@#@#@@@@######
##########@@@+****+++++*++*@@@@##@@@*@@@@@@@@@#####
##@@@@@@****++...+....++++++*@@@@@@#@@@****@@####
@@@@@@@@*.+...+++++++.++++.+****@@@#@@@***@@@@###
@@@@@@**++++++++*+++++++++***********@@@@*@@@@@@@@
*****++++*****+*+++++++*****@@@****++++***+++++*++
+++++++++***+*+++++*+++++@@@@***@@@***+++++++++++
+++++.++*****@*****+..+*@@@@@*+@@@*++++++++++++++
++++*+++******+++.+++. ++++*@***+*@@@*+++++++++++
+++++++++*@**+*.       .+++*+..*@@@@*+++++++++++++
+++++++++**@@@*.       ...++++++.+@@*++++++++++++
+++++++++@@@@@+        ..++++.+****+.+.   .+++++++++
+.....+***@@@+     ..+++++. .+....... ++    .+++++++
+..++++***@@*+          . ..+***   .++.+++
+.++****@****+.           .. .+...+@@+.     .....+
++++++***@*...         .++..++++*++.++.       .....
+++++**@@@###+.        ..+...*******+*+         ++++
++++++***@*@#+..       ...+++++++++**@+......  .++***
+++++++++****@+     ....++....+++..*@+*.+...+******.
++++++...+****+.    .+****......+++**.*.*..++*+ ... .
+.....     ....     ....*********++**+*....*+**.
..                   ....+.++++.. .++++..+*+*++++++.
 ..                   ......++. ...++++.. . .+.....
                       ........ .. .++ .  ...
                                 .. . .... . .. ++++
$ _
```

18.7.2 Coursework: Encoding binary in text

Have you ever wondered how it is that you can send a **binary file**, such as an image, as an attachment inside an email message, when in fact an email is actually an **ASCII**[9] **text file**? The answer is simple: the binary file is coded as ASCII text when the email is constructed, and decoded back to binary again when the email is opened at the other end.

Search on the Internet to find out about a program called uuencode and how it codes sequences of 3 **bytes**, each using all 8 **bit**s as in a binary file, into sequences of 4 ASCII **character**s, each using only 6 bits. ($3 \times 8 = 4 \times 6$.) Or, if you are using Unix then there is a good chance the program is already installed and you can find out about it using man -a uuencode.

Write your own program called Uuencode which performs this function. Its **command line argument** should be the name of the **file** to be encoded, and the result should go to **standard output**. You should handle **exception**s using the same style as the example in this section. You can test your program by converting a binary file to ASCII, converting it back to binary again using a standard uudecode program (take care not to replace the original with the decoded one!), and comparing that result with the original. uudecode is available from the Internet or is probably installed if you are using Unix. You could use your CheckSum program to undertake the comparison (or on Unix you could use the cmp program).

The following **pseudo code** might help (after you have found out about the format that uuencode produces).

```
write the header -- assume file mode 600
create an array to hold the bytes for one line (partially filled)
read next byte
while next byte is not -1
  process a line of bytes and read next byte
output a line representing zero number of bytes
output the trailer line
```

We can refine this to the following.

```
write the header -- assume file mode 600
create an array to hold the bytes for one line (partially filled)
read next byte
while next byte is not -1
  while next byte is not -1 and array is not full
    put next byte in the array
    read next byte
  end-while
  output the number of bytes on this line
  loop over the line array in groups of 3 bytes
    calculate the 4 output bytes for those 3 bytes
    output the 4 output bytes
  end-loop
  output an end of line
end-while
output a line representing zero number of bytes
output the trailer line
```

You will also find the following code fragments helpful!

```
...
009:    // Write a single result byte as a printable character.
010:    // Each byte is 6-bit, i.e. range 0..63.
011:    // Thus adding 32 makes it printable, except for 0 which would become space
012:    // and so we add 96 instead -- a left single quote (').
013:    private static void writeByteAsChar(int thisByte)
014:    {
015:        System.out.print((char) (thisByte == 0 ? 96 : thisByte + 32));
016:    } // writeByteAsChar
...
056:            // Calculate 4 result bytes from the 3 input bytes.
057:            int byte1 = lineBytes[byteGroupIndex] >> 2;
058:            int byte2 = (lineBytes[byteGroupIndex] & 0x3) << 4
059:                        | (lineBytes[byteGroupIndex + 1] >> 4);
060:            int byte3 = (lineBytes[byteGroupIndex + 1] & 0xf) << 2
061:                        | lineBytes[byteGroupIndex + 2] >> 6;
062:            int byte4 = lineBytes[byteGroupIndex + 2] & 0x3f;
```

478

```
063:             // Now write those result bytes.
064:             writeByteAsChar(byte1);
065:             writeByteAsChar(byte2);
066:             writeByteAsChar(byte3);
067:             writeByteAsChar(byte4);
...
```

Optional extra: Write the Uudecode program too!

18.8 Example: Contour points

AIM: To show an example of writing and reading **binary files** where we choose the **data** format, using DataOutputStream and DataInputStream **classes**.

Assume we wish to build an application that manipulates contour points in a model of a terrain surface. We do not present the whole program here, indeed we do not even identify its full requirements! However, we assume that the program will process and generate a large amount of **data**, which we wish to store in a **binary file format** so that it is more compact. Here we simply present an early stage of the program development, as a vehicle for exploring writing to and reading from **binary files**, where we have chosen the data format.

We shall use the **classes** DataOutputStream and DataInputStream to respectively write to and read from a binary file.

Concept **File IO API: DataOutputStream.** If we wish to write values of any **primitive type**, rather than just **byte**, to a **binary file**, we can use the java.io.DataOutputStream **class**. This is a **subclass** of java.io.OutputStream and an **instance** of it is also a wrapper around an OutputStream (including its subclasses such as java.io.FileOutputStream). For example, a DataOutputStream **object** which writes to the **file** out.dat can be **construct**ed with the following code.

```
DataOutputStream out = new DataOutputStream(new FileOutputStream("out.dat"));
```

DataOutputStream has **instance method**s to write all the kinds of primitive type, such as writeInt() to write an **int** value in four **byte**s, and writeShort() to write a **short** value in two bytes. The *most* significant byte of numbers is written first, although if we intend to read the **data** back using the corresponding readXXX() instance method of java.io.DataInputStream, we do not really need to worry about the byte order.

Instances of java.lang.String can also be written, using the writeUTF() instance method. This records the information in (a slight variant of) a **file encoding** known as **8-bit Unicode Transformation Format**. **UTF-8** allows for all **Unicode**[20] **character**s to be represented.

Concept **File IO API: DataInputStream.** If we wish to read values from a **binary file** which was written using a DataOutputStream, we can use the java.io.DataInputStream **class**. This is a **subclass** of java.io.InputStream and an **instance** of it is also a wrapper around an InputStream (including its subclasses such as java.io.FileInputStream). For example, a DataInputStream **object** which reads from the **file** in.dat can be **construct**ed with the following code.

```
DataInputStream in = new DataInputStream(new FileInputStream("in.dat"));
```

DataInputStream has **instance method**s to read all the kinds of **primitive type**, such as readInt() to read an **int** value from four **byte**s, and readShort() to read a **short** value from two bytes. The *most* significant byte of numbers is read first, although if we are just reading **data** back which was written using the corresponding writeXXX() instance method of DataOutputStream, we do not really need to worry about the byte order.

Instances of java.lang.String which were written using writeUTF() of DataOutputStream, can be read using the readUTF() instance method.

Coffee time: 18.8.1   Why could we *not* have used DataInputStream to read the four **byte** integer values for width and height, from the input image binary file in the last example?

Our early stage of development of the program is all contained in the ContourPoint class. Assume a contour point can be modelled on a two-dimensional grid, with a four-digit number for each of the X and Y dimensions, together with an **integer** height above sea level (including negative heights for those below it). We shall use **short** values for the X and Y dimensions, and an **int** for the height.

```
001: import java.io.DataInputStream;
002: import java.io.DataOutputStream;
003: import java.io.FileInputStream;
004: import java.io.FileOutputStream;
005: import java.io.IOException;
006:
007: // Representation of a contour point with X,Y grid reference
008: // and height above sea level.
009: public class ContourPoint
010: {
011:   // gridX and gridY are in the range 0-9999, so a short will do nicely.
012:   private final short gridX, gridY;
013:
014:   // Height has a wider range, but int is plenty.
015:   private final int height;
016:
017:
018:   // Construct a ContourPoint with the given dimensions.
019:   public ContourPoint(int requiredGridX, int requiredGridY, int requiredHeight)
020:   {
021:     gridX = (short) requiredGridX;
022:     gridY = (short) requiredGridY;
023:     height = requiredHeight;
024:   } // ContourPoint
```

We have a second **constructor method** which reads the dimensions from a given DataInputStream **object**. These are assumed to be in the same form as produced by the following write() **instance method**, otherwise an IOException may be **thrown**.

```
027:   // Construct a ContourPoint, by reading the dimensions
028:   // from the given DataInputStream.
029:   public ContourPoint(DataInputStream in) throws IOException
030:   {
031:     gridX = in.readShort();
032:     gridY = in.readShort();
033:     height = in.readInt();
034:   } // ContourPoint
```

The write() instance method writes the three dimensions of the ContourPoint to a given DataOutputStream object, in the form expected by the above constructor method.

```
037:   // Write the three dimensions to a given DataOutputStream
038:   // so that it can be read back into the above constructor.
039:   public void write(DataOutputStream out) throws IOException
040:   {
041:     out.writeShort(gridX);
042:     out.writeShort(gridY);
043:     out.writeInt(height);
044:   } // write
```

The class has **accessor methods** for the **instance variables**.

```
047:   // Accessor for gridX.        054:   // Accessor for gridY.        061:   // Accessor for height.
048:   public short getGridX()       055:   public short getGridY()       062:   public int getHeight()
049:   {                             056:   {                             063:   {
050:     return gridX;               057:     return gridY;               064:     return height;
051:   } // getGridX                 058:   } // getGridY                 065:   } // getHeight
```

One of the features of the class is to generate an **array**, of a given length, of ContourPoint objects. These **new** ContourPoints are linearly interpolated between this one and a given other one. That is, we **construct** a point in each array position, such that they are all evenly spaced between this point and the given other one.

```
068:   // Linear interpolation between this and a given other point.
069:   public ContourPoint[] interpolate(ContourPoint endPoint, int noOfSteps)
070:   {
071:     ContourPoint[] result = new ContourPoint[noOfSteps];
072:
073:     for (int stepCount = 1; stepCount <= noOfSteps; stepCount++)
074:     {
075:       short newGridX = (short) (gridX + stepCount * (endPoint.gridX - gridX)
076:                                         / (noOfSteps + 1));
077:       short newGridY = (short) (gridY + stepCount * (endPoint.gridY - gridY)
078:                                         / (noOfSteps + 1));
079:       // Cast stepCount to long, to avoid int overflow.
080:       int newHeight = (int) (height + (long) stepCount
081:                                     * (endPoint.height - height)
082:                                     / (noOfSteps + 1));
083:       result[stepCount - 1] = new ContourPoint(newGridX, newGridY, newHeight);
084:     } // for
085:     return result;
086:   } // interpolate
```

The class has a toString() instance method.

```
089:   // Return a String representing the point.
090:   @Override
091:   public String toString()
092:   {
093:     return "(" + gridX + "," + gridY + "," + height + ")";
094:   } // toString
```

Finally, we have a **main method**, purely for the purpose of testing during development. This creates two points, and various interpolations between them, which it writes to the binary file test.dat. Then it reads this data back from the **file** and prints it to **standard output**.

```
097:   // Purely for testing during development, and so does not catch exceptions.
098:   public static void main(String[] args) throws Exception
099:   {
100:     ContourPoint point1 = new ContourPoint(0, 0, 0);
101:     ContourPoint point2 = new ContourPoint(9999, 9999, 100000000);
102:
103:     DataOutputStream output
104:       = new DataOutputStream(new FileOutputStream("test.dat"));
```

The test will try three interpolation steps (i.e. numbers of generated intermediate points) between point1 and point2.

481

```
106:     // Test the following interpolation steps.
107:     int[] trySteps = {0, 10, 100};
```

We write the number of **lists** of points to the test file.

```
109:     // Write the number of lists.
110:     output.writeByte(trySteps.length);
```

Then we write the lists of points. For each we write how many points there are – including the original pair, and then we write the details of each point.

```
112:     for (int tryStep : trySteps)
113:     {
114:       ContourPoint[] interpolation = point1.interpolate(point2, tryStep);
115:       // Write the length of this list,
116:       // plus 2 to include the original points.
117:       output.writeInt(interpolation.length + 2);
118:       // Now write the first point.
119:       point1.write(output);
120:       // Now write each interpolated point.
121:       for (ContourPoint aPoint : interpolation)
122:         aPoint.write(output);
123:       // Now write the last point.
124:       point2.write(output);
125:     } // for
126:
127:     output.close();
```

Finally, we read the information back in the same order we wrote it, and print it to **standard output**.

```
129:     DataInputStream input
130:       = new DataInputStream(new FileInputStream("test.dat"));
131:
132:     // Read the number of lists.
133:     int noOfLists = input.readByte();
134:     for (int count = 1; count <= noOfLists; count++)
135:     {
136:       // Read the length of this list.
137:       int length = input.readInt();
138:       ContourPoint[] pointArray = new ContourPoint[length];
139:
140:       // Now read each point.
141:       for (int pointIndex = 0; pointIndex < length; pointIndex++)
142:         // Construct a point from the file.
143:         pointArray[pointIndex] = new ContourPoint(input);
144:
145:       // Now print them out.
146:       for (int pointIndex = 0; pointIndex < length; pointIndex++)
147:         System.out.println(pointIndex + " " + pointArray[pointIndex]);
148:       System.out.println();
149:     } // for
150:
151:     input.close();
152:   } // main
153:
154: } // class ContourPoint
```

18.8.1 Trying it

We **run** the program and check its output is correct.

The size of the **binary file** produced by the test program, test.dat, is considerably less than it would be if the **data** was stored as a **text file**. If we take the **standard output** from the test program, strip off everything except the text inside the brackets and then count the **character**s we should get a good approximation of the minimum size that would be needed to store the data as text. We can compare that with the size of test.dat.

On Unix we can achieve the above text filtering and character counting with the following 'magic'.

```
                    Console Input / Output
$ java ContourPoint | cut -f2 -d"(" | cut -f1 -d ")" | wc -c
2135
$ ls -l test.dat
-rw-------  1 jtl jtl 941 Mar 30 12:30 test.dat
$ _
```

We can see that the binary file is less than half the size of a text file containing the same information. Each **short** takes only two **byte**s, instead of up to four as text (one for each digit), and each **int** takes four bytes, instead of a typical eight (for this data). There is no need for a separator byte (e.g. comma) between each component of a point, nor (e.g. new line) between each point, as each component is a fixed size.

```
         Console Input / Output
$ java ContourPoint
0 (0,0,0)
1 (9999,9999,100000000)

0 (0,0,0)
1 (909,909,9090909)
2 (1818,1818,18181818)
3 (2727,2727,27272727)
4 (3636,3636,36363636)
5 (4545,4545,45454545)
6 (5454,5454,54545454)
7 (6363,6363,63636363)
8 (7272,7272,72727272)
9 (8181,8181,81818181)
10 (9090,9090,90909090)
11 (9999,9999,100000000)

0 (0,0,0)
1 (99,99,990099)
2 (198,198,1980198)
(... lines removed to save space.)
99 (9801,9801,98019801)
100 (9900,9900,99009900)
101 (9999,9999,100000000)

$ _
```

18.8.2 Coursework: Saving greedy children

Copy the GreedyChild and IceCreamParlour **class**es from Section 11.3 starting on page 201 and add code so they can be written to a DataOutputStream and read back from a DataInputStream. You do not need to save the IceCreamParlour that a GreedyChild is in – so when a GreedyChild is read back, he or she will always not be in a parlour. Test your new features with a program called TestGreedyChildrenIO.

Optional extra: Figure out how to save and restore the IceCreamParlour that a GreedyChild is in. Perhaps each IceCreamParlour could have a unique ID number? Maybe that number would also be an **array index**? You may want to ensure that all IceCreamParlours are read (and hence written) before any GreedyChild is read.

Optional extra: (Challenge!) Find out about ObjectInputStream and ObjectOutputStream and use those instead.

18.9 Concepts covered in this chapter

Here is a list of the concepts that were covered in this chapter, each with a self-test question. You can use this to check you remember them being introduced, and perhaps re-read some of them before going on to the next chapter.

Expression	
– arithmetic: shift operators (p.473)	<< is to * like >> is to /, or is it vice versa?
– arithmetic: integer bitwise operators (p.474)	What is the value of each of the following expressions? 1. 16 & 8 & 4 & 2 & 1 2. 16 | 8 | 4 | 2 | 1

File IO API	
– `PrintWriter` (p.463)	What possible values are given to the method(s) used for writing data? Bytes? Characters? Lines?
– `PrintWriter: checkError()` (p.464)	What result is returned by this instance method if something has gone wrong?
– `PrintWriter:` versus `PrintStream` (p.468)	What does `PrintWriter` not have that `PrintStream` does? Is that something we want to generally use?
– `PrintWriter:` can also wrap an `OutputStream` (p.468)	What is flushing and automatic flushing?
– `IOException` (p.450)	Is this a subclass of `Exception` or `RuntimeException`? Is it a checked or unchecked exception type?
– `InputStream` (p.451)	What possible values are returned from the method used for reading data? Bytes? Characters? Lines? Some other value?
– `InputStreamReader` (p.456)	What possible values are returned from the instance method used for reading data? Bytes? Characters? Lines? Some other value?
– `BufferedReader` (p.459)	What possible values are returned from the method used for reading data? Bytes? Characters? Lines? Some other value?
– `FileInputStream` (p.462)	What is the superclass of this class?
– `FileReader` (p.462)	This class is merely a convenience for something. What?
– `OutputStream` (p.462)	What possible values are given to the method(s) used for writing data? Bytes? Characters? Lines?
– `OutputStreamWriter` (p.462)	What possible values are given to the method(s) used for writing data? Bytes? Characters? Lines?
– `FileOutputStream` (p.463)	What is the superclass of this class?
– `FileWriter` (p.463)	This class is merely a convenience for something. What?
– `File` (p.469)	How do we use this to check for the existence of a file?
– `DataOutputStream` (p.479)	In what order are bytes of a number written?
– `DataInputStream` (p.479)	In what order are bytes of a number read?
Standard API	
– `System: err:` is an `OutputStream` (p.468)	The type of `System.out` and `System.err` is actually a subclass of `OutputStream` – which one?
– `System: in:` is an `InputStream` (p.452)	This allows access to the standard input, as bytes or characters?
– `System: out:` is an `OutputStream` (p.468)	Does this allows access to the standard output as bytes, characters or both?
Statement	
– assignment statement: is an expression (p.450)	What is the significance of the associativity of the assignment operator? Is it left or right?
– try statement: with finally (p.451)	Under what circumstances is the finally block executed?
Variable	
– initial value (p.453)	Why is it generally a good idea not to rely on initial values of variables? Which kinds of variables are we forced to initialize?

Chapter 19

Generic classes

He who does not label his boxes
can expect surprises when he opens them!

19.1 Chapter aims

There are many situations in which we wish to have an **object** contained or embedded within another. For example, we may wish to have a whole collection of items grouped into one object, such as a **list** or **set**, etc.. If, as is often the case, we want our collections to be able to contain *any* kind of object, we run the risk of forgetting what kind of thing we have put in them – rather like sealing up a box without labelling it with a list of contents.

This chapter introduces the simple idea of us being able to apply such labels, which we call **type argument**s, when we create the container. But first we explore the problems we have if we don't use such labelling.

(The related topic of **generic method**s is covered in Section 20.4.2 on page 522.)

The chapter contains the following sections.

Section	Aims	Associated Coursework
19.2 A pair of any objects (p.486)	To explore potential problems of having a container **object** that can hold **instances** of any **class**, in particular that we need protection against us erroneously getting the **type** wrong when we extract items from the container. We also introduce the idea of **boxing** an `int` within an `Integer`.	Write a **class** that can store a triple of **objects**, and use it. (p.490)
19.3 A generic pair of specified types (p.490)	To introduce the idea of **generic class**es, and show how it can be used to avoid the problems explored in the previous section.	Write a **generic class** that can store a triple of specific kinds of **objects**, and use it. (p.494)
19.4 Autoboxing and auto-unboxing of primitive values (p.494)	To expose Java's implicit conversion between values of **primitive type**s and **instances** of the corresponding wrapper **classes**.	Write a **generic class** that can store a triple of specific kinds of **objects**, and use it; this time using **autoboxing** and **auto-unboxing**. (p.495)

Section	Aims	Associated Coursework
19.5 A conversation of persons (p.496)	To introduce the idea of a **bound type parameter**, in particular, one that must **extend** some other **type**.	Write a **generic class** that can store a collection of a particular kind of MoodyPerson **object**s, from the Notional Lottery example, and make them all happy or unhappy at the same time. (p.500)
19.6 What we cannot do with type parameters (p.501)	To briefly explore some of the things we might like to do with **type parameters** but cannot.	(None.)
19.7 Using a generic class without type parameters (p.502)	To briefly explore what happens when we use a **generic class** without **type parameters**.	(None.)

19.2 Example: A pair of any objects

AIM:
To explore potential problems of having a container **object** that can hold **instance**s of any **class**, in particular that we need protection against us erroneously getting the **type** wrong when we extract items from the container. We also introduce the idea of **boxing** an **int** within an Integer.

This first section introduces the example which we shall use in the next section to look at the concept of **generic class**es.

The idea is to have a pair of **object**s which needs no more functionality than having two items paired together, which can be later extracted apart. There are a number of places where such a thing would be useful, but perhaps the most obvious ones are those times when it is desirable for a **method** to **return** two results, rather than just one. In such situations, many programmers introduce **class variables** or **instance variables** which have no other use than to receive the results from the method. Indeed, you have no doubt seen examples of that approach in earlier chapters. Some programmers make the method return an **array** of length two, containing the two results. The problem with this is its lack of robustness – the code that calls the method could accidentally be written to extract the third item in the array, which would cause an error, but only at **run time** rather than **compile time**. Using a pair does not have that problem, and is arguably more elegant.

19.2.1 The Pair class

The **class** has a **constructor method** which takes (**reference**s to) the two **object**s and stores them in **instance variable**s.

```
001: // Two Objects grouped into a pair.
002: public class Pair
003: {
004:   // The two objects.
005:   private final Object first, second;
006:
007:
008:   // Constructor is given the two objects.
009:   public Pair(Object requiredFirst, Object requiredSecond)
010:   {
011:     first = requiredFirst;
012:     second = requiredSecond;
013:   } // Pair
```

Then it merely has two **accessor method**s.

```
016:    // Return the first object.
017:    public Object getFirst()
018:    {
019:      return first;
020:    } // getFirst
021:
022:
023:    // Return the second object.
024:    public Object getSecond()
025:    {
026:      return second;
027:    } // getSecond
028:
029: } // class Pair
```

19.2.2 The longest argument program

To illustrate the use of our Pair **class**, we shall consider a contrived but attractively simple program that finds the longest string in the **command line argument**s and reports it together with its position (counting from one). More precisely, it will find the first occurrence of a longest string, if there are two or more strings of the same greatest length.

To promote future flexibility, we shall write a general purpose **class method** to find the longest string from an **array** and put it into a separate class called LongestString. We shall call this from the **main method** in the class LongestArgument.

19.2.3 The LongestString class

```
001: // Contains a method to find the position of the longest string in an array.
002: public class LongestString
003: {
```

The **class method** to search the **array** of Strings will **return** a Pair consisting of the longest string and its **array index** in the array. One slight snag is that the index will be an **int**, which is a **primitive type**, whereas the Pair **class** requires both of the elements to be Objects. The typical solution to this common problem, when we wish to treat a primitive value as though it is an **object**, is to wrap up, or **box**, the primitive value *inside* an object. For an **int** we would use an Integer object.

Concept **Standard API: Integer: as a box for int.** In addition to containing **class method**s to manipulate **integer** related values, the standard **class** java.lang.Integer can be used to wrap up **int** values as **objects**. One of the **constructor method**s of the class may be given an **int**, and this makes an **instance** of Integer wrapping up, or boxing, that number. The **instance method** intValue() can then later be used to retrieve the boxed number from the object. This effectively allows an **int**, which is a **primitive type**, to be treated as though it is an **object**.

Here is the findLongestString() class method. Notice how longestIndex is **box**ed inside an Integer before being placed into the Pair.

```
004:    // Find the longest string in the given array.
005:    // Return a Pair containing it and its position.
006:    // Throw IllegalArgumentException if array is null or empty.
```

```
007:    public static Pair findLongestString(String[] array)
008:                        throws IllegalArgumentException
009:    {
010:      if (array == null || array.length == 0)
011:        throw new IllegalArgumentException("Array must exist and be non-empty");
012:
013:      String longestString = array[0];
014:      int longestIndex = 0;
015:      for (int index = 1; index < array.length; index++)
016:        if (longestString.length() < array[index].length())
017:        {
018:          longestString = array[index];
019:          longestIndex = index;
020:        } // if
021:
022:      return new Pair(longestString, new Integer(longestIndex));
023:    } // findLongestString
024:
025: } // class LongestString
```

Coffee time: 19.2.1 What would happen if we swapped the **operands** of the **conditional or operator** in the first **if statement** above?

Coffee time: 19.2.2 Our Pair **constructor method** expects to be given two Objects but we are supplying a String and an Integer. Is that okay?

19.2.4 The LongestArgument class

Our **main method** simply calls LongestString.findLongestString() passing it the **command line argument**s. It then extracts the two components of the resulting Pair. The first one needs **cast**ing from Object to String – inside the Pair it is only known to be an Object, whereas we know it actually **is a** String and need to treat it as such. The second component needs to be cast into an Integer and then have its **boxed int** retrieved via intValue().

To avoid getting distracted, we do not bother to **catch exception**s caused by there being no command line arguments in this example.

```
001: // Find the longest command line argument and report it and its position.
002: // (Warning: this program does not catch RuntimeExceptions.)
003: public class LongestArgument
004: {
005:    public static void main(String[] args) throws RuntimeException
006:    {
007:      Pair result = LongestString.findLongestString(args);
008:      String longestArg = (String) result.getFirst();
009:      int longestIndex = ((Integer)result.getSecond()).intValue();
010:
011:      System.out.println("A longest argument was '" + longestArg + "'");
012:      System.out.println("of length " + longestArg.length());
013:      System.out.println("found at position " + (longestIndex + 1));
014:    } // main
015:
016: } // class LongestArgument
```

19.2.5 Trying it

This is not a thorough set of tests.

```
Console Input / Output
$ java LongestArgument A stitch in time saves nine
A longest argument was 'stitch'
of length 6
found at position 2
$ _
```

```
Console Input / Output
$ java LongestArgument A stitch in time will become very painful
A longest argument was 'painful'
of length 7
found at position 8
$ _
```

Coffee time: 19.2.3
What other tests should we perform?

19.2.6 The `LongestArgumentOops` class

Here is another version of the program, called `LongestArgumentOops` because it has a simple mistake in it.

```
001: // Find the longest command line argument and report it and its position.
002: // (Warning: this program does not catch RuntimeExceptions.)
003: public class LongestArgumentOops
004: {
005:   public static void main(String[] args)
006:   {
007:     Pair result = LongestString.findLongestString(args);
008:     int longestIndex = ((Integer)result.getFirst()).intValue();
009:     String longestArg = (String) result.getSecond();
010:
011:     System.out.println("A longest argument was '" + longestArg + "'");
012:     System.out.println("of length " + longestArg.length());
013:     System.out.println("found at position " + (longestIndex + 1));
014:   } // main
015:
016: } // class LongestArgumentOops
```

Coffee time: 19.2.4
Can you spot the simple mistake?

Let us **compile** the program.

```
Console Input / Output
$ javac LongestArgumentOops.java
$ _
```

It compiles okay – despite the simple mistake. The **compiler** has no choice but to believe us when we say that those two **type cast**s will work. The snag is, we as programmers are not infallible, and we have made a mistake. Now let us **run** the program.

```
Console Input / Output
$ java LongestArgumentOops A stitch in time saves nine
Exception in thread "main" java.lang.ClassCastException: java.lang.String cannot
 be cast to java.lang.Integer
        at LongestArgumentOops.main(LongestArgumentOops.java:8)
$ _
```

We get a **run time error**, of course.

Coffee time: 19.2.5
How common do you expect this sort of simple mistake is? Are you happy that the error is only detected at **run time**? What if the error was made in an obscure part of the code that only **execute**s under highly unusual circumstances that were unfortunately not tested for; perhaps during an emergency, such as a sudden close proximity of another aircraft in an auto pilot control program?

The next section introduces Java concepts that enable us to seriously reduce the possibility of making this kind of mistake.

19.2.7   Coursework: A triple

Write a **class** called `Triple`, similar to `Pair`, except that its **instance**s each store three **object**s.

Write a class called `IntArrayStats` containing a **class method** `getStats()` which takes an **array** of `int`s and **returns** a `Triple` containing the maximum **integer** in the array, the minimum, and also the mean of all the values. You will need to **box** the first two inside `Integer` objects, and the third inside a `Double`.

Test your work with the following program which measures how much the mean of a **set** of numbers differs from the average of its minimum and maximum.

```
001: // Program to measure how much the mean of the integer command line arguments
002: // differs from the average of their minimum and maximum.
003: // (Warning: this program does not catch RuntimeExceptions.)
004: public class MeanMinMaxMinusMean
005: {
006:   public static void main(String[] args) throws RuntimeException
007:   {
008:     int[] array = new int[args.length];
009:     for (int index = 0; index < args.length; index++)
010:       array[index] = Integer.parseInt(args[index]);
011:
012:     Triple stats = IntArrayStats.getStats(array);
013:     int max = ((Integer)stats.getFirst()).intValue();
014:     int min = ((Integer)stats.getSecond()).intValue();
015:     double mean = ((Double)stats.getThird()).doubleValue();
016:     System.out.println((min + max) / 2.0 - mean);
017:   } // main
018:
019: } // class MeanMinMaxMinusMean
```

If you **run** the program with a set of consecutive numbers, the result should come out as `0.0`.

 Coffee time: `19.2.6`   What common **bug** could cause the result to be `0.5` when the program is given a list of consecutive numbers of a length which is even?

Experiment to see what happens when you make the same kind of mistake in the above program as we did in the example in this section.

19.3   Example: A generic pair of specified types

AIM:
To introduce the idea of **generic classes**, and show how it can be used to avoid the problems explored in the previous section.

In this section we introduce the topic which this chapter is really about. We have just seen that we can make ourselves a general purpose `Pair` **class** and use it appropriately. But there is something a little unsatisfactory about it. When we build an **instance** of `Pair` the **compiler** knows what **type**s of **object** are going into it, but when we take them out we have to tell the compiler to **cast** them from `Object` to whatever **subclass** we need them to be – typically whatever they were known as when they were put into the pair. A type cast is checked at **run time** – the **virtual machine** checks that the object really **is** an **instance** of the class it is being cast into, and **throws** a `ClassCastException` if it is not. As we saw at the end of the last section, we are not infallible, and we should be worried that our simple mistakes can become **bug**s.

Wouldn't it be nice if there was a way of allowing the compiler to already know that the items in the pair are of the type we want? What this boils down to, in our `Pair` example, is the desire to be able to say what *kind* of pair we have, rather than just that we have a pair. Since Java 5.0 we have the ability to write **generic class**es and this gives us the power we are looking for.

Concept **Class: generic class.** A **generic class** is a **class** which has one or more **type parameter**s written within angled brackets (<>) just after its name in the class heading. When an **instance** of a generic class is made, specific **type**s are supplied as **type argument**s for the type parameters, in a similar way that **method argument**s are supplied for **method parameter**s in a **method call**.

In the following symbolic example, `T1` and `T2` are type parameters.

```
public class MyGenericClass<T1, T2>
{
    ... Typical class stuff here,
    ... but using T1 and T2 as though they are types
    ... (in permitted ways).
    T1 someVariable = ...
    T2 someOtherVariable = ...
    ...
} // class MyGenericClass
```

When we make an instance of `MyGenericClass`, or delare a **variable** of that type, we supply a specific type for each type parameter, as in the following example.

```
MyGenericClass<String, Date> myVariable = new MyGenericClass<String, Date>();
```

A class is a **type**. However, the intention with a generic class is that we supply specific type arguments for the type parameters before we use it, and in doing so, we identify a **parameterized type**. For example, from the generic class `MyGenericClass` we can have parameterized types such as `MyGenericClass<String, Date>`, `MyGenericClass<Integer, String>`, etc., including ones involving **arrays**, like `MyGenericClass<String[], Integer>`, and so on.

A parameterized type almost behaves as though we have made a textual copy of the generic class, and replaced each type parameter with its corresponding type argument. But not quite. Instead, due to the way Java actually implements generic classes, there are some restrictions. In particular, type arguments must be **reference type**s, such as classes and arrays. This means they cannot be **primitive type**s.

19.3.1 The `Pair` class

We can improve our `Pair` **class** from the previous section by defining it as a **generic class** which takes two **type parameter**s, one for the **type** of the first element of each pair, and the other for the second. This enables us to identify a **parameterized type** for any particular kind of pair we wish to have.

```
001: // Two Objects grouped into a pair.
002: public class Pair<FirstType, SecondType>
003: {
```

Instead of having two **instance variable**s, both of type `Object`, the new class has one of each of the two type parameters.

```
004:     // The first object.
005:     private final FirstType first;
006:
```

```
007:   // The second object.
008:   private final SecondType second;
```

The **constructor method** takes two **method parameters**, but instead of both of these being (**references** to) **objects** of type Object, each one is (a reference to) an object of the appropriate type parameter.

```
011:   // Constructor is given the two objects.
012:   public Pair(FirstType requiredFirst, SecondType requiredSecond)
013:   {
014:     first = requiredFirst;
015:     second = requiredSecond;
016:   } // Pair
```

The class has **accessor method**s as before, but their **return type**s are specific to the corresponding type parameter, rather than being Object as in the previous version. It is this aspect of the generic class that means we will not have to write **cast**s for the **return**ed values – the compiler will already know what the types are.

```
019:   // Return the first object.
020:   public FirstType getFirst()
021:   {
022:     return first;
023:   } // getFirst
024:
025:
026:   // Return the second object.
027:   public SecondType getSecond()
028:   {
029:     return second;
030:   } // getSecond
031:
032: } // class Pair
```

19.3.2 The LongestString class

Now that we have a **generic class** version of the Pair **class**, we can modify the **class method** findLongestString() from the previous section so that it **return**s a value of the **parameterized type** for the specific kind of pair, that is, (a **reference** to) an **instance** of the **type** Pair<String, Integer>.

```
001: // Contains a method to find the position of the longest string in an array.
002: public class LongestString
003: {
004:   // Find the longest string in the given array.
005:   // Return a Pair containing it and its position.
006:   // Throw IllegalArgumentException if array is null or empty.
007:   public static Pair<String, Integer> findLongestString(String[] array)
008:                                       throws IllegalArgumentException
009:   {
010:     if (array == null || array.length == 0)
011:       throw new IllegalArgumentException("Array must exist and be non-empty");
012:
013:     String longestString = array[0];
014:     int longestIndex = 0;
015:     for (int index = 1; index < array.length; index++)
016:       if (longestString.length() < array[index].length())
017:       {
018:         longestString = array[index];
019:         longestIndex = index;
020:       } // if
021:
022:     return new Pair<String, Integer>(longestString, new Integer(longestIndex));
023:   } // findLongestString
024:
025: } // class LongestString
```

Coffee time: Compare this latest version of LongestString with the original in Section 19.2.3 on page 487.

19.3.3   The `LongestArgument` class

Finally in this section, we can rewrite the **main method** in the `LongestArgument` program from the previous section so that it uses our new `findLongestString()` **class method**.

```
001: // Find the longest command line argument and report it and its position.
002: // (Warning: this program does not catch RuntimeExceptions.)
003: public class LongestArgument
004: {
005:    public static void main(String[] args) throws RuntimeException
006:    {
007:       Pair<String, Integer> result = LongestString.findLongestString(args);
008:       String longestArg = result.getFirst();
009:       int longestIndex = result.getSecond().intValue();
010:
011:       System.out.println("A longest argument was '" + longestArg + "'");
012:       System.out.println("of length " + longestArg.length());
013:       System.out.println("found at position " + (longestIndex + 1));
014:    } // main
015:
016: } // class LongestArgument
```

Note that we do not need to write **cast**s for the two elements, into `String` and `Integer` respectively, because the **compiler** already knows they are of those **type**s.

19.3.4   Trying it

The new version works just like the previous in Section 19.2.5 on page 489.

19.3.5   The `LongestArgumentOops` class

The real power of **generic class**es is shown when we make the same kind of mistake as we did in the previous section.

```
001: // Find the longest command line argument and report it and its position.
002: // (Warning: this program does not catch RuntimeExceptions.)
003: public class LongestArgumentOops
004: {
005:    public static void main(String[] args)
006:    {
007:       Pair<Integer, String> result = LongestString.findLongestString(args);
008:       int longestIndex = result.getFirst().intValue();
009:       String longestArg = result.getSecond();
010:
011:       System.out.println("A longest argument was '" + longestArg + "'");
012:       System.out.println("of length " + longestArg.length());
013:       System.out.println("found at position " + (longestIndex + 1));
014:    } // main
015:
016: } // class LongestArgumentOops
```

 Coffee time: 19.3.2 Do you agree that the above program contains the equivalent error to the one in Section 19.2.6 on page 489?

Let us compile the program.

Console Input / Output

`$ javac LongestArgumentOops.java`
`LongestArgumentOops.java:7: incompatible types`
`found   : Pair<java.lang.String,java.lang.Integer>`
`required: Pair<java.lang.Integer,java.lang.String>`
`    Pair<Integer, String> result = LongestString.findLongestString(args);`
`                                                          ^`
 	
`1 error`
`$ _`

Now the same error becomes a **compile time error** which is much better than it being a **run time error** because it does not rely on us performing the right tests to find it. What is more, the **compiler** is, in its own slightly cryptic way, telling us exactly what we have done wrong.

Coffee time:
19.3.3
While this new power is wonderful to protect against many trivial mistakes, can you think of situations where the accidental swapping of the pair elements would not be detected by the compiler?

Coffee time:
19.3.4
What do you think would happen if we had not made the changes to the `LongestString` and `LongestArgument` **class**es, but tried to **compile** the original ones from the last section with the generic class version of `Pair`? Try it! Surprised? Can you figure out why it behaves like that?

19.3.6   Coursework: A generic triple

Rewrite your **class**es from Section 19.2.7 on page 490 so that `Triple` becomes a **generic class**, and the other classes are altered appropriately.

(If you have read ahead, please do not use **autoboxing** – you will learn more by saving that for a separate task.)

19.4   Autoboxing and auto-unboxing of primitive values

AIM:
To expose Java's implicit conversion between values of **primitive types** and **instances** of the corresponding wrapper **class**es.

As we saw in Section 19.2.3 on page 487, the Java standard **class**es provide a simple mechanism for wrapping up an **int** as an `Object`. And as you might expect, there are similar classes for other **primitive types**.

Coffee time: 19.4.1
In addition to `Integer`, you have already met *two* other of these wrapper classes, although we have not yet seen them used to wrap up a value. Which two are they?

Because the use of these wrappers is widespread, since Java 5.0 they have been made even more convenient via the **auto-boxing** and **auto-unboxing** of primitive values.

Concept **Standard API: `Integer`: as a box for `int`: autoboxing.** Use of the standard **class** `java.lang.Integer` to wrap up **int** values as **object**s is so common, that since Java 5.0 the **compiler** can make their use implicit by providing **autoboxing** and **auto-unboxing**. Whenever an **int** value is given where an `Integer` is required, the **int** is automatically **boxed** (wrapped up) into a **new** `Integer` object. And whenever (a **reference** to) an `Integer` is given where an **int** is required, the `intValue()` **instance method** is automatically used to unbox the **int** value.

For example, here is some code that explicitly wraps up and extracts an `int`.

```
Integer anInteger = new Integer(10);
int anInt = anInteger.intValue() + 1;
System.out.println(anInt);
```

The following code would have exactly the same effect – both would print out 11.

```
Integer anInteger = 10;
int anInt = anInteger + 1;
System.out.println(anInt);
```

Whilst this convenience can often make the `int` and `Integer` **type**s work seamlessly together, it is important to remember the difference between them. `int` is a **primitive type**, whereas `Integer` is a **reference type**. So, for example, an **array** of ten `int` values would take as much memory as ten times the space of one `int` value (plus a little). By contrast, an array of ten `Integer` objects would hold ten **reference**s, each referring to an object storing an `int` value.

Coffee time: 19.4.2   Draw a diagram of an **array** of ten `int`s, and another of an array of ten `Integer`s.

Coffee time: 19.4.3   Do you think autoboxing and auto-unboxing has been applied to the other primitive type wrapper classes? What would be the easiest way to find out?

Here are fragments of `LongestString` and `LongestArgument` showing the differences from the previous version if we use autoboxing and auto-unboxing.

First **autoboxing**: `longestIndex` is automatically **box**ed within an `Integer`.

```
001: // Contains a method to find the position of the longest string in an array.
002: public class LongestString
003: {
...
022:     return new Pair<String, Integer>(longestString, longestIndex);
...
025: } // class LongestString
```

And **auto-unboxing**: the **return type** of `getSecond()` is `Integer`, so `intValue()` is automatically applied for us.

```
001: // Find the longest command line argument and report it and its position.
002: // (Warning: this program does not catch RuntimeExceptions.)
003: public class LongestArgument
004: {
...
009:     int longestIndex = result.getSecond();
...
016: } // class LongestArgument
```

19.4.1   Coursework: A generic triple, used with autoboxing

Rewrite your **class**es from Section 19.3.6 on page 494 so that **autoboxing** and **auto-unboxing** is used appropriately.

19.5 Example: A conversation of persons

AIM:
To introduce the idea of a **bound type parameter**, in particular, one that must **extend** some other **type**.

Recall the Notional Lottery game from Section 16.2 on page 372. Suppose we wished to add the feature of having a conversation between Persons. This is essentially a wrapper around an **array** of Person with an **instance method**, speak(), which makes one of the Persons speak, in such a way that if the instance method is called repeatedly, each Person speaks in turn.

Note that a conversation is a kind of *collection* of persons, and this observation has some significance; perhaps the times when we are most likely to write a **generic class** are when we are implementing a collection of things. For this reason, we shall speak in this section, perhaps strangely, as having a conversation *of* persons.

Suppose further, we wished to have the ability to specify that a particular Conversation comprises only persons of a particular **subclass** of Person, such as AudienceMember, whilst some other Conversation is made up from only some other subclass, such as TVHost, and so on. To achieve this, we make Conversation a **generic class**, but give it a **type parameter** which is a **bound type parameter** specifying that it must be a kind of Person.

Concept **Class: generic class: bound type parameter.** The **type parameter**s of a **generic class** may be **bound type parameter**s, which means we specify certain restrictions for the **type argument**s that can be supplied when a **parameterized type** is identified.

Concept **Class: generic class: bound type parameter: extends some class.** One kind of restriction we can specify for a **bound type parameter** is that the type argument must **extend** some known **class**. This is done by following the name of the **type parameter** with the **reserved word extends** and then the known class. When a type argument is supplied, the **compiler** checks that it is either the known class, or a **subclass** of it.

For example, in the context of some vehicle simulation program, the following is a class that has a type parameter, VehicleType, for which any corresponding **type argument** must be Vehicle or a subclass of it.

```
public class ServiceCentre<VehicleType extends Vehicle>
{
    ... Etc., using VehicleType as a type (in permitted ways)
    ... but knowing that it is a Vehicle
    ... and so using some Vehicle methods, etc..

    public void service(VehicleType vehicle)
    {
      if (! vehicle.isRoadworthy())
      {
        ...
      } // if
    } // service

    ...
} // class ServiceCentre
```

This would allow us to make ServiceCentre **object**s for particular kinds of Vehicle.

```
ServiceCentre<Car> garage = new ServiceCentre<Car>();
Car car = new Car(...);
Lorry lorry = new Lorry(...);
```

```
garage.service(car);
garage.service(lorry);
garage.service("car");
```

The last two lines above would each cause a **compile time error**.

19.5.1 The Conversation class

Our `Conversation` **class** has one **type parameter** which **extend**s `Person`.

```
001: // Representation of a group of lottery people talking in turn.
002: public class Conversation<PersonType extends Person>
003: {
```

This means the **type argument** which can be given when a **parameterized type** is identified, must be a **subclass** of `Person`, or be `Person` itself.

An **instance** of the class stores (a **reference** to) a **partially filled array** of `Person` **object**s in an **instance variable**. This **array** will be grown on demand using **array extension**.

```
004:    // Initial size and resize factor.
005:    private static final int INITIAL_ARRAY_SIZE = 2, ARRAY_RESIZE_FACTOR = 2;
006:
007:    // The array, together with the number of Person objects in it.
008:    private Person[] persons = new Person[INITIAL_ARRAY_SIZE];
009:    private int noOfPersons = 0;
```

 Coffee time: 19.5.1   Are you wondering why the array is of type `Person[]` rather than `PersonType[]`? Would that be better?

There is no work for the **constructor method**, but we write one anyway to make it clear that we have not overlooked it.

```
012:    // Empty constructor, nothing needs doing.
013:    public Conversation()
014:    {
015:    } // Conversation
```

The `addPerson()` **instance method** is given (a reference to) an object of **type** `PersonType`. This is stored in the `Person` array, which is allowed because `PersonType` extends `Person` – we know that it **is a** `Person` as well as being an instance of a subclass of `Person`.

```
018:    // Add given Person to the Conversation (extend array as required).
019:    public void addPerson(PersonType newPerson)
020:    {
021:      if (noOfPersons == persons.length)
022:      {
023:        Person[] biggerArray = new Person[persons.length * ARRAY_RESIZE_FACTOR];
024:        for (int index = 0; index < persons.length; index++)
025:          biggerArray[index] = persons[index];
026:        persons = biggerArray;
027:      } // if
028:      persons[noOfPersons] = newPerson;
029:      noOfPersons++;
030:    } // addPerson
```

The fact that the **method argument** supplied to addPerson() must be of type PersonType means that the **compiler** will complain if we try to add the wrong kind of Person to an instance of a parameterized type version of the class.

Coffee time: 19.5.2 Are you getting tired of seeing code that copies from one array to another? Take a look in the **API** documentation for the System class to find something that might be of interest to you.

Another instance method in our Conversation class reveals how many persons are in the conversation.

```
033:   // Return the number of people in the conversation.
034:   public int getSize()
035:   {
036:     return noOfPersons;
037:   } // getSize
```

The instance method speak() chooses one of the **array element**s and invokes the instance method of the same name on it.

```
040:   // Used to keep track of whose turn it is to speak.
041:   private int nextToSpeak = 0;
042:
043:
044:   // Make the next person speak and update who is next after that.
045:   public void speak()
046:   {
047:     if (noOfPersons > 0)
048:     {
049:       persons[nextToSpeak].speak();
050:       nextToSpeak = (nextToSpeak + 1) % noOfPersons;
051:     } // if
052:   } // speak
```

Finally, we have a toString() instance method, mainly for testing the class.

```
055:   // Mainly for testing.
056:   @Override
057:   public String toString()
058:   {
059:     String result = noOfPersons == 0 ? "" : "" + persons[0];
060:     for (int index = 1; index < noOfPersons; index++)
061:       result += String.format("%n%s", persons[index]);
062:     return result;
063:   } // toString
064:
065: } // class Conversation
```

19.5.2 The TestConversation class

To test the Conversation **class**, we create some Conversations, add some Persons to them, and invoke speak(), once for each Person, printing out the Conversation in between. This is not a thorough test.

```
001: // Create conversations of persons and make them speak.
002: public class TestConversation
003: {
004:   public static void main(String[] args)
005:   {
```

We can have a conversation in which all the persons *must* be AudienceMembers by supplying a **type argument** which is AudienceMember.

```
006:     // A conversation of AudienceMembers.
007:     Conversation<AudienceMember> audienceChat
008:       = new Conversation<AudienceMember>();
```

Then we can add some Persons to it. The **compiler** will check that we do not accidentally add the wrong kind of Person.

```
009:     audienceChat.addPerson(new AudienceMember("AM 1"));
010:     audienceChat.addPerson(new AudienceMember("AM 2"));
011:     audienceChat.addPerson(new AudienceMember("AM 3"));
```

Then we can make the Persons speak and print out the Conversation.

```
012:     System.out.printf("%s%n%n", audienceChat);
013:     for (int count = 1; count <= audienceChat.getSize(); count++)
014:     {
015:       audienceChat.speak();
016:       System.out.printf("%s%n%n", audienceChat);
017:     } // for
```

But, if we wish to have a Conversation that consists of different types of Person, we can still do that too, by supplying Person itself as the type argument.

```
019:     // A conversation of any kind of person.
020:     Conversation<Person> anyChat = new Conversation<Person>();
021:     anyChat.addPerson(new TVHost("TVH 1"));
022:     anyChat.addPerson(new AudienceMember("AM 4"));
023:     System.out.printf("%s%n%n", anyChat);
024:     for (int count = 1; count <= anyChat.getSize(); count++)
025:     {
026:       anyChat.speak();
027:       System.out.printf("%s%n%n", anyChat);
028:     } // for
029:   } // main
030:
031: } // class TestConversation
```

19.5.3   Trying it

The program works as expected.

Console Input / Output

```
$ java TestConversation
(Output shown using multiple columns to save space.)
Audience Member AM 1 true I am AM 1      Audience Member AM 2 true Oooooh!
Audience Member AM 2 true I am AM 2      Audience Member AM 3 true Oooooh!
Audience Member AM 3 true I am AM 3
                                         TV Host TVH 1 true I am TVH 1
Audience Member AM 1 true Oooooh!        Audience Member AM 4 true I am AM 4
Audience Member AM 2 true I am AM 2
Audience Member AM 3 true I am AM 3      TV Host TVH 1 true Welcome, suckers!
                                         Audience Member AM 4 true I am AM 4
Audience Member AM 1 true Oooooh!
Audience Member AM 2 true Oooooh!        TV Host TVH 1 true Welcome, suckers!
Audience Member AM 3 true I am AM 3      Audience Member AM 4 true Oooooh!

Audience Member AM 1 true Oooooh!
$ _
```

19.5.4 The `TestConversationOops` class

Let's see what happens if we put the wrong kind of `Person` in a `Conversation`.

```
001: // Create conversations of people and make them speak.
002: public class TestConversationOops
003: {
004:   public static void main(String[] args)
005:   {
006:     // A conversation of AudienceMembers.
007:     Conversation<AudienceMember> audienceChat
008:       = new Conversation<AudienceMember>();
009:     audienceChat.addPerson(new AudienceMember("AM 1"));
010:     audienceChat.addPerson(new TVHost("TVH 1"));
011:     System.out.printf("%s%n%n", audienceChat);
012:     for (int count = 1; count <= audienceChat.getSize(); count++)
013:     {
014:       audienceChat.speak();
015:       System.out.printf("%s%n%n", audienceChat);
016:     } // for
017:   } // main
018:
019: } // class TestConversationOops
```

Coffee time: 19.5.3
Recall the full `Person` hierarchy from Section 16.13 on page 416. How could we have a `Conversation` in which all the persons must be `MoodyPersons`, but can be any kind of moody person?

Console Input / Output

```
$ javac TestConversationOops.java
TestConversationOops.java:10: addPerson(AudienceMember) in Conversation<Audience
Member> cannot be applied to (TVHost)
    audienceChat.addPerson(new TVHost("TVH 1"));
                          ^
1 error
$ _
```

Coffee time: 19.5.4
Recall that within the `Conversation` **class**, we had an **array** of **type** `Person[]`, in which only `PersonType` **objects** were stored. It would have been nicer to declare the array as `PersonType[]`. So, why didn't we? Try it to find out!

19.5.5 Coursework: A moody group

This coursework is set in the context of the Notional Lottery game from Section 16.2 on page 372.

Write a **generic class** called `MoodyGroup` that contains a collection of some **subclass** of `MoodyPerson` **objects**, rather like the `Conversation` **class** does with `Person`. However, instead of a `speak()` **instance method**, `MoodyGroup` should have `setHappy()`. This will take a **boolean** and pass it to the instance method of the same name belonging to each of the `MoodyPersons` in the group. You will recall that only `MoodyPersons` have the `setHappy()` instance method, whereas the more general `Person` does not.

Test your class with a program called `TestMoodyGroup`. This will do the following.

- Create an **instance** of `MoodyGroup<Teenager>` and populate it with a small number of `Teenagers`.
- Invoke `setHappy()` with **false** and print out the group.
- Invoke `setHappy()` with **true** and print out the group again.
- Create a second moody group which can contain any kind of `MoodyPerson`, and populate it with a `Worker` and one of the *same* `Teenagers` which was put into the first group.
- Invoke `setHappy()` on the second group with **true** and print out the group.
- Invoke `setHappy()` on the second group with **false** and print out the group.
- Print out the first group one more time to show that the teenager which is in both groups stands out from the others.

19.6 What we cannot do with type parameters

AIM: To briefly explore some of the things we might like to do with **type parameters** but cannot.

Whilst **type parameters** are generally a powerful mechanism, there are certain restrictions on what we can do with them.

Concept **Class: generic class: where type parameters cannot be used.** Each **type parameter** of a **generic class** may be treated as a **type** within the generic class, except for certain restrictions, which fall into two categories.

The first is about the meaning of type parameters. A **type argument** is supplied for each of these to identify a **parameterized type**, which is then ready for **instances** of it to be made. The type arguments only mean anything in the context of creating instances, and make no sense in the **static context** of the generic class (which is not part of the type). So, we cannot refer to the type parameters in `static` parts, that is, in **class variable** and **class method** declarations.[1]

The second set of restrictions are associated with the way Java implements generic classes. In particular, we cannot create any **instances** of a type parameter, nor create any **arrays** whose **array elements** are of that type. (Essentially, the generic features of a **class** is an entirely **compile time** artifact – to enable the **compiler** to undertake more type checking than it otherwise could. At **run time**, the **virtual machine** has no knowledge of the type parameters, and so cannot *create* instances of the correct type.)

For example, we cannot have the following handy mechanism to make **objects** of a certain **type** whilst counting how many have been made. Pity?

```
001: // Create instances of ObjectType, and count them.
002: public class CountingFactory<ObjectType>
003: {
004:   // The number of instances made so far.
005:   private int constructionCount = 0;
006:
007:
008:   // Empty constructor, nothing needs doing.
009:   public CountingFactory()
010:   {
011:   } // CountingFactory
012:
013:
014:   // Return the number of objects that have been made up to now.
015:   public int getConstructionCount()
016:   {
017:     return constructionCount;
018:   } // getConstructionCount
019:
020:
021:   // Create an ObjectType and count it.
022:   public ObjectType newObject()
023:   {
024:     constructionCount++;
025:     return new ObjectType();
026:   } // newObject
```

---

[1] There is actually a separate mechanism for putting type parameters on class methods.

```
027:
028: } // class CountingFactory
```

19.6.1 Trying it

Console Input / Output

$ **javac CountingFactory.java**
CountingFactory.java:25: unexpected type
found   : type parameter ObjectType
required: class
    return new ObjectType();
                ^
 	
1 error
$ _

19.7 Using a generic class without type parameters

AIM:
To briefly explore what happens when we use a **generic class** without **type parameters**.

And finally, what happens if we attempt to make **instance**s of a **generic class** without supplying any **type argument**s?

Concept **Class: generic class: used as a raw type.**   A **generic class** is still a **class** and hence a **type**, and actually it
can be used directly to make **instance**s of it without supplying **type argument**s. This is due to legacy issues: generic
classes were added in Java 5.0, and **type parameter**s were added to many standard **application program interface**
(**API**) classes at that time. Obviously there already existed millions of Java programs that use those classes, and it
would be unacceptable for them all to suddenly stop working!

Java refers to the type of the generic class without type parameters as the **raw type** for the class. If we use the raw
type, then the **compiler** assumes the best known actual type for each of its type parameters, and gives us warnings,
about types being unchecked. But it goes ahead and makes the **byte code** anyway. This way, programmers are
encouraged to use the generic classes properly for new code and gradually change legacy code to do so. The best
known type assumed by the compiler for a type parameter which **extend**s some concrete type is that concrete type,
and for ones that do not it is java.lang.Object.

Let us try using Conversation without type arguments, by 'accidentally' adding a TVHost into the conversation that was
intended to be for AudienceMembers, but without us having told Java that it was.

```
001: // Create conversations of people and make them speak.
002: public class TestConversationOops
003: {
004:   public static void main(String[] args)
005:   {
006:     // A conversation of AudienceMembers.
007:     Conversation audienceChat = new Conversation();
008:     audienceChat.addPerson(new AudienceMember("AM 1"));
009:     audienceChat.addPerson(new TVHost("TVH 1"));
010:     System.out.printf("%s%n%n", audienceChat);
011:     for (int count = 1; count <= audienceChat.getSize(); count++)
012:     {
013:       audienceChat.speak();
014:       System.out.printf("%s%n%n", audienceChat);
015:     } // for
016:   } // main
017:
018: } // class TestConversationOops
```

19.7.1 Trying it

We get no **compile time error**s for the program, but we do get some **compile time warning**s.

```
                    Console Input / Output
$ javac TestConversationOops.java
Note: TestConversationOops.java uses unchecked or unsafe operations.
Note: Recompile with -Xlint:unchecked for details.
$ _
```

The **compiler** does not tell us the details of the warnings by default, just that there are some. But we can ask for details by supplying the -Xlint:unchecked compiler option.

```
                    Console Input / Output
$ javac -Xlint:unchecked TestConversationOops.java
TestConversationOops.java:8: warning: [unchecked] unchecked call to addPerson(Pe
rsonType) as a member of the raw type Conversation
    audienceChat.addPerson(new AudienceMember("AM 1"));
                          ^
TestConversationOops.java:9: warning: [unchecked] unchecked call to addPerson(Pe
rsonType) as a member of the raw type Conversation
    audienceChat.addPerson(new TVHost("TVH 1"));
                          ^
2 warnings
$ _
```

We should not write new code that generates warnings like this, if we can avoid it – always supply **type argument**s when we use **generic class**es.

Of course, and most worryingly, our erroneous program **run**s without error too!

```
                    Console Input / Output
$ java TestConversationOops
Audience Member AM 1 true I am AM 1
TV Host TVH 1 true I am TVH 1

Audience Member AM 1 true Oooooh!
TV Host TVH 1 true I am TVH 1

Audience Member AM 1 true Oooooh!
TV Host TVH 1 true Welcome, suckers!

$ _
```

19.7.2 The `TestConversationMajorOops` class

Having defined the **type parameter** of `Conversation` as `PersonType` **extends** `Person` then Java knows that the missing **type argument** for a **raw type** is at least `Person` or a **subclass** of it. So we get a **compile time error** if we try to add an **object** which is not a `Person`.

```
001: // Create conversations of people and make them speak.
002: public class TestConversationMajorOops
003: {
004:   public static void main(String[] args)
005:   {
006:     // A conversation of AudienceMembers.
007:     Conversation audienceChat = new Conversation();
008:     audienceChat.addPerson("AM 1");
```

```
009:        System.out.printf("%s%n%n", audienceChat);
010:        for (int count = 1; count <= audienceChat.getSize(); count++)
011:        {
012:            audienceChat.speak();
013:            System.out.printf("%s%n%n", audienceChat);
014:        } // for
015:    } // main
016:
017: } // class TestConversationMajorOops
```

Console Input / Output

`$ javac TestConversationMajorOops.java`
`TestConversationMajorOops.java:8: addPerson(Person) in Conversation cannot be ap`
`plied to (java.lang.String)`
`        audienceChat.addPerson("AM 1");`
`                      ^`
 	
`1 error`
`$ _`

19.8   Concepts covered in this chapter

Here is a list of the concepts that were covered in this chapter, each with a self-test question. You can use this to check you remember them being introduced, and perhaps re-read some of them before going on to the next chapter.

Class	
– generic class (p.491)	What do we add to the name of a generic class in order to get a parameterized type?
– generic class: bound type parameter (p.496)	What is the purpose of this?
– generic class: bound type parameter: extends some class (p.496)	What is the difference between the following? 1. `public class C <T> { ... }` 2. `public class C <T extends Vehicle>` `{ ... }`
– generic class: where type parameters cannot be used (p.501)	Why can we not refer to type parameters in static methods of a generic class? What else can we not do with type parameters?
– generic class: used as a raw type (p.502)	What is the raw type of a generic class, and why does Java allow it to be used?

Standard API	
– Integer: as a box for int (p.487)	What is the difference between the following? 1. `10` 2. `new Integer(10)`

– Integer: as a box for int: autoboxing (p.494)	Where is autoboxing and auto-unboxing occurring in the following?
	`Integer anInteger = 10;`
	`Integer anotherInteger = anInteger + 1;`
	`System.out.println(anotherInteger - anInteger);`

Chapter 20

Interfaces, including generic interfaces

Just as not all that glistens is gold,
not all that can be opened is a door!

20.1 Chapter aims

Sometimes our programs need to work in a problem area which requires **multiple inheritance**, that is we would like a **class** to be a **subclass** of more than one **superclass**. However, as we have already seen, each class in Java has only one superclass. Instead, multiple inheritance is permitted in a limited way through the use of **interfaces**. The job of this chapter is to explore this idea, including the use of **generic interfaces**. We also look at **generic methods**.

The chapter contains the following sections.

Section	Aims	Associated Coursework
20.2 Summing valuables (p.506)	To introduce the idea of **multiple inheritance** and take a proper look at **interfaces**. We look closely at what it means for a **class** to be a **type**, compare this with **interfaces**, and revisit **method implementation**.	(None.)
20.3 Sorting a text file using an array (p.516)	To introduce the idea of **total order** and the Comparable **interface**. We also meet the Arrays **class**.	Implement the program to **sort a text file**. (p.519)
20.4 Translating documents (p.519)	To explore **generic interfaces**, observe that Comparable is generic, see that String **implement**s it, meet equals() from Object and talk about consistency with compareTo(). We also introduce **generic methods**, **binary search**, revisit Arrays and note that an **interface** can **extend** another.	Write a **generic method** to find the minimum and maximum items in an **array** of Comparable items. (p.530)
20.5 Sorting valuables (p.530)	To introduce the idea that a **class** can **implement** many **interfaces**, and explore what it means for an **interface** to **extend** another. We also take another look at having consistency between compareTo() and equals().	Undertake an analysis of previous uses of compareTo() and equals() **instance methods**. (p.534)

20.2 Example: Summing valuables

AIM:
> To introduce the idea of **multiple inheritance** and take a proper look at **interface**s. We look closely at what it means for a **class** to be a **type**, compare this with **interfaces**, and revisit **method implementation**.

In this section we look at an example which requires us to think about **multiple inheritance** – the possibility that we might like a **class** to be a **subclass** of more than one **superclass**. We present only an outline of the example here, to avoid the detail of it being a distraction away from its interesting aspect.

Suppose we wished to write a program that can keep track of the valuables of a person, and say, calculate the total worth of their assets. The major things that people typically own are houses, cars and maybe things like jewellery and artwork, etc.. Suppose also, thanks to some other unrelated project, we have an existing **inheritance hierarchy** which models buildings, including the subclass House. Also, let us imagine we have another inheritance hierarchy, from yet another previous project, which models vehicles, including the subclass Car. As it happens, the classes House and Car contain much information which is of use to us in our new project, and so, following the principle of **software reuse**, we decide to share these classes in the new project.

20.2.1 The Building class and its subclasses

Here is a skeleton of the Building class and two of its **subclass**es.

```
001: // Representation of an abstract building.
002: public abstract class Building
003: {
004:
005:   // ... Lots of stuff here about buildings in general.
006:
007: } // class Building
```

An OfficeBlock **is a** Building.

```
001: // Representation of an office block.
002: public class OfficeBlock extends Building
003: {
004:
005:   // ... Lots of stuff here specific to an office block.
006:
007: } // class OfficeBlock
```

A House also **is a** Building. In reality there would probably be many more **instance variable**s and more than just the number of bedrooms given to the **constructor method**.

```
001: // Representation of a house.
002: public class House extends Building
003: {
004:   // The number of bedrooms in the house.
005:   private int noOfBedrooms;
006:
007:
008:   // Construct a house with a given number of bedrooms.
009:   public House(int requiredNoOfBedrooms)
010:   {
```

```
011:    noOfBedrooms = requiredNoOfBedrooms;
012:  } // House
013:
014:
015:   // Return the number of bedrooms in the house.
016:   public int getNoOfBedrooms()
017:   {
018:    return noOfBedrooms;
019:   } // getNoOfBedrooms
020:
021:
022:   // ... Lots more stuff here specific to a house.
023:
024: } // class House
```

20.2.2 The `Vehicle` class and its subclasses

Now, here is a skeleton of the `Vehicle` **class** and two of its **subclass**es.

```
001: // Representation of an abstract vehicle.
002: public abstract class Vehicle
003: {
004:
005:   // ... Lots of stuff here about vehicles in general.
006:
007: } // class Vehicle
```

A `Tractor` **is a** `Vehicle`.

```
001: // Representation of a tractor.
002: public class Tractor extends Vehicle
003: {
004:
005:   // ... Lots of stuff here specific to a tractor.
006:
007: } // class Tractor
```

A `Car` also **is a** `Vehicle`. In reality there would probably be many more **instance variable**s and more than just the number of doors given to the **constructor method**.

```
001: // Representation of a car.
002: public class Car extends Vehicle
003: {
004:   // The number of doors on the car.
005:   private final int noOfDoors;
006:
007:
008:   // Construct a car with a given number of doors.
009:   public Car(int requiredNoOfDoors)
010:   {
011:    noOfDoors = requiredNoOfDoors;
012:   } // Car
013:
014:
```

```
015:   // Return the number of doors on the car.
016:   public int getNoOfDoors()
017:   {
018:     return noOfDoors;
019:   } // getNoOfDoors
020:
021:
022:   // ... Lots more stuff here specific to a car.
023:
024: } // class Car
```

20.2.3   The `ValuableHouse` and `ValuableCar` classes

Despite containing lots of information that can be used in calculating the value of things, let us assume that the other projects, which involved modelling buildings and vehicles, were not actually interested in the value of such items, and hence did not provide a `value()` **instance method** in those **class**es. So, we decide to add one to the classes which we are going to reuse. Of course, we do not change the existing classes, as that would possibly interfere with the previous projects. Instead, we naturally make new **subclass**es of `House` and `Car`, which we call `ValuableHouse` and `ValuableCar` respectively.

This leads us to a situation shown in the following **UML class diagram**.

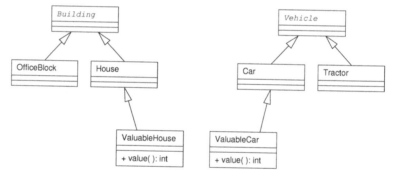

Additionally we would have classes for modelling other kinds of valuables, such as `ValuableBoat`, `ValuableArtWork` and `ValuableJewellery`. Now we have the capability to calculate the value of a house and a car, but we do not have the right relationship between them, and also between them and other kinds of valuable items. In order to calculate the total value of some valuables, we would like to have an **array** of **object**s, each of which models a valuable item, and each of which has a `value()` instance method. As it stands, the **type** of such an array would have to be `Object[]`, as the class `Object` is the only link between `ValuableHouse` and `ValuableCar`. But, of course, not every **instance** of `Object` has a `value()` instance method! So, code which is designed to add up the values of items in such an array would have to look something like this.

```
...
099: Object[] valuables;
100: // Code here to create and populate this array. ...
...
199: int total = 0;
200: for (Object someValuable : valuables)
201:   if (someValuable instanceof ValuableHouse)
202:     total += ((ValuableHouse)someValuable).value();
203:   else if (someValuable instanceof ValuableCar)
204:     total += ((ValuableCar)someValuable).value();
```

```
205:    else if (someValuable instanceof ValuableArtWork)
206:      total += ((ValuableArtWork)someValuable).value();
207:    else if // One of these for every kind of valuable, ho hum! ...
...
```

Coffee time: `20.2.1` Does this surprise you? Would it be a nice idea to be able to say to the **compiler** in some simple way "trust me, someValuable has got a `value()` instance method, and I want to use it"? Or even more liberal, would it be nice if the compiler trusted us in the first place and just allowed us to write code to invoke the `value()` instance method of someValuable without moaning at us that the class Object does not have such an instance method?!

Every time we add a new kind of valuable item to our program, we would have to remember to add another bit of code in all places like the above – that is not an acceptable position at all.

20.2.4 The **Valuable** class

What we want instead is a `Valuable` class, and then we can store our `Valuable` **objects** in an **array** of **type** `Valuable[]`. The question is, where should `Valuable` live in the **inheritance hierarchy**? We could consider changing our approach completely, and put the `Valuable` class at the top of `Building` and `Vehicle` (and above any other inheritance hierarchies which contain some **subclass** we wish to use).

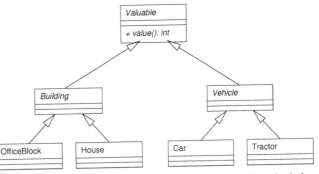

This idea has removed the need for the classes `ValuableHouse` and `ValuableCar`, but there are two things bad about it. The *second* bad thing is that we now have to consider what it means for an `OfficeBlock` and a `Tractor`, and all the other subclasses not shown on the diagram, to have a `value()` instance method, while in fact, we only care about the value of `House` and `Car` in those hierarchies.

Coffee time: `20.2.2` What is the *first* bad thing about this proposed inheritance hierarchy? (Hint: it would require us to do something which we have previously said we do not want to do.)

So, let us go back to the idea of having the classes `ValuableHouse` and `ValuableCar`. To get these to be related in the most appropriate way, we would really like to make them subclasses of `Valuable`, while not doing this for the other subclasses of `Building` and `Vehicle`. This leads to the following diagram.

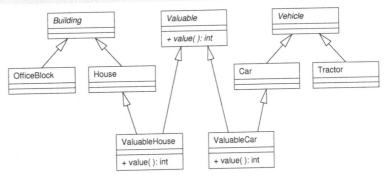

The idea that a class may have more than one **superclass** is known as **multiple inheritance**.

Concept **Inheritance: multiple inheritance.** By saying that a **class** is a **subclass** of another we are modelling the **is a** relationship. Sometimes, it can appear natural to view a class as being a subclass of more than one **superclass**. This results in the subclass **inherit**ing properties from each of its superclasses, which is known as **multiple inheritance**.

Whilst the idea can sound attractive, it brings with it a complication when two or more of these superclasses contain an **instance method** with the same name and **method parameter**s. This problem is best illustrated by an abstract example. Suppose we have the class Super1, with the instance method methodA().

```
public class Super1
{
  ...
  public void methodA()
  {
    ...
  } // methodA
  ...
} // class Super1
```

Suppose we, quite separately, have the class Super2, which also has an instance method methodA().

```
public class Super2
{
  ...
  public void methodA()
  {
    ...
  } // methodA
  ...
} // class Super2
```

At some later date, somebody could make a subclass, Sub, of both Super1 and Super2.

```
public class Sub extends Super1, Super2
{
  ...
  public void methodB()
  {
    ...
    methodA();
    ...
  } // methodB
  ...
} // class Sub
```

There are two, related, issues here. The first is about ambiguity: which methodA() should the call inside methodB() invoke? Many people regard the potential for this problem as being the basis for the view that multiple inheritance is a bad idea – it leads to problematic **inheritance hierarchy** designs. No doubt when the class Super1 was written, the name methodA was a good name for the **method**. And the same was true when Super2 was being written. But the two methods may have completely unrelated functions, written by different people at different times.

The second issue is concerned with **run time** efficiency. When the **virtual machine** is performing **dynamic method binding** for a **method call**, it needs to search the inheritance hierarchy for every superclass, to find the method, perhaps hoping there is no conflict, but somehow dealing with it if there is. This takes more time than searching up the tree in a single inheritance hierarchy.

In practice, *full* multiple inheritance is not very often required anyway. So, for all these reasons, Java does not permit a class to have more than one superclass. Every class, except java.lang.Object, has exactly one superclass, and Object has none because it is at the top of the inheritance hierarchy.

20.2.5 The `Valuable` interface

So, how can we implement our design? Well, whilst Java does not permit full **multiple inheritance**, it does permit *partial* multiple inheritance, through a mechanism that we have already met in the context of **graphical user interface**s (if you studied that chapter).

Coffee time: 20.2.3   You may recall that in Section 13.7 on page 260 we had a class `StopClock` that was both a `JFrame` and an `ActionListener`. How was that multiple inheritance achieved?

Let us think about our **class** `Valuable`. It contains just one instance method, `value()`. The way we calculate the value of a house will be very different to the way we do so for a car. One would expect this to be true of all the potential subclasses of `Valuable`, and so `value()` will be an **abstract method**. This means `Valuable` would have to be an **abstract class**. Java has a special kind of piece of code, as an alternative to an abstract class that contains *only* abstract methods, called an **interface**.

Concept **Interface: definition.** An **interface** is like a **class**, except all the **instance method**s in it must be **abstract method**s, that is, they have no bodies.[1] Only the **method interface**s are declared, i.e. the **method signature**s and **return type**s. The **method implementation**s must be provided by each non-**abstract class** that **implements** the interface. For example, the following code says that the class `StopClock` is both a **subclass** of `JFrame` and implements `ActionListener`.

```
import java.awt.event.ActionListener;
import javax.swing.JFrame;

public class StopClock extends JFrame implements ActionListener
{
  ...
  public void actionPerformed(ActionEvent event)
  {
    ...
  } // actionPerformed
  ...
} // class StopClock
```

This means that an **instance** of `StopClock` is **polymorphic** – it **is a** `StopClock`, **is a** `JFrame` and also **is an** `ActionListener`.

The definition of an interface has the **reserved word `interface`** in its heading, instead of the reserved word **`class`**. It can contain a list of instance method headings, each of which has no body – just a semi-colon (`;`). If we wish, we can write the reserved word **abstract** in the heading of the interface, like we would for an **abstract class**. We can also write it in the instance method headings, like we would for abstract methods appearing in abstract classes. However, we are discouraged from doing so by the Java language standard[5], because all the instance methods *must* be abstract methods. Similarly, all the instance methods *must* be **public**, and so we do not need to write that visibility **modifier** either, and are discouraged from doing so.

The following is what you might expect the `ActionListener` interface to look like.

```
public interface ActionListener
{
  void actionPerformed(ActionEvent e);
} // interface ActionListener
```

---

[1] Actually, Java 8 introduced **default methods** into interfaces to solve problems with legacy APIs. You should ignore them for now.

An interface cannot contain **constructor method**s nor **class method**s (`static method`)s. What is more, if it has any **variable**s defined, they must be **public**, `static` and **final variable**s, although we can omit those modifiers if we wish.

There can be no **private** instance methods or variables in an interface – obviously.

Coffee time: [20.2.4] Obviously? Why would it not make sense to have a **private** instance method or **variable** in an interface?

Before moving on, let us look at the relationship between a class and an interface, in terms of them both being **type**s.

Concept **Class: is a type: and has three components.** Whilst a **type** is essentially a **set** of values, it also has two other components. These are the operations which can be performed on those values, and the **operation interface** to those operations. For example, the type `int` is a collection of numbers, with operations such as **addition** and **multiplication**, and each operation has an **operator** as its operation interface, such as + and *.

The distinction between operation and operation interface is subtle, and may even seem pedantic, but nevertheless, they are not the same thing. For example, one could imagine the **design**ers of Java one day permitting a proper multiplication symbol ($\times$) to be used as an alternative to the * operator, without altering the meaning of the multiplication operation.

Each **class** is a type, the set of all (**references** to) **object**s that can be created which are **instance**s of that class. It has operations, which are the **method implementation**s of the **instance method**s of the class, and each of these operations has an operation interface, which is the **method interface**.

Concept **Interface: is a type.** An **interface** is a type, the **set** of all (**references** to) **object**s that can be created which are **instance**s of any **class** that **implements** the interface. It has operations, which are the **method implementation**s of the **instance method**s of the interface, provided by each class which implements the interface. And each of these operations has an **operation interface**, which is the **method interface** defined in the interface (and, in effect, redefined in each class that implements the interface).

So, an interface defines only the operation interfaces of the type, not the actual operations. That is why this code construct is called an *interface*. We can think of it as being an **interface contract** – any class that claims to implement it is obliged to supply operation implementations.

So, rather than us having a **class** called `Valuable` it shall instead be an **interface**. We declare it to contain the **abstract method** `value()` and nothing else.

```
001: // Objects which have a value obtained via a value() method.
002: public interface Valuable
003: {
004:   // The value of this Valuable.
005:   int value();
006:
007: } // interface Valuable
```

So any non-**abstract class** that **implements** `Valuable` must supply a **method implementation** of `value()`.

20.2.6 The `ValuableHouse` class

Our **class** ValuableHouse shall be a **subclass** of House and shall also **implement** Valuable. For brevity, we have only a tongue-in-cheek implementation of the class here!

```
001: // Representation of a Valuable which is a house.
002: public class ValuableHouse extends House implements Valuable
003: {
004:    // A measure of the value of the area the house is in.
005:    private double locationDesirabilityIndex;
006:
007:
008:    // Construct a ValuableHouse with a given number of bedrooms
009:    // and location desirability.
010:    public ValuableHouse(int requiredNoOfBedrooms,
011:                         double requiredLocationDesirabilityIndex)
012:    {
013:      super(requiredNoOfBedrooms);
014:      locationDesirabilityIndex = requiredLocationDesirabilityIndex;
015:    } // ValuableHouse
```

We provide a **method implementation** of value() which is (tongue-in-cheek) appropriate to calculating the value of a house. (In reality, the calculation would include many other details about houses too.)

Concept **Interface: method implementation.** A non-**abstract class** which **implement**s an **interface** must supply **method implementation**s for the **abstract method**s defined in that interface. As when making an **override** of an **instance method** defined in a **superclass**, there is a danger of getting a **method parameter type** wrong, and introducing an **overloaded method** instead, or mistyping the method name. The **override annotation**, @Override, introduced in Java 5.0, was extended in Java 6.0 to enable us to tell the **compiler** that we believe an instance method is an override or an implementation of one from a superclass *or* an interface. One situation this detects is when we have indeed got the method implementation correct, but forgot to say that our **class** implements the interface we had in mind!

```
018:    // Calculate and return the value of this valuable item.
019:    @Override
020:    public int value()
021:    {
022:      return (int) (getNoOfBedrooms() * 50000 * locationDesirabilityIndex);
023:    } // valuable
024:
025:
026:    // Return a short description of this as a valuable item.
027:    @Override
028:    public String toString()
029:    {
030:      return "House worth " + value();
031:    } // toString
032:
033: } // class ValuableHouse
```

513

20.2.7 The ValuableCar class

Similarly, our **class** ValuableCar shall be a **subclass** of Car and **implement** Valuable.

```
001: // Representation of a Valuable which is a car.
002: public class ValuableCar extends Car implements Valuable
003: {
004:   // A measure of the value of the car in general.
005:   private double streetCredibilityIndex;
006:
007:
008:   // Construct a ValuableCar with a given number of doors
009:   // and general desirability.
010:   public ValuableCar(int requiredNoOfDoors,
011:                      double requiredStreetCredibilityIndex)
012:   {
013:     super(requiredNoOfDoors);
014:     streetCredibilityIndex = requiredStreetCredibilityIndex;
015:   } // ValuableCar
```

Just as we did with ValuableHouse, we supply a **method implementation** for value(), which is (tongue-in-cheek) appropriate to calculating the value of a car. (In reality, the calculation would include many other details about cars too.)

```
018:   // Calculate and return the value of this valuable item.
019:   @Override
020:   public int value()
021:   {
022:     return (int) (getNoOfDoors() * 2000 * streetCredibilityIndex);
023:   } // valuable
024:
025:
026:   // Return a short description of this as a valuable item.
027:   @Override
028:   public String toString()
029:   {
030:     return "Car worth " + value();
031:   } // toString
032:
033: } // class ValuableCar
```

20.2.8 The Valuables class

Finally, let us have a **class** that stores a **set** of Valuable **objects**, using an **array** of **type** Valuable[].

```
001: // Representation of a collection of Valuables.
002: public class Valuables
003: {
004:   // The Valuables, stored in a partially filled array, together with size.
005:   private final Valuable[] valuableArray;
006:   private int noOfValuables;
007:
008:
009:   // Create a collection with the given maximum size.
010:   public Valuables(int maxNoOfValuables)
011:   {
012:     valuableArray = new Valuable[maxNoOfValuables];
013:     noOfValuables = 0;
014:   } // Valuables
```

For simplicity in this example, we shall just ignore any attempt to add a Valuable when the array is full.

```
017:    // Add a given Valuable to the collection (ignore if full).
018:    public void addValuable(Valuable valuable)
019:    {
020:      if (noOfValuables < valuableArray.length)
021:      {
022:        valuableArray[noOfValuables] = valuable;
023:        noOfValuables++;
024:      } // if
025:    } // addValuable
```

We want an **instance method** that **return**s the total value of the Valuable **objects**. Notice that we do not have to do any **cast**ing here – all the objects (which have **reference**s) stored in the array are definitely of type Valuable no matter what else they also are.

```
028:    // Calculate and return the total value of the collection.
029:    public int totalValue()
030:    {
031:      int result = 0;
032:      for (Valuable valuable : valuableArray)
033:        result += valuable.value();
034:      return result;
035:    } // totalValue
```

Our toString() instance method returns a String representing the **list** of Valuables.

```
038:    // Return a short description of the collection.
039:    @Override
040:    public String toString()
041:    {
042:      if (noOfValuables == 0)
043:        return "Nothing valuable";
044:
045:      String result = valuableArray[0].toString();
046:      for (int index = 1; index < noOfValuables; index++)
047:        result += String.format("%n%s", valuableArray[index]);
048:      return result;
049:    } // toString
```

For testing the program so far, we write a **main method** in this class. Notice that we can add **instance**s of ValuableHouse and ValuableCar via the addValuable() instance method, which has a **method parameter** of type Valuable. This reminds us that an instance of ValuableHouse **is a** Valuable, as is an instance of ValuableCar.

```
052:    // Create a Valuables collection, add Valuable items and show result.
053:    // Purely for testing during development.
054:    public static void main(String[] args)
055:    {
056:      Valuables valuables = new Valuables(5);
057:
058:      // My first house -- I was so proud of its spare bedroom
059:      // and 'value for money' area.
060:      valuables.addValuable(new ValuableHouse(2, 0.5));
061:
062:      // My first car, not quite a 'head turner',
063:      // but its third door was handy when the main 2 got stuck.
064:      valuables.addValuable(new ValuableCar(3, 0.25));
```

```
065:
066:         // It was nice to have a new car when I started work.
067:         valuables.addValuable(new ValuableCar(4, 1.0));
068:
069:         // Then I won the lottery! (Yeah, right.)
070:         valuables.addValuable(new ValuableHouse(6, 2.0));
071:         valuables.addValuable(new ValuableCar(12, 4.0));
072:
073:         System.out.println("My valuables are worth " + valuables.totalValue());
074:
075:         System.out.println(valuables);
076:     } // main
077:
078: } // class Valuables
```

20.2.9 Trying it

```
                          Console Input / Output
$ java Valuables
My valuables are worth 755500
House worth 50000
Car worth 1500
Car worth 8000
House worth 600000
Car worth 96000
$ _
```

20.3 Example: Sorting a text file using an array

AIM:
To introduce the idea of **total order** and the Comparable **interface**. We also meet the Arrays **class**.

In this section, we develop a program that takes an input **text file** and produces the text, **sort**ed line by line, into another text file. This could be useful if, for example, we had a text file of examination results which are sorted by merit, but we wished to produce a version sorted by name, and it happens that the student name is the first item in each line.

Rather than write yet another implementation of a sort **algorithm** specific to this program, we are here going to generalize the idea of sorting, and employ something which can be used to sort any **array** of any items which can be sorted!

An array of **data** can be sorted if there is a **total order** over the data, so that any item may be compared with any other.

Concept **Design: Sorting a list: total order.** A **total order** over some **data** is a relationship between pairs of that data which enables it to be **sorted**. For example, **less than or equal** is a total order over numbers: we can choose to sort a **list** of numbers into ascending order. So, **greater than or equal** is also a total order – we can sort into descending order. We can sort strings using a **lexicographic order**ing (i.e. into dictionary order). A child might sort sweets into order by colour – unwittingly defining a total order of colours in the process.

More formally, every total order, $\preceq$, has three properties, for all values x, y and z:

[Antisymmetric:]   if $x \preceq y$ and $y \preceq x$, then $x = y$
[Transitive:]   if $x \preceq y$ and $y \preceq z$, then $x \preceq z$
[Total:] $x \preceq y$ or $y \preceq x$

516

One way of modelling a total order is to provide a **function** that takes any pair, (x, y), of the data and yields one of three states as follows.

- x comes before y.

- x and y have the same placing.

- x comes after y.

In Java the function is typically implemented by an **instance method** compareTo() which compares the current **instance** (x) with a given other (y), and yields an **int** that is negative, zero, or positive to represent the three states respectively.

20.3.1 The Sortable interface?

To enable an implementation that can **sort** any **array**, we could provide a **type**, in the form of an **interface**, for all the kinds of things that can be sorted. Each **class** that **implement**s the interface would provide its own implementation for comparing pairs of that particular kind.

This is what the code could look like.

```
001: // A type for all things which can be sorted.
002: public interface Sortable
003: {
004:    // This method must provide a total order, and return:
005:    //        a negative number if this is less than the given other,
006:    //        zero if they have the same ordering or
007:    //        a positive number if this is greater than the given other.
008:    int compareTo(Sortable other);
009:
010: } // interface Sortable
```

20.3.2 The SortArray class?

Our next step would be to write a general sorting **class** so that it can **sort** the items in any kind of **array** of **object**s, as long as they all **implement** the Sortable interface. We might call the class SortArray and have it contain a **class method** called sort. This would take an array of Sortable objects, together with a number saying how many of the **array element**s contain data to be sorted – thus permitting the sorting of **partially filled array**s. The **bubble sort** algorithm could be used.

This is what the code could look like. It is similar to previous sorting code, such as in JobAnalysis from Section 14.4.2 on page 304.

```
001: // Provides a class method for sorting an array of any Sortable objects.
002: public class SortArray
003: {
004:    // Sort the given array from indices 0 to noOfItemsToSort - 1.
005:    public static void sort(Sortable[] anArray, int noOfItemsToSort)
006:                    throws NullPointerException, ArrayIndexOutOfBoundsException
007:    {
008:       // Each pass of the sort reduces unsortedLength by one.
009:       int unsortedLength = noOfItemsToSort;
010:       boolean changedOnThisPass;
```

```
011:    do
012:    {
013:      changedOnThisPass = false;
014:      for (int pairLeftIndex = 0;
015:           pairLeftIndex < unsortedLength - 1; pairLeftIndex++)
016:      {
017:        if (anArray[pairLeftIndex].compareTo(anArray[pairLeftIndex + 1]) > 0)
018:        {
019:          Sortable thatWasAtPairLeftIndex = anArray[pairLeftIndex];
020:          anArray[pairLeftIndex] = anArray[pairLeftIndex + 1];
021:          anArray[pairLeftIndex + 1] = thatWasAtPairLeftIndex;
022:          changedOnThisPass = true;
023:        } // if
024:      } // for
025:      unsortedLength--;
026:    } while (changedOnThisPass);
027:  } // sort
028:
029: } // SortArray
```

Notice the **method parameter** of **type** Sortable[] and the **variable** of type Sortable in the sort() **class method**. This reminds us that an **interface** is a type.

Coffee time: Any **class** could implement Sortable, and obviously objects of different classes are different sizes. So, how does the **compiler** know how big to make a variable of type Sortable? (A tricky question, or a trick one?)

This idea of having an interface for any type of object that can be sorted is such a good one that you should not be surprised to discover that Java already has a similar thing in its standard **application program interface** (**API**), although it is called Comparable rather than Sortable. So, there's no need for us to write our own Sortable interface. The ordering provided by compareTo() in a class that implements Comparable, is known as the **natural ordering** for that class.

What is more, Java has beaten us to the great idea of having a class method to sort an array of any Comparable items.

Concept **Standard API: Arrays.** The standard **class** java.util.Arrays provides various **class methods** to perform complex manipulations of **arrays**.

Concept **Standard API: Arrays: sort().** One of the **class methods** in java.util.Arrays is called sort, and it takes an **array** of Objects which it **sorts** into their **natural ordering**. For this to work without **throwing** an **exception**, the items in the array must all be of **type** Comparable and be **mutually comparable**. The **algorithm** used is called **merge sort**. This is much more efficient than **bubble sort**.

In fact, the **class** also contains several more class methods called sort, one for each array of a **primitive type**, such as int[], etc.. There is even a second version for each type which takes three **method parameters**: an array, and a pair of **int** indices, *from* and *to*. These sort all the items in the array which have an **array index** $\geq from$ and $< to$. This enables **partially filled arrays** to be sorted by making $from = 0$ and $to =$ the number of **array elements** used.

The version of Arrays.sort() that allows us to specify the range of indices containing data to be sorted is similar to our own suggestion in SortArray, if anything it is a little more flexible. It is also more efficient than ours, so we shall use Arrays.sort() rather than implement our own.

518

20.3.3 The `Sort` class

We are now ready to develop the program which **sort**s a **text file**. It works by reading the lines from the input into an **array** of `String`s, sorting the array, then printing them to the output text file. We can use `Arrays.sort()` to sort the array because, as we shall see in the next section, the **class** `String` **implement**s `Comparable`. We shall employ the version which is suitable for use with **partially filled array**s.

As we do not know how big the file is, we shall use the **array extension** technique when storing the lines. Much of the program is similar to `LineNumber` from Section 18.5 on page 465, and the **array extension** part of it is similar to previous examples using that technique, such as `JobList` in Section 14.5.3 on page 313. In fact, the code is so similar to previous examples, that we do not show it here – we leave it as a coursework instead!

20.3.4 Trying it

Let us try the program with a small **file** of examination results. This is not a thorough test.

20.3.5 Coursework: Sort a text file

Write the program `Sort` as described in the example for this section. The following fragments may help you.

```
...
006: import java.util.Arrays;
...
055:     Arrays.sort(lineArray, 0, noOfLinesReadSoFar);
...
```

Console Input / Output
`$ cat input.txt`
`Bear,Rupert     13.7%`
`Smith,James     51.5%`
`Brown,Margaret  68.2%`
`Jones,Stephen   87.9%`
`Jackson,Helen   100%`
`$ java Sort input.txt output.txt`
`$ cat output.txt`
`Bear,Rupert     13.7%`
`Brown,Margaret  68.2%`
`Jackson,Helen   100%`
`Jones,Stephen   87.9%`
`Smith,James     51.5%`
`$ _`

20.4 Example: Translating documents

AIM: To explore **generic interfaces**, observe that `Comparable` is generic, see that `String` **implement**s it, meet `equals()` from `Object` and talk about consistency with `compareTo()`. We also introduce **generic methods**, **binary search**, revisit `Arrays` and note that an **interface** can **extend** another.

The example program in this section is capable of translating documents written in any language into any other language! Well, okay, it simply changes each word for a corresponding one, according to a dictionary **file**. The program is divided into the following classes.

Class list for Translate	
Class	**Description**
`Translate`	The main class containing the **main method**. It makes an **instance** of `Dictionary`, from the file named as the first **command line argument**, then reads the input document from the file named as the second argument, and outputs the translated document to the file named by the third.
`DictionaryEntry`	This contains a pair of words, the first is in the source language, and the second is its translation in the target language.
Continued...	...

\...continued: **Class list for Translate**	
Class	**Description**
Dictionary	This contains an **array** of DictionaryEntry objects, and provides an **instance method** to translate a single word.
SearchArray	This contains a **class method** to search any kind of Comparable array – it is used by Dictionary to find the DictionaryEntry corresponding to a word that needs translating.

20.4.1   The DictionaryEntry class

An instance of the DictionaryEntry **class** pairs two words together. The first is from the source language and the second is the corresponding translation. The Dictionary class is going to use an efficient search mechanism which requires the **array** of DictionaryEntry **objects** to be **sort**ed, and so DictionaryEntry needs to **implement** Comparable. Since Java 5.0, Comparable is a **generic interface**.

Concept **Interface: generic interface.**   A **generic interface** is an **interface** which has one or more **type parameters** written within angled brackets (<>) just after its name in the interface heading. Such type parameters may be used as **type**s in the declaration of the **abstract method**s in the interface. The feature works in the same way as for **generic class**es: the generic interface itself is a **raw type** and when we supply **type arguments** for the type parameters, we identify a **parameterized type**.

Concept **Standard API: Comparable interface.**   The standard **interface** java.lang.Comparable provides a **type** for **objects** which can be compared with similar items. Having one type for this notion enables general **algorithm**s to be implemented, such as ones for **sort**ing and efficient searching of **arrays**. It was introduced in Java 1.2, but at Java 5.0 it became a **generic interface**. It contains just one **instance method** definition.

```
public interface Comparable<T>
{
  int compareTo(T o);
} // Comparable
```

Any non-**abstract class** that **implements** this interface, must contain a **method implementation** of compareTo() which provides a **total order** for its objects. The **type parameter**, T, is for the **type** of objects that can be compared and **classes** that (directly) implement Comparable typically supply their own class name as the **type argument**. For example, if we say that class SomeClass implements Comparable<SomeClass> we are stating that SomeClass provides an **instance method** compareTo(), enabling a SomeClass object to compare itself with a given other one.

If a class implements Comparable, then the order defined by compareTo() is known as the **natural ordering** of that class.

Concept **Standard API: String: implements Comparable.**   The standard **class** java.lang.String **implements** java.lang.Comparable, with an implementation of compareTo() which provides a **lexicographic ordering**. This means it orders the strings in dictionary order based on the values of the **characters** in them.

Since Java 5.0, when Comparable became a **generic interface**, String actually implements Comparable<String>.

```
public final class String implements Comparable<String>
{
  ...
```

```
         @Override
         public int compareTo(String other)
         {
           ...
         } // compareTo
         ...
      } // class String
```

Coffee time: Why do you think that String is a **final class**? [20.4.1]

Thanks to Comparable being a generic interface, the **method parameter** of compareTo() in String is defined to be a String, and so the **compiler** checks that any argument supplied for it is a String. So, for example, if we accidentally tried to compare a String with an Integer we would get a **compile time error**. Whereas prior to Java 5.0, compareTo() could only test at **run time** that the argument was a String, using a **cast**.

We define our DictionaryEntry class to **implement** Comparable<DictionaryEntry>, which is saying that DictionaryEntry objects can be compared with each other, and the comparison provides a **total order**. Of course, we have to provide the implementation within the class. In addition, as each DictionaryEntry is essentially a pair of Strings, we can make the class **extend** Pair<String, String> using Pair from Section 19.3.1 on page 491.

```
001: // A word from one language, paired with the equivalent one from another.
002: public class DictionaryEntry extends Pair<String, String>
003:                             implements Comparable<DictionaryEntry>
004: {
005:   // Constructor is given the words.
006:   public DictionaryEntry(String sourceLanguageWord, String targetLanguageWord)
007:   {
008:     super(sourceLanguageWord, targetLanguageWord);
009:   } // DictionaryEntry
```

We must provide a **method implementation** of compareTo(), which here is based merely on the first word in the pair, i.e. the one in the source language. This is because every word in the input document will be searched for in the Dictionary, and that search requires the DictionaryEntry objects to be sorted by the words we may be looking for, so it can be efficient. To compare the two first words from two DictionaryEntrys, we can use compareTo() from String, because the two first words are each a String, and String implements Comparable<String>.

```
012:   // Return negative if this first word is less than other's first word,
013:   // zero if they are the same, or positive if this one is the greater.
014:   @Override
015:   public int compareTo(DictionaryEntry other)
016:   {
017:     return getFirst().compareTo(other.getFirst());
018:   } // compareTo
```

The compareTo() **instance method** will be used to help efficiently find the location of a certain DictionaryEntry in the sorted **list**, but we shall also have equals().

Concept **Standard API: Object: equals().** The standard **class** java.lang.Object contains an **instance method** equals() which is designed to model the notion of **equivalence** between two **objects**. The definition is as follows.

```
   public boolean equals(Object other)
   {
     return this == other;
   } // equals
```

This is **inherit**ed by all other classes, and so by default all **object**s have this *finest* notion of equivalence: two objects are **equivalent** if and only if they are **equal**, i.e. are the same object. This is often too fine, and so, many classes **override** this definition with one which models the appropriate notion of equivalence for that particular class.

Concept **Standard API: Comparable interface: `compareTo()` and `equals()`.** A **class** that **implements** `java.lang.Comparable` should have a **method implementation** of `compareTo()` which is consistent with `equals()`, wherever this is possible. By consistent, we mean that

$$x.equals(y)$$

always gives the same value as the following.

$$x.compareTo(y) == 0$$

We shall follow the recommendation to have a notion of **equivalence**, implemented via `equals()`, which is consistent with `compareTo()`. Two `DictionaryEntry` objects are **equivalent** if and only if their first words are equivalent, regardless of the values of their second words – which is exactly (and deliberately) the circumstances for obtaining a zero from `compareTo()`.

```
021:    // Return true if and only if this and other have the same first word.
022:    // Unless other is not a DictionaryEntry,
023:    // in which case delegate to superclass.
024:    @Override
025:    public boolean equals(Object other)
026:    {
027:      if (other instanceof DictionaryEntry)
028:        return compareTo((DictionaryEntry)other) == 0;
029:      else
030:        return super.equals(other);
031:    } // equals
032:
033: } // class DictionaryEntry
```

Coffee time:
`20.4.2`
If we changed the **method parameter** of `equals()` to be of **type** `DictionaryEntry` instead of `Object`, would it still **override** the one from `Object` as we intended? Or would it instead be an **overloaded method**? What have we written that would cause a **compile time error** if we made that mistake?

20.4.2 The `Dictionary` class

The `Dictionary` **class** uses a **partially filled array** to store the `DictionaryEntry` **object**s. The **data** for these pairs is read from a `BufferedReader` passed to the **constructor method**.

Some of the code is similar to examples you have seen before, for reading from a `BufferedReader` and using **array extension**. However, this time we shall use the **generic method** `Arrays.copyOf()` to make a **new** bigger **array** when our existing one is full.

Concept **Method: generic methods.** A **generic method** is a **method** which has one or more **type parameters** written within angled brackets (`<>`) just before the **return type** in the method heading. These are used in a similar way to type parameters of a **generic class**, but apply only to the method. When we write a **method call** for a generic method, we can supply **type arguments** for the type parameters. Generic methods may be defined inside a generic or non-generic class, and may be **instance methods** or **class methods**. However, they are of most use as **class methods**, because generic features of instance methods are *usually* best achieved via type parameters for the whole **class**.

The following symbolic example is a class method with two type parameters.

```
public static <T1, T2> void myGenericMethod(T1[] anArray, T2 aValue)
{
    ... Code here that uses T1 and T2 as types.
    ... Some restrictions apply,
    ... such as we cannot make instances of T1, or T2.
} // myGenericMethod
```

This takes (a **reference** to) an **array** of some **type**, T1[] and also (a reference to) an **object** of type T2. The actual types for T1 and T2 can be supplied as type arguments when the method is called. For example, assuming the above is defined in a class called MyClassWithGenericMethod, then the following could be a call to it.

```
Date[] aDateArray = ...
String aString = ...

MyClassWithGenericMethod.<Date, String>myGenericMethod(aDateArray, aString);
```

Notice that the type arguments are written, within angled brackets (<>), *after* the dot (.) separating the class name from the method name – they are not class type parameters, and so are not written after the class name, but instead they occur before the method name. There is also a peculiarity to watch out for. Normally, if we call a class method from within the class where it is defined, we do not need to prepend the class name and a dot(.), but if we are going to supply type arguments then we must. And for a generic instance method, we must similarly use the **this reference** and prepend **this** and a dot.

However, the good news is that we can *omit* the type arguments completely when we call a generic method, and in nearly all cases the **compiler** is able to work them out from the types of the **method arguments**.

Concept **Standard API: Arrays: copyOf().** The standard **class** java.util.Arrays provides, since Java 6.0, another **class method** called copyOf which makes a copy of an **array**. It is a **generic method** and so can handle any kind of **reference type** array. The **new** array returned can be bigger or smaller than the original, and the **array elements** will be the same as in the original for the **array index** positions they have in common.

```
public static <T> T[] copyOf(T[] original, int newLength)
{
    T[] result = ... make a new array of length newLength,
             ... where result[i] = original[i]
             ...    for all 0 <= i < min(original.length, newLength)
    return result;
} // copyOf
```

The single **type parameter**, T, specifies the **type** of the array elements, and the two **method parameters** are the original array of type T[], and an **int** required length for the copy. It **return**s a new array of type T[]. (The method uses reflection – an advanced topic not covered by this book – to get around the restrictions on the use of type parameters.)

In fact, the class also contains several more class methods called copyOf, one for each array of a **primitive type**, such as **int**[], etc..

These methods are particularly useful for **array extension**.

```
SomeType[] myArray = new SomeType[INITIAL_SIZE];
...
if ... myArray is now full and I need more room
    myArray = Arrays.copyOf(myArray, myArray.length * RESIZE_FACTOR);
...
```

Here is our `Dictionary` code.

```
001: import java.io.BufferedReader;
002: import java.io.IOException;
003: import java.util.Arrays;
004:
005: // Reads a translation dictionary from a given BufferedReader,
006: // and provides a translateWord method.
007: public class Dictionary
008: {
009:   // We store the DictionaryEntries in a partially filled array,
010:   // and use array extension as required.
011:   // The initial size and resize factor of that array.
012:   private static final int INITIAL_ARRAY_SIZE = 50, ARRAY_RESIZE_FACTOR = 2;
013:
014:   // The array for storing the entries, and a count of the number of them.
015:   private final DictionaryEntry[] dictionaryEntries;
016:   private final int noOfDictionaryEntries;
```

The constructor method reads lines from a given `BufferedReader`. Each of these should contain a pair of words, separated by a **tab character**. The first word is in the same language which the input document is expressed in, and the second word is the corresponding translation in the other language. (For brevity, let us assume the format of that **file** can be trusted.)

```
019:   // Read lines from the given BufferedReader, split each into tab separated
020:   // pairs, create a DictionaryEntry for it and add to dictionaryEntries.
021:   public Dictionary(BufferedReader input) throws IOException, RuntimeException
022:   {
023:     DictionaryEntry[] dictionaryEntriesSoFar
024:       = new DictionaryEntry[INITIAL_ARRAY_SIZE];
025:     int noOfDictionaryEntriesSoFar = 0;
026:     String currentLine;
027:     while ((currentLine = input.readLine()) != null)
028:     {
029:       String[] lineInParts = currentLine.split("\t");
030:       DictionaryEntry dictionaryEntry
031:         = new DictionaryEntry(lineInParts[0], lineInParts[1]);
032:       if (noOfDictionaryEntriesSoFar == dictionaryEntriesSoFar.length)
033:         dictionaryEntriesSoFar
034:           = Arrays.copyOf(dictionaryEntriesSoFar,
035:                           dictionaryEntriesSoFar.length * ARRAY_RESIZE_FACTOR);
036:       dictionaryEntriesSoFar[noOfDictionaryEntriesSoFar] = dictionaryEntry;
037:       noOfDictionaryEntriesSoFar++;
038:     } // while
039:
040:     // Sort the array to allow for efficient searching of it.
041:     Arrays.sort(dictionaryEntriesSoFar, 0, noOfDictionaryEntriesSoFar);
042:     noOfDictionaryEntries = noOfDictionaryEntriesSoFar;
043:     dictionaryEntries = dictionaryEntriesSoFar;
044:   } // Dictionary
```

Note that the **compiler** was able to figure out the **type parameter** for the **generic method**, and our **method call** above was equivalent to the following.

```
dictionaryEntriesSoFar
  = Arrays.<DictionaryEntry>copyOf
            (dictionaryEntriesSoFar,
             dictionaryEntriesSoFar.length * ARRAY_RESIZE_FACTOR);
```

Coffee time: 20.4.3 Why did we use two **local variables** in the constructor method which we copied into the **instance variables** at the end of it – could we instead have used the instance variables directly throughout the constructor method?

Finally for `Dictionary`, we have the **instance method** to translate a given word. This needs to perform an **array search**, to look for a `DictionaryEntry` which has a matching word in its first place. If one is found, it shall **return** the paired second word, or, if not then the given word is returned with square brackets around it. The process of efficiently searching an **array** can be generalized to work for an array of any `Comparable` **type**. So, we write that part of the program in a separate reusable class, called `SearchArray`. This will contain a **class method**, `search()`, which takes three **method parameters**: an array, the number of items stored in that array, and an entry to be searched for. It will return either the **array index** of an object matching the given one, or a negative number if there is no such object in the array. For this efficient searching to work, the array *must* already be **sort**ed into the **natural ordering** of its **array elements**. We ensured this was so at the end of the **constructor method**.

```
047:   // Translate one word.
048:   public String translateWord(String word)
049:   {
050:     int dictionaryEntryIndex
051:       = SearchArray.search(dictionaryEntries, noOfDictionaryEntries,
052:                            new DictionaryEntry(word, null));
053:     if (dictionaryEntryIndex < 0)
054:       return "[" + word + "]";
055:     else
056:       return dictionaryEntries[dictionaryEntryIndex].getSecond();
057:   } // translateWord
058:
059: } // class Dictionary
```

`SearchArray.search()` will use `compareTo()` and `equals()` from `DictionaryEntry` to help find and confirm finding the matching `DictionaryEntry`. Notice the `DictionaryEntry` we create for these instance methods to compare against: it has the **null reference** as its second word, but this is fine because the comparisons are based solely on the first word.

20.4.3 The `SearchArray` class

The `SearchArray` **class** provides a single **class method** which performs an efficient **array search** using a **binary search algorithm**.

Concept **Design: Searching a list: binary search.** When searching for a particular item in a **list** of items we can seriously improve efficiency compared with performing a **linear search** if the items are already **sort**ed into a known **total order** and we use a **binary search**. However, this more efficient approach is also more complicated than the simple, but slow, linear search. This exhibits the unfortunately typical trade-off between speed and simplicity.

In a binary search we have two indices `low` and `high` which start off as **index**ing the first and last elements of the **data** in the list. At any time, the item we are looking for lies somewhere between `low` and `high`, or it is not present. So we look at the item half way between them. If it is the one we are looking for, then the process is over. If it is **less than** the one we want, we move the `low` index up to that half way point plus one, otherwise we move the `high` index down to one less than it. If `low` and `high` meet or cross over then we can stop looking – the item is not there.

```
list = ... items are stored in the list in ascending order
searchItem = .. the item we wish to find in list
int lowIndex = 0
int highIndex = list.length - 1
int midIndex = (lowIndex + highIndex) / 2
```

```
while lowIndex < highIndex && list[midIndex] != searchItem
  if list[midIndex] < searchItem
    lowIndex = midIndex + 1
  else
    highIndex = midIndex - 1
  midIndex = (lowIndex + highIndex) / 2
end-while
if list[midIndex] == searchItem
  ... you found it
else
  ... searchItem is not in the list
```

Our class method to search an **array** is intended to handle any type of Comparable items, so we write it as a **generic method** with a single **type parameter** called ArrayType. We shall need to specify that any **type argument** supplied (or implied) for it is a **class** or **interface** that **implements** or **extends** the Comparable **interface**.

Concept **Interface: extending another interface.** An **interface** can **extend** another interface. This means that the **abstract methods** and **class constants** specified in the **superinterface** are **inherited** in the **subinterface**. From a **polymorphism** point of view, it also means that (references to) **instances** of a **class** which **implements** the subinterface, are members of the **type** denoted by the superinterface in addition to the type denoted by the subinterface.

Unlike **classes** which can only extend one other class, interfaces can extend many other interfaces.

Concept **Class: generic class: bound type parameter: extends some interface.** The **type parameters** of a **generic class** (or **generic interface**, or **generic method**) may be declared to **extend** some known **type**. The known type may be a **class** or an **interface**. Perhaps surprisingly, we use the **reserved word extends** even if the known type is an interface. This is in recognition of the idea that an **interface** is a **type** in just the same way that a class is. One type can be an **extension** of another through **inheritance**, either by being a **subclass** of another class, a **subinterface** of another interface, or by being a class that **implements** an interface.

If the known type is an interface, then when a **type argument** is supplied for the type parameter, the **compiler** checks that it is a class which implements that interface, or is that interface or an interface that extends it.

Concept **Method: generic methods: bound type parameter.** The **type parameters** of a **generic method** can be **bound type parameters** as they can be with **generic classes**. For example, here is a **class method** that **returns** the largest element, according to **natural ordering**, of an **array** of items which are Comparable with themselves.

```
public class MaxArray
{
  public static <ArrayType extends Comparable<ArrayType>>
                ArrayType getMax(ArrayType[] anArray)
                throws IllegalArgumentException
  {
    try
    {
      ArrayType result = anArray[0];
      for (int index = 1; index < anArray.length; index++)
        if (result.compareTo(anArray[index]) < 0)
          result = anArray[index];
      return result;
    } // try
```

```
        catch (ArrayIndexOutOfBoundsException e)
        { throw new IllegalArgumentException("Array must be non-empty", e); }
        catch (NullPointerException e)
        { throw new IllegalArgumentException("Array must exist", e); }
    } // getMax

  } // class MaxArray
```

This could be used as follows.

```
    String[] aStringArray = { "the", "cat", "vaporized", "on", "the", "mat" };
    String maxInAStringArray = MaxArray.getMax(aStringArray);
```

The **compiler** was able to figure out the **type argument**, and so our **method call** above is equivalent to the following.

```
    String maxInAStringArray = MaxArray.<String>getMax(aStringArray);
```

Coffee   Why 'vaporized' and not 'sat'? (There is a good reason – look at the 'test data' carefully.)
time: 20.4.4

Our generic method to efficiently search an array, has one type parameter, `ArrayType`, which must be a **type** of **object** which can be compared with others of the same type. So we write `<ArrayType extends Comparable<ArrayType>>` – this means any **type argument** supplied, or figured out by the **compiler**, will need to be `Comparable` with itself.

```
001: // Provides an efficient search for a Comparable in a sorted Comparable[].
002: public class SearchArray
003: {
004:    // Use binary search to find searchItem in anArray which must be sorted.
005:    // Returns a negative number if not present, or array index.
006:    public static <ArrayType extends Comparable<ArrayType>>
007:          int search(ArrayType[] anArray, int noOfItems, ArrayType searchItem)
008:          throws IllegalArgumentException
009:    {
010:      if (anArray == null)
011:        throw new IllegalArgumentException("Array must exist");
012:      if (noOfItems > anArray.length)
013:        throw new IllegalArgumentException("Data length > array length: "
014:                                          + noOfItems + " " + anArray.length);
015:      if (noOfItems == 0)
016:        return -1;
017:
018:      int lowIndex = 0;
019:      int highIndex = noOfItems - 1;
020:      int midIndex = (lowIndex + highIndex) / 2;
021:      while (lowIndex < highIndex && ! anArray[midIndex].equals(searchItem))
022:      {
023:        if (anArray[midIndex].compareTo(searchItem) < 0)
024:          lowIndex = midIndex + 1;
025:        else
026:          highIndex = midIndex - 1;
027:        midIndex = (lowIndex + highIndex) / 2;
028:      } // while
029:      if (anArray[midIndex].equals(searchItem))
030:        return midIndex;
```

```
031:      else
032:         return -1;
033:   } // search
034:
035: } // SearchArray
```

20.4.4 The Translate class

Finally for this program, we have the **class** containing the **main method**. This accepts the three **command line argument**s, makes a Dictionary from the **file** named in the first one, and translates the text in the file named by the second argument into that named by the third.

The parts of it for reading from a BufferedReader and writing to a PrintWriter, are similar to LineNumber from Section 18.5 on page 465.

```
001: import java.io.BufferedReader;
002: import java.io.FileReader;
003: import java.io.FileWriter;
004: import java.io.IOException;
005: import java.io.PrintWriter;
006:
007: // Program to translate a document from one language to another.
008: // Translation dictionary file is first argument.
009: // Input file is the second argument, output is the third.
010: public class Translate
011: {
012:    // The main method reads lines from the dictionary and stores them,
013:    // via the Dictionary constructor. Then it reads lines from the input file,
014:    // translates each word and writes it to the output file.
015:    public static void main(String[] args)
016:    {
017:       BufferedReader input = null;
018:       PrintWriter output = null;
019:       try
020:       {
021:          if (args.length != 3)
022:             throw new IllegalArgumentException
023:                         ("There must be exactly three arguments:"
024:                            + " dictfile infile outfile");
025:
026:          // The dictionary.
027:          Dictionary dictionary
028:             = new Dictionary(new BufferedReader(new FileReader(args[0])));
029:
030:          input = new BufferedReader(new FileReader(args[1]));
031:          output = new PrintWriter(new FileWriter(args[2]));
032:
033:          // Read the lines and translate each word.
034:          String currentLine;
035:          while ((currentLine = input.readLine()) != null)
036:          {
037:             String wordDelimiter = "";
038:             for (String word : currentLine.split(" "))
039:             {
040:                output.print(wordDelimiter);
041:                if (! word.equals(""))
042:                   output.print(dictionary.translateWord(word));
043:                wordDelimiter = " ";
```

```
044:          } // for
045:          output.println();
046:        } // while
047:
048:      } // try
049:      catch (Exception exception)
050:      {
051:        System.err.println(exception);
052:      } // catch
053:      finally
054:      {
055:        try { if (input != null) input.close(); }
056:        catch (IOException exception)
057:          { System.err.println("Could not close input " + exception); }
058:        if (output != null)
059:        {
060:          output.close();
061:          if (output.checkError())
062:            System.err.println("Something went wrong with the output");
063:        } // if
064:      } // finally
065:    } // main
066:
067: } // class Translate
```

Coffee time: [20.4.5] The **binary search** idea was a good one – it is so much faster than the **linear search** we used in earlier chapters. Do you think that the idea has already made it to the Java **API**? Check out the Arrays class.

20.4.5 Trying it

For a bit of fun, instead of translating a document from one language to another, why not use a 'dictionary of opposites'? To show that the **sort**ing by first word is working, we here deliberately store the opposites sorted by the second word.

Our input document is made from some well known cliches.

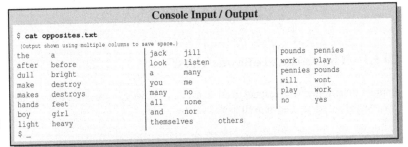

```
                      Console Input / Output

$ cat opposites.txt
(Output shown using multiple columns to save space.)
the       a            jack     jill              pounds  pennies
after     before       look     listen            work    play
dull      bright       a        many              pennies pounds
make      destroy      you      me                will    wont
makes     destroys     many     no                play    work
hands     feet         all      none              no      yes
boy       girl         and      nor
light     heavy        themselves   others
$ _
```

```
                      Console Input / Output

$ cat input.txt
all work and no play makes jack a dull boy
      while many hands make light work

if you look after the pennies
the pounds will look after themselves
$ _
```

Here is the resulting 'translation'.

```
                      Console Input / Output

$ java Translate opposites.txt input.txt output.txt
$ cat output.txt
none play nor yes work destroys jill many bright girl
    [while] no feet destroy heavy play

[if] me listen before a pounds
a pennies wont listen before others
$ _
```

Coffee time: [20.4.6]
Would it be difficult to improve the program by making it able to handle capitalization and punctuation?

20.4.6 Coursework: Minimum and maximum `Comparable`

Write a **class** called `MinMaxArray` which has one **class method** that takes an **array**. It will be a **generic method** with one **type parameter** that is comparable with itself, and the array shall have that **array base type**. It will **return** an **instance** of the **generic class** `Pair` from Section 19.3.1 on page 491, comprising the minimum and the maximum items from the array, based on the **natural ordering** of the items. It should **throw** an `IllegalArgumentException` if the array is empty or non-existent.

Test your class with a program called `TestMinMaxArray`.

20.5 Example: Sorting valuables

AIM:
To introduce the idea that a **class** can **implement** many **interfaces**, and explore what it means for an **interface** to **extend** another. We also take another look at having consistency between `compareTo()` and `equals()`.

In this final section, we revisit the valuables example from Section 20.2.5 starting on page 512, and assume we wish to add an **instance method** to the **class** `Valuables`, which **sort**s the **array** into descending order by value.

The **classes**, `Building`, `Car`, `House`, `OfficeBlock`, `Tractor` and `Vehicle` are the same as in the previous version of the program.

20.5.1 The `ValuableHouse` class?

In order to be sorted with respect to other `Valuables`, we can state that the `ValuableHouse` **class implements** the **interface** `Comparable<Valuable>` as well as `Valuable`.

Concept **Interface: a class can implement many interfaces.** A **class** can **extend** at most one other class, but is permitted to **implement** any number of **interfaces**. The implemented interfaces are listed, with commas between, after the **reserved word** `implements`.

For example, we could imagine a `StopClock` program, which automatically stopped and started the clock when the mouse is moved out of and back in to the window. This would probably implement `MouseListener` as well as `ActionListener`.

```
import java.awt.ActionListener;
import java.awt.MouseListener;
import javax.swing.JFrame;
...
public class StopClock extends JFrame
                       implements ActionListener, MouseListener
{
  ...
  // actionPerformed is specified in the interface ActionListener
  public void actionPerformed(ActionEvent event)
  {
    ...
  } // actionPerformed
```

```
        ... Various methods here, as specified in MouseListener.

      } // class StopClock
```

We want a `ValuableHouse` to be comparable with any other (or even the same) `Valuable`, so we say it implements `Comparable<Valuable>` and give it a definition of `compareTo()`.

```
001: // Representation of a Valuable which is a house.
002: public class ValuableHouse extends House
003:                                      implements Valuable, Comparable<Valuable>
004: ...
```

Wait a minute – this isn't going to work!

20.5.2   The `Valuable` interface

How does Java know that *every* `Valuable` **implements** `Comparable<Valuable>`? Even after going through and making that change to all our `Valuable` classes, there is no guarantee: sometime in the future another class could be written that implements `Valuable` but not `Comparable<Valuable>`.

Instead we want to state that every `Valuable` also implements `Comparable<Valuable>`. So, let us make `Valuable` **extend** `Comparable<Valuable>`.

```
001: // Objects which have a value obtained via a value() method.
002: public interface Valuable extends Comparable<Valuable>
003: {
004:   // The value of this Valuable.
005:   int value();
006:
007: } // interface Valuable
```

From now on, every **class** that implements `Valuable` must also provide a **method implementation** for `compareTo()`.

20.5.3   The `ValuableHouse` class

Here is the new version of `ValuableHouse`. The first part of the class is the same as in the previous version of the program.

```
001: // Representation of a Valuable which is a house.
002: public class ValuableHouse extends House implements Valuable
003: {
004:   // A measure of the value of the area the house is in.
005:   private double locationDesirabilityIndex;
006:
007:
008:   // Construct a ValuableHouse with a given number of bedrooms
009:   // and location desirability.
010:   public ValuableHouse(int requiredNoOfBedrooms,
011:                        double requiredLocationDesirabilityIndex)
012:   {
013:     super(requiredNoOfBedrooms);
014:     locationDesirabilityIndex = requiredLocationDesirabilityIndex;
015:   } // ValuableHouse
016:
017:
018:   // Calculate and return the value of this valuable item.
019:   @Override
020:   public int value()
021:   {
022:     return (int) (getNoOfBedrooms() * 50000 * locationDesirabilityIndex);
023:   } // valuable
```

```
024:
025:
026:    // Return a short description of this as a valuable item.
027:    @Override
028:    public String toString()
029:    {
030:        return "House worth " + value();
031:    } // toString
```

The `compareTo()` **instance method** subtracts the value of this `Valuable` from that of the given other one. This will provide a **total order**ing by *descending* value.

```
034:    // Return negative if this value is greater than other's value,
035:    // zero if they are the same, or positive if this value is the lesser.
036:    @Override
037:    public int compareTo(Valuable other)
038:    {
039:        return other.value() - value();
040:    } // compareTo
```

You will recall the recommendation that **method implementation**s of `compareTo()` are consistent with `equals()`. So we here **override** `equals()` from `Object` with one that is consistent with `compareTo()`. Notice that the **method parameter type** has to be `Object`, rather than `Valuable` – otherwise we would not be overriding the instance method, but making a new **overloaded method**. Also notice that we are regarding two `Valuable` items as being **equivalent** if they have the same value, regardless of the the the kind of valuable, let alone their inner details. This is the desired effect for this program – a house with three bedrooms worth £100,000 is equivalent to one with four bedrooms also worth that amount, and both are equivalent to a car of that value. Similar classes written for a different program may well have a different implementation of `equals()` and `compareTo()`.

```
043:    // Return true if and only if this and other have the same value.
044:    // Unless other is not a Valuable, in which case delegate to superclass.
045:    @Override
046:    public boolean equals(Object other)
047:    {
048:        if (other instanceof Valuable)
049:            return compareTo((Valuable)other) == 0;
050:        else
051:            return super.equals(other);
052:    } // equals
053:
054: } // class ValuableHouse
```

The above code is a simple way of ensuring that `equals()` is consistent with `compareTo()` for `Valuable`, whilst it **in-herit**s the same properties as in the **superclass** for other types. For example, if we compare `ValuableHouse` with another `Valuable` then they are equivalent if they have the same value; but if we compare a `ValuableHouse` with, say, an `OfficeBlock`, then we will get the definition of **equivalence** from (probably) the class `Building`.

20.5.4 The `ValuableCar` class

The same modifications are made to the `ValuableCar` **class**, and the rest of it is left as in the previous version of the program. This also applies to any other **class**es that **implement** `Valuable`, such as `ValuableBoat`, `ValuableArtWork`, `ValuableJewellery` etc..

20.5.5 The `Valuables` class

To **sort** the **array** inside the `Valuables` **class**, we will use `Arrays.sort()`. Here is the code for the new version – the first part is the same as previously, except for an **import statement**.

```
001: import java.util.Arrays;
002:
003: // Representation of a collection of Valuables.
004: public class Valuables
005: {
006:   // The Valuables, stored in a partially filled array, together with size.
007:   private Valuable[] valuableArray;
008:   private int noOfValuables;
009:
010:
011:   // Create a collection with the given maximum size.
012:   public Valuables(int maxNoOfValuables)
013:   {
014:     valuableArray = new Valuable[maxNoOfValuables];
015:     noOfValuables = 0;
016:   } // Valuables
017:
018:
019:   // Add a given Valuable to the collection (ignore if full).
020:   public void addValuable(Valuable valuable)
021:   {
022:     if (noOfValuables < valuableArray.length)
023:     {
024:       valuableArray[noOfValuables] = valuable;
025:       noOfValuables++;
026:     } // if
027:   } // addValuable
028:
029:
030:   // Calculate and return the total value of the collection.
031:   public int totalValue()
032:   {
033:     int result = 0;
034:     for (Valuable valuable : valuableArray)
035:       result += valuable.value();
036:     return result;
037:   } // totalValue
038:
039:
040:   // Return a short description of the collection.
041:   @Override
042:   public String toString()
043:   {
044:     if (noOfValuables == 0)
045:       return "Nothing valuable";
046:
047:     String result = valuableArray[0].toString();
048:     for (int index = 1; index < noOfValuables; index++)
049:       result += String.format("%n%s", valuableArray[index]);
050:     return result;
051:   } // toString
```

The `sort()` **instance method** uses a `sort()` **class method** from the `Arrays` class.

```
054:   // Sort the collection into order by value.
055:   public void sort()
056:   {
057:     Arrays.sort(valuableArray, 0, noOfValuables);
058:   } // sort
```

This will work because the **array element**s of `valuableArray` are **mutually comparable**.

Finally, we add an extra **statement** to our test code, to invoke the `sort()` instance method.

```
060:    // Create a Valuables collection, add Valuable items, sort, and show result.
061:    // Purely for testing during development.
062:    public static void main(String[] args)
063:    {
064:      Valuables valuables = new Valuables(5);
065:
066:      // My first house -- I was so proud of its spare bedroom
067:      // and 'value for money' area.
068:      valuables.addValuable(new ValuableHouse(2, 0.5));
069:
070:      // My first car, not quite a 'head turner',
071:      // but its third door was handy when the main 2 got stuck.
072:      valuables.addValuable(new ValuableCar(3, 0.25));
073:
074:      // It was nice to have a new car when I started work.
075:      valuables.addValuable(new ValuableCar(4, 1.0));
076:
077:      // Then I won the lottery! (Yeah, right.)
078:      valuables.addValuable(new ValuableHouse(6, 2.0));
079:      valuables.addValuable(new ValuableCar(12, 4.0));
080:
081:      System.out.println("My valuables are worth " + valuables.totalValue());
082:
083:      valuables.sort();
084:
085:      System.out.println(valuables);
086:    } // main
087:
088: } // class Valuables
```

20.5.6   Trying it

```
                        Console Input / Output
$ java Valuables
My valuables are worth 755500
House worth 600000
Car worth 96000
House worth 50000
Car worth 8000
Car worth 1500
$ _
```

20.5.7   Coursework: Analysis of `compareTo()` and `equals()`

We saw examples of `compareTo()` and `equals()` **instance method**s in various **class**es before this chapter. Now that you know about the `Comparable` **interface** and the `equals()` instance method from the `Object` class – which takes (a **reference** to) an `Object` as a **method parameter**, find all those previous places and identify the changes we should make. Record them in your logbook.

20.6   Concepts covered in this chapter

Here is a list of the concepts that were covered in this chapter, each with a self-test question. You can use this to check you remember them being introduced, and perhaps re-read some of them before going on to the next chapter.

Class	
– generic class: bound type parameter: extends some interface (p.526)	What is perhaps surprising about the way we say that a type argument of a generic class or interface or generic method, must implement a particular interface?
– is a type: and has three components (p.512)	What are the three components of a type? In what way does a class have these things?

Design	
– Searching a list: binary search (p.525)	What typical trade-off is being shown when we compare this with the simplest way to search a list?
– Sorting a list: total order (p.516)	What is the instance method that implements a total order in Java typically called? What parameters does it take and what result does it produce?

Inheritance	
– multiple inheritance (p.509)	Which of the following, if any, are examples of multiple inheritance? 1. An instance of class A is a B and has a C. 2. An instance of class A is a B and also is a C, but a B is not a C nor vice versa. 3. An instance of class A is a B which in turn is a C. 4. An instance of class A has a B and is a C. In Java, what is the maximum number of (direct) superclasses that a class can have? What is the minimum?

Interface	
– definition (p.511)	What is the main difference between an interface and a class? What can interfaces not contain?
– is a type (p.512)	Which of the three components of a type are provided by an interface, and which are provided by the classes that implement the interface?
– method implementation (p.513)	What simple errors might we make, and what can we write to protect us from them?
– generic interface (p.520)	If we do not supply type arguments for a generic interface when we use it, then what is it we are using?
– extending another interface (p.526)	How many other interfaces can an interface extend? How many classes can an interface extend?
– a class can implement many interfaces (p.530)	How do we state that a class implements several interfaces?

Method	
– generic methods (p.522)	When might we want to have a generic method rather than a generic class? How do we call a generic method – where do we write the type argument(s)? Do we actually have to write them anyway?
– generic methods: bound type parameter (p.526)	What do we mean by bound type parameter?

Standard API	
– Arrays (p.518)	What is the purpose of this class?
– Arrays: sort() (p.518)	What must be true about the argument if it is an array of objects?
– Arrays: copyOf() (p.523)	What is this especially useful for? What is its type parameter?
– Comparable interface (p.520)	What instance method must be provided by any non-abstract class that implements this?
– Comparable interface: compareTo() and equals() (p.522)	What should be the relationship between these two methods?
– Object: equals() (p.521)	What notion of equivalence is implemented in Object?
– String: implements Comparable (p.520)	Exactly what parameterization of Comparable does String implement?

Chapter 21

Collections

Harvest only what you need
and store it well.
So you neither starve
nor choke.

21.1   Chapter aims

The need to handle **collections** of **object**s is quite common, and previously we have seen that an **array** can be used to store things in an **index**ed **list**. In this chapter we explore the Java **collections framework**, which is a group of **class**es and **interface**s providing a variety of mechanisms for storing collections, all of which are more convenient to use than arrays. For example, one of the collections, called ArrayList, is essentially a wrapped up array which automatically handles **array extension** when it is full.

We will look at Lists, Sets and Maps. These different kinds of collection are in fact specified as **interface**s, and are **implement**ed by ArrayList, LinkedList, TreeSet, HashSet, TreeMap and HashMap (and other classes that we do not look at here).

The chapter contains the following sections.

Section	Aims	Associated Coursework
21.2 Reversing a text file (p.538)	To introduce the Java **collections framework**, and in particular the idea of **list collection**s, the List **interface** and the ArrayList **class**.	Write a program to **sort** election information leaflets into delivery order. (p.541)
21.3 Sorting a text file using an ArrayList (p.542)	To reinforce the use of ArrayList, in particular, showing uses of the set() **instance method** of a List. We also note that an **array** can be created from a List, and vice versa. Finally, we look at the Collections **class** and observe that it has a sort() **generic method**.	Write a program to **sort** election information leaflets into delivery order, using a compareTo() **instance method**. (p.545)
21.4 Prime numbers (p.546)	To introduce the idea of **set collection**s, the Set **interface** and the HashSet **class**. For this we explore **hash tables** and meet hashCode() from Object. We also see that the class Integer **implements** Comparable<Integer>.	Write a program to detect people voting more than once in voting records. (p.551)

Section	Aims	Associated Coursework
21.5 Sorting a text file using a `TreeSet` (p.552)	To introduce the `TreeSet` **class**, for which we explore **ordered binary trees** and **tree sort**. We also meet the `Iterator` **interface**, together with how it is used on a `List` and a `Set`, especially a `TreeSet`.	Write a program to **sort** election information leaflets into delivery order, using a `TreeSet`. (p.555)
21.6 Summary of lists and sets (p.555)	To summarize the **collections framework** explored so far, and introduce the `Collection` **interface** and the `LinkedList` **class**, for which we explore **linked lists**. We also revisit `List`.	(None.)
21.7 Word frequency count (p.559)	To introduce the idea of **maps**, the `Map` **interface** and the `TreeMap` **class**. In particular we observe that a `TreeMap` makes it easy to obtain the values from the map in **key** order. We also see that the **for-each loop** can be used with **collections**.	(None.)
21.8 Word frequency count sorted by frequency (p.565)	To introduce the `HashMap` **class**, and the fact that a **collection** can be built to initially contain the same values as some other collection. We also take a look at how we can go about making a good **override** of the `hashCode()` **instance method** of `Object`.	Write a program to detect people voting more than once in voting records, using a `HashMap`. (p.569)
21.9 Collections of collections (p.569)	To explore the idea that the elements of a **collection** can themselves be collections, and so quite complex **data structures** can be built.	Write a program to detect people voting more than once, using a `HashMap` of **objects** containing a `LinkedList`. (p.569)

21.2 Example: Reversing a text file

AIM: To introduce the Java **collections framework**, and in particular the idea of **list collections**, the `List` **interface** and the `ArrayList` **class**.

In this first example, we present a program that reads the lines of a **text file** and outputs them in reverse to a second text file. That is, the first line is output last, and the last line is output first. This could be useful if, for example, we had a file of examination results in ascending order of merit, and we wished to present it in descending order.

In order to achieve the result, the program will read the **data** in, line by line, store it all, and then output the lines in reverse order. We could use an **array** for this, but we do not know in advance how many lines there will be, and so how big to make the array. Rather than use the strategy of **array extension**, we shall instead use an `ArrayList` **object**.

Concept **Collections API.** The need to store **collections** of **data** is very common in programming, and so in addition to the **array type** built-in to Java, the standard Java **application program interface** (**API**) provides the **collections framework**. This is a group of **classes** and **interfaces** designed to store collections of data in various different ways. These collections typically allow elements to be added to them without us worrying about memory allocation – that is, they automatically grow big enough to hold the elements that are added to them.

Concept **Collections API: Lists.** One of the kinds of **collection** supported by the **collections framework** is the **list collection**. These are collections of **data** which are essentially **lists** or sequences. This means that duplicate elements are permitted, they are stored in some order, and each element occurs at a particular **list index** position, starting at index zero. Lists are, in principle, similar to **arrays**.

Concept **Collections API: Lists: `List` interface.** The **interface** `java.util.List` is part of the **collections framework**. It specifies the **instance methods** needed to support a **list collection**. These include the following.

Method	Return	Arguments	Description
size	int		Returns the size of this List, that is, the number of elements in it.
add	boolean	Object	Appends the given Object to the end of the List. Returns **true**.
get	Object	int	Returns the Object at the specified **list index**, which must be legal (0 <= index < size()) to avoid an IndexOutOfBoundsException.
set	Object	int, Object	Overwrites an existing element with a new one: i.e. it replaces the Object at the given int list index with the given other Object. Returns the original Object. The index must be legal to avoid an IndexOutOfBoundsException.

Method definitions in interface List (some of them).

Since Java 5.0, List is a **generic interface** with a single **type parameter** representing the **type** of **object**s that can be stored in it. So, when we use a **parameterized type** of List rather than its **raw type**, all the occurrences of Object in the above table of instance methods are replaced by the **type argument**.

Concept **Collections API: Lists: ArrayList.** The **class** java.util.ArrayList is part of the **collections framework**, and is one **implement**ation of a **list collection**. It **implement**s the java.util.List **interface**. As the name suggests, this kind of **list** is implemented using a **private instance variable**, which is an **array** of **type** java.lang.Object[]. This array is grown (by **array extension**) automatically as required.

Since Java 5.0, ArrayList, and the other classes in the collections framework are **generic class**es. The **type parameter** of an ArrayList is the **type** of **object**s that can be stored in it.

```
public class ArrayList<E> implements List<E>
{ ... }
```

Here is our Reverse program. It uses an ArrayList of Strings, that is, an **instance** of ArrayList<String>. Much of it is similar to previous programs that have read lines from a BufferedReader and written to a PrintWriter, such as LineNumber from Section 18.5 on page 465.

```
001: import java.io.BufferedReader;
002: import java.io.FileReader;
003: import java.io.FileWriter;
004: import java.io.IOException;
005: import java.io.PrintWriter;
006: import java.util.ArrayList;
007: import java.util.List;
008:
009: // Program to read lines of a file, line by line, and write them in reverse
010: // order to another. Input file is the first argument, output is the second.
011: public class Reverse
012: {
013:   public static void main(String[] args)
014:   {
015:     BufferedReader input = null;
016:     PrintWriter output = null;
017:     try
018:     {
019:       if (args.length != 2)
020:         throw new IllegalArgumentException
021:                   ("There must be exactly two arguments: infile outfile");
022:
023:       input = new BufferedReader(new FileReader(args[0]));
024:       output = new PrintWriter(new FileWriter(args[1]));
025:
```

```
026:      // The List for storing the lines.
027:      List<String> lineList = new ArrayList<String>();
028:
029:      // Read the lines into lineList.
030:      String currentLine;
031:      while ((currentLine = input.readLine()) != null)
032:        lineList.add(currentLine);
033:
034:      // Now output them in reverse.
035:      for (int index = lineList.size() - 1; index >= 0; index--)
036:        output.println(lineList.get(index));
037:    } // try
038:    catch (Exception exception)
039:    {
040:      System.err.println(exception);
041:    } // catch
042:    finally
043:    {
044:      try { if (input != null) input.close(); }
045:      catch (IOException exception)
046:        { System.err.println("Could not close input " + exception); }
047:      if (output != null)
048:      {
049:        output.close();
050:        if (output.checkError())
051:          System.err.println("Something went wrong with the output");
052:      } // if
053:    } // finally
054:  } // main
055:
056: } // class Reverse
```

Notice the **type** of our `lineList` **variable** – this reminds us that an **interface** is a **type**.

Coffee time:	Why does the `add()` **instance method** of `List` always **return true**? You can find the answer to this by looking at the **API** on-line documentation for `List` and observe that it **extends** the `Collection` **interface**.

21.2.1

21.2.1   Trying it

We test our program with a **text file** containing the examination results of 5 students.

And now again, with an **empty file** – the Unix device /dev/null is a handy one (just nul on Microsoft Windows).

```
                    Console Input / Output
$ cat input.txt
Bear,Rupert        13.7%
Smith,James        51.5%
Brown,Margaret     68.2%
Jones,Stephen      87.9%
Jackson,Helen      100%
$ java Reverse input.txt output.txt
$ cat output.txt
Jackson,Helen      100%
Jones,Stephen      87.9%
Brown,Margaret     68.2%
Smith,James        51.5%
Bear,Rupert        13.7%
$ _
```

```
                    Console Input / Output
$ java Reverse /dev/null output.txt
$ ls -l output.txt
-rw-------   1 jtl jtl 0 Mar 30 12:30 output.txt
$ _
```

21.2.2 Coursework: Sorting election leaflets

Being disillusioned with the main political parties, you have recently joined the newly formed "Sort it out" party. As an election is looming, they have asked you to distribute campaign material in your area. They have sent you a stack of leaflets for each street, each with a label on the front showing the names of its recipients. Here are examples of two labels.

```
Augustus Belcher,
Regents Crescent
```

```
Joanne Smith and Lionel Brown,
Regents Crescent
```

How 'sorted out', *they* think. That is, until you tell them they have failed to print the house numbers on the leaflets, only the street names! They quickly email you a **text file** for each street, containing the recipient names for each house, in house number order. For example, the **file** for Regents Crescent is called regents-crescent.txt, and contains the following.

Console Input / Output
`$ cat regents-crescent.txt` 1 Joanne Smith and Lionel Brown 2 Augustus Belcher 3 Fatima Bacon and Gaynor White 4 Celina Simmons and Rupert Rodgers-Smythe 5 Ahmed Hussain 6 Samuel Peacock and Sarah Peacock 7 Hsin Cheng Liu 8 Blanche Peacock and Harry Peacock $ _

The first line is the names of the people who live at number one Regents Crescent, the second is the names for number two, and so on. The party officials tell you to **sort** the leaflets into this order before delivering them.

However, you are cleverer than that. You will write a program to sort a file into delivery order, that is, the order of walking up one side of the street and down the other. As it happens, you know that all the streets in your area are symmetrical, with odd numbered houses on the left, and even numbered ones on the right, both ascending in the same direction.[1]

In this task you will write the delivery order sorting program, calling it StreetOrder. It should take two **command line arguments**, the name of the original file, and the sorted file to be created. It should work by reading the lines from the input file into an ArrayList of Strings. Then it should **loop** forwards through all the even indices of the **list**, printing the lines to the output file. That will be the details for the odd numbered houses. Finally it should loop *backwards* through the odd indices of the list and print those lines. So the output for the above input would be as follows.

Console Input / Output

`$ java StreetOrder regents-crescent.txt regents-crescent-sorted.txt`
`$ cat regents-crescent-sorted.txt`
1 Joanne Smith and Lionel Brown
3 Fatima Bacon and Gaynor White
5 Ahmed Hussain
7 Hsin Cheng Liu
8 Blanche Peacock and Harry Peacock
6 Samuel Peacock and Sarah Peacock
4 Celina Simmons and Rupert Rodgers-Smythe
2 Augustus Belcher
$ _

The program should be able to handle files which have an odd number of lines – some of the streets are a cul-de-sac of detached houses with one in the middle at the bottom.

Let us next devise a reasonable set of **test cases** for the program.

---

[1] In this simplistic world, obviously the houses on the outer curve of Regents Crescent have bigger gardens than those across the road!

#	Test case description
1	No command line arguments.
2	Only one command line argument.
3	An input file that does not exist.
4	An output file that has a leading directory that does not exist.
5	An output file that has a leading directory which is not writable (e.g. the root directory on Unix, /).
6	An input file with no odd numbered houses and no even numbered houses (e.g. /dev/null or nul).
7	An input file with one odd numbered house and no even numbered houses (i.e. one line).
8	An input file with one odd numbered house and one even numbered house (i.e. two lines).
9	An input file with two odd numbered houses and one even numbered house (i.e. three lines).
10	An input file with two odd numbered houses and two even numbered houses (i.e. four lines).
11	An input file with three odd numbered houses and two even numbered houses (i.e. five lines).
12	An input file with three odd numbered houses and three even numbered houses (i.e. six lines).

As usual, devise **test data**, before **design**ing the program, and create input files ready for testing. Record this in your logbook.

Now design and implement the program. You should handle **exceptions** in the same way as we did for the example in this section. After implementation, **run** the program with the tests you designed beforehand. Record in your logbook the outcome and any unexpected results together with their cause and how you fixed any **bug**s.

21.3 Example: Sorting a text file using an `ArrayList`

AIM:
To reinforce the use of `ArrayList`, in particular, showing uses of the `set()` **instance method** of a `List`. We also note that an **array** can be created from a `List`, and vice versa. Finally, we look at the `Collections` **class** and observe that it has a `sort()` **generic method**.

Recall the program to **sort** the lines of a **text file**, from Section 20.3.3 on page 519 where we solved the problem using an **array** with explicit code for **array extension**. (Actually, it was you who wrote the full program, for your coursework there.) In this section we present another version of the program, this time using an `ArrayList` instead.

We could adopt the approach of first developing a separate **class** that can sort a `List` of `Comparable` items, as we nearly did previously for an **array** of `Sortables` (in Section 20.3.2 on page 517).

21.3.1 The `SortList` class?

We would write our general **sorting class**, `SortList` so that it contains a **class method** to sort `Comparable` items in *any* kind of `List`, not just an `ArrayList`. This **generic method**, would have a **type parameter**, `ListType`, which is comparable with itself, and take a `List<ListType>` as a **method parameter**. It is similar to the code we wrote (and then didn't use) for sorting an **array** of `Sortables` in Section 20.3.2 on page 517 except this is a generic method because `Comparable` is a **generic interface**.

```
001: import java.util.List;
002:
003: // Provides a class method for sorting a List of any Comparable objects.
004: public class SortList
005: {
```

```
006:    public static <ListType extends Comparable<ListType>>
007:            void sort(List<ListType> list)
008:    {
009:      // Each pass of the sort reduces unsortedLength by one.
010:      int unsortedLength = list.size();
011:      boolean changedOnThisPass;
012:      do
013:      {
014:        changedOnThisPass = false;
015:        for (int pairLeftIndex = 0;
016:             pairLeftIndex < unsortedLength - 1; pairLeftIndex++)
017:        {
018:          if (list.get(pairLeftIndex).compareTo(list.get(pairLeftIndex + 1)) > 0)
019:          {
020:            ListType thatWasAtPairLeftIndex = list.get(pairLeftIndex);
021:            list.set(pairLeftIndex, list.get(pairLeftIndex + 1));
022:            list.set(pairLeftIndex + 1, thatWasAtPairLeftIndex);
023:            changedOnThisPass = true;
024:          } // if
025:        } // for
026:        unsortedLength--;
027:      } while (changedOnThisPass);
028:    } // sort
029:
030: } // class SortList
```

Notice the use of the set() **instance method** when swapping adjacent List elements during the **bubble sort**. Also observe that the items obtained from the List, via the get() instance method, are known by the **compiler** to be of **type** ListType. Thus no **cast** is needed for them.

So, we *could* write our SortList class as above, but another way would be to turn our List into an **array**, sort it with Arrays.sort() and turn it back into a List. It shouldn't surprise you that the Java **application program interface (API)** contains the **method**s we would need for such an approach.

However, we don't even need to do that, because yet again the Java **application program interface (API)** has beaten us to a great idea.

Concept **Collections API:** Collections **class.** The standard **class** java.util.Collections provides various **class method**s to perform complex manipulations of **collection**s. One of these is called sort, and takes a List of Objects which it **sort**s into their **natural ordering**. For this to work without **throw**ing an **exception**, the items in the List must all be of **type** java.lang.Comparable and be **mutually comparable**. The **algorithm** used is called **merge sort**, which is far more efficient than **bubble sort** (but less simple).

Since Java 5.0, many of the class methods in Collections have become **generic method**s. The sort() **class** method has a single **type parameter** which is the **type** of the items in the given List. These must be Comparable with themselves, and so you would probably expect the heading of the class method to be as follows.

```
    public static <T extends Comparable<T>>
                void sort(List<T> list)
```

In fact, it is defined in this way instead.

```
    public static <T extends Comparable<? super T>>
                void sort(List<T> list)
```

The code <? super T> means "any type that is T or a **superclass** (or **superinterface**) of it (or an **interface** implemented by it)". So here, this means any *class* supplied as the **type argument** must **implement** Comparable with itself, or a superclass of itself. Many of the **type parameter**s in the standard **application program interface (API)** are expressed in that sort of way, because it leads to more flexibility and convenience.

Coffee *Warning – this one is subtle stuff.* If a class, A, implements `Comparable<A>`, and a class B **extend**s
time: A, then B also implements `Comparable<A>`. But, does it **implement** `Comparable<B>` as well? You
 might think it does, because any B can be compared with any other B, via the **instance method**
defined in A. However, perhaps surprisingly, Java regards that it does not: `Comparable<B>` is not
'implied' from `Comparable<A>` in the same way that `int compareTo(B other)` would not **override** `int compareTo(A other)` – it would be an **overloaded method** instead. This has surprising
implications. For example, suppose we have the following **generic method**.

```
public static <T extends Comparable<T>>
                void sort(List<T> list) { ... }
```

Then the last line of the code below will not **compile** because B does not implement `Comparable<B>`
and so cannot match T.

```
List<A> a = new ArrayList<A>();
List<B> b = new ArrayList<B>();
sort(a);
sort(b);
```

The code `<T extends Comparable<? super T>>` gets around this problem. B implements
`Comparable<A>`, and `<A>` matches `<? super B>`, thus B implements `Comparable<? super B>`.
If none of that makes any sense at the moment, then you can happily ignore it for now!

21.3.2 The Sort class

Now we develop the program which **sort**s a **text file**. This is similar to the version described in Section 20.3.3 on page 519
which stored the lines in an **array**, except, of course, we do not need to worry about **array extension**. It is also similar to
`Reverse` from Section 21.2 on page 539.

```
001: import java.io.BufferedReader;
002: import java.io.FileReader;
003: import java.io.FileWriter;
004: import java.io.IOException;
005: import java.io.PrintWriter;
006: import java.util.ArrayList;
007: import java.util.Collections;
008: import java.util.List;
009:
010: // Program to sort lines of a file, line by line, and write to another.
011: // Input file is the first argument, output is the second.
012: public class Sort
013: {
014:   public static void main(String[] args)
015:   {
016:     BufferedReader input = null;
017:     PrintWriter output = null;
018:     try
019:     {
020:       if (args.length != 2)
021:         throw new IllegalArgumentException
022:                     ("There must be exactly two arguments: infile outfile");
023:
024:       input = new BufferedReader(new FileReader(args[0]));
025:       output = new PrintWriter(new FileWriter(args[1]));
026:
027:       // The List for storing the lines.
028:       List<String> lineList = new ArrayList<String>();
029:
```

```
030:        // Read the lines into lineList.
031:        String currentLine;
032:        while ((currentLine = input.readLine()) != null)
033:          lineList.add(currentLine);
034:
035:        // Sort lineList.
036:        Collections.sort(lineList);
037:
038:        // Now output them.
039:        for (int index = 0; index < lineList.size(); index++)
040:          output.println(lineList.get(index));
041:      } // try
042:      catch (Exception exception)
043:      {
044:        System.err.println(exception);
045:      } // catch
046:      finally
047:      {
048:        try { if (input != null) input.close(); }
049:        catch (IOException exception)
050:          { System.err.println("Could not close input " + exception); }
051:        if (output != null)
052:        {
053:          output.close();
054:          if (output.checkError())
055:            System.err.println("Something went wrong with the output");
056:        } // if
057:      } // finally
058:    } // main
059:
060: } // class Sort
```

21.3.3   Trying it

The program has the same behaviour as the one from Section 20.3.3 on page 519 so we do not need to show it **run**ning here.

21.3.4   Coursework: Sorting election leaflets, with `compareTo()`

In this task you will write the same program as in the coursework for Section 21.2.2 on page 541, but in a different way.

Create a **class** called `DeliveryHouseDetails`, which is `Comparable` with itself. This will store a house number in an **instance variable**, and the person name details (including the house number) in another. It will have an **accessor method** to obtain the person names. It will also have another **instance method**, `compareTo()`, which orders `DeliveryHouseDetails` **object**s by delivery order. Here is some **pseudo code**.

```
compareTo (other)
{
  if both house numbers are odd
    return this house number minus the other one
  else if both house numbers are even
    return the other house number minus this one
  else if this house number is odd
    return -1
  else
    return 1
}
```

This will cause a `List` of `DeliveryHouseDetails` objects, when processed by `Collections.sort()`, to be **sort**ed into the required delivery order, as described in the coursework for Section 21.2.2 on page 541. Convince yourself this is true and write notes about it in your logbook.

Copy your `StreetOrder` class from the previous version, and modify it so that it creates a `DeliveryHouseDetails` object for each input line and stores it in the `ArrayList`. You can simply count the lines to obtain the house number – there is no need to extract it from the details on the line. After loading the details the program will use `sort()` from the `Collections` class to sort them, then it can print them out by **loop**ing through them all, and extracting the person details.

Implement the `DeliveryHouseDetails` class. Note, you should also include an `equals()` instance method which is consistent with `compareTo()`. The following code should do the trick.

```
...
043:   // Equivalence test, consistent with compareTo.
044:   @Override
045:   public boolean equals(Object other)
046:   {
047:     if (other instanceof DeliveryHouseDetails)
048:       return houseNumber == ((DeliveryHouseDetails)other).houseNumber;
049:     else
050:       return super.equals(other);
051:   } // equals
...
```

After implementation, **run** the program with the same tests you used for the first version, and record the results in your logbook. Now, think about which approach is best, and write notes in your logbook.

21.4 Example: Prime numbers

AIM:
To introduce the idea of **set collections**, the `Set` **interface** and the `HashSet` **class**. For this we explore **hash tables** and meet `hashCode()` from `Object`. We also see that the class `Integer` **implements** `Comparable<Integer>`.

You will recall that a **prime number** is a positive **integer** which can be divided without remainder by only itself and one. The pursuit and understanding of such numbers has been a holy grail for many mathematicians over the ages. In this section we develop a program to output all the prime numbers which are **less than or equal** to a given **command line argument**.

The approach we take is simple, and yet fast to **execute**. The program maintains a **set** of all the multiples of the prime numbers found so far, starting with an empty set. It considers all the numbers from two up to the given maximum. If the number is not a multiple of a prime number previously found, then it is a prime number, so we print it out and add all its multiples, up to the maximum, to the set. This **algorithm** is based on the Sieve of Eratosthenes[19].

Concept **Collections API: Sets.** Another of the kinds of **collection** supported by the **collections framework** is the **set collection**. These are collections of **data** which are essentially **set**s, which means that adding an element to them has no effect if the set already contains an element that is **equivalent** to the new one. Also, the order in which the elements are added to the collection is *not* preserved.

For the purposes of determining whether two `Object`s are equivalent, sets are intended to use the `equals()` **instance method** of the elements in them.

Concept **Collections API: Sets: Set interface.** The **interface** `java.util.Set` is part of the **collections framework**. It specifies the **instance methods** needed to support a **set collection**. These include the following.

	Method definitions in interface `Set` (some of them).		
Method	**Return**	**Arguments**	**Description**
`size`	**int**		Returns the size of this `Set`, that is, the number of elements in it.
`add`	**boolean**	`Object`	Inserts the given `Object` into the `Set`, unless an **equivalent** one is already present. Returns **true** if it gets added, **false** otherwise.
`contains`	**boolean**	`Object`	Return **true** if the `Set` contains an `Object` which is equivalent to the given one, **false** otherwise.

Since Java 5.0, `Set` is a **generic interface**. The **type parameter** of a `Set` is the **type** of **object**s that can be stored in it. So, when we use a **parameterized type** of `Set` rather than its **raw type**, all the occurrences of `Object` in the above table of instance methods are replaced by the **type argument**.

In this program we are going to use a `HashSet`, the implementation of which is based on the use of a **hash table**.

Concept **Design: Storing data.** Collections of **data** which need to be stored in the **computer memory** at **run time** are placed in a **data structure**. Perhaps the most obvious example is the **array**, in which data might be stored in an arbitrary or specific order. One common thing we want to do with stored data is find it, using some kind of search **algorithm** such as a **linear search** (see Section 14.6.2 on page 323) or a **binary search** (see Section 20.4.3 on page 525). The latter requires the data to be sorted in a particular order, using a **sort algorithm** such as **bubble sort** (see Section 14.3 on page 296).

Concept **Design: Storing data: hash table.** One way of storing **data** so that it can be retrieved quickly is to use a **hash table**. This **data structure** places (**references** to) items in an **array**, where the **array index** is based on a **hash code** provided by each item that might need to be stored. The idea is that data items which are **equivalent** *must* have the same hash code, and items which are not equivalent try to have different hash codes. To insert an item into the structure, we take its hash code, which is an **integer**, and divide it by the size of the array we are using for the hash table, take the remainder and place the item at that array index. To see if an item is already in the hash table, we compute the corresponding array index and check the array.

The following diagram shows a hash table of size eleven, holding five items with hash codes 22, 223, 38, 30 and 119.

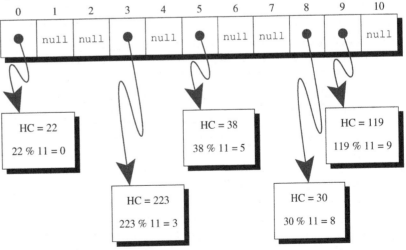

We may of course have clashes, caused by two items which are not equivalent having the same array index, and there are various strategies for coping with that, such as merely finding the next available free slot in the array.

547

However that leads to a partial **linear search** to find such items later. To get the best efficiency from the hash table, it is important to minimize the occurrence of clashes, so we typically make the size of the array a **prime number** and, when **design**ing the **function** which computes the hash code of an element, we try to make non-equivalent items get different hash codes.

For items to work properly in a `HashSet`, they need to have an appropriate definition of `hashCode()`.

Concept **Standard API: `Object`: `hashCode()`.** Every object has an **instance method** called `hashCode`, defined in the `java.lang.Object` **class**, which is designed to help with classes that use a **hash table** to store **object**s, such as `java.util.HashSet`. The definition in `Object` is such that distinct objects have a distinct **hash code**, (usually) based on the memory address of the **reference** at **run time**. Classes that **override** `equals()` should really also override `hashCode()` with one that **return**s the same hash code for objects that are **equivalent**, rather than distinct, and yet tend to return a different code for those that are not equivalent. This is so that they will work properly if needed to be used as elements of a `HashSet`, etc..

```
MyClass v1 = new MyClass(...);
MyClass v2 = new MyClass(...);

if (v1.equals(v2) && v1.hashCode() != v2.hashCode())
  System.out.println("Your hash tables will not work!");
else if (! v1.equals(v2) && v1.hashCode() == v2.hashCode())
  System.out.println("Your hash tables may operate slowly.");
```

Concept **Collections API: Sets: `HashSet`.** The **class** `java.util.HashSet` is part of the **collections framework**, and is one implementation of a **set collection**. It **implements** the `java.util.Set` **interface**. This kind of **set** uses a **hash table**, with the **hash codes** being obtained from the `hashCode()` **instance method** of the items stored in it. For this to work, any **objects** which are **equivalent** *must* have the same hash code, otherwise multiple copies of equivalent items will be allowed in the set! For efficiency, non-equivalent objects should tend to have different hash codes.

Since Java 5.0, `HashSet`, and the other classes in the collections framework are **generic class**es. The **type parameter** of a `HashSet` is the **type** of **object**s that can be stored in it.

```
public class HashSet<E> implements Set<E>
{ ... }
```

We want to put **`int`** values into a `HashSet`, but the **collections** in the **collections framework** all expect to hold **objects**, not values of **primitive types**. We shall, of course, **box** the **`int`** values in **instances** of `Integer`.

Concept **Standard API: `Integer`: as a box for `int`: works with collections.** The standard **class** `java.lang.Integer` **implements** `java.lang.Comparable<Integer>`, and provides the instance methods `compareTo()`, and also `equals()` and `hashCode()` in such a way that `Integer` **objects** behave properly as `Comparable`s and in **hash table**s, etc..

Here is our prime number program.

```
001: import java.util.HashSet;
002: import java.util.Set;
003:
004: // List all the prime numbers less than or equal to the command line argument.
005: // (Warning: this program does not catch RuntimeExceptions.)
006: public class Primes
007: {
```

```
008:    public static void main(String[] args)
009:    {
010:      // The maximum number we need to consider.
011:      int maxPossiblePrime = Integer.parseInt(args[0]);
012:
013:      // The set of all multiples of prime numbers found so far.
014:      // These are therefore not prime numbers.
015:      Set<Integer> multiplesOfPrimesFound = new HashSet<Integer>();
016:
017:      // Consider every number from 2 up to maximum,
018:      // it is a possible prime, output and count it if it is.
019:      int primeNumberCount = 0;
020:      for (int possiblePrimeNumber = 2;
021:           possiblePrimeNumber <= maxPossiblePrime; possiblePrimeNumber++)
022:        if (! multiplesOfPrimesFound.contains(possiblePrimeNumber))
023:        {
024:          // possiblePrimeNumber really is a prime number.
025:          primeNumberCount++;
026:          System.out.println(primeNumberCount + " : " + possiblePrimeNumber);
027:          // Now add multiples of possiblePrimeNumber to multiplesOfPrimesFound.
028:          for (int primeMultiple = possiblePrimeNumber * 2;
029:               primeMultiple <= maxPossiblePrime;
030:               primeMultiple += possiblePrimeNumber)
031:            multiplesOfPrimesFound.add(primeMultiple);
032:        } // if
033:    } // main
034:
035:  } // class Primes
```

Coffee time: 21.4.1
Did you notice the *two* places where **autoboxing** wraps an **int** inside an Integer?

Coffee time: 21.4.2
What do you imagine is the **hash code** for an Integer object containing the number *n*?

Coffee time: 21.4.3 Suppose the implementers of the Integer **class** had forgotten to **override** hashCode(), so that every Integer object had a *unique* hash code. What would be the effect of our Primes program?

Coffee time: 21.4.4 Find all the places where we previously wrote an equals() **instance method** and devise a suitable hashCode() instance method to go with each one.

21.4.1 Trying it

Let us obtain the **prime numbers** up to 100.

Console Input / Output

```
$ java Primes 100
(Output shown using multiple columns to save space.)
1 : 2        6 : 13       11 : 31      16 : 53      21 : 73
2 : 3        7 : 17       12 : 37      17 : 59      22 : 79
3 : 5        8 : 19       13 : 41      18 : 61      23 : 83
4 : 7        9 : 23       14 : 43      19 : 67      24 : 89
5 : 11      10 : 29       15 : 47      20 : 71      25 : 97
$ _
```

How many **prime numbers** are there up to 1 thousand?

```
                              Console Input / Output
$ java Primes 1000
(Output shown using multiple columns to save space.)
1 : 2       25 : 97     49 : 227    73 : 367    97 : 509    121 : 661   145 : 829
2 : 3       26 : 101    50 : 229    74 : 373    98 : 521    122 : 673   146 : 839
3 : 5       27 : 103    51 : 233    75 : 379    99 : 523    123 : 677   147 : 853
4 : 7       28 : 107    52 : 239    76 : 383    100 : 541   124 : 683   148 : 857
5 : 11      29 : 109    53 : 241    77 : 389    101 : 547   125 : 691   149 : 859
6 : 13      30 : 113    54 : 251    78 : 397    102 : 557   126 : 701   150 : 863
7 : 17      31 : 127    55 : 257    79 : 401    103 : 563   127 : 709   151 : 877
8 : 19      32 : 131    56 : 263    80 : 409    104 : 569   128 : 719   152 : 881
9 : 23      33 : 137    57 : 269    81 : 419    105 : 571   129 : 727   153 : 883
10 : 29     34 : 139    58 : 271    82 : 421    106 : 577   130 : 733   154 : 887
11 : 31     35 : 149    59 : 277    83 : 431    107 : 587   131 : 739   155 : 907
12 : 37     36 : 151    60 : 281    84 : 433    108 : 593   132 : 743   156 : 911
13 : 41     37 : 157    61 : 283    85 : 439    109 : 599   133 : 751   157 : 919
14 : 43     38 : 163    62 : 293    86 : 443    110 : 601   134 : 757   158 : 929
15 : 47     39 : 167    63 : 307    87 : 449    111 : 607   135 : 761   159 : 937
16 : 53     40 : 173    64 : 311    88 : 457    112 : 613   136 : 769   160 : 941
17 : 59     41 : 179    65 : 313    89 : 461    113 : 617   137 : 773   161 : 947
18 : 61     42 : 181    66 : 317    90 : 463    114 : 619   138 : 787   162 : 953
19 : 67     43 : 191    67 : 331    91 : 467    115 : 631   139 : 797   163 : 967
20 : 71     44 : 193    68 : 337    92 : 479    116 : 641   140 : 809   164 : 971
21 : 73     45 : 197    69 : 347    93 : 487    117 : 643   141 : 811   165 : 977
22 : 79     46 : 199    70 : 349    94 : 491    118 : 647   142 : 821   166 : 983
23 : 83     47 : 211    71 : 353    95 : 499    119 : 653   143 : 823   167 : 991
24 : 89     48 : 223    72 : 359    96 : 503    120 : 659   144 : 827   168 : 997
$ _
```

How fast is this **algorithm**? Let's find the primes up to 1 million. We can time it using the Unix `time` command to **run** the program and then tell us how long it took to run.[a] (In case you are interested, this was run on a 2Gig Hertz Athlon XP 2600+ processor.) We redirect the output to a **file**, using >, so that displaying the numbers does not seriously slow down the program.

---

[a]Unfortunately, there is no simple way of doing this using standard commands in a Microsoft Command Prompt.

```
                    Console Input / Output
$ time java Primes 1000000 > primes.txt

real    0m5.307s
user    0m3.831s
sys     0m1.370s
$ cat primes.txt
1 : 2
2 : 3
(... lines removed to save space.)
78496 : 999961
78497 : 999979
78498 : 999983
$ _
```

Ah, but it does require a lot of space to store all those non-prime numbers – let's try up to 10 million.

```
                    Console Input / Output
$ time java Primes 10000000 > primes.txt
Exception in thread "main" java.lang.OutOfMemoryError: Java heap space
        at java.util.HashMap.addEntry(HashMap.java:753)
        at java.util.HashMap.put(HashMap.java:385)
        at java.util.HashSet.add(HashSet.java:200)
        at Primes.main(Primes.java:31)

real    0m57.465s
user    0m56.014s
sys     0m1.038s
$ cat primes.txt
1 : 2
2 : 3
$ _
```

Coffee time: 21.4.5	The `Primes` program has been a suitable introduction to the use of **set collection**s, but actually, there may be a better way to implement the same algorithm. Consider this: the **set** contains all the non-prime numbers up to the maximum, and as the maximum gets bigger, the difference between this set and *all* the numbers up to the maximum, gets proportionally smaller. With this in mind, what even simpler way could we use to implement the set of non-primes?

21.4.2 Coursework: Finding duplicate voters

The government have been encouraging more people to vote, and one of the features of a new system is that voters are allowed to do so in any polling station within a certain radius of their home, rather than just one. The idea is that more people can vote at lunch time, near to where they work. Unfortunately, this opens up additional potential for multiple voting, by people visiting more than one station! The officials have collected **data** from across the region, and want you to write a program to detect multiple votes. The input is in the form of a **text file** consisting of two lines per vote. The first line uniquely identifies the voter by their name, house number and post code. The second line records the time and location of the vote cast. The location is the name of a polling station, in the form of an area name and an identity number, such as `Manchester 538`. For example, here is a (cut down) set of data.

```
Console Input / Output
$ cat voting.txt
(Output shown using multiple columns to save space.)
Rupert Rodgers-Smythe, 4, M25 7QZ      Sarah Peacock, 6, M25 7QZ
07:37 Manchester 538                   14:59 Manchester 537
Fatima Bacon, 3, M25 7QZ               Joanne Smith, 1, M25 7QZ
10:01 Manchester 538                   15:09 Manchester 538
Samuel Peacock, 6, M25 7QZ             Giles Schubert, 3, M19 4FK
10:25 Manchester 538                   16:19 Manchester 189
Sarah Peacock, 6, M25 7QZ             Blanche Peacock, 8, M25 7QZ
10:25 Manchester 538                   16:37 Manchester 538
Phillip Jones, 13, M1 0KY              Ahmed Hussain, 5, M25 7QZ
10:32 Manchester 605                   17:21 Manchester 538
Lionel Brown, 1, M25 7QZ              Gaynor White, 3, M25 7QZ
11:17 Manchester 538                   18:50 Manchester 538
Margaret Chopin, 9, M37 9MP            Sarah Peacock, 6, M25 7QZ
12:14 Manchester 299                   19:01 Manchester 539
Rupert Rodgers-Smythe, 4, M25 7QZ    Annette Longbridge, 8, M9 6QP
12:27 Manchester 099                   19:07 Manchester 314
John Bach, 11, M2 9WQ                 Harry Peacock, 8, M25 7QZ
13:27 Manchester 308                   19:21 Manchester 538
Hsin Cheng Liu, 7, M25 7QZ            Margaret Chopin, 9, M37 9MP
13:27 Manchester 538                   19:30 Manchester 308
Celina Simmons, 4, M25 7QZ            Augustus Belcher, 2, M25 7QZ
14:12 Manchester 538                   20:59 Manchester 538
Gregory Beethoven, 5, M17 8XJ         Sarah Peacock, 6, M25 7QZ
14:22 Manchester 009                   20:59 Manchester 540
$ _
```

They simply want your program to detect and report duplicate voter identifications, followed by the number of duplicates found. So, the output for the above input would be as follows.

```
Console Input / Output
$ java DuplicateVoters voting.txt voting-duplicates.txt
$ cat voting-duplicates.txt
Rupert Rodgers-Smythe, 4, M25 7QZ
Sarah Peacock, 6, M25 7QZ
Sarah Peacock, 6, M25 7QZ
Margaret Chopin, 9, M37 9MP
Sarah Peacock, 6, M25 7QZ
There were 5 duplicate votes
$ _
```

Your program should use a `HashSet` to store the voter identifications, i.e. the first line of each pair of lines. (It will just skip over and ignore the second line of each pair – in this version.) If when adding to this **set**, using `add()`, the result of the addition is **false**, then the voter was already present and so the voter identification being added must be a duplicate.

The program should be called `DuplicateVoters`, and take two **command line arguments**, the first being the name of the input file, the second being the name of the resulting report file.

To save time, you may test your program using just the above sample data.

21.5   Example: Sorting a text file using a `TreeSet`

AIM:
To introduce the `TreeSet` **class**, for which we explore **ordered binary tree**s and **tree sort**. We also meet the `Iterator` **interface**, together with how it is used on a `List` and a `Set`, especially a `TreeSet`.

We have covered two ways of **sorting** a **text file**: using an **array** (Section 20.3.3 on page 519) and using an `ArrayList` (Section 21.3.2 on page 544). Here we use a `TreeSet`, and this causes an interesting twist: multiple copies of a line in the input will produce only one copy in the output.

Concept **Design: Storing data: ordered binary tree.**   An **ordered binary tree** (**OBT**) is a **data structure** which allows for quick storage and retrieval of **data**. The structure is so named because the data is stored in a tree, with each branch having a possible left subtree and/or a right subtree (binary) and the data is kept in some **total order** from left to right across the tree. That is, for every item in the tree, all items in its left subtree are **less than** it (according to whatever total order is being used) and all items in its right subtree are **greater than** it.

For example, the following diagram shows an OBT containing the ten **integer**s 12, 17, 19, 27, 34, 49, 53, 75, 81 and 99.

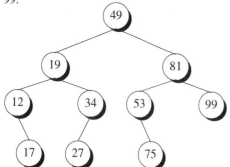

Because the data is ordered, we do not have to search the entire tree to find an item. Instead we start at the top and, if we have not yet found it, we go left if the item we want is less than the item where we are, or right otherwise, and repeat these steps until we either find the item or reach the bottom.

Searching an OBT has similar efficiency to a **binary search** (see Section 20.4.3 on page 525) because we (essentially) halve the search space at each stage as we proceed down the tree. Although this is not as fast as using a **hash table** with a *good* (and quick) **hash code function**, an OBT is useful in situations where we wish to retrieve the data from it in order.

Concept **Collections API: Sets: `TreeSet`.**   The **class** `java.util.TreeSet` is part of the **collections framework**, and is another implementation of a **set collection**. It **implements** the `java.util.Set` **interface**. This kind of **set** uses an **ordered binary tree** and so it has to be possible to order the elements which are stored in it. The simplest way of providing such an ordering is to ensure that the **class** of the elements implements `java.lang.Comparable`.

Since Java 5.0, `TreeSet`, and the other classes in the collections framework are **generic classes**. The **type parameter** of a `TreeSet` is the **type** of **objects** that can be stored in it.

```
public class TreeSet<E> implements Set<E>
{ ... }
```

Our program will work by inserting all the lines into a `TreeSet`, and then obtaining an `Iterator` for these elements, which supports sequential access to them in the order we desire.

Concept **Collections API: `Iterator` interface.**   The **interface** `java.util.Iterator` is part of the **collections framework**. It specifies the **instance method**s needed to support a way of accessing all the elements in a **collection** one by one.

	Method definitions in interface `Iterator` (some of them).		
Method	**Return**	**Arguments**	**Description**
`hasNext`	`boolean`		Returns **`true`** if the **iteration** has more elements, **`false`** otherwise.
`next`	`Object`		Returns the next element in the iteration, and moves the iteration on to the element following that one.

When a **new** `Iterator` **object** is obtained from a collection, `hasNext()` will **return `true`**, unless the collection is empty. The first time we call `next()`, we get the first element from the iteration if there is one, then the second time we get the second element, and so on. Sooner or later `hasNext()` will return **`false`** because we have called `next()` as many times as there are elements. Typically we use `hasNext()` to control a **loop** and call `next()` inside the loop only if there is another element.

All **list collection**s and **set collection**s support the instance method `iterator()` which returns some **object** that is an **instance** of some **class** that **implements** `Iterator`. The object returned supports an iteration through the elements of the collection, in an order which depends on the kind of collection.

Since Java 5.0, `Iterator` is a **generic interface**. The **type parameter** of an `Iterator` is the **type** of objects that are stored in the corresponding collection. In other words, if the collection was given a **type argument**, then the `next()` instance method of an `Iterator` over that collection returns an object of that type.

Concept **Collections API: Lists: `List` interface: `iterator()`.**   The **instance method** `iterator()`, specified in the **interface** `java.util.List`, **return**s an **object** that **implements** `java.util.Iterator`, supporting an **iteration** of the elements in the `List`, in ascending order of their **list index** in the `List`.

For example, the following code prints out all the elements of a `List`, from the one indexed by zero, up to the last one, indexed by `size()` minus one.

```
public static <ListType> void printList(List<ListType> list)
{
  Iterator<ListType> iterator = list.iterator();
  while (iterator.hasNext())
  {
    ListType item = iterator.next();
    System.out.println(item);
  } // while
} // printList
```

For an `ArrayList`, this way of scanning through the elements is just as efficient as using the list index of each element. However, for some kinds of `List`s, accessing by index is not efficient, whereas scanning using an `Iterator` always will be, because it is designed for that purpose. So, as a rule of thumb, whenever you need to scan through the elements of a **list** in an arbitrary order, or from first to last, you should use an `Iterator` rather than the indices.

Coffee time: `21.5.1`   Identify all the places in this chapter before this point, where we used indices to scan through the elements of a `List`, and devise the changes needed to make them use an `Iterator` instead.

Concept **Collections API: Sets: Set interface: iterator().** The **instance method** iterator(), specified in the **interface** java.util.Set, **returns** an **object** that **implements** java.util.Iterator, supporting an **iteration** of the elements in the Set. The order of the iteration will depend on the kind of **set**, and may be in some arbitrary order.

Concept **Collections API: Sets: TreeSet: iterator().** The iterator() **instance method** of the java.util.TreeSet **class returns** an **object** that **implements** java.util.Iterator, which supports an **iteration** through the elements in the order they appear in the tree, from left to right. With the simplest use of a TreeSet we thus get the **natural ordering** of elements as provided by **method implementations** of compareTo().

As a rule of thumb, java.util.HashSet should be used in preference to TreeSet when it is not desired to obtain the values from the **set collection** in a specific order. If there is little or no **hash code** clashing, a HashSet operates in nearly constant time per addition and membership test. By contrast, a TreeSet operates in time which is proportional to the logarithm of the size of the **set**.

Concept **Design: Sorting a list: tree sort.** Another **algorithm** for **sorting** is known as **tree sort**. In this approach, the items from the **list** are inserted into an **ordered binary tree**, and then the tree is scanned from left to right, that is smallest item to largest (according to the **total order** being used), to produce the result.

If the **data** to be sorted has no duplicates, or if it is desired to not include such multiple elements in the result, then in Java a tree sort can be achieved by using an **instance** of java.util.TreeSet. This is because its iterator() **instance method** produces an Iterator which gives access to the elements in order from smallest to largest. Any duplicate items will not appear in the result because a **set** is not changed by an attempt to add an element which is **equivalent** to one that is already present.

Here is our third and final visit to the Sort program. Much of it is similar to the one from Section 21.3.2 on page 544.

```
001: import java.io.BufferedReader;
002: import java.io.FileReader;
003: import java.io.FileWriter;
004: import java.io.IOException;
005: import java.io.PrintWriter;
006: import java.util.Iterator;
007: import java.util.TreeSet;
008:
009: // Program to sort lines of a file, line by line, and write to another.
010: // Input file is the first argument, output is the second.
011: // Duplicate lines are removed.
012: public class Sort
013: {
014:   public static void main(String[] args)
015:   {
016:     BufferedReader input = null;
017:     PrintWriter output = null;
018:     try
019:     {
020:       if (args.length != 2)
021:         throw new IllegalArgumentException
022:                    ("There must be exactly two arguments: infile outfile");
023:
024:       input = new BufferedReader(new FileReader(args[0]));
025:       output = new PrintWriter(new FileWriter(args[1]));
026:
027:       // The Set for storing the lines: TreeSet so it has an ordered Iterator.
028:       TreeSet<String> lineSet = new TreeSet<String>();
029:
030:       // Read the lines into lineSet.
031:       String currentLine;
032:       while ((currentLine = input.readLine()) != null)
033:         lineSet.add(currentLine);
```

```
034:
035:         // Now output them in natural ordering.
036:         Iterator<String> iterator = lineSet.iterator();
037:         while (iterator.hasNext())
038:           output.println(iterator.next());
039:       } // try
040:     catch (Exception exception)
041:     {
042:       System.err.println(exception);
043:     } // catch
044:     finally
045:     {
046:       try { if (input != null) input.close(); }
047:       catch (IOException exception)
048:         { System.err.println("Could not close input " + exception); }
049:       if (output != null)
050:       {
051:         output.close();
052:         if (output.checkError())
053:           System.err.println("Something went wrong with the output");
054:       } // if
055:     } // finally
056:   } // main
057:
058: } // class Sort
```

Coffee time: What do you think our `Sort` program would do, if we used a `HashSet` instead of a `TreeSet`?

21.5.2

21.5.1 Trying it

The program **sort**s its input and also removes any duplicate lines.

```
Console Input / Output
$ cat input.txt
Smith, James      87.9%
Jackson, Helen    100%
Jones, Stephen    51.5%
Jackson, Helen    100%
$ java Sort input.txt output.txt
$ cat output.txt
Jackson, Helen    100%
Jones, Stephen    51.5%
Smith, James      87.9%
$ _
```

21.5.2 Coursework: Sorting election leaflets, using a `TreeSet`

In this task you will write the same program as in Section 21.2.2 on page 541 in a third way. You will use your `DeliveryHouseDetails` **class** again, but instead of building a `List` of the **object**s, you will insert them into a `TreeSet`. Then, instead of **sort**ing them using `sort()` from the `Collections` class, you will access the elements via the `Iterator` of the `TreeSet`.

Copy your `StreetOrder` class from the previous version, and modify it. After implementation, **run** the program with the same tests you used for the previous versions, and record the results in your logbook. If all three programs are working, then their outputs should be identical – there are, of course, no duplicate lines in the input **data**.

21.6 Summary of lists and sets

AIM: To summarize the **collections framework** explored so far, and introduce the `Collection` **interface** and the `LinkedList` **class**, for which we explore **linked list**s. We also revisit `List`.

So far we have met the **interface** `List`, with `ArrayList` as one **implement**ation, and the interface `Set` implemented by `HashSet` and `TreeSet`. There is a common **type** of which all **list collection**s and **set collection**s are members, which is the interface `Collection`.

Concept **Collections API: `Collection` interface.** The **interface** `java.util.Collection` is part of the **collections framework**. It specifies the **instance method**s needed to support a **collection**, such as a **list collection** or a **set collection**. These include the following.

Method definitions in interface `Collection` (some of them).			
Method	**Return**	**Arguments**	**Description**
`size`	**int**		Returns the size of this `Collection`, that is, the number of elements in it.
`add`	**boolean**	`Object`	Ensures that this `Collection` contains the given `Object`, or an **equivalent** one if appropriate. It **returns true** if the `Collection` was modified, **false** otherwise. For example, a `List` always appends the element on the end and returns **true**, whereas a `Set` will do nothing if it already contains an equivalent element.
`remove`	**boolean**	`Object`	Removes one element equivalent to the given `Object`, and returns **true** if the `Collection` was changed (i.e. there was at least one element matching the given one).
`addAll`	**boolean**	`Collection`	Adds all the elements of the given `Collection` to this one, and returns **true** if this collection was changed. (E.g. the given collection could be empty, or this one could be a `Set` and already contain the elements.)
`removeAll`	**boolean**	`Collection`	Removes all the elements of the given `Collection` from this one, and returns **true** if this collection was changed.
`retainAll`	**boolean**	`Collection`	Removes all elements of this collection which are *not* contained in the given `Collection`, and returns **true** if this collection was changed.
`contains`	**boolean**	`Object`	Returns **true** if the `Collection` contains at least one `Object` which is equivalent to the given one, **false** otherwise.
`containsAll`	**boolean**	`Collection`	Returns **true** if this `Collection` contains at least one equivalent `Object` for each element in the given collection, **false** otherwise.
`iterator`	Iterator		Returns an **object** that **implements** `java.util.Iterator`, giving access to all the elements of the `Collection`. The order depends on the kind of collection.

Since Java 5.0, `Collection` is a **generic interface** with a single **type parameter** which represents the **type** of **object**s that can be stored in it. So, when we use a **parameterized type** of `Collection` rather than its **raw type**, all occurrences of `Object` in the above table of instance methods are replaced by the **type argument**.

The interfaces `List` and `Set` both **extend** the interface `Collection`.

Concept **Collections API: Lists: `List` interface: extends `Collection`.** The **interface** `java.util.List` is an **extension** of the more general interface `java.util.Collection`.

```
public interface List<E> extends Collection<E>
{
  ...
} // interface List
```

Concept **Collections API: Sets: Set interface: extends Collection.** The **interface** java.util.Set is an **extension** of the more general interface java.util.Collection.

```
public interface Set<E> extends Collection<E>
{
  ...
} // interface Set
```

So, an **instance** of ArrayList<T> **is an** ArrayList<T>, but also **is a** List<T> and **is a** Collection<T>.

Coffee time: **21.6.1** Consider the instance methods addAll(), removeAll() and retainAll() as they apply to Sets. What is the relationship between these and the notions of **set union**, **set intersection** and **set difference**?

Lists also have instance methods which are not specified in Collection, based on the use of a **list index**. We have already seen get() and set().

Concept **Collections API: Lists: add(index) and remove(index).** The **interface** java.util.List specifies **instance method**s for adding and removing an element at a particular **list index**, in addition to those defined in java.util.Collection for adding an element (at the end in **list**s), or removing an element **equivalent** to a given one.

Method definitions in interface **List** (some more of them).			
Method	**Return**	**Arguments**	**Description**
add		**int**, Object	Inserts the given Object at the specified list index, shifting any elements after that position up by one place. To avoid an IndexOutOfBoundsException, the index must be legal (0 <= index <= size()).
remove	Object	**int**	Removes the element at the given list index, shifting elements after that position down by one place. To avoid an IndexOutOfBoundsException, the index must be legal (0 <= index < size()).

There is another kind of List, called a LinkedList.

Concept **Design: Storing data: linked list.** A **linked list** is a **data structure** which holds **data** in a chain of link **object**s, each containing a (**reference** to) one data element, and a reference to the next link object.

In a **doubly linked list**, such as the one shown in the following diagram, each link also has a reference to the previous link.

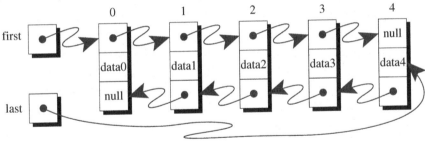

References are kept to the first and last links in the chain. To access an element at a particular **list index**, the chain must be followed from the front counting links until that index is reached, or from the back if that is nearer. So, this kind of **list** is not very efficient if many **random access**es of elements are needed. It can, however, be more efficient than using an **array** in other situations, such as adding at the back without ever having to use **array extension**, and adding or removing at the front or middle, without the need to shuffle the existing elements along.

Concept **Collections API: Lists: LinkedList.** The **class** java.util.LinkedList is part of the **collections frame-work**, and is another implementation of a **list collection**. It **implement**s the java.util.List **interface** by using a **doubly linked list**.

Since Java 5.0, LinkedList, and the other classes in the collections framework are **generic class**es. The **type parameter** of a LinkedList is the **type** of **object**s that can be stored in it.

```
public class LinkedList<E> implements List<E>
{ ... }
```

Coffee time: 21.6.2
Could we have used a LinkedList for our Reverse program from Section 21.2 on page 539? How about if we had added each line at the front of the **list**, using add(0)? Would we still use a **list index** for printing the result?

The following diagram helps show the **class** and interface **inheritance hierarchy** we have looked at so far. This does not show all the **instance methods**, just *some* of those we have already seen.

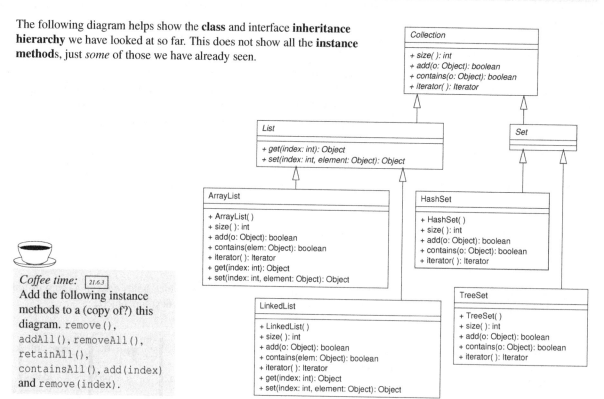

Coffee time: 21.6.3
Add the following instance methods to a (copy of?) this diagram. remove(), addAll(), removeAll(), retainAll(), containsAll(), add(index) and remove(index).

Coffee time: 21.6.4
Why do you think that Collection, List and Set are interfaces, rather than **abstract classes**?

21.7 Example: Word frequency count

AIM: To introduce the idea of **maps**, the Map **interface** and the TreeMap **class**. In particular we observe that a TreeMap makes it easy to obtain the values from the map in **key** order. We also see that the **for-each loop** can be used with **collection**s.

In this section we develop a program to read in a **text file** and produce, on **standard output**, an alphabetically **sort**ed list of all the words in the input (i.e. using **lexicographic order**ing), each together with the number of times it appears in the input. To achieve this, we shall use a **map**.

> *Concept* **Collections API: Maps.** Another kind of **collection** supported by the **collections framework** is the **map**. One view of **arrays** and **list collection**s is that they are functions from a **key** to a corresponding element, where the key is the **array index** or **list index**. A map is more general, in the sense that the key can be any **type** of **object**, rather than always an **int index**. For every key in the map, there is an associated value. Two different keys may map on to the same value, but every possible key maps on to at most one value. To put it another way, you can think of a map as being a **set** of pairs, each containing a key and a value. The keys are all unique within a particular map – every pair has a key which is not **equivalent** to the key in any other pair. By contrast, the values may be duplicated – any number of different pairs may have values which are equivalent. Thus, a map is a **many-to-one association**, otherwise known in Mathematics as a **function**.

Our program will separate the input into words, and build a map from each word on to an **object** that pairs the word with the count of its frequency found so far. At the heart of this, then, is a **class** that stores a word together with its frequency.

21.7.1 The `WordWithFrequency` class

Each **instance** of WordWithFrequency stores a word and its frequency.

```
001: // A pairing of a word with its frequency count (so far).
002: public class WordWithFrequency
003: {
004:    // The word, occurrences of which are being counted.
005:    private final String word;
006:
007:    // The frequency count of this word (so far).
008:    private int frequency;
```

The **constructor method** stores the given word, and sets the frequency to one – this is because we only create a WordWithFrequency when we find the first occurrence of the word in the input. At that point in time, its frequency is one.

```
011:    // Create a pairing with the given word, and frequency of one.
012:    public WordWithFrequency(String requiredWord)
013:    {
014:       word = requiredWord;
015:       frequency = 1;
016:    } // WordWithFrequency
```

When we find subsequent occurrences of the word, we need to increment its associated frequency count.

```
019:    // Count another occurrence of this word.
020:    public void incrementFrequency()
021:    {
022:      frequency++;
023:    } // incrementFrequency
```

Finally, we have a `toString()` **instance method**.

```
026:    // A String showing the word and its frequency.
027:    @Override
028:    public String toString()
029:    {
030:      return word + " " + frequency;
031:    } // toString
032:
033: } // class WordWithFrequency
```

21.7.2 The `WordFrequencyMap` class

The `WordFrequencyMap` **class** is the part of the program that stores the mapping of each word on to its `WordWithFrequency`. To achieve this, the class has an **instance variable** of **type** `TreeMap`.

Concept **Collections API: Maps: Map interface.** The **interface** `java.util.Map` is part of the **collections framework**. It specifies the **instance methods** needed to support a **map**. These include the following.

Method definitions in interface `Map` (some of them).			
Method	**Return**	**Arguments**	**Description**
put	Object	Object, Object	Takes a **key** and a value, and adds that association to the map. If the map previously contained a mapping for this key (or an **equivalent** one), the old value is replaced with the new one. Returns the **null reference**, if this is a new key, or **returns** the old value otherwise.
get	Object	Object	Takes a key and returns the value associated with it, or the null reference if the map does not contain a mapping with a key which equivalent to the given one.
values	Collection		Returns a `Collection` of the values (not keys) in the map. The `iterator()` **instance method** of the resulting `Collection` may support iterating through the values in a particular order, or not, depending on the kind of `Map`.
keySet	Set		Returns a `Set` of the keys (not values) in the map.

Since Java 5.0, `Map` is a **generic interface**. There are *two* **type parameters** for a `Map`, first the **type of objects** that can be used as keys, and then the type of objects that can be used as values. So, when we use a **parameterized type** of `Map` rather than its **raw type**, occurrences of `Object` in the above table of instance methods are replaced by the corresponding **type argument** as appropriate.

Concept **Collections API: Maps: `TreeMap`.** The **class** `java.util.TreeMap` is part of the **collections framework**, and is one implementation of a **map**. It **implements** the `java.util.Map` **interface**. This kind of map is implemented using an **ordered binary tree**. This means that there must be an ordering on the **keys** of the map, and the simplest way of providing such an ordering is to ensure that the keys implement `java.util.Comparable`.

The `values()` **instance method** of `TreeMap` gives a `Collection`; the `iterator()` of this gives an **object** that **implement**s `java.util.Iterator`, and supports **iteration** over the values of the map in key order.

Since Java 5.0, `TreeMap`, and the other classes in the collections framework are **generic class**es. There are *two* **type parameter**s for a `TreeMap`, first the **type** of **object**s that can be used as keys, and then the type of objects that can be used as values.

```
public class TreeMap<K, V> implements Map<K, V>
{ ... }
```

(Actually `TreeMap` implements an interface called `java.util.SortedMap` which **extend**s `Map`.)

Here is the `WordFrequencyMap` code. The **instance variable** `wordToWordWithFrequency` will contain a **reference** to a `TreeMap` which will **map** each word on to its corresponding `WordWithFrequency`.

```
001: import java.util.Collection;
002: import java.util.TreeMap;
003:
004: // A map from word to WordWithFrequency.
005: public class WordFrequencyMap
006: {
007:   // The map uses a TreeMap, so that we can obtain the values in natural
008:   // ordering of the keys. I.e., in order by word.
009:   private final TreeMap<String, WordWithFrequency>
010:     wordMappedToWordWithFrequency = new TreeMap<String, WordWithFrequency>();
011:
012:
013:   // Empty constructor, nothing needs doing.
014:   public WordFrequencyMap()
015:   {
016:   } // WordFrequencyMap
```

The `countWord()` **instance method** will be called for each occurrence of a word in the input **text file** of the program. It works by first attempting to find an existing `WordWithFrequency` for the word. If one exists, then its frequency is incremented. Otherwise, a **new** one is created and added to the `TreeMap`. Notice that the result **return**ed by `get()` is known to be a `WordWithFrequency` and so we do not need to write a **cast** for it.

```
019:   // Count an occurrence of the given word by either incrementing the
020:   // frequency of an existing WordWithFrequency or creating a new one if
021:   // this is the first occurrence of the word.
022:   public void countWord(String word)
023:   {
024:     WordWithFrequency wordWithFrequency
025:       = wordMappedToWordWithFrequency.get(word);
026:     if (wordWithFrequency != null)
027:       wordWithFrequency.incrementFrequency();
028:     else
029:     {
030:       wordWithFrequency = new WordWithFrequency(word);
031:       wordMappedToWordWithFrequency.put(word, wordWithFrequency);
032:     } // else
033:   } // countWord
```

The `toString()` instance method of `WordFrequencyMap` exploits the fact that the `values()` instance method of a `TreeMap` yields a `Collection` which has an `Iterator` that presents the elements in **key** order. In other words, the `Iterator` will go through the values from this TreeMap in **lexicographic order** (alphabetical/dictionary order) of the words used as keys.

Instead of explicitly creating this Iterator and using a **for loop** to go through it, we shall here use a **for-each loop**.

Concept **Statement: for-each loop: on collections.** The **enhanced for statement** introduced in Java 5.0 and more commonly known as the **for-each loop**, can be used with **collections** as well as **arrays**. Suppose we have some Collection for which we want to process each of the elements using its Iterator.

```
Collection<T> c = ...

Iterator<T> i = c.iterator();
while (i.hasNext())
   ... Statement with one use of i.next().
```

If, as in the above abstract example, we wish to process all the elements of the collection in the same **loop**, then we can use a for-each loop, as follows.

```
Collection<T> c = ...

for (T e : c)
   ... Statement using e.
```

This is a shorthand for precisely the following **for loop**.

```
Collection<T> c = ...

for (Iterator<T> i = c.iterator(); i.hasNext(); )
{
  T e = i.next();
  ... Statement using e.
} // for
```

As with arrays, the for-each loop is only suitable if we want to process all the elements using the one loop.

```
036:   // Show the words and frequencies in word order.
037:   @Override
038:   public String toString()
039:   {
040:     // Obtain the WordWithFrequency values in word iterable order.
041:     Collection<WordWithFrequency> wordWithFrequencyValues
042:       = wordMappedToWordWithFrequency.values();
043:
044:     String result = "";
045:     for (WordWithFrequency wordWithFrequency : wordWithFrequencyValues)
046:       result += String.format("%s%n", wordWithFrequency);
047:
048:     return result;
049:   } // toString
050:
051: } // class WordFrequencyMap
```

As you can see, the for-each loop is shorter code than the long way of writing it.

```
Iterator<WordWithFrequency> iterator = wordWithFrequencyValues.iterator();
while (iterator.hasNext())
  result += String.format("%s%n", iterator.next());
```

We could have made it even shorter if we wanted to, by eliminating the **variable** wordWithFrequencyValues.

```
for (WordWithFrequency wordWithFrequency
       : wordMappedToWordWithFrequency.values())
    result += String.format("%s%n", wordWithFrequency);
```

21.7.3 The WordFrequency class

The WordFrequency **class** contains the **main method** of the program. This reads the input **text file** one **character** at a time and builds characters into groups. Each group is either a sequence of letters and/or apostrophe, and thus is to be counted as a word, or it is a sequence of non-letters, which we ignore. We use the isLetter() **class method** of the Character class to determine whether a given character is a letter or not. Character groups which consist of letters and/or apostrophe, are added to the WordFrequencyMap, but first we turn all the upper case letters into their corresponding lower case ones, using the toLowerCase() **instance method** of the String class. We have a minor issue about comparing a character from the input with an apostrophe, which is of course the same character as a single quote, used to denote a **character literal** in Java. In Section 9.2.2 on page 146 we saw how we can use an **escape sequence** to describe a literal quote character.

Here is the WordFrequency program code.

```
001: import java.io.FileReader;
002: import java.io.IOException;
003:
004: // Read a text document from the file named by the first argument,
005: // and report frequency count of each word on standard output.
006: public class WordFrequency
007: {
008:   public static void main(String[] args)
009:   {
010:     // We see the data as a character stream.
011:     FileReader input = null;
012:     try
013:     {
014:       if (args.length != 1)
015:         throw new IllegalArgumentException
016:                   ("There must be exactly one argument: input-file");
017:
018:       input = new FileReader(args[0]);
019:
020:       // A store of all the words found so far.
021:       WordFrequencyMap wordFrequencyMap = new WordFrequencyMap();
022:
023:       // Remember whether we are reading a word or characters between words.
024:       boolean currentGroupIsAWord = false;
025:
026:       // The group of characters we are currently reading.
027:       String currentGroup = "";
028:
029:       int currentCharAsInt;
030:       while ((currentCharAsInt = input.read()) != -1)
031:       {
032:         char currentChar = (char)currentCharAsInt;
033:
```

```
034:          // We change group if the kind of the current character
035:          // is not the same as the kind of the current group.
036:          if ( (Character.isLetter(currentChar) || currentChar == '\'')
037:               != currentGroupIsAWord )
038:          {
039:            // We are starting a new group.
040:            if (currentGroupIsAWord)
041:              wordFrequencyMap.countWord(currentGroup.toLowerCase());
042:            currentGroup = "";
043:            currentGroupIsAWord = !currentGroupIsAWord;
044:          } //if
045:          // Whether new or old group, add the current character to it.
046:          currentGroup += currentChar;
047:        } // while
048:
049:        // We have a trailing word if the last character was a letter or '.
050:        if (currentGroupIsAWord && ! currentGroup.equals(""))
051:          wordFrequencyMap.countWord(currentGroup.toLowerCase());
052:
053:        // The toString of wordFrequencyMap already has a new line at the end.
054:        System.out.print(wordFrequencyMap);
055:      } // try
056:      catch (Exception exception)
057:      {
058:        System.err.println(exception);
059:      } // catch
060:      finally
061:      {
062:        try { if (input != null) input.close(); }
063:        catch (IOException exception)
064:          { System.err.println("Could not close input " + exception); }
065:      } // finally
066:    } // main
067:
068: } // class WordFrequency
```

> *Coffee time:* `21.7.1` Are you happy with the **condition** of the first **if statement** inside the **while loop**? How would you have written that? Also, for the if statement after the while loop, could we replace the condition with just `currentGroupIsAWord`?

21.7.4 Trying it

Let us try the program with the piece of Shakespeare[8], that we saw in Section 18.5.1 on page 467 – assume it is stored in the **file** RomeoAndJuliet.txt.

```
                           Console Input / Output
$ java WordFrequency RomeoAndJuliet.txt
  (Output shown using multiple columns to save space.)
'tis 1        belonging 1   foot 1       my 1        owes 1          sweet 1       to 1
a 4           but 1         for 1        myself 1    part 2          take 1        we 1
all 1         by 1          hand 1       name 6      perfection 1    that 4        were 1
and 1         call 1        he 2         no 1        retain 1        thee 1        what's 2
any 2         call'd 1      in 1         nor 5       romeo 3         thou 1        which 3
arm 1         dear 1        is 3         not 2       rose 1          though 1      without 1
art 1         doff 1        it 1         o 1         smell 1         thy 3         would 2
as 1          enemy 1       man 1        of 1        so 1           thyself 1
be 1          face 1        montague 2   other 3     some 1          title 1
$ _
```

 Coffee time: `21.7.2` Now that you know about `TreeMap`, can you think how we could have a **tree sort** that does not lose duplicate input items?

21.8 Example: Word frequency count sorted by frequency

AIM: To introduce the HashMap **class**, and the fact that a **collection** can be built to initially contain the same values as some other collection. We also take a look at how we can go about making a good **override** of the hashCode() **instance method** of Object.

The program developed in this section is essentially the same as the one from the previous, except that we now want the words to be presented in descending order of frequency.

21.8.1 The WordWithFrequency class

To achieve the new ordering by frequency, we will need to compare WordWithFrequency **object**s with each other. So we make the **class implement** Comparable, and add a compareTo() **instance method** which orders by frequency and then by word.

```
001: // A pairing of a word with its frequency count (so far).
002: public class WordWithFrequency implements Comparable<WordWithFrequency>
003: {
```

The next part of the class is the same as previously.

```
004:   // The word, occurrences of which are being counted.
005:   private final String word;
006:
007:   // The frequency count of this word (so far).
008:   private int frequency;
009:
010:
011:   // Create a pairing with the given word, and frequency of one.
012:   public WordWithFrequency(String requiredWord)
013:   {
014:     word = requiredWord;
015:     frequency = 1;
016:   } // WordWithFrequency
017:
018:
019:   // Count another occurrence of this word.
020:   public void incrementFrequency()
021:   {
022:     frequency++;
023:   } // incrementFrequency
024:
025:
026:   // A String showing the word and its frequency.
027:   @Override
028:   public String toString()
029:   {
030:     return word + " " + frequency;
031:   } // toString
```

The compareTo() instance method orders by highest frequency first, and if two frequencies are the same, it orders alphabetically by word.

```
034:   // Compare this with the given other, returning negative, zero or positive.
035:   // Order first on descending frequency, then on ascending word.
036:   @Override
037:   public int compareTo(WordWithFrequency other)
038:   {
039:     if (frequency != other.frequency)
040:       return other.frequency - frequency;
```

```
041:    else
042:      return word.compareTo(other.word);
043:  } // compareTo
```

Coffee time: How would we change this to make it order by descending frequency?
21.8.1

Also, we **override** equals() with one that defines an appropriate notion of **equivalence** for this class.

```
046:  // Return true if and only if the given object is equivalent to this one.
047:  @Override
048:  public boolean equals(Object other)
049:  {
050:    if (other instanceof WordWithFrequency)
051:      return compareTo((WordWithFrequency)other) == 0;
052:    else
053:      return super.equals(other);
054:  } // equals
```

Finally, even though we do not strictly need to for this program, we shall override hashCode() to ensure that two WordWithFrequency objects have the same **hash code** if they are **equivalent**, but will tend to be different for non-equivalent ones.

> *Concept* **Standard API: Object: hashCode(): making a good definition.** Classes that **override** equals() ought to also override hashCode() with one that **return**s the same value for **equivalent objects**. Thus, the **function** should be based on the same **instance variables** that are used to define **equivalence** in equals(). A good **hash code** function should tend to give different hash codes for objects that are not equivalent, otherwise **hash tables** that use them will have too many clashes. One way of achieving a good spread of numbers in a hash code, is to turn these instance variables into numbers, if they are not already so (e.g. by using their own hashCode()) and multiply each by a different, arbitrarily chosen, **prime number**, before adding the products together.

Here we shall take the frequency, multiply it by the **prime number** 29, and add that to the hash code of the word (effectively multiplying the latter by the prime number 1).

```
057:  // A hash code for this object: equivalent ones have the same hash code.
058:  @Override
059:  public int hashCode()
060:  {
061:    return frequency * 29 + word.hashCode();
062:  } // hashCode
063:
064: } // class WordWithFrequency
```

Many professional Java programmers make every class have an equals() and a matching hashCode(), and, if the class **implements** Comparable, a matching compareTo(). They do this even if they are not intending to need them right now, just in case they are needed in some future version of the program, or in another program that reuses the class. Failing to implement these properly at initial implementation time could lead to strange **bug**s at that later time.

Coffee time: In some previous examples we had an equals(), but no hashCode(). Are you tempted to go
21.8.2 back and add one in?

21.8.2 The WordFrequencyMap class

In this version of WordFrequencyMap, we still have a **map** from words onto WordWithFrequency **object**s, but we do not use the **natural ordering** of the word **key**s to obtain the toString() result. For this reason, we use the more efficient HashMap instead of a TreeMap.

Concept **Collections API: Maps: HashMap.** The **class** `java.util.HashMap` is part of the **collections framework**, and is another implementation of a **map**. It **implements** the `java.util.Map` **interface**. This kind of map is implemented using a **hash table** and so each **key** must have an appropriate implementation of `hashCode()` so that the `HashMap` works correctly.

The `values()` **instance method** of `HashMap` gives a `Collection` containing the values of the map, which can yield an **object implementing** `java.util.Iterator` that supports **iteration** over these values in no specific order.

As a rule of thumb, `HashMap` should be used in preference to `java.util.TreeMap` when it is not desired to obtain the values from the map in **key** order. If there is little or no **hash code** clashing, a `HashMap` operates in nearly constant time per look up and addition. By contrast, a `TreeMap` operates in time which is proportional to the logarithm of the size of the map.

Since Java 5.0, `HashMap`, and the other classes in the collections framework are **generic class**es. There are *two* **type parameters** for a `HashMap`, first the **type** of **object**s that can be used as keys, and then the type of objects that can be used as values.

```
public class HashMap<K, V> implements Map<K, V>
{ ... }
```

Here is the `WordFrequencyMap` code. The main difference in the first part is the use of `HashMap`.

```
001: import java.util.Collection;
002: import java.util.HashMap;
003: import java.util.Map;
004: import java.util.TreeSet;
005:
006: // A map from word to WordWithFrequency.
007: public class WordFrequencyMap
008: {
009:   // The map uses a HashMap to efficiently store the WordWithFrequency objects.
010:   private final Map<String, WordWithFrequency>
011:     wordMappedToWordWithFrequency = new HashMap<String, WordWithFrequency>();
012:
013:   // Empty constructor, nothing needs doing.
014:   public WordFrequencyMap()
015:   {
016:   } // WordFrequencyMap
017:
018:
019:   // Count an occurrence of the given word by either incrementing the
020:   // frequency of an existing WordWithFrequency or creating a new one if
021:   // this is the first occurrence of the word.
022:   public void countWord(String word)
023:   {
024:     WordWithFrequency wordWithFrequency
025:       = wordMappedToWordWithFrequency.get(word);
026:     if (wordWithFrequency != null)
027:       wordWithFrequency.incrementFrequency();
028:     else
029:     {
030:       wordWithFrequency = new WordWithFrequency(word);
031:       wordMappedToWordWithFrequency.put(word, wordWithFrequency);
032:     } // else
033:   } // countWord
```

In the `toString()` **instance method**, instead of obtaining the values from the map in key order, we build a **new** `TreeSet` containing the values, and then iterate through those in the natural ordering of those values. This will use the `compareTo()` instance method of the `WordWithFrequency` class, and so the values will be covered in descending order of frequency.

We can make an **instance** of a **collection** class, such as `TreeSet`, by using its **constructor method** which takes an existing `Collection` as a **method argument**.

Concept **Collections API: `Collection` interface: constructor taking a `Collection`.** The **application program interface (API)** documentation of the `java.util.Collection` **interface** states that any **class** which **implements** it should provide two **constructor methods**, one which takes no **method arguments** and builds an empty `Collection`, and one which takes an existing `Collection` and builds a **new** one containing the same elements.

Interestingly, there is no way for this requirement to be enforced in Java, as interfaces cannot specify constructor methods! It could be argued that this is a deficiency in the use of interfaces as a means of contractual obligation.

Anyway, all the standard implementations of `java.util.Collection` do satisfy the requirement.

Here is the `toString()` instance method of our latest version of `WordFrequencyMap`.

```
036:   // Show the words and frequencies in frequency order.
037:   @Override
038:   public String toString()
039:   {
040:     // Obtain the WordWithFrequency values in an unpredictable order,
041:     // and put them into a TreeSet so we can extract them in frequency order.
042:     TreeSet<WordWithFrequency> wordWithFrequencyValues
043:       = new TreeSet<WordWithFrequency>(wordMappedToWordWithFrequency.values());
044:
045:     String result = "";
046:     for (WordWithFrequency wordWithFrequency : wordWithFrequencyValues)
047:       result += String.format("%s%n", wordWithFrequency);
048:
049:     return result;
050:   } // toString
051:
052: } // class WordFrequencyMap
```

21.8.3   The `WordFrequency` class

The `WordFrequency` **class** is the same as in the previous version of the program in Section 21.7.3 on page 563.

Coffee time: [21.8.3]
What would happen if `String` did not **override** `hashCode()` — would our program here work? What would it do instead?

21.8.4   Trying it

Let us **run** the program with the same input **data** as the previous version.

Console Input / Output

```
$ java WordFrequency input.txt
(Output shown using multiple columns to save space.)
name 6      he 2         and 1          call'd 1    it 1        retain 1     though 1
nor 5       montague 2   arm 1          dear 1      man 1       rose 1       thyself 1
that 5      not 2        art 1          doff 1      my 1        smell 1      title 1
a 4         part 2       as 1           enemy 1     myself 1    so 1         to 1
is 3        thy 2        be 1           face 1      no 1        some 1       we 1
other 3     what's 2     belonging 1    foot 1      o 1         sweet 1      were 1
romeo 3     would 2      but 1          for 1       of 1        take 1       without 1
which 3     'tis 1       by 1           hand 1      owes 1      thee 1
any 2       all 1        call 1         in 1        perfection 1 thou 1
$ _
```

Coffee time: [21.8.4]
Now that you know about **maps**, are you tempted to re-implement some of the program for translating documents, perhaps in particular the way that `Dictionary` works, in Section 20.4.2 on page 524?

21.8.5 Coursework: Finding duplicate voters, using a `HashMap`

The election officials are very pleased with your work from the task in Section 21.4.2 on page 551 but they have found so many duplicate votes that they would now like you to modify the way the results are presented, to make them easier to process!

All they ask is that each time a duplicate vote is found, your program outputs it, together with the time and location of the duplicate *and* the time and location of the *first* occurrence of the naughty voter. So, the output for the input shown in Section 21.4.2 on page 551 would be as follows.

```
            Console Input / Output
$ java DuplicateVoters voting.txt voting-duplicates.txt
$ cat voting-duplicates.txt
Rupert Rodgers-Smythe, 4, M25 7QZ
  Duplicate: 12:27 Manchester 099
  First occurrence: 07:37 Manchester 538
Sarah Peacock, 6, M25 7QZ
  Duplicate: 14:59 Manchester 537
  First occurrence: 10:25 Manchester 538
Sarah Peacock, 6, M25 7QZ
  Duplicate: 19:01 Manchester 539
  First occurrence: 10:25 Manchester 538
Margaret Chopin, 9, M37 9MP
  Duplicate: 19:30 Manchester 308
  First occurrence: 12:14 Manchester 299
Sarah Peacock, 6, M25 7QZ
  Duplicate: 20:59 Manchester 540
  First occurrence: 10:25 Manchester 538
There were 5 duplicate votes
$ _
```

Your program should use a `HashMap` to store the voter identifications processed so far, each mapped on to their *first* occurring time and location. So, the voter identifications will be **keys**, and the time and locations will be values in the map. Your program will read through the **file** as before, but this time it will not ignore the time and location lines. For each vote, it will check in the `HashMap` to see if that voter identification is already present – by using `get()` to try and retrieve the time and location of their first vote. If this is the first occurrence of the voter identification (i.e. the result from `get()` is the **null reference**) then all is well, and the voter identification mapped to the time and location is `put()` into the **map**. If on the other hand the voter identification is already in the map, then it is to be printed, along with the new time and location and the first time and location (retrieved from the map).

21.9 Collections of collections

AIM: To explore the idea that the elements of a **collection** can themselves be collections, and so quite complex **data structures** can be built.

There's no example here, just an idea. And some coursework. The idea might be a bit obvious to you, but just in case, let us explore it. Collections can contain any kinds of **object** – including **collections**. So, for example, an `ArrayList` of `ArrayLists` is the **collections framework**'s answer to a **two-dimensional array**. You could have a `TreeMap` of `LinkedLists`, if you were, for example, making an index of all occurrences of identifiers in a directory (folder) of Java **source code files**. And so on.

21.9.1 Coursework: Finding duplicate voters, using a `HashMap` of `LinkedLists`

The election officials are very sorry to bother you again, but they have a new idea to make the processing of duplicate voting even more easy. They now would like the results grouped by fraudulent voter! (Of course, if you had been given the opportunity, you may well have pointed this out during requirements analysis at the start!)

This version of the program should produce the following results from the **data** shown in Section 21.4.2 on page 551.

```
                     Console Input / Output
$ java DuplicateVoters voting.txt voting-duplicates.txt
$ cat voting-duplicates.txt
Rupert Rodgers-Smythe, 4, M25 7QZ
    07:37 Manchester 538
    12:27 Manchester 099
Sarah Peacock, 6, M25 7QZ
    10:25 Manchester 538
    14:59 Manchester 537
    19:01 Manchester 539
    20:59 Manchester 540
Margaret Chopin, 9, M37 9MP
    12:14 Manchester 299
    19:30 Manchester 308
$ _
```

The order of the voters might be different. Also note that your customers no longer desire to have a count of the duplicate votes.

Your program should use a HashMap to store the voter identifications, each mapped on to an **object** which contains a LinkedList of all the time and location lines for that voter identification. Once the input **file** has been read, your program will iterate through the values of this **map** looking for ones which have more than one vote, and reporting those it finds.

A LinkedList is arguably better than an ArrayList for storing the vote details of each voter, as each **list** just gets items added on the end, and then finally scanned via its Iterator. This means we do not get the inefficiency of LinkedList, because we are not accessing its elements in a random order, but we do benefit from each one being the exact size needed – most of them will contain only one item, and there will be very many of them.

The elements of the HashMap should be **instance**s of a **class** called VoterRecord, which you will write. This will contain two **instance variables**, the identity of a voter, and a LinkedList of his or her voting times and locations, in the order found in the file. Its **constructor method** will be given the identity of the voter. It will have an **instance method** to add a voting time and location. Another instance method will **return** the number of times the person has voted. The toString() instance method should give a multi-line String representing the VoterRecord object, including the identity of the voter and the times and locations of voting, ready for use in the output of the program.

To obtain the efficiency of using LinkedLists, you must use an Iterator when scanning through the LinkedList in a VoterRecord to build the result of its toString(), rather than accessing each element by its **list index**.

Optional extra: Predict the effect of changing your HashMap to a TreeMap, and try it.

21.10 Concepts covered in this chapter

Here is a list of the concepts that were covered in this chapter, each with a self-test question. You can use this to check you remember them being introduced, and perhaps re-read some of them before going on to the next chapter.

Collections API	
Collections API (p.538)	Although there are different kinds of collection, what particular convenience do they all have in common?
– Collection interface (p.556)	Name four methods from this interface. Which collections have these methods?
– Collection interface: constructor taking a Collection (p.568)	What deficiency arguably exists in the use of interfaces as a means of contractual obligation?
– Lists (p.538)	What features characterize a collection as being a list?
– Lists: List interface (p.538)	What is the type parameter of a List used for?
– Lists: List interface: iterator() (p.553)	What order does this present the elements in?

Collections API	
– Lists: List interface: extends Collection (p.556)	If we have ArrayList al = **new** ArrayList(); what type is the object referenced by the variable al – is it ArrayList, List, Collection or Object?
– Lists: ArrayList (p.539)	How is this collection implemented?
– Lists: add(index) and remove(index) (p.557)	For which implementation of List will these instance methods be slow, and for which will they be fast?
– Lists: LinkedList (p.558)	How is this collection implemented?
– Maps (p.559)	What features characterize a collection as being a map?
– Maps: Map interface (p.560)	What are the type parameters of a Map used for?
– Maps: TreeMap (p.560)	How is this collection implemented?
– Maps: HashMap (p.567)	How is this collection implemented?
– Sets (p.546)	What features characterize a collection as being a set?
– Sets: Set interface (p.546)	What is the type parameter of a Set used for?
– Sets: Set interface: iterator() (p.554)	What order does this present the elements in?
– Sets: Set interface: extends Collection (p.557)	If we have HashSet hs = **new** HashSet(); what type is the object referenced by the variable hs – is it HashSet, Set, Collection or Object?
– Sets: TreeSet (p.552)	How is this collection implemented?
– Sets: TreeSet: iterator() (p.554)	What order does this present the elements in?
– Sets: HashSet (p.548)	How is this collection implemented?
– Collections class (p.543)	Name a generic class method that is provided in this class. What restrictions are placed on its List method argument?
– Iterator interface (p.553)	What two abstract methods does this have?

Design	
– Sorting a list: tree sort (p.554)	What two stages are involved in this?
– Storing data (p.547)	What is data stored in at run time? What kinds of things might we want to do with such stored data?
– Storing data: hash table (p.547)	What is the consequence of clashes, and how is their occurrence minimized?
– Storing data: ordered binary tree (p.552)	Why is this data structure called an OBT?
– Storing data: linked list (p.557)	For what circumstances is this better than using an array?

Standard API	
– Integer: as a box for int: works with collections (p.548)	What three instance methods does Integer have in order for it to behave properly in the collections classes?
– Object: hashCode() (p.548)	What is hashCode() used for, and what properties should it have?
– Object: hashCode(): making a good definition (p.566)	What property must it have, and what property should it have? How can we achieve this?

Statement	
– for-each loop: on collections (p.562)	When should we use a for-each loop with collections?

Chapter 22

Recursion

How long is a piece of string, you ask?
To find out, you should cut off from it as much as you can measure
and add that number to the length of the piece that remains!

22.1   Chapter aims

The principle of **recursion** is the centuries old idea of regarding something as being comprised of other instances of the same thing. For example, a positive whole number might be seen as being one more than a smaller whole number. Or a large river could be viewed as a collection of its tributaries, which are themselves rivers.

So a **recursive definition** is one in which we define something in terms of itself – an idea we explore here, mainly in relation to **recursive methods**. We shall see that recursion is related to **iteration** (i.e. **loop**ing) in the sense that the latter is really just a special case of the former. After a brief introduction, we look at two **recursive algorithms** which have nothing to do with Java, and then a progression of Java programs that use recursion, from a simple one through to much more complex ones. Along the way, we address the common problems that often cause students to misunderstand recursion.

Our final example is one which embodies a **recursive data structure**.

The chapter contains the following sections.

Section	Aims	Associated Coursework
22.2 What is recursion? (p.574)	To introduce the idea of **recursion**, together with the notions of **base case** and **recursive case**.	(None.)
22.3 Lecture attendance (p.576)	To introduce the idea of a **recursive algorithm**, with an example of one that is not intended for use on a computer.	Describe a **recursive algorithm** to be followed by humans. (p.577)
22.4 Sum of ages of descendants (p.577)	To reinforce the idea of a **recursive algorithm**, with another example of one that is not intended for use on a computer. This one would not be easy to perform **iteratively**.	Attempt to write an **iterative algorithm** that does the same work as a complex **recursive algorithm**. (p.578)
22.5 Factorial (p.579)	To introduce the idea of a **recursive method**, present a simple example and talk about common misunderstandings. We also look at what it means for a recursive method to be **well defined** and compare **recursion** with **iteration**.	Write a program to copy **standard input** to **standard output** but with the lines in reverse order, so that the first input line comes out last. (p.584)

Section	Aims	Associated Coursework
22.6 Fibonacci (p.585)	To show an example of a **recursive method** which has **multiple recursion**.	Implement Fibonacci using an **array** to remember the results. (p.589)
22.7 Number puzzle (p.590)	To solve a problem, using a **recursive method** with **multiple recursion**, which would be quite tricky to solve **iteratively**. Along the way, we look at the process of *designing* a **recursive algorithm**.	Add two more **recursive method calls** to a **doubly recursive method**. (p.594)
22.8 Dice combinations (p.594)	To show an example of a **recursive method** which has **multiple recursion** with **recursive method calls** inside a **loop**.	Write a program to output all the anagrams of a word given as a **command line argument**. (p.597)
22.9 Vowel movements (p.597)	To present another example of a **recursive method** which has **multiple recursion** with **recursive method calls** inside a **loop**. We also meet **anonymous arrays**.	(None.)
22.10 Tower of Hanoi (p.601)	To devise a remarkably short **recursive method** solution to a seemingly very tricky puzzle.	Extend a Hanoi solving program to show the state of the pegs. (p.602)
22.11 Friend book (p.603)	To show an example of **recursion** based on walking through a **recursive data structure**. We also have a **private constructor method**.	Write a program to model family ancestry. (p.609)
22.12 Summary (p.610)	To summarize our coverage of **recursion**.	(None.)

22.2 What is recursion?

AIM:
To introduce the idea of **recursion**, together with the notions of **base case** and **recursive case**.

In this introduction we explore what we mean by **recursion**, before putting the idea into practice in the sections that follow.

Concept **Recursion.** The principle of **recursion** is a centuries old mathematical concept. It is the simple idea that one can define something in terms of that same thing. For example, consider the **factorial function** which is defined for all **natural numbers**, that is, **integers** which are **greater than or equal** to zero.

$fact\ 0 = 1$
$fact\ 1 = 1 \times 1$
$fact\ 2 = 2 \times 1 \times 1$
$fact\ 3 = 3 \times 2 \times 1 \times 1$
$\dots$
$fact\ n = n \times (n-1) \times (n-2) \times \dots \times 3 \times 2 \times 1 \times 1$

This definition is somewhat unsatisfactory in that the occurrences of "..." have to be read as "and so on", which is really just as vague as saying "you know what I mean". Mathematicians and programmers prefer a more precise way of describing the **function**, such as the following **recursive definition**.

$fact\ 0 = 1$
$fact\ n = n \times fact(n-1)$ where $n > 0$

This is a recursive definition of $fact$, because we define it in terms of itself.

$thing = \dots thing \dots$

Let us take a closer look at the **recursive definition** of $fact$ by evaluating an example application of it. We start with $fact$ 4, and expand it using the $fact$ definition, but replacing n with 4.

$fact$ 4
$= 4 \times (fact\ 3)$

Let us do the expansion for $fact$ 3 too.

$fact$ 4
$= 4 \times (fact\ 3)$
$= 4 \times (3 \times (fact\ 2))$

Let us do it for the whole lot, until we cannot expand any more, and then evaluate the answer.

$fact$ 4
$= 4 \times (fact\ 3)$
$= 4 \times (3 \times (fact\ 2))$
$= 4 \times (3 \times (2 \times (fact\ 1)))$
$= 4 \times (3 \times (2 \times (1 \times (fact\ 0))))$
$= 4 \times (3 \times (2 \times (1 \times 1)))$
$= 4 \times (3 \times (2 \times 1))$
$= 4 \times (3 \times 2)$
$= 4 \times 6$
$= 24$

See how the **expression** expands until it reaches the part of the definition that requires no more expansion, and then it contracts as the result is calculated.

What happens if the argument is negative?

$fact\ -1$
$= -1 \times (fact\ -2)$
$= -1 \times -2 \times (fact\ -3)$
$= -1 \times -2 \times (-3 \times (fact\ -4))$
$= -1 \times -2 \times (-3 \times (-4 \times (fact\ -5)))$
$= -1 \times -2 \times (-3 \times (-4 \times (-5 \times (fact\ -6)))) \ldots$

Clearly this expansion will proceed forever, and we will never get to the point where we can start contracting the expression. This is why the **function** $fact$ is only defined for **natural number** (non-negative integer) arguments.

It is, on the other hand, defined for *all* natural numbers, and we can convince ourselves of this.

Concept **Recursion: base and recursive cases.** The **factorial function** is defined for *all* **natural number** (non-negative integer) arguments, n. Let us see why. For any given n, there are only two possibilities.

- n could be 0 – the result is defined to be 1.

  $fact\ 0 = 1$

  This is known as a **base case** – a part of the definition that does not contain a reference to the thing being defined.

- All other (non-negative integer) n are bigger than 0, and so we can subtract 1 from n only a finite number of times before reaching 0.

$$fact\ n = n \times fact(n-1)$$

This is known as a **recursive case** – a part of the definition that contains a reference to the thing being defined.

The **function** *fact* has one base case and one recursive case. More generally, a **recursive definition** can have one or more base cases, and one or more recursive cases.

In the next sections we shall see various examples which use the principle of recursion by having **recursive algorithm**s.

 Coffee time: 22.2.1   What do you think a recursive algorithm is?

22.3 Example: Lecture attendance

AIM:
To introduce the idea of a **recursive algorithm**, with an example of one that is not intended for use on a computer.

In this section we present an example of a **recursive algorithm**, for humans to follow.

Concept **Recursion: recursive algorithm.** An **algorithm** is a procedure for undertaking some task. For example, every **method** in Java is an implementation of some particular algorithm to achieve the desired purpose. We do not have to express algorithms in Java code of course, we can instead use **pseudo code**, or even just natural language – especially if the algorithm is not intended to be followed by a computer!

A **recursive algorithm** is one which is expressed in terms of itself. This means that somewhere in the instructions of the algorithm, there is a requirement to perform the same algorithm again, probably just on some *part* of the overall **data** which is being processed.

Imagine you are a student sitting in a lecture theatre along with lots of other students, and for some reason, the lecturer wishes to know how many students are in the room, but doesn't wish to stand there and count each one. Let us assume that all those present are cooperative, and, being rather clever, can understand simple instructions. The lecturer could pass the following instructions to the left-most person in the front row, and wait for the answer.

```
Stand up.
Count the number of people in your row (including you), and remember it.
If there are no non-empty rows behind your row then:
  Your row count is your answer.
Else
  Pass these instructions to the left-most person
    in the nearest non-empty row behind yours, and wait.
  Take the result from that person behind you, add it to your row count,
    -- that is your answer.
End if
Pass your answer to whomever asked you to follow these instructions.
```

Coffee time: 22.3.1   Would this work? Is it a **recursive algorithm**?

Here are some key points to observe about this **algorithm**.

- Each person following the instructions has his or her own *separate* notion of the following things.

  - Who called upon him or her to follow the instructions.

  - His or her row count.

  - Who he or she calls upon from the row behind, if any.

  - The result got back from who he or she called.

- The result **return**ed by any person is always the number of people in his or her row, plus all those in rows behind.

- So the result returned by the first person is the count from all the rows.

Could we have used **iteration** instead of **recursion**? Yes, of course! For example, the lecturer could have done all the counting, essentially (and perhaps subconsciously) obeying the following instructions.

```
Start your counter at zero.
For every row containing any people, from front to back
  For every person in that row, from left to right
    Add one to your counter.
  End for
End for
Your counter is the result.
```

That may well have been simpler, but probably less fun. (Probably.) The real point is that you now know we have a choice of doing it **iterative**ly or **recursive**ly. For this particular example, the iterative way of doing it is more straightforward. However, in the next section we shall meet an example where this is not so.

Coffee time: 22.3.2   But before we go there, how could we *simply* change our recursive instructions to exploit the inherent parallelism in the room, to get the answer more quickly? Well anyway, concurrent programming is not a topic of this book! ;-)

22.3.1 Coursework: Finding the most populated row

Describe a **recursive algorithm** for finding from the lecture theatre the size of the row which contains the most people.

Optional extra: Also find the number of the row with most people in it – assume the rows are numbered from one, from front to back, and that every row has at least one person in it. (You cannot just assume the answer is the back row... !)

22.4 Example: Sum of ages of descendants

AIM: To reinforce the idea of a **recursive algorithm**, with another example of one that is not intended for use on a computer. This one would not be easy to perform **iterative**ly.

577

In this section we appeal to fantasy! Imagine there is an isolated, if a little crowded, island where people live for thousands of years, because they eat so well and look after themselves. One day, a very old, very rich woman wants to give a present to all her descendants, to mark her retirement from running her gold mine for the past 2000 years.

She wants to give to each descendant, a piece of gold for each year of his or her age. She does not know how many descendants she has, let alone their ages. She does, of course, know her own children. In order to figure out how many pieces of gold to get out of her safe, she asks her children for the sum of the ages of their descendants.... (Oh, by the way, there is never any incest on this island, and people never die before their parents do.)

She simply asks herself to follow these instructions.

```
result = 0
For each child you have (if any):
  Ask him/her to follow these instructions, wait for the result.
  result += result from child.
End for
result += your age.
Pass your result to whomever asked you.
```

 Coffee time: 22.4.1   Would this work? (What if there was some incest, perish the thought?)

Could this result be easily obtained using **iteration** rather than **recursion**? The answer is no, because each person following the instructions may have more than one child, and so having got a result **recursively** from one child there is still more work left to do. It is fundamentally a more complex problem than the lecture attendance count, because it uses **multiple recursion**.

 Coffee time: 22.4.2   Check carefully – does the **algorithm** *really* work, or does it produce a slightly wrong answer?

Correct – it does not quite work, because she has included her own age in the sum of all the ages! Maybe the following instructions would have been better?

```
result = 0
For each child you have (if any):
  Ask him/her to follow these instructions, wait for the result.
  result += result from child.
  result += age of that child.
End for
Pass your result to whomever asked you.
```

22.4.1 Coursework: An iterative sum of ages algorithm

Attempt to write an **iterative** version of the instructions to obtain the sum of the ages of the woman's descendants. It has to be instructions that would really work (albeit the woman herself only exists in fantasy). Hint: try hard, but be prepared to give up.

22.5 Example: Factorial

AIM: To introduce the idea of a **recursive method**, present a simple example and talk about common misunderstandings. We also look at what it means for a recursive method to be **well defined** and compare **recursion** with **iteration**.

In this section we present our first example program with **recursion** in it. This is an implementation of factorial, using a **recursive method**.

Concept **Recursion: recursive method.** A **recursive definition** is one which refers to the thing being defined. So, given that the definition of a **method** is its body, then a **recursive method** is one which contains one or more **method calls** to itself.

Any route through the method that does not involve a method call to the same method is known as a **base case**. Any route which does involve such a call is known as a **recursive case**.

First we present the program using 'fairy steps' which makes it easier to grasp how it works, and then in the following subsection we show a compact version of it.

22.5.1 Factorial with fairy steps

In this first version we store intermediate results in **local variables** before using them.

```
001: // Contains a class method to calculate factorial.
002: public class Factorial
003: {
004:   // Find the factorial of n which must be non-negative.
005:   public static int factorial(int n)
006:   {
007:     int result;
008:     // Base case when n is 0 or 1.
009:     if (n <= 1)
010:       result = 1;
011:     else
012:     {
013:       // Recursive case when n > 1.
014:       int factNMinus1 = factorial(n - 1);
015:       result = n * factNMinus1;
016:     } // else
017:     return result;
018:   } // factorial
019:
020: } // class Factorial
```

Notice the **base case** which occurs when n has the value 0 or 1 and the **recursive case** for values **greater than** 1.

It is easy to misunderstand recursion when it is first met, so let us deal with some common learning obstacles.

Concept **Recursion: recursive method: avoid misunderstanding.** Students new to **recursive methods** often make one or both of the following two mistakes which lead to difficulty understanding the concept.

1. Misconception: A **recursive method call** makes execution go back to the start of the **method**. So **recursion** is an odd form of **iteration**. This is not the case – a recursive method call starts another separate occurrence of the method execution.

2. Assumption: There is one copy of each **method variable** belonging to a method. This also is not the case – each call to a method causes a set of method variables to be created for use during the method execution. So, each occurrence of a recursive method call has its own separate set of method variables.

In order to understand that the code will work for any given non-negative **integer**, you should observe that each **method call** to factorial() has its own *separate* notions of the following.

- The **method parameter** n.

- The **local variable** result.

- The local variable factNMinus1.

- Where it was called from (e.g. which other invocation of the recursive method).

- Where it is up to.

The following diagram shows the execution of the **method** for an original **method argument** of 3.

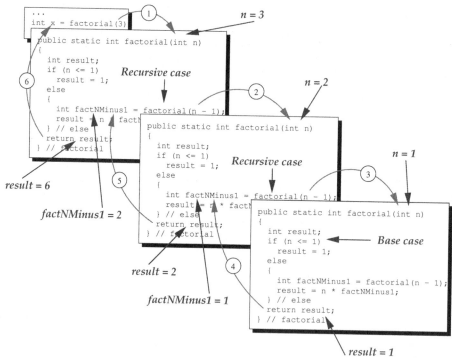

The first method call is given the method argument 3, so the method parameter n of the first method invocation has the value 3. As this is a recursive case, this causes a second method call to the same method, with the method argument n - 1 which is 2. The second method invocation has its own method parameter n with the value 2. This also is a recursive case, and so a third method call to the same method is **executed**, with the method argument n - 1 which is 1. At this point there are three invocations of the method, each with a different method parameter called n.

The third method invocation executes the base case, sets its local variable called `result` to 1 and **return**s that value. Execution transfers back to the place where the third method call was made, which is in the second method invocation. This places the returned value in its local variable called `factNMinus1`. That value is then multiplied by n, which in this second method invocation has the value 2, and the resulting value, 2, is placed in the local variable `result` belonging to this second method invocation. This then ends with that value being passed into the local variable called `factNMinus1` belonging to the first method invocation. Next this is multiplied by n, which here is 3, to yield 6, and this is finally returned to the code which started it all off.

To be convinced that it will work for *all* non-negative integers, we need to be sure that it is **well defined**.

Concept **Recursion: recursive method: well defined.** To be **well defined**, also known as **well founded**, a **recursive method** must have the following properties.

- Have a clearly identified range of **method argument**s for which it is meant to work.

- For all possible method arguments for which it is meant to work:

  – Have at least one **base case**, which does not cause a **recursive method call**.

  – In all **recursive case**s, the arguments passed to a recursive method call make progress in some way towards a base case, so there can be no **infinite recursion**. Often, especially when there is only one base case, this means such arguments are values which are nearer to the base case than the **method parameter** values were.

Our factorial method is well defined because:

- It is supposed to work only for non-negative integers.

- For all non-negative integers

  – The arguments 0 and 1 are the base cases.

  – All other non-negative integers, n, are greater than 1, and so the argument passed to the **recursive method call**, n − 1, is nearer to 1 than n is.

22.5.2 Factorial without fairy steps

Here we shall present another version of factorial that does not have the 'fairy steps' in it. But first, we shall take a closer look at the relationship between **recursion** and **iteration**.

Concept **Recursion: recursive method: versus iteration.** At first glance, **recursion** can look like another form of **iteration** – execution appears to 'jump back' to the start of the **recursive method**. Please be warned that is a dangerously wrong view of what is actually happening!

Indeed many recursive methods could (and perhaps should) be easily implemented using a **loop** instead. But many cannot easily be implemented **iteratively**. Recursion is a more powerful, more general tool, than iteration.

Iteration is in fact merely an optimized implementation of *simple* uses of recursion, known as **tail recursion**, that is, the kind of recursion for which the **recursive method call** is always the last thing done.

Please avoid any temptation at this stage to not take recursion seriously because iteration feels 'more straightforward'. Very soon we shall meet examples where this is not the case, and you should take the opportunity to get to grips with recursion now while the examples are still simple.

Can factorial be implemented **iteratively**? Our `factorial()` **method** does not use simple **tail recursion**, because the result from the **recursive method call** needs to be multiplied by n. However, that **multiplication** could be done as we expand the recursion, rather than as we contract it; causing the answer to be calculated in the opposite order but still getting the same result. So it should be fairly easy to implement `factorial()` iteratively – no-one would really implement it using **recursion**, would they?

On the other hand, the **recursive** version is more 'obviously correct' with respect to the mathematical definition of factorial. This is especially so when the method is expressed as follows (removing the 'fairy steps').

```
001: // Contains a class method to calculate factorial.
002: public class FactorialCompact
003: {
004:   // Find the factorial of n which must be non-negative.
005:   public static int factorial(int n)
006:   {
007:     if (n <= 1) return 1;
008:     else        return n * factorial(n - 1);
009:   } // factorial
010:
011: } // class FactorialCompact
```

Observe that the recursion is now occurring while an **expression** is being **evaluated**.

Coffee time: 22.5.1	Convince yourself that the compact version of factorial really is the same as the one with 'fairy steps'.	

Coffee time: 22.5.2	Write a version of factorial that uses tail recursion (hint – have an extra **method parameter** which is the 'result so far', starting with 1). Compare it with the mathematical definition – is it '*obviously* correct'?	

Coffee time: 22.5.3	Write an iterative version of factorial. Compare it with the recursive mathematical definition – is it '*obviously* correct'?	

Coffee time: 22.5.4	Did the lecture attendance count **algorithm** use tail recursion? Did it almost do so? What about the sum of the ages algorithm?	

22.5.3 Factorial with tracing

Here is a third version of factorial which presents a trace of what it is doing on **standard output**. We might use this as a means to help us understand **recursion**.

```
001: // Program to demonstrate factorial, using tracing.
002: // (Warning: this program does not catch RuntimeExceptions.)
```

```
003: public class FactorialTrace
004: {
005:    // Find the factorial of n which must be non-negative.
006:    // Output tracing at each recursion level.
007:    private static int factorial(int n,
008:                                 int recursionLevel,
009:                                 String recursionLevelIndentation)
010:    {
011:       // We output tracing as we do each part of the task.
012:       System.out.println(recursionLevelIndentation
013:                          + "Entered recursion level " + recursionLevel
014:                          + " with n=" + n);
015:
016:       int result;
017:       // Base case when n is 0 or 1.
018:       if (n <= 1)
019:       {
020:          System.out.println(recursionLevelIndentation
021:                             + "Arrived at base case, n=" + n);
022:          result = 1;
023:       } // if
024:       else
025:       {
026:          // Recursive case when n > 1.
027:          System.out.println(recursionLevelIndentation
028:                             + "Calling factorial with argument " + (n - 1));
029:          int factNMinus1 = factorial(n - 1,
030:                                       recursionLevel + 1,
031:                                       recursionLevelIndentation + "|   ");
032:          System.out.println(recursionLevelIndentation
033:                             + "Back from recursion: n=" + n
034:                             + ", factNMinus1=" + factNMinus1);
035:          System.out.println(recursionLevelIndentation + "Multiplying n=" + n
036:                             + " by factNMinus1=" + factNMinus1);
037:          result = n * factNMinus1;
038:       } // else
039:
040:       System.out.println(recursionLevelIndentation
041:                          + "Exiting recursion level " + recursionLevel
042:                          + " with result=" + result);
043:       return result;
044:    } // factorial
```

We shall have a **main method** so that we can run factorial with various **method arguments**.

```
047:    // Output factorial of first argument, with tracing.
048:    public static void main(String[] args) throws RuntimeException
049:    {
050:       int argument = Integer.parseInt(args[0]);
051:       System.out.println("Calling factorial with argument " + argument);
052:       int factorialOfArgument = factorial(argument, 1, "|   ");
053:       System.out.println("The factorial of " + argument
054:                          + " is " + factorialOfArgument);
055:    } // main
056:
057: } // class FactorialTrace
```

22.5.4 Trying it

When we **run** our program, it will produce output which should help us understand **recursion**.

Study this to ensure you appreciate that, for example, each invocation of factorial has its own notion of n.

22.5.5 Coursework: Reversing lines

Write a program called `ReverseLines` to copy **standard input** to **standard output** but with the lines in reverse order, so that the first input line comes out last. Your **main method** will set up a `BufferedReader` and a `PrintWriter`, and pass these as **method arguments** to another **class method**, which shall be a **recursive method**.

The recursive method will read the input lines and output them. It will *not* use **tail recursion**, in that it will perform some work *after* the **recursive method call**.

Think of an abstract sequence, seq, as either being empty, or being a head, seq.head, followed by a tail, seq.tail, itself a possibly empty sequence.

```
                         Console Input / Output
$ java FactorialTrace 7
Calling factorial with argument 7
|   Entered recursion level 1 with n=7
|   Calling factorial with argument 6
|   |   Entered recursion level 2 with n=6
|   |   Calling factorial with argument 5
|   |   |   Entered recursion level 3 with n=5
|   |   |   Calling factorial with argument 4
|   |   |   |   Entered recursion level 4 with n=4
|   |   |   |   Calling factorial with argument 3
|   |   |   |   |   Entered recursion level 5 with n=3
|   |   |   |   |   Calling factorial with argument 2
|   |   |   |   |   |   Entered recursion level 6 with n=2
|   |   |   |   |   |   Calling factorial with argument 1
|   |   |   |   |   |   |   Entered recursion level 7 with n=1
|   |   |   |   |   |   |   Arrived at base case, n=1
|   |   |   |   |   |   |   Exiting recursion level 7 with result=1
|   |   |   |   |   |   Back from recursion: n=2, factNMinus1=1
|   |   |   |   |   |   Multiplying n=2 by factNMinus1=1
|   |   |   |   |   |   Exiting recursion level 6 with result=2
|   |   |   |   |   Back from recursion: n=3, factNMinus1=2
|   |   |   |   |   Multiplying n=3 by factNMinus1=2
|   |   |   |   |   Exiting recursion level 5 with result=6
|   |   |   |   Back from recursion: n=4, factNMinus1=6
|   |   |   |   Multiplying n=4 by factNMinus1=6
|   |   |   |   Exiting recursion level 4 with result=24
|   |   |   Back from recursion: n=5, factNMinus1=24
|   |   |   Multiplying n=5 by factNMinus1=24
|   |   |   Exiting recursion level 3 with result=120
|   |   Back from recursion: n=6, factNMinus1=120
|   |   Multiplying n=6 by factNMinus1=120
|   |   Exiting recursion level 2 with result=720
|   Back from recursion: n=7, factNMinus1=720
|   Multiplying n=7 by factNMinus1=720
|   Exiting recursion level 1 with result=5040
The factorial of 7 is 5040
$ _
```

Here is **pseudo code** for printing such an abstract sequence, `inputSeq`, in reverse.

```
if inputSeq is not empty
  recursively output inputSeq.tail
  output inputSeq.head
end-if
```

In this case, you are using a `BufferedReader` to obtain the sequence of lines, line by line, and the act of reading a line tells you whether you have read them all, and if not, moves the input onto the remaining lines, i.e. the tail. You will need a **variable** to save the head line. So we can recast the above general pseudo code as follows.

```
String head line
if trying to read the head line does not yield null
  recursively read and output the tail lines
  output the head line
end-if
```

For brevity, you may be skimpy with **exception** handling – just declare that each **method throws** Exception.

584

22.6 Example: Fibonacci

AIM: To show an example of a **recursive method** which has **multiple recursion**.

In 1202, the Italian mathematician Leonardo Bonacci of Pisa introduced into Western mathematics a sequence of numbers[4] which ancient Indian mathematicians had recognized as playing a central role in nature. In the 19th century he became nicknamed as Fibonacci by mathematicians of that time. The simple relationship between the Fibonacci numbers, as they have come to be known, is that each one is the sum of the previous two, except for the first two which are both 1.

Assuming n is a positive **integer**, then the nth Fibonacci number is $fib\ n$, defined as follows.[1]

$fib\ 1 = 1$
$fib\ 2 = 1$
$fib\ n = fib(n-1) + fib(n-2)$ where $n > 2$

One popular 'use' of this definition is to solve the following puzzle about the breeding patterns of rabbits, posed by Fibonacci. Assume that

- Rabbits never die.

- From one month old a pair of rabbits can mate (every pair is one of each gender).

- One month later they produce one more pair of rabbits.

- They continue this monthly pattern forever.

If we start with one pair of new-born rabbits, how many pairs will we have at the start of month n?[2] The answer is $fib\ n$: you have all the rabbits you had last month, $fib(n-1)$, because they never die, plus as many as the month before that, $fib(n-2)$, because that many have bred another pair.

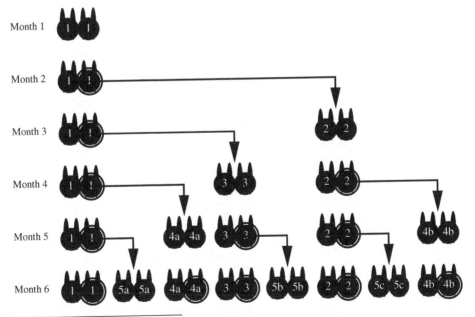

---

[1] Some modern definitions of the Fibonacci sequence start with n being 0 where $fib\ 0 = 0$.
[2] There are modern variations of this puzzle which amount to the same principle.

Let us see an expansion of *fib* 5.

$$
\begin{array}{lllll}
& fib\ 5 & & & \\
= & fib(5-1) & & & +fib(5-2) \\
= & fib\ 4 & & & +fib(5-2) \\
= & (fib(4-1) & & +fib(4-2)) & +fib(5-2) \\
= & (fib\ 3 & & +fib(4-2)) & +fib(5-2) \\
= & ((fib(3-1) & +fib(3-2)) & +fib(4-2)) & +fib(5-2) \\
= & ((fib\ 2 & +fib(3-2)) & +fib(4-2)) & +fib(5-2) \\
= & ((1 & +fib(3-2)) & +fib(4-2)) & +fib(5-2) \\
= & ((1 & +fib\ 1) & +fib(4-2)) & +fib(5-2) \\
= & ((1 & +1) & +fib(4-2)) & +fib(5-2) \\
= & (2 & & +fib(4-2)) & +fib(5-2) \\
= & (2 & & +fib\ 2) & +fib(5-2) \\
= & (2 & & +1) & +fib(5-2) \\
= & 3 & & & +fib(5-2) \\
= & 3 & & & +fib(5-2) \\
= & 3 & & & +fib\ 3 \\
= & 3 & & & +(fib(3-1) & +fib(3-2)) \\
= & 3 & & & +(fib\ 2 & +fib(3-2)) \\
= & 3 & & & +(1 & +fib(3-2)) \\
= & 3 & & & +(1 & +fib\ 1) \\
= & 3 & & & +(1 & +1) \\
= & 3 & & & +2 \\
= & 5 & & &
\end{array}
$$

Here is another view of the same expansion, this time just showing the links between the 'levels' of **recursion**.

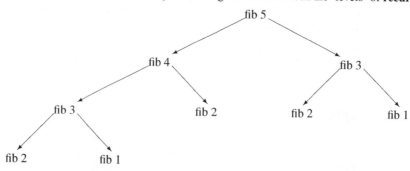

The work involved in computing *fib* 6 is significantly more – notice that *fib* 4 is computed twice, and *fib* 3 three times.

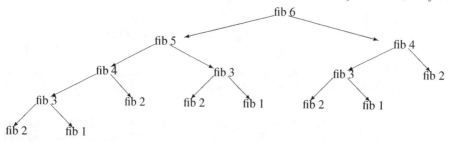

Coffee time: [22.6.1]   How many more 'nodes' would we need to add to get the diagram for *fib* 7?

22.6.1 Fibonacci with fairy steps

Here is Java code for a version that uses **local variable**s to store intermediate results.

```
001: // Contains a class method to calculate Fibonacci.
002: public class Fibonacci
003: {
004:    // Find the Fibonacci of n which must be positive.
005:    public static int fibonacci(int n)
006:    {
007:      int result;
008:      // Base case when n is 1 or 2.
009:      if (n == 1 || n == 2)
010:        result = 1;
011:      else
012:      {
013:        // Recursive case when n > 2.
014:        int fibNMinus1 = fibonacci(n - 1);
015:        int fibNMinus2 = fibonacci(n - 2);
016:        result = fibNMinus1 + fibNMinus2;
017:      } // else
018:      return result;
019:    } // fibonacci
020:
021: } // class Fibonacci
```

Our `fibonacci()` **method** does not use **tail recursion**: in fact it has **multiple recursion** – more than one **recursive method call** within the method. Consequently, it is not immediately obvious how to implement it **iterative**ly (but see shortly).

22.6.2 Fibonacci without fairy steps

Just as we did with the previous example, let us present a more compact version of `fibonacci()`.

```
001: // Contains a class method to calculate Fibonacci.
002: public class FibonacciCompact
003: {
004:    // Find the Fibonacci of n which must be positive.
005:    public static int fibonacci(int n)
006:    {
007:      if (n == 1 || n == 2) return 1;
008:      else                  return fibonacci(n - 1) + fibonacci(n - 2);
009:    } // fibonacci
010:
011: } // class FibonacciCompact
```

 Coffee time: [22.6.2] Convince yourself that the compact version of `fibonacci()` really has the same effect as the one with 'fairy steps'.

22.6.3 Fibonacci with tracing

And finally, we have a third version that outputs a trace of what it is doing on the **standard output**, which we might use as another means to help us understand **recursion**. It uses a similar tracing 'mechanism' as did `FactorialTrace` on Section 22.5.3 on page 582, except we do not show the recursion level here, to keep the output a little smaller.

```
001: // Program to demonstrate Fibonacci, using tracing.
002: // (Warning: this program does not catch RuntimeExceptions.)
003: public class FibonacciTrace
004: {
005:    // Find the Fibonacci of n which must be positive.
006:    // Output tracing at each recursion level.
007:    private static int fibonacci(int n, String recursionLevelIndentation)
008:    {
009:      int result;
010:      // Base case when n is 1 or 2.
011:      if (n == 1 || n == 2)
012:      {
013:        System.out.println(recursionLevelIndentation + "n = " + n + ": "
014:                         + "Arrived at base case, result = 1");
015:        result = 1;
016:      } // if
017:      else
018:      {
019:        // Recursive case when n > 2.
020:        System.out.println(recursionLevelIndentation + "n = " + n + ": "
021:                         + "Calling fibonacci with argument n - 1 = "
022:                         + (n - 1));
023:        int fibNMinus1 = fibonacci(n - 1, recursionLevelIndentation + "|    ");
024:        System.out.println(recursionLevelIndentation + "n = " + n + ": "
025:                         + "Calling fibonacci with argument n - 2 = "
026:                         + (n - 2));
027:        int fibNMinus2 = fibonacci(n - 2, recursionLevelIndentation + "|    ");
028:        result = fibNMinus1 + fibNMinus2;
029:        System.out.println(recursionLevelIndentation + "n = " + n + ": "
030:                         + "Adding " + fibNMinus1 + " to " + fibNMinus2
031:                         + ", result = " + result);
032:      } // else
033:      return result;
034:    } // fibonacci
```

As in the previous example, we shall have a **main method** so that we can **run** it.

```
037:    // Output Fibonacci of first argument, with tracing.
038:    public static void main(String[] args) throws RuntimeException
039:    {
040:      int argument = Integer.parseInt(args[0]);
041:      System.out.println("Calling fibonacci with argument " + argument);
042:      int fibonacciOfArgument = fibonacci(argument, "|    ");
043:      System.out.println("The fibonacci of " + argument
044:                       + " is " + fibonacciOfArgument);
045:    } // main
046:
047: } // class FibonacciTrace
```

22.6.4 Trying it

Let us **run** the program with the value 7. Observe that there are 25 calls to fibonacci(), including 13 **base case**s.

```
                    Console Input / Output
$ java FibonacciTrace 7
Calling fibonacci with argument 7
|  n = 7: Calling fibonacci with argument n - 1 = 6
|  |  n = 6: Calling fibonacci with argument n - 1 = 5
|  |  |  n = 5: Calling fibonacci with argument n - 1 = 4
|  |  |  |  n = 4: Calling fibonacci with argument n - 1 = 3
|  |  |  |  |  n = 3: Calling fibonacci with argument n - 1 = 2
|  |  |  |  |  |  n = 2: Arrived at base case, result = 1
|  |  |  |  |  n = 3: Calling fibonacci with argument n - 2 = 1
|  |  |  |  |  |  n = 1: Arrived at base case, result = 1
|  |  |  |  |  n = 3: Adding 1 to 1, result = 2
|  |  |  |  n = 4: Calling fibonacci with argument n - 2 = 2
|  |  |  |  |  n = 2: Arrived at base case, result = 1
|  |  |  |  n = 4: Adding 2 to 1, result = 3
|  |  |  n = 5: Calling fibonacci with argument n - 2 = 3
|  |  |  |  n = 3: Calling fibonacci with argument n - 1 = 2
|  |  |  |  |  n = 2: Arrived at base case, result = 1
|  |  |  |  n = 3: Calling fibonacci with argument n - 2 = 1
|  |  |  |  |  n = 1: Arrived at base case, result = 1
|  |  |  |  n = 3: Adding 1 to 1, result = 2
|  |  |  n = 5: Adding 3 to 2, result = 5
|  |  n = 6: Calling fibonacci with argument n - 2 = 4
|  |  |  n = 4: Calling fibonacci with argument n - 1 = 3
|  |  |  |  n = 3: Calling fibonacci with argument n - 1 = 2
|  |  |  |  |  n = 2: Arrived at base case, result = 1
|  |  |  |  n = 3: Calling fibonacci with argument n - 2 = 1
|  |  |  |  |  n = 1: Arrived at base case, result = 1
|  |  |  |  n = 3: Adding 1 to 1, result = 2
|  |  |  n = 4: Calling fibonacci with argument n - 2 = 2
|  |  |  |  n = 2: Arrived at base case, result = 1
|  |  |  n = 4: Adding 2 to 1, result = 3
|  |  n = 6: Adding 5 to 3, result = 8
|  n = 7: Calling fibonacci with argument n - 2 = 5
|  |  n = 5: Calling fibonacci with argument n - 1 = 4
|  |  |  n = 4: Calling fibonacci with argument n - 1 = 3
|  |  |  |  n = 3: Calling fibonacci with argument n - 1 = 2
|  |  |  |  |  n = 2: Arrived at base case, result = 1
|  |  |  |  n = 3: Calling fibonacci with argument n - 2 = 1
|  |  |  |  |  n = 1: Arrived at base case, result = 1
|  |  |  |  n = 3: Adding 1 to 1, result = 2
|  |  |  n = 4: Calling fibonacci with argument n - 2 = 2
|  |  |  |  n = 2: Arrived at base case, result = 1
|  |  |  n = 4: Adding 2 to 1, result = 3
|  |  n = 5: Calling fibonacci with argument n - 2 = 3
|  |  |  n = 3: Calling fibonacci with argument n - 1 = 2
|  |  |  |  n = 2: Arrived at base case, result = 1
|  |  |  n = 3: Calling fibonacci with argument n - 2 = 1
|  |  |  |  n = 1: Arrived at base case, result = 1
|  |  |  n = 3: Adding 1 to 1, result = 2
|  |  n = 5: Adding 3 to 2, result = 5
|  n = 7: Adding 8 to 5, result = 13
The fibonacci of 7 is 13
$ _
```

Coffee time: 22.6.3
How many **method calls** and base cases would there be if the initial **method argument** was 8? What is the relationship between the resulting answer and the number of base cases arrived at? Can you explain that?

As you can see, this **doubly recursive method** implementation of fibonacci() is not very efficient – the work done involves repeating a lot of work that has already been done. The following table shows this.

n	fib n	# of method calls	# of base cases
1	1	1	1
2	1	1	1
3	2	3	2
4	3	5	3
5	5	9	5
6	8	15	8
7	13	25	13
8	21	41	21
9	34	67	34
10	55	109	55
11	89	177	89
12	144	287	144

Coffee time: 22.6.4
Why is the number of base cases the same as the result? Can you spot the pattern in the number of method calls? How many calls are needed to calculate *fib n*?

With some serious thought, you might be able to find a wholly different way of implementing it, which has **linear time complexity**, that is, the time taken to run is proportional to n. What is more, when this alternative approach is expressed recursively, it does in fact use only **tail recursion**, and so can easily be implemented in a **loop**.

Coffee time: 22.6.5 Find that solution! (Hint: remember the last two values computed.) Was it easy to find? Is it 'obviously correct' with respect to the mathematical definition of the **function**, compared with the implementation in FibonacciCompact?

22.6.5 Coursework: A more efficient Fibonacci

Write a version of the Fibonacci **class** with a **recursive method** that has the same structure as the one here, but is made efficient by storing the result for *fib n* in an **array** at **array index** n. This technique to avoid recomputing results is sometimes known as a **memo function**.

22.7 Example: Number puzzle

AIM:
To solve a problem, using a **recursive method** with **multiple recursion**, which would be quite tricky to solve **iteratively**. Along the way, we look at the process of *designing* a **recursive algorithm**.

Imagine that you have been asked to solve puzzles. Each one consists of a sequence of positive whole numbers separated by question marks, then an **equal sign** and another positive whole number, which is the target. The idea is for you to try and make the sequence equal to the target by replacing each question mark with either an **addition** or a **division operator**. There can be no use of brackets. Also, **operator precedence** is ignored – the evaluation works in simple (non scientific) calculator order from left to right.

For example, you might be asked to solve the following puzzles.

```
1    ?  2  ?  3   ?  4  ?  5   =  1
24   ?  4  ?  59  ?  5  ?  87  =  100
```

 Coffee time: 22.7.1 Stop a moment and think how you would go about solving these puzzles without the use of a computer.

In this section we develop a **recursive method** designed to solve a number puzzle given to it as **method arguments**. If there is at least one solution, it will **return** its description as a String. For example, here is our developed program, which uses this recursive method, being asked to solve the second of the two puzzles above.

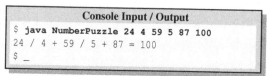

```
Console Input / Output
$ java NumberPuzzle 24 4 59 5 87 100
24 / 4 + 59 / 5 + 87 = 100
$ _
```

Why are we not including the **subtraction** and **multiplication** operators in the puzzle? Well it's your job in the coursework to extend the solution for those two! But, perhaps luckily for you, whether we allow two or four operators does not fundamentally affect the design of the solution.

Concept **Recursion: recursive algorithm: design.** The key to **design**ing a **recursive algorithm** is to identify three things.

1. What are the **base cases**? Overall the recursive algorithm is solving problems of a particular type. Some of these problems can be solved easily, maybe even trivially. These are the base cases.

2. What are the **recursive cases**? In order to deal with an occurrence of the problem which cannot be solved easily, we must find another occurrence of the *same* kind of problem, which is simpler ...

3. ... and such that the solution to this simpler problem helps solve the given one.

To put this more formally, for every problem, *p*, which is not covered by a base case, we find another problem, *p'*, such that

- *p'* is simpler than *p*, in the sense of being nearer to a base case,
- and *p'* can easily be derived from *p*,
- and the result of solving *p'* can easily be processed into a solution of *p*.

Each characterization of *p* paired with *p'* is a recursive case.

For example, a recursive algorithm for factorial recognizes that the factorial of one is trivial – it is always one – and so that is the base case. Then, given a problem *p* which is the desire to have the factorial of some whole positive *n*, not covered by the base case, we note that the problem p', which is finding the factorial of $n-1$, is both nearer the base case and is useful in that its solution can be processed to solve p: the factorial of $n-1$ when multiplied by n yields the factorial of n.

Let us **design** a **recursive algorithm** for solving our number puzzles. We are given a sequence of numbers and a target. The sequence must be non-empty, otherwise the puzzle is meaningless.

What are the **base cases**? If the sequence contains just one number, then the puzzle is trivial – that number is either **equal** to the target, or it is not. So, this is the base case for our recursive method.

What are the **recursive cases**? If there is more than one number in the sequence, then we need to find a new puzzle with the following properties.

- It must have less numbers.

- If we can solve it, then its solution must be part of the solution of the one we are given.

For example, suppose we want to solve the following.

24 ? 4 ? 59 ? 5 ? 87 = 100

There are two simpler problems that could help us, each found by ignoring one of the numbers and adjusting the target.

1: 24 ? 4 ? 59 ? 5 = 100 − 87
2: 24 ? 4 ? 59 ? 5 = 100 × 87

The first sub-puzzle is found by removing the 87 from the sequence and treating the last question mark as an **addition** operator, so we subtract 87 from the target. If we are able to find a solution to this, then we can solve our main puzzle by simply adding the 87.

The second sub-puzzle is found by removing the 87 and treating the last question mark as a **division** operator, so we multiply the target by 87. If we can find a solution to this, then we can solve our main puzzle – we simply divide by the 87.

So we have two recursive cases, representing the two sub-puzzles found by ignoring the last number from the sequence and adjusting the target in each of the two simple ways. As we are trying to find just one solution (rather than them all), we attempt to solve the first sub-puzzle, and only try the second if the first was not solved.

The following diagram shows the steps in solving our example.

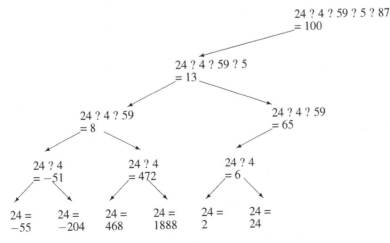

The left arrows represent trying a sub-puzzle with an addition operator before the number being ignored, and the right arrows show trying a division operator. In the former case the target for the sub-puzzle is adjusted by subtracting the number being ignored, and in the latter by multiplying.

591

The sub-puzzles at the bottom of the tree correspond to the base cases, each containing just one number and a target. The first five of these are not equal, and so do not find a solution. The sixth one is, and so the path back up the tree is the solution to each sub-puzzle at each stage, right up to the original puzzle at the top.

$$24 \ / \ 4 \ + \ 59 \ / \ 5 \ + \ 87 \ = \ 100$$

The following table is another way of analysing the process and shows the steps in solving our example.

Step	Puzzle											Target value	Base case
Given	24	?	4	?	59	?	5	?	87	=	100	100	
1	24	?	4	?	59	?	5	=	100	−	87	13	
1.1	24	?	4	?	59	=	100	−	87	−	5	8	
1.1.1	24	?	4	=	100	−	87	−	5	−	59	−51	
1.1.1.1	24	=	100	−	87	−	5	−	59	−	4	−55	Yes: false
1.1.1.2	24	=	100	−	87	−	5	−	59	×	4	−204	Yes: false
1.1.2	24	?	4	=	100	−	87	−	5	×	59	472	
1.1.2.1	24	=	100	−	87	−	5	×	59	−	4	468	Yes: false
1.1.2.2	24	=	100	−	87	−	5	×	59	×	4	1888	Yes: false
1.2	24	?	4	?	59	=	100	−	87	×	5	65	
1.2.1	24	?	4	=	100	−	87	×	5	−	59	6	
1.2.1.1	24	=	100	−	87	×	5	−	59	−	4	2	Yes: false
1.2.1.2	24	=	100	−	87	×	5	−	59	×	4	24	Yes: true

Study the patterns carefully – do you see what is happening on either side of the **equal sign** in the puzzle? Look just at the base cases – the first one corresponds to the four question marks being $++++$ and the second to $+++/$.

Here is the code. The **main method** reads the **command line arguments**, the last one of which is the target, creates an **instance** of NumberPuzzle and asks for its solution.

```
001: // Program for solving number puzzles presented as command line arguments.
002: // (Warning: this program does not catch RuntimeExceptions.)
003: public class NumberPuzzle
004: {
005:   public static void main(String[] args) throws RuntimeException
006:   {
007:     // The last argument is the target.
008:     int target = Integer.parseInt(args[args.length - 1]);
009:     // And the preceding ones are the numbers to match the target.
010:     int[] puzzleNumbers = new int[args.length - 1];
011:     for (int index = 0; index < puzzleNumbers.length; index++)
012:       puzzleNumbers[index] = Integer.parseInt(args[index]);
013:
014:     // Now create a NumberPuzzle with those numbers.
015:     NumberPuzzle puzzle = new NumberPuzzle(puzzleNumbers, target);
016:     // And solve it.
017:     System.out.println(puzzle.solve());
018:   } // main
```

The numbers and the target are stored as **instance variables** which are initialized by the **constructor method**.

```
021:   // The list of numbers is supplied as an array of int.
022:   private final int[] puzzleNumbers;
023:
024:   // The required target.
025:   private final int target;
026:
```

```
027:
028:    // Constructor is given puzzle numbers and target.
029:    public NumberPuzzle(int[] requiredPuzzleNumbers, int requiredTarget)
030:    {
031:      puzzleNumbers = requiredPuzzleNumbers;
032:      target = requiredTarget;
033:    } // NumberPuzzle
```

We have a **public instance method** which returns a `String` representing the solution. The search for the solution is done by a **private** instance method.

```
036:    // Find a solution, if possible, and return it as a String.
037:    public String solve()
038:    {
039:      String solution = solveUpto(puzzleNumbers.length, target);
040:      if (solution == null) return "There is no solution";
041:      else                  return solution + " = " + target;
042:    } // solve
```

The private **doubly recursive method** is given a count of how many numbers to use from `puzzleNumbers` and a target.

```
045:    // Find a solution, if possible, and return it as a String.
046:    // But only use the first noOfNumbersToUse puzzle numbers,
047:    // with the given target. If no solution then return null.
048:    private String solveUpto(int noOfNumbersToUse, int target)
049:    {
050:      // This means there were none to start with!
051:      if (noOfNumbersToUse < 1)
052:        return null;
053:
054:      // Proper base case: only one number, which = or != the target.
055:      else if (noOfNumbersToUse == 1)
056:        if (puzzleNumbers[0] == target) return "" + target;
057:        else                            return null;
058:
059:      // Recursive cases: at least two numbers.
060:      else
061:      {
062:        // We shall ignore the last number and try sub-puzzles.
063:        int numberToIgnore = puzzleNumbers[noOfNumbersToUse - 1];
064:
065:        // Try an ADD before the ignored number.
066:        String subPuzzleResult
067:          = solveUpto(noOfNumbersToUse - 1, target - numberToIgnore);
068:        if (subPuzzleResult != null) // Success!
069:          return subPuzzleResult + " + " + numberToIgnore;
070:
071:        // Try a DIVIDE before the ignored number.
072:        subPuzzleResult
073:          = solveUpto(noOfNumbersToUse - 1, target * numberToIgnore);
074:        if (subPuzzleResult != null) // Success!
075:          return subPuzzleResult + " / " + numberToIgnore;
076:
077:        // Both sub-puzzles failed.
078:        return null;
```

```
079:    } // else
080:  } // solveUpto
081:
082: } // class NumberPuzzle
```

22.7.1   Trying it

```
                      Console Input / Output
$ java NumberPuzzle 1 1
1 = 1
$ java NumberPuzzle 1 2 3 4 5 1
1 + 2 / 3 + 4 / 5 = 1
$ java NumberPuzzle 24 4 59 5 87 100
24 / 4 + 59 / 5 + 87 = 100
$ java NumberPuzzle 24 4 59 5 87 99
There is no solution
$ _
```

Can `solve()` be implemented **iteratively**? Our `solveUpto()` **instance method** does not use **tail recursion**, so it is not obvious how to implement it iteratively.

Coffee time: 22.7.2
Have a go at finding an iterative solution!

22.7.2   Coursework: Extending `NumberPuzzle`

Extend our `NumberPuzzle` program so that the other two **arithmetic operator**s are included. Hint: for **multiplication**, there is no point making a **recursive method call** if the target is not divisible by the number being ignored – in fact doing so would lead to erroneous solutions (due to **integer** truncation).

Optional extra: For a real challenge, why not allow brackets in the sequence?

22.8   Example: Dice combinations

AIM:
To show an example of a **recursive method** which has **multiple recursion** with recursive method calls inside a loop.

Do you recall the example from Section 6.7 on page 104 which printed out all the combinations of three dice? It used three **nested loop**s, each taking their **iteration** from 1 to 6. What if we wanted there to be four dice? Ten? Any number chosen at **run time**?

In this section we have a **recursive method** that uses **multiple recursion** to generate all the combinations of any number of dice, where the number is given as a **command line argument**.

Here is the key **design** to the solution. We work through all the dice, from first to last. The **base case** is when we have reached the end of the **list** of dice. The **recursive case**s are based on printing out the combinations of all the dice to the right of the point we are at, each preceded by whatever combination we have set up to the left of where we are at. So, in order to print out all the combinations, we make the first die go through all its possible numbers, and for *each* value, **recursively** find all the combinations of the dice to the right of it. We do this using an **array** with as many **array element**s as there are dice.

The following diagram illustrates this with three dice. The arrow shows the die we are currently considering (i.e. an **array index**), and the little number next to the arrow shows the step count – the first step is to make the first die have the value 1, the second is to set the second die to 1, etc.. The base cases happen when this arrow has moved beyond the end of the array, which first happens in step four in the diagram. (Not all steps are shown – of course!)

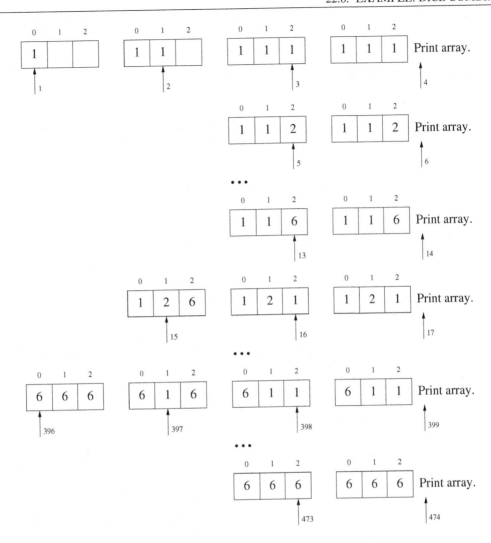

Here is the code.

```
001: // Program to output all combinations of any number of six sided dice.
002: // (Warning: this program does not catch RuntimeExceptions.)
003: public class DiceThrows
004: {
005:   public static void main(String[] args) throws RuntimeException
006:   {
007:     int noOfDice = Integer.parseInt(args[0]);
008:     diceValues = new int[noOfDice];
009:     printDiceCombinations(0);
010:   } // main
011:
012:
013:   // The array of dice, length is number of dice (command line argument).
014:   private static int[] diceValues;
015:
```

```
016:
017:    // Generate all combinations of dice in diceValues
018:    // from indices currentDieNumber to diceValues.length - 1.
019:    // Each is preceded by whatever is already generated
020:    // at indices 0 to currentDieNumber - 1.
021:    private static void printDiceCombinations(int currentDieNumber)
022:    {
023:      // Base case when we have reached the end of the array.
024:      if (currentDieNumber == diceValues.length)
025:      {
026:        // Calculate the sum of the dice.
027:        int sumOfDice = 0;
028:        for (int dieValue : diceValues) sumOfDice += dieValue;
029:        // Output sum and combination.
030:        System.out.print(sumOfDice + " from");
031:        for (int dieValue : diceValues) System.out.print(" " + dieValue);
032:        System.out.println();
033:      } // if
034:      else
035:        // Recursive cases: take dice at currentDieNumber from 1 to 6
036:        // and recurse from the next index for each value.
037:        for (diceValues[currentDieNumber] = 1;
038:             diceValues[currentDieNumber] <= 6;
039:             diceValues[currentDieNumber]++)
040:          printDiceCombinations(currentDieNumber + 1);
041:    } // printDiceCombinations
042:
043: } // class DiceThrows
```

Notice the use of an array element as the control **variable** for a **for loop**.

22.8.1 Trying it

We try the program with two dice.

```
Console Input / Output

$ java DiceThrows 2
(Output shown using multiple columns to save space.)
2 from 1 1    | 5 from 2 3 | 8 from 3 5 | 6 from 5 1 | 9 from 6 3
3 from 1 2    | 6 from 2 4 | 9 from 3 6 | 7 from 5 2 | 10 from 6 4
4 from 1 3    | 7 from 2 5 | 5 from 4 1 | 8 from 5 3 | 11 from 6 5
5 from 1 4    | 8 from 2 6 | 6 from 4 2 | 9 from 5 4 | 12 from 6 6
6 from
7 from
3 from
4 from
$ _
```

Let's **run** the program with 6 dice, and pipe the output through our LineNumber program from Section 18.6 on page 469.[a]

[a]Or, on Unix, we could just use cat -n.

```
Console Input / Output

$ java DiceThrows 6 | java LineNumber
(Output shown using multiple columns to save space.)
00001 6 from 1 1 1 1 1 1    | 46643 33 from 6 6 6 6 4 5
00002 7 from 1 1 1 1 1 2    | 46644 34 from 6 6 6 6 4 6
00003 8 from 1 1 1 1 1 3    | 46645 30 from 6 6 6 6 5 1
00004 9 from 1 1 1 1 1 4    | 46646 31 from 6 6 6 6 5 2
00005 10 from 1 1 1 1 1 5   | 46647 32 from 6 6 6 6 5 3
00006 11 from 1 1 1 1 1 6   | 46648 33 from 6 6 6 6 5 4
00007 7 from 1 1 1 1 2 1    | 46649 34 from 6 6 6 6 5 5
(...lines removed to save space.)         | 46650 35 from 6 6 6 6 5 6
46637 32 from 6 6 6 6 3 5   | 46651 31 from 6 6 6 6 6 1
46638 33 from 6 6 6 6 3 6   | 46652 32 from 6 6 6 6 6 2
46639 29 from 6 6 6 6 4 1   | 46653 33 from 6 6 6 6 6 3
46640 30 from 6 6 6 6 4 2   | 46654 34 from 6 6 6 6 6 4
46641 31 from 6 6 6 6 4 3   | 46655 35 from 6 6 6 6 6 5
46642 32 from 6 6 6 6 4 4   | 46656 36 from 6 6 6 6 6 6
$ _
```

Coffee time: 22.8.1
What is the value of 6^6?

Can `printDiceCombinations()` be implemented **iteratively**? It does not use **tail recursion**, so it is not obvious how to do so.

Coffee time: Have a go at finding an **iterative** solution – not just for a fixed number of dice, like the **nested loops** approach. You can do it, if you approach the problem in a wholly different way. (Hint: count from 0 to $6^N - 1$ in base 6, where N is the number of dice.) Is the iterative solution (significantly) more efficient? Is it shorter or longer code? Is it easier or harder to see that it is correct?

22.8.2 Coursework: `Anagrams`

Write a program called `Anagrams` which outputs all the permutations of a string given as a **command line argument**. The **main method** will, for efficiency, turn the first (and only) command line argument into a **char array**, using the `toCharArray()` **instance method** of the `String` **class**. It will also set up two other arrays of the same length, one, of **type** `char[]` to build the current permutation, and another, of type `boolean[]`, to record whether **characters** from the given string have been used so far in the permutation being constructed. It will then call a **recursive method** to print all the permutations.

Here is **pseudo code** for the recursive method.

```
printPermutations(int currentIndex)
{
  if currentIndex has gone past the end of the permutation array
    print out the permutation
  else
    for each index in the char array made from the given string
      if the character at that index is not already used in the permutation
        mark it as being in use (using the boolean array)
        put that character in the permutation at currentIndex
        printPermutations(currentIndex + 1)
        mark the character as NOT being used in the permutation
      end-if
    end-for
  end-else
}
```

Note that if the given string contains duplicate characters, then there will be duplicate permutations produced. This is fine.

Optional extra: Do it in a different **recursive** way, which does not need the **boolean** array nor a second **char** array. (Hint: swap the character at the given **array index** with each other one at a greater index, in turn.)

Optional extra: Do it without using **recursion**.

22.9 Example: Vowel movements

AIM: To present another example of a **recursive method** which has **multiple recursion** with **recursive method calls** inside a **loop**. We also meet **anonymous arrays**.

In this section we have a program that takes a word as a **command line argument**, in which some or all of the vowels have been replaced by asterisks. The program produces all possible 'words' where each asterisk is replaced by every vowel in turn. So, if we have one asterisk in the input, there would be five 'words' in the output, two would generate 25 and three would yield 125.

```
                        Console Input / Output
$ java VowelMovements '*l*s*n'

(Output shown using multiple columns to save space.)
alasan      elasan      ilasan      olasan      ulasan
alasen      elasen      ilasen      olasen      ulasen
alasin      elasin      ilasin      olasin      ulasin
alason      elason      ilason      olason      ulason
alasun      elasun      ilasun      olasun      ulasun
alesan      elesan      ilesan      olesan      ulesan
alesen      elesen      ilesen      olesen      ulesen
alesin      elesin      ilesin      olesin      ulesin
aleson      eleson      ileson      oleson      uleson
alesun      elesun      ilesun      olesun      ulesun
alisan      elisan      ilisan      olisan      ulisan
alisen      elisen      ilisen      olisen      ulisen
alisin      elisin      ilisin      olisin      ulisin
alison      elison      ilison      olison      ulison
alisun      elisun      ilisun      olisun      ulisun
alosan      elosan      ilosan      olosan      ulosan
alosen      elosen      ilosen      olosen      ulosen
alosin      elosin      ilosin      olosin      ulosin
aloson      eloson      iloson      oloson      uloson
alosun      elosun      ilosun      olosun      ulosun
alusan      elusan      ilusan      olusan      ulusan
alusen      elusen      ilusen      olusen      ulusen
alusin      elusin      ilusin      olusin      ulusin
aluson      eluson      iluson      oluson      uluson
alusun      elusun      ilusun      olusun      ulusun
$ _
```

The key **design** to the vowel movements solution is actually very similar to that for dice combinations. We work through all the **characters**, from first to last. The **base case** is when we have reached the end of the word – we print it out. The **recursive case**s are based on printing out the combinations of all the characters to the right of the point we are at, each prepended with what we have so far in the word. So, in order to print out all the 'words', if the character at the current position is '*' we set it in turn to every vowel, and for *each* vowel, **recursive**ly find all the 'words' to the right of it.

Here is the code. The **main method** obtains the command line argument and turns it into an **array** of characters. Then it calls the **recursive method** with an initial scan position of zero.

```
001: // Program to generate all words from argument, where * becomes a,e,i,o,u.
002: // (Warning: this program does not catch RuntimeExceptions.)
003: public class VowelMovements
004: {
005:   // The argument, stored as characters for easy processing.
006:   private static char[] inputChars;
007:
008:   // Store the argument as chars and invoke the recursion.
009:   public static void main(String[] args) throws RuntimeException
010:   {
011:     inputChars = args[0].toCharArray();
012:     outputVowelMovements(0);
013:   } // main
```

The recursive method deals with three possibilities. The **base case** is when the scan position has gone past the end of the array. A second, **recursive case**, is when the character at the scan position is not an asterisk – we simply recurse right. And the third, also recursive case, is when we have found an asterisk. Here we need to replace the asterisk with each vowel, and for each recurse right. In order to **loop** through the five vowels, we shall use an **anonymous array**.

Concept **Array: array creation: anonymous array.** When we create an **array** in Java using the **reserved word new**, we can provide a **list** of the elements we wish to be placed into the array instead of just saying how big it is. Such an array is known as an **anonymous array**, because it can be used to avoid us needing to declare a **variable** to **reference** the newly created array.

The **syntax** is as follows.

```
new Type[] { value1, value2, ... valueN }
```

This is very similar to an **array initializer**, but can be used in any **expression**, rather than just in an array **variable declaration**. To show the similarity, here is an **array variable** declared and initialized with an array initializer.

```
String[] daysOfTheWeek
    = { "Mon", "Tue", "Wed", "Thu", "Fri", "Sat", "Sun" };
```

And here is the same effect using an anonymous array instead.

```
String[] daysOfTheWeek
    = new String[] { "Mon", "Tue", "Wed", "Thu", "Fri", "Sat", "Sun" };
```

You should regard the array initializer as a shorthand for using an anonymous array, when we are declaring the variable and creating the array in one go. As the name suggests though, an anonymous array is most useful in situations where we do not wish to declare a variable to hold a reference it.

For example, consider the following code.

```
for (boolean haveUmbrella : new boolean { true, false })
  for (boolean isRaining : new boolean { true, false })
  {
    System.out.println("It is" + (isRaining ? "" : " not") + " raining.");
    System.out.println
        ("You have " + (haveUmbrella ? "an" : "no") + " umbrella.");
    if (isRaining && !haveUmbrella)
      System.out.println("You get wet!");
    else
      System.out.println("You stay dry.");
    System.out.println();
  } // for
```

```
016:    // Generate all words in inputChars
017:    // from indices scanPosition to inputChars.length - 1.
018:    // Each is preceded by whatever is already generated
019:    // at indices 0 to scanPosition - 1.
020:    private static void outputVowelMovements(int scanPosition)
021:    {
022:      // scanPosition is where we are up to in our scan from left to right.
023:      // If we have reached the end, we can print the string and return.
024:      if (scanPosition >= inputChars.length)
025:        System.out.println(inputChars);
026:
027:      // If we have not found '*' then move on to the next.
028:      else if (inputChars[scanPosition] != '*')
029:        outputVowelMovements(scanPosition + 1);
030:
031:      // Otherwise change '*' to 'a', 'e', 'i', 'o', 'u'
032:      // and for each move on.
033:      else
034:      {
035:        for (char vowel : new char[] {'a', 'e', 'i', 'o', 'u'})
036:        {
037:          inputChars[scanPosition] = vowel;
038:          outputVowelMovements(scanPosition + 1);
039:        } // for
```

```
040:        // Put the asterisk back to restore the value,
041:        // which is needed for later calls past this point.
042:        inputChars[scanPosition] = '*';
043:      } // else
044:   } // outputVowelMovements
045:
046: } // class VowelMovements
```

Coffee time: `22.9.1` What would happen if we forgot to replace the asterisk after the loop that goes through the five vowels? If we had two asterisks in the input, how many output 'words' would we get?

Our `outputVowelMovements()` recursive method does not use **tail recursion**, so it is not obvious how to implement it **iteratively**.

 Coffee time: `22.9.2` Have a go at finding an iterative solution! You can do it, if you approach the problem in a wholly different way – similar to what you did for the dice combinations. Is the iterative solution (significantly) more efficient? Is it shorter or longer code? Is it easier or harder to see that it is correct?

22.9.1 Trying it

Console Input / Output

```
$ java VowelMovements 'El*zabeth'
```
(Output shown using multiple columns to save space.)

Elazabeth	Elezabeth	Elizabeth	Elozabeth	Eluzabeth

`$ _`

Console Input / Output

```
$ java VowelMovements Elizabeth
Elizabeth
$ _
```

Console Input / Output

```
$ java VowelMovements 'El*z*beth'
```
(Output shown using multiple columns to save space.)

Elazabeth	Elezabeth	Elizabeth	Elozabeth	Eluzabeth
Elazebeth	Elezebeth	Elizebeth	Elozebeth	Eluzebeth
Elazibeth	Elezibeth	Elizibeth	Elozibeth	Eluzibeth
Elazobeth	Elezobeth	Elizobeth	Elozobeth	Eluzobeth
Elazubeth	Elezubeth	Elizubeth	Elozubeth	Eluzubeth

`$ _`

Console Input / Output

```
$ java VowelMovements '*****' | java LineNumber
```
(Output shown using multiple columns to save space.)

00001 aaaaa	00018 aaaoi	03109 uuueo
00002 aaaae	00019 aaaoo	03110 uuueu
00003 aaaai	00020 aaaou	03111 uuuia
00004 aaaao	00021 aaaua	03112 uuuie
00005 aaaau	00022 aaaue	03113 uuuii
00006 aaaea	00023 aaaui	03114 uuuio
00007 aaaee	00024 aaauo	03115 uuuiu
00008 aaaei	00025 aaauu	03116 uuuoa
00009 aaaeo	(...lines removed to save space.)	03117 uuuoe
00010 aaaeu	03101 uuuaa	03118 uuuoi
00011 aaaia	03102 uuuae	03119 uuuoo
00012 aaaie	03103 uuuai	03120 uuuou
00013 aaaii	03104 uuuao	03121 uuuua
00014 aaaio	03105 uuuau	03122 uuuue
00015 aaaiu	03106 uuuea	03123 uuuui
00016 aaaoa	03107 uuuee	03124 uuuuo
00017 aaaoe	03108 uuuei	03125 uuuuu

`$ _`

22.10 Example: Tower of Hanoi

AIM: To devise a remarkably short **recursive method** solution to a seemingly very tricky puzzle.

The Tower of Hanoi puzzle was invented by the French mathematician Edouard Lucas in 1883[3].

There are three pegs, Left, Middle and Right. Stacked on the left peg there are a number of discs, with holes in them which the peg goes through. The discs vary in size with the largest one at the bottom, and each other disc sitting on top of a larger one. The puzzle is simply to move the stack of discs from the Left peg to the Right one.

However there are rules: you can only pick up one disc at a time, you are only allowed to move the top disc from one peg to another, and you cannot put it on top of any smaller disc. But you can use all three pegs.

The job of moving N discs from Left to Right consists of moving the top $N-1$ discs to Middle, moving the bottom disc to Right and finally moving the $N-1$ discs from Middle to Right.

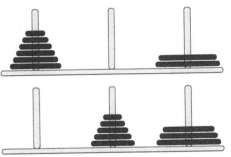

The job of moving $N-1$ discs from, say, Middle to Right consists of moving the top $N-2$ discs to Left, moving the bottom disc to Right and finally moving the $N-2$ discs from Left to Right.

The job of moving $N-2$ discs from, say, Left to Right consists of moving the top $N-3$ discs to Middle, moving the bottom disc to Right and finally moving the $N-3$ discs from Middle to Right.

And so on.

Whenever we move discs from one peg to another, we use the third peg as a temporary storage area. The following program prints out the instructions for moving any given number of discs from Left to Right. Remarkably, we do not actually need to model the towers in order to do this.

```
001: // Program to compute the moves for a Tower of Hanoi with the number of discs
002: // given as an argument.
003: // (Warning: this program does not catch RuntimeExceptions.)
004: public class Hanoi
005: {
006:    public static void main(String[] args) throws RuntimeException
007:    {
008:       int towerSize = Integer.parseInt(args[0]);
009:       moveCount = 0;
010:       showMoves(towerSize, 'L', 'R', 'M');
011:    } // main
```

The showMoves() **class method** is given four **method parameter**s. The first is an **int** saying how many discs are to be moved, and the remaining three are each a **char** representing one of the three towers: 'L', 'M' or 'R'. The first of these is the source peg – where the discs that need moving are currently located. The second tower named is the destination peg – where the discs should be moved to. And the third named tower is the one that can be used for temporary storage of discs during the overall movement. The initial call asks for as all the discs to be moved from 'L' to 'R' using 'M' as temporary storage.

```
014:  // We count the moves as they are made.
015:  private static int moveCount;
016:
017:
018:  // Show moving noOfDiscsToMove from sourcePeg to destinationPeg
019:  // using temporaryPeg as the temporary space.
020:  private static void showMoves(int noOfDiscsToMove, char sourcePeg,
021:                                char destinationPeg, char temporaryPeg)
022:  {
023:    // Nothing to do unless noOfDiscsToMove > 0.
024:    if (noOfDiscsToMove > 0)
025:    {
026:      // Show moving all but the bottom disc from sourcePeg to temporaryPeg.
027:      showMoves(noOfDiscsToMove - 1, sourcePeg, temporaryPeg, destinationPeg);
028:      // Now show moving the bottom disc to destinationPeg.
029:      moveCount++;
030:      System.out.println(moveCount + ": "
031:                         + sourcePeg + " -> " + destinationPeg);
032:      // Show moving the other discs from temporaryPeg to destinationPeg.
033:      showMoves(noOfDiscsToMove - 1, temporaryPeg, destinationPeg, sourcePeg);
034:    } // if
035:  } // showMoves
036:
037: } // class Hanoi
```

22.10.1 Trying it

```
                      Console Input / Output
$ java Hanoi 1
1: L -> R
$ java Hanoi 2
(Output shown using multiple columns to save space.)
1: L -> M     | 2: L -> R     | 3: M -> R
$ java Hanoi 3
(Output shown using multiple columns to save space.)
1: L -> R     | 3: R -> M     | 5: M -> L     | 7: L -> R
2: L -> M     | 4: L -> R     | 6: M -> R
$ _
```

```
                           Console Input / Output
$ java Hanoi 4
(Output shown using multiple columns to save space.)
1: L -> M   | 4: L -> M   | 7: L -> M   | 10: M -> L   | 13: L -> M
2: L -> R   | 5: R -> L   | 8: L -> R   | 11: R -> L   | 14: L -> R
3: M -> R   | 6: R -> M   | 9: M -> R   | 12: M -> R   | 15: M -> R
$ _
```

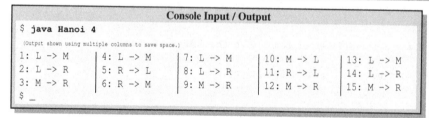

You should check these instructions work by using four coins of differing sizes – mark the three peg positions on a piece of paper, pile the coins on the left position and go.

Coffee time: 22.10.1   How many moves are needed for five discs? Six? *N*?

22.10.2 Coursework: Tower of Hanoi with peg values

Write a version of the Tower of Hanoi program which actually models the discs on the pegs and prints them out at each move. You should have a separate **class** called Peg which models the actual discs on a particular peg. The disc sizes could be stored in a **partially filled array**, the value at **array index** *i* being the size of the disc at location *i* on the peg. Or you could perhaps find out about the standard **class** java.util.Stack, and make a **subclass** of that.

Here is sample output from **run**ning the program with a **command line argument** of 4.

```
                            Console Input / Output
$ java Hanoi 4
   0    Start:      L=< 4 3 2 1 >      M=< >        R=< >
   1    L to M:     L=< 4 3 2 >       M=< 1 >       R=< >
   2    L to R:     L=< 4 3 >        M=< 1 >       R=< 2 >
   3    M to R:     L=< 4 3 >        M=< >         R=< 2 1 >
   4    L to M:     L=< 4 >        M=< 3 >         R=< 2 1 >
   5    R to L:     L=< 4 1 >       M=< 3 >        R=< 2 >
   6    R to M:     L=< 4 1 >       M=< 3 2 >       R=< >
   7    L to M:     L=< 4 >        M=< 3 2 1 >       R=< >
   8    L to R:     L=< >        M=< 3 2 1 >       R=< 4 >
   9    M to R:     L=< >        M=< 3 2 >       R=< 4 1 >
  10    M to L:     L=< 2 >        M=< 3 >        R=< 4 1 >
  11    R to L:     L=< 2 1 >       M=< 3 >        R=< 4 >
  12    M to R:     L=< 2 1 >       M=< >         R=< 4 3 >
  13    L to M:     L=< 2 >        M=< 1 >        R=< 4 3 >
  14    L to R:     L=< >        M=< 1 >        R=< 4 3 2 >
  15    M to R:     L=< >        M=< >         R=< 4 3 2 1 >
$ _
```

22.11   Example: Friend book

AIM: To show an example of **recursion** based on walking through a **recursive data structure**. We also have a **private constructor method**.

This final program allows us to model friendships between people – who is friends with whom. We will have a **text file** of **data** containing the groups of friends – each line of this represents one group of friends by containing their names separated by spaces. Every person in such a group is friends with every other person in the group. Some people may be in more than one group.

Here is an example of the text file.

```
                            Console Input / Output
$ cat friend-book.txt
(Output shown using multiple columns to save space.)
tom dick harry                    | harry sally
alice white-rabbit                | jack sarah
mad-hatter white-rabbit           | jack jill
cinderella prince-charming        | alice jill harry
$ _
```

When we **run** the program, we supply the name of one person and it prints out his or her friends, each with their friends and so on.

```
                    Console Input / Output
$ java FriendBook cinderella
+--cinderella has 1 friend(s): prince-charming
|    +--prince-charming has 1 friend(s): cinderella
|    |    +--cinderella
$ _
```

So, starting from cinderella, we print a **list** of her friends, which is just one, prince-charming. Then for each of her friends we do the same thing, which leads us back to cinderella. On this second visit to her, we do not list her friends and so on – otherwise the process would never stop!

Let's try it with someone more sociable, who is not just half of a couple with no other friends.

```
                        Console Input / Output
$ java FriendBook jack
+--jack has 2 friend(s): jill sarah
|   +--jill has 3 friend(s): alice harry jack
|   |   +--alice has 3 friend(s): harry jill white-rabbit
|   |   |   +--harry has 5 friend(s): alice dick jill sally tom
|   |   |   |   +--alice
|   |   |   |   +--dick has 2 friend(s): harry tom
|   |   |   |   |   +--harry
|   |   |   |   |   +--tom has 2 friend(s): dick harry
|   |   |   |   |   |   +--dick
|   |   |   |   |   |   +--harry
|   |   |   |   +--jill
|   |   |   |   +--sally has 1 friend(s): harry
|   |   |   |   |   +--harry
|   |   |   |   +--tom
|   |   |   +--jill
|   |   |   +--white-rabbit has 2 friend(s): alice mad-hatter
|   |   |   |   +--alice
|   |   |   |   +--mad-hatter has 1 friend(s): white-rabbit
|   |   |   |   |   +--white-rabbit
|   |   +--harry
|   |   +--jack
|   +--sarah has 1 friend(s): jack
|   |   +--jack
$ _
```

Notice that each time we arrive at somebody we have visited before we do not list their friends again.

We will have two **class**es in the program.

Class list for FriendBook	
Class	**Description**
FriendBook	The main class containing the **main method**. It will read the data text file and make **instances** of Friend.
Friend	An instance of this will represent a person, together with the **set** of friends he or she has.

22.11.1 The Friend class

Friend has some **import statements** and **implements** Comparable.

```
001: import java.util.Map;
002: import java.util.Set;
003: import java.util.HashMap;
004: import java.util.HashSet;
005: import java.util.TreeSet;
006:
007: // Representation of a person who is a friend and has some friends.
008: public class Friend implements Comparable<Friend>
009: {
```

We need to be able to find the corresponding Friend **object** for any given String name of a friend. To do this we have a Map from String to Friend and a **class method** to look in this Map and add a **new** Friend if the one we want is not there yet.

```
010:    // A map of all friends, from name(String) to Friend.
011:    // We use this to ensure each Friend is created only once.
012:    private static Map<String, Friend> allFriends
013:      = new HashMap<String, Friend>();
014:
015:
016:    // Get existing, or create new Friend with the given name.
017:    public static Friend getFriend(String name)
018:    {
019:      // Attempt to find an existing Friend with that name.
020:      Friend friend = allFriends.get(name);
021:      if (friend == null)
022:      {
023:        // Create a new one and store it in the map.
024:        friend = new Friend(name);
025:        allFriends.put(name, friend);
026:      } // if
027:      return friend;
028:    } // getFriend
```

Coffee time: Could we have used `TreeMap` instead of `HashMap` above? Which is better for this purpose?

22.11.1

The class has two **instance variable**s.

```
031:    // The name of this friend.
032:    private final String name;
033:
034:    // The set of friends this person has.
035:    // We use TreeSet so we can iterate through them in name order.
036:    private final Set<Friend> friends = new TreeSet<Friend>();
```

The **constructor method** is given the name of the Friend. We want to ensure that no two Friend objects have the same name, and this requires that every Friend object is properly stored in the Map **referenced** from allFriends declared above. In other words, we must ensure that all Friend objects are created via the getFriend() class method. So we make the constructor method **private**.

Concept **Method: constructor methods: private.** Most of the time when we write **constructor method**s we declare them to be **public** because we want to permit code from other **class**es to be able to **construct objects**. However, occasionally we want the creation of objects to be tightly controlled by the class itself. This might be to fix the number of objects created, or to ensure there are no duplicates, etc.. In such cases we make the constructor method **private**. And if we want code outside the class to be able to make objects indirectly, we provide a public **class method** for the job.

```
039:    // Create a friend with the given name. This is private so we can ensure
040:    // each friend is created only once, via getFriend().
041:    private Friend(String requiredName)
042:    {
043:      name = requiredName;
044:    } // Friend
```

We provide the three standard **instance method**s for **natural ordering**, **equivalence** and **hash code**, necessary to ensure that **collection**s of Friends work properly.

```
047:    // Compare this friend with the given other, using the names.
048:    @Override
049:    public int compareTo(Friend other)
050:    {
051:      return name.compareTo(other.name);
052:    } // compareTo
053:
054:
055:    // Equivalence test, consistent with compareTo().
056:    @Override
057:    public boolean equals(Object other)
058:    {
059:      if (other instanceof Friend)
060:        return compareTo((Friend)other) == 0;
061:      else
062:        return super.equals(other);
063:    } // equals
064:
065:
066:    // Hash code, consistent with equals() -- using the hashCode of the name.
067:    @Override
068:    public int hashCode()
069:    {
070:      return name.hashCode();
071:    } // hashCode
```

Friendships are always two-way arrangements, but we make sure a friend is not friends with him or herself. When adding a friendship, we check that the **this reference** does not have the same value as other.

```
074:    // Add the given other as a friend to this, and vice versa.
075:    public void addFriend(Friend other)
076:    {
077:      if (other != this)
078:      {
079:        friends.add(other);
080:        other.friends.add(this);
081:      } // if
082:    } // addFriend
```

We have an instance method to print the tree of friendship for a Friend object. This uses a **private recursive method** which itself needs to keep track of which friends in the structure have already been, or are in the process of being, printed.

```
085:    // Used to avoid infinite recursion:
086:    // as we start to print the details of a friend we add it to this set.
087:    private Set<Friend> friendsStartedToBePrinted;
088:
089:
090:    // Show all the friends of this friend, and their friends, etc..
091:    public void printAllFriends()
092:    {
093:      // Start with a new, empty, set of friends being printed.
094:      friendsStartedToBePrinted = new HashSet<Friend>();
095:      // Show the friends, starting from this.
096:      printAllFriends(this, "");
097:    } // printAllFriends
```

Our recursive method takes two **method parameter**s, the `Friend` object it is currently working on (initially the **this reference**) and an indentation `String` to be printed at the front of all result lines (initially `""`).

The **recursion** here is a process of walking over the **recursive data structure** representing the relationships between `Friend`s.

Concept **Recursion: recursive data structure.** A **recursive data structure** (in Java) is one which consists of **objects** that contain (**references** to) other objects of the same **type**. For example a **binary tree** might be modelled using `BinTreeNode` objects, each of which has `left` and `right` **instance variables** which are of type `BinTreeNode`.

```
public class BinTreeNode
{
  private BinTreeNode left, right;

  private SomeClass nodeData;


  ...

} // class BinTreeNode
```

This permits arbitrary structures to be built, which would not be possible if Java did not use **references** to access **objects**, i.e. if instead objects were somehow stored directly in **variables**.

`Friend` is a recursive data structure because a `Friend` object contains a (**reference** to a) `Set` of other `Friend` objects.

The **basic method** of our recursive `printAllFriends()` is as follows: first print out the name of the `Friend` we are on, then **recursively** process each of the friends of that `Friend`. However, this would continue forever because friendships are two-way, and we also typically have chains of friends. So, we use the `Set`, `friendsStartedToBePrinted` to tell us whether we have already started to print details for a particular `Friend`.

Our **base case** occurs when the `Friend` we are given is already in the set of those started to be printed – we merely print out his or her name. For the **recursive case** we add the given `Friend` to that set, print out his or her name and list of friends, and then recursively process each of those friends, with an increased indentation.

```
100:    // Show the friends starting from the given friend.
101:    // Indentation helps with layout, and increases with each nested level.
102:    private void printAllFriends(Friend from, String indentation)
103:    {
104:      // Base case: from is already being printed.
105:      if (friendsStartedToBePrinted.contains(from))
106:        System.out.println(indentation + "+--" + from.name);
107:      else
108:      {
109:        // Recursive case: print name and list of friends.
110:        friendsStartedToBePrinted.add(from);
111:        System.out.print(indentation + "+--" + from.name
112:                           + " has " + from.friends.size() + " friend(s):");
113:        for (Friend other : from.friends)
114:          System.out.print(" " + other.name);
115:        System.out.println();
116:
117:        // Now recursively process each friend.
118:        for (Friend other : from.friends)
119:          printAllFriends(other, indentation + "|    ");
120:      } // if
121:    } // printAllFriends
```

```
122:
123: } // class Friend
```

Coffee time: Is our definition of `equals()` adequate? For example, what if we had two Friends with the same name but different friends? Or is that not possible?

What would happen if we had completely forgotten to **override** `equals()` anyway? Normally this would break things – would it do so here?

What would happen if we had forgotten to override `hashCode()`?

What if we had missed out **implements** `Comparable<Friend>`?

22.11.2 The `FriendBook` class

One job of this **class** is to read the **data text file**. For brevity we are ignoring the processing of **exceptions** here.

```
001: import java.io.BufferedReader;
002: import java.io.FileReader;
003:
004: // Program to read a network of friends from friend-book.txt,
005: // and then show the 'tree' of friends from the one named as an argument.
006: // (Warning: this program does not catch Exceptions.)
007: public class FriendBook
008: {
009:   // Read the file and build the data structure of Friends.
010:   private static void readFriendBook() throws Exception
011:   {
012:     BufferedReader inputBufferedReader
013:       = new BufferedReader(new FileReader("friend-book.txt"));
014:     String currentLine;
015:     while ((currentLine = inputBufferedReader.readLine()) != null)
016:     {
017:       String[] friendList = currentLine.split(" ");
018:       for (String oneName : friendList)
019:       {
020:         Friend oneFriend = Friend.getFriend(oneName);
021:         for (String otherName : friendList)
022:         {
023:           Friend otherFriend = Friend.getFriend(otherName);
024:           oneFriend.addFriend(otherFriend);
025:         } // for
026:       } // for
027:     } // while
028:   } // readFriendBook
```

Finally, the **main method** finds the `Friend` corresponding to the **command line argument** and uses its **instance method** to output the result.

```
031:   // Read the file, get the first argument and print the friends of him/her.
032:   public static void main(String[] args) throws Exception
033:   {
034:     readFriendBook();
035:     Friend startFriend = Friend.getFriend(args[0]);
036:     startFriend.printAllFriends();
037:   } // main
038:
039: } // class FriendBook
```

22.11.3 Trying it

We have already seen some sample **run**s of the program earlier on page 603. What happens if we try a friend who does not appear in the **file**?

```
                              Console Input / Output
$ java FriendBook norman
+--norman has 0 friend(s):
$ _
```

22.11.4 Coursework: Family trees

Write a program that enables the ancestry of people to be stored and printed out. You will want **object**s of **type** Person with a name and a **set** of other persons who are that person's immediate children. There's no need to model marriage (after all in modern life, many family 'tree's are not that simple). So if we wish to store two parents of a collection of children then we have those children contained separately in each of the parent's objects. (This permits the two parents of one child to have different sets of children.)

Your other **class**, containing the **main method** should be called FamilyTree.

The **data** should be stored in a **text file** called parent-children.txt. Each line consists of the name of a parent, followed by a **list** of his or her children, all separated by spaces.

The program should read this text file and take the name of a person as the first **command line argument**. It will then print out that person and his or her descendants as a 'family tree'. In theory the data should not contain any cycles (a person being their own descendant), however it might – so you should ensure the **recursion** cannot attempt to proceed forever.

To avoid distraction, you may ignore **exception catching** if you wish.

Here is some sample data (based on the UK Royal Family[14]).

```
                              Console Input / Output
$ cat parent-children.txt
George-V Edward-VIII George-VI Mary Henry George John
Victoria-Mary Edward-VIII George-VI Mary Henry George John
Edward-VIII
Wallis-Simpson
George-VI Elizabeth-II Margaret
Elizabeth-Bowes-Lyon Elizabeth-II Margaret
Elizabeth-II Charles Anne Andrew Edward
Philip Charles Anne Andrew Edward
Charles William Harry
Diana William Harry
$ _
```

And here is the corresponding output for George-V.

```
                              Console Input / Output
$ java FamilyTree George-V
+--George-V has 6 child(ren): Edward-VIII George George-VI Henry John Mary
|   +--Edward-VIII has 0 child(ren):
|   +--George has 0 child(ren):
|   +--George-VI has 2 child(ren): Elizabeth-II Margaret
|   |   +--Elizabeth-II has 4 child(ren): Andrew Anne Charles Edward
|   |   |   +--Andrew has 0 child(ren):
|   |   |   +--Anne has 0 child(ren):
|   |   |   +--Charles has 2 child(ren): Harry William
|   |   |   |   +--Harry has 0 child(ren):
|   |   |   |   +--William has 0 child(ren):
|   |   |   +--Edward has 0 child(ren):
|   |   +--Margaret has 0 child(ren):
|   +--Henry has 0 child(ren):
|   +--John has 0 child(ren):
|   +--Mary has 0 child(ren):
$ _
```

Optional extra: What simple change could you make so that the children of a person are listed in the order they were added (which would probably be the order of birth), rather than alphabetically by name? (Hint: look at the **application program interface** (**API**) documentation for java.util.LinkedHashSet.)

22.12   Summary

AIM:
   To summarize our coverage of **recursion**.

This chapter has shown that **recursion** is a powerful tool, more powerful than **iteration** which is just an optimized implementation of **tail recursion**. It is true that some students shy away from it because it can seem a bit tricky. However, you should strive to get comfortable with it, and then you will have the ability to choose when to use it for the right reasons.

Factorial is really best done using **iteration**. Fibonacci is best done with the more efficient **algorithm** which is easily implemented using iteration. But there are many cases where recursion is the best tool for the job, such as the other program examples here.

22.13   Concepts covered in this chapter

Here is a list of the concepts that were covered in this chapter, each with a self-test question. You can use this to check you remember them being introduced, and perhaps re-read some of them before going on to the next chapter.

Array	
– array creation: anonymous array (p.598)	What is the difference between an array initializer and an anonymous array?

Method	
– constructor methods: private (p.605)	In what circumstances would we have a private constructor method?

Recursion	
Recursion (p.574)	What is a recursive definition?
– recursive algorithm (p.576)	What is a recursive algorithm?
– recursive algorithm: design (p.590)	What three things do we need to identify in order to design a recursive algorithm?
– recursive method (p.579)	What does a recursive method contain?
– recursive method: avoid misunderstanding (p.580)	What are the common misconceptions that lead to a failure to understand recursive methods?
– recursive method: well defined (p.581)	What three things must be true for a recursive method to be well defined?
– recursive method: versus iteration (p.581)	What is the relationship between recursion and iteration?
– base and recursive cases (p.575)	Can a recursive definition have any number of base and recursive cases?
– recursive data structure (p.607)	Give two examples of a recursive data structure.

Chapter 23

The end of the beginning

Tomorrow
is a brand new day.

23.1 Looking back

Here you are at the end. If you got through all that, and it mostly made sense, and you did most of the coursework then you're *definitely* a programmer now. And even though we didn't cover all of the language and the application program interface, you are a Java programmer.

Just stop a moment and think how far you have come, especially if you hadn't programmed before starting this book; HelloWorld might seem like another planet now! In the introduction we met some very basic stuff – remember the dog machine? Then came sequential execution and different kinds of errors, followed by types, variables and expressions. Adding conditional execution, and then repeated execution allowed you to write some non-trivial programs, especially when we added in the idea of nesting control statements in loops. We looked at some less commonly used control statements before examining the merits of using separate methods and meeting the logical operators: thus completing our coverage of programming without objects.

And that's where the real power began, first we studied the basic technology of objects, and then we started looking at how to use them properly. We took note of the vast array of classes available in the API, and saw how reusable classes should be documented.

At this point we were ready to write programs with graphical user interfaces – if you missed out that chapter then don't forget to visit it some day.

As our programming was maturing, we studied how to use arrays to store and retrieve data. Maturing still further, we discovered how to make our programs cleanly deal with exceptional circumstances, before visiting the amazing idea of inheritance and polymorphism. We then started making our own exception classes after which we took a tour around Java's file handling techniques.

This lead us on to the fantastic topic of generic classes followed by a coverage of multiple inheritance through the use of interfaces, including generic interfaces, and then finally we were ready to embrace Java's collections framework.

We finished by grasping the awesome power of recursion.

That journey has probably taken you a while. Do you know how many different terms you have seen? Or how many concepts you read through? How many coffee times did you chew over? And how many example programs did you see?

This is how much you have achieved!

Number of terms	423
Number of concepts	391
Number of coffee times	285
Number of Java examples[1]	107

23.2 Looking forwards

So where do you go from here? There are four places to visit – perhaps in parallel.

- Bits of Java that we didn't cover. For example, did you end up wondering how `System.out.printf()` and `String.format()` are able to be given a variable length list of method arguments of arbitrary types? Such use of **variable arity** (or **varargs**), which arrived in Java 5.0, is essentially a shorthand for defining an anonymous array of `Object`s, and that combined with autoboxing does the trick. Oh, now I've gone and told you most of it!

  Well, what about making our own threads so our program can do more than one thing at the same time? Or more advanced graphical user interface features? Take a look at the book's website for some more material.

- More algorithms. For example, you have seen bubble sort, and heard mention of some other sorting algorithms. You might take a look at those.

- Other programming languages. Programming is largely a transferable skill, so now that you can do it you'll find it much easier to learn your next language. It's rather like wanting to be a good foreign language novelist – which is hardest: learning how to write good novels, or learning the foreign language?

- Practising your skill. Yes, you are a programmer now, but you'll get better and quicker the more you practice. Find interesting problems and solve them for yourself – get into the habit of writing software rather than buying it!

Well, wherever you go next, I hope you enjoy the rest of your journey.

---

[1]Excluding the many minor ones inside concept sections!

References and further reading

[1] W. W. Rouse Ball and H. S. M. Coxeter. *Mathematical Recreations and Essays*, pages 50–52. Dover Publications Inc, 13th edition, 1987.
After writing the three weights coursework, I found the puzzle of determining weights to weigh values from 1 to 40 was posed by Bachet. It is explored here.

[2] W. W. Rouse Ball and H. S. M. Coxeter. *Mathematical Recreations and Essays*, page 14. Dover Publications Inc, 13th edition, 1987.
The curio of numbers which are equal to the sum of the cubes of their digits briefly appears here, apparently from *Sphinx* Journal, Brussels, 1937. The task of finding them has seemingly appeared in many programming courses since then.

[3] W. W. Rouse Ball and H. S. M. Coxeter. *Mathematical Recreations and Essays*, pages 316–317. Dover Publications Inc, 13th edition, 1987.
The Tower of Hanoi puzzle was 'brought out' in 1883 by Edouard Lucas.

[4] Leonardo Fibonacci and Laurence E. Sigler. *Fibonacci's Liber Abaci*, pages 404–405. Springer, 2003.
A modern translation of Fibonacci's work, including the original rabbit breeding example from which we have the 'Fibonacci numbers'.

[5] James Gosling, Bill Joy, Guy Steele, Gilad Bracha, and Alex Buckley. *The Java Language Specification, Java SE 8 Edition*. Addison Wesley, 2014.
The official definition of Java, but not an easy read for new programmers!

[6] Leslie Lamport. *LaTeX: A Document Preparation System*. Addison-Wesley, 1986.
This discusses one of the tools used to produce the book, without which the production would have been seriously painful!

[7] John Miano. *Compressed Image File Formats: JPEG, PNG, GIF, XBM, BMP*, pages 23–30. ACM Press/Addison Wesley, 1999.
This gives more information about the BMP file format (but so do many web pages).

[8] William Shakespeare and Brian Gibbons (ed). *Romeo and Juliet*, page 129. Arden Shakespeare (Thompson Learning), 1980.
A piece of text used as test data. From Act 2, Scene 2: ... a rose by any other name ....

[9] ASCII - Wikipedia, the free encyclopedia.
http://en.wikipedia.org/wiki/ASCII (access September 2014).
American Standard Code for Information Interchange (ASCII) defines codes for 128 characters, including 33 control codes. It is replaced nowadays with Unicode which uses the same codes for those 128 characters, but includes very many more.

[10] BSD checksum - Wikipedia, the free encyclopedia.
`http://en.wikipedia.org/wiki/BSD_checksum` (access September 2014).
A simple algorithm for checking file contents.

[11] Caesar cipher - Wikipedia, the free encyclopedia.
`http://en.wikipedia.org/wiki/Caesar_cipher` (access September 2014).
One of the simplest forms of encryption, allegedly used by Julius Caesar.

[12] George Boole - Wikipedia, the free encyclopedia.
`http://en.wikipedia.org/wiki/George_Boole` (access September 2014).
The inventor of Boolean logic.

[13] Gregorian calendar - Wikipedia, the free encyclopedia.
`http://en.wikipedia.org/wiki/Gregorian_calendar` (access September 2014).
A correction to the Julian calendar, introduced in 1582 and adopted in many countries by 1753.

[14] House of Windsor - Wikipedia, the free encyclopedia.
`http://en.wikipedia.org/wiki/House_of_Windsor` (access September 2014).
Starting source for our example family tree data.

[15] Leibniz formula for π - Wikipedia, the free encyclopedia.
`http://en.wikipedia.org/wiki/Leibniz_formula_for_pi` (access September 2014).
Leibniz re-discovered this formula to compute π.

[16] Overview (Java Platform SE 6)
or Overview (Java Platform SE 7)
or Overview (Java Platform SE 8).
`http://download.oracle.com/javase/6/docs/api/` (access September 2014)
or `http://download.oracle.com/javase/7/docs/api/` (access September 2014)
or `http://download.oracle.com/javase/8/docs/api/` (access September 2014).
The doc comment documentation for the standard API classes.

[17] The Perl Programming Language - www.perl.org.
`http://www.perl.org/` (access September 2014).
Perl is a programming language which can execute string data as program code, and also may have inspired Java's 'for each' statement.

[18] Pythagorean theorem - Wikipedia, the free encyclopedia.
`http://en.wikipedia.org/wiki/Pythagorean_theorem` (access September 2014).
Pythagoras' theorem tells us the distance between two points.

[19] Sieve of Eratosthenes - Wikipedia, the free encyclopedia.
`http://en.wikipedia.org/wiki/Sieve_of_Eratosthenes` (access September 2014).
The method of finding prime numbers created by the ancient Greek Eratosthenes. This page includes a simple animation.

[20] Unicode Consortium.
`http://unicode.org/` (access September 2014).
The replacement for (or perhaps extension of) ASCII that intends to include all characters used in all human languages.

Index

The End!!

```
System.exit(0);
```

Colour shades for publisher's use.

This box is 0.05 This box is 0.05 This box is 0.05	This box is 0.06 This box is 0.06 This box is 0.06	This box is 0.07 This box is 0.07 This box is 0.07	This box is 0.08 This box is 0.08 This box is 0.08
This box is 0.09 This box is 0.09 This box is 0.09	This box is 0.10 This box is 0.10 This box is 0.10	This box is 0.11 This box is 0.11 This box is 0.11	This box is 0.12 This box is 0.12 This box is 0.12
This box is 0.13 This box is 0.13 This box is 0.13	This box is 0.14 This box is 0.14 This box is 0.14	This box is 0.15 This box is 0.15 This box is 0.15	This box is 0.16 This box is 0.16 This box is 0.16
This box is 0.17 This box is 0.17 This box is 0.17	This box is 0.18 This box is 0.18 This box is 0.18	This box is 0.19 This box is 0.19 This box is 0.19	This box is 0.20 This box is 0.20 This box is 0.20
This box is 0.21 This box is 0.21 This box is 0.21	This box is 0.22 This box is 0.22 This box is 0.22	This box is 0.23 This box is 0.23 This box is 0.23	This box is 0.24 This box is 0.24 This box is 0.24
This box is 0.25 This box is 0.25 This box is 0.25	This box is 0.26 This box is 0.26 This box is 0.26	This box is 0.27 This box is 0.27 This box is 0.27	This box is 0.28 This box is 0.28 This box is 0.28
This box is 0.29 This box is 0.29 This box is 0.29	This box is 0.30 This box is 0.30 This box is 0.30	This box is 0.31 This box is 0.31 This box is 0.31	This box is 0.32 This box is 0.32 This box is 0.32
This box is 0.33 This box is 0.33 This box is 0.33	This box is 0.34 This box is 0.34 This box is 0.34	This box is 0.35 This box is 0.35 This box is 0.35	This box is 0.36 This box is 0.36 This box is 0.36
This box is 0.37 This box is 0.37 This box is 0.37	This box is 0.38 This box is 0.38 This box is 0.38	This box is 0.39 This box is 0.39 This box is 0.39	This box is 0.40 This box is 0.40 This box is 0.40
This box is 0.41 This box is 0.41 This box is 0.41	This box is 0.42 This box is 0.42 This box is 0.42	This box is 0.43 This box is 0.43 This box is 0.43	This box is 0.44 This box is 0.44 This box is 0.44
This box is 0.45 This box is 0.45 This box is 0.45	This box is 0.46 This box is 0.46 This box is 0.46	This box is 0.47 This box is 0.47 This box is 0.47	This box is 0.48 This box is 0.48 This box is 0.48
This box is 0.49 This box is 0.49 This box is 0.49	This box is 0.50 This box is 0.50 This box is 0.50	This box is 0.51 This box is 0.51 This box is 0.51	This box is 0.52 This box is 0.52 This box is 0.52